COMPUTER SYSTEMS

Architecture, Organization, and Programming

COMPUTER SYSTEMS

Architecture, Organization, and Programming

◆

ARTHUR B. MACCABE

Department of Computer Science
The University of New Mexico

IRWIN
Homewood, IL 60430
Boston, MA 02116

Cover image: © Elissa Dorfman/VAGA. New York 1992

Richard D. Irwin, Inc., recognizes that certain terms in the book are trademarks, and we have made every effort to reprint these throughout the text with the capitalization and punctuation used by the holders of the trademark.

© RICHARD D. IRWIN, INC., 1993

Senior sponsoring editor: Bill Stenquist
Editorial assistant: Christine Bara
Marketing manager: Robb Linsky
Project editor: Margaret Haywood
Production manager: Bob Lange
Cover designer: Mercedes Santos
Compositor: Technique Typesetting
Typeface: 10/12 Times Roman
Printer: R. R. Donnelley & Sons Company

Library of Congress Cataloging-in-Publication Data

Maccabe, Arthur B.
    Computer systems : architecture, organization, and programming / Arthur B. Maccabe.
       p.   cm.
    ISBN 0-256-11456-0 (alk. paper)
    1. Computer architecture.   2. Computer organization.
QA76.9.A73M33   1993
004.2'2—dc20   92–27699

Printed in the United States of America
1 2 3 4 5 6 7 8 9 0 DOC 0 9 8 7 6 5 4 3

To Linda, my companion for life.

As the curricula in computer science and engineering continue to evolve, many of the traditional classes need to be compressed to make room for new material. Given the current set of topics that must be covered in these curricula, the computing disciplines can no longer afford to offer introductory courses in computer organization, assembly language programming, and the principles of computer architecture. This book integrates these areas in a unified presentation with an emphasis on parallelism and the principles underlying the RISC approach to computer architecture. In particular, the text introduces and motivates the load/store architecture, instruction scheduling and delay slots, limitations in addressing modes, and the instruction interpretation pipeline.

This text was developed to serve as an introduction to computing systems. The primary goal is to introduce and motivate the principles of modern computer architecture (instruction set design) and organization (instruction set implementation) through assembly language programming. This goal is reflected in the structure and organization of the text. The secondary goal is to convey the spirit of design used in the development of modern computing systems. The design of modern computing systems is based on a variety of solutions that have been implemented in previous systems. In writing this text, I have emphasized the concepts underlying modern computing systems, believing that students must have a strong foundation in basic concepts before they can understand and appreciate the empirical studies that currently dominate the design of systems.

Unlike many other areas of computing, there are few definitive answers in the design of computing systems. The most important answers are solutions that fit a set of constraints. The constraints are frequently determined by the current state of the technology and our understanding of the technology. As such, the constraints (and solutions) represent a moving target. In this context, it is important to emphasize general concepts so that students will understand the limits of the current solutions. Given an understanding of the limits, students will be in a better position to anticipate and appreciate the inevitable changes in future systems.

The concepts presented in this text cannot be learned in sufficient depth by studying general principles in isolation. To learn this material, students need to experiment with and learn the entire instruction set of a specific machine. In learning the details of a specific machine, students will see how one set of solutions imposes constraints on other solutions. Importantly, they will see a computing system as an integrated set of solutions—not merely a collection of independent solutions.

In writing this text, I have sought a balance between an emphasis on concepts presented as independent solutions and the need to provide students with hands-on experience and detailed understanding of a specific computing system. The body of the text emphasizes general principles and independent solutions to problems. This presentation is augmented with case studies to highlight specific aspects of different computing systems. In addition, the text has been organized so that laboratory exercises, providing the necessary hands-on experience, can be integrated with the material presented in the text.

COVERAGE

The text begins with a concise coverage of the material that provides a foundation for the remainder of the text: basic data representation (including an introductory presentation of 2's complement representation); logic design (covering combinational and sequential circuits); and the components (including memory organization, basic concepts of the CPU, and bus structures). The coverage in this part of the text is introductory; later portions of the text expand on this material.

The second part of the text covers the principles of computer architecture by considering arithmetic calculations, addressing modes (data organization), and subroutine calling mechanisms. This material appears early in the text so that students can begin writing simple assembly language programs early in the course.

The third part of the text expands on the material presented in the first chapter by considering the representation of numbers. This part of the text includes a careful coverage of integer and floating point representations. The goal is to provide students with the background needed to understand and reason about numeric representations.

The fourth part of the text considers instruction representation, expanding on the concepts introduced in the first and second parts of the text. This part of the text includes a discussion of instruction set implementation—including direct implementation of instruction sets, instruction pipelining, and microprogramming. In addition, this part of the text considers the translation process—assembly, linking, and loading.

The fifth part of the text considers the foundations of operating systems: the mechanisms associated with resource use and protection. This part of the text begins with a discussion of resource protection and the trap mechanism found in modern machines. It concludes by considering interrupt and device structures.

The final part of the text presents the concepts underlying parallel machines. Parallelism is a fundamental concept integrated throughout the earlier parts of this text. This part of the text provides students with a view of the future and an integration of the issues associated with parallelism.

PREREQUISITES

Prior to studying the material in this text, students should have completed a one-semester course in procedural programming using a structured language like Ada, Pascal, or C. Students should be familiar with basic data types and type constructors (arrays, structures/records, and pointers), basic control structures (if-then-else statements, loops, and case/switch statements), and subroutines and parameter passing. In addition, familiarity with recursion would be helpful but is not required.

FOUNDATION

In most curricula, the material presented in this text is not important in isolation but is important in providing a foundation for many of the core classes in the curriculum. In particular, the material presented in this text is intended to provide a foundation for classes in operating system principles, modern computer architecture, the foundations of modern programming languages, and compiler construction. For the operating systems class, students need to learn about the memory heirarchy, asynchrony, concurrency, exceptions, interrupts, and traps. For the architecture class, students need to learn about the design of instruction sets for sequential machines. For the languages and compiler construction classes, students need to learn about instruction sets, memory addressing, and the linkage process.

GENERAL ORGANIZATION

The body of the text is presented in 6 parts, 13 chapters, and 4 appendixes. It is expected that the instructor will select a subset of these chapters for careful coverage and may select other chapters for lighter coverage. The set of chapters covered will vary with the background of the students and the courses that follow this one. More specifically, the organization has been designed to accommodate at least three course organizations. In curricula where students do not have a background in data representation or logic design, a one semester course should be able to cover the material in Chapters 1–6 in detail, with selected coverage of material in Chapters 7–12. In curricula where students have a background in data representation and logic design, a one semester course should be able to cover Chapters 3–6 in detail, with complete (but lighter) coverage of the material in Chapters 7–12. In curricula where students have a background in the foundations and the course is followed by a hands-on course in operating system design and implementation, a one semester course should be able to cover Chapters 3–10 in detail.

The following diagram presents the prerequisite structure for the chapters in the text:

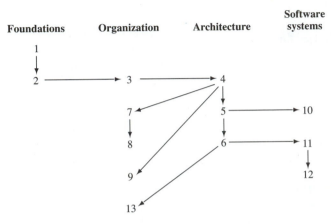

FEATURES

- **Foundations:** The text begins by covering the principles of data representation and logic design. The coverage of logic design is concise and to the point. The goal is to provide students with the background needed to design and understand simple combinational and sequential circuits. To maintain the brevity of this presentation, several topics (including Karnaugh maps and optimization) have been omitted.

- **Assembly language:** While this is not a text on assembly language programming, assembly language is used as a tool for exploring the principles of modern computer architecture. Throughout the text architectural principles are introduced using assembly language constructs and code fragments.

- **Load/store architecture:** The assembly language used in the text is based on the load/store architecture that provides the basis for modern computing systems. This feature makes it easier for students to apply the principles presented in the text to an actual architecture in laboratory exercises.

- **Pipelining:** The principles of pipelined instruction execution are integrated throughout the text. The early chapters introduce overlapped instruction execution and instruction delay slots. Later chapters consider issues related to pipeline design along with the superpipelining and superscalar approaches.

- **Case studies:** Numerous case studies covering aspects of real architectures are integrated into the body of the text. While these case studies emphasize the SPARC and HP Precision architectures, they also cover aspects of other modern machines including the IBM RS/6000, the MIPS R4000, the Intel i860, and the Motorola 88100.

- **Laboratory support:** The text has been carefully organized to support laboratory exercises that explore the details of a particular architecture. The early chapters on computer architecture provide students with the background needed to write a variety of assembly language programs. While students are working on programming assignments, the text considers the details of instruction set implementation and translation. Later chapters introduce exceptions and interrupts. These chapters provide students with the background needed to write simple interrupt handlers and explore the foundations of operating system structures.

- **Parallelism:** The principles of parallel execution are emphasized throughout the text. The first 12 chapters introduce parallelism in circuit design (conditional-sum and carry-lookahead adders), coprocessors (overlap of floating point operations), and instruction interpretation (pipelining). The final chapter presents a unified and comprehensive treatment of parallel execution with an emphasis on massively parallel machines.

- **Rigorous treatment of number representations:** An initial treatment of integer representations in the first chapter emphasizes the consequences of integer representations, providing students with the background needed to understand the operations provided by modern machines. Chapter 7 presents a rigorous treatment of integer representations, providing students with the tools needed to reason about these representations. Additionally, Chapter 8 provides a thorough treatment of floating point representations with an emphasis on the IEEE 754 floating point standard.

PEDAGOGICAL AIDS

- **Terminology:** Terminology and concepts are closely related. Most of the concepts introduced in this text have very specific names and differences in terminology reflect variations in concepts. To assist students in their efforts to learn the terminology, Appendix D of the text contains a glossary of over 150 terms. In addition, margin notes throughout the text identify the introduction of new terms in the body of the text.

- **Visual presentation:** The text contains over 200 illustrations and more than 60 tables. The illustrations and tables provide an important graphical summary of the material presented in the text.

- **Chapter summaries:** Each chapter concludes with a summary of the important concepts introduced in the chapter. Each of these summaries includes a section on additional reading that tells students where they can find more material on the topics introduced in the chapter. Each summary also includes a list of the important terms introduced in the chapter and a collection of review questions.

- **Examples:** Over 250 examples are integrated with the presentation to illustrate specific skills or topics. While they flow with the body of the text, the examples are set apart from the text by horizontal rules to make them easy to spot for review or further study.

- **Exercises:** There are approximately 250 exercises at the end of the chapters. These exercises are designed to reinforce and, in some cases, extend the material presented in the chapter.

TEACHING AIDS

- **Instructor's manual:** Mark Boyd at the University of North Carolina–Asheville has developed an instructor's manual that includes solutions to all of the exercises in the text.
- **SPARC emulator:** A group of students at the University of New Mexico, led by Jeff Van Dyke, have developed an emulator for the SPARC architecture. The emulator provides a convenient environment for developing and debugging assembly language programs. Using this emulated environment, students can take advantage of the full complement of Unix tools and easily develop programs that require supervisor privileges (i.e., interrupt and exception handlers). The emulator package includes a complete emulation of the SPARC integer unit and a small collection of devices. Currently the emulator runs on Unix workstations and uses X11 for the graphic oriented devices.

    This emulator can be obtained via anonymous ftp. To obtain the emulator and associated documentation, ftp to

    ftp.cs.unm.edu

    and login as anonymous. The emulator is in the directory

    pub/maccabe/SPARC

- **Laboratory manuals:** We are developing a collection of laboratory manuals to ease the integration of the material presented in the text with the details of a particular architecture. These laboratory manuals will cover the details of specific machines and provide programming assignments to reinforce the material presented in the text. We are currently developing the first of these laboratory manuals, a laboratory manual for the SPARC architecture that covers the SPARC emulator and devices included in the SPARC emulator package. This manual should be available by August 1993.

ACKNOWLEDGMENTS

First, I would like to thank my colleagues in the computer science department at the University of New Mexico. In the four years I spent writing this book, I found hundreds of questions that I couldn't answer. In every case, I had a colleague who was willing to take the time to answer my question or point me in the direction of an answer. Thanks.

Second, I would like to thank my graduate advisor, Richard LeBlanc. A long time ago, in a city far far away, Richard thought it was worth his time and effort to teach me how to write. Believe me, this was not a small task. Thanks, Richard.

Third, I would like to thank Bill Stenquist, the editor who originally sponsored this project. Bill found a great set of reviewers and managed to get me the resources that I needed so that I could concentrate on writing. Thanks, Bill.

Fourth, I would like to thank Mark Boyd, Harold Knudsen, Jeff Van Dyke, and the few hundred students who have used early drafts of this text in their classes. I know that it is very difficult to use an unfinished book in a class. Thanks for the feedback.

Fifth, I would like to thank Anne Cable and Wynette Richards who read and commented on several of the early chapters.

Sixth, I would like to thank the people who helped in the final stages of development. Tom Casson was a great help in polishing the edges. Margaret Haywood managed to keep the whole process close to the impossible schedule we needed to get the book out on time. The folks at Technique Typesetting did an excellent job of transforming my LaTeX files into the book you see. Thanks.

Finally, I would like to acknowledge the efforts of people who reviewed this text as it was in progress. The reviewers were exceptional. Their comments were honest, insightful, clear, and concise: What more could an author want! The following individuals participated in the reviewing process:

- Keith Barker, University of Connecticut
- Anthony Baxter, University of Kentucky
- Mark Boyd, University of North Carolina–Asheville
- Roger Camp, Cal Poly–San Luis Obispo
- Yaohan Chu, University of Maryland
- Dave Hanscom, University of Utah
- Olin Johnson, University of Houston
- Brian Lindow, University of Wisconsin–Eau Claire
- Fabrizio Lombardi, Texas A&M University
- Thomas Miller, University of Idaho
- William Morritz, University of Washington
- Taghi Mostafavi, University of North Carolina-Charlotte
- Chris Papachristow, Case Western Reserve University
- John Passafiume, Clemson University
- Keshav Pingali, Cornell University
- Steve Schack, Vanderbilt University
- Thomas Skinner, Boston University Metropolitan College
- M.D. Wagh, Lehigh University
- Gloria Wigley, University of Arkansas–Monticello
- William Ziegler, SUNY–Binghamton

Thank you, one and all.

ERRATA

In spite of the careful reviewing and my best intentions, I am certain that a number of errors remain in the text. If you find an error, a section of the text that is misleading, an omission in the glossary, or an omission in the index, please drop me a note. I'd like to hear from you. My email address is:

maccabe@unmvax.cs.unm.edu

Barney Maccabe

CONTENTS

FOUNDATIONS

BASIC DATA REPRESENTATION

We begin our study by introducing the principles of data representation. In particular, we discuss the issues related to the representation of numbers and characters. Before considering the details of number and character representations, it is helpful if we take a moment to introduce some fundamental concepts associated with representations.

As intelligent beings, we can devise and manipulate representations of physical and imaginary objects. We frequently exploit this ability to save time and effort. As an example, suppose you have to rearrange the furniture in your apartment. You could hire a couple of football players for the day and have them move the furniture until you like the arrangement. This might get a bit expensive: you have to pay the football players for their time, and your furniture may get damaged by all the moving. You can save time and effort by drawing a floor plan for your apartment and making a paper cutout for each piece of furniture that you own. Using your floor plan and paper cutouts, you can experiment with different furniture arrangements before inviting the football players over to do the real work. In this example, the floor plan is a representation of your apartment and each paper cutout represents a piece of furniture.

Every representation emphasizes a set of properties while ignoring others. In other words, representations *abstract* essential properties while hiding unnecessary details. The paper cutouts used to represent your furniture emphasize the width and depth of each piece, but do not reflect the height or weight. This *abstraction* is reasonable if the floor of your apartment is sound enough to support any arrangement of your furniture and the ceiling is a constant height. In other words, the abstraction is valid if floor space is the essential consideration in evaluating different arrangements of your furniture.

Abstract

Abstraction

It should be obvious that you could devise many different representations for an object. If you are planning to move across the country, you might choose to represent each piece of furniture by its weight (professional movers use weight and distance to calculate shipping charges). Given two or more representations for an object, you must consider the expected uses before you can determine which is the most appropriate. Importantly, different representations simplify different uses.

Symbolic
representation

Alphabet

In this text, we will only consider *symbolic representations*, that is, representations constructed from a fixed alphabet. An *alphabet* is a set of symbols. As an example, the sentence that you are reading is an instance of a symbolic representation. The representation uses the symbols in the alphabet of the English language. We use many different alphabets in our representations. Table 1.1 presents several other alphabets.

Table 1.1 Sample alphabets

Name	Symbols	Example
Roman numerals	{ I, V, X, L, C, D, M }	XIV
Decimal digits	{ 0, 1, 2, 3, 4, 5, 6, 7, 8, 9 }	14
Binary digits	{ 0, 1 }	1110
Greek letters	{ $\alpha, \beta, \gamma, \delta, \ldots, \psi, \omega$ }	$\tau\varepsilon\chi$

Our restriction to symbolic representations is not as much of a limitation as it may seem. It is easy to construct a symbolic representation for most objects. For example, the floor plan for your apartment can be represented by a set of line segments and dimensions. Each line segment can be described by a symbolic equation. A photograph can be represented by a two-dimensional grid of very small colored dots (called *pixels*). Here the colors in the photograph define the alphabet used in the representation.[1]

Encoding

A fundamental result from information theory is that every symbolic representation can be converted into a symbolic representation based on the binary alphabet. The term *encoding* refers to a representation based on the binary alphabet. In the remainder of this chapter, we consider strategies for constructing encodings for numbers and characters. We begin by considering different number systems with an emphasis on positional number systems. After discussing positional number systems, we will consider strategies for encoding numbers and characters. We conclude this chapter with a brief discussion of errors. In particular, we discuss the detection and correction of errors that may occur during the transmission of an encoded value.

1.1 POSITIONAL NUMBER SYSTEMS

In this section we consider simple techniques for representing numbers. Our goal is to discuss positional number systems. Before we introduce positional number systems, we will consider three other number systems: stick numbers, grouping systems, and the roman numeral system.

It is helpful to take a moment to consider what numbers are before we consider specific techniques for representing numbers. Numbers are not physical objects,

---

[1] We should note that the technique used to construct a symbolic representation of the photograph only approximates the actual photograph. The grid is only an approximation of the actual space occupied by the image. Moreover, the colors identified during the construction of the representation are only an approximation of the actual colors used in the actual image.

they are abstract objects. They are frequently used in the description of physical objects. For example, in describing an apple tree, I might say that the tree has 56 apples. If I need to represent an orchard of apple trees, I might choose to represent each apple tree by the number of apples on the tree. As such, when we discuss the representation of numbers we are, in effect, discussing the representation of a representation.

1.1.1 Stick Numbers

In a stick number system, a set of sticks represents a number. Usually, each stick represents a physical object. For example, a sheepherder might use one stick for every sheep in the flock. The advantages of this representation scheme should be obvious—sticks are easier to manipulate than sheep.

In the terms of symbolic representations, stick numbers use an alphabet consisting of one symbol—the stick. This symbol is called the *unit symbol*.

Unit symbol

Simple operations, like addition, subtraction, and comparison, are easy to implement in stick number systems. However, this representation technique is not very good when you need to represent large numbers.

1.1.2 Simple Grouping Systems

In simple grouping systems, the alphabet contains *grouping symbols* along with the unit symbol. Each grouping symbol represents a collection of units. Coins are a good example of a simple grouping system. In the American coin system, the penny is the unit symbol. Nickels, dimes, quarters, half-dollars, and dollars are grouping symbols.

Grouping symbol

Grouping systems simplify the representation of large numbers because fewer symbols need to be communicated. However, simple operations like addition and subtraction are more complicated in simple grouping systems.

We should note that simple grouping systems do not provide unique representations for every value. As an example, consider the American coin system and the value 49. There are several possible representations for this value: four dimes and nine pennies; one quarter, four nickels, and four pennies; 49 pennies, and so forth. If we are required to use the larger grouping symbols whenever possible, the representation of every number is unique. Moreover, the representation will use the smallest number of symbols. Using this rule, 49 would be represented by one quarter, two dimes, and four pennies.

1.1.3 Roman Numerals

The roman numeral system is essentially a grouping system. Along with a set of grouping symbols, the roman numeral system has a subtractive rule. The subtractive rule further reduces the number of symbols needed in the representation of large numbers.

6 Chapter 1 Basic Data Representation

Table 1.2 presents the grouping symbols used in the roman numeral system. Because symbols are defined for each power of 10 (I, X, C, and M), the roman numeral system is essentially a decimal grouping system. We call the symbols I, X, C, and M decimal symbols. In addition to the decimal symbols, the roman numeral system defines three midpoint symbols, V, L, and D.

Table 1.2 Symbols used in roman numerals

Symbol	Meaning	Group
I	Basic unit	Ones
V	5 I's	
X	10 I's	Tens
L	50 I's	
C	100 I's	Hundreds
D	500 I's	
M	1,000 I's	thousands

In simple grouping systems, the order in which you write the symbols is not important. The representation of a number is simply a set of symbols. However, in the roman numeral system, the order of the symbols is important. The symbols used in the representation of a number are usually sorted by the number of units each symbol represents. As such, XXII is the representation for the number 22 and not IXIX or XIIX. When the *subtraction rule* is used, a symbol representing a smaller number of units is written in front of a symbol representing a larger number of units. The combined symbol represents the difference between the number of units represented by the two symbols. The use of the subtraction rule in the roman numeral system is subject to two additional restrictions. First, the rule is only defined for a pair of symbols; that is, the string IXC is *not* a valid representation of 89. Second, the first symbol in a subtraction pair must be a decimal symbol. Table 1.3 presents the combined symbols introduced by the subtractive rule.

Table 1.3 Subtractive symbols used in roman numerals

Combined symbol	Meaning
IV	4 I's
IX	9 I's
XL	40 I's
XC	90 I's
CD	400 I's
CM	900 I's

1.1.4 Positional Number Systems

Grouping systems, with the subtractive rule, make it easier to represent large numbers. However, large numbers still require the communication of many symbols and/or a large alphabet. Positional number systems make it easier to represent large numbers.

Every positional number system has a radix and an alphabet. The *radix* (or *base*) is a positive integer. The number of symbols in the alphabet is the same as the value of the radix. Each symbol in the alphabet is a grouping symbol called a *digit*.[2] Each digit is a grouping symbol that corresponds to a different integer in the range from zero[3] to the value of the radix minus one. For example, the binary number system uses a radix of two and an alphabet of two digits. One digit corresponds to zero and the other corresponds to one. The digits used in the binary number system are frequently called *bits*, a contraction of the phrase *binary digit*. In the remainder of this text, we will emphasize four different number systems: binary (base 2), octal (base 8), decimal (base 10), and hexadecimal (base 16).

Radix (base)

Digit

Bit (binary digit)

When a number system has 10 or fewer symbols, we use the initial digits of the decimal number system as the digits for the number system. For example, the octal number system uses the symbols "0" through "7". When a number system has more than ten symbols, we will use the initial letters in the English alphabet to represent values greater than nine. For example, the hexadecimal number system uses the symbols "0" through "9" and the symbols "A" through "F".

In a positional number system, a sequence of digits is used to represent an integer value. When the digits are read from right to left, each digit counts the next power of the radix starting from 0. For example, the value two hundred and thirty-eight is represented by the sequence 238, that is, the digit "2", followed by the digit "3", followed by the digit "8". If we read the digits from right to left, the sequence indicates that the value has eight 1's ($1 = 10^0$), three 10's ($10 = 10^1$), and 2 100's ($100 = 10^2$). In general, the sequence:

$$d_{n-1} \ldots d_2 d_1 d_0$$

represents the value

$$d_{n-1} \cdot r^{n-1} + \cdots + d_2 \cdot r^2 + d_1 \cdot r^1 + d_0 \cdot r^0$$

where r is the radix.

In discussing the representation of a number in a positional number system, we frequently speak of the significance of a digit. The significance of a digit is based on its position in the representation. Digits further to the left are more significant because they represent larger powers of the radix. The rightmost digit is the *least significant digit*, while the leftmost (nonzero) digit is the *most significant digit*.

Least significant digit

Most significant digit

The fact that different number systems use the same symbols creates a bit of a problem. For example, if you write down 101, is it a number written in

---

[2] If there is a possibility of confusion in using the term *digit,* it may be preceded by the name of the number system to avoid confusion; for example, the phrase *decimal digit* refers to a digit in the decimal number system.

[3] We should note that the symbol that corresponds to zero is not really a grouping symbol. This symbol represents the absence of any objects and is used as a placeholder in modern positional number systems.

decimal notation or binary notation? We will use a simple convention to avoid this problem. When we write a number in a number system other than the decimal number system, we will follow the digits by a subscript (base 10) number. The subscript number indicates the radix of the number system used to construct the representation. For example, 101_2 is a number written in binary notation, while 101_8 is a number written in octal notation.

1.1.5 Converting between Bases

When you are working with several number systems, you will frequently need to convert representations between the different number systems. For example, you might need to convert the binary representation of a number into its decimal representation or vice versa.

Converting a representation into the decimal number system from any other number system is relatively easy. Simply perform the arithmetic calculation presented earlier.

Example 1.1   *Convert 564_8 into its decimal equivalent.*

$$564_8 = 5 \cdot 8^2 + 6 \cdot 8^1 + 4 \cdot 8^0$$
$$= 5 \cdot 64 + 6 \cdot 8 + 4 \cdot 1$$
$$= 320 + 48 + 4$$
$$= 372$$

We could use the same technique to convert a representation from the decimal number system into any other number system. However, this approach requires that you carry out the arithmetic in the target number system. Because most of us are not very good at performing arithmetic in other number systems, this is not a particularly good approach.

Example 1.2   *Convert 964 into its octal equivalent (the hard way).*

$$964 = 9 \cdot 10^2 + 6 \cdot 10^1 + 4 \cdot 10^0$$
$$= 11_8 \cdot 12_8^2 + 6_8 \cdot 12_8^1 + 4_8 \cdot 12_8^0$$
$$= 11_8 \cdot 144_8 + 6_8 \cdot 12_8 + 4_8 \cdot 1$$
$$= 1604_8 + 74_8 + 4_8$$
$$= 1704_8$$

Luckily there is an algorithm that allows us to use decimal arithmetic for the needed calculations. In presenting this algorithm, we begin by considering an example.

Example 1.3   *Convert 964 into its octal representation.*

If you divide 964 by 8, you will get a quotient of 120 and a remainder of 4. In other words,

$$964 = \frac{964 \cdot 8}{8} = 120 \cdot 8 + 4 \cdot 8^0$$

In this manner, you have determined the least significant digit in the octal representation. Continuing in this fashion yields the following derivation:

$$
\begin{aligned}
964 &= \frac{964 \cdot 8}{8} \\
&= 120 \cdot 8^1 + 4 \cdot 8^0 \\
&= \frac{120 \cdot 8}{8} \cdot 8^1 + 4 \cdot 8^0 \\
&= (15 \cdot 8 + 0) \cdot 8^1 + 4 \cdot 8^0 \\
&= 15 \cdot 8^2 + 0 \cdot 8^1 + 4 \cdot 8^0 \\
&= \frac{15 \cdot 8}{8} \cdot 8^2 + 0 \cdot 8^1 + 4 \cdot 8^0 \\
&= (1 \cdot 8 + 7) \cdot 8^2 + 0 \cdot 8^1 + 4 \cdot 8^0 \\
&= 1 \cdot 8^3 + 7 \cdot 8^2 + 0 \cdot 8^1 + 4 \cdot 8^0 \\
&= 1704_8
\end{aligned}
$$

In general, you can divide by the radix of the target number system to determine the digits of the result. The rightmost digit of the representation is the remainder that results from dividing the original value by the radix. In subsequent steps, the next digit is the remainder that results from dividing the quotient of the previous step by the radix. This process is repeated until the quotient is zero.

Example 1.4   *Given this algorithm, the calculations performed in Example 1.3 can be summarized as*

Step	Division	Quotient	Remainder	Result
1	964/8	120	4	4_8
2	120/8	15	0	04_8
3	15/8	1	7	704_8
4	1/8	0	1	1704_8

If you need to convert a representation between two different number systems, it is usually easier if you convert the representation into decimal and then into the target number system. This approach allows you to use decimal arithmetic for the required calculations.

There are special cases when it is easy to perform a direct conversion between different number systems (without going through the decimal number system along the way). For example, Table 1.4 presents the information you need to perform direct conversions between binary and octal representations. If you need to convert from octal to binary, you can simply replace each octal digit with the corresponding binary pattern shown in Table 1.4. The inverse conversion is performed by partitioning the binary representation into groups of three digits, starting from the right. (You may need to add leading zeros to the representation to ensure that the leftmost group has three digits.) You can then replace every group of three binary digits with the corresponding octal digit shown in Table 1.4.

Table 1.4   Binary and octal

Binary	Octal
000	0
001	1
010	2
011	3
100	4
101	5
110	6
111	7

Example 1.5   *Convert 1704_8 into binary.*

$$1704_8 = 001\ 111\ 000\ 100_2 = 1111000100_2$$

Example 1.6   *Convert 11010100001_2 into octal.*

$$11010100001_2 = 011\ 010\ 100\ 001_2 = 3241_8$$

Conversions between binary and hexadecimal are also simple. Table 1.5 presents the information you need to perform these conversions.

Table 1.5   Binary and hexadecimal

Binary	Hex	Binary	Hex	Binary	Hex	Binary	Hex
0000	0	0100	4	1000	8	1100	C
0001	1	0101	5	1001	9	1101	D
0010	2	0110	6	1010	A	1110	E
0011	3	0111	7	1011	B	1111	F

Example 1.7   *Convert $1BF_{16}$ into binary.*

$$1BF_{16} = 0001\ 1011\ 1111_2 = 110111111_2$$

Example 1.8   *Convert 11010100001_2 into hexadecimal.*

$$11010100001_2 = 0110\ 1010\ 0001_2 = 6A1_{16}$$

1.1.6 Fractional Values

Positional number systems can also be used to represent fractional values. Fractional values are expressed by writing digits to the right of a *radix point*. You may   Radix point
be used to calling this symbol a decimal point because you are most familiar with
the decimal number system. Digits written after the radix point represent smaller
and smaller powers of the radix, starting with -1. In other words,

$$.d_1 d_2 d_3 \ldots d_n$$

represents the value

$$d_1 \cdot r^{-1} + d_2 \cdot r^{-2} + d_3 \cdot r^{-3} + \cdots + d_n \cdot r^{-n}$$

For example,

$$.782 = 7 \cdot 10^{-1} + 8 \cdot 10^{-2} + 2 \cdot 10^{-3} = 7/10 + 8/100 + 2/1000$$

To convert a fractional representation from any number system into decimal,
you simply carry out the arithmetic.

Example 1.9   *Convert $.662_8$ into decimal.*

$$.662_8 = 6/8 + 6/64 + 2/512$$
$$= .75 + .09375 + .00390625$$
$$= .84765625$$

The inverse conversion is not nearly as simple. You could "carry out the arithmetic." However, the arithmetic must be performed in the target number system.
As was the case for whole numbers, there is an easier algorithm. We introduce
this algorithm by considering a simple example.

Example 1.10   *Convert .6640625 into octal.*

If you multiply .6640625 by 8 you will get 5.3125, that is,

$$.6640625 = .6640625 \cdot \frac{8}{8} = \frac{5.3125}{8} = 5/8 + \frac{.3125}{8}$$

In this manner, you have determined the most significant digit in the octal representation. Continuing in this fashion results in the following derivation:

$$.6640625 = .6640625 \cdot \frac{8}{8}$$
$$= \frac{5.3125}{8}$$
$$= 5/8 + \frac{.3125}{8}$$
$$= 5/8 + \frac{.3125}{8} \cdot \frac{8}{8}$$
$$= 5/8 + \frac{2.5}{8^2}$$
$$= 5/8 + 2/8^2 + \frac{.5}{8^2}$$
$$= 5/8 + 2/8^2 + \frac{.5}{8^2} \cdot \frac{8}{8}$$
$$= 5/8 + 2/8^2 + \frac{4.0}{8^3}$$
$$= 5/8 + 2/8^2 + 4/8^3$$
$$= .524_8$$

In principle, the algorithm is simple. You start by multiplying the fraction by the radix of the target number system. The integer part that results from the multiplication is the next digit of the result. The fractional part remains to be converted.

Example 1.11   *Convert .3154296875 into hexadecimal.*

Step	Multiplication	Result
1	$0.3154296875 \cdot 16 = 5.046875$	$.5_{16}$
2	$.046875 \cdot 16 = 0.75$	$.50_{16}$
3	$.75 \cdot 16 = 12$	$.50C_{16}$ ($12_{10} = C_{16}$)

While the algorithm is simple, it may never terminate. If the algorithm does not terminate, it will result in a number followed by a repeating sequence of digits.

When this happens, we use a bar over a sequence of digits to indicate that the sequence repeats.

Example 1.12 *Convert .975 into octal.*

Step	Multiplication	Result
1	$.975 \cdot 8 = 7.8$	$.7_8$
2	$.8 \cdot 8 = 6.4$	$.76_8$
3	$.4 \cdot 8 = 3.2$	$.763_8$
4	$.2 \cdot 8 = 1.6$	$.7631_8$
5	$.6 \cdot 8 = 4.8$	$.76314_8$

After step 5, we will repeat the multiplications shown in steps 2 through 5. Each repetition of these steps will add the sequence of digits 6314 to the end of the octal representation. As such, the result is:

$$.975 = .7\overline{6314}_8$$

You can combine whole numbers and fractional numbers by concatenating their representations. The concatenation represents the sum of the whole value and the fractional value. For example, 34.78 represents $34 + .78$. You may have noticed that we used this fact when we developed the algorithm for converting a decimal fraction into another number system.

1.2 ENCODING NUMBERS

In Chapters 7 and 8, we will consider the issues related to strategies for encoding integers in detail. In this section, we limit our consideration to three simple encoding strategies: signed magnitude, binary-coded decimal, and 2's complement.

A simple encoding technique for signed integers involves using 1 bit for the sign followed by the binary representation of the magnitude. We will use 0 as the *sign bit* for nonnegative values and 1 as the sign bit for negative values. We call this encoding technique *signed magnitude* because it encodes the sign of the number and the magnitude of the number separately.

Sign bit

Signed magnitude

Example 1.13 *Give the signed magnitude representation for 23.*

010111

Notice that we did not use a subscript in writing the representation. This is a representation, not a number in the binary number system!

Example 1.14   *Give the signed magnitude representation for −23.*

110111

Binary-coded decimal (BCD) is the second encoding technique that we will consider. To construct a BCD encoding, you start with the decimal representation of the number. Given the decimal representation for a number, BCD encodes each digit using its 4-bit binary representation. Table 1.6 presents the encoding used for each digit. In examining this table, notice that each digit is encoded in 4 bits. Because there are only 10 digits in the decimal number system and 16 different patterns consisting of 4 bits, there are 6 patterns that are not used to encode digits (1010, 1011, 1100, 1101, 1110, and 1111). We use one of these patterns, 1010, to encode the plus sign and another, 1011, to encode the minus sign. Positive numbers do not need to have an explicit plus sign; therefore, our encoding for the plus sign is not strictly necessary. It is only included for completeness.

Table 1.6   Encodings used in BCD

Digit	Encoding	Symbol	Encoding
0	0000	+	1010
1	0001	−	1011
2	0010		
3	0011		
4	0100		
5	0101		
6	0110		
7	0111		
8	1000		
9	1001		

Example 1.15   *Give the BCD encoding for 23.*

0010 0011

Example 1.16   *Give the BCD encoding for −23.*

1011 0010 0011

Example 1.17   *Give the value represented by the BCD encoding 1001 0111.*

97

The signed magnitude encoding for a number is usually shorter than the BCD encoding for the same number. The primary advantage of the BCD encoding scheme is that it is easy to convert between a BCD encoding and a decimal representation.

Most digital computers use a technique called 2's complement to encode signed integer values. This encoding scheme is actually a family of encodings. Every 2's complement encoding uses a fixed number of bits. Different members of the family use different numbers of bits to encode values. For example, there is an 8-bit 2's complement encoding that uses 8 bits to encode values. Because the number of bits is fixed by the encoding, not every integer value can be encoded by a 2's complement encoding. For example, only the values from -128 to 127 (inclusive) can be encoded using the 8-bit 2's complement encoding.

In this discussion we will use n to denote the number of bits used to encode values. The n-bit 2's complement encoding can only encode values in the range -2^{n-1} to $2^{n-1} - 1$ (inclusive). Nonnegative numbers in the range 0 to $2^{n-1} - 1$ are encoded by their n-bit binary representation. A negative number, x, in the range -2^{n-1} to -1 is encoded as the binary representation of $2^n + x$. (Notice that $2^n + x$ must be between $2^n - 1$ and 2^{n-1} because x is between -1 and -2^{n-1}.)

Example 1.18 *Give the 8-bit 2's complement representation of 14.*

Because 14 is nonnegative, we use the 8-bit binary representation of 14, that is,

$$00001110$$

Example 1.19 *Give the 8-bit 2's complement representation of -14.*

Because -14 is negative, we use the 8-bit binary representation of $2^8 - 14$, which is $256 - 14$, which is 242, that is,

$$11110010$$

We will consider 2's complement encoding in much more detail in Chapter 7. However, there are three aspects of the 2's complement representation that we should note before leaving this discussion.

First, given an encoded value, the leftmost bit of the encoded value indicates whether the value is negative. If the leftmost bit is 1, the value is negative; otherwise, the value is nonnegative. This bit is frequently called a sign bit. We should note that this sign bit is a *consequence* of the representation. In contrast, the sign bit used in the signed magnitude representation is defined by the representation.

Second, there is an easy way to negate a number in the 2's complement representation: invert the bits and add one.

Example 1.20   *Find the 8-bit 2's complement negation of 00001110.*

The encoding for 14	00001110
Invert the bits	11110001
Add 1	+1
The encoding for −14	11110010

Sign extend

Third, if you need to increase the number of bits used in the 2's complement representation of a number, you can replicate the sign bit in the higher order bits. This operation is called *sign extend*.

Example 1.21   *Convert the following patterns from 4-bit 2's complement to 8-bit 2's complement representations using the* sign extend *operation: 1010, 0011.*

1010	→	11111010
0011	→	00000011

1.3 CHARACTER ENCODINGS

Characters are the symbols that we use in written communication. Because we use so many symbols and we can easily create new symbols, machines cannot provide a direct representation for every character that we use. Instead, each machine provides representations for a limited set of characters called the *character set* of the machine. In the early days of computing, different manufacturers devised and used different character sets. Now, almost every manufacturer uses the ASCII character set. ASCII is an acronym that stands for American Standard Code for Information Interchange. We begin this section by considering the ASCII character set. Then we consider another encoding technique, Huffman encoding. Huffman encoding can be used to reduce the number of bits needed in the representation of long sequences of characters.

Character set

Before we consider the issues related to character encodings, we need to introduce a bit of terminology. As we have noted, an *encoding* is a symbolic representation based on the binary alphabet, that is, a sequence of 1's and 0's. The *length* of an encoding is the number of bits in the encoding. For example, the encoding 01100 has a length of five. A *code* is a set of encodings. For example, the set { 110, 001, 101, 011 } is a code that has four encodings. Because each encoding has the same length, this is a *fixed-length code*. *Variable-length codes* have encodings with different lengths.

Encoding

Length

Code

Fixed-length code

Variable-length code

1.3.1 ASCII

Table 1.7 presents the ASCII character set with the encoding for each symbol. ASCII is an example of a fixed-length code with a code length of seven. When we refer to the bits in the representation of a character, we number the bits from right to left. For example, the representation of "B" is 100 0010; therefore, the first bit in the representation is 0, the second is 1, the third is 0, and so forth.

There are two subsets in the ASCII character set: the control characters and the printable characters. The *control characters* include the first 32 characters and the last character (delete). The remaining characters are the *printable characters*.

Control character

Printable character

You can generate the printable characters by typing the appropriate keys on most computer keyboards. You can generate the control characters by holding down the control key while typing a single character. Table 1.7 shows the keystroke needed to generate each control character using a two-symbol sequence: the caret symbol (^) followed by the symbol for the key. You should read the caret symbols as "control." For example, you should read the sequence ^C as "control C."

All of the printable characters (except the space character) have graphical symbols associated with them. In contrast, the control characters are not associated with graphical symbols. These characters are not intended for display. Instead, they are used to control devices and the communication between devices. For example, there is a control character that can be used to acknowledge the receipt of a message (ACK), another that can be used to cancel the transmission of a message (CAN), and another that can be used to separate records (RS) during the transfer of a file.

There are several control characters that you should become familiar with. The bell character (^G) will usually cause a terminal to beep (audible bell) or blink (visual bell). The backspace character (^H) is used to back up one character, that is, move one character to the left. The horizontal tab character (^I) is used to move to the next tab stop. The line feed character (^J) is used to move down one line. The carriage return character (^M) is used to return to the beginning of the line.

In examining the encodings for the printable characters, there are several aspects of the ASCII encoding that are worth noting. First, notice that the last 4 bits of the encoding for each digit (0–9) are the binary representation of the digit. This aspect of the encoding is useful if you ever need to convert sequences of decimal digits into binary. In addition, notice that the upper- and lowercase letters only differ in the 6th bit position. For example, the encoding of "K" is 100 1011, while the encoding of "k" is 110 1011.

Because modern memory systems provide access to 8-bit storage units, you will usually use 8 bits to store characters. When you store an ASCII character using 8 bits, the leftmost bit is set to zero. The designers of the IBM PC knew they were going to store character representations using 8 bits. Rather than waste a bit in every character, they decided to use the 8th bit to extend the ASCII character set. In this extended character set, the 8th bit of the standard ASCII characters is set to 0, and the extended characters have their 8th bit set to 1. The new characters

Table 1.7 The ASCII character set

Binary	Name	Key	Meaning	Binary	Name	Key	Meaning
000 0000	NUL	^@	NULl	001 0000	DLE	^P	Data Link Escape
000 0001	SOH	^A	Start Of Header	001 0001	DC1	^Q	Device Control 1
000 0010	STX	^B	Start of TeXt	001 0010	DC1	^R	Device Control 2
000 0011	ETX	^C	End of TeXt	001 0011	DC1	^S	Device Control 3
000 0100	EOT	^D	End Of Trans.	001 0100	DC1	^T	Device Control 4
000 0101	ENQ	^E	ENQuire	001 0101	NAK	^U	Negative ACK
000 0110	ACK	^F	ACKnowledge	001 0110	SYN	^V	SYNchronize
000 0111	BEL	^G	BELl	001 0111	ETB	^W	End of Trans. Block
000 1000	BS	^H	BackSpace	001 1000	CAN	^X	CANcel
000 1001	HT	^I	Horizontal Tab	001 1001	EM	^Y	End of Medium
000 1010	LF	^J	Line Feed	001 1010	SUB	^Z	SUBstitute
000 1011	VT	^K	Vertical Tab	001 1011	ESC	^[	ESCape
000 1100	FF	^L	Form Feed	001 1100	FS	^\	File Separator
000 1101	CR	^M	Carriage Return	001 1101	GS	^]	Group Separator
000 1110	SO	^N	Shift Out	001 1110	RS	^^	Record Separator
000 1111	SI	^O	Shift In	001 1111	US	^_	Unit Separator

Binary	Symbol	Binary	Symbol	Binary	Symbol	Binary	Symbol
010 0000	space	011 1000	8	100 1111	O	110 0111	g
010 0001	!	011 1001	9	101 0000	P	110 1000	h
010 0010	"			101 0001	Q	110 1001	i
010 0011	#	011 1010	:	101 0010	R	110 1010	j
010 0100	$	011 1011	;	101 0011	S	110 1011	k
010 0101	%	011 1100	<	101 0100	T	110 1100	l
010 0110	&	011 1101	=	101 0101	U	110 1101	m
010 0111	'	011 1110	>	101 0110	V	110 1110	n
010 1000	(	011 1111	?	101 0111	W	110 1111	o
010 1001	)	100 0000	@	101 1000	X	111 0000	p
010 1010	*			101 1001	Y	111 0001	q
010 1011	+			101 1010	Z	111 0010	r
010 1100	,	100 0001	A			111 0011	s
010 1101	–	100 0010	B	101 1011	[	111 0100	t
010 1110	.	100 0011	C	101 1100	\	111 0101	u
010 1111	/	100 0100	D	101 1101	]	111 0110	v
		100 0101	E	101 1110	^	111 0111	w
		100 0110	F	101 1111	_	111 1000	x
011 0000	0	100 0111	G	110 0000	`	111 1001	y
011 0001	1	100 1000	H			111 1010	z
011 0010	2	100 1001	I	110 0001	a		
011 0011	3	100 1010	J	110 0010	b	111 1011	{
011 0100	4	100 1011	K	110 0011	c	111 1100	|
011 0101	5	100 1100	L	110 0100	d	111 1101	}
011 0110	6	100 1101	M	110 0101	e	111 1110	~
011 0111	7	100 1110	N	110 0110	f	111 1111	delete

include graphical characters that can be used to draw simple graphical objects, and some symbols from the Greek alphabet.

Because ASCII is a fixed-length code, it is easy to decode sequences of encoded characters. You begin by breaking the sequence into subsequences consisting of 7 bits. Then you match each subsequence to a character using Table 1.7.

Example 1.22   *Decode the ASCII string 1001000110010111011001101111.*

Step 1. Break the string into 7-bit subsequences

1001000	1100101	1101100	1101100	1101111

Step 2. Decode each subsequence

1001000	1100101	1101100	1101100	1101111
H	e	l	l	o

1.3.2 Huffman Codes

While the fixed-length aspect of the ASCII code is an advantage in decoding, it is a disadvantage when you need to transmit long sequences of characters. Fixed-length codes do not reflect the frequency of character usage. To illustrate the advantage of a variable-length code, we consider a simple example.

Example 1.23   *The following table presents a fixed-length code and a variable-length code for the symbols α, β, γ, and δ. How many bits will it take to encode the message $\alpha\alpha\alpha\beta\alpha\beta\gamma$ using each of these codes?*

Symbol	Fixed length	Variable length
α	00	1
β	01	01
γ	10	001
δ	11	000

Using the fixed-length code, $\alpha\alpha\alpha\beta\alpha\beta\gamma$ will be encoded as 00 00 00 01 00 01 10, which uses 14 bits.

Using the variable-length code, $\alpha\alpha\alpha\beta\alpha\beta\gamma$ will be encoded as 1 1 1 01 1 01 001, which only uses 11 bits.

An important characterization for a variable-length code is the expected code length. The *expected code length (ecl)* is the sum of the lengths of the encodings

Expected code length (ecl)

Expected frequency

in a code weighted by the expected frequency for the encoding. The *expected frequency* for an encoding is expressed as a fraction of the total uses of all encodings in the code. Figure 1.1 presents a formula for calculating the expected code length.

$$ecl = \sum_{l \in C} freq(l) \cdot length(l)$$

Notes:

C	The code
freq(l)	The expected frequency of the letter l
length(l)	The length of the encoding for l

Figure 1.1   Expected code length

Example 1.24   *Suppose that 50% of the characters that you send are α, 25% are β, 15% are γ, and 10% are δ. Calculate the expected code length for the variable-length code presented in Example 1.23.*

$$ecl = .50 \cdot 1 + .25 \cdot 2 + .15 \cdot 3 + .10 \cdot 3$$
$$= .50 + .50 + .45 + .30$$
$$= 1.75$$

Therefore, we expect to use 1.75 bits to encode a character.

Given our definition of the expected code length, it makes sense to ask if a code has the minimum expected code length. Before we consider this question, we need to introduce an important property: the prefix property. Variable-length codes complicate the decoding process because it is not as easy to determine where the encoding for one character ends and the next one begins. In codes that have the prefix property, the encoding for one symbol is not the prefix for the encoding of another symbol. Codes that have the prefix property are called *prefix codes*. Messages encoded using a prefix code can be decoded using a left-to-right scan of the encoded message. Thus, when you recognize the encoding of a character, you know you have recognized that character. You do not need to be concerned that the bits may be the prefix for another encoding. The variable-length code presented in Example 1.23 is an example of a prefix code.

Prefix code

Decode tree

A *decode tree* is a binary tree that can be used to simplify the decoding process for messages encoded using a prefix code. Every node in a decode tree is either a leaf (with no children), or it has two children. We label the leaves of a decode tree with the characters in the character set. We use the symbol "1" to label the arcs that connect a parent to its left child and "0" to label the arcs that connect a parent to its right child. Given a decode tree, you can read encoding for a character by reading the arc labels on the path from the root to the leaf labeled by the character.

Example 1.25 *Show the decode tree for the variable-length code presented in Example 1.23.*

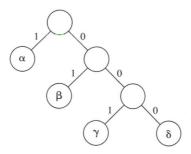

To decode a message using a decode tree, you need to keep a pointer into the tree. Initially, this pointer points to the root of the tree. The decoding process examines the message one bit at a time. On each iteration, the next bit of the message is used to advance the tree pointer—if this bit is a 1, the tree pointer is moved to the left subtree; otherwise, it is moved to the right subtree. When the tree pointer reaches a leaf, the decoding process reports the character associated with the leaf.

In the remainder of this section, we present an algorithm that constructs a prefix code with the minimum expected code length. This algorithm was developed by David Huffman; thus, codes produced by the algorithm are called Huffman codes.

Huffman's algorithm builds a decode tree. To construct the decode tree, the algorithm maintains a set of binary trees (a forest). With each iteration, the algorithm removes two trees and adds a new one. The algorithm terminates when only one tree remains in the set.

The set of binary trees is initialized with a simple tree for each character in the alphabet. Each tree has a single node that is labeled by the expected frequency of the character. With each iteration, the algorithm removes two trees with the smallest labels. These trees are replaced by a new tree that has one tree as its left child and the other as its right child. The new tree is labeled by the sum of the labels for the trees that were removed.

Example 1.26 *The following table presents the relative frequencies of letters in the English language. Using the frequencies presented in this table, construct a Huffman code for the first six letters of the English alphabet.*

Letter	Freq.	Letter	Freq.	Letter	Freq.	Letter	Freq.	Letter	Freq.
A	.0781	G	.0139	M	.0262	S	.0646	Y	.0151
B	.0128	H	.0585	N	.0728	T	.0902	Z	.0009
C	.0293	I	.0677	O	.0821	U	.0277		
D	.0411	J	.0023	P	.0215	V	.0100		
E	.1305	K	.0042	Q	.0014	W	.0149		
F	.0288	L	.0360	R	.0664	X	.0030		

Step 0. We begin by constructing a trivial tree for each character.

Step 1. Because the trees for B and F have the smallest labels, we merge these trees.

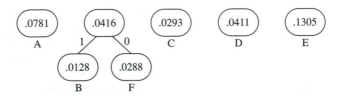

Step 2. Next, we merge the trees for C and D.

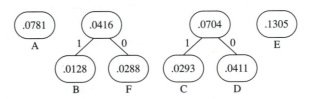

Step 3. Next, we merge the trees for (B,F) and (C,D).

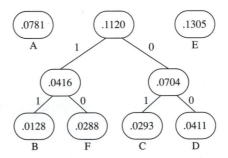

Step 4. Next, we merge the tree for A with the tree for [(B,F),(C,D)].

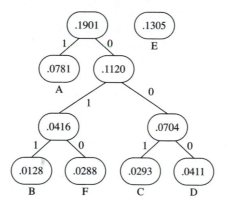

Step 5. Finally, we merge the tree for E with the tree for {A,[(B,F),(C,D)]}.

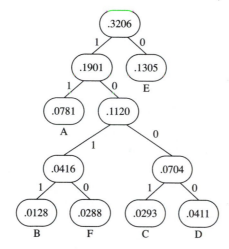

This construction results in the following code.

Symbol	Encoding
A	11
B	1011
C	1001
D	1000
E	0
F	1010

1.4 ERROR DETECTION/CORRECTION

Error detection

Error correction

Error masking

In this section, we consider the possibility that the storage or transmission of an encoded value incorrectly changes the value. In particular, we consider how you can use an error detection strategy or an error correction strategy to limit the scope of these changes. In *error detection*, the goal is to detect errors that occur. In contrast, the goal of *error correction* is to correct any errors that occur during transmission. Error correction is frequently called *error masking* because the errors that occur are not visible to any part of the system other than the receiver.

In reading this section, it is important to note that any technique used to detect or correct errors may miss an error. The best we can do is to reduce the likelihood that an error escapes detection or correction.

Bit flip

To simplify the presentation, we limit our consideration to fixed-length codes. Given this restriction, we only consider errors that change individual bits. In particular, we ignore the possibility that transmission errors insert or delete bits. Changes to bits are frequently called *bit flips* because the change flips the bit from 0 to 1 or from 1 to 0.

Example 1.27 *Suppose that you send the ASCII encoding for the character "S" (101 0011). Show the different values that a receiver will receive if a single bit is flipped during transmission.*

Bit flipped	Received pattern	Received symbol
none	101 0011	S
0	101 0010	R
1	101 0001	Q
2	101 0111	W
3	101 1011	[
4	100 0011	C
5	110 0011	c
6	001 0011	^S

Hamming distance

Before we present error detection/correction techniques, we need to introduce a simple metric, Hamming distance. Named for its inventor, Richard Hamming, the *Hamming distance* defines a distance between two encodings of the same length. To compute the Hamming distance between two encodings, you count the number of bits in the first encoding that need to be changed to result in the second encoding.

Example 1.28   *What is the Hamming distance between 101 1001 and 101 1010?*

To convert the first pattern to the second, we need to change the first and second bits in the first pattern. As such, the Hamming distance between the two patterns is 2.

We generalize the Hamming distance to a code by considering the elements of the code in a pairwise fashion. Given a fixed-length code, the Hamming distance for the code is the minimum Hamming distance between any two encodings in the code.

Example 1.29   *What is the Hamming distance of the following code?*

$$\{ 1010, 1101, 0110 \}$$

$$dist\,(1010, 1101) = 3$$
$$dist\,(1010, 0110) = 2$$
$$dist\,(1101, 0110) = 3$$

As such, the Hamming distance is 2.

The Hamming distance for a code reflects the degree of redundancy in the code. A code with a Hamming distance of one lacks redundancy. If a code has a Hamming distance of two, changing a single bit in any of the encodings will result in a bit pattern that is not in the code. Thus, when the Hamming distance of a code is two, you can decide if an error introduced a single bit flip.

Parity provides a simple way to ensure that the Hamming distance of a code is at least two. The *parity* of a binary pattern is determined by counting the number of 1's in the pattern. If the number of 1's is even, the pattern has *even parity*; otherwise, the pattern has *odd parity*.

Parity

Even parity

Odd parity

Example 1.30   *What is the parity of the pattern 101 0011?*

Because the pattern has 4 1's, it has even parity.

If every encoding in a code has the same parity (either even or odd), the code must have a Hamming distance of at least two. In particular, if you flip a single bit in an encoding, the number of 1's in the encoding will increase or decrease by one. This will change the parity of the encoding.

Parity bit

To ensure that every encoding has the same parity, we add a bit, called the *parity bit*, to each encoding. Given an encoding, we set the parity bit to 1 or 0 to make sure that the resulting bit pattern has the desired parity. When we add a parity bit to the ASCII code, the parity bit is the 8th bit in the encoding.

Example 1.31   *Show even and odd parity bits for the ASCII encodings of the decimal digits.*

Symbol	ASCII	Even parity	Odd parity
0	011 0000	0011 0000	1011 0000
1	011 0001	1011 0001	0011 0001
2	011 0010	1011 0010	0011 0010
3	011 0011	0011 0011	1011 0011
4	011 0100	1011 0100	0011 0100
5	011 0101	0011 0101	1011 0101
6	011 0110	0011 0110	1011 0110
7	011 0111	1011 0111	0011 0111
8	011 1000	1011 1000	0011 1000
9	011 1001	0011 1001	1011 1001

The sender and receiver must agree on the type of parity (even or odd) when they use this technique to detect errors. Before sending a message, the sender computes the parity bit. The sender sends the message and the parity bit to the receiver. The receiver checks the parity of any message it receives. If the parity is wrong, the receiver announces that it has detected an error. Otherwise, the receiver discards the parity bit and uses the remaining bits as the body of the message.

It is important to note that a parity bit only enables the detection of errors that result from changing a single bit. If an error changes an even number of bits, the resulting bit pattern will have the expected parity. In this case, the receiver will not detect the error. Moreover, when a receiver detects an error, a simple parity bit does not provide enough information to decide which bit was changed. In other words, the simple parity scheme provides us with enough information to detect simple errors, but not enough to correct them.

Two-dimensional parity

Data block

Horizontal parity bit

Longitudinal parity bit

We can use a simple two-dimensional parity scheme to support error correction. In *two-dimensional parity,* we encode each message as a two-dimensional bit pattern. We call this bit pattern the *data block*. To support error correction, we add a parity bit to each row and each column. We call the parity bits for the rows *horizontal parity bits* and the parity bits for the columns *longitudinal parity bits*. Figure 1.2 illustrates two-dimensional (even) parity for a simple message.

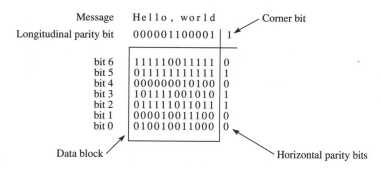

Figure 1.2   Two-dimensional (even) parity

In addition to the data block and vertical and longitudinal parity bits, Figure 1.2 also includes a "corner bit." This bit does not check any of the bits in the data block; instead it checks the parity bits. Here it is worth noting that a single bit can be used to affect the parity of two different sets of bits (the longitudinal parity bits and the vertical parity bits).

To see how this two-dimensional parity scheme can be used to detect and correct errors, suppose that a single bit in the data block changes. When this happens, the parity for the row and the column of the changed bit will be incorrect. Because the row and column identify a unique bit in the data block, we can correct the error.

As was the case for simple parity, our two-dimensional error correction scheme is only guaranteed to work for single-bit errors. If two bits in the same column (or row) are changed, the parity for the column (or row) will be correct. As such, the receiver will not be able to decide which bits in the data block were changed. Notice that the receiver will be able to detect the error but will not be able to correct it. In practice, the receiver can frequently correct more than one error. If the changed bits do not share a common row or column, the receiver will be able to detect and correct the changed bits.

Our two-dimensional parity scheme is frequently called vertical redundancy check/longitudinal redundancy check (*VRC/LRC*). This scheme is also associated   VRC/LRC with the phrase "detect 2, correct 1" because it can detect any 2-bit error and can correct any 1-bit error.

If the data block has m rows and n columns, our two-dimensional parity scheme uses $m + n + 1$ parity bits. Richard Hamming devised an error correction scheme that only requires $\lceil \log_2(n + m + 1) \rceil$ parity bits. The main advantage that Hamming's scheme introduces is that every combination of parity bits identifies a unique bit in the data block. Our two-dimensional scheme has redundancy because a pair of horizontal (or vertical) parity bits does not identify a single bit in the data block.

There are several issues related to error detection and correction that we have not addressed in this brief overview. An important issue that we have ignored involves the selection of data block sizes, that is, the number of bits in a data block. In general, it is reasonable to assume that the probability of errors increases as the size of the data block increases. Because we have only considered single-bit errors, we must ensure that the data block size is small enough that the probability of 2 bits changing is acceptably small. Determining this probability requires a detailed model of the communication system and is beyond the scope of this discussion.

Another issue that we have ignored is the possibility of error correction and detection with a variable-length code. When we use a variable-length code, we cannot easily dismiss the possibility that bits are inserted or deleted during the transmission. As such, devising techniques to deal with errors is far more complicated. Many communication systems avoid the problems associated with variable-length codes by dividing each message into fixed-length units called *packets*. Because packets are fixed length, we can use the techniques that we have discussed.

Packets

1.5 SUMMARY

Our goal in this text is to explore the principles that underlie the design and implementation of digital computers. In this chapter, we have introduced one of the most fundamental issues—data representation. Data is anything that needs to be manipulated. For example, in rearranging the furniture in your apartment, the furniture is the data. Data representation involves identifying which properties should be emphasized and which should be ignored. Given a physical object, there are several representations that can be used to represent the object. Selection of the appropriate representation must be based on the manipulations that will be performed on the representation.

There are two important terms that we have introduced in this chapter: representation and encoding. As we have noted, a representation is an abstraction of an object that emphasizes some properties of the object and de-emphasizes or ignores others. Representations can be constructed from anything: words, equations, photographs, paper cutouts, and so forth. Symbolic representations are representations that are constructed from an alphabet, that is, a fixed set of symbols. Encodings are symbolic representations constructed from the binary alphabet (the symbols "0" and "1"). In other words, every encoding is a symbolic representation. As such, we can refer to 2's complement as an encoding scheme or a representation scheme. To make matters a bit more confusing, we frequently use the term "encode" as a verb, meaning the act of constructing the encoded value for an object.

In a practical sense, we have introduced three important topics in this chapter: 2's complement representation, ASCII encoding, and parity bits. We will return to these topics several times throughout the remainder of this text. In addition to these topics, we discussed basic number systems and Huffman codes. These topics were introduced to provide necessary background and to provide contrasts to the primary topics.

We discussed number systems to provide the background needed to understand number encodings. Numbers are such an integral part of our lives that we frequently take their representation and manipulation for granted. It is easy to believe that the base 10 positional number system is the only representation for numbers and that the addition, subtraction, multiplication, and division algorithms that we use are the only possible algorithms. Historically, positional number systems did not evolve until there was a need to represent very large numbers.

We discussed Huffman codes as a contrast to ASCII encoding. Huffman codes are variable-length codes that are motivated by the desire to minimize the number of bits that need to be transmitted when sending a message.

We concluded this discussion by considering an important aspect of encodings. Many different encodings may result in the same string of bits. For example, the string 1010101 could be the result of encoding the character "U" using the ASCII encoding, or the result of encoding -43 using the 7-bit 2's complement encoding, or the result of encoding -21 using the signed magnitude representation.

1.5.1 Additional Reading

If you are interested in learning more about number systems, you should consult books that cover the history of mathematics. Among these books I recommend *An Introduction to the History of Mathematics* by Eves (Holt, Rinehart & Winston, 1969).

Huffman codes are covered in virtually every text on data structures. Among these presentations, I recommend the presentations in *Structure and Interpretation of Computer Programs* by Abelson and Sussman (McGraw-Hill, 1985) and *Fundamental Algorithms* by Knuth (Addison-Wesley, 1973).

Error detection and recovery techniques are typically covered in books that cover computer organization and books that cover computer networks. If you are looking for a more in-depth coverage of Hamming codes, I recommend the presentation in *Structured Computer Organization* by Tanenbaum (Prentice Hall, 1990, 1984, 1976).

1.5.2 Terminology

- Abstract, Abstraction
- Representation, Symbolic representation, Encoding, Alphabet
- Stick numbers, Unit symbol, Grouping symbol, Roman numerals, Subtractive rule
- Positional number system, Radix, Base, Digit, Bit
- Least significant digit, Most significant digit
- Radix point, Decimal point
- Signed magnitude, Binary-coded decimal (BCD), 2's complement
- Character set
- Fixed-length encoding, Variable-length encoding
- Control characters, Printable characters
- Expected code length
- Prefix property, Decode tree
- Error detection, Error correction, Hamming distance

- Bit flip
- Parity, Even parity, Odd parity
- Two-dimensional parity, Horizontal parity, Vertical parity

1.5.3 Review Questions

1. What is an abstraction?
2. What is an alphabet?
3. What is the difference between a representation and an encoding?
4. What is the difference between a unit symbol and a grouping symbol?
5. What is a digit?
6. What is the most significant bit? What is the least significant bit?
7. What is a sign bit?
8. Why is the signed magnitude encoding called signed magnitude?
9. Why is the binary-coded decimal encoding called binary-coded decimal?
10. What is a code?
11. What are control characters used for?
12. What is the primary advantage of a fixed-length code?
13. What is the primary disadvantage of a fixed-length code?
14. What is the prefix property?
15. What is the primary motivation for Huffman codes?
16. How is a decode tree used?
17. What is the difference between error detection and error correction?
18. How is the parity for a string of bits computed?
19. What is a parity bit?
20. Given two binary strings with the same length, how is the Hamming distance for the two strings computed?
21. Given two fixed-length codes with the same lengths, how is the Hamming distance for the codes computed?

1.6 EXERCISES

1. Describe three different representations for each of the following objects. For each of these representations, describe when the representation might be useful.

    a. A house plant.

    b. An automobile.

    c. An employee.

    d. A student.

2. For each of the following operations, give an algorithm (pseudocode) that describes how to implement the operation on stick numbers. In writing these algorithms, you may use simple operations involving sticks and sets (e.g., create an empty set called X, add a stick to the set called Z, remove a stick from the set called Y, test to see if the set called X is empty, and so forth). You should assume that you have an infinite supply of sticks.

   The first three operations result in a stick number, while the last operation results in the value *true* or the value *false*.

   a. Addition.

   b. Multiplication.

   c. Subtraction (you may assume that the first stick number is larger than the second).

   d. The relational operation $>$.

3. In discussing simple grouping systems, we noted that our rule requiring the use of larger grouping symbols whenever possible would result in a representation with the fewest number of symbols. Using mathematical induction, prove that this rule minimizes the number of coins needed when using the American coin system.

4. Using roman numerals, give the representation for 1994:

   a. Without using the subtractive rule.

   b. Using the subtractive rule.

5. Repeat the previous exercise for 1944.

6. Explain why it would not make sense to have the combined symbol VX in the roman numeral system.

7. For each of the following strings, if the string is a valid roman numeral, give the decimal representation for the roman numeral; otherwise, explain why it is not a valid roman numeral.

   a. IXIV.

   b. XIVI.

   c. ILC.

   d. XXXIC.

8. Write an addition table for the

   a. Octal number system.

   b. Hexadecimal number system.

9. Write a multiplication table for the

   a. Octal number system.

   b. Hexadecimal number system.

10. Convert each of the following numbers into decimal:

   a. 101_2, 101_8, 101_{16}.

     b. 457_8, 234_8, 701_8.

     c. AF_{16}, $C1D_{16}$, $2FB_{16}$.

11. Convert each of the following numbers into binary:

     a.   876, 924, 1023.

     b. 724_8, 640_8.

     c. $D3A_{16}$, $A7B_{16}$.

12. Convert the following numbers into octal:

     a. 110101011_2.

     b. 10110011_2.

13. Convert the following numbers into hexadecimal:

     a. 10101011_2.

     b. 100110011_2.

14. Convert the following numbers into decimal:

     a. 10.011_2, 1.101_2, $.010_2$.

     b. 2.7_8, 1.23_8.

     c. 1.2_{16}, $D.E1_{16}$.

15. Convert the following decimal values into binary:

     a.   7.25.

     b.   8.55.

     c.   9.23.

     d.   7.65.

16. Give the signed magnitude representation for each of the following values:

     a.   43, -12, 13.

     b. -27, 25, -2.

17. Give the BCD representation for each of the following values:

     a.   43, -12, 13.

     b. -27, 25, -2.

18. Give the 8-bit 2's complement representation for each of the following values:

     a.   43, -12, 13.

     b. -27, 25, -2.

19. For each of the following bit patterns, identify the integer value that would be encoded into this bit pattern using the 8-bit 2's complement representation:

     a.   00110011.

     b.   00010111.

     c.   10000010.

d. 10101010.

e. 11111111.

20. Decode each of the following ASCII messages; that is, give a symbolic version for each of these messages using the English alphabet:

a. 11101001100101111100111110100.

b. 11001101110101110111001111111.

21. In considering Table 1.7 (on page 18) note that the control keys are denoted using uppercase letters, for example ^B. Because you do not have to hold down the SHIFT and CONTROL keys to type a control character, it might seem that it would be better to use the lowercase letters to denote the control characters, for example ^b. Explain why you think the uppercase characters are used.

22. Compute the expected code length for the code presented in Example 1.26 (starting on page 21).

23. For each set of letters, construct a Huffman code using the frequencies presented in Example 1.26 (starting on page 21). In presenting your answer, show the tree that results from Huffman's algorithm as well as the encoding for each letter.

a. { E, F, G, H }.

b. { E, F, G, H, I, J }.

c. { L, C, F, U, M, P, Y, W }.

d. { E, T, Z, Q, U, M }.

24. For each pair of encodings, give the Hamming distance:

a. 10011, 11001.

b. 00101, 11011.

c. 11100, 00001.

25. In defining the Hamming distance for a code, we chose to use the minimum (Hamming) distance between any two encodings in the code. Explain why it would not be better to use the maximum or average distance.

26. For each of the following codes, give the Hamming distance of the code:

a. { 0001, 1001, 0101, 1110 }.

b. { 11100, 00011, 01010, 10101, 11011 }.

c. { 01010, 10101, 11111, 00000, 00110 }.

27. For each of the following codes, add a parity bit to the code. The parity bit should be the leftmost bit in each of the encodings and should be used to ensure that each encoding has even parity:

a. { 110, 010, 011, 111 }.

b. { 1010, 0111, 1110, 1011, 0011 }.

c. { 0011, 1010, 1100, 0000, 1111, 0101 }.

28.   Give a list of all of the binary patterns of length 5 that have even parity.

29.   Suppose you have to devise a code with even parity in which every encoding is n bits. What is the maximum number of distinct encodings that you can have in your code?

30.   Suppose you are working with a particularly unreliable system in which 1 or 2 bits frequently get flipped in the transmission of a 7-bit ASCII character. Your friend suggests that you add 2 "parity" bits to the encoding for each character. In this scheme, the first 7 bits are used for the ASCII character while the last 2 bits ensure that the number of 1's is a multiple of 3. Give an example that illustrates why this scheme will not work.

31.   For each of the following messages, construct the ASCII encoding with two-dimensional even parity:

   a.   Test.

   b.   soda.

   c.   Sam I am.

32.   Each of the following blocks contains a (short) message that was encoded using ASCII and two-dimensional even parity. Moreover, each message has had 1 bit altered during transmission. Identify the bit that was altered during transmission. (Do not attempt to decode these messages, they are meaningless.)

   a.   1010 0011
         0010 0101
         0110 0011
         1110 0001

   b.   1010 0011
         1010 0101
         0010 0011
         0110 0101

   c.   1010 0011
         1010 0101
         1110 0011
         0110 0101

33.   In considering our two-dimensional parity scheme, explain why the vertical and longitudinal parity bits must have the same parity. (Hint: Every possible data block can be generated by starting from the pattern that is all 0's and selectively setting bits to 1. You should consider a proof by induction on the number of 1's in the data block.)

LOGIC DESIGN

CHAPTER 2

In this chapter, we consider the techniques that are commonly used to describe the most fundamental operations of a digital computer. We begin by considering simple combinational circuits—circuits in which the output is completely determined by the input values. In the second section, we consider sequential circuits. In contrast to combinational circuits, sequential circuits have memory. As such, the outputs produced by sequential circuits can be determined by previous input values as well as the current input values.

2.1 COMBINATIONAL CIRCUITS

We begin our study of logic design by introducing combinational circuits. Combinational circuits are an important technique used to describe the implementation of digital computers. A combinational circuit maps a set of binary inputs to a set of binary outputs. We frequently use the term *signal* to refer to the input or output of a combinational circuit.   Signal

The fundamental property of combinational circuits is that the outputs constantly reflect the inputs. Whenever the input values change, the output values reflect the new input values after a short delay. We call this the *propagation delay* because   Propagation delay it represents the time it takes for an input signal to propagate through the circuit.

Combinational circuits are purely functional, the output values are completely determined by the input values. Combinational circuits do not have any state and cannot alter their behavior based on previous inputs.

You can specify the behavior of a simple function with binary inputs and binary outputs using a table. If the function has n inputs, the table used to specify its behavior will have 2^n rows. Each row specifies the output for a different combination of input values.

Example 2.1   *Use a table to specify the behavior of a function that tests for even parity. Your function should have four binary inputs and produce a single binary output. The output*

should be 1 whenever an even number of the inputs are 1; otherwise, it should be 0. (A receiver might use this function to test the parity of the values it receives.)

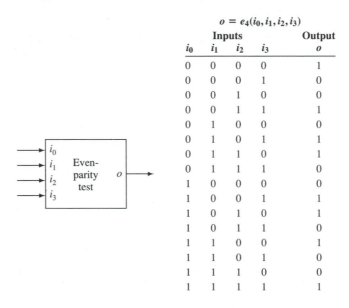

$$o = e_4(i_0, i_1, i_2, i_3)$$

Inputs				Output
i_0	i_1	i_2	i_3	o
0	0	0	0	1
0	0	0	1	0
0	0	1	0	0
0	0	1	1	1
0	1	0	0	0
0	1	0	1	1
0	1	1	0	1
0	1	1	1	0
1	0	0	0	0
1	0	0	1	1
1	0	1	0	1
1	0	1	1	0
1	1	0	0	1
1	1	0	1	0
1	1	1	0	0
1	1	1	1	1

In addition to the table, we present a graphical representation for the function.

Graphical Convention
When we illustrate a function (as in Example 2.1), we use a box to represent the function. We represent inputs to the function by arrows pointing to the box and outputs by an arrow pointing out from the box. Labels for the inputs and outputs are usually written inside the box.

While tabular descriptions are adequate for expressing the behavior of simple functions, this description technique has two significant drawbacks. First, when functions have more than a few inputs, the tables become very large. For example, a function with 10 inputs would require a table with 1,024 lines (over 10 pages)! Second, the tabular approach does not provide any way to determine the costs associated with a function. In this text, we measure costs in terms of time and space.

Function composition   We can avoid the first problem (the size of the table) by using *function composition*. Function composition uses the outputs of one function as the inputs of other functions.

Example 2.2 *Show how the four-input even-parity test can be implemented using the two-input even-parity test and function composition.*

$$e_4(i_0, i_1, i_2, i_3) = e_2(e_2(i_0, i_1), e_2(i_2, i_3))$$

The following circuit diagram presents a graphical illustration of this solution:

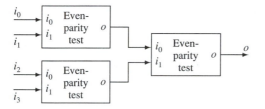

Inputs		Output
i_0	i_1	o
0	0	1
0	1	0
1	0	0
1	1	1

$o = e_2(i_0, i_1)$

Graphical Convention

The graphical representation shown in Example 2.2 is a *circuit diagram*. Circuit diagrams are a graphical tool used to illustrate function composition. In a circuit diagram, directed line segments connect the outputs of functions to the inputs of other functions. In concept, the arcs illustrate the paths that signals follow. In this text, we use directed arcs to show the direction that a signal travels. This convention is common but not universal.

Function composition also provides us with a foundation for measuring costs. For example, our implementation of the four-input even-parity function uses three instances of the two-input parity function. Moreover, this implementation requires twice as much time to update its outputs as the two-input parity function.

2.1.1 Gates and Boolean Expressions

Saying that our implementation of the four-input even-parity function requires three instances of the two-input even-parity function is comparable to saying that one farble is equal to two frobats. It tells us something about the relationship between the two objects, but it does not tell us how these objects relate to other objects. If we are going to make meaningful statements about the costs associated with the implementation of a function, we need a basic unit of measurement.

In logic design, we measure both time and space in *gates*. Gates are simple Boolean functions that can be used to construct more complex functions. Each

Gate

gate requires roughly the same amount of space and the same amount of time for propagation delay when implemented in hardware.[1]

We use four basic gates in this text: *and, or, xor* (exclusive or), and *not* (complement). Table 2.1 presents these gates. Notice that we use tables to specify the functions implemented by these gates.

Table 2.1 Simple gates

Operation name	Graphical symbol	Function implemented			Boolean expression
		x	y	z	
and		0	0	0	$z = x \cdot y$
		0	1	0	
		1	0	0	
		1	1	1	
		x	y	z	
or		0	0	0	$z = x + y$
		0	1	1	
		1	0	1	
		1	1	1	
		x	y	z	
xor		0	0	0	$z = x \oplus y$
		0	1	1	
		1	0	1	
		1	1	0	
		x		z	
not		0		1	$z = \bar{x}$
		1		0	

It is common to interpret the value "1" as the logical value *true* and the value "0" as the logical value *false*. Given these interpretations, gates reflect the operations used in logical expressions. For example, the *and* gate only produces an output of 1 (true) when both of its inputs are 1 (true); otherwise, this gate produces an output of 0 (false). This relation to logical expressions is the source of the term *logic design*.

Logic design

Boolean expression

Table 2.1 also presents a *Boolean expression* for each gate. In terms of expressive power, Boolean expressions are equivalent to circuit diagrams. In other words, every circuit diagram constructed using the gates shown in Table 2.1 has an equivalent set of Boolean expressions and vice versa. Circuit diagrams are

---

[1] The *xor* function requires much more space than the other gates. For this reason, some people do not consider this function to be a simple gate. Also, the *not* function is much simpler than the other gates. We will not count *not* gates in our calculations.

graphical representations and are generally easier to read and understand. Boolean expressions are algebraic representations and are easier to manipulate and analyze. For example, we can simplify Boolean expressions using standard algebraic manipulations. Moreover, we can use simple algebraic manipulations to decide if two Boolean expressions are equivalent. You need to become familiar with both representations. In the remainder of this text, we will use the representation technique that best suits our needs. In the remainder of the section, we will use both techniques to describe the functions that we present.

Example 2.3 *Show how to use the gates presented in Table 2.1 to implement the four-input even-parity test.*

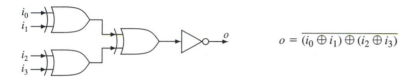

$$o = \overline{(i_0 \oplus i_1) \oplus (i_2 \oplus i_3)}$$

Two observations provide the basis for this implementation. First, the *xor* function is equivalent to the two-input odd-parity test. Second, even parity is the complement of odd parity. (It may take you a while to convince yourself that this implementation is indeed correct.)

This implementation uses four gates (three *xor* gates and one *not* gate). It will generate an output after three gate delays (two *xor* delays and one *not* delay).

Example 2.4 *Give an alternative implementation of the four-input even-parity function.*

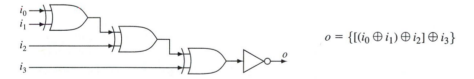

$$o = \overline{\{[(i_0 \oplus i_1) \oplus i_2] \oplus i_3\}}$$

Like the earlier implementation, this implementation uses four gates (three *xor* gates and a *not* gate). However, this implementation requires four gate delays to produce an output (three *xor* delays and one *not* delay). With this analysis, we conclude that this implementation is not as good as the previous implementation.

You can use a table to determine the function that a circuit diagram implements. If the circuit has *n* inputs, the table will have 2^n rows. Each row represents a different combination of the input values. The table has a column for every input signal and a column for each gate used in the circuit. The values in the gate columns reflect the output of the gate given the combination of input values determined by the row.

Example 2.5   *Using a table, prove that the circuit diagram presented in Example 2.3 implements the four-input even-parity test.*

The following table shows that the circuit produces the input/output (I/O) behavior specified in Example 2.1. The first four columns in the table enumerate the possible combinations of input values. The next three columns present the outputs produced by each *xor* gate. The next to the last column presents the output produced by the *not* gate. The last column presents the value of the four-input even-parity function. Notice that the last two columns are identical.

i_0	i_1	i_2	i_3	$t_0 = i_0 \oplus i_1$	$t_1 = i_2 \oplus i_3$	$t_2 = t_0 \oplus t_1$	$\overline{t_2}$	$e_4(i_0, i_1, i_2, i_3)$
0	0	0	0	0	0	0	1	1
0	0	0	1	0	1	1	0	0
0	0	1	0	0	1	1	0	0
0	0	1	1	0	0	0	1	1
0	1	0	0	1	0	1	0	0
0	1	0	1	1	1	0	1	1
0	1	1	0	1	1	0	1	1
0	1	1	1	1	0	1	0	0
1	0	0	0	1	0	1	0	0
1	0	0	1	1	1	0	1	1
1	0	1	0	1	1	0	1	1
1	0	1	1	1	0	1	0	0
1	1	0	0	0	0	0	1	1
1	1	0	1	0	1	1	0	0
1	1	1	0	0	1	1	0	0
1	1	1	1	0	0	0	1	1

So far, we have used the four-input even-parity test to motivate our discussion. While this is a useful function, it may seem a bit artificial. To correct this situation, we conclude our introduction of the simple gates by presenting a circuit that implements binary addition. We begin by introducing the half adder. A *half adder* is a function that takes two inputs and produces two outputs. The two outputs reflect the sum of the two inputs.

Half adder

Example 2.6   *Design a circuit that implements a half adder.*

In the following circuit, the c (carry) output reflects the most significant bit of the sum, while the z output reflects the least significant bit of the sum.

$$c = x \cdot y$$
$$z = x \oplus y$$

Inputs		Outputs	
x	y	c	z
0	0	0	0
0	1	0	1
1	0	0	1
1	1	1	0

Graphical Convention

In examining the circuit shown in Example 2.6, note that both of the input signals go to both of the gates. We use a black dot over the intersection of two arcs to show that both arcs carry the same signal. Frequently, arcs that carry different values need to cross. In some cases, a small break in one arc indicates that the arcs carry different signals. However, the absence of a black dot is sufficient to indicate that the two lines carry independent signals.

A half adder only performs half the job needed in a true binary addition. A *full adder* needs to accept a *carry-in* input along with the two input values.

Full adder
Carry-in

Example 2.7   *Design a circuit that implements a full adder.*

The following circuit implements a full adder using two half adders and an *or* gate. One half adder adds two of the inputs, x and y. The other half adder adds the least significant bit of this addition with the carry input, c_i. If either of the half adders generates a carry-out, the full adder generates a carry-out.

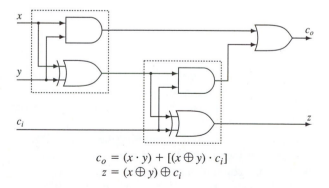

$$c_o = (x \cdot y) + [(x \oplus y) \cdot c_i]$$
$$z = (x \oplus y) \oplus c_i$$

2.1.2 Negation and Universal Gates

The need to negate values arises frequently and the explicit use of *not* gates is cumbersome. For these reasons, a shorthand notation has evolved that is comparable to the use of contractions in the English language. In this shorthand, a bubble (open circle) can be placed on the input or output of any of the simple gates (*and*, *or*, or *xor*). When present, the bubble negates the value entering or leaving the gate. These bubbles are called *negation bubbles* or *inversion bubbles*.

Negation bubbles

Inversion bubbles

In counting gates and gate delays, we count gates with bubbles as simple gates. In other words, there is no cost associated with negating a value.

Three of the gates that use negation bubbles are used so frequently that they have special names: *nand* (not and), *nor* (not or), and *equiv* (not xor). Table 2.2 presents these gates.

Table 2.2   Negating gate outputs

Operation name	Graphical symbol	Function implemented			Boolean expression
		x	y	z	
nand		0	0	1	$z = \overline{x \cdot y}$
		0	1	1	
		1	0	1	
		1	1	0	
		x	y	z	
nor		0	0	1	$z = \overline{x + y}$
		0	1	0	
		1	0	0	
		1	1	0	
		x	y	z	
equiv		0	0	1	$z = x \equiv y$
		0	1	0	
		1	0	0	
		1	1	1	

Note that our symbol for the *not* gate has a negation bubble on its output (see Table 2.1). Removing the negation bubble results in a *buffer*. Buffers do not alter the value of their input signals, but they do introduce a slight propagation delay.

Buffer

In some circuits, buffers are used to amplify the signal. The need to amplify signals is a practical consideration. Discussion of the situations that require amplification is beyond the scope of this text.

The *nand* and *nor* gates are of particular interest for two reasons. From an implementation perspective, they are of interest because they have simple implementations using transistors (see section 2.1.5). From the perspective of descriptions, these gates are of interest because they are universal. In other words, any circuit implemented using the simple gates can be implemented using only *nand* gates or only *nor* gates.

Example 2.8 *Show how to implement the* not, or, and *and functions using only* nand *gates.*

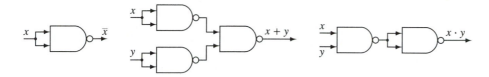

2.1.3 Generalized *and* and *or* Gates

Table 2.3 presents generalized forms of the basic *and* and *or* gates. These gates accept several inputs and produce a single output. The generalized *and* gate produces 1 if all of its inputs are 1; otherwise, it produces 0. The generalized *or* gate produces 1 if any of its inputs is 1; otherwise, it produces 0.

Table 2.3 Generalized gates

Operation name	Graphical symbol	Boolean expression
and	y_n ... y_1 y_0 → x	$x = y_0 \cdot y_1 \cdot \cdots \cdot y_n$
or	y_n ... y_1 y_0 → x	$x = y_0 + y_1 + \cdots + y_n$

The propagation delay introduced by a generalized gate is the same as the delay introduced by a basic gate. However, the space required by a generalized gate is directly proportional to the number of inputs. For example, an *or* gate with four inputs requires twice as much space as a simple *or* gate with two inputs.

Example 2.9   *Using the generalized gates, design a circuit that implements a full adder.*

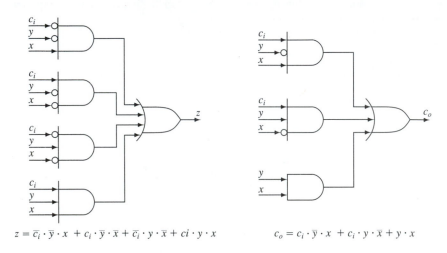

$$z = \overline{c_i} \cdot \overline{y} \cdot x + c_i \cdot \overline{y} \cdot \overline{x} + \overline{c_i} \cdot y \cdot \overline{x} + ci \cdot y \cdot x$$

$$c_o = c_i \cdot \overline{y} \cdot x + c_i \cdot y \cdot \overline{x} + y \cdot x$$

Example 2.9 presents an alternate implementation of the full adder shown in Example 2.7. Our earlier implementation uses five gates (two *xor* gates, two *and* gates, and one *or* gate) and requires three gate delays to produce the c_o output. The newer implementation only requires two gate delays to produce valid outputs. However, this implementation uses the space of approximately 13 simple gates (count the number of gate inputs and divide by 2).

This simple example illustrates a trade-off between time and space. The first implementation is slower than the second but does not use as much space. The trade-off between time and space is perhaps the most fundamental problem in computing. This type of trade-off is frequently called a "cost-performance trade-off" because you can trade a cost (space) for performance (time).

You may notice that we have omitted parentheses in the Boolean expressions shown in Example 2.9. In omitting these parentheses we are relying on the *precedence and associativity* of · and +. In Boolean expressions, · has precedence over +. Moreover, both · and + are associative; therefore, expressions involving only one of these operators can be evaluated in any order.

Precedence and associativity

2.1.4 Boolean Algebra and Normal Forms

If you study the circuits shown in Examples 2.7 and 2.9 long enough, you can convince yourself that both circuits implement the same function. If the circuits are just a bit more complicated, it may be very difficult to convince yourself that two different circuits implement the same function. To remove any nagging doubts, you need to prove to yourself that two circuits really do implement the same function.

As we have already discussed, you can use a table to prove that two circuits have the same I/O behavior. However, table construction is tedious and error prone. It is usually easier if you start with the Boolean expressions for the two circuits and use algebraic transformations to demonstrate that these expressions are equivalent. Table 2.4 summarizes the identities that we use from Boolean algebra. These identities are easy to prove using the tabular approach.

Table 2.4 Identities from Boolean algebra

And	Or	Law
$1 \cdot x = x, x \cdot 1 = x$	$0 + x = x, x + 0 = x$	Identity
$0 \cdot x = 0, x \cdot 0 = 0$	$1 + x = 1, x + 1 = 1$	Null (zero)
$x \cdot x = x$	$x + x = x$	Idempotent
$x \cdot \bar{x} = 0, \bar{x} \cdot x = 0$	$x + \bar{x} = 1, \bar{x} + x = 1$	Complement
$x \cdot y = y \cdot x$	$x + y = y + x$	Commutative
$x \cdot (y \cdot z) = (x \cdot y) \cdot z$	$x + (y + z) = (x + y) + z$	Associative
$x + (y \cdot z) = (x + y) \cdot (x + z)$	$x \cdot (y + z) = x \cdot y + x \cdot z$	Distributive
$\overline{x \cdot y} = \bar{x} + \bar{y}$	$\overline{x + y} = \bar{x} \cdot \bar{y}$	De Morgan
$x \cdot (x + y) = x$	$x + x \cdot y = x$	Absorption
	$\bar{\bar{x}} = x$	Double negative
	$x \oplus y = \bar{x} \cdot y + x \cdot \bar{y}$	Definition of $\oplus$
	$x \equiv y = x \cdot y + \bar{x} \cdot \bar{y}$	Definition of $\equiv$

In examining Table 2.4, notice that the identities have two forms: an *and* form and an *or* form. To transform the *and* form of a law to its *or* form, simply replace every 1 with a 0, every 0 with a 1, every $\cdot$ with a +, and every + with $\cdot$. This relationship is called *duality*.

Duality

Example 2.10 *Using the identities presented in Table 2.4, show that the circuits presented in Examples 2.7 and 2.9 produce the same value for c_o.*

$c_o = x \cdot y + (x \oplus y) \cdot c_i$	Example 2.7
$= (x \oplus y) \cdot c_i + x \cdot y$	Commutative law
$= (x \oplus y) \cdot c_i + y \cdot x$	Commutative law
$= c_i \cdot (x \oplus y) + y \cdot x$	Commutative law
$= c_i \cdot (\bar{x} \cdot y + x \cdot \bar{y}) + y \cdot x$	Definition of $\oplus$
$= c_i \cdot (x \cdot \bar{y} + \bar{x} \cdot y) + y \cdot x$	Commutative law
$= c_i \cdot (\bar{y} \cdot x + \bar{x} \cdot y) + y \cdot x$	Commutative law
$= c_i \cdot (\bar{y} \cdot x + y \cdot \bar{x}) + y \cdot x$	Commutative law
$= c_i \cdot \bar{y} \cdot x + c_i \cdot y \cdot \bar{x} + y \cdot x$	Distributive law

Disjunctive normal
form

Terms

Factors

Sum of products

Conjunctive normal
form

Product of sums

Fan-out problem

The final expression in Example 2.10 is an example of an expression in *disjunctive normal form*. Expressions in disjunctive normal form contain *terms* that are or'ed together. There are three terms in the final expression of Example 2.10: $c_i \cdot \overline{y} \cdot x$, $c_i \cdot y \cdot \overline{x}$, and $y \cdot x$. Each term contains *factors* that are and'ed together. There are three factors in the first term: c_i, $\overline{y}$, and x. Finally, each factor is a simple variable (e.g., c_i) or the negation of a simple variable (e.g., $\overline{y}$).

Every Boolean expression can be written in disjunctive normal form. We frequently use the phrase *sum of products* to refer to expressions in disjunctive normal form. This terminology stems from our use of the plus symbol to denote *or* and the product symbol to denote *and*. In addition to disjunctive normal form, every Boolean expression can be written in *conjunctive normal form*. In conjunctive normal form, the expression is written as a *product of sums*.

Expressions written in disjunctive normal form have a very simple gating structure. These expressions represent a collection of *and* gates leading into a single *or* gate. Example 2.9 illustrates this structure. From this observation it may seem that every Boolean expression can be evaluated in two gate delays. To a limited extent this is true. However, there is a limit on the number of gates that can use a signal before the signal must be amplified. We call this the *fan-out problem*. (If you straighten out the signal lines leading to the different gates, they look like the ribs in a fan.)

2.1.5 Transistors

Up to this point, we have emphasized the use of combinational circuits as a tool for the description of binary functions. We conclude our coverage of combinational circuits by discussing two practical concerns: transistors and integrated circuits. We begin by considering transistors. Our goal is to motivate the accounting procedures (time and space) that we introduced earlier in this discussion.

The ability to construct a controllable switch is the basis of digital logic. In the past, mechanical relays provided the switching. In the future, we may use chemical reactions. Currently, we use electronic transistors.

Figure 2.1 presents the graphical representation of a transistor. The name transistor is a contraction of TRANsfer reSISTOR. A transistor has three points of access: the base, the collector, and the emitter. When a small, positive voltage is applied to the base, the transistor lets electrons flow from the emitter to the collector. When a zero voltage is applied to the base, the transistor acts as a resistor of infinite capacity and electrons cannot flow from the emitter to the collector. Put simply, the transistor acts as a switch that is controlled by the voltage applied to the base.

In thinking about using transistors to implements gates, it is helpful to remember that electrons flow from the ground (up) to a voltage source. In other words, voltage represents a potential to draw electrons from the ground. Things get a bit confusing because the arrow (from the base to the emitter) in the illustration of a transistor indicates the direction of current (which is the opposite direction of electron flow).

Collector

Base

Emitter

Figure 2.1   A transistor

Example 2.11   *Show how a transistor can be used to implement a* not *gate.*

+5 V

Resistor

V_o

V_i

Electrons

Ground

V_i	V_o
0 V	+5 V
+5 V	0 V

This implementation has a single input voltage, V_i, and a single output voltage, V_o. When the input voltage, V_i, is positive, electrons flow from the ground to the voltage source and the output voltage, V_o, is zero. (In this case, the resistor between the voltage source and transistor limits the current drawn through the transistor.) On the other hand, when the input voltage is zero, the transistor acts as an open circuit and the output voltage, V_o, is positive.

Example 2.12   *Show how to construct a* nor *gate using transistors.*

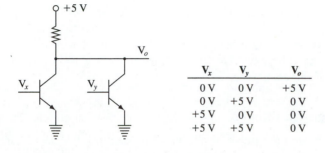

+5 V

V_o

V_x V_y

V_x	V_y	V_o
0 V	0 V	+5 V
0 V	+5 V	0 V
+5 V	0 V	0 V
+5 V	+5 V	0 V

This implementation has two inputs, V_x and V_y, and a single output, V_o. If either of the input voltages is positive, electrons flow from the ground to the voltage source and the output voltage is zero. Otherwise, there is no electron flow from the ground to the voltage source, and the output voltage is positive.

Example 2.13   *Show how to construct a* nand *gate using transistors.*

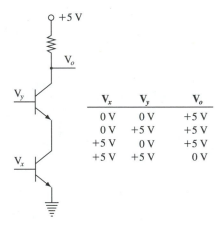

V_x	V_y	V_o
0 V	0 V	+5 V
0 V	+5 V	+5 V
+5 V	0 V	+5 V
+5 V	+5 V	0 V

As in the implementation of the *nor* gate, there are two inputs, V_x and V_y, and a single output, V_o. Here both input voltages must be positive before electrons can flow from the ground to the voltage source. Otherwise, there is no electron flow from the ground to the voltage source, and the output voltage is positive.

We can now review our basic accounting procedures. First, we note that the negated gates (*not, nand,* and *nor*) are the easiest to construct. Combining this with the fact that negation requires only one additional transistor, we have chosen to ignore the costs associated with negating the input or output of any gate. In considering the structure of the *nand* and *nor* gates, our accounting policies for the generalized gates should be more apparent.

Notice that we have not shown how to implement the *xor* or *equiv* functions. These functions require seven transistors in their implementation (more than twice as many transistors as the other gates). For this reason, some people do not consider these functions to be gates. We will continue to use *xor* and *equiv* as gates for the remainder of this text.

2.1.6 Integrated Circuits

Even if we count the number of transistors needed to implement a circuit, we still will not have a complete accounting of the costs associated with constructing a circuit. Designers do not construct circuits from individual transistors or individual gates. Instead, they use integrated circuits. An integrated circuit is a prepackaged collection of circuits or gates.

Integrated circuits are commonly called *chips* or *ICs*. The name *chip* refers to the fact that integrated circuits are constructed on a small "chip" of silicon. The failure rate limits the size of a chip. Larger pieces of silicon are more likely to have flaws and, as such, yield too many defective circuits.

Chip

IC

An IC is packaged by attaching it to a (relatively large) piece of plastic or ceramic material. Metal pins that protrude from the packaging material carry the input and output signals of the IC. This packing strategy makes it possible to "plug" an IC into a larger circuit. Figure 2.2 illustrates the packaging of an integrated circuit.

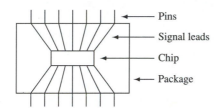

Figure 2.2 Packaging an integrated circuit

The package shown in Figure 2.2 is called a *dual in-line package (DIP)* because it has two parallel rows of pins. Many chips are packaged with a single row of pins. These packages are called *single in-line packages (SIPs)*. In addition, some chips are packaged with pins on all four sides of the packaging material. Microprocessors commonly use this packaging strategy.

Dual in-line package (DIP)

Single in-line package (SIP)

The signal leads shown in Figure 2.2 are very thin wire filaments that connect the signal pads of the IC to the pins of the package. Using current packaging techniques, the signal leads are not shielded and, as such, cannot cross. (If two signal leads touch, they must carry the same signal.) This means that the maximum number of signal leads that can be connected to an IC is directly proportional to the circumference of the IC. In contrast, the number of gates that can be placed on a chip is directly proportional to the area of the chip. Thus, the number of gates on a chip grows at a much faster rate than the number of leads used to transmit signals to and from the chip. This difference in growth rates is frequently called the *pin-limitation problem*.

Pin-limitation problem

In considering integrated circuits, we distinguish four degrees of integration: small-scale integration (SSI), medium-scale integration (MSI), large-scale integration (LSI), and very large scale integration (VLSI). Historically, SSI and MSI were introduced in the late 1960s, LSI was introduced in the early 1970s, and VLSI was introduced in the late 1970s. Table 2.5 contrasts these degrees of integration based on the number of gates in a chip.

Table 2.5 Degrees of integration

Scale of integration	Number of gates
Small	1–10
Medium	10–100
Large	100–10,000
Very large	10,000–1,000,000

The numbers given in Table 2.5 are rough approximations, and there is very little consensus about where the lines should be drawn. Our interest is not so much in the numbers but the consequences of the numbers. The pin-limitation problem implies that the complexity of the function implemented on an IC must increase as the number of gates increases. Importantly, chips with more gates are not simply more of the same thing. In the remainder of this section we consider an example of the functionality provided by each scale of integration.

SSI—*Nand* Gates   In SSI each IC implements a small collection of independent logic gates. Typically, the packages used for SSI chips have between 8 and 20 pins. One pin carries a common ground (GND) and another carries a common voltage source (V_{cc}). As an example, Figure 2.3 presents a schematic for an SSI chip with a collection of 2-input *nand* gates. This chip has four gates and 14 signal leads. Other SSI chips might provide a collection of *nand* gates or a generalized *or* gate.

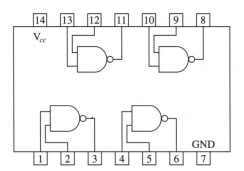

Figure 2.3   Small-scale integration

MSI—Multiplexers   In MSI each IC implements a general-purpose function. For example, a single medium-scale IC might implement a 4-bit adder. Another example of MSI is the 8-input multiplexer (MUX). Figure 2.4 illustrates an 8-input MUX. An 8-input multiplexer has 8 input lines, labeled i_0 to i_7; three select lines, labeled s_0, s_1, and s_2; and a single output line, labeled o. The select lines determine which of the input signals is mapped to the output of the multiplexer. We leave the design of a circuit that implements the multiplexer function as an exercise.

An interesting aspect of the 8-input multiplexer is that it can be used to implement any 3-input, 1-output binary function. All you need to do is set the inputs to 1 or 0, depending on the value that the function is supposed to compute. For

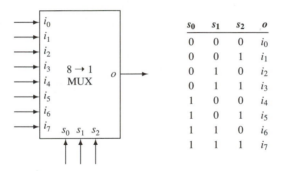

s_0	s_1	s_2	o
0	0	0	i_0
0	0	1	i_1
0	1	0	i_2
0	1	1	i_3
1	0	0	i_4
1	0	1	i_5
1	1	0	i_6
1	1	1	i_7

Figure 2.4   An 8-input multiplexer

example, if the function produces a 1 when all the inputs are 0, you should set the i_0 input of the multiplexer to 1. Using this strategy, you could implement the full adder shown in Example 2.7 using two 8-input multiplexers: one to compute the z output and another to compute the c_o output. Considering that there is a single MSI chip that adds two 4-bit numbers, this is not a particularly good way to implement a full adder. However, this may be a reasonable implementation technique for 3-input functions that do not have a more direct implementation.

LSI—Programmable Logic Arrays   We examine the structure of programmable logic arrays (PLAs) as an example of LSI. Other examples of LSI include 8-bit microprocessors and universal asynchronous receiver/transmitters (UARTs).

The observation that every Boolean expression can be written in disjunctive normal form provides the motivation for PLAs. As you will recall, the circuits for expressions written in disjunctive normal form have a simple structure: an array of *and* gates (with optional negation bubbles) leading to a single *or* gate. Example 2.9 illustrates this structure.

Figure 2.5A presents the basic structure of the gates in a programmable logic array. Starting from the lower left side of this diagram, the circuit copies and negates each input signal. This provides every factor you might need in the construction of an expression. Next, the circuit gates each of the factors into an array of *and* gates. When you program a PLA, you fix the inputs for each of the *and* gates. In particular, every input to the *and* signal leading into the *and* gates can be left in as shown or broken. Any signal that is broken is treated as a logical one. In this way, the *and* gates can provide any terms that you might need. Next, the circuit gates the terms into an array of *or* gates. Again, this gating can be selected when you program the PLA. In this case, a broken signal line is treated as logical zero. The output of each *or* gate represents a different Boolean expression.

Figure 2.5B presents an abstract representation of the PLA shown in Figure 2.5A. In this abstraction, the vertical lines on the left represent the inputs and their negations. The horizontal lines represent the *and* gates. The vertical lines on the right represent the *or* gates. We indicate selections for gate inputs by placing a black dot over the intersection of a signal and a gate.

A. The gate structure

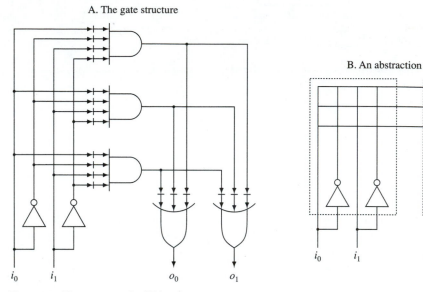

B. An abstraction

Figure 2.5   The structure of a PLA

Example 2.14   *Show how the two expressions used in a full adder can be implemented using a PLA.*

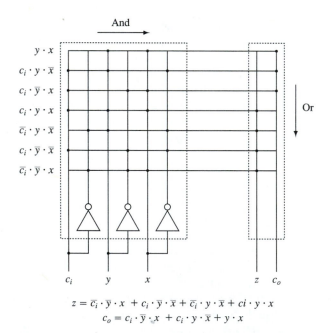

$$z = \overline{c}_i \cdot \overline{y} \cdot x + c_i \cdot \overline{y} \cdot \overline{x} + \overline{c}_i \cdot y \cdot \overline{x} + ci \cdot y \cdot x$$
$$c_o = c_i \cdot \overline{y} \cdot x + c_i \cdot y \cdot \overline{x} + y \cdot x$$

Actual PLAs are characterized by three parameters: the number of inputs, the number of outputs, and the number of *and* gates. For example, a single PLA might have 12 inputs, 6 outputs, and 50 *and* gates.

VLSI—The Microprocessor   Very large scale integration is used to implement sophisticated logic functions. For example, microprocessors and I/O controllers are frequently constructed using VLSI. We consider the structures of these devices throughout this text.

2.2 SEQUENTIAL CIRCUITS

Sequence is an important technique that we use in the description of computations. In hardware design, sequence can be used to reduce the cost of hardware while providing the same functionality. As an example, suppose that you need to add three numbers. You could design a circuit that takes the three numbers and produces the result. What if you also need to add four numbers? Each time you need to add more numbers, the circuit becomes more complex and more costly. We can avoid these problems by introducing the notion of sequence. Using sequence, we can design a circuit that adds two numbers to implement the addition of three numbers or a list of numbers.

Example 2.15   *Suppose that you know how to add two numbers. Present an algorithm that can be used to add three numbers.*

1.   Add two of the numbers.
2.   Add the third number to the result obtained in the first step.

There are two important aspects of the algorithm presented in Example 2.15. First, the algorithm has two discrete steps. Because both steps use the same adder, the first step must be completed before the second step can begin. Second, the algorithm relies on memory. You must store the result of the first step so that you can use it during the second step.

Example 2.16   *Give a graphical illustration of the algorithm presented in Example 2.15.*

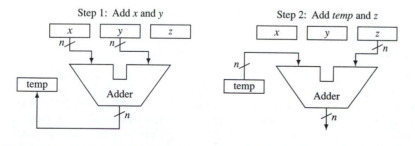

The adder shown in Example 2.16 is a combinational circuit that implements the addition function for two (binary) numbers. The box labeled *temp* represents the storage required to implement the algorithm. In the remainder of this section, we consider the hardware components needed to implement this algorithm.

Graphical Convention
When more than one signal follows the same path, we cross the path with a slash and use a number to indicate the number of signals that follow the path. Example 2.16 uses this convention. Here the paths carry *n* signals.

2.2.1 Controlling Data Paths—Tri-State Devices and Buses

In examining Example 2.16, note that we enable different data paths during different steps. In the first step, we enable the data path from the x input to the left input of the adder. In the second step, we enable the data path from temp to the left input of the adder.

Example 2.17   *Given the signals step 1 and step 2, show how you can control the left input of the adder in Example 2.16.*

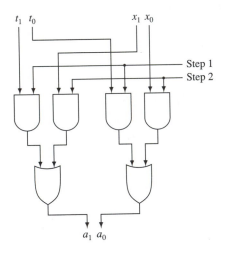

The outputs a_1 and a_0 are the inputs for the left side of the adder.

In discussing sequential circuits, we frequently distinguish two types of signals: data signals and control signals. *Data signals* represent the values manipulated by the circuit. *Control signals* control the paths taken by the data values. In our example, the two control signals, step 1 and step 2, control which data signals are sent to

Data signals

Control signals

the adder. The distinction between data signals and control signals is simply a matter of perspective. Control signals, like data signals, always have a value of 0 or 1.

The approach presented in Example 2.17 requires that all of the data signals be close together *before* gating them onto the common data path. The logical structure needed to bring all of the data signals together is awkward and complicates the logic of the circuit. The notion of a bus simplifies the logic and makes many circuits more flexible. A *bus* is a collection of data lines. Data values can be gated onto and off the bus at different points.

Bus

Implementation of a bus requires a new gate called a tri-state device. Figure 2.6 presents a graphical illustration of a tri-state device. A *tri-state device* has two inputs and a single output. One input signal is a data signal, the other is a control signal. When the control value is 1, the tri-state device acts as a simple buffer (the tri-state device does not alter the signal, but does introduces a gate delay). When the control signal is 0, the output of the tri-state devices does not produce an output signal. Instead, the tri-state device enters a high-impedance state that does not interfere with other signals on a shared bus.

Tri-state device

Control	Data in	Data out
0	0	–
0	1	–
1	0	0
1	1	1

Data in
Control
Data out

Figure 2.6 A tri-state device

Example 2.18 *Show how you can use tri-sate devices and the concept of a bus to implement the gating presented in Example 2.16.*

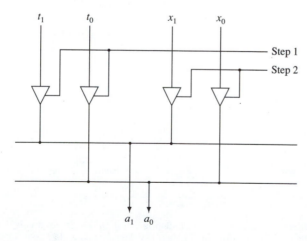

In this illustration, the two horizontal lines constitute the bus.

2.2.2 Storage—Flip-Flops and Registers

D flip-flop

Figure 2.7 A flip-flop

Edge-triggered

Latch

Level-triggered

Figure 2.8 A latch

Flip-flops are the basic storage devices used in digital circuits. There are several types of flip-flops. We limit our consideration to a particular type of flip-flop: the *D flip-flop*. Figure 2.7 presents the graphical illustration of a D flip-flop. Every D flip-flop has two inputs, labeled D and CK, and a single output, labeled Q. The label D stands for data and the label CK stands for clock. The CK signal controls the storage operation performed by the flip-flop. Whenever the CK signal changes from 0 to 1, the flip-flop stores the current value of the D input. The single output signal, Q, simply propagates the value that was most recently stored in the flip-flop.[2] It should be noted that a D flip-flop can be constructed from the simple gates that we introduced in the previous section. We will not consider this aspect of flip-flops in this text.

Flip-flops are *edge-triggered* devices. This means that the value stored in a flip-flop is only changed when the value of the CK signal changes from 0 to 1. In contrast, a *latch* is a *level-triggered* device. Figure 2.8 presents the graphical representation of a latch. A latch has two inputs, D and CK, and a single output, Q. The behavior of a latch is similar to that of a flip-flop. However, there is an important difference: The latch constantly stores the value of the D input while the CK input is 1. In other words, a latch acts as a combinational circuit while the CK signal is 1. If the value of the D signal changes while the CK signal is 1, a latch and a flip-flop produce different outputs.

Example 2.19 *Present timing diagrams to illustrate the difference between a latch and a flip-flop.*

In the following timing diagrams, the value of the D input changes from 1 to 0 while the CK input is 1. Note that the final value for the latch is 0, while the final value for the flip-flop is 1.

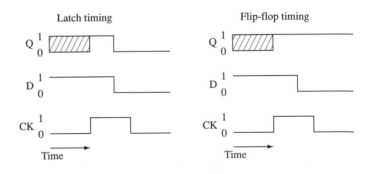

---

[2] You may wonder why the output of a D flip-flop is called Q. The D flip-flop is derived from the clocked SR flip-flop. The clocked SR flip-flop has three inputs: a clock signal called CK, a set signal called S, and a reset signal called R. The name Q seems to be based on alphabetic proximity.

Graphical Convention

The illustrations shown in Example 2.19 are called *timing diagrams*. We use timing diagrams to illustrate the relationship among the individual signals in a collection. These illustrations show how a change in the clock signal affects the Q signal.

Note that the Q signal is initially shaded. We use this type of shading to indicate that the value of a signal is not important and may be changing. The initial value of the Q signal is not important. The timing diagram emphasizes the fact that the value of this signal is fixed when the clock signal goes from 0 to 1.

Example 2.20   *Show how you can use flip-flops to implement the storage needed in Example 2.16.*

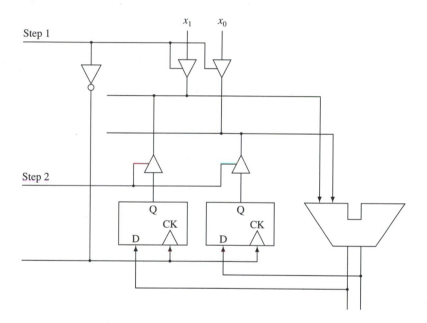

Registers   A register is a collection of flip-flops with a common control signal. The register used in Example 2.20 simply stores values. Other types of registers may take a more active role in the construction of values. For example, a shift register shifts the bits that it stores (to the left or right) every time the control signal goes from 0 to 1.

Example 2.21   *Design a 4-bit shift register that implements a right shift. Along with the clock and data inputs, your circuit should accept a* load/$\overline{\text{shift}}$ *signal. This signal controls* the activities of the shift register. When the load/$\overline{shift}$ signal is 1, the register should load a new value; otherwise, it should perform a shift.

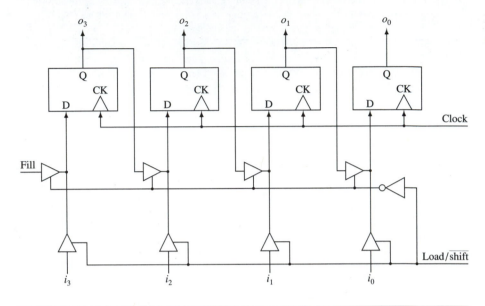

Feedback Loops   Suppose that we need to add four numbers instead of just three. We could still use the circuit presented in Example 2.20; however, we would need to add control signals for a new step, step 3. Now, at the start of step 2, we route the current value of the temp register into the adder. Moreover, we store the result of the addition into the temp register at the end of the second step. This is an example of a simple feedback loop. In a feedback loop, the output of a storage unit (flip-flop or latch) is used to determine the next value to be stored.

Example 2.22   *Using a feedback loop, design a circuit that changes its output value (a single bit) every time a clock signal changes from 0 to 1.*

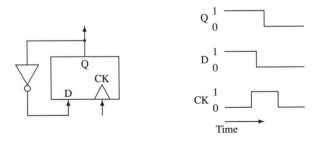

Example 2.23   *Up to this point, it may seem that there is no significant difference between flip-flops and latches; however, latches can create problems when used in feedback loops.*

The following timing diagram shows what might happen if we replace the flip-flop in the previous example by a latch. Here the clock pulse is long enough that the latch manages to invert the value of its output twice and ends with the same output.

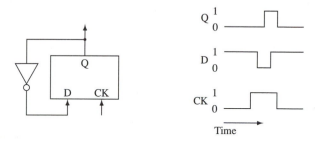

2.2.3 Control and Timing Signals

To complete our running example, we need to generate the two control signals (step 1 and step 2) used in Example 2.20. We define these control signals in terms of a common timing signal. A *timing signal* is a signal that repeats a 1 to 0, 0 to 1 transition pattern at regular intervals. The *period* of a timing signal is the length of time that it takes to repeat the pattern. The time in which the signal has a value of 1 is called a *pulse*. The *leading edge* is the 0 to 1 transition just before the pulse. Similarly the *trailing edge* is the 1 to 0 transition that follows each pulse. Figure 2.9 illustrates the terms associated with timing signals.

Timing signal

Period

Pulse

Leading edge

Trailing edge

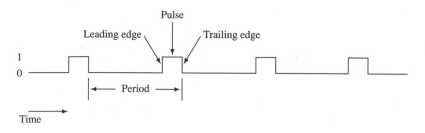

Figure 2.9   A sample timing signal

Timing signals like the one shown in Figure 2.9 are derived from crystal oscillators. Figure 2.10A illustrates the logical signal produced by a crystal oscillator. In contrast to a timing signal, the clock signal is symmetric; that is, the pulses are the same length as the time between pulses. To generate a timing signal with a shorter pulse, we can feed the basic clock signal through a circuit with a known delay resulting in the signal shown in Figure 2.10B. When the basic clock signal and the delayed clock signal are and'ed together, a timing signal results (Figure 2.10C).

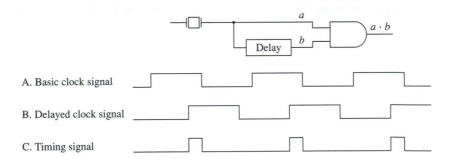

A. Basic clock signal

B. Delayed clock signal

C. Timing signal

Figure 2.10   The generation of a timing signal

As we noted earlier, we define the control signals needed for a sequential circuit in terms of a common timing signal. Each control signal is asserted for one or more periods in the timing signal. Because we have defined a period in terms of trailing edges of the timing signal, we start activities on the trailing edge of a clock pulse and store the results of these activities on the trailing edge of a later pulse. In other words, the leading edge of a control signal coincides with the trailing edge of a timing pulse, and the trailing edge of the control pulse coincides with the trailing edge of a later timing pulse. The number of timing pulses is determined by the time needed to complete the activities controlled by the control signal. Besides providing a time frame for a control signal, we can also use a common timing signal to establish a temporal relationship between different control signals.

Example 2.24   *Given a timing signal, show the relationship between the control signals step 1 and step 2 needed to complete our running example. You may assume that each control signal lasts for a single period of the timing signal.*

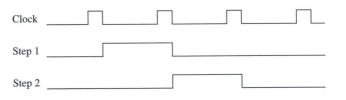

Clock

Step 1

Step 2

2.3 COMPONENTS

We conclude this chapter by discussing four types of components: multiplexers, demultiplexers, decoders, and encoders. These components represent basic building blocks frequently used in the design of more complicated circuits. In this section, we only discuss the functionality of these components; we leave their implementations as exercises.

2.3.1 Multiplexers and Demultiplexers

We introduced multiplexers as an example of medium scale integration (MSI). At that time, we pointed out that an 8-input multiplexer could be used to implement any 3-input, 1-output function. While this is true, multiplexers are more typically used to control signal routing. Figure 2.11 presents a graphical representation of a $2^n \rightarrow 1$ multiplexer (MUX). This MUX can selectively place any of its 2^n input signals onto its output signal.

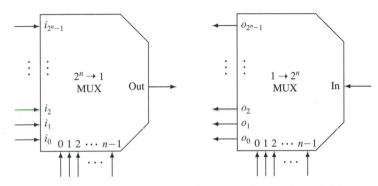

Figure 2.11   A $2^n \rightarrow 1$ multiplexer   **Figure 2.12**   A $1 \rightarrow 2^n$ (de)multiplexer

A demultiplexer performs the inverse operation of the multiplexer. These components have a single data input, n control inputs, and 2^n data outputs. The control inputs are used to select one of the data output signals. The input signal is gated to the selected output. Figure 2.12 presents a graphical representation for a demultiplexer. It is common to use the name multiplexer when referring to multiplexers or demultiplexers.

Simple (1-input) multiplexers and (1-output) demultiplexers can be combined when the data paths that need to be routed are greater than 1 bit wide. In particular, it is easy to construct a $k2^n \rightarrow k$ multiplexer from k, $2^n \rightarrow 1$ multiplexers.

2.3.2 Decoders and Encoders

An $n \rightarrow 2^n$ decoder is a combinational circuit that has n inputs and 2^n outputs. Following our standard conventions, the inputs are labeled i_0 through i_{n-1} and the outputs are labeled o_0 through o_{2^n-1}. The decoder interprets its inputs as a binary number and outputs a 1 on the output line labeled by the value of the input while setting all of the other outputs to zero.

An encoder performs the inverse operation of a decoder. Given 2^n inputs, labeled i_0 through i_{2^n-1}, an encoder produces an n-bit output, that is the binary representation of the first input with a nonzero value. If none of the inputs has a nonzero value, the output signals do not have a defined value. Figure 2.13 presents graphical representations for a decoder and an encoder.

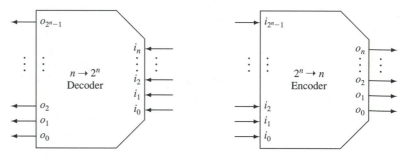

Figure 2.13   A decoder and an encoder

2.4 SUMMARY

We have covered a great deal of material in this chapter, from transistors to simple sequential circuits. We will use this material throughout the remainder of this text. In particular, you need to be comfortable with the use of the basic logic gates, tri-state devices, flip-flops, and registers before moving on to the later chapters. In addition to the logic gates, registers, and tri-state devices, we discussed Boolean expressions and algebra, transistors, and integrated circuits. Boolean algebra provides a mechanism that we can use to reason about the functions used in a digital computer. In particular, we can use Boolean algebra to determine if two circuits implement the same function. Transistors represent a basic unit of measure in evaluating the costs (both space and time) associated with a circuit. We discussed integrated circuits to present the practical considerations that must be dealt with in the construction of computing systems. In particular, we noted the pin-limitation problem. This is a fundamental problem in the implementation of computing systems. We will encounter this problem again in the next chapter when we consider memory organization.

2.4.1 Additional Reading

There are entire textbooks dedicated to the topic of logic design. It goes without saying that these books provide a much more in-depth presentation of the subject matter presented in this chapter. In addition to the books on logic design, most books on computer organization or computer architecture provide an overview of logic design.

2.4.2 Terminology

For the most part, the terminology introduced in this chapter is universal. However, there are some minor variations that you should be aware of. As we introduced flip-flops, we introduced another type of storage device called a *latch*. When the term *latch* is used as noun, it refers to the storage cell that we described. However, the term *latch* is frequently used as a verb. In these contexts, it means to store a value. For example, it is common to talk about "latching a value into a register." In addition, timing pulses are frequently referred to as *strobes* because, like the strobe on your camera, they do not have a very long duration.

- Propagation delay
- Function composition
- Gate
- Half adder, Full adder, Carry in, Carry out
- Inversion bubbles, Buffers
- Generalized gates
- Precedence and associativity
- Boolean algebra, Duality, Normal forms
- Sum of products, Disjunctive normal form
- Product of sums, Conjunctive normal form
- Fan-out
- Transistors, Base, Collector, Emitter
- Integrated circuits, ICs, Chips
- Pins, Signal leads, Package
- DIP, SIP
- Pin-limitation problem
- SSI, MSI, LSI, VLSI
- PLA
- Multiplexer, Demultiplexer, Encoder, Decoder
- Tri-state device, Bus
- Flip-flop, Latch
- Edge-triggered, Level-triggered
- Feedback loop
- Register
- Control signal, Data signal, Timing signal
- Period, Pulse
- Leading edge, Trailing edge

2.4.3 Review Questions

1. Explain the relationship between function composition and circuit diagrams.
2. What is propagation delay?
3. For each of the following gates, define the function that it implements: *and, or, xor, not, nand, nor,* and *equiv.*
4. Explain the differences between a full adder and a half adder.
5. What is an inversion bubble? Explain why we do not account for inversion bubbles when we count the time and space required for a circuit.
6. Explain what it means when we say that a gate is universal.
7. Explain why we use the number of inputs to count the size of a generalized gate but only count them as a single gate delay when counting time.
8. What is the basis of the pin-limitation problem?
9. Explain the essential difference among the different levels of integration.
10. Explain what tri-state devices are used for.
11. Explain the difference between control signals and data signals.
12. What is the difference between a latch and a flip-flop?
13. What is a feedback loop?
14. What does the term *register* mean?

2.5 EXERCISES

1. Consider the full adder shown in Example 2.7. How long will it take, in terms of gate delays, for this circuit to produce output values?
2. The following table presents the 16 binary functions that can be defined for two inputs. You should recognize f_1 (and), f_6 (xor), f_7 (or), f_8 (nand), f_9 (equiv), and f_{14}.

x	y	f_0	f_1	f_2	f_3	f_4	f_5	f_6	f_7	f_8	f_9	f_{10}	f_{11}	f_{12}	f_{13}	f_{14}	f_{15}
0	0	0	0	0	0	0	0	0	0	1	1	1	1	1	1	1	1
0	1	0	0	0	0	1	1	1	1	0	0	0	0	1	1	1	1
1	0	0	0	1	1	0	0	1	1	0	0	1	1	0	0	1	1
1	1	0	1	0	1	0	1	0	1	0	1	0	1	0	1	0	1

For each of the following functions, show how the function can be implemented using one of the simple gates with negation bubbles:

a. f_2.
b. f_4.
c. f_{11}.
d. f_{13}.

3. Suppose that you only have a collection of *or* and *not* gates. Design a circuit that implements the *and* function.

4. Using only *nand* gates, design a circuit that implements the *xor* function (it will probably be helpful to use the definition of *xor* given in Table 2.4).

5. Using only *nor* gates, design a circuit that implements the
    a. *not* function.
    b. *or* function.
    c. *and* function.

6. Construct a 4-bit adder using four full adders. Your 4-bit adder should accept a carry input labeled c_i and two 4-bit inputs labeled x_0 through x_3 and y_0 through y_3. In addition, your adder should produce a carry output labeled c_o and a 4-bit output labeled z_0 through z_3.

7. Consider the specification and implementation of a full subtractor. (In this case, the development follows the development of the full adder presented in the text.)
    a. Using a table, specify the I/O behavior of a half subtractor. This function should accept two inputs called x and y and should produce two outputs, z (the difference) and b (the borrow). The borrow is set to 1 if the subtraction needs to "borrow a one" from the next most significant bit.
    b. Using the logic gates presented in Table 2.1 and negation bubbles, design a circuit that implements the half subtractor that you specified in part *a*. Try to minimize the number of gates and the propagation delay.
    c. Using a table, specify the I/O behavior of a full subtractor. In addition to the inputs, x and y, a full subtractor accepts a borrow input, b_i. Like the half subtractor, the full subtractor produces the result, z, and a borrow output, b_o.
    d. Design a circuit that implements the full subtractor, using two half subtractors. Be certain to identify both of the half subtractors in your solution.

8. Consider the relationship between binary addition and binary subtraction.
    a. Using a table, prove that the following circuit implements a full subtractor for the expression $x - y$. (Note the similarity between this circuit and the fuller adder presented in Example 2.7.

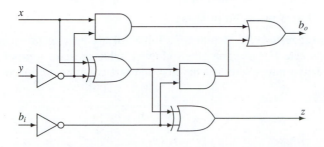

b. Suppose that you have a 4-bit binary adder as shown in the following diagram. Show how you could adapt this adder (by adding gates to the lines leading into or out of the adder) to construct a circuit that implements 4-bit binary subtraction. Note: You are not allowed to alter the internal structure of the 4-bit binary adder. (Make sure that the subtractor produces a valid borrow output.)

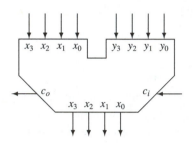

9. Consider the specification and implementation of a four-input function that counts the number of 1's in the four inputs. The inputs should be labeled x_0 through x_3 and the outputs should be labeled y_0, y_1, and y_3.

a. Using a table, specify the I/O behavior of this function.

b. Implement this function using logic gates.

10. Design a circuit that takes two 2-bit inputs and produces a 2-bit output that is the larger of the inputs when they are interpreted as binary numbers. Your inputs should be labeled x_1, x_0, y_1, and y_0, where x_1 and y_1 are most significant bits of the input values. Your outputs should be labeled z_1 and z_0 where z_1 is the most significant bit.

11. The circuits shown in Example 2.8 are really assertions. For example, the first circuit asserts that $\bar{x} = \overline{x \cdot x}$. To demonstrate that the *nand* gate is universal, you need to prove that these assertions are in fact true.

For each of the following assertions

- $\bar{x} = \overline{x \cdot x}$
- $x + y = \overline{\overline{x \cdot x} \cdot \overline{y \cdot y}}$
- $x \cdot y = \overline{\overline{x \cdot y} \cdot \overline{x \cdot y}}$

a. Prove the assertion using the tabular approach.

b. Prove the assertion using a derivation.

12. As suggested, the identities in Table 2.4 are easy to prove using the table approach. For example, the following table presents a proof of the double negative law. (Note that the first and last columns are identical.)

x	$\bar{x}$	$\bar{\bar{x}}$
0	1	0
1	0	1

Prove (all forms) of the following laws using the tabular approach:

a. Identity.

b. Null.

c. Complement.

d. Idempotent.

e. Commutative.

f. Associative.

g. Distributive.

h. De Morgan.

i. Absorption.

13. Implement the following (gate) expressions using three or fewer transistors. (Hint: You will need to use De Morgan's laws.)

a. $\bar{x} + \bar{y}$.

b. $\bar{x} \cdot \bar{y}$.

c. $\bar{x} + y$.

d. $\bar{x} \cdot y$.

14. Implement the following (gate) functions using eight or fewer transistors:

a. $x \equiv y$.

b. $x \oplus y$.

15. Implement the following (gate) functions using eight or fewer transistors:

a. $\bar{x} \equiv y$.

b. $\bar{x} \oplus y$.

16. Recall the $8 \rightarrow 1$ multiplexer shown in Figure 2.4. Design a combinational circuit that implements this function.

17. Using an $8 \rightarrow 1$ multiplexer, implement a function that computes the z output of a full adder, given the c_i, x, and y inputs.

18. Using an $8 \rightarrow 1$ multiplexer, implement a function that computes the c_o output of a full adder, given the c_i, x, and y inputs.

19. Use a PLA to implement the four-input even-parity function.

20. How many simple gates would you need to implement a PLA with 12 inputs, 50 *and* gates, and 6 outputs? Remember, the number of simple gates needed for a generalized *and* or *or* gate is the number of inputs for the gate. Show and justify each step in your calculation.

21. Design a combinational circuit that implements a $1 \rightarrow 8$ (de)multiplexer.

22. Given three $4 \rightarrow 1$ multiplexers, show how you could construct a $12 \rightarrow 3$ multiplexer, that is, a $3 \times (4 \rightarrow 1)$ multiplexer.

23. Using a collection of $4 \rightarrow 1$ multiplexers, construct a single $16 \rightarrow 1$ multiplexer.

24. Design a combinational circuit that implements a $3 \rightarrow 8$ decoder.

25. Design a combinational circuit that implements an $8 \rightarrow 3$ encoder. In designing this circuit, assume that exactly one of the inputs is 1 while the other inputs are 0.

26. Design a combinational circuit that implements modulo 8 incrementation of a 3-bit input value (in modulo 8 incrementation, $7 + 1 = 0$). Your circuit should have three inputs and three outputs.

27. Design a sequential circuit that increments a 3-bit register. Your circuit should accept two input signals, an increment/reset signal, and a control signal. Whenever the increment/reset signal is 0 on the leading edge of a pulse on the control signal, your circuit should clear the value of the register (to 0). If the increment/reset signal is 1 on the leading edge of a pulse on the control signal, your circuit should increment the value in the register.

    Your circuit should provide three output signals—the three bits of the register. In designing this circuit, assume that you have been given an incrementer meeting the specifications stated in exercise 27.

28. Design a sequential circuit that has two 3-bit registers and a single 3-bit incrementer. Your circuit should accept three inputs: an increment/reset signal, a select signal, and a control signal. If the increment/reset signal is 0 on the leading edge of a pulse on the control signal, your circuit should clear both of the 3-bit registers. The select signal is used to determine which 3-bit register is incremented. If the increment/reset signal is 1 on the leading edge of a pulse on the control signal, the 3-bit register selected by the select signal should be incremented. Assume that the select signal does not change during the increment.

    Your circuit should provide six output signals—one for the current value of each register bit. In designing this circuit, assume that you have been given an incrementer meeting the specifications stated in exercise 27.

29. Implement a model of a baseball game. In particular, implement a circuit that uses a 3-bit register to keep track of the baserunners in a baseball game. Each bit of the 3-bit register represents one of the bases. If the value of the bit is 1, there is a runner on the base; otherwise, the base is empty. In addition to the three output signals (from the register), your circuit needs to accept three input signals: a reset signal, a control signal, and a runner signal. Whenever there is a significant event in the baseball game—either an out or a runner reaches first base—your circuit will receive a pulse on the control signal. The runner signal is used to indicate whether a runner reached first base or made an out. In this simple model, runners can only reach first base (no doubles, triples, or home runs). Moreover, runners advance to the next base whenever a runner reaches first base but not when an out is scored. After every three outs, the bases should be cleared. The reset signal is used to reset the game. If the reset signal is active on the leading edge of a pulse on the control signal, the bases should be cleared and the number of outs should be set to zero.

30. Implement a set of four 3-bit registers. Your circuit should have three data inputs, three data outputs, and three control inputs. Two of the control inputs are used to select the appropriate 3-bit register—these signals should be labeled A_0 and A_1. The three data output signals should always reflect the current value of the register identified by the values of A_0 and A_1. The third control signal should be labeled *store*. Whenever the *store* signal goes through a 0 to 1 transition, the value on the data input signals should be stored into the register identified by the values of A_0 and A_1. In designing this circuit, use any components (multiplexers, decoders, encoders, and so forth) that you need.

BASIC COMPONENTS

CHAPTER 3

In this chapter, we consider the basic components used in the construction of modern computing systems. Modern digital computers are constructed from three types of components: processors, memories, and I/O devices. Memories store programs and data values. Central processing units (CPUs) interpret programs, that is, manipulate data. I/O devices provide the means by which a computing system can sense or affect its environment. The components are connected by one or more buses. Buses provide a medium for transferring values between the components.

Figure 3.1 illustrates a simple organization for a simple computing system. This organization uses two buses: a memory bus and an I/O bus. The memory bus supports transfers between the CPU and the memory. The I/O bus supports transfers between the CPU and the I/O devices.

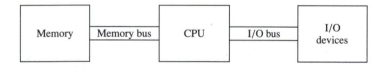

Figure 3.1   The basic components

Our goal in this chapter is to introduce the basic components. While we present a fairly thorough coverage of memory, we only introduce the CPU and I/O devices. We consider the functionality provided by the CPU in Chapters 4, 5, and 6. We consider implementation of the CPU in Chapter 9. We consider I/O devices in more depth in Chapters 11 and 12.

3.1 MEMORY

In the previous chapter, we introduced the flip-flop (and latch) as a basic unit of storage. As you will recall, a flip-flop provides one bit of storage. A register is a collection of flip-flops that share a common control signal. In this section, we discuss the organization of primary memory. In contrast to simple flip-flops and registers, primary memories provide millions of bits of storage.

3.1.1 Basic Characteristics

Primary memory is a collection of independent storage units. Each unit stores a single multi-bit value. The number of bits in a storage unit is a constant for all storage units in the memory system. We call this constant the *memory width*.

Memory width

Addresses are used to access the storage units in a memory system. Each storage unit has a unique address. Usually, the addresses for a memory system are a range of nonnegative integers starting with 0 (i.e., 0 through $n - 1$). If each storage unit holds a byte, the memory is *byte addressable* because each address identifies a byte of memory. Similarly, the term *bit addressable* refers to a memory whose width is 1.

Byte addressable

Bit addressable

Figure 3.2 presents a graphical representation for a memory with n storage units and width w. The memory shown in Figure 3.2 is called an $n \times w$ memory because it has n rows and w columns.

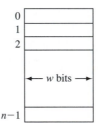

Figure 3.2 An $n \times w$ memory

At first, the choice of values used for addresses may appear to be arbitrary. After all, addresses are simply labels that identify storage units in the memory. However, viewing addresses as integers is frequently convenient. Addresses are frequently the objects of calculations. As a simple example, suppose you need to send a letter to every address in a city. If there were an effective way to enumerate all the valid addresses for a city, you could simply write a program to generate your address labels. Your task will be complicated because there is no easy way to determine which street numbers are valid.

Write

Read

Memory systems define two operations: read and write. The *write* operation stores a value in a storage unit. The *read* operation retrieves a previously stored value. The value obtained by the read operation is always the value most recently stored by the write operation. The same value may be read any number of times. Table 3.1 summarizes these operations. While we use the names read and write to denote the memory access operations, they are frequently called *fetch and store*.

Fetch and store

Table 3.1 Memory operations

Operation	Semantics
void write(mem_value v, address a);	Store the value v in the storage unit associated with address a.
mem_value read(address a);	Return the value most recently stored in the storage unit associated with address a. If no value has been stored in this unit, the result of the operation is undefined.

Some memory systems impose restrictions on the write operation. For example, *read-only memory (ROM)* does not provide a write operation. You cannot alter the values stored in ROM. *Programmable read-only memory (PROM)* imposes a slightly different restriction on the write operation. PROMs initially have the same value in every storage unit (either all 0's or all 1's). You can set the values in the units of a PROM using a PROM programmer. The process of programming a PROM is destructive, so you can only program a PROM once. In contrast to PROM, you can erase and reprogram an *erasable PROM (EPROM)*. Erasing an EPROM requires a special process (usually exposure to ultraviolet light). Like EPROM, you can erase *electrically erasable PROM (EEPROM)*. However, you do not need to remove EEPROM from the computing system to erase and reprogram its values.

Read-only memory (ROM)

Programmable read-only memory (PROM)

Erasable PROM (EPROM)

Electrically erasable PROM (EEPROM)

By now it should be clear that erasing and reprogramming an EEPROM is equivalent to writing values into the units of the memory. You may wonder then about the distinction between EEPROM and standard memory that provides both read and write operations. The essential difference is the time it takes to erase and reprogram EEPROM. In standard read/write memory, both operations take roughly the same amount of time. In EEPROMs the erase/reprogram operation may take 1,000 times as long as a read operation.

Besides the restrictions on the write operation, memory systems can be characterized by their access pattern and volatility. There are essentially two types of access patterns: sequential access and random (or direct) access. In *sequential access memories*, the memory system must be accessed sequentially. In particular, the time needed to access a storage unit depends on the address of the previous access. Magnetic tape is an example of a sequential access memory system. In a *random access memory (RAM)*, the access time for a storage unit is independent of its address. Random refers to the fact that arbitrary (random) addresses have the same access time. RAMs are often called *direct access* memories because the storage units can be accessed directly (without needing to access intermediate units).

Sequential access memories

Random access memory (RAM)

Direct access

Finally, volatility refers to the fact that some memory systems do not retain the values stored in the memory with a loss of power. A *volatile* memory system does not retain its values in the absence of power. Using current technology, most read/write memory systems are volatile, while the variations on ROM are nonvolatile. This introduces another important distinction between standard read/write memory and EEPROM.

Volatile

3.1.2 Operational Characteristics

Address port

Data port

Control port

CS (chip select)

R/$\overline{W}$ (read/not write)

Three ports provide access to the storage units in a memory system: an address port, a data port, and a control port. Figure 3.3 illustrates these ports. The value on the *address port* identifies the storage unit being accessed. We label the lines in the address port with the labels A_0 through A_{n-1} where n is the number of bits in an address. The *data port* transmits values to and from the memory subsystem. We label the lines in the data port with the labels D_0 through D_{w-1} where w is the width of the memory. The *control port* controls the operations performed by the memory subsystem. This port contains two lines: CS and R/$\overline{W}$. The *CS (chip select)* line selects the memory subsystem. When the CS line is low, the memory subsystem does not perform any operation. When the CS signal is high, the *R/$\overline{W}$ (read/not write)* line indicates the operation to be performed. A 1 indicates a read operation; 0 indicates a write operation. Figure 3.4 presents the steps performed during a read or write operation.

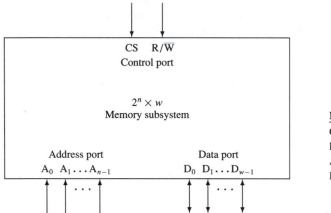

Figure 3.3   Memory ports

A.	Steps during a read operation	B.	Steps during a write operation
1.	Put the address value on $A_0 \ldots A_{n-1}$ and raise R/$\overline{W}$.	1.	Put the address value on $A_0 \ldots A_{n-1}$ and the data value on $D_0 \ldots D_{w-1}$.
2.	Raise CS.	2.	Raise CS.
3.	Wait.	3.	Wait.
4.	Read the value on $D_0 \ldots D_{w-1}$.	4.	Drop CS.
5.	Drop CS and R/$\overline{W}$.		

Figure 3.4   Steps to perform memory operations

We use two measures to characterize memory operations: access time and cycle time. *Access time* is the time from the start of a read operation until the requested value is available. *Cycle time* is the time from the start of an operation (read or write) until the next operation can begin. Cycle time may be larger than the access time when the memory system needs to perform housekeeping activities after an operation.

Access time

Cycle time

In considering access time and cycle time, we distinguish two types of memory: static RAM and dynamic RAM. *Static RAM (SRAM)* is implemented using transistors. While it has power, static RAM retains its values. In contrast, *dynamic RAM (DRAM)* is implemented using capacitors. Because capacitors slowly lose their charge, memory systems implemented using DRAM must include *refresh logic* that refreshes the capacitors regularly. Without this logic, the values stored in the memory would be lost. In addition to the refresh logic, dynamic RAMs have a complicated read operation. The basic DRAM read operation is destructive. Reading a DRAM storage cell destroys the value stored in the cell. To provide a nondestructive read operation, the DRAM system must include additional *rewrite* logic that restores the value in a storage unit whenever it is read. (Here we should note that the refresh and rewrite aspects of DRAM systems are performed "behind the scenes." Users of DRAM systems are presented with the basic *read* and *write* operations described at the beginning of this section.)

Static RAM (SRAM)

Dynamic RAM (DRAM)

Refresh logic

Static RAMs are typically faster than dynamic RAMs. Currently, static RAMs have an access time of about 20 nanoseconds while dynamic RAMs have an access time of about 80 nanoseconds. The distinction in access times is narrowing. The more significant distinctions seem to be associated with manufacturing costs and densities. Dynamic RAMs are much less expensive to manufacture, and it is possible to fit many more bits of dynamic memory on a single chip. Table 3.2 summarizes the differences between DRAM and SRAM.

Table 3.2 Dynamic versus static RAM

	Bits/chip	Access time	Cycle time	Disadvantage
DRAM	~4M	~80ns	~165ns	Refresh/rewrite logic
SRAM	~256K	~20ns	~20ns	High cost, low density

3.1.3 Memory Organization

Figure 3.5 presents a graphical representation of a dynamic memory cell. This cell stores a single bit. The cell has an input control line, S, and a bi-directional data line, D. When its S line is zero, the D line of the memory cell is in a high impedance state. In this state, the memory cell will not interfere with other signals on a common line. When its S line is 1, the memory cell goes through a two-step process. During the first step, the cell places its value on its D output. During the second step, the cell reads a new value from its D input.

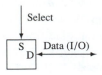

Figure 3.5 A dynamic memory cell

Example 3.1 *Give the steps needed to store a bit in a dynamic memory cell.*

1. Select the cell.
2. Wait while the cell puts its current value on the D line.
3. Put the new value on the D line.

Example 3.2 *Give the steps needed to read the bit stored in a dynamic memory cell.*

1. Select the cell.
2. Sense and store value on the D line.
3. Put the saved value on the D line.

Words

Word select lines

Bit lines

Figure 3.6 illustrates the construction of a $2^n \times 4$ memory system using dynamic memory cells. The horizontal rows of memory cells represent *words* in the memory system. We call the horizontal control lines *word select lines* because they select the word. We call the vertical lines in Figure 3.6 *bit lines* because they carry bit values between the memory cells and the sense/write logic components.

Note that several memory cells share the same bit line. If two or more of these cells try to assert a value on the bit line at the same time, the value on the bit line will be unpredictable. However, the structure of the memory ensures that only one memory cell is selected per bit line. Only this cell asserts a value on the bit line. Other cells remain in their high impedance state while the memory operation is in progress.

The sense/write logic senses the outputs of the selected memory cells during the first phase of a memory access. This logic also sets the values of the selected memory cells during the second phase. In a read operation, these components store the output values produced by the first phase and use these values to restore the cells during the second phase.

2D organization

Because the memory cells are arranged in rows and columns, we call the organization of memory cells shown in Figure 3.6 the *2D organization*. In principle, we

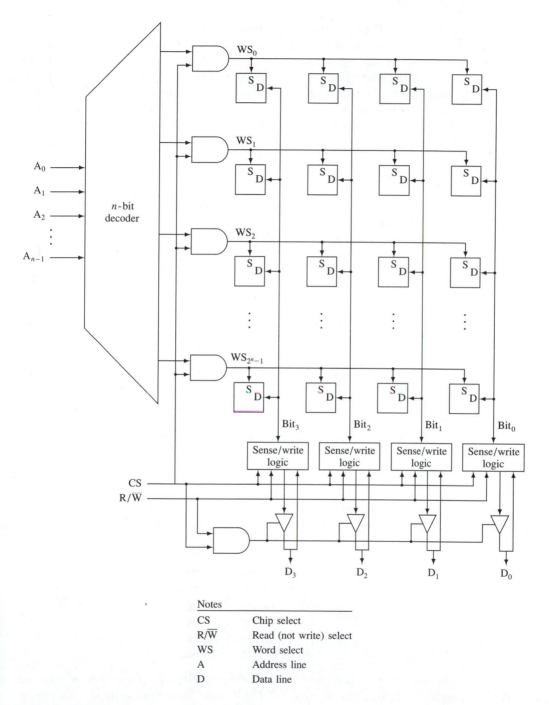

Figure 3.6 The 2D organization of a $2^n \times 4$ memory

Pin count

could use the 2D organization to implement a memory with an arbitrary number of rows and columns. However, there are two important factors that limit the applicability of this organization: the complexity of the address decoder and the *pin count*. The address decoder requires at least one *and* gate for each output line. In other words, the address decoder requires 2^n *and* gates. In terms of pin counts, the 2D organization requires $n + w + 4$ pins to implement a $2^n \times w$ memory: n pins for the address; w lines for the data; four lines for the control, voltage, and ground signals.

Example 3.3   *How many pins would you need to construct a 1024 $\times$ 8 memory using the 2D organization?*

22 pins: 10 address pins ($1024 = 2^{10}$), 8 data pins, a CS pin, an R/$\overline{\text{W}}$ pin, a ground pin, and a common voltage pin.

Table 3.3 shows the relations between the costs for implementing memories with 4 Kbits (1 K is 1024, so 4 Kbits is 4096 bits). In examining this table, note that the more closely square the memory is, the lower the cost of the decoder but the greater the number of pins. Figure 3.7 presents an organization that makes a physically square (64×64) memory appear to be rectangular (4096×1). Because the memory appears to be rectangular, the number of pins used to implement the memory is small. Because the memory is actually square, this organization minimizes the cost of the decoder. Besides the decoder, this organization uses a $1 \rightarrow 64$ MUX and a $64 \rightarrow 1$ MUX. We use these components to select the bit within the 64-bit word. The organization shown in Figure 3.7 is called a *2½ D organization*.

2½D organization

Table 3.3   Pin and decoder costs for 2D memories

Size	Address pins	Data pins	Total pins	Decoder gates
64 $\times$ 64	6	64	74	64
128 $\times$ 32	7	32	43	128
256 $\times$ 16	8	16	28	256
512 $\times$ 8	9	8	21	512
1024 $\times$ 4	10	4	18	1024
2048 $\times$ 2	11	2	17	2048
4096 $\times$ 1	12	1	17	4096

Physical word size

Logical word size

In discussing 2½D memories, we distinguish between physical word size and logical word size. The *physical word size* is the number of cells in each row of the memory. The memory shown in Figure 3.7 has a 64-bit physical word. In contrast, *logical word size* is determined by the permitted access. The memory

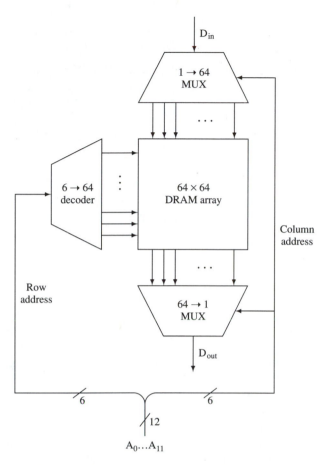

Figure 3.7 The 2½D organization of a 4096 × 1 memory

shown in Figure 3.7 only permits access to 1 bit values and, as such, has a 1-bit logical word.

While the 2½D organization offers a partial solution to the pin count problem, this solution does not extend to very large memories. Current manufacturing technology makes it possible to put up to 4 megabits on a single chip. Using the techniques that we have discussed, these chips would require at least 27 pins.[1] We can use another technique called *multiplexing* to reduce the number of pins needed to carry the address value into the chip. In multiplexing, the same pins transmit different values at different times. Multiplexing slows down memory access and cycle times but permits much higher densities of memory cells.

Multiplexing

---

[1] 22 address pins, 1 data pin, 2 control pins, and 2 common pins (one for voltage and another for ground).

Example 3.4   *Suppose that you have a $2^{20} \times 1$ memory. Explain how you could use multiplexing to reduce the number of pins needed for this memory.*

Using simple pin connections, this memory system would require 20 pins for address lines. However, if we divide the address into a row address and a column address (off chip), we only need 10 pins for address lines. Transmitting the address value to the chip becomes a two-step process. The row address is transmitted during the first step, and the column address is transmitted during the second step.

Memory systems are frequently constructed using collections of memory chips. For example, we might use sixteen 64K $\times$ 1 chips to construct a 128K $\times$ 8 memory system. We will explore this aspect of memory systems in the exercises.

3.1.4 Memory Units (Bytes and Words)

Perhaps the most important trade-off in the design of a memory system involves the determination of (logical) word size. The problem is that computations need to manipulate different types of data items. Different types of data items frequently have different size requirements for their representations. For example, a single program may need to compute the annual income of all employees and list this information by employee name in alphabetical order. In computing the annual income, the program will need to use numbers. In alphabetizing the employee names, the program will need to access the individual characters in the names of the employees.

We usually use 8 bits to store characters, while numbers frequently require 16 or more bits for their representation. If the memory subsystem provides 8-bit words, your program will need to read or write two values every time it needs to manipulate a 16-bit value. On the other hand, if the memory subsystem provides 16-bit values, you face a difficult decision—do you store characters as 16-bit values, or do you pack two 8-bit characters into a single 16-bit value? If you select the first alternative, you waste 8 bits of storage for every 8-bit value in your program. If you take the second alternative, you need to write code to pack and unpack 8-bit values into 16-bit units. This code is not difficult to write, but it will affect the speed of your program.

Memory Banks   In modern machines, the memory system typically provides access to byte (8-bit), halfword (16-bit), and word (32-bit) values. Figure 3.8 illustrates how a memory system can be organized to provide efficient access to both 8- and 16-bit values. Besides the standard control signals, this organization
Size
uses a *size* signal that indicates the size of the memory unit to manipulate (8- or 16-bit). Internally, the memory system has two memory banks. Each bank acts as an independent $2^{n-1} \times 8$ memory. Accessing a 16-bit value involves accessing an 8-bit value from each bank.

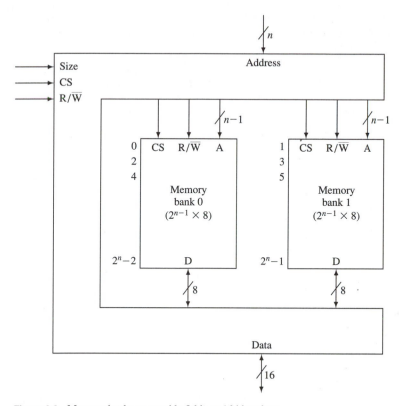

Figure 3.8 Memory banks to provide 8-bit or 16-bit values

Graphical Convention
In examining Figure 3.8, note that a component drawn in the shape of a "C" surrounds
the memory banks. This convention is useful for illustrating control components. Here
the control component can use any of the input signals to control different parts of
the memory banks. In particular, it may use the address and size signals to control
the routing of the data signals.

When discussing this organization, there are three sets of addresses that we
need to consider: the set of *global addresses* and two sets of *relative addresses*   Global addresses
(one set for each bank). The global addresses range from 0 to $2^n - 1$, while the
relative addresses for each bank range from 0 to $2^{n-1} - 1$ (Figure 3.8 only shows   Relative addresses
the global addresses). Converting a global address is straightforward. The least
significant bit of the global address identifies the bank, while the most significant
$n - 1$ bits specify the relative address.

Example 3.5   *Where would you find the 8-bit value with global address 32? The 8-bit
value with address 33?*

The 8-bit value that has global address 32 is stored in location 16 in bank 0. The 8-bit value that has global address 33 is also stored in location 16, but here the address is relative to bank 1.

Example 3.6 *Where would you find the 16-bit value with global address 48? The 16-bit value with address 63?*

The 16-bit value that has the global address 48 is stored in memory location 24 of bank 0 and location 24 of bank 1. Similarly, the 16-bit value that has the global address 63 is stored in location 31 of bank 1 and location 32 of bank 0.

Interleaved addressing

Notice that the global addresses in Figure 3.8 alternate between the two memory banks. This arrangement is called *interleaved addressing* because the addresses are interleaved between the memory banks. We could just as easily allocate the global addresses 0 through 2^{n-1} to bank 0 and addresses 2^{n-1} through $2^n - 1$ to bank 1. This might appear to simplify the memory subsystem, but would make access to 16-bit values inefficient. Recall that 16-bit values occupy adjacent memory locations. Because addresses are interleaved between the banks, all 16-bit values span both banks. Hence, interleaving means that both parts of the 16-bit value can be accessed during the same memory cycle. If we arranged the memory banks so that consecutive addresses are in the same bank, access to a 16-bit value would require two memory cycles (one for each 8-bit portion).

Suppose you request a one-byte value from memory. Will the memory system put the value on data lines D_0 through D_7 or D_8 through D_{15}? The answer may depend on the value of the address. In particular, if it is an even address, the value may end up on one set of lines, while values with odd addresses end up on another set of lines. If the memory system has a *justified* data port, it will always place byte values on the same lines (presumably D_0 through D_7).

Justified

Suppose you need to access a 16-bit value. If the value begins on an even address, the operation is straightforward. Both of the memory banks use the same relative address: the value specified on lines A_1 through A_{n-1}. Moreover, the data path simply splits between the two memory banks: bank 0 gets D_0 through D_7 and bank 1 gets D_8 through D_{15}. On the other hand, if a 16-bit value starts on an odd address, the situation is significantly more complicated. The first complication involves the fact that the address sent to the memory banks will be different. Bank 1 will still get the address specified on lines A_1 through A_{n-1}; bank 0 needs to get one plus the value specified on lines A_1 through A_{n-1}. Besides the addressing difficulties, the data lines must be "crossed." Bank 0 gets lines D_8 through D_{15}, while bank 1 gets lines D_0 through D_7. Because of these difficulties, many memory systems only permit access to 16-bit values stored at even addresses. We say these memory systems are *aligned* systems because they force 16-bit values to be aligned on even addresses.

Aligned

Byte Ordering Consider the 16 boxes shown in Figure 3.9. Suppose you are to label these boxes with the integers in the range 0–15. If I tell you that the boxes represent an array of 16 integers, which one would you label with 0? Which would you label with 15? If I change my mind and tell you that the boxes represent the bits in a 16-bit integer, would your answer change? If you're like most of us, your answer probably changes. Most of us label arrays from left to right and bits from right to left. Why does our labeling depend on the context of what we are labeling? The left-to-right labeling is undoubtedly due to the fact that we write left to right and, therefore, naturally label objects left to right. The right-to-left labeling of bits is based on powers of two. If we want to be consistent in our labeling, we should always label the boxes from left to right or right to left, independent of the context.[2]

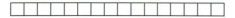

Figure 3.9 Boxes to be labeled

In a similar vein, suppose I ask you which is the first digit of 235, 2 or 5? If you are thinking about writing the number, 2 is clearly the first digit. However, if you are planning to add 235 to another number, you might consider 5 to be the first digit. After all, 5 is the first digit that you need when you perform the addition.

Well, that was an interesting digression, but what does it have to do with memory organization? If you always access memory one byte at a time, nothing. However, if you want to access bytes and words, the way that you chose to label memory is important. Suppose you have stored a two-byte (16-bit) integer at memory location 0. Is the most significant byte stored in location 0 or location 1? Before we consider this question, let us establish a simple convention—we always write numbers with the most significant part to the left. In addition, recall that addresses for multiple memory units always start with the lower numbered address. Now, the answer depends on how you choose to label memory locations. If you label the memory locations from left to right, you will store the most significant byte in location 0; that is, the most significant byte is in the lower address. On the other hand, if you label the memory locations from right to left you will store the most significant byte in location 1; that is, the most significant byte is in the higher address. Figure 3.10 illustrates these possibilities.

---

[2] If you know that our positional numbering system comes from the Arabs and that Arabic is written from right to left, you might be tempted to conclude that the "inconsistency" is due to the differences in orientations of our written language—I was. However, our numbering system was developed by the Hindus and transmitted to us through the Arabs. Hindi, the language of the Hindus, is written from left to right as is English.

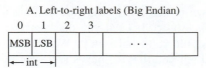
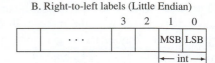

Figure 3.10   Byte orderings

By now, you may wonder which byte-ordering scheme is best. Unfortunately, neither is better than the other. Labeling the memory locations from left to right is consistent with the way we order horizontal information. Labeling memory locations from right to left is consistent with the powers of 256. It is unfortunate that there is no best approach because it means that different machines use different approaches. When you are working with a particular machine, the different approaches do not present any difficulty; you can easily adapt to the approach taken by the machine. However, if you need to deal with both types of machines regularly or if you ever have to transfer data between different types of machines, the difference becomes something more than an annoyance.

Because there is no best approach, the debate frequently takes on the characteristics of a religious dispute. This has caused the debate to be called "Big Endians and Little Endians," referring to a war described in *Gulliver's Travels*. Gulliver describes a war based on a controversy involving which end of the egg should be broken. One group, the Little Endians, believe that the smaller end should be broken, while the Big Endians maintain that the larger end should be broken. Jonathan Swift used the absurdity of this war to satarize Catholic and Protestant disputes in his day.

Beyond pointing out the arbitrary nature of the differences between byte ordering schemes, the title also characterizes the two factions. If we consider the most significant byte to be the "big end" and the least significant byte to be the "little end," then it is reasonable to call machines that store the most significant byte in location 0 *Big Endians*. Here, the big end is the first part of the value encountered when traversing memory. Similarly, we call machines that store the least significant byte in memory location 0 *Little Endians*.

If you recall the start of this discussion, I asked you to label an array of integers and an array of bits. At the time, I pointed out that your natural inclination is most likely inconsistent—left to right for integers and right to left for bits. As we have seen, this inconsistency enables designers to justify a left-to-right or right-to-left labeling of memory locations, whichever they prefer. Along the way, we dropped the issue of labeling the bits in a byte (or integer). Well, it is time to reconsider the bits!

If you chose to label memory locations from right to left, you are unlikely to consider labeling the bits in a byte from left to right. This would introduce an inconsistency with no real justification. Thus, you would naturally label the bits from right to left also. However, if you chose to label memory locations from left to right, you have another decision to make. Labeling the bits from right to left

Big Endians

Little Endians

is inconsistent with the labeling of memory locations, but it is consistent with our conventions. Labeling the bits from left to right is consistent with the labeling of memory locations; however, it is inconsistent with our conventions. Moreover, this labeling introduces a minor inconvenience because bit labels do not represent powers of two.

In almost every context, the ordering of bytes is far more important than the ordering of bits. Hence, we classify machines by the way that they order bytes. We use the adjective *inconsistent* when the byte and bit orderings differ. Table 3.4 summarizes the possibilities.

Table 3.4 Big versus Little Endian

Name	Byte ordering	Bit ordering	Sample machine
Consistent Little Endian	Right to left	Right to left	Intel 80x86
Consistent Big Endian	Left to right	Left to right	TI 9900
Inconsistent Little Endian	Right to left	Left to right	*None*
Inconsistent Big Endian	Left to right	Right to left	Motorola 68000

Many newer machines avoid these difficulties by providing flexibility. For example, the MIPS R2000 processor can be set to be a Big Endian or Little Endian machine as it is started up. Once started, the mode cannot be changed until the machine is restarted. The Intel i860 processor provides an instruction that switches between Big Endian and Little Endian addressing.

Graphical Convention

By now, you realize that there is at least one issue regarding the orientation of a diagram—left to right versus right to left. As a rule, the illustrations in this book follow the customs of our language. This means that the diagrams are consistent with an inconsistent Big Endian.

There is another minor inconsistency that you may or may not be aware of. If I ask you where the first line on this page is, you are likely to point toward the top of the page. This is natural because we read from the top of the page to the bottom. Unfortunately, this convention means that lower numbered lines appear higher on the page and higher numbered lines appear lower on the page. Usually, this does not present a problem because we do not usually talk about lines of text using adjectives like "higher" and "lower." However, we do frequently talk about memory locations using adjectives like "low" and "high." Whenever memory is illustrated using a vertical orientation, lower numbered memory locations appear toward the top of the page.

3.2 THE CPU

The CPU is responsible for the interpretation of programs (i.e., the manipulation of data). In this section, we consider the operation of the CPU. In particular, we examine a very simple machine in some detail. We have simplified the machine that we discuss in this section to the point that it is not particularly realistic. However, our implementation of this machine does illustrate the basic techniques used in the implementation of actual machines. In Chapter 9, we consider more advanced techniques used in implementing CPUs (e.g., microprogramming, instruction pipelining, and caching).

We begin by presenting an instruction set for our simple machine. After we present the instruction set, we consider an implementation of the machine (i.e., a realization of the instruction set). We present the implementation in two parts. In the first part, we present the registers and data paths used in the machine. In the second part, we present the interpretation of instructions.

3.2.1 A Simple Instruction Set

Accumulator machine

You are undoubtedly familiar with simple calculators and adding machines. Logically these machines maintain a value to which other values can be added, subtracted, multiplied, and so forth. Because the result accumulates in a register, we call these devices *accumulator machines*. Accumulator machines have a very simple and regular instruction set. For these reasons, accumulator machines have simple implementations. The machine that we examine in the remainder of this section is an accumulator machine.

Example 3.7   *Describe how to carry out the calculation 47 * 82 + 91 on an accumulator machine.*

1. LOAD 47 into the accumulator.
2. MULTIPLY the accumulator by 82.
3. ADD 91 to the accumulator.
4. EXAMINE the value in the accumulator.

The descriptions of the operations in Example 3.7 are rather verbose. Note that we mention accumulator in every instruction. We can reduce the description by removing the explicit references to the accumulator. With this reduction, every instruction has an operation and, at most, one explicit operand.

Example 3.8   *Rewrite the instructions given in Example 3.7 without any explicit references to the accumulator.*

LOAD   47
MULTIPLY   82

ADD   91
EXAMINE

Table 3.5 presents a simple set of instructions for an accumulator machine. In contrast to our previous instructions, these instructions use values stored in memory instead of constant values.

Table 3.5   Instructions for a simple machine

Symbolic	Semantics
ADD *addr*	Add the value in memory cell *addr* to the value in the accumulator.
SUB *addr*	Subtract the value in memory cell *addr* from the value in the accumulator.
MPY *addr*	Multiply the value in memory cell *addr* by the value in the accumulator. Load the accumulator with the least significant 8 bits of the result.
DIV *addr*	Divide the value in the accumulator by the value in memory cell *addr*. Load the accumulator with the integer portion of the result.
LOAD *addr*	Load the accumulator with the value in memory cell *addr*.
STORE *addr*	Store the value of the accumulator into memory cell *addr*.

Example 3.9   *Using the instructions presented in Table 3.5, show how to evaluate the expression $c = a * b + c * d$. In writing your instructions you should use memory locations 20, 21, 22, and 23 for the variables a, b, c, and d, respectively. Moreover, you should use memory location 30 to hold intermediate results.*

LOAD	20;	$acc = a$
MPY	21;	$acc = a * b$
STORE	30;	$temp = a * b$
LOAD	22;	$acc = c$
MPY	23;	$acc = c * d$
ADD	30;	$acc = a * b + c * d$
STORE	22;	$c = a * b + c * d$

In a *stored program computer*, the instructions used to evaluate expressions are stored in memory with the data values that they manipulate. To store instructions, we must devise a scheme for encoding them into binary. Each instruction in Table 3.5 has an operation (e.g., LOAD or STORE) and an address. As such, we need to encode the operation and the address for each instruction. Encoding the address is straightforward; simply use the binary representation of the address. Encoding the operation is also straightforward. Table 3.6 presents a possible encoding for the operations.

Stored program computer

Table 3.6 Operation codes
for the simple machine

Operation	Encoding
ADD	000
SUB	001
MPY	010
DIV	011
LOAD	100
STORE	101

If we assume that our memory system provides access to 8-bit values, Figure 3.11 presents a reasonable format for instruction encodings. This format uses the most significant 3 bits to store the encoding of the operation. This field is called the *OPCODE (OPeration CODE)*. The remaining 5 bits encode the address of the explicit operand.

OPCODE (OPeration CODE)

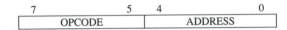

Figure 3.11 Instruction format for the simple machine

Assembly

Assembler

Assembly language

We use the term *assembly* to refer to the process of encoding a symbolic program (like the one shown in Example 3.9). A program that implements the assembly process is called an *assembler*. The input to an assembler defines a language, called *assembly language*. The program shown in Example 3.9 is an example of an assembly language program. We will discuss assemblers and assembly language programming in the next few chapters.

Example 3.10   *Hand assemble the code fragment presented in Example 3.9.*

10010100	LOAD	20;	*acc = a*
01010101	MPY	21;	*acc = a * b*
10111110	STORE	30;	*temp = a * b*
10010110	LOAD	22;	*acc = c*
01010111	MPY	23;	*acc = c * d*
00011110	ADD	30;	*acc = a * b + c * d*
10110110	STORE	22;	*c = a * b + c * d*

3.2.2 Data Paths and Control Points

Figure 3.12 presents an organization of registers, logic components, and data paths that we could use to implement our simple machine. All data paths in this illustration are 8 bits wide. A shared bus is the foundation for this organization. The bus supports the transmission of values among the other components of the computer system.

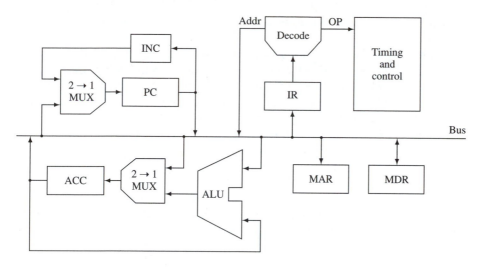

Registers	Combinational circuits
ACC (accumulator)	ALU (arithmetic and logic unit)
IR (instruction register)	Decode (instruction decoder)
MAR (memory address register)	INC (incrementer)
MDR (memory data register)	MUX (multiplexer)
PC (program counter)	Timing and control

Figure 3.12 Internal data paths in an accumulator machine

In addition to the shared bus, this organization uses six combinational and sequential circuits and five registers. We begin by considering the registers. The register labeled ACC is the accumulator for the machine. The registers labeled *MAR (memory address register)* and *MDR (memory data register)* support access to memory. A memory access starts by storing the address of the word in the MAR. The MDR holds the data value associated with the memory access (either the value read from or written to the memory). The *PC (program counter)* stores the address of the next instruction to be executed. In some contexts, the PC is called the *instruction counter* because it identifies an instruction. As we will see, the PC gets incremented on a regular basis, so it makes sense to refer to this register as a counter. The remaining register shown in Figure 3.12, the *IR (instruction register)* holds the instruction during instruction interpretation.

In considering the circuits used in Figure 3.12, we begin by considering the four simple combinational circuits. The two MUXs control the inputs to the PC and ACC. The *ALU (arithmetic and logic unit)* is a combinational circuit that implements the arithmetic and logical operations needed by the machine. Here the ALU needs to provide the four arithmetic operations (addition, subtraction, multiplication, and division) in our instruction set. The *INC (incrementer)* is a combinational circuit used to increment the value of the PC. We will discuss the remaining circuits, *decode* and *timing and control,* after we discuss the principles of instruction interpretation.

Table 3.7 presents the *control points* needed to control the registers shown in Figure 3.12. Our organization requires 15 independent control points. Each register requires a control signal to control when the register loads a new value. Table 3.7 assigns the numbers 1, 3, 4, 5, and 7 to these control points. In addition, every data path that leads to the shared bus must have a control signal that controls when the value on the data path is gated onto the shared bus. Table 3.7 assigns the numbers 0, 2, 6, and 12 to these control points.

Table 3.7   Control points in the accumulator machine

Number	Operation performed	Number	Operation performed
0	ACC→bus	8	ALU→ACC
1	load ACC	9	INC→PC
2	PC→bus	10	ALU operation
3	load PC	11	ALU operation
4	load IR	12	Addr→bus
5	load MAR	13	CS
6	MDR→bus	14	R/$\overline{\text{W}}$
7	load MDR		

Example 3.11   *Show how the control points presented in Table 3.7 can be used to control the activities of the accumulator.*

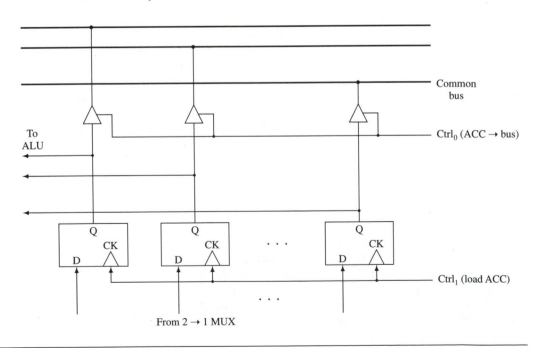

The remaining control points control the activities of the memory system and the combinational circuits shown in Figure 3.12. Control points 8 and 9 control the two MUXs. For example, when control point 8 is set to 1, the output of the ALU is gated to the input of the ACC; otherwise, the value on the shared bus is gated to the input of the ACC. Control points 10 and 11 control the function performed by the ALU. Finally, control points 13 and 14 control the activities of the memory system.

3.2.3 The ifetch Loop

Figure 3.13 presents a flowchart of an *ifetch (instruction fetch/execute) loop* for our simple machine. The rectangles shown in the flowchart represent the states that the machine can enter. When the machine enters one of these states, it asserts the

Ifetch (instruction fetch/execute) loop

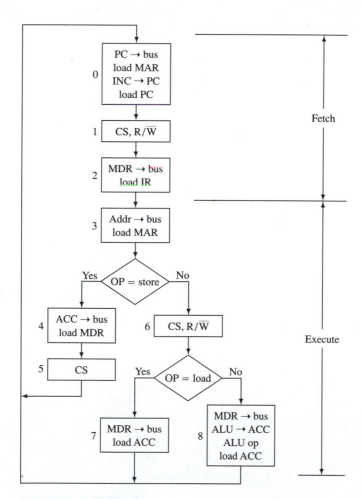

Figure 3.13 An ifetch loop

signals indicated in the rectangle. The machine continues to assert these signals until it leaves the state. Notice that we have numbered the states shown in Figure 3.13. These numbers provide a point of reference for the remainder of our discussion.

The flowchart starts by fetching (reading) the next instruction from the memory of the machine. To accomplish this task the flowchart starts by copying the value of the PC into the MAR and incrementing the PC (state 0). Then the control logic initiates a memory read operation (state 1). After the memory read is complete, the machine leaves state 1 and enters state 2, where the control logic copies the value in the MDR to the IR where it can be decoded. This completes the instruction fetch component of the ifetch loop.

Because every instruction contains a memory address, the execute component of the ifetch loop begins by moving the address field of the instruction into the MAR (state 3). The control logic then examines the OPCODE field of the instruction. If the OPCODE field indicates that this is a store instruction, the control logic copies the current value of the ACC into the MDR (state 4) and initiates a memory write operation (state 5). These steps store the current value of the ACC into the memory of the machine. Otherwise, if the instruction is not a store instruction, the control logic initiates a memory read (state 6) to fetch the value of the explicit operand. When this memory operation is complete, the control logic reexamines the value of the OPCODE field. If it is a load instruction, the control logic simply copies the value read from the memory into the ACC (state 7). Otherwise, the control passes the memory value (in the MDR) and the current value of the ACC through the ALU and loads the result in the ACC (state 8).

Given a flowchart like the one shown in Figure 3.13, constructing a hardware interpreter for the flowchart is relatively simple. Figure 3.14 presents the basic structure of such an interpreter. The interpreter takes two types of inputs: a set of condition signals and a clock signal. The *condition signals* control the flow of

Condition signals

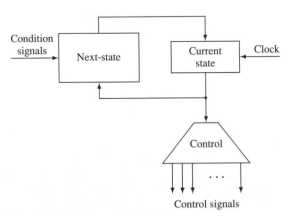

Figure 3.14 State machine interpretation

execution within the machine. The clock signal provides the timing for changes in state. Using these inputs, the interpreter produces a set of control signals as outputs.

Internally, the interpreter uses a register and two combinational circuits to perform its tasks. The register, called *current state*, holds the current value of the state. Every pulse on the clock signal initiates a *processor cycle*. At the start of the cycle, the current state register loads a new value, thus establishing a new value for the current state. Given the current state, the *control* logic produces the control signals needed to control the activities of the registers. The *next-state* logic uses the current state and the condition signals to determine the next state. This cycle repeats with the next pulse on the clock signal. We begin by considering the encoding and timing of the current state signal. We then consider the structure of the next-state logic. After we have discussed this component, we consider the structure of the control logic.

Because our machine only has nine states, we will use a separate signal for each state. We use the labels s_0 through s_8 for these signals. At any time, exactly one of these signals has the value 1, the rest have the value 0. If our machine had hundreds or thousands of states, we might choose to encode the current state to reduce the number of lines needed to carry the current state information.

Figure 3.15 illustrates the timing of a state signal. In this illustration *state* refers to a state signal that is active during the processor cycle—it could be any one of the nine state signals. As we will see, all of the control signals are derived from the state signals.

Current state
Processor cycle

Control
Next-state

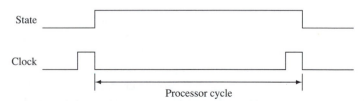

Figure 3.15   Control signals for our simple machine

In considering the next-state logic, we need to specify the condition signals used by this component. For our machine, we need the OPCODE field of the instruction register and a *memory done (MD)* signal as condition signals. The memory system uses the memory done signal to indicate when an access is complete. This signal can be generated by the memory system, or it may be generated by a simple counter that counts a fixed number of pulses in a timing signal. Given these condition signals and the current state, you can design circuits that determine the value of the next state. In the next two examples, we present the logic needed to determine if the machine is in state 1, 2, or 4. We consider the remaining states in the exercises (see exercise 10).

Example 3.12   *Design a circuit that determines when the next state is state 4.*

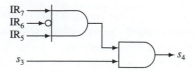

In words, the next state is state 4 if the current state is 3 and the OPCODE is 101.

Example 3.13   *Design a circuit that determines when the next state is 1 or 2.*

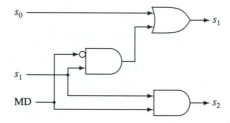

This circuit illustrates how the memory done signal (MD) inhibits the transition from state 1 to state 2 while the memory operation is in progress.

We conclude this presentation of our accumulator machine by considering the generation of control signals. In examining the control points presented in Table 3.7, there are two types of control signals that we need to consider: control signals that control the function performed by a combinational circuit, and control signals that are used to load registers. For example, control points 10 and 11 control the function performed by the ALU, while control point 1 loads the ACC.

The control signals associated with the control points on combinational circuits should be asserted as long as the machine is a state that asserts these control points. In other words, the control signals for these control points should coincide with the appropriate state signals.

Example 3.14   *Design a circuit that produces the memory control signals, CS (chip select) and $R/\overline{W}$.*

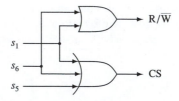

In words, the CS control signal should be asserted whenever the machine is in state 1, 5, or 6 and the R/$\overline{\text{W}}$ signal should be asserted whenever the machine is in state 1 or 6.

The control signals associated with the control points used to load values into registers must be handled in a different fashion. Values should be loaded into registers at the end of a processor cycle—as the processor is leaving one state and entering the next.

Example 3.15 *Design a circuit that generates the control signal used to load the ACC.*

$$s_7 \longrightarrow \!\!\!\!\!\!\!\!\!\!\!\!\!\!\!\!\! \text{)o} \longrightarrow \text{load ACC}$$
$$s_8 \longrightarrow$$

In words, the machine should load the ACC when it is leaving state 7 or 8.

3.3 I/O DEVICES

I/O devices provide the means by which a computing system can sense or affect its environment. There are I/O devices that print characters, measure temperatures, light lights, store vast quantities of data, read characters, and so on. We will discuss I/O devices and I/O structures at length in Chapter 11. In this chapter, we present a simple model of how I/O devices work.

To make our discussion more concrete, we consider the operation of a simple device like a printer. The printer itself is not part of the computer. Rather, the printer is a separate entity. A component called the *controller* controls the activities of   Controller
the printer. Figure 3.16 illustrates the relationships between the CPU, the printer controller, and the printer.

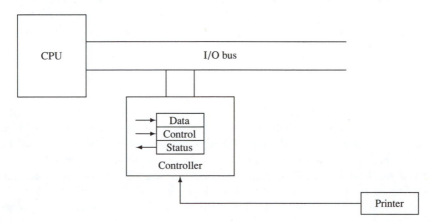

Figure 3.16 Controllers and devices

Data register

Control register

Status register

I/O port

Memory-mapped I/O

Isolated I/O

The printer controller defines three registers: a data register, a control register, and a status register. The values in these registers control the activities of the controller and, in turn, the activities of the printer. The *data register* holds the value to be sent to the printer. The *control register* tells the controller which operation the CPU is requesting; for example, send the value in the data register to the printer. The CPU establishes the value in the data and control registers. The controller uses the *status register* to report the status of the last requested operation. For example, when the controller has sent the value to the printer, it sets a bit in the status register to indicate that the operation is complete. We use the term *I/O port* to refer to the set of registers defined by a device controller.

Some machines map the I/O ports into the set of addresses used by the memory system. In these machines, you can access the I/O registers using the memory transfer operations (*load* and *store* in our simple machine). This strategy is called *memory-mapped I/O*. Other machines provide a separate address space for the I/O ports. These machines have special instructions for accessing the I/O port registers. This strategy is called *isolated I/O*.

Suppose you want to send a value to the printer. To complete this task, you need to perform the following sequence of subtasks:

- Wait for the controller to finish the last command.
- Place a value in the data register.
- Set the control register to initiate the transfer.

You can implement the waiting required in the first step by repeatedly reading the status register. You are done with this step when the value in this register indicates that the controller has finished the previous operation. You can implement the remaining subtasks by writing values to the appropriate registers.

At this point, you might be interested in what happens with the values that get sent to the printer. That depends on the printer. Some values control the actions of the printer, for example, the formfeed character (control-L) may cause the printer to eject the current page. Other values are simply printed at the current position on the page (they have very simple control actions). In many cases, control codes are sent as *escape sequences*, sequences in which the values have nonstandard interpretations.

Escape sequences

3.4 BUSES

Internal bus

External bus

Buses transmit values between the components of a computing system. In this discussion, we distinguish two types of buses: internal buses and external buses. An *internal bus* is internal to the CPU, while an *external bus* is external to the CPU. Figure 3.17 illustrates the distinction between these types of buses. We distinguish internal and external buses because they have different management strategies. As we have seen, the control logic of the CPU controls the activities of an internal bus. The control logic determines which components place values on the internal buses and which components use these values. In contrast, external buses rely on *self-selection* to complete data transfers among their components. This strategy makes it relatively easy to add (or remove) components to (or from) an external bus.

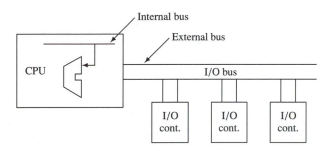

Figure 3.17   Internal versus external buses

A data transfer using an external bus is called a *bus transaction*. Every bus transaction involves two components: the initiator of the transaction, called the *master*, and the target of the transaction, called the *slave*. It is important to recognize that the master/slave relationship only lasts for a single transaction. Some components, like memory, are usually slaves. Other components, like the CPU, are usually masters. Some components perform different roles depending on the context of the transaction. For example, a disk controller acts as a slave when the CPU requests that the controller read in a block of data. The same controller acts as a master when it transfers the data into the memory of the machine. We use the terms *transaction master* and *transaction slave* to emphasize the transitive nature of the master/slave relationship. In addition, we use the term *bus master* to refer to any component that can act as a transaction master.

Buses usually support two types of transactions: read transactions and write transactions. In a read transaction, the transaction master issues a request to obtain a value from another component. In a write transaction, the transaction master issues a request to send a value to another component. These transactions should remind you of the read and write operations that we defined as we considered memory access. We can also use these operations to access the registers of a device controller. As such, these are the only operations that a simple bus needs to support. Some buses permit the transmission of several values in a single transaction. These transactions are called *burst-mode transactions*.

Bus transaction

Master

Slave

Transaction master

Transaction slave

Bus master

Burst-mode transactions

3.4.1 Synchronous Bus Protocols

Table 3.8 presents a set of signals that can be used to implement the read and write transactions on a synchronous bus. The existence of a shared timing signal,

Clock

Synchronous bus

Asynchronous bus

clock, is the distinguishing characteristic of a *synchronous bus*. In contrast, an *asynchronous bus* does not use a common timing signal. Asynchronous buses have more complicated protocols than synchronous buses. However, asynchronous buses can accommodate a wider variety of devices and are usually faster than synchronous buses.

Table 3.8 Bus lines

Line/signal	Established by
Start	Master
Data	Master/slave
Address	Master
R/$\overline{\text{W}}$	Master
Done	Slave
Clock	Bus

Address lines

Data lines

Start

Done

Wait states

Figure 3.18 presents a simple protocol for the read and write transactions using the signals presented in Table 3.8. Both types of transactions take two clock cycles to complete their activities. We use the names T_1 and T_2 to refer to the two cycles. Edges in these clock cycles provide important reference points for the communication between the transaction master and slave. In particular, the leading edge of T_1 signifies the start of a transaction, while the trailing edge of T_2 is used to confirm the completion of the transaction.

Both types of transactions begin on the leading edge of T_1. On the leading edge of T_1, the transaction master establishes the value on the *address lines* and R/$\overline{\text{W}}$ lines. In a write transaction, the transaction master also establishes the value on the *data lines*. After these signals are stable on the bus (a parameter of the bus), the transaction master asserts the *start* signal.

When the transaction master asserts the start signal, the other components on the bus check the address lines. Each component is preconditioned to respond to a set of addresses. Whenever a component recognizes one of its addresses on the address lines, it becomes the slave for the current transaction. As the slave, the component initiates the requested operation. When it completes the requested operation, the slave asserts the *done* signal. This signal indicates that the transaction is complete. In a read transaction, the slave also establishes the value on the data lines as it signals that the operation is complete.

It is important to note that the transaction master only examines the done signal on the trailing edge of a clock pulse. If the slave is unable to respond fast enough to be certain that the done signal is stable by the trailing edge of the next clock cycle, it must wait an entire clock cycle to signal the completion of the transaction. There may be any number of clock cycles between the T_1 and T_2 cycles shown in Figure 3.18. These cycles are called *wait states* because the transaction master

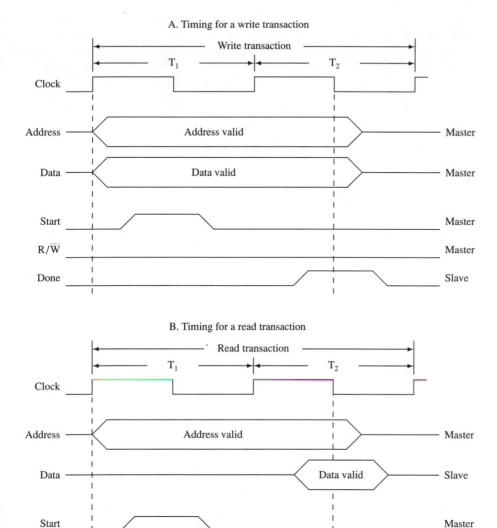

Figure 3.18 Bus timings

is waiting for the slave to complete the transaction. Figure 3.19 illustrates the introduction of a wait state in a write transaction.

Because the done signal must be synchronized with the trailing edge of the clock signal, synchronous buses are generally slower than asynchronous buses.

To meet this synchronization constraint, the transaction master must frequently wait an additional clock cycle to recognize the completion of a transaction. In an asynchronous bus, the transaction master responds to the done signal when it is signaled. However, the protocol must be extended to include an acknowledgment by the transaction master that it has seen the done signal.

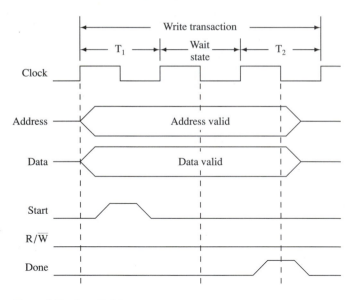

Figure 3.19   A wait state

Synchronous buses may be characterized by the rate of the common clock signal. As such, you may hear that a particular bus operates at 20 Mhertz. Synchronous buses operate in the 5 to 50 Mhertz range. While the clock rate is a useful characterization of a synchronous bus, this is not a meaningful measure for asynchronous buses. A more useful measure is the *bandwidth* of the bus. Bandwidth characterizes the rate at which information can flow through the bus.

Bandwidth

We measure bandwidth in bytes per second. For example, a bus may have a bandwidth of 20,000 bytes per second.

3.4.2 Timing Considerations

At this point, it is helpful if we take a closer look at the timing associated with our simple bus protocols. In particular, we consider the factors that contribute to the need for wait states. In essence there are two factors to be considered in determining the need for wait states: transaction access time and transaction cycle time. We introduced the terms *access time* and *cycle time* when we discussed the memory subsystem. In a bus transaction, *transaction access time* is the interval from the time the slave recognizes the operation until it responds by asserting the done signal. The *transaction cycle time* is the interval that must elapse between consecutive requests. The transaction access and cycle times depend on the transaction slave and the requested operation. For example, we can expect that the transaction access time for a memory read operation is about 80 nanoseconds[3] (the access time for DRAM). On the other hand, the transaction access time for a memory write operation might be on the order of 10 to 20 nanoseconds, just enough time to latch the address and data values on the bus.

> Transaction access time
>
> Transaction cycle time

We begin by considering the impact of transaction access time. If the bus timing does not provide enough time to complete the access, the transaction slave needs to introduce wait states. To simplify our calculations, we assume that every bus signal stabilizes within s nanoseconds of the time it is introduced on the bus. This means that the slave can identify itself and begin the requested operation within $2s$ nanoseconds of the leading edge of T_1 (s nanoseconds for the address to stabilize and s nanoseconds for the start signal to stabilize). Moreover, the operation must be completed within s nanoseconds of the trailing edge of T_2 (to allow the done signal to stabilize on the bus). Given these parameters, we have the following relationship

$$a \leq 1.5 \cdot b + w \cdot b - 3 \cdot s$$

where b is the cycle time for the bus clock, w is the number of wait states, and a is the transaction access time. This relationship is illustrated in Figure 3.20. Rearranging terms we get:

$$w \geq \frac{a - 1.5 \cdot b + 3 \cdot s}{b}$$

Thus, given the stabilization time, the access time, and the bus cycle time, we can determine the number of wait states needed by a particular device.

---

[3] A nanosecond is 10^{-9} second.

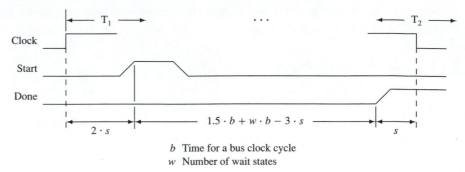

b Time for a bus clock cycle
w Number of wait states

Figure 3.20 Bus timing

Example 3.16 *Suppose that the bus clock is running at a rate of 16.67 MHertz (i.e., 16,670,000 cycles per second) and the bus stabilization time is 10 nanoseconds. If the slave device has an access time of 80 nanoseconds, how many wait states will the slave need?*

We begin by computing the time for a bus cycle.

$$\frac{1}{16,670,000}\frac{sec}{cycle} = \frac{1,000,000,000}{16,670,000}\frac{nanosec}{cycle} \approx 60\frac{nanosec}{cycle}$$

In this case, each bus cycle takes 60 nanoseconds, and the memory needs one wait state:

$$w \geq \frac{80 - 1.5 \cdot 60 + 30}{60} = \frac{20}{60}$$

$$\Rightarrow w = 1$$

Example 3.17 *Now suppose that the bus clock is running at a rate of 12.5 MHertz; that is, each cycle takes 80 nanoseconds. How many waits states will the memory require?*

In this case, the memory does not require any wait states:

$$w \geq \frac{80 - 1.5 \cdot 80 + 30}{80} = \frac{-10}{80}$$

$$\Rightarrow w = 0$$

We can use this calculation to determine the minimum number of wait states needed to access a device. To determine the maximum number of wait states, we need to consider the transaction cycle time. In considering the transaction cycle time, we need to ensure that the slave has completed the previous operation before it starts the next one. An easy way to do this is to introduce enough wait states at the end of the current transaction to ensure that the next operation cannot be requested before the current operation has been completed.

Example 3.18   *As an example, suppose that the bus has a stabilization time of 10 nanoseconds and is running at a rate of 25 MHertz, that is, 40 nanoseconds per cycle. Moreover, suppose that the memory has a write access time of 20 nanoseconds and a write cycle time of 160 nanoseconds. How many wait states will the memory need?*

Using the access time, we conclude that we do not need any wait states to complete the access:

$$ w \geq \frac{20 - 1.5 \cdot 40 + 30}{20} = \frac{-10}{20} $$

However, the next operation could be requested within two cycles (or 80 nanoseconds) after the start of the current operation. To make sure that the current operation is completed before the next one is requested, we need to wait for at least 80 additional nanoseconds, two wait states, before the memory subsystem asserts the done signal.

This strategy is simple, but it may introduce wait states when they are not needed. In particular, if the next bus transaction is not a memory request or if there are idle bus cycles, the transaction master is detained unnecessarily. A better strategy is to have the slave respond to the request as soon as possible and introduce wait states as needed during later requests.

3.4.3 Bus Arbitration

If there is more than one bus master, it is possible that two bus masters will want to initiate bus transactions at the same time. When this happens, both attempt to become transaction masters for the same bus transaction. If two or more bus masters attempt to initiate a bus transaction during the same clock cycle, they clash in their independent uses of the address lines. To avoid this problem bus masters must go through a *bus arbitration* protocol before using the bus. Any bus master that needs to use the bus can initiate the bus arbitration protocol. The bus arbitration protocol results in the selection of a single bus master that becomes the transaction master for the next bus transaction. If there is already a transaction in progress, the bus arbitration protocol is *overlapped* with the current transaction so   Overlapped that the next transaction can begin as soon as the current transaction completes. We will discuss bus arbitration techniques in Chapter 11 when we consider I/O devices in more depth.

3.5 SUMMARY

In this chapter, we have covered the basic components that are used in a computing system. We will expand on the issues that we have introduced in this chapter throughout the remainder of this text.

3.5.1 Additional Reading

If you are interested in more information on the topics covered in this chapter, you should consult books on computer organization. Among these books, I highly recommend *Computer Organization* by Hamacher, Vranesic, and Zaky (McGraw-Hill, 1990, 1984, and 1978).

3.5.2 Terminology

- Memory width, Word size, Bit/Byte addressable memory
- Address, Control and Data ports
- Read, Write, Fetch, Store
- ROM, PROM, EPROM, EEPROM
- Random access, Sequential access, Direct access
- Volatile
- CS, R/$\overline{\text{W}}$
- Memory access time, Memory cycle time
- Static RAM, Dynamic RAM
- Refresh, Destructive read
- 2D organization, 2½D organization
- Word select line, Bit line
- Physical word size, Logical word size
- Multiplexing
- Memory bank, Interleaved addressing, Data port justification, Alignment
- Big Endian, Little Endian
- Accumulator machine, Load, Store
- Stored program computer
- OPCODE
- Assembler, Assembly language
- MAR, MDR, PC, IR
- Program counter, Instruction counter
- ALU
- Ifetch loop, Flowchart
- Control points, Control logic
- Processor cycle
- I/O controller
- Data, Control, and Status registers, I/O port
- Memory-mapped I/O, Isolated I/O
- Internal bus, External bus

- Bus transaction, Transaction master, Transaction slave, Bus master
- Asynchronous bus, Synchronous bus
- Bandwidth
- Wait state
- Transaction access time, Transaction cycle time
- Bus arbitration

3.5.3 Review Questions

1. In the context of memory cells, what does the term *destructive read* mean? What type of memory has a destructive read operation?
2. Explain the difference between volatile memory and dynamic memory.
3. Discuss the relationship between signals and pins. Be certain to consider multiplexing.
4. Why is it important to interleave addresses in the organization shown in Figure 3.8?
5. In a Big Endian machine, is the most significant byte stored in the larger or smaller address?
6. In the memory organization shown in Figure 3.6, are the read/sense components constructed using combinational logic or sequential logic? Explain.
7. Explain the relationship between multiplexing and the pin-limitation problem.
8. What is an OPCODE? What is the purpose of an instruction format?
9. What does an assembler do?
10. What are the MAR and MDR used for?
11. What is a program counter?
12. What are the three activities that must be performed during each processor cycle?
13. What is an I/O port?
14. What does the term *memory-mapped I/O* mean? What is the important consequence of memory-mapped I/O?
15. What is the difference between memory-mapped I/O and isolated I/O?
16. Discuss the differences between internal and external buses.
17. What is the difference between a synchronous bus and an asynchronous bus?
18. How is the bandwidth of a bus defined?
19. What are the factors that contribute to the need for wait states?
20. What is the purpose of bus arbitration?

3.6 EXERCISES

1. The memory organization shown in Figure 3.6 uses dynamic RAM for the individual cells. Redesign this organization using flip-flops in place of the dynamic RAM cells.

2. For the following memory sizes, describe how you would implement the memory using the 2½D strategy. Your description should be a diagram like the one shown in Figure 3.7.

    a. 1M $\times$ 1.

    b. 2048 $\times$ 1.

3. Design a 1M $\times$ 4 memory system using four

    a. 512K $\times$ 2 memory chips.

    b. 256K $\times$ 4 memory chips.

    c. 128K $\times$ 8 memory chips.

    d. 64K $\times$ 16 memory chips.

4. Some of the 4M $\times$ 4 memory chips are packaged using 16 pins.

    a. Describe the signals that are needed to implement a 4M $\times$ 4 memory.

    b. Explain how you could use 16 pins to carry these signals onto the memory chip.

5. Consider the details of the organization shown in Figure 3.8. Assume that the memory system is *aligned* and that a 0 on the Size signal indicates a byte operation.

    a. Using the signals available to the memory system, design a circuit that outputs a 1 if a request meets the requirements of alignment and a 0 otherwise.

    b. Design a circuit that routes the address, CS, and R/$\overline{\text{W}}$ to the internal memory banks of the memory system.

    c. Assuming that the data port is justified (i.e., that byte values are always transmitted along lines D_0 through D_7), design a circuit that routes the data inputs/outputs of the memory banks to the correct lines of the data port. (To simplify your illustration, assume that the memory is 4 bits wide and that each bank is 2 bits wide.)

6. Consider the implementation of an unaligned memory. As in exercise 5, assume that a 0 on the Size signal is used to indicate a byte operation.

    a. Design a circuit that routes the address, CS, and R/$\overline{\text{W}}$ to the internal memory banks of the memory system.

    b. Assuming that the data port is justified, design a circuit that routes the data inputs/outputs of the memory banks to the correct lines of the data port. (Assume that the memory is 4 bits wide and that each bank is 2 bits wide.)

7. Consider the details of the following organization. Like the organization
    shown in Figure 3.8, this organization can support access to 8-bit and 16-bit
    values.

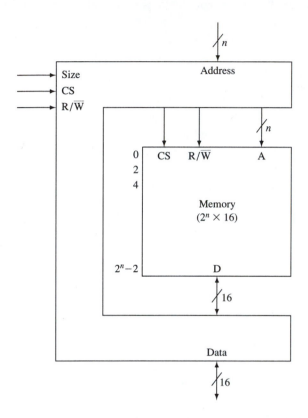

    Assume that a 0 on the Size line is used to indicate a byte operation and
    that 16-bit memory accesses must be aligned.

    a. Design a circuit that will correctly route the data output signals from
        the internal memory assuming that the data port is justified.

    b. This organization is inefficient when you need to store a single byte.
        It is difficult to make sure that you only write over the correct byte
        of the memory word. One solution is to use two steps whenever you
        need to write a single byte. During the first step the current value of
        the appropriate word is read into a register. During the second step, the
        value in the register is combined with the input byte and written back to
        the memory. Design a sequential circuit that implements this solution.
        In designing this circuit, assume that the two clock signals (step 1 and
        step 2) are provided.

8. For each of the following C statements, give a sequence of instructions,
    from those described in Table 3.5 that will evaluate the statement. In writing

the code sequences, assume that the values for *a, b, c, d,* and *e* are stored in memory locations 20, 21, 22, 23, and 24, respectively. In addition, you may assume that memory locations 28, 29, 30, and 31 can be used to store intermediate results as needed. (Note: % is the **mod** operator of C.)

a.   e = a + b * d;

b.   e = a − b * c;

c.   e = −a;

d.   e = a % b;

9.   Translate your code sequences from exercise 8 into binary using the encoding presented in Table 3.6 and Figure 3.11.

10.   In the text, we only illustrated the next-state function for states 1, 2, and 4 (see Examples 3.12 and 3.13). Design a circuit that will compute the next-state function for

    a.   States 5 and 0.

    b.   States 6, 7, and 8.

11.   Using your solution to exercise 10 and the examples in the text, give a complete circuit for determining the next state from the current state and the condition signals.

12.   For each of the following control points, design a circuit that could be used to activate the control point:

    a.   ACC→bus (control point 0).

    b.   PC→bus (control point 2).

    c.   MDR→bus (control point 6).

    d.   ALU→ACC (control point 8).

    e.   INC→PC (control point 9).

    f.   Addr→bus (control point 12).

    g.   load PC (control point 3).

    h.   load IR (control point 4).

    i.   load MAR (control point 5).

    j.   load MDR (control point 7).

13.   Explain how you would generate the control signals needed to control the function of the ALU (i.e., control points 10 and 11).

14.   Our implementation of the simple CPU does not provide any means to alter the value of the program counter (PC) other than the incrementation in the ifetch loop. Suppose that the OPCODE 110 is used to set the PC to the value stored in the address field of the instruction.

    a.   Describe how you would alter the flowchart shown in Figure 3.13 to accommodate this new instruction.

    b.   Explain how your changes impact the next-state logic. Give circuits that illustrate changes in the generation of the next state.

15. In the text, we assumed that the ALU could perform multiplication and division directly. In this question, we only assume that the ALU can perform addition and subtraction. To implement multiplication and division, we need to extend the basic organization by adding three "scratch" registers, two constant values, and two additional condition signals. We call the scratch registers TMP1, TMP2, and TMP3. Each of these registers can store the value on the shared bus. Moreover, the value of each register can be gated onto the shared bus. We also need to use the constant values 0 and 1. Thus, we presume that we can gate either of these values onto the shared bus. Finally, we need to be able to branch based on whether the value in the accumulator is zero or nonzero and whether the value in the accumulator is negative or nonnegative. Therefore, we introduce two new condition signals, zero and negative, that are passed to the control logic.

   a. Adapt Figure 3.12 to show the new data paths that we have introduced. In particular, add the "scratch" registers and constant values.

   b. Identify the new control points that our modifications have introduced.

   c. Show how you could implement the zero condition signal.

   d. Assuming that the ALU implements two's complement arithmetic, show how you could implement the negative condition signal.

   e. Design a flowchart, similar to the flowchart in Figure 3.13, that could be used to implement multiplication. In designing this flowchart, assume that the value being multiplied by the accumulator is a nonnegative number, so the multiplication can be implemented by adding the accumulator to itself the appropriate number of times. Also assume that the result of the multiplication is less than 256.

   f. Design a flowchart that could be used to implement division. In designing this flowchart, assume that the accumulator and the number that the accumulator is to be divided by are both positive (nonzero) numbers.

16. Suppose you have a synchronous bus that uses the read and write protocols shown in Figure 3.18 with a clock operating at r cycles per second and $8n$ data lines. Derive a formula for calculating the bandwidth of the bus.

17. Suppose the CPU clock operates at a frequency of 25 MHertz and the memory subsystem has an 80-nanosecond access time. For each of the following bus clock frequencies, calculate the minimum number of CPU cycles that the CPU will spend in state 1 of Figure 3.13. (In performing these calculations consider only wait states introduced due to access time, do not consider wait states due to cycle time.)

   a. 10 MHertz.

   b. 12.5 MHertz.

   c. 16.67 MHertz.

   d. 25 MHertz.

   e. 50 MHertz.

18. Repeat exercise 17 assuming that the memory access time is 20 nanoseconds.

19. In the text, we discussed two different strategies for dealing with the wait states that might be needed to accommodate transaction cycle time (one strategy always introduces wait states at the end of the bus transaction; the other only introduces wait states when they are needed). Consider the differences between these strategies. Suppose that the bus clock operates at a frequency of 16.67 MHertz. Moreover, suppose the memory write access time is 20 nanoseconds and the memory cycle time is 160 nanoseconds. For each of the strategies, how many wait states will the memory system need to introduce if there are

  a. Two consecutive memory writes?

  b. Three consecutive memory writes?

  c. Four consecutive memory writes?

  Be certain to justify your answers.

20. Given the assumptions stated in exercise 19, derive a formula for the number of wait states that will be needed for each memory access.

21. Suppose you have an I/O device with a single 8-bit register. Design a circuit that will interface the 8-bit register with an I/O bus. The I/O bus has eight data lines and eight address lines in addition to the Clock, Start, $R/\overline{W}$, and Done lines. The device should respond to the address 00001001_2. In designing this circuit, assume that the device does not need any wait states.

22. Repeat exercise 21, assuming that the register requires a single wait state (for any type of access).

23. In discussing the CPU, we used a memory done signal to indicate when the memory operation is complete. By now you realize there is no memory done signal. Instead there is a done signal associated with the (memory) bus. Design a circuit that takes the done and Clock signals from the bus along with any state signals that you need and produces the memory done signal. Because you cannot assume that the processor clock and bus clock are synchronized, you will need to use a flip-flop (or latch) to store the value of the done signal. Be certain to show how this memory cell is cleared.

24. The multiplication operation for our simple machine only retains the least significant 8 bits of the result. If you multiply two unsigned 8-bit values, the result could require 16 bits. One way to deal with this problem is to add another operation, MPYH, that stores the most significant 8 bits of the multiplication in the accumulator. Discuss how this approach affects the design of our simple machine. Be certain to address the following issues:

   ■ Instruction encoding.

   ■ Data paths.

   ■ Control points.

   ■ Ease of programming.

25. We could also resolve the multiplication problem by having the ALU produce a 16-bit result and store this value in two 8-bit registers. Discuss how this approach affects the design of our simple machine. Be certain to address the following issues:

    - New operations needed to access the added register.
    - Instruction encoding.
    - Data paths.
    - Control points.
    - Ease of programming.

COMPUTER ARCHITECTURE

PART TWO

SIMPLE CALCULATIONS

With this chapter, we begin our study of computer architecture. We cover the basics of computer architecture in three chapters. Chapter 4 considers simple calculations. Our goal is to introduce the types of instructions used to describe calculations. Chapter 5 covers basic data organization, introducing the techniques used to specify memory addresses. Chapter 6 covers subroutine calling mechanisms, introducing the basic mechanisms used to implement subroutines (procedures and functions) in high-level programming languages.

Before we consider the details of computer architecture, we need to discuss the two most prominent approaches to architectural design: CISC and RISC. *RISC* is an acronym that stands for *reduced instruction set computer*. In contrast, *CISC* stands for *complex instruction set computer*. The "reduced" in RISC refers to the complexity of individual instructions. For the most part, the individual instructions of a RISC machine perform a single, well-defined operation (e.g., add two values and store the result). In contrast, a single instruction on a CISC machine may perform several operations (e.g., a single CISC instruction might add two values, store the result, and increment one or two registers).

RISC (reduced instruction set computer)

CISC (complex instruction set computer)

Historically, the CISC approach was developed to support the assembly language programmer. Because a single CISC instruction can perform several operations, assembly language programmers do not need to write as many instructions to accomplish a large task. In contrast, the RISC approach assumes that the vast majority of programming will be done in high-level languages (like C or Pascal). Given this perspective, there is little incentive to reduce the number of instructions that the programmer needs to write. Instead, the emphasis shifts to improving the efficiency of each instruction.

At the risk of oversimplifying the situation, the debate between RISC and CISC boils down to one important issue: Is it better to complete a large task by doing many small but simple tasks (RISC) or by doing several medium-sized tasks (CISC)? It may seem that the division among tasks is arbitrary. The CISC approach reduces the number of instructions but increases the complexity of the processor. The RISC approach increases the number of instructions but simplifies the structure of the processor. By carefully controlling complexity of the processor,

RISC architects have been able to optimize the performance of these processors. Currently, the trade-offs favor the RISC approach.

This analysis of the RISC versus CISC debate is admittedly very shallow. As we introduce different aspects of computer architecture, we will point out contrasts between the RISC and CISC approaches.

Having introduced the RISC versus CISC debate, we are ready to begin the topic for this chapter: the description of simple calculations. To describe simple calculations, we need three basic types of operations: data transfer operations, data manipulation operations, and control flow operations. We use *data transfer* operations to transfer data values among the components (primarily memory and the CPU) of a computing system. We use *data manipulation* operations to compute new data values (addition and multiplication are examples of data manipulation operations). We use *control flow* operations to control which operations are performed.

The remainder of this chapter is organized as follows: The first section introduces the types of instructions used for data manipulation operations by considering the number of addresses in an instruction. In this section, we also introduce several data transfer operations. The second section introduces data registers. Data registers are internal to the CPU and their use may improve the execution time of a program. Moreover, data registers have shorter addresses than words in primary memory, which may decrease the number of bits needed to encode an instruction. In the third section, we consider the techniques that are used to specify the sizes of the operands used in data manipulation instructions. The fourth section discusses constant (immediate) values. We consider flow of control operations and the condition code register in the fifth section. The sixth section of this chapter presents a description of several bit-oriented data manipulation operations. We conclude this chapter with a brief discussion of a real architecture, the Sun Microsystems SPARC.

(margin notes: Data transfer, Data manipulation, Control flow)

4.1 HOW MANY ADDRESSES?

Consider the following assignment statement:

$$a = a * b + c * d * e;$$

While you and I immediately understand the meaning of this statement, we are basing our understanding on the rules of precedence and associativity. Because these rules are part of "common knowledge," it is reasonable that high-level languages like FORTRAN, C, and Pascal incorporate these rules. However, it is a bit unreasonable to expect that a machine can apply these rules directly.

To simplify the interpretation of our programs, we begin by requiring that every statement specify the application of a single operation. This rule simplifies interpretation by eliminating the need for the associativity and precedence of operators. The only rule we need is *sequence*. We use sequence to identify the next instruction.

(margin note: Sequence)

Example 4.1　*Show how you can implement the statement* $a = a * b + c * d * e$ *using a single operation per statement.*

$$a = a * b;$$
$$t1 = c * d;$$
$$t1 = t1 * e;$$
$$a = a + t1;$$

Note that you only need to know what each operator does and how sequencing works to understand the fragment presented in this example. Further, note that we introduced a new variable, *t1*, in the statements shown in Example 4.1. We call variables like *t1* *temporaries* because they hold intermediate results, temporarily, while we calculate other results. There are three intermediate results needed in our running example:

$$a * b, \ c * d, \ \text{and} \ (c * d) * e.$$

In Example 4.1, we used the variable *a* to hold the first intermediate result, and the temporary *t1* to hold the other two. As such, we did not need to introduce a new variable for each temporary result. If you know that the program does not use the current value of *b*, you can use *b* instead of *t1*. In compiler construction, it is common to call improvements like these *optimizations*.[1]

Consider our definition of operation. What is the operation in the first statement of Example 4.1? Perhaps the most obvious answer is multiplication. While this answer is essentially correct, it is not technically correct. Besides multiplication, the first statement specifies where the result should be stored. To avoid confusion, we call this operation *multiply-and-store*. While multiplication is a binary operation, multiply-and-store is a *ternary operation*. This operation has the two operands needed for the multiplication and an operand that specifies where to store the result. We call the operand that specifies where to store the result the *destination operand*. We call the operands that specify the values for the underlying binary operation *source operands*.

The two operations used in Example 4.1, multiply-and-store and add-and-store, are both ternary operations. Besides the other obvious ternary operations, there are several binary operations, for example, copy ($a = b$) and negation ($a = -b$). There is one common unary operation, **goto**, whose single operand specifies the address of the next instruction. As we will see, most machines also provide a collection of constant operations.

By now, it should be apparent that sequential machines add a new operand to each operation—the destination. When we count the destination, unary operations

Temporary

Optimization

Multiply-and-store

Ternary operation

Destination operand

Source operand

---

[1] Optimization is not really an appropriate choice of words—we do not claim to have the best possible solution, just a better one. In this context, optimization really means improvement.

become binary operations and binary operations become ternary operations. For the present, we will not consider operations with three or more operands. These operations are not nearly as common as binary or unary operations. We consider operations with three or more operands when we consider subroutine calling conventions in Chapter 6.

In the remainder of this section, we consider four approaches for providing common arithmetic operations: 3-address machines, 2-address machines, 1-address machines, and 0-address machines. As you read these descriptions, bear in mind that this is a gross classification of machines. Like any classification scheme, it is not perfect. Most real machines do not fit cleanly into any one of these categories.

You may notice that we jumped from operands to addresses. For the remainder of this section, we will use addresses to specify operands. The destination operand must specify a location to store the result and, as such, this convention is appropriate for the destination operand. On the other hand, the source operands specify the values used in the calculation. It might seem more appropriate to specify these values directly. Frequently, however, we use the result of an earlier operation as an operand. In these cases, we will not know the value of the operand, just the location of the result from the earlier operation. Given this context, using addresses instead of values provides us with a greater degree of flexibility. Later, in section 4.4, we will discuss notational conventions that allow you to specify the source operands using values instead of memory locations. For the present, we must specify source operands indirectly by giving the address of a memory location that holds the value.

4.1.1 3-Address Machines

In a 3-address machine, all three operands are explicit in each instruction. Table 4.1 presents sample instructions for a 3-address machine.

Table 4.1 Sample instructions for a 3-address machine

Symbolic instruction	Semantics
ADD $dest, src_1, src_2$	Add the value stored in memory location src_1 to the value stored in memory location src_2, and store the result in memory location $dest$. $M[dest] = M[src_1] + M[src_2]$
MPY $dest, src_1, src_2$	Multiply the value stored in memory location src_1 by the value stored in memory location src_2, and store the result in memory location $dest$. $M[dest] = M[src_1] * M[src_2]$

Coding Convention—Destination First

Note that we list the destination as the first operand of each instruction. This convention is common but not universal. Some machines list the destination as the last operand. Listing the destination as the last operand is consistent with the verbal descriptions given in Table 4.1. In contrast, listing the destination operand first is consistent with the assignment statements written in high-level languages (see the comments in Example 4.2).

Example 4.2   *Show how you can use the instructions shown in Table 4.1 to evaluate the statement* a = a ∗ b + c ∗ d ∗ e. *You should assume that the variables* a, b, c, d, *and* e *are associated with the memory locations 100, 104, 108, 112, and 116, respectively. In addition, you may assume that memory location 200 is available for use as a temporary.*

```
MPY   100, 100, 104    ; a = a * b;
MPY   200, 108, 112    ; tl = c * d;
MPY   200, 200, 116    ; tl = tl * e;
ADD   100, 200, 100    ; a = a + tl;
```

Coding Convention—Line Oriented

In examining the code fragment shown in Example 4.2, notice that every line is a statement and every statement is on a separate line. In other words, there is a direct relationship between lines and statements. This is a common requirement of assemblers and, consequently, assembly language programming. We call this requirement *line oriented*. In contrast, free-format languages (like C and Pascal) do not impose a similar restriction. In these languages, you can have several statements on a single line or a single statement that spans several lines.

Because assembly languages are line oriented, they typically have very simple *comment conventions*. Lines that only have white space characters (space, tab, newline, and so forth) are comments and, as such, ignored. Further, anything on a line that follows a semicolon (including the semicolon) is a comment and, as such, ignored.

4.1.2 2-Address Machines

As you examine the instructions in Example 4.2, notice that three of the four instructions repeat an address. Only the second instruction uses three distinct addresses. This situation arises frequently. In 2-address machines, instructions only have two explicit addresses. One address doubles as the address of a source operand and the address of the destination.

Table 4.2 Sample instructions for a 2-address machine

Symbolic instruction	Semantics
ADD *dest, src*	Add the value stored in memory location *src* to the value stored in memory location *dest,* and store the result in memory location *dest.* M[*dest*] = M[*dest*] + M[*src*]
MPY *dest, src*	Multiply the value stored in memory location *src* by the value stored in memory location *dest,* and store the result in memory location *dest.* M[*dest*] = M[*dest*] * M[*src*]
MOVE *dest, src*	Copy the value stored in memory location *src* to memory location *dest.* M[*dest*] = M[*src*]

MOVE

Table 4.2 presents sample instructions for a 2-address machine. In examining Table 4.2, notice that the first address doubles as a source operand and the destination operand in the ADD and MPY instructions. Besides the data manipulation operations (ADD and MPY), Table 4.2 includes a data transfer operation—*MOVE*.

Example 4.3   *Show how you can use the instructions shown in Table 4.2 to evaluate the statement* a = a * b + c * d * e. *You should assume that the variables* a, b, c, d, *and* e *are associated with the memory locations 100, 104, 108, 112, and 116, respectively. In addition, you may assume that memory location 200 is available for use as a temporary.*

```
MPY     100, 104      ; a *= b;
MOVE    200, 108      ; tl = c;
MPY     200, 112      ; tl *= d;
MPY     200, 116      ; tl *= e;
ADD     100, 200      ; a += tl;
```

> **C Programming Convention**
> In examining Example 4.3, you may be surprised by the notation used in the comments. In the C programming language, a statement of the form $a\ +=\ tl$ is equivalent to the statement $a = a + tl$.

Note how we use the MOVE instruction to initialize the value of the temporary, *tl*. We used the fact that multiplication and addition are commutative in writing the program fragment shown in Example 4.3. If the original statement used division and subtraction, we might need to rearrange parts of the calculation or use more instructions to calculate the result.

4.1.3 1-Address Machines (Accumulator Machines)

In a 1-address (or accumulator) machine, the accumulator doubles as the destination operand and one of the source operands. As such, you only need to specify one explicit operand, the address of the other source operand, in each instruction. There is, of course, an exception to the rule that the accumulator is the destination operand. In the STORE instruction, the accumulator is the source operand, the single explicit address specifies the destination.

In Chapter 3, we presented a simple accumulator machine. Table 4.3 reproduces a portion of the instruction set for that machine.

Table 4.3 Sample instructions for a 1-address machine

Symbolic instruction	Semantics
ADD *addr*	Add the value stored in memory location *addr* with the value in the accumulator, and store the result in the accumulator. *accum = accum +* M[*addr*]
MPY *addr*	Multiply the value stored in memory location *addr* with the value in the accumulator, and store the result in the accumulator. *accum = accum ∗* M[*addr*]
LOAD *addr*	Load the accumulator with the value stored in memory location *addr*. *accum =* M[*addr*]
STORE *addr*	Store the value in the accumulator into memory location *addr*. M[*addr*] *= accum*

Example 4.4 *Show how you can use the instructions shown in Table 4.3 to evaluate the statement* a = a ∗ b + c ∗ d ∗ e. *You should assume that the variables* a, b, c, d, *and* e *are associated with the memory locations 100, 104, 108, 112, and 116, respectively.*

```
LOAD   100     ; acc = a;
MPY    104     ; acc *= b;
STORE  100     ; a = acc;
LOAD   108     ; acc = c;
MPY    112     ; acc *= d;
MPY    116     ; acc *= e;
ADD    100     ; acc += a;
STORE  100     ; a = acc;
```

Note that there is no explicit temporary, *t1*, in Example 4.4. In effect, the accumulator acts as the needed temporary. The accumulator can only act as a single temporary. More complicated expressions may require explicit temporaries.

4.1.4 0-Address Machines (Stack Machines)

At first it may seem impossible to consider a machine in which instructions do not have explicit addresses. However, all that is required is that we know where to find both of the operands and where to store the result. Perhaps the most common example of a stack machine is an HP calculator. Values that you enter are pushed onto an internal stack. Operations take values from the stack and push their results back onto the stack (where they are available for future calculations).

To contrast stack machines with the other machines we have been discussing, we will assume that variables are associated with memory cells. As such, we need two special operations to transfer values between memory cells and the stack. As you have probably guessed, we call these operations PUSH and POP. Table 4.4 presents sample instructions for a stack machine. Note that the PUSH and POP instructions both have explicit addresses, even though we call this a 0-address machine.

Table 4.4 Sample instructions for a 0-address machine

Symbolic instruction	Semantics
ADD	Pop the top two values off of the stack, add them together, and push the result back onto the stack. push(pop + pop)
MPY	Pop the top two values off of the stack, multiply them, and push the result back onto the stack. push(pop * pop)
PUSH addr	Push the value stored in memory location addr onto the top of the stack. push(M[addr])
POP addr	Pop the top value off of the stack, and store it into memory location addr. M[addr] = pop

---

Example 4.5   *Show how you can use the instructions shown in Table 4.4 to evaluate the statement* a = a * b + c * d * e. *You should assume that the variables* a, b, c, d, *and* e *are associated with the memory locations 100, 104, 108, 112, and 116, respectively.*

```
PUSH   100     ; ⟨a⟩
PUSH   104     ; ⟨a⟩⟨b⟩
MPY            ; ⟨a * b⟩
PUSH   108     ; ⟨a * b⟩⟨c⟩
PUSH   112     ; ⟨a * b⟩⟨c⟩⟨d⟩
MPY            ; ⟨a * b⟩⟨c * d⟩
PUSH   116     ; ⟨a * b⟩⟨c * d⟩⟨e⟩
MPY            ; ⟨a * b⟩⟨c * d * e⟩
ADD            ; ⟨a * b + c * d * e⟩
POP    100
```

As was the case for the accumulator machine, there is no need for an explicit temporary in the code shown in Example 4.5. Unlike the accumulator, the stack can hold any number of temporaries;[2] therefore, you never need explicit temporaries on a stack machine.

---

[2] The number of temporaries is, of course, limited by the actual size of the stack.

4.1.5 Contrasts

Every machine has instructions for evaluating standard binary operations and storing the result. We call these ternary operations because three operands need to be specified: the two operands for the binary operation and a third operand that specifies where the result should be stored. In a 3-address machine, all three operands are explicit in the instruction. In a 2-address machine, one address specifies a source operand and the destination. In a 1-address machine, the accumulator is the second source operand as well as the destination. In a 0-address machine, the stack provides both source operands as well as the destination.

You may have noticed that we did not discuss any binary operations (copy, negate, and so forth) in the context of 3-address machines. In a 3-address machine, these operations might be provided by instructions with only two addresses. Saying that a machine is an n-address machine does not imply that every instruction for the machine must have n explicit addresses, nor does it imply that instructions have at most n addresses. As we saw with the 0-address machines, it is possible to have instructions that have an explicit address and still classify the machine as a 0-address machine. The classification scheme is based on how many addresses are explicitly stated in most of the "important" arithmetic instructions.

If you compare the code sequences shown in Examples 4.2, 4.3, 4.4, and 4.5, you may notice two trends. First, the number of instructions needed seems to increase as we decrease the number of explicit operands in each instruction. Second, the size of each instruction seems to decrease as we decrease the number of addresses in each instruction (because you do not need to specify as many addresses). While there are exceptions to these rules, they are in general valid observations.

4.2 REGISTERS

When compared with the speed of the CPU, memory access is slow. To compensate for this difference, many machines provide a small set of registers that are internal to the CPU. Like the words in primary memory, each register has a unique address. You can use these registers for storing intermediate results. Because they are internal to the CPU, accessing a register does not incur the additional time of a memory access.

Besides the savings in time, using registers can frequently save space. Because the number of registers is much smaller than the number of words in primary memory, the address of a register is smaller than the address of a memory word. This saving is reflected in the instruction encoding.

In considering how code fragments might be improved, it is helpful to count the number of memory accesses needed to execute the fragment. The more memory accesses required, the longer it takes to execute the code. To simplify our accounting, we assume that the encoding for every instruction uses a single memory word. As such, every instruction fetch requires a single memory access. This is not necessarily a reasonable assumption. The number of words used to encode an instruction frequently depends on the number and types of the explicit addresses in the instruction.

It is common to refer to operations that move values from memory locations into registers as *load operations* because these operations "load" the registers before starting a calculation. Operations that move values from registers to memory locations are called *store operations* because they "store" the results in memory when the calculation is complete. Note that these names are consistent with the LOAD and STORE instructions that we introduced with the accumulator machines.

Load operations

Store operations

4.2.1 Registers on a 3-Address Machine

Execution of an ADD or MPY instruction on a 3-address machine requires four memory accesses: one to fetch the instruction, two to fetch the source operands, and one to store the result. We can reduce the number of memory accesses by using registers for the source or destination operands. If an instruction uses registers for all of its operands, the processor only needs one memory access to execute the instruction (the access needed to fetch the instruction).

Example 4.6   *Show how you can use registers to improve the code fragment presented in Example 4.2.*

	Original sequence			Using registers	
MPY	100, 100, 104	; 4 refs.	MPY	R2, 100, 104	; 3 refs.
MPY	200, 108, 112	; 4 refs.	MPY	R3, 108, 112	; 3 refs.
MPY	200, 116, 200	; 4 refs.	MPY	R3, 116, R3	; 2 refs.
ADD	100, 200, 100	; 4 refs.	ADD	100, R3, R2	; 2 refs.
		; 16 refs.			; 10 refs.

Note that the original version required 16 memory references, while the register version only requires 10 memory references—a significant savings in the number of memory accesses.

Coding Convention—Register Notation
In writing assembly language programs, we use the notation R*n* (where *n* is a small unsigned integer) to distinguish register addresses from memory addresses. In Example 4.6, we used R2 and R3 to denote registers 2 and 3, respectively.

4.2.2 Registers on a 2-Address Machine

On a 2-address machine, execution of a standard arithmetic operation may require four memory accesses; the accounting is just as it was for the 3-address machine. If the source operand is a register, you will save a memory access. If the destination is a register, you will save two memory accesses. Binary operations (e.g., MOVE) may require one, two, or three memory accesses.

Example 4.7   *Show how you can use registers to improve the code fragment shown in Example 4.3.*

Original sequence			Using registers		
MPY	100, 104	; *4 refs.*	MPY	100, 104	; *4 refs.*
MOVE	200, 108	; *3 refs.*	MOVE	R2, 108	; *2 refs.*
MPY	200, 112	; *4 refs.*	MPY	R2, 112	; *2 refs.*
MPY	200, 116	; *4 refs.*	MPY	R2, 116	; *2 refs.*
ADD	100, 200	; *4 refs.*	ADD	100, R2	; *3 refs.*
		; *19 refs.*			; *13 refs.*

Note that the code that uses registers only requires 13 memory accesses, while the original code sequence requires 19 memory accesses.

---

1 1/2-Address Machines   Some 2-address machines require that one operand be a register. Usually, the destination must be a register; however, there are exceptions to this rule. These machines are similar to accumulator machines—with multiple accumulators. They are somewhere between general 2-address machines and simple accumulator machines. You have an explicit second address; however, one address must identify an accumulator. For this reason, these machines are called 1 1/2-address machines.

Example 4.8   *Show how you would rewrite the code given in Example 4.7 for a 1 1/2-address machine.*

MOVE	R2, 100	; *2 refs.*
MPY	R2, 104	; *2 refs.*
MOVE	R3, 108	; *2 refs.*
MPY	R3, 112	; *2 refs.*
MPY	R3, 116	; *2 refs.*
ADD	R2, R3	; *1 ref.*
MOVE	100, R2	; *2 refs.*
		; *13 refs.*

4.2.3 Registers on an Accumulator Machine

In an accumulator machine, the accumulator is *the* register. Like the registers on a 2- or 3-address machine, the accumulator is internal to the CPU. Therefore, access to the accumulator does not incur an additional memory access. Here, it is reasonable to assume that every instruction requires two memory accesses—one to fetch the instruction and another to fetch the explicit operand or store the result. Additional registers could be used to save intermediate results that cannot be stored in the accumulator.

Example 4.9   *Show how you can use registers to improve the code fragment shown in Example 4.4.*

Original sequence			Using registers		
LOAD	100	; *2 refs.*	LOAD	100	; *2 refs.*
MPY	104	; *2 refs.*	MPY	104	; *2 refs.*
STORE	100	; *2 refs.*	STORE	R2	; *1 refs.*
LOAD	108	; *2 refs.*	LOAD	108	; *2 refs.*
MPY	112	; *2 refs.*	MPY	112	; *2 refs.*
MPY	116	; *2 refs.*	MPY	116	; *2 refs.*
ADD	100	; *2 refs.*	ADD	R2	; *1 refs.*
STORE	100	; *2 refs.*	STORE	100	; *2 refs.*
		; *16 refs.*			; *14 refs.*

4.2.4 Registers on a Stack Machine

Stack depth

In a stack machine, a small part of the stack is internal to the CPU; the remaining values are in memory. The details of stack management are beyond the scope of our discussion. For the present, it is important to recognize that the number of values on the stack, called the *stack depth*, can influence the execution time of programs. If you push several values onto the stack, you may exceed the number of values stored in the CPU. When this happens, the push operation incurs additional memory references as the deeper values in the stack need to be moved from the CPU to the memory. Subsequent arithmetic operations also incur additional costs as they need to return these values from memory to the CPU. Clearly, minimizing stack depth is an important aspect of code optimization for a stack machine.

If we assume that the depth of the stack never exceeds the number of values maintained in the CPU, it is reasonable to assume that the push and pop operations require two memory accesses: one access to fetch the instruction and another to manipulate the operand. It is also reasonable to assume that arithmetic operations only require a single memory access. Here, we use the access to fetch the instruction. Applying these accounting procedures, we conclude that the code shown in Example 4.5 requires 16 memory accesses (6 push and pop operations + 4 arithmetic operations).[3]

There is no need to add explicit (data) registers to a stack machine. The stack provides a source of implicit registers. If the internal portion of the stack is not large enough (and requires memory accesses), the solution is to increase the size of the internal stack—not to introduce registers.

4.2.5 The Load/Store Architecture—RISC Machines

The load/store architecture is the basis for the RISC machines. Like 1 1/2-address machines, the load/store architecture imposes a restriction on the use of memory addresses: the operands for the data manipulation operations must be in registers. As such, you must explicitly load data values into registers before you can manipulate them. Table 4.5 presents sample instructions for a load/store architecture. In examining these instructions, note that the data manipulation instructions use three (register) addresses.

Table 4.5 Sample instructions for a load/store architecture

Symbolic instruction	Semantics
ADD Rd, Rs_1, Rs_2	Add the value stored in register Rs_1 with the value stored in register Rs_2, and store the result in Rd. $R[Rd] = R[Rs_1] + R[Rs_2]$
SUB Rd, Rs_1, Rs_2	Add the value stored in register Rs_1 with the value stored in register Rs_2, and store the result in Rd. $R[Rd] = R[Rs_1] - R[Rs_2]$
MPY Rd, Rs_1, Rs_2	Multiply the value stored in register Rs_1 with the value stored in register Rs_2 and store the result in Rd. $R[Rd] = R[Rs_1] * R[Rs_2]$
LOAD Rd, addr	Load register Rd with the value stored in memory location addr. $R[Rd] = M[addr]$
STORE addr, Rs	Store the value in register Rs in memory location addr. $M[addr] = R[Rs]$

Example 4.10 *Show how you can use the instructions shown in Table 4.5 to evaluate the statement* a = a * b + c * d * e. *You should assume that the variables* a, b, c, d, *and* e *are associated with the memory locations 100, 104, 108, 112, and 116, respectively.*

[3] Our accounting procedures are actually a bit unfair to stack machines. In particular, to simplify our accounting, we have assumed that each instruction can be encoded in a single word. Instructions for 2- and 3-address machines frequently require more than one word. In contrast, several instructions may fit into a single word on a stack machine. As such, the number of memory accesses we obtain for a 2-address machine is low, while the number for a stack machine is high.

```
LOAD      R2, 100      ; load a                    2 refs.
LOAD      R3, 104      ; load b                    2 refs.
LOAD      R4, 108      ; load c                    2 refs.
LOAD      R5, 112      ; load d                    2 refs.
LOAD      R6, 116      ; load e                    2 refs.
MPY       R2, R2, R3   ; R2 = a * b;               1 ref.
MPY       R3, R4, R5   ; R3 = c * d;               1 ref.
MPY       R3, R3, R6   ; R3 = (c*d) * e;           1 ref.
ADD       R2, R2, R3   ; R2 = a*b + (c*d)*e;       1 ref.
STORE     100, R2                                  2 refs.
                                                  ─────────
                                                  16 refs.
```

RISC

The load/store architecture is a common characteristic of *RISC* machines. As we have noted, the "reduced" in RISC refers to complexity of individual instructions. The load/store architecture simplifies instruction interpretation because only the load and store instructions need to access memory.

> **Coding Convention—Load/Store Architecture**
> Because it is the basis for most of the newer machines, we use the load/store architecture in the code examples that we present in the remainder of this text.

In examining the code fragment shown in this example, note that the load/store fragment requires 16 memory references. In contrast, the fragment for the 3-address machine only required 10 memory references (see Example 4.6), while the fragments for the 2-address and 1 1/2-address machines only required 13 memory references (see Examples 4.7 and 4.8). To see the advantages of the load/store architecture, we must look deeper than simple memory reference counts.

Instruction overlapping

Memory latency

An important benefit of the load/store architecture is that it simplifies *instruction overlapping*. Because memory systems are relatively slow, there is a time lag between the time the processor initiates a memory read and the time that the value is available. This time lag is frequently called *memory latency*. If the processor simply waits for the memory to respond with the requested value, it is wasting time when it could be doing useful work. To avoid wasting time, the processor may attempt to overlap instruction executions when possible. For example, the processor may be able to execute several instructions while it is executing a single LOAD instruction. To accommodate this overlap, the CPU initiates a memory read and continues executing instructions. Later, when the memory value is available, the CPU completes the LOAD operation by moving the memory value into the destination register.

Masked

If the instructions following the LOAD instruction do not use the value being read from memory, the processor will be kept busy and the memory latency will not be apparent. In this case, we have effectively *masked*, that is, hidden, the memory latency. If an instruction needs the value being loaded before the memory read completes, the processor needs to delay its execution. This delay is called a

Register interlock

register interlock.

Because this type of overlapping is limited to LOAD instructions, it is relatively easy to implement. In contrast, if a single instruction can include zero, one, two, or three memory references with an arithmetic manipulation, keeping track of which instructions have completed becomes an almost impossible task.

We should note that instruction overlapping requires that the instructions be stored in a high-speed memory—memory that does not have a significant latency. Without this high-speed memory, the processor could not possibly fetch and execute an instruction while it waits for a value from the memory. We discuss the techniques associated with instruction overlap in Chapter 9.

To take advantage of the instruction execution overlap, you need to be careful about the way you order the instructions in your program. In particular, it is a good idea to put at least one instruction between a LOAD instruction and any instructions that use the loaded value. Note that the code shown in Example 4.10 uses this strategy. Rearranging instructions to improve program execution is called *instruction scheduling*.

Instruction scheduling

We should note that some RISC machines (in particular the MIPS R3000 processor) require that the processor execute at least one instruction between a LOAD instruction and the first instruction that uses the loaded value. The instruction slot following the LOAD instruction is called the *load delay slot*. This term refers to the fact that the processor delays the effect of the load until it executes the instruction in the load delay slot. In these machines you can use a special instruction, *NOP (no operation)*, when you do not have any useful work to do before using the loaded value. We discuss these aspects of RISC machines at greater length in Chapter 9.

Load delay slot

NOP (no operation)

The term *instruction slot* reflects an interesting aspect of the RISC perspective. In this perspective, (instruction) memory is a collection of slots that hold instructions. The CPU looks in each slot and executes the instruction it finds.

Instruction slot

Note that the data manipulation operations in Table 4.5 use three addresses. This is also a common characteristic of RISC machines. Most RISC machines use 3-address instructions for all data manipulation or transfer operations. This introduces an interesting problem: How can you copy a value from one register to another? How can you negate the value in a register? On a RISC machine, you can copy register values using addition with the value zero. Similarly, you can implement negation using subtraction from zero. To support these operations, many RISC machines hardwire *R0* (register 0) to the value zero.

Example 4.11   *Write a code fragment that copies the value in R3 into R4 and negates the value in R5. Assume that R0 holds the value zero.*

```
ADD   R4, R0, R3    ; COPY R3 to R4
SUB   R5, R0, R5    ; negate the value in R5
```

While these instructions may not seem very intuitive, they are efficient. Remember, an addition or a subtraction only requires a single processor cycle.

> **Coding Convention—R0 = 0**
> In the remainder of this text, we will assume that the register R0 always holds the value zero.

Pseudo-op

Constructs like those in Example 4.11 make assembly code particularly difficult to read. In these instructions, the name of the operation does not convey the goal of the instruction. To avoid this problem, many assemblers provide special operations, called pseudo-operations (or *pseudo-ops*), that better reflect the operation implemented by an instruction. A pseudo-op is any operation that is not directly implemented by the machine but is recognized by the assembler.[4] As an example, the assembler might provide a MOVE operation. If the machine does not provide a MOVE operation, the assembler could translate instructions using the MOVE operation into instructions like the one shown in Example 4.11.

> **Coding Convention—Pseudo-Ops**
> In the remainder of this text we will assume that the assembler provides the following pseudo-ops:
>
> | Symbolic instruction | Semantics |
> | --- | --- |
> | CLEAR *Rd* | Clear register *Rd* to zero.
R[*Rd*] = 0 |
> | MOVE *Rd, Rs* | Copy register *Rs* to register *Rd*.
R[*Rd*] = R[*Rs*] |
> | NEG *Rd, Rs* | Store the negation of *Rs* in *Rd*.
R[*Rd*] = −R[*Rs*] |

4.3 OPERAND SIZES

In Chapter 3, we discussed the fact that modern memory systems provide access to a variety of unit sizes. Most memories are *byte addressable,* meaning that the smallest memory unit that can be addressed is one byte. As such, you can manipulate memory values in units of one byte, two bytes (halfword), or four bytes (word). This introduces a bit of a problem. Suppose you write the following instruction:

LOAD R0, 24

Does this mean to load the byte, halfword, or word value at memory location 24 into register 0?

Assemblers for the Intel 80x86 machines usually handle this problem by requiring an explicit size specifier on one operand. For example, AX and AL are both

---

[4] Pseudo-ops are also called *synthetic* operations.

names for the A register: AX denotes the 16-bit quantity stored in the A register, while AL denotes the lower 8 bits. As such, you can distinguish between adding the byte at memory location 24 and adding the halfword at memory location 24 by the name that you use for the A register. If you use the name AX, the 8086 performs a 16-bit addition. If you use the name AL, the 8086 performs an 8-bit addition.

Most assemblers associate the size specifier with the operation. In particular, it is common to use an operator suffix to denote the size of the operand(s). For example, the instruction:

LOAD.h R0, 24

specifies the halfword value stored at location 24.

Coding Convention—Operand Size

We will use an operator suffix to denote size of the operands. The following table summarizes the suffixes used in this text.

Suffix	Name	Number of bytes
.b	byte	1
.h	halfword	2
.w	word	4

RISC machines limit the use of size specifiers to the load and store operations. All data manipulation operations use the full register value. On these machines, values are expanded to the size of a register during the load operation and contracted to the appropriate size during a store operation. This expansion may be performed using *sign extension* or by setting the most significant bits to zero.

Most CISC machines are more flexible in the uses of size specifiers. On these machines, you can use size specifiers on the data manipulation operations in addition to the data transfer operations.

4.4 IMMEDIATE VALUES—CONSTANTS

So far, our instructions can manipulate the contents of memory cells and registers. In essence, we can evaluate any expression that involves simple arithmetic operations and variables. What about constants? Suppose you need to add 1 to a variable, assign the value 0 to a variable, or divide a variable by 5. How can this be accomplished? You could arrange to have all the constants that you need stored in memory locations. For example, you might arrange to have the value 5 stored in the memory location 102. Now, when you need to multiply by 5, you simply multiply by the value stored in memory location 102. The memory locations used in this fashion constitute a *constant table*.

Constant table

The problem with the constant table is that the constant value must be fetched from the table, adding a memory reference. Memory accesses are only useful if we expect that the value stored in the memory might change. If the value never changes (as is the case with constants), the address in effect specifies the value. This line of reasoning has lead to the inclusion of *immediate operands* on many machines. An immediate operand is an operand whose value (not address) is stored in the instruction. Thus, when the instruction is fetched, the value of the operand is immediately available and does not need to be fetched from memory.

Assemblers use two techniques to distinguish immediate operands from addresses: an operator suffix notation or an operand prefix. The name ADDI (add immediate) is an example of the operator suffix approach. In this case, the operator, ADD, has a suffix, I, to indicate that one operand is an immediate value (and not an address). Using the operand prefix approach, an operand may be prefixed with the symbol # to indicate that the operand is a value and not an address.

Coding Convention—Address Prefixes

So far, we have discussed three types of "addresses": memory addresses, register addresses, and immediate values. In every case, we use unsigned integers to distinguish the objects in these sets. By default, the number used to specify an operand is interpreted as a memory address. We distinguish the other possible interpretations by using prefixes: R for registers, and # for immediate values. The following table summarizes these conventions.

Prefix	Example	Meaning
⟨none⟩	24	Memory address
R	R4	Register address
#	#32	Immediate value

4.5 FLOW OF CONTROL

Suppose the machine you are using does not have a division operation. How would you provide the necessary calculation? Knowing how to write programs, you might sketch out the code fragment shown in Figure 4.1.

```
temp = y;
x = 0;
while( temp >= z ){
    x = x + 1;
    temp = temp − z;
}
```

Figure 4.1   A code fragment to implement $x = y/z$

From our previous discussions, you know (in principle) how to translate the initializing statements and body of this loop into assembly language. However, you do not know how to translate the control structure (the **while** loop). In this section, we present the basic mechanisms used to express flow of control in assembly language programs.

Before discussing machine-level mechanisms, we consider a version of our code that uses simpler control mechanisms, in particular, one that does not use a **while** loop. Figure 4.2 presents a code fragment that only uses **goto**'s and a simple **if** statement. In this code fragment, the **if** statement simply specifies the conditional execution of a **goto**.

```
        temp = y;
        x = 0;
top:
    if( temp < z ) goto bottom
        x = x + 1;
    temp = temp − z;
    goto top
bottom:
```

Figure 4.2 Using conditional and unconditional **goto**'s

This version is more difficult to read than the previous version because the mechanisms used, conditional and unconditional **goto**'s, are more primitive. These are the basic mechanisms used to control program execution on sequential machines. All control structures provided by high-level languages, **if-else** statements, **while** loops, **do-until** loops, **for** loops, and so forth, can be implemented using only these simple mechanisms.

4.5.1 Labels and Unconditional Transfers

In Chapter 3, we presented the ifetch loop. As you will recall, each iteration of the loop involves three steps: fetch the next instruction, increment the program counter, and interpret the instruction. The processor uses the value of the program counter to determine the instruction to fetch in the first step. Because the processor increments the program counter on each iteration of the ifetch loop, the next instruction is, by default, in the memory location following the current instruction. Control transfer instructions change the value of the program counter, thus changing the location of the next instruction.

An unconditional transfer simply assigns a new value to the program counter. We use the name BRANCH to refer to this operation (this operation may also be called JUMP). BRANCH is a single-address instruction. The address specifies the target of the branch, that is, the new value for the program counter.

When you use a BRANCH instruction, you know the instruction that you would like to branch to but you probably do not know where the assembler will place that instruction. Moreover, even if you did know, you might need to change the addresses specified in your branch statements when you add or delete an instruction.

Fortunately, most assemblers provide symbolic labels so you can avoid these difficulties. The following conventions are common among assemblers:

- A label is an identifier (and follows the standard rules for identifier formation).
- The definition of a label occurs when the label appears as the first nonwhite space item on a line followed by a colon (":").
- Each label can have at most one definition.
- The value of the label is the address of the next instruction (which may be on the same line as the label).
- Whenever you use a label in a nondefining context, the assembler substitutes the value of the label for the label.
- You may use a label before you give its definition.

Example 4.12   *Using labels and the BRANCH instruction, show how you can translate the program fragment shown in Figure 4.2. Do not attempt to translate the conditional* **goto** *used in this code. You should assume that* x, y, *and* z *are in memory locations 100, 104, and 108, respectively.*

```
        LOAD.w    R2, 104        ; temp = y; (R2 is temp)
        LOAD.w    R3, 108        ; R3 is z
        CLEAR     R4             ; x = 0; (R4 is x)
top:
        ?????     ????           ; if( temp < z ) goto bottom
        ADD       R4, R4, #1     ; x = x + 1;
        SUB       R2, R2, R3     ; temp = temp − z;
        BRANCH    top            ; goto top
bottom:
        STORE.w   100, R4        ; store the result
```

This code fragment uses two labels: *top* and *bottom*. Besides the labels, there are three aspects of this code fragment that merit further comment:

- Note the use of an immediate value in the fifth statement.
- Note the size specifiers on the LOAD and STORE instructions.
- Note that the code begins by loading the needed memory values; this may improve the efficiency of the code.

4.5.2 Compare and Branch

We began our study of arithmetic expressions by describing how complex expressions could be broken into a sequence of simple statements. Similarly, all conditional expressions can be transformed into sequences of simple relational operations. As such, we only need to consider relational operations when we consider conditional branching mechanisms. For the moment, we only consider conditional branches that involve a single relational operation—just enough to complete the translation of our code fragment. After we consider these simple branches, we will discuss a technique for reducing more complex conditional expressions into sequences of simple relational operations.

Every relational operation takes two operands and produces a Boolean value (*true* or *false*). Conditional branching instructions have a third operand—the *target*. If the relation is *true,* the target specifies the new value of the program counter, that is, the address of the next instruction. If the relation is *false,* the processor does not change the value of the program counter; that is, the processor uses simple sequencing to determine the next instruction. In other words, the program counter "falls through" to the next instruction if the relation does not hold. This is exactly the behavior of the **if** statement in our division code fragment (Figure 4.2).

Target

Table 4.6 presents a collection of conditional branching instructions. These instructions use an explicit statement of all three operands.

Table 4.6 Compare and branch operations

Symbolic instruction	Semantics
BRLT R_1, R_2, *target*	PC $\leftarrow$ *target* if R_1 is **less than** R_2.
BRLE R_1, R_2, *target*	PC $\leftarrow$ *target* if R_1 is **less than or equal to** R_2.
BREQ R_1, R_2, *target*	PC $\leftarrow$ *target* if R_1 is **equal to** R_2.
BRNE R_1, R_2, *target*	PC $\leftarrow$ *target* if R_1 is **not equal to** R_2.
BRGE R_1, R_2, *target*	PC $\leftarrow$ *target* if R_1 is **greater than or equal to** R_2.
BRGT R_1, R_2, *target*	PC $\leftarrow$ *target* if R_1 is **greater than** R_2.

Example 4.13   *Using the conditional branching instructions in Table 4.6, show how you can complete the translation of the program fragment shown in Figure 4.2.*

```
        LOAD.w    R2, 104          ; temp = y; (R2 is temp)
        LOAD.w    R3, 108          ; R3 is z
        CLEAR     R4               ; x = 0; (R4 is x)
top:
        BRLT      R2, R3, bottom   ; if( temp < z ) goto bottom
        ADD       R4, R4, #1       ; x = x + 1;
        SUB       R2, R2, R3       ; temp = temp − z;
        BRANCH    top              ; goto top
bottom:
        STORE.w   100, R4          ; store the result
```

4.5.3 Comparison to Zero

Since the instructions shown in Table 4.6 have three addresses, you might suspect that these instructions are best suited to a 3-address machine. This might lead you to consider how you could eliminate an explicit operand. In presenting the arithmetic instructions, we eliminated an explicit operand by using one operand as both a source and destination. This technique will not work for the conditional branching operations. The value stored at the target address is an instruction—hardly a meaningful value on which to base a comparison. However, we can eliminate an explicit operand by using the value 0 as an implicit operand. Table 4.7 presents a collection of conditional branching instructions based on comparisons to zero.

Table 4.7 Compare-to-zero operations

Symbolic instruction	Semantics
BRLT R, target	PC ← target if R is **less than** 0.
BRLE R, target	PC ← target if R is **less than or equal to** 0.
BREQ R, target	PC ← target if R is **equal to** 0.
BRNE R, target	PC ← target if R is **not equal to** 0.
BRGE R, target	PC ← target if R is **greater than or equal to** 0.
BRGT R, target	PC ← target if R is **greater than** 0.

Example 4.14   *Using the conditional branching instructions in Table 4.7, show how you can complete the translation of the program fragment shown in Figure 4.2.*

```
        LOAD.w    R2, 104      ; temp = y; (R2 is temp)
        LOAD.w    R3, 108      ; R3 is z
        CLEAR     R4           ; x = 0; (R4 is x)
top:
        SUB       R5, R2, R3   ; R5 = temp - z
        BRLT      R5, bottom   ; if( R5 < 0 ) goto bottom
        ADD       R4, R4, #1   ; x = x + 1;
        SUB       R2, R2, R3   ; temp = temp − z;
        BRANCH    top          ; goto top
bottom:
        STORE.w   100, R4      ; store the result
```

The code shown in Example 4.14 represents a direct translation of the original program. This translation uses the fact that the relation $temp \leq z$ is equivalent to the relation $temp - z \leq 0$.

Note that the two subtractions in Example 4.14 are almost identical. It is not necessarily bad to have two similar subtractions in a program. However, when both are in the same loop, you should see if they can be merged into a single instruction. If you know that the value of *temp* will not be used after the loop—the name *temp* seems to suggest this possibility—you can reduce the number of subtractions performed inside the loop.

Example 4.15   *Show how you can improve the code fragment presented in Example 4.14.*

```
          LOAD.w    R2, 104       ; temp = y; (R2 is temp)
          LOAD.w    R3, 108       ; R3 is z
          CLEAR     R4            ; x = 0; (R4 is x)
top:
          SUB       R2, R2, R3    ; temp = temp − z;
          BRLT      R2, bottom    ; if( temp < 0 ) goto bottom
          ADD       R4, R4, #1    ; x = x + 1;
          BRANCH    top           ; goto top
bottom:
          STORE.w   100, R4       ; store the result
```

Notice that this version iterates until the value of *temp* is less than 0 (the original iterates until *temp* is less than *z*).

In examining the code in Example 4.15, you may spot another possible optimization. Because the subtraction occurs just before the start of each iteration, we can merge the two subtractions into a single statement. This statement should appear just after the *top* label and before the BRLT instruction. While the previous optimization improves the execution speed of the program, this optimization simply reduces the number of instructions used in the description of the program.

Even with these improvements, another improvement is possible. Currently, the unconditional branch at the bottom of the loop jumps to the top of the loop to determine if it should branch to the end of the loop. It would be better to move the label *top* just below the conditional branch and change the unconditional branch into a conditional branch. With these changes, execution of the program only reaches the top of the loop if the body of the loop is going to be executed. This improvement is important because it reduces the number of instructions in the body of the loop. Our previous version had two branch instructions in the loop—a conditional branch at the top of the loop and an unconditional branch at the bottom of the loop. The suggested version only has a conditional branch at the bottom of the loop. The unconditional branch has been moved outside of the loop.

Example 4.16   *Show how you can apply the suggested improvements to the code fragment shown in Example 4.15.*

```
          LOAD.w    R2, 104       ; temp = y; (R2 is temp)
          LOAD.w    R3, 108       ; R3 is z
          CLEAR     R4            ; x = 0; (R4 is x)
          BRANCH    test          ; goto test
```

```
top:
        ADD     R4, R4, #1      ; x = x + 1;
test:
        SUB     R2, R2, R3      ; temp = temp − z;
        BRGE    R2, top         ; if( temp ≥ 0 ) goto top
        STORE.w 100, R4         ; store the result
```

4.5.4 Condition Codes

As you look at the code in the previous examples, notice that we use an arithmetic operation to "set up" the conditional branch. In particular, we compare the result of a subtraction to zero in a later instruction. We can avoid the need to name the result of the arithmetic operation if we base conditional operations on the result of the last arithmetic operation. In particular, if we store two bits of information—one to indicate if the result was negative and another to indicate if the result was zero—we can use comparison of the result of the last arithmetic result to zero as the basis of conditional branches. The bits saved after every arithmetic operation constitute the *condition code register*. Use of the condition code register means that conditional branch instructions only need one explicit operand—the target address. The other operands are implicit—one source operand is the result of the last operation, the other is the value zero.

Condition code register

Table 4.8 presents a collection of conditional branch instructions based on a condition register. In these descriptions, we use N for the name of the bit that indicates if the result was negative and Z for the bit that indicates if the result was zero. The Boolean expressions that specify the conditions for branching should be rather obvious. For example, the BRGT instruction branches to the target address if the result of the previous operation was greater than zero—in other words if the result was not negative and not zero.

Table 4.8 Condition code branching operations

Symbolic instruction	Semantics
BRLT *target*	PC ← *target* if N.
BRLE *target*	PC ← *target* if $N \lor Z$.
BREQ *target*	PC ← *target* if Z.
BRNE *target*	PC ← *target* $\bar{Z}$.
BRGE *target*	PC ← *target* if $\bar{N}$.
BRGT *target*	PC ← *target* if $\bar{N} \land \bar{Z}$.

The standard arithmetic operations update the bits in the condition code register. On some machines, the data transfer operations also update the bits in the condition code register. Some of the newer machines provide two versions of the standard arithmetic operations: one set that updates the condition code register and another set that does not.

Example 4.17   *Show how you can write the code fragment shown in Example 4.16 using the conditional branch instructions in Table 4.8.*

```
        LOAD.w    R2, 104      ; temp = y; (R2 is temp)
        LOAD.w    R3, 108      ; R3 is z
        CLEAR     R4           ; x = 0; (R4 is x)
        BRANCH    test         ; goto test
top:
        ADD       R4, R4, #1   ; x = x + 1;
test:
        SUB       R2, R2, R3   ; temp = temp − z;
        BRGE      top          ; if( temp ≥ 0 ) goto top
        STORE.w   100, R4      ; store the result
```

Coding Convention—CMP

In many cases, you need to compare two values, but do not need to subtract them (and store the result of the subtraction). In this text we will assume that the assembler provides a comparison operation, CMP, that can be used to set the condition codes.

Symbolic	Semantics	Possible implementation
CMP *Ra, Rb*	Compare registers *Ra* and *Rb*	SUB R0, *Ra, Rb*

Coding Convention—Condition Codes

In the remainder of this text, we will describe conditional branching in terms of condition codes.

4.5.5 Definite Iteration—Special Looping Instructions

The example that we have been discussing involves *indefinite iteration*—iteration in which the number of iterations is not easily determined prior to the execution of the loop. Indefinite iteration is typically specified using a **while** or **do-while** (**repeat**) loop in a high-level language. In *definite iteration*, you can easily determine the number of iterations that a loop will execute without executing the loop. Definite iteration is typically expressed using a **for** loop. Figure 4.3 presents a code fragment that uses definite iteration. In this example, the body of the loop will be executed y times.

Indefinite iteration

Definite iteration

```
x = 0
for( temp = y ; temp > 0 ; temp−− ){
   x = x + z;
}
```

Figure 4.3   A code fragment to implement
$x = y * z$

C Programming Convention

The **for** loop in C has a header and a body. The header has three parts: the initializer, the loop test, and the increment. These parts of the header are separated by semi-colons. The initializer is executed before the first iteration of the loop. The test is performed before each iteration and determines if the body of the loop is executed. The increment is executed at the completion of each iteration.

In Figure 4.3, the initializer sets *temp* to the value of *y*. The test specifies that the body of the loop is only executed if *temp* is greater than 0. Upon the completion of every iteration, the value of *temp* is decremented by 1.

Example 4.18   *Translate the code fragment in Figure 4.3 into assembly code. You should assume that the variables* x, y, *and* z *are associated with the memory locations 100, 104, and 108, respectively.*

```
        LOAD.w    R2, 104        ; temp = y; (R2 is temp)
        LOAD.w    R3, 108        ; (R3 is z)
        CLEAR     R4             ; x = 0; (R4 is x)
        ADD       R2, R2, #1     ; set up for decrement
        BRANCH    test           ; test the loop condition
top:
        ADD       R4, R4, R3     ; x = x + z;
test:
        SUB       R2, R2, #1     ; temp--
        BRGT      top            ; test loop condition
        STORE.w   100, R4        ; store x
```

Note that the last two instructions in the body of the loop involve a decrement and a conditional branch. Every **for** loop can be translated so that the body of the loop ends with a decrement followed by a conditional branch. Many machines provide a special-purpose *looping instruction* that combines the decrement and conditional branch in a single instruction.

Looping instruction

4.5.6 More Complex Conditional Expressions

Having covered simple relational operations, we turn our attention to the translation of more complicated conditional expressions. In particular, we consider the evaluation of expressions that use the operators *and* (&&) and *or* (||). In this section, we consider a particular technique called *positional evaluation*. Positional evaluation is an appropriate technique when you need to evaluate a conditional expression to implement conditional branching.

Positional evaluation

When you use positional evaluation, you do not obtain a value for the expression. Instead, you ensure that the program counter will be at one location if the expression is *true* and another if it is *false*. When we discuss the bitwise logical operations (AND and OR) in the next section, we consider another approach that generates the value of the result.

Example 4.19   *Show you can implement the following statement using* positional evaluation:

```
if( a < b && b ≤ c )
    goto true_lab;
else
    goto false_lab;
```

In writing this code, you should assume that the values for a, b, *and* c *are in registers R2, R3, and R4, respectively.*

```
BRGE      R2, R3, false_lab    ; a ≥ b?
BRGT      R3, R4, false_lab    ; b > c?
BRANCH    true_lab
```

Note that we do not need to evaluate $b \leq c$ if we determine that $a \geq b$. We call this technique *short-circuit evaluation*. In short-circuit evaluation, we transfer control to the appropriate location in the code as soon as we determine the result. We do not necessarily evaluate the entire expression.

Short-circuit evaluation

Two observations provide the basis for short-circuit evaluation. If the first operand of an *and* operation evaluates as *false,* the entire expression is *false*; otherwise, we must evaluate the second operand. In contrast, if the first operand of an *or* operation is *true,* the entire expression is *true*; otherwise, the second operand determines the value of the expression.

C requires short-circuit evaluation of conditional expressions. Other languages, like Pascal, require evaluation of the entire expression even after the result is known. Usually there is no observable difference between short-circuit evaluation and complete evaluation. As you write assembly language programs, you need to decide if the possibility of short-circuit evaluation is acceptable or whether you need to ensure complete evaluation.

4.5.7 Branch Delay Slots

We conclude our presentation of basic control mechanisms by considering an interesting aspect of overlapped instruction execution. As you will recall, an important aspect of RISC machines is that they overlap the execution of instructions. Overlapped execution is not limited to LOAD instructions. The processor may begin the execution of the next instruction before it completes the execution of the current instruction. Usually this execution strategy does not affect the way in which you write code; however, it has an important consequence when combined with branching instructions.

Consider how the execution of a (conditional or unconditional) branch interacts with an overlapped instruction execution. When the processor completes the execution of the branch instruction, it has already begun execution of the next instruction. In other words, the processor has fetched and begun execution of the instruction following the branch instruction, before it changes the value of the program counter. This means that the instruction following the branch instruction is **Branch delay slot**   always executed. The instruction slot after a branch instruction is called the *branch delay slot*, which refers to the fact that the processor delays the effect of the branch until it completes the execution of the instruction in the branch delay slot.

In considering the branch delay slot, it is useful to imagine that the CPU maintains two program counters: PC and nPC. The program counter, PC, identifies the current instruction; the next program counter, nPC, identifies the next instruction to be executed. RISC machines fetch the instruction identified by nPC while they **Instruction prefetch**   are executing the current instruction. This overlap is called *instruction prefetch*. Because of instruction prefetch, the processor assigns the current value of nPC to PC. In most cases, the processor also increments the value of nPC (by four— remember, each instruction occupies 4 bytes) so that it is pointing to the next instruction to be fetched. Branching instructions always change the value of nPC to affect a control transfer.

Example 4.20   *Consider the following program fragment. Suppose that the first instruction is stored in memory location 1000 and that every instruction requires four bytes. Show how the PC and nPC are updated during the execution of this code fragment.*

```
        CLEAR   R4              ; x = 0; (R4 is x)
        ADD     R2, R2, #1      ; set up for decrement
        BRANCH  test            ; test the loop condition
top:
        ADD     R4, R4, R3      ; x = x + z;
test:
        SUB     R2, R2, #1      ; temp− −
        BRGT    top             ; test loop condition
```

In this case, the label *top* is associated with memory location 1012 and *test* is associated with location 1016. In considering the following table, notice that the BRANCH has no effect.

PC	nPC	Executing	Fetching
1000	1004	CLEAR R4	ADD R2, R2, #1
1004	1008	ADD R2, R2, #1	BRANCH 1016
1008	1012	BRANCH 1016	ADD R4, R4, R3
1012	1016	ADD R4, R4, R3	SUB R2, R2, #1
1016	1020	SUB R2, R2, #1	BRGT 1012

Example 4.21 *Consider the following (revised) program fragment. Suppose that the first instruction is stored in memory location 1000 and that every instruction requires four bytes. Show how the PC and nPC are updated during the execution of this code fragment.*

```
         CLEAR    R4              ; x = 0; (R4 is x)
         BRANCH   test            ; test the loop condition
         ADD      R2, R2, #1      ; set up for decrement
top:
         ADD      R4, R4, R3      ; x = x + z;
test:
         SUB      R2, R2, #1      ; temp--
         BRGT     top             ; test loop condition
```

As before, the label *top* is associated with memory location 1012 and *test* is associated with location 1016. In this case, the BRANCH instruction causes the processor to skip the instruction at location 1012.

PC	nPC	Executing	Fetching
1000	1004	CLEAR R4	BRANCH 1016
1004	1008	BRANCH 1016	ADD R2, R2, #1
1008	1016	ADD R2, R2, #1	SUB R2, R2, #1
1016	1020	SUB R2, R2, #1	BRGT 1012

The branch delay slot (the instruction slot following a branch or conditional branch instruction) must hold an instruction. In most cases, you can move the instruction that occurs just before the branch into the branch delay slot. When this cannot be done, you need to fill the branch delay slot with a NOP instruction.

Example 4.22 *Modify the code fragment presented in Example 4.18 to account for branch delay slots.*

```
         LOAD.w   R2, 104         ; temp = y; (R2 is temp)
         LOAD.w   R3, 108         ; (R3 is z)
         CLEAR    R4              ; x = 0; (R4 is x)
         BRANCH   test            ; test the loop condition
         ADD      R2, R2, #1      ; MOVED—branch delay slot
top:
         ADD      R4, R4, R3      ; x = x + z;
test:
         SUB      R2, R2, #1      ; temp--
         BRGT     top             ; test loop condition
         NOP                      ; branch delay slot
         STORE.w  100, R4         ; store x
```

In this example, we filled the branch delay slot for the unconditional branch with the instruction that was just before the branch. However, we did not fill the branch delay slot for the conditional branch with a useful instruction. The instruction just before the conditional branch sets the condition code register for the conditional branch and, as such, must stay in front of the conditional branch.[5]

The situation illustrated by this example arises frequently—every time you use definite iteration in your program. Because this situation arises frequently, many RISC machines provide special versions of the conditional branching instructions. Besides providing a conditional branch, these instructions conditionally cancel the effect of the instruction in the branch delay slot. In particular, these conditional branch instructions *nullify* the effect of the instruction in the branch delay slot when the conditional branch is *not* taken.

Nullify

Example 4.23 *Show how you can use the conditional branch with nullify instructions to improve the code presented in the previous example.*

```
        LOAD.w    R2, 104        ; temp = y; (R2 is temp)
        LOAD.w    R3, 108        ; (R3 is z)
        CLEAR     R4             ; x = 0; (R4 is x)
        ADD       R2, R2, #1     ; MOVED—branch delay slot
top:
        SUB       R2, R2, #1     ; temp− −
        BRGT*     top            ; test loop condition
        ADD       R4, R4, R3     ; x = x + z; (may be canceled)
        STORE.w   100, R4        ; store x
```

Coding Convention—Conditional Nullify
We will use the operator suffix * to indicate nullification. Note that this convention is used in the BRGT operation in Example 4.23.

Our example seems tailor-made for this version of the conditional branch instructions. Moving the ADD instruction into the branch delay slot eliminated the need to branch around this instruction on the first iteration of the loop. This is a single example, and you should not assume that you can improve every loop to this extent by using a conditional branch with nullify instruction.

The semantics of the conditional branch with nullify instructions are well suited to looping structures. You can always put a useful instruction in the delay slot following the conditional branch at the end of a loop. You start by making two

---

[5] In this example, you could move the STORE instruction into the branch delay slot. The final execution of this instruction, after the loop exits, stores the correct value. However, this solution is not appropriate because it introduces an unnecessary memory access in every iteration of the loop.

copies of the first instruction in the loop. Place one copy in the branch delay slot and the other just before the start of the loop. The copy before the start of the loop ensures that the instruction is executed on the first iteration of the loop. The copy in the branch delay slot ensures that the instruction is executed on every other iteration of the loop.

Coding Convention—No Branch Delay Slots!
We will not use an explicit branch delay slot in the code fragments that we write in the remainder of this text. Inclusion of branch delay slots would make our code unnecessarily difficult to read. Moreover there are RISC machines (e.g., the IBM RIOS) that do not use an explicit branch delay slot.

4.6 BIT MANIPULATION

In this section, we introduce a collection of data manipulation operations that provide for direct manipulation of the bits in a memory word or register. There are three general types of bit manipulation operations. The *bitwise* operations manipulate an entire register one bit at a time. The *direct bit access* operations allow you to manipulate or test bits within registers. The *shift* and *rotate* operations provide a mechanism for shifting bits.

Bitwise

Direct bit access

Shift

Rotate

4.6.1 Bitwise Operations

The Boolean operations *and*, *or*, *xor*, and *not* provide the basis for the bitwise operations. The bitwise operations generalize the simple binary operations to sequences of bits by performing the simple operation on the corresponding bits from both sequences. Table 4.9 presents a collection of symbolic instructions for specifying the bitwise operations. The last two instructions, ANDN and ORN, implement the *and not* and *or not* operations, respectively.

Table 4.9 Bitwise operations

Symbolic instruction	Semantics
AND Rd, Rs_1, Rs_2	Each bit of the value in register Rs_1 is *and*ed with the corresponding bit of the value in Rs_2. The result is stored in Rd. $R[Rd] = R[Rs_1]$ & $R[Rs_2]$
OR Rd, Rs_1, Rs_2	Each bit of the value in register Rs_1 is *or*ed with the corresponding bit of the value in Rs_2. The result is stored in Rd. $R[Rd] = R[Rs_1]$ | $Rs_2]$
XOR Rd, Rs_1, Rs_2	Each bit of the value in register Rs_1 is *xor*ed with the corresponding bit of the value in Rs_2. The result is stored in Rd. $R[Rd] = R[Rs_1]$ ^ $R[Rs_2]$
ANDN Rd, Rs_1, Rs_2	Bitwise *and* of the value in Rs_1 with the bitwise inverse of the value in Rs_2. $R[Rd] = R[Rs_1]$ & $\sim R[Rs_2]$
ORN Rd, Rs_1, Rs_2	Bitwise *or* of the value in Rs_1 with the bitwise inverse of the value in Rs_2. $R[Rd] = R[Rs_1]$ | $\sim R[Rs_2]$

Coding Convention—NOT

Note that the operations in Table 4.9 do not include an operation that implements bitwise inversion, for example, NOT. Like NEG and MOVE, this operation does not map directly into the 3-address instructions used in the load/store architecture. As such, you can expect that the assembler provides a pseudo-op that implements this operation. The assembler may implement this pseudo-op using R0 and the ORN operation.

Example 4.24   *Suppose your registers hold 8-bit values and that R2 holds the value 10011011 and R3 holds the value 00001111. Describe what each of the following statements does:*

AND	R4, R2, R3
OR	R5, R2, R3
XOR	R6, R2, R3
ANDN	R7, R2, R3
ORN	R8, R2, R3

	10011011 (R2)		10011011 (R2)		10011011 (R2)
AND	00001111 (R3)	OR	00001111 (R3)	XOR	00001111 (R3)
	00001011 (R4)		10011111 (R5)		10010100 (R6)

	10011011 (R2)		10011011 (R2)
ANDN	00001111 (R3)	ORN	00001111 (R3)
	10010000 (R7)		11111011 (R8)

Mask

We frequently use the bitwise operations to clear, set, or invert selected bits in a register. Selecting the bits to be altered involves the use of a *mask*. We use the term *mask* in the sense of masking tape. You use masking tape to protect the things that you do not want changed when you are painting your car or a room in your house. The mask value is similarly used to protect bit positions that should not be changed by a bitwise operation.

Bits can be cleared (to zero) using a bitwise AND operation and a mask with zeros in the positions that are to be cleared and ones in the other positions. Bits can be set (to one) using a bitwise OR operation and a mask with ones in the positions that are to be changed. Bits can be inverted using a bitwise XOR operation and a mask with ones in the positions that are to be altered.

The bitwise operations can also be used to implement complex Boolean expressions. In contrast to *positional evaluation,* this approach is appropriate when you are working with Boolean values. To implement Boolean expressions using these operations, you must first determine appropriate representations for the Boolean values *true* and *false*. We use bytes to store Boolean values; we use the value 00000000 to represent the value *false* and the value 11111111 to represent the value *true*.

Example 4.25   *Show how you could implement the statement:*

$x = (x \ \& \ y) \ | \ z$

In writing this code, you should assume that the values for x, y, *and* z *are in locations 100, 104, and 108, respectively.*

```
LOAD.b    R2, 100      ; R2 is x
LOAD.b    R3, 104      ; R3 is y
LOAD.b    R4, 108      ; R4 is z
AND       R2, R2, R3   ; R2 = x & y
OR        R2, R2, R4   ; R2 = (x & y) | z
STORE.b   100, R2
```

4.6.2 Direct Bit Access

In this discussion, our goal is to introduce the direct bit access operations. These operations provide direct access to the bits in the values stored in registers. There is perhaps more variation on these operations than any other type of operation. As such, we keep our operations as simple as possible. You should expect to find much more sophisticated versions of these operations on actual machines.

Table 4.10 presents a simple collection of direct bit access operations. The first operation, BB (bit branch), tests the value of the *n*th bit and branches if the value of this bit is one. In this and the remaining direct access operations, the meaning of *n*th is intentionally vague. Depending on the machine, it could mean the *n*th most significant or least significant bit of the operand. Besides the BB operation, many machines provide operations that allow you to set or clear a bit field in a register. In Table 4.10, we call these operations BSET and BCLR.

Table 4.10   Direct bit access operations

Symbolic instruction	Semantics
BB *Rs, n, target*	Branch to *target* if the *n*th bit of register *Rs* is 1.
BSET *Rd, n, m*	Sets the *n*th through *m*th bits of register *Rd* to 1.
BCLR *Rd, n, m*	Sets the *n*th through *m*th bits of register *Rd* to 0.

4.6.3 Shift and Rotate Instructions

Shift operations involve moving each bit in a value to the left or right by a specified number of bit positions. Machines that have condition code registers usually store

Carry bit

the last bit shifted out of the value in the condition code register. Usually, the *carry bit* is used for this purpose. We discuss the carry bit at greater length in Chapter 7.

When you use a shift instruction, you need to specify the value to be used when the vacated bit positions are filled in addition to the direction and number of bit positions in the shift. Figure 4.4 illustrates six common shift operations. The box labeled "C" denotes the carry bit in the condition code register. In the *zero-fill* variations, the vacated bit positions are filled with zeros. In the *one-fill* variations, these positions are filled with ones. In the *rotate* versions, the bits that would otherwise be lost are used to fill the vacated bit positions.

Zero-fill

One-fill

Rotate

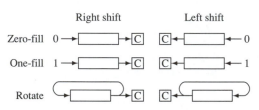

Figure 4.4   Shift operations

Table 4.11 presents a collection of symbolic instructions for specifying the shift operations. Table 4.11 only presents the left shifts; the instructions corresponding to the right shifts should be obvious.

Table 4.11   Left-shift operations

Symbolic instruction	Semantics
SLZ *Rd, Rs, n*	Shift the value in register *Rs* to the left by *n* bit positions, filling the vacated positions with zeros. Store the result in register *Rd*.
SLO *Rd, Rs, n*	Shift the value in register *Rs* to the left by *n* bit positions, filling the vacated positions with ones. Store the result in register *Rd*.
ROTL *Rd, Rs, n*	Rotate the value in register *Rs* to the left by *n* bit positions. Store the result in register *Rd*.

Arithmetic shift

In addition to the shift operations presented in this section, most machines provide a collection of *arithmetic shift* operations. We defer discussion of these operations until Chapter 7 when we discuss number representations.

4.7 CASE STUDY: INSTRUCTION ENCODING ON THE SPARC

We conclude this chapter by considering instruction encoding on the SPARC. SPARC is an acronym for *scalable processor architecture*. The SPARC architecture descends from the RISC I and RISC II processors developed at the University of California at Berkeley. This architecture is the basis for the SUN/4 workstations marketed by SUN Microsystems. Sun Microsystems developed the SPARC architecture. Instead of making the architecture proprietary, Sun Microsystems has decided to make SPARC an open architecture. Any vendor can build an implementation of the SPARC architecture. In adopting this strategy, Sun Microsystems hopes that the SPARC architecture will become the next industry standard.

In this section, we only present those aspects of the SPARC architecture needed to understand basic instruction encoding. We consider other aspects of this architecture in later chapters.

The SPARC architecture has 32 general-purpose registers; each register is 32 bits wide. Memory is byte addressable. Each memory address is 32 bits. Instructions are 32 bits and must be aligned on word boundaries.

Instruction encoding uses the three basic formats shown in Figure 4.5: the general format, the call format, and the branch/SETHI format. We distinguish basic formats by the positions of the fields in the instruction. Two of the basic formats (general and branch/SETHI) have variations. We distinguish variations by minor changes in the fields and changes in the interpretation of the fields. For example, bit 13, the immediate bit (*i*), in the first two variations of the general format specifies how to interpret the remaining 13 bits of the instruction. If this bit is 1, the remaining bits represent an immediate value. Otherwise, the remaining bits represent two fields, asi and rs2.

4.7.1 Load/Store Operations

We begin by considering the load and store operations. The SPARC architecture provides operations to load and store byte, halfword, word, and double word values. The double word operations use two successive registers and must start with an even numbered register (e.g., R2 and R3 could be used as a double word register pair). Every load instruction sets all 32 bits of the destination register(s). When you load a byte or halfword value, you must use a *signed* or *unsigned* load operation. Unsigned loads set the most significant bits in the destination register to zero. Signed loads extend the sign bit of the value loaded.

Load and store instructions are encoded using the first two variations of the general format. The op and op3 fields encode the operation. The operation encoding specifies the size of the operation and, in the case of the load operations, whether the operation is signed or unsigned. The rd field specifies the destination register. The remaining fields specify the address of the value to load or store. We will discuss the nature of these fields in the next chapter when we consider addressing structures in more detail.

4.7.2 Data Manipulation Instructions

The SPARC architecture provides a variety of data manipulation operations. All data manipulation instructions are encoded using a variation of the general instruction format. Floating point and coprocessor operations are encoded using the third

General format

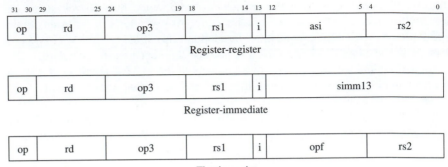

Register-register

Register-immediate

Floating point

Call format

Call instructions

Branch / SETHI format

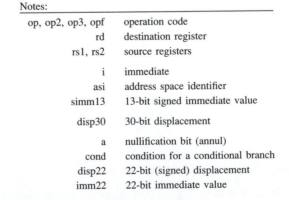

Branch instructions

SETHI instruction

Notes:

op, op2, op3, opf	operation code
rd	destination register
rs1, rs2	source registers
i	immediate
asi	address space identifier
simm13	13-bit signed immediate value
disp30	30-bit displacement
a	nullification bit (annul)
cond	condition for a conditional branch
disp22	22-bit (signed) displacement
imm22	22-bit immediate value

Figure 4.5 Instruction formats on the SPARC

variation. In these instructions, the op, op3, and opf fields encode the operation. The rs1 and rs2 fields encode the source registers, while the rd field encodes the destination.

Integer and bit manipulation operations are encoded using the first two variations of the general instruction format. The first variation is for instructions that use two source registers. The processor ignores the asi field of these instructions. The second variation is for instructions that use an immediate value as one of the source operands. During the execution of an arithmetic operation, the processor sign extends the immediate value encoded in the simm13 field to a 32-bit value. In bit-oriented operations, the processor simply fills the most significant bits with zero when constructing a 32-bit value from the value in the simm13 field. Note that this encoding limits the range of the immediate values that can be used in these instructions. The assembler must be able to encode the immediate value in 13 bits.

4.7.3 Control Transfer Instructions

The SPARC architecture provides two types of control transfer operations: a subroutine call operation and a branching operation. Both types of operations have a branch delay slot. In addition, the branching operation can conditionally nullify the next instruction. The SPARC uses a condition code register for its branching operations. The condition code register has four bits: *zero, negative, overflow,* and *carry.*

Subroutine call instructions are encoded using the CALL format. This format encodes the operation in the op field and a program counter displacement in the disp30 field. Though the disp30 field is only 30 bits long, it represents a full 32-bit value. Because instructions must be aligned on word boundaries, the two least significant bits of every instruction address must be zero. As such, these bits do not need to be explicitly stored in the instruction encoding.

Other branching instructions are encoded using the first variation of the Branch/SETHI format. The op and op2 fields encode the operation. The cond field encodes the condition of the branch (one encoding specifies that the branch is always taken). The a field specifies whether the next instruction is conditionally nullified (in SPARC terminology, this is the annul bit, hence the name a). Finally, the disp22 field contains a 22-bit signed displacement. When the processor executes a branch instruction, it concatenates two zeros onto the end of the 22-bit displacement and sign extends the 24-bit result to 32 bits. The processor completes the branch operation by adding this 32-bit value to the program counter.

4.7.4 The SETHI Instruction

The last instruction format, the second variation of the Branch/SETHI format, is only used for the *SETHI (set high)* operation. This operation sets the most significant 22 bits in a register. The op and op2 fields encode the operation, the rd

SETHI (set high)

field encodes the destination register, and the imm22 field encodes a 22-bit value. During the execution of a SETHI operation, the processor clears the low-order 10 bits of the destination register and copies the bits in the imm22 field into the high-order 22 bits.

The SETHI operation supports the manipulation of 32-bit values. The SPARC is a 32-bit machine; however, there is no direct support for 32-bit immediate values. (The only instruction that includes a 32-bit value is the CALL instruction, and this instruction relies on a bit of a trick.) Setting all 32 bits in a register requires two instructions. The first instruction is a SETHI operation to set the most significant bits. The second instruction is an OR operation with an immediate value to set the least significant bits. To make it easier to write these instructions, SPARC assemblers provide the unary operations *lo* and *hi*. The lo operation extracts the 10 least significant bits of a value, while the hi operation extracts the 22 most significant bits.

Example 4.26   *Show how you can use the SETHI instruction to load R2 with the value 0x12345678. (The 0x prefix denotes a hexadecimal constant—in this case we have a 32-bit number expressed in hexadecimal notation.)*

SETHI	R2, #hi(0x12345678)	*; set the high-order 22 bits*
OR	R2, R2, #lo(0x123454678)	*; set the low-order 10 bits*

Note: The SPARC assembler puts the destination as the last operand in an instruction. To assemble these instructions for a SPARC, you will need to reverse the order of the operands.

Coding Convention—The Pseudo-op MOVE
We will assume that the assembler provides a pseudo-op, MOVE, that allows us to store immediate values in registers. If the immediate value is small, we expect that the assembler will use an ADD operation with R0. Otherwise, we expect that the assembler will use a two-instruction sequence like the one shown in Example 4.26.

The problem addressed by the SETHI operation is a fundamental problem in computer architecture. Most architectural designs start by fixing the size of a word. (Currently, 32 bits is the standard word size.) Given a fixed word size, it is impossible to fit a word-sized value and the other fields needed in an instruction into a single word.

The CISC approach involves the use of *extension words*. A single CISC instruction may span several words. The first word of the instruction is called the *primary instruction word*. The remaining words in the instruction are called *extension words*, that is, they extend the primary instruction. Because the extension words are words, they can easily store word-sized values.

In contrast to the CISC approach, RISC designers insist on a single instruction per word and do not use extension words. Here the RISC designers contend that extension words complicate instruction interpretation. The SETHI operation is typical of the solutions found in RISC machines.

Primary instruction word

Extension words

4.8 SUMMARY

In this chapter, we have discussed the mechanisms that are provided for the evaluation of simple expressions. We have approached this material from the perspective of translating a statement or code fragment from a high-level language into assembly language. As you write assembly language programs, you should adhere to this approach. Always write your algorithm in a high-level language before you begin to write assembly language. You already know how to write programs in high-level languages, and as you are undoubtedly aware, the mere act of writing a program frequently uncovers holes in your understanding of the problem to be solved. By the time you start to write code in assembly language, you need to be certain that you understand the problem you are trying to solve!

Part of the presentation in this chapter has dealt with the topic of optimization. While it is important to understand how your programs might be improved, it is far more important that your programs work correctly. "Premature optimization" is regarded as a significant problem in the design of systems. The problem exists at all levels—in the design of machines, in the design of algorithms, in the design of small programs, and in the design of large systems—but seems to be particularly acute among assembly language programmers. We have taken a stepwise approach to introducing optimizations, always being certain that we understand the simple version of our program before introducing optimizations. This approach is important. Do not try to optimize your code before you are certain that you understand it in its entirety!

4.8.1 Additional Reading

If you want more information about expression translation and optimization, you should consult the books listed under the headings "Compiler Construction" and "Programming Language Surveys."

If you want more information about control transfer operations, you should consult the books listed under the headings "Architecture and Organization" and "Assembly Language." In addition, you should consult the Programmer's Reference Manual for any machines that are available to you.

Finally, I highly recommend the books by Jon Bentley (under the heading "Programming" and the C programming language books (either edition) by Kernighan and Ritchie (also listed under the heading "Programming") if you want good examples of how you should optimize your programs.

4.8.2 Terminology

- RISC, CISC
- Precedence, Associativity, Sequence
- Temporary
- Optimization/improvement of code
- Multiply-and-store, Add-and-store
- Source, Destination
- Line oriented, Free-format
- Registers
- Stack, Stack depth
- Load/store architecture
- Memory latency, Masking memory latency
- Overlapped execution, Instruction scheduling, Register interlock
- Instruction slot, Load delay slot, NOP
- Pseudo-operations
- Size specifier
- Constant table, Immediates
- Operator suffix, Operand prefix
- Branch, Jump, Target
- Compare and branch, Compare to zero, Condition code register
- Definite iteration/indefinite iteration
- Positional evaluation, Short-circuit evaluation
- Branch delay slots, Instruction prefetch, Conditional nullify, Annul
- Bitwise operations
- Primary instruction word, Extension words

4.8.3 Review Questions

1. How many differences can you identify between the RISC and CISC approaches?
2. What is the difference between an instruction and an operation?
3. Contrast the term *line oriented* with the term *free-format*.
4. If you use a calculator, what do you do when you need a temporary?
5. Explain the significance of the term *instruction slot*. What is the *load delay slot?*

6. What is a *pseudo-operation?* Give an example.

7. Why are constants called immediates?

8. What does the term *positional evaluation* mean?

9. What does the term *short-circuit evaluation* mean?

10. What is the difference between definite iteration and indefinite iteration?

11. What is a branch delay slot? When is a conditional nullify useful?

4.9 EXERCISES

1. Assuming the *a* is associated with memory location 100, *b* with location 101, and so on, write a code fragment that will evaluate the statement:

   a. $a = a * (b + c)$

   b. $a = b - (a + c)$

   c. $a = a/b$

   d. $a = a/b - c/d/e$

   on a:

   a. 3-address machine.

   b. 2-address machine.

   c. 1-address machine.

   d. 0-address machine.

   Do not use any registers.

2. For each of the statements in exercise 1, show how the statement could be translated using registers for a

   a. 3-address machine.

   b. 2-address machine.

   Try to minimize the number of memory accesses required in your code sequences. Show the number of memory accesses needed by your improved code contrasted with the number of accesses needed when registers are not used.

3. For each of the statements in exercise 1, show how the statement could be translated for a machine based on the load/store architecture.

4. Write an expression that requires an explicit temporary on an accumulator machine. Be certain to explain why your expression requires an explicit temporary.

5. Suppose that a stack machine maintains four values in the CPU. Is it possible to write an expression that needs more than four values on the stack? If so, show the expression and explain why it needs more than four stack values. If not, explain why four stack values are enough for any expression.

6. The code fragment in Example 4.18 uses the condition code instructions for conditional branching. Rewrite this code fragment using the compare and branch instructions for conditional branching.

7. In Example 4.19, we used the compare and branch instructions for conditional branching. Rewrite this code using the condition code instructions for conditional branching.

8. Consider the following program fragment (assume that c is initialized before entering this code):

```
b = 0;
for( a = 0 ; a < c ; a++ ){
   b = b + a;
}
```

As you may have guessed this fragment computes the sum of the digits from zero to $c - 1$ ($b = \sum_{a=0}^{c-1} a$).

Provide a direct translation of this loop. Do not improve the code. Moreover, in writing the assembly language fragments, assume that the machine does not have a branch delay slot.

a. In C, using **goto**'s as in Figure 4.2.

b. In assembly language, using compare and branch as in Example 4.13.

c. In assembly language, using compare to zero as in Example 4.14.

d. In assembly language, using condition codes as in Example 4.17.

9. Now improve your code. Translate the loop given in exercise 8 into better code based on the same algorithm. Do not use the fact that $\sum_{a=0}^{c-1} a = (c - 1)c/2$. Moreover, in writing the assembly language fragments, assume that the machine does not have a branch delay slot.

a. In C, using **goto**'s.

b. In assembly language, using compare and branch.

c. In assembly language, using compare to zero.

d. In assembly language, using condition codes.

In each case, be certain to justify your improvements to the direct translation.

10. Now consider branch delay slots. Repeat exercise 9 b, c, and d, assuming that your machine has a branch delay slot. Also assume that your machine provides versions of the conditional branching instruction that conditionally nullify the instruction in the branch delay slot.

11. The conditional branch with nullify operation nullifies the effect of the next instruction if the branch is *not* taken. We could just as easily have specified that the effect of the next instruction is nullified *if* the conditional branch is taken. Discuss the advantages and disadvantages of the two definitions. Be certain to consider the impact on looping structures.

12. Consider the following code fragment:

    i1:   *nonbranch*
    i2:   BRANCH   i5
    i3:   BRANCH   i7
    i4:   *nonbranch*
    i5:   *nonbranch*
    i6:   *nonbranch*
    i7:   *nonbranch*

    Give a list of the instructions that the machine will execute starting from instruction *i1*.

13. Consider the following code fragment:

    i1:   *nonbranch*
    i2:   BRANCH   i5
    i3:   BRGT*   i7
    i4:   *nonbranch*
    i5:   *nonbranch*
    i6:   *nonbranch*
    i7:   *nonbranch*

    Give a list of the instructions that the machine will execute if the conditional branch in instruction *i3*

    a.   Is taken.

    b.   Is *not* taken.

14. Consider the following code fragment:

    i1:   *nonbranch*
    i2:   BRGT   i5
    i3:   BRANCH   i7
    i4:   *nonbranch*
    i5:   *nonbranch*
    i6:   *nonbranch*
    i7:   *nonbranch*

    Give a list of the instructions that the machine will execute if the conditional branch in instruction *i2*

    a.   Is taken.

    b.   Is *not* taken.

15. Consider the following code fragment:

    i1:   *nonbranch*
    i2:   BRGT*   i5
    i3:   BRANCH   i7
    i4:   *nonbranch*
    i5:   *nonbranch*
    i6:   *nonbranch*
    i7:   *nonbranch*

Give a list of the instructions that the machine will execute if the conditional branch in instruction *i2*

a.   Is taken.

b.   Is *not* taken.

16.   Describe how you can use the ORN operation and the fact that R0 holds the value 0 to implement a NOT pseudo-op.

17.   As we noted in the discussion of the SPARC architecture, the immediate value used in a data manipulation operation is limited to values that can be encoded in 13 bits. Explain how you would write the instruction ADD   R2, #0x45678 for a machine based on the SPARC architecture. Assume that R1 is available for use as a temporary if you need to use an additional register.

18.   The following instructions use pseudo-ops. For each of these instructions, show the instructions that an assembler for the SPARC architecture might generate. (We use the SPARC architecture to fix the number of bits that can be used in an immediate value.) Here it is worth noting that the SPARC architecture uses 2's complement encoding for signed integer values.

a.   CLEAR   R5

b.   MOVE   R5, #42

c.   MOVE   R5, #−42

d.   MOVE   R5, #0x4567

e.   MOVE   R5, #−0x4567

ADDRESSING MODES AND DATA ORGANIZATION

Our goal in this chapter is to discuss how basic data structures can be realized in assembly language. To this end, we consider a fairly substantial collection of basic data structures: pointers, records, arrays, strings, and stacks. As we begin our coverage of data structures, it is helpful to realize that there are only two important issues that we need to consider: declaration and access. Recall your first exposure to arrays. The first thing you needed to learn was how to declare an array. The second thing you had to learn was how to access the individual elements of the array. After that there was nothing new to learn—arrays elements are just like simple variables.

To present the data structures, we need to discuss the assembly process and assembler directives. In particular, we need to introduce symbolic constants, static allocation, initialization, assembler segments, and assembler expressions. We begin this chapter by considering the assembly process and assembler directives. After we have covered these topics, we will cover the central topic of this chapter—data structures and addressing modes. The next two sections cover topics that are related to addressing modes: the LEA instruction and branch tables. The chapter concludes with a discussion of the differences between addresses and integers.

5.1 ASSEMBLER DIRECTIVES

In the previous chapter, we presented a number of code fragments written in "assembly language." At the time, we did not discuss the structure of assembly language programs in much depth. So far, we know that an assembly language program is line oriented and that each statement specifies a fairly simple operation. To discuss data structure declarations, we need to consider the structure of an assembly language program and the assembly process in more detail. We begin by summarizing the basic rules of assembly language programs:

- A *space* is equivalent to any number of spaces or tabs. Spaces cannot appear in the middle of a number or identifier; otherwise, unless specifically required

Space

or prohibited, spaces are optional and may be inserted to improve the readability of your programs.

Comment

- A semicolon (";") and anything on the same line after the semicolon is a *comment*. Comments are ignored by the assembler.

Identifier

- An *identifier* is a letter followed by any number of letters and digits (and perhaps other special characters like "_").

Label definition

- A *label definition* is an identifier followed by a colon (":").

Instruction

- An *instruction* is an operation name followed by a list of operands. There must be a space between the operation name and the operand list.

Operand list

- An *operand list* is a comma-separated list of operands. The number of operands in the list depends on the operation.

Line

- A *line* may be:

  Empty (i.e., white space).

  A label definition.

  An instruction.

  A label definition followed by an instruction.

Program

- A *program* is a sequence of lines.

Assembler directives

In the remainder of this section, we introduce several *assembler directives*.[1] Like an instruction, an assembler directive is specified on a single line and may be preceded by a label definition. Moreover, an assembler directive consists of a directive name followed by a list of parameters. As we will see, the structure of the parameter list varies from directive to directive.

Because they have similar syntactic structures, the difference between instructions and assembler directives is frequently confusing. In contrasting instructions and directives, it may be helpful to remember that instructions are used to specify computations; directives are used to specify how the assembler translates instructions. That is, directives direct the translation process.

Coding Convention—Assembler Directives

In contrast to instruction names (that always start with a letter), directive names always start with a period ("."). To further emphasize the difference between directives and instructions, we use uppercase letters for instructions (e.g., MPY) and lowercase letters for assembler directives (e.g., .equate).

As we introduce new assembler directives, we will discuss how these directives impact the translation process. Figure 5.1 presents a graphical representation of the

Data flow diagram

translation process using a *data flow diagram*. In a data flow diagram, rectangular

---
[1] Assembler directives are sometimes called pseudo-operations.

boxes represent data structures, while the oval-shaped *bubbles* represent processes. The arcs connecting the boxes and bubbles indicate the flow of information. In this case, the diagram is fairly simple: the "translator" process obtains information from the *source-code* data structure (a file) and adds information to the *object-code* data structure (also a file).

Source code

Object code

Figure 5.1   The translation process

To have your source-code programs translated into object-code files, you need to invoke the assembler. To execute your program after it has been translated, you need to invoke an operating system utility called the *loader*. The loader allocates enough space in the memory of the machine to hold your program and then copies the values in the object-code file into the memory space it has allocated. As we discuss in Chapter 10, the loader may actually do more than copy the values from the object-code file into the memory; however, this simple model is sufficient for our present purposes. After it loads your program, the loader transfers control to the first instruction in your program. This operation is frequently called a *load-and-go* because it combines the loading of the program and the start of its execution in a single step. These two steps may be distinct in some systems. It is unlikely that you will need to separate them, so we will consider the loading and subsequent execution of your programs as a single operation.

Loader

Load-and-go

5.1.1 The Location Counter

While the assembler is processing the source file and producing the object file, it maintains an internal variable called the *location counter*. The assembler initializes the location counter to zero when it starts translating a program. After translating each instruction, the assembler adds the size of the encoded instruction (in bytes) to the location counter. In this way, the assembler uses the location counter to maintain the location of the next instruction as an offset from the start of the object-code file. If your program is loaded at memory location zero, this offset can be interpreted as the address of the instruction. In Chapter 10 we discuss a technique, called *relocation*, that makes it appear as though the loader loaded your program at memory location zero. For the remainder of this discussion, we will assume that the loader loads every program at memory location zero. We will ignore the distinction between the address of an instruction and its offset in the object-code file.

Location counter

Relocation

There are two counters that we associate with instructions: the *location counter* and the *program counter.* The distinction between these counters is frequently a source of confusion. The location counter is only defined during the translation of an assembly language program, while the program counter is only defined during the execution of the program. These two counters never exist at the same time. Further, the values assigned to the location counter form a strictly increasing sequence. Each time the location counter is assigned a new value, the new value is strictly larger than the previous value. In contrast, the program counter can be assigned a value that is less than its current value. As an example, consider a conditional branch from the bottom of a loop to the top of the loop—if the branch is taken, the program counter is assigned a value that is less than the current value of the program counter.

5.1.2 The Symbol Table—Labels and Equates

Symbol table

In Chapter 4, we introduced labels to provide a level of naming between the symbolic instructions in the source code and the addresses of the instructions in the object code. During the translation process, the assembler stores labels and their associated values in a *symbol table*. The symbol table is nothing more than a collection of ordered pairs. Each pair in the symbol table has the form: ⟨*label,address*⟩. Abstractly, the symbol table is defined by two operations, *insert* and *lookup*. When the assembler recognizes a label definition, it inserts the label and the current value of the location counter into the symbol table. Later, when the assembler encounters a use of the label, it uses the lookup operation to find the value associated with the label. In this way, the assembler can replace every use of the label with its value.

Figure 5.2 illustrates the translation process, including the symbol table. Note that the symbol table is shown as a dashed box. The dashed box indicates that the symbol table is a transient data structure. It only exists as a separate entity during the translation process.

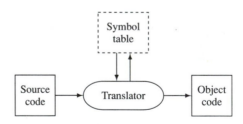

Figure 5.2   The symbol table

Symbolic constants

In addition to labels, most assemblers provide a mechanism for defining and using *symbolic constants*. Symbolic constants are a convenience, but an important one. Definition of a symbolic constant involves the association of a name with a value. After the definition has been established, every use of the name is replaced by the associated value. When the assembler encounters the definition of a symbolic constant, it adds a new ⟨*name,value*⟩ pair to the symbol table. As such, whenever the assembler subsequently encounters the *name,* it will find the ⟨*name,value*⟩ pair in the symbol table and can replace the occurrence of *name* by the associated value. In essence, the definition of a symbolic constant establishes an equivalence between the name and the value. For this reason, definitions of symbolic constants are frequently called *equates*.

Equates

Coding Convention—Equate

We use an equate directive to define symbolic constants. Our equate directive has two arguments, the name of the constant and its value. For example, the following directive equates the name *const* with the value 15:

.equate   const, 15

You can use symbolic constants to avoid *magic numbers*—numbers that appear, as if by magic, in the middle of a program. The meaning of some numbers, like 3.141592654, is apparent from the number itself; however, most numbers, like 16, could mean many different things. By associating a meaningful name with each different use of a number in your program, you can make your program easier to read and modify. When someone reads your code they will not have to deduce the meaning of the number 16; the name tells them what you intend. If you have to modify the program, you only need to change the definition of the symbolic constant.

Magic numbers

Consider the code fragments that we discussed in Chapter 4. Every code fragment was predicated by a statement of the form: "assume that the variables *x, y,* and *z* are associated with memory locations 100, 104, and 108, respectively." Because these assumptions were not explicit in the code, you had to recall these assumptions every time you saw the number 100 in the code fragment. Then you had to decide if the number was really a reference to the variable *x*. (I expect that the comments made this task a bit easier, but you should not rely on the accuracy of comments!) Using the equate directive, we can explicitly document many of the assumptions used in an assembly language program.

Example 5.1   *Show how you can improve the readability of the code fragment presented in Example 4.17 using the equate directive.*

```
        .equate    loc_x, 100      ; x is associated with location 100
        .equate    loc_y, 104      ; y is associated with location 104
        .equate    loc_z, 108      ; z is associated with location 108

        LOAD.w     R2, loc_y       ; temp = y; (R2 is temp)
        LOAD.w     R3, loc_z       ; R3 is z
        CLEAR      R4              ; x = 0; (R4 is x)
        BRANCH     test            ; goto test
top:
        ADD        R4, R4, #1      ; x = x + 1;
```

test:
```
        SUB      R2, R2, R3      ; temp = temp − z;
        BRGE     top             ; if( temp ≥ 0 ) goto top
        STORE.w  loc_x, R4       ; store the result
```

The new version of the code is not only easier to read, it is also easier to modify. Suppose you need to move the variable x from location 100 to location 200. Using the new version, you only need to change the equate that defines the value of *loc_x*. You do not need to look through the code and find each occurrence of the number 100 to determine if it needs to be changed to 200.

As we have seen, labels and symbolic constants are closely related. The definition of either a label or a symbolic constant adds an ordered pair of the form ⟨*name,value*⟩ in the symbol table. The most important difference is the way that the assembler determines the value part of the pair. In the case of a label, the assembler uses the current value of the location counter. In the case of a symbolic constant, the assembler uses the value explicitly stated in the definition. Beyond this difference, most assemblers require that you define symbolic constants before using them. Assemblers do not impose a similar restriction on labels. Consider the code fragment shown in Example 5.1. In particular, consider the instruction

Forward reference

"BRANCH test." The reference to the symbol *test* is called a *forward reference* because the label *test* has not been defined at this point. Using the notion of a forward reference, we can restate the difference as follows: Most assemblers do not allow forward references to symbolic constants but do allow forward references to labels.

Finally, there is a stylistic issue that we should consider before moving onto the next topic: equate directives do not have a direct effect on the construction of the object-code file. They simply add entries to the symbol table that can be used during the remainder of the translation. As such, you can mix instructions and equate directives in any way you like, as long as you make sure that all symbolic constants are defined before they are used. When you write (assembly language) programs, you should collect definitions and place them at the beginning of the program whenever possible. By following this rule, you will find that your programs are easier to read, understand, and modify.

5.1.3 Allocation, Initialization, and Alignment

Up until this point, we have assumed that we know the memory location of every variable and temporary used in our programs. In the previous discussion, we showed how we could integrate these assumptions into our code using the equate directive, but this ignores an important question. Why do we care which memory locations are associated with the variables in our programs? All we want to do is to ensure that each variable is associated with a unique memory location that is not used to store an instruction. Beyond the inconvenience of having to know which memory locations are associated with the variables in our code, there is a potential problem that we have ignored. How do we know that the assembler will not store an instruction in a memory location that we are using for a variable?

Before we discuss the assembler directives that allow us to avoid these difficulties, we need to adopt a simple convention regarding the execution sequence for our programs. We will be able to drop this convention when we discuss assembler segments, but for the moment we need to assume that the assembler recognizes a special label, *START*. We further assume that the assembler arranges to have the execution of the program begin with the instruction labeled by this special label.

START

In almost every context, the special label START labels the first instruction in the source code. As such, the assembler will not use memory locations before START to store instructions and can be used for variables. All that we need is a way to tell the assembler how much space to reserve for each variable.

Coding Convention—Reserve

We use the reserve directive to allocate the space needed for variables. This directive requires a single parameter, an integer value, that specifies the number of bytes to be reserved. For example the following directive reserves 2 bytes:

.reserve 2

Example 5.2 *Show how you can use the reserve directive to allocate the space needed for the variables used in Example 5.1.*

```
    x:   .reserve    4           ; x needs 4 bytes
    y:   .reserve    4           ; y needs 4 bytes
    z:   .reserve    4           ; z needs 4 bytes

START:
         ⋮                       ; other instructions
         LOAD.w    R2, y         ; temp = y; (R2 is temp)
         LOAD.w    R3, z         ; R3 is z
         CLEAR     R4            ; x = 0; (R4 is x)
         BRANCH    test          ; goto test
  top:
         ADD       R4, R4, #1    ; x = x + 1;
  test:
         SUB       R2, R2, R3    ; temp = temp − z;
         BRGE      top           ; if( temp ≥ 0 ) goto top
         STORE.w   x, R4         ; store the result
```

In examining Example 5.2, note that every block of reserved space is labeled. The assembler does not distinguish between labels that are associated with instructions and labels that are associated with memory blocks. As such, you could include an instruction that branches to *x* in your program. Moreover, you could include an instruction that stores a register into memory location *top*. The assembler will not prevent you from including either of these instructions in your program, even though execution of either instruction is likely to lead to disaster.

Unlike the equate directive introduced earlier, the reserve directive does have an effect on the object-code file. When the assembler encounters a reserve directive, it leaves an uninitialized block of memory in the object-code file. In essence, the assembler implements the reserve directive by incrementing the location counter.

Noting that the space allocated using the reserve directive is not initialized, you might wonder if there is a way to initialize space in the object-code file as it is allocated. Most assemblers provide a small collection of directives that can be used to initialize locations in the object-code file with data values (note: the primary task of an assembler is to initialize locations in the object-code file with instruction values). The different initialization directives are distinguished by the size of the memory block they initialize.

Coding Convention—Initialization Directives

An initialization directive consists of the directive name followed by a comma-separated list of initial values. Every value in the list is stored in a separate memory block of the size associated with the directive name.

The following table summarizes the initialization directives that we use in this text:

Name	Size
.byte	1 byte
.halfword	2 bytes
.word	4 bytes

For example, the following directive initializes three bytes of memory in the object-code file with the ASCII representation for the letters 'a', 'b', and 'c'.

.byte 'a', 'b', 'c'

Most assemblers issue a warning message if a value specified in an initialization directive is too large to fit in the memory block associated with the directive name. For example, the number 290 cannot be represented in 8 bits (one byte) of memory; if you attempt to use this value with a byte directive, the assembler will issue a warning message. Values that are clearly too small do not cause the assembler any problem. For example, the assembler will not complain if you issue the directive ".word 'B'." In this case, the assembler simply converts the symbolic representation ('B') into an 8-bit binary number and stores this number in a 32-bit block of memory.

Example 5.3   *Consider the following C variable declarations. Assuming that a character is one byte, a short integer is two bytes, and an integer is four bytes, write directives that could be used to allocate and initialize the memory space required by this set of declarations. (In case you are not familiar with C declarations, this collection declares five variables: ch_one, short_one, ch_two, int_one, and short_two. Moreover, it specifies the space that needs to be associated with each of these variables. The variables ch_one and ch_two need enough space to hold a character value, the variables short_one and short_two need enough space to hold a short integer value, and the variable int_one needs enough space to hold an integer value. Moreover, each variable is given an initial value. For example, the variable short_two is initialized to the value 33.)*

short int	short_one = 22;
char	ch_one = 'a';
short int	short_two = 33;
char	ch_two = 'A';
int	int_one = 0;

			Address	Contents
short_one:	.halfword	22	$n-1$	
ch_one:	.byte	'a'	n	short_one
short_two:	.halfword	33	$n+1$	
ch_two:	.byte	'A'	$n+2$	ch_one
int_one:	.word	0	$n+3$	short_two
			$n+4$	
			$n+5$	ch_two
			$n+6$	
			$n+7$	int_one
			$n+8$	
			$n+9$	
			$n+10$	

This brings us to the topic of *memory alignment*. When we discussed memory structures in Chapter 3, we introduced the concept of memory alignment. Many machines require that you store halfword values at even addresses and word values at addresses that are a multiple of four. Assemblers for these machines provide directives that you can use to specify alignment.

Memory alignment

Coding Convention—Align
The align directive has a single argument, an integer, that specifies the required alignment. For example, if the argument is 2, it specifies that the location counter must be brought to an even value. If the location counter is odd when the assembler encounters the directive ".align 2," it will increment the location counter by one.

Example 5.4   *Show how you can use the align directive to ensure that halfword values are aligned on even addresses and that word values are aligned on addresses that are multiples of four for the declarations in Example 5.3.*

			Address	Contents
	.align	2	$n-2$	
short_one:	.halfword	22	n	short_one
ch_one:	.byte	'a'	$n+2$	ch_one ///////
	.align	2	$n+4$	short_two
short_two:	.halfword	33	$n+6$	ch_two ///////
ch_two:	.byte	'A'	$n+8$	//////////////////
	.align	4	$n+10$	int_one
int_one:	.word	0	$n+12$	
			$n+14$	

The graphical representation in Example 5.4 assumes that the value of the location counter is even but not a multiple of four when the assembler processes these directives. Note that we could reduce the amount of wasted memory by reorganizing the allocation directives. To avoid wasting memory, it is usually a good idea to start with the allocation that has the largest alignment requirement—word allocations in our example.

5.1.4 Assembler Segments

Assembler segments

Text

Data

bss

As you write assembly language programs, it is important to keep your code and data separate. As a rule, you do not want to execute your data, and you do not want to modify your instructions. Most assemblers provide *assembler segments* to help you maintain a distinction between code and data. Each segment holds a subset of the objects in a program. Typically the assembler provides one segment, the *text* segment, to hold the instructions of the program and two segments, the *data* and *bss* segments, to hold the data values. Figure 5.3 illustrates the translation process with these segments. As it translates an assembly language program, the assembler deposits values into the segments. The assembler maintains a separate location counter for each segment. When the assembler completes the translation of a program, it concatenates the segments to construct the object-code file.

Figure 5.4 shows the structure of an object-code file and how the loader maps this structure into memory. The object file includes a header along with the contents of the text and data segments. The assembler uses the header of the object file to store information that the loader uses. For example, the header has fields that record the size of each segment.

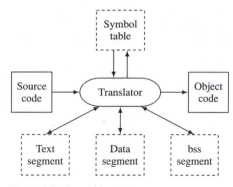

Figure 5.3 Assembler segments

In examining the object-code file shown in Figure 5.4, note that the bss segment is not explicitly stored in this file. The bss segment stores *uninitialized* data space, and, as such, the loader only needs to know the size of this segment. When the loader allocates space for your program, it allocates space for the bss segment (along with the other segments). Some loaders initialize the space for the bss segment to zero; others leave this space uninitialized.[2]

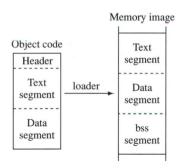

Figure 5.4 The loading process

When the assembler is translating a program, how does it know which segment to use? If you think about the kinds of things the assembler encounters in a source

---

[2] You may be curious about the name bss. It is an acronym that stands for "block started by symbol." Originally, bss was the name of a directive and not an assembler segment. According to one rumor, bss was an assembler directive for the IBM 360. According to another rumor, bss stands for block storage save. In either case, the directive was similar to our reserve directive. The purpose of the reserve directive is to reserve a block of memory. If you consider the semantics of the reserve directive, it should be apparent that it does not make much sense to have a reserve directive that is not labeled—how else will you refer to the block of memory that you have allocated? A label is really a symbol, and hence, we have a *block* of memory that is *started by* a *symbol*.

file, it is easy to identify the appropriate segment by the type of the object encountered. For example, the assembler should place instructions in the text segment. It should use the data segment for initialized data values, that is, values established using the byte, halfword, or word directives. Finally, uninitialized data space, that is, space allocated using the reserve directive, should be associated with the bss segment.

While it would be simple to implement this *implicit segment identification* scheme in an assembler, most assemblers require *explicit segment identification*. Assemblers typically base segment identification on the use of a *current segment*. Every action that the assembler performs is relative to the current segment. One of the segments (typically the text segment) is the default current segment when the assembler starts. The current segment can be changed during the assembly with the directives text, data, and bss. Each directive causes the named segment to become the current segment. For example, after you issue a data directive, the data segment is the current segment until you issue a text or bss directive.

Current segment

Coding Convention—Assembler Segments

In this text, we use the following directives to identify assembler segments:

Name	Directive	Primary use
Text	.text	Program instructions
Data	.data	Initialized data
Block data	.bss	Uninitialized data

Example 5.5 *Show how you can use the assembler segment directives in the code fragment presented in Example 5.2.*

```
        .bss                    ; switch to the bss segment
x:      .reserve    4           ; x needs 4 bytes
y:      .reserve    4           ; y needs 4 bytes
z:      .reserve    4           ; z needs 4 bytes

        .text                   ; switch to the text segment

        :                       ; other instructions
        LOAD.w   R2, y          ; temp = y; (R2 is temp)
        LOAD.w   R3, z          ; R3 is z
        CLEAR    R4             ; x = 0; (R4 is x)
        BRANCH   test           ; goto test
top:
        ADD      R4, R4, #1     ; x = x + 1;
test:
```

```
SUB        R2, R2, R3      ; temp = temp − z;
BRGE       top             ; if( temp ≥ 0 ) goto top
STORE.w    x, R4           ; store the result
```

This code fragment begins by switching to the bss segment. After allocating space for the variables used in the code, it switches to the text segment. In this case, we do not have any initialized variables, so there is no need to switch to the data segment.

Because the assembler reorganizes our program, putting the text segment at the start of the object-code file, we no longer need the START label that we introduced earlier. As such, the code shown in Example 5.5 does not include a definition for the label START.

The assembler may restrict your requests based on the current segment—announcing an error whenever you make an illegal request. For example, your assembler may announce an error if you try to deposit a value (instruction or data value) into the bss segment. The assembler may also permit some requests that seem to be clear violations of the intended use for a segment, for example, depositing a data value in the code segment or an instruction value in the data segment.

5.1.5 Constant Expressions

Most assemblers will let you use the constant expression $2 * 14$ in place of the simple constant 28. When this facility is combined with the symbolic constants, it is especially useful. For example, suppose you are a writing a program that simulates automobile traffic. Suppose further that your representation of an automobile requires 14 bytes. In this context, you might choose to include the following directive in your code:

.equate CarSize, 14

Now, if you need to reserve enough space for 20 automobiles, you only need to issue the following directive:

.reserve 20 * CarSize

5.2 ADDRESSING MODES

In this section, we introduce a collection of addressing modes. The collection is not intended to be complete. There are many addressing modes that are not presented in this discussion. The collection presented is sufficiently diverse that you should have no trouble learning the addressing modes that are provided by an actual machine once you have learned the addressing modes presented in this section.

We covered a small collection of addressing modes in Chapter 4. Before we start our discussion of the modes to be introduced in this section, we should review

Direct-memory
addressing

Direct-register
addressing

Immediate addressing

the ones that we have already discussed. In assembly language, every operand is specified by a number. Addressing modes specify how a number identifies an operand. In *direct-memory addressing*, the number is the address of the memory cell. In our notation, direct-memory addressing is the default addressing mode; that is, we interpret a number as a direct-memory address. In *direct-register addressing*, the number is the address of the register. In our notation, we use a prefix of R to denote direct-register addressing. In *immediate addressing*, the number is the value of the operand. In our notation, we use a prefix of # to denote immediate addressing.

The addressing modes that we introduce in the remainder of this section identify memory locations. As such, these addressing modes can only be used in the LOAD and STORE operations of a RISC machine. CISC machines, in contrast, typically permit a much greater flexibility in the use of addressing modes.

One of the characteristics of the earlier RISC architectures (MIPS and SPARC in particular) was the limited number of addressing modes provided by the architecture. More recent RISC machines, like the HP Precision architecture, include a variety of powerful addressing modes.

5.2.1 Pointers—Indirect Addressing

Pointers provide a mechanism for using variables (instead of names) to refer to objects (other variables). In their actual implementation, pointers are nothing more than variables whose values are addresses. Before we discuss the assembly language notations associated with pointers, we should review the concepts and notations used by high-level languages. In Pascal, a pointer is declared using the prefix "↑." For example, the following declares the variable *ptr* as a pointer to a character:

ptr: ↑char;

Pascal provides three ways to assign a value (an address) to a pointer variable: *(a)* a pointer may be assigned value **nil**, *(b)* a pointer may be assigned a copy of an existing pointer value, or *(c)* a pointer may be assigned a new pointer value using the predefined function *new*. The only way to construct a pointer in Pascal is by invoking the predefined function *new*.

Once a pointer variable has been assigned a value, you can access the location that it refers to using the symbol ↑ as a suffix. For example, the following statement assigns the letter 'A' to the location pointed to by *ptr*:

ptr↑ := 'A';

In C, a pointer is declared using the symbol "*" as a prefix of the variable. For example, the following declares *ptr* as a pointer to a character:

char *ptr;

Unlike Pascal, C provides a very flexible (and potentially dangerous) mechanism for constructing pointer values. In C, the symbol "&" is used to denote the unary

operator *address of*. For example, if *ch1* has been declared as a character variable,   Address of
the following statement assigns the address of *ch1* to *ptr*:

ptr = &ch1;

Once a pointer variable has been assigned a value, you can access the location
that *ptr* points to using the symbol * as a prefix. For example, the following
statement assigns the value 'A' to the location pointed to by *ptr*:

*ptr = 'A';

In addition to the linguistic notations provided by high-level languages, we have
a graphical notation for representing the logical structures created by assignments
to pointer variables. Figure 5.5 illustrates the logical structure created by the
assignment *ptr = &ch1*.

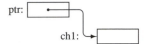

Figure 5.5   Graphical representation
of a pointer

Coding Convention—Pointer Size
In this text, we assume that every address is 32 bits, that is, one word.

Example 5.6   *Show how you can translate the following C code fragment in assembly
language:*

char *ch1, *ptr;*
ptr = &ch1;

```
        .bss
        .align    4
ptr:    .reserve  4              ; an address is 32 bits

        ⋮

ch1:    .reserve  1              ; a character is one byte


        ⋮

        .text
        LOAD.w    R2, #ch1       ; R2 = &ch1
        STORE.w   ptr, R2        ; store it in ptr
```

Note that this code fragment uses immediate addressing to load the address of the variable *ch1* into register R2. Had we (accidentally) neglected the "#," we would have loaded the current value of *ch1* into R2 instead of its address. Figure 5.6 presents a graphical illustration of the relationship established by the code fragment in Example 5.6.

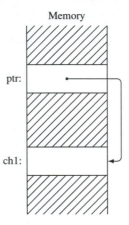

Figure 5.6 A pointer in assembly language

Indirect addressing

Memory-indirect addressing

Register-indirect addressing

Once you have loaded an address value into a memory location or register, you can access the memory location that this value references using *indirect addressing.* When you use *direct addressing,* the address in the instruction is the address of the operand. In contrast, when you use *indirect addressing,* the basic address is the address of a location that holds the address of the operand. In other words, an indirect address is actually the address of the address of the operand. In *memory-indirect addressing*, the basic address is a memory address. Most machines do not support memory-indirect addressing. However, almost every machine supports *register-indirect addressing.* In register-indirect addressing, the basic address is a register address instead of a memory address.

Coding Convention—Indirect Addressing
We use the symbol @ as an address prefix to denote indirect addressing. For example, the address expression *@R2* denotes the memory location identified by the value in R2.

Example 5.7   *Show how you could translate the following C statement into assembly language, using register-indirect addressing:*

*ptr = 'a';

```
LOAD.w    R2, ptr        ; R2 gets a copy of ptr
MOVE      R3, #'a'       ; R3 has the value 'a'
STORE.b   @R2, R3
```

This code sequence begins by loading the current value of *ptr* into register R2. It concludes by storing the least significant byte of R3 in the location pointed to by R2. Figure 5.7 illustrates the logical structure constructed by the first statement in this code sequence.

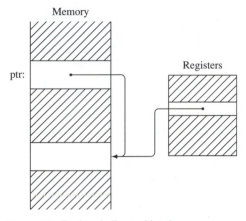

Figure 5.7   Register-indirect addressing

An important aspect of indirect addressing and the other addressing modes we present in this section is that the basic address in the instruction is not the address of the operand. The actual address of the operand is called the *effective address*. The operation needed to transform the basic address into the effective address is called the *effective address calculation*. In the case of indirect addressing, the effective address calculation is particularly simple—fetch the value stored in the location identified by the address in the instruction.

Effective address

Effective address calculation

5.2.2 Arrays—Indexed Addressing

In C, the following declaration can be used to declare *int_arr* to be the name of an array of 24 integers:

int int_arr[24];

Arrays are always zero based in C. As such, the elements of the array *int_arr* are associated with the indexes 0 through 23. You can access the elements of *int_arr* using the (addressing) expressions *int_arr[0]*, *int_arr[1]*, ..., *int_arr[23]*.

Example 5.8   *Show how you can translate the following C declaration into assembly language:*

int int_arr[24];

```
        .bss
        .align    4
int_arr:    .reserve    24 * 4; 4 bytes per integer
```

These directives simply allocate a block of 96 bytes. There is no further structure that results from these directives. We have not constructed a new set of names based on the name *int_arr*. An important aspect of assembly language programming is that data structures are defined by the way that your code accesses memory, not by a declaration. As you write code to access the elements of an array, you need to have a clear understanding of the logical structure that provides the basis for your code.

Figure 5.8 illustrates the logical structure of an array. Note that array elements are allocated in adjacent memory locations. As such, if you know that the array has been allocated space starting at memory location 1000, you know that memory locations 1000 through 1003 are used to store the value of int_arr[0], memory locations 1004 through 1007 are used for int_arr[1], and so on. In general, you can determine the starting address of an element using the following formula:

$$addr = base + elem\_size * index \qquad (5.1)$$

where *base* is the starting address of the array, *elem_size* is the size of each array element (in bytes), and *index* is the index of the element for which we need an

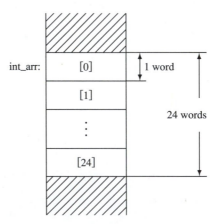

Figure 5.8 Array layout

address. In our example, the starting address is 1000 and the element size is 4. Therefore, the address of the element with index 20 is 1080. If you have a variable, *i*, that specifies the index, the address of int_arr[i] can be calculated using the expression: $1000 + 4 * i$. The expression on the right side of equation 5.1 is called a *scaled addition* because the value of the index is scaled by the element size (the multiplication) before being added to the base address.

Scaled addition

Example 5.9   *Translate the following C statement into assembly language:*

int_arr[5] = 47;

```
MOVE      R2, #47              ; need the value 47 in a register
STORE.w   int_arr+4*5, R2      ; store the value
```

Note that the STORE instruction uses a constant expression to formulate the address of the element. In this case the index, 5, is scaled by the element size, 4, and added to the base address int_arr.

Example 5.10   *Translate the following C statement into assembly language:*

int_arr[i] = 47;

```
MOVE      R2, #47       ; need the value 47 in a register
LOAD.w    R3, i
MPY       R3, R3, #4    ; scale the value of R2
MOVE      R4, #int_arr  ; #int_arr is a 32 bit value
ADD       R3, R3, R4    ; R2 holds the address
STORE.w   @R3, R2       ; store the value
```

The second and third instructions in this sequence calculate the offset of the element from the start of the array and store this value in R3. In other words, R3 holds the address of the element relative to the start of the array. The fourth and fifth instructions transform this *relative address* into an actual memory address. The need to transform relative addresses into actual addresses arises frequently— especially when you are working with arrays. Because they arise frequently, many machines provide an *indexed addressing* mode so you can use relative addresses more easily in your programs.

Relative address

Indexed addressing

Coding Convention—Indexed Addressing

We use the notation $addr_1[addr_2]$ to denote an indexed address. The first address ($addr_1$) is the *base address* and the second ($addr_2$) is the *index address*. The base address specifies the start of the memory block that has been allocated for the array. The index address specifies the location of the *index value*. The index value is interpreted as an offset from the base address.

If the index address is a register address we use the term *register-indexed* addressing. In *memory-indexed* addressing, the index address is a memory address. Most machines do not support memory-indexed addressing.

Example 5.11   *Show how you can rewrite the code fragment presented in Example 5.10 using indexed addressing.*

```
MOVE      R2, #47          ; need the value 47 in a register
LOAD.w    R3, i
MPY       R3, R3, #4       ; scale the value of R2
STORE.w   int_arr[R3], R2  ; store the value
```

Figure 5.9 presents a graphical representation of indexed addressing. As shown on the right side of the figure, the value of the index specifies the distance from the base address to the desired element. The left side of the figure illustrates the effective address calculation: the value of the base address is added to the contents of the index resulting in the effective address.

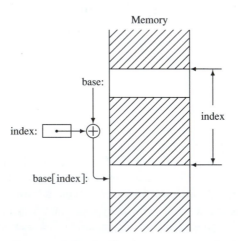

Figure 5.9   Indexed addressing

Note that we used a separate instruction to scale the index value in the code fragment presented in Example 5.11. In this instance, we use a multiplication by the value 4 to implement the scaling operation. Some machines avoid the need for an explicit multiplication by providing an addressing mode that implicitly scales the index value used in an indexed address. In this addressing mode, the index is scaled by the size of the object being accessed. Figure 5.10 presents a graphical illustration of this addressing mode.

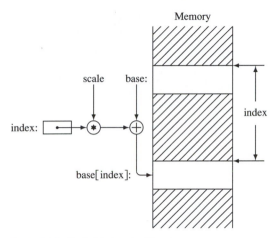

Figure 5.10   Scaled indexed addressing

Example 5.12   *Show how you can rewrite the code fragment presented in Example 5.11 using indexed addressing, assuming that indexed addresses are scaled.*

```
MOVE     R2, #47              ; need the value 47 in a register
LOAD.w   R3, i
STORE.w  int_arr[R3], R2      ; store the value
```

Nonzero-Based Array Indexes   So far, we have used zero-based arrays in our examples. If you need to use an array with a nonzero lower bound, you need to alter the formula used to determine the starting address of an element in the array. The following formula allows you to use a nonzero lower bound for the indexes of an array. In this formula, *lower* is the lower bound for the array indices.

$$addr = base + elem\_size * (index - lower) \qquad (5.2)$$

The subtraction, *index − lower*, transforms a nonzero-based index into a zero-based index. This is frequently called *normalization*. As equation 5.2 is written,   Normalization it may appear that you need to perform the normalization during execution, just before the index is scaled by the element size. However, using algebraic manipulations, we can transform equation 5.2 into the following formula:

$$addr = (base - elem\_size * lower) + elem\_size * index \qquad (5.3)$$

Note that the first term on the right side of the equation only uses constant values. As such, this term can be computed prior to execution.

Example 5.13   *Suppose you have an application that requires an array of integers with a lower bound of 15 and an upper bound of 34. Show how to declare the space needed for this array. Moreover, show the code needed to set the element with index* i *to the value 432.*

```
                .bss
                .align      4
        i:      .reserve    4
 real_base:     .reserve    (34-15+1)*4              ; 4 bytes per integer
                .equate     my_arr, real_base - 15*4

                .text
                 :
                 :
                MOVE        R2, #432
                LOAD.w      R3, i
                MPY         R3, R3, #4               ; scale the index
                STORE.w     my_arr[R3], R2
```

Note that we associate the name *real_base* with the space that we allocate, but use the name *my_arr* to access the elements of the array. Figure 5.11 presents a graphical representation of this technique.

Multidimensional Arrays   This brings us to the topic of *multidimensional arrays*. Multidimensional arrays can be thought of as simple arrays with elements that are arrays. In other words, a multidimensional array is just an *array of arrays*. This is the basis for multidimensional arrays in C and Pascal. For example, the C declaration:

int two_arr[5][3];

declares *two_arr* to be the name of an array of five elements. Each element in the array *two_arr* is itself an array of three elements. Each of these elements is a simple integer. Figure 5.12 presents the natural memory layout for this declaration. We call this layout strategy *row major* order because the array is stored as an array of rows. Row major order is the layout strategy used by Pascal and C. In contrast, FORTRAN uses a *column major* layout strategy.

Multidimensional
arrays

Array of arrays

Row major

Column major

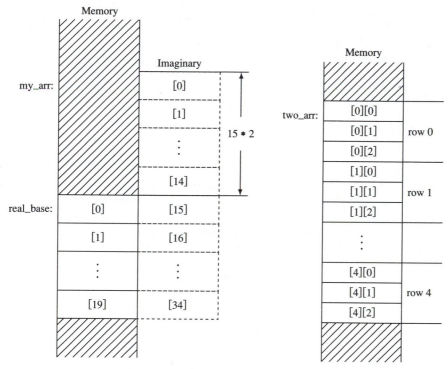

Figure 5.11 Nonzero-based arrays

Figure 5.12 A two-dimensional array

Example 5.14 *Translate the following C declarations and assignment statement into assembly language:*

int *i, j;*
int *two_arr[5][3];*

⋮

two_arr[i][j] = 47;

```
        .bss
two_arr: .reserve   (5*3)*4          ; 5 arrays of 3 elements of 4 bytes
     i: .reserve   4
     j: .reserve   4

        .text
        ⋮
        MOVE     R2, #47
        LOAD.w   R3, i
        MPY      R3, R3, #(3*4)       ; R3 is the row offset
```

```
LOAD.w    R4, j
MPY       R4, R4, #4        ; R4 is the column offset
ADD       R3, R3, R4
STORE.w   two_arr[R3], R2
```

5.2.3 Structures—Displacement Addressing

In C, you can use structures to collect related pieces of information in a single unit. A structure declaration is a sequence of *field* declarations. Each field declaration is a type specification followed by a list of the fields that have the specified type. You can access a field in a structure using a period ("."") between the name of the structure variable and the name of the field. Given a pointer to a structure, you can access a field using the symbol "→" between the pointer and the field name. (These conventions are similar to the conventions of Pascal.)

Figure 5.13 illustrates the declaration and use of structures in C. This fragment begins by declaring the structure *person*. Each instance of the structure *person* has a field called *name,* which is an array of characters and two integer fields called *age* and *salary.* The next two statements declare that *joe* is a variable of type *person* and that *sam* is a pointer to a *person.* The first executable statement sets the *age* field of the structure called *joe* to the value 25. The last statement sets the *age* field of the structure pointed to by *sam* to the value 32.

```
struct person {              /* declare a structure */
   char name[15];
   int salary, age;
};

struct person joe;           /* joe is a structure variable */
struct person *sam;          /* sam is a pointer to a structure */

/* initialize what sam points to */

joe.age = 25;                /* joe is 25 */
sam→age = 32;                /* sam is 32 */
```

Figure 5.13 Declaring and using structures in C

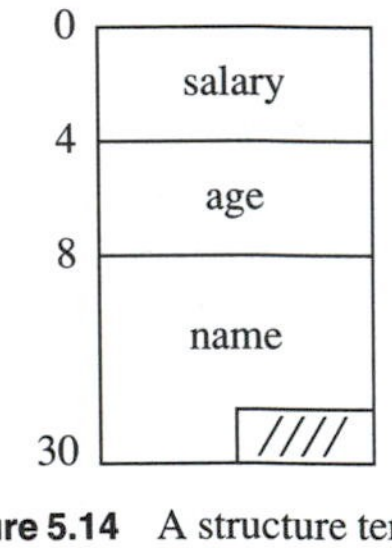

Figure 5.14 A structure template

A structure (or record) declaration defines a template for memory usage. Figure 5.14 presents a graphical representation of the template defined by the structure *person.* Note that we have rearranged the fields. In particular, we have moved the integer fields to the start of the structure. This organization should simplify alignment considerations.

In assembly language, a structure is simply a block of memory. Fields are offsets from the start of the block allocated for the structure. You can make your assembly language programs easier to read if you define symbolic constants for the field offsets.

Example 5.15   *Translate the C fragment shown in Figure 5.13 into assembly language using the structure template shown in Figure 5.14*

```
         ; defines for the structure person
         .equate     SALARY, 0      ; the salary field starts at offset 0
         .equate     AGE, 4         ; the age field starts at offset 4
         .equate     NAME, 8        ; the name field starts at offset 8
         .equate     P_SIZE, 32     ; each structure is 32 bytes

         ; declare the variables
         .bss
         .align      4
joe:     .reserve    P_SIZE         ; joe is a structure
sam:     .reserve    4              ; sam is a pointer

         ; executable statements
         .text
         :
         :
         MOVE        R2, #25
         STORE.w     joe+AGE, R2    ; joe.age = 25

         MOVE        R2, #32
         LOAD.w      R3, sam        ; R3 points to the structure
         ADD         R3, R3, #AGE   ; R3 points to the age field
         STORE.w     R3, R2
```

Note that the first assignment statement uses a constant expression to calculate the address of the field. The second assignment statement must use an ADD instruction to determine the address of the field. In effect, the value AGE is a displacement for the address value held in register R3.

Many machines provide a *displaced addressing* mode. In displaced addressing, you specify an address and a displacement. The address is interpreted as an indirect address and the displacement is interpreted as a constant value. The *effective address* is calculated by adding the constant displacement with the value stored in the address.

Displaced addressing

Effective address

> **Coding Convention—Displaced Addressing**
>
> We use the notation *addr* → *disp* to denote displaced addressing. Most machines require that *addr* be a register address. In these machines, this addressing mode may be called *register-displaced addressing* or *register-indirect with displacement.*

Example 5.16   *Show how you can translate the last assignment statement in Figure 5.13 using register-displaced addressing.*

```
MOVE     R2, #32
LOAD.w   R3, sam              ; R3 points to the structure
STORE.w  R3→AGE, R2
```

Unlike the code in the previous example, this code does not change the value stored in R3. The value in R3 is simply used during the effective address calculation—it is not changed by the effective address calculation. A graphical representation of displacement addressing is shown in Figure 5.15.

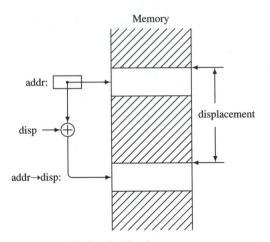

Figure 5.15   Displaced addressing

5.2.4 Strings—Auto-Increment Addressing

In this section, our goal is to motivate the auto-increment addressing modes by considering simple string processing applications. However, before we consider these applications, we need to digress to consider representation strategies for strings, that is, ways to store strings in memory.

Representing Strings   There are two common strategies for storing strings in memory. In the first, the length of the string is stored in the first byte followed by the characters of the string. We refer to this strategy as *length-plus-value* because it stores the length of the string followed by the value of the string. In the second strategy, the characters in the string are stored in memory followed by a special character to mark the end of the string. Typically, the character whose value is zero

Length-plus-value

is used to mark the end of the string. This character is frequently called NULL, and, as such, we refer to strings stored using this strategy as *NULL terminated strings*.

Neither of these strategies is the best for all applications. The length-plus-value strategy establishes a maximum string length (because we encode the length in a single byte, a string can have at most 255 characters). On the other hand, the NULL terminated strategy makes simple operations like length and concatenation (appending to the end of a string) more expensive in terms of time.

Coding Convention—String Constants

You can expect that your assembler provides some support for string constants. In our examples, we assume that the assembler treats a directive of the form:

.byte "hello"

as a shorthand for

.byte 'h','e','l','l','o'

Example 5.17   *Show how you can construct a NULL terminated representation for the string "Hello, world." using the byte directive.*

```
my_str:   .byte   "Hello, world.", 0
```

Constructing string constants that are based on the length-plus-value strategy involves a bit of a trick. At first, you might suspect that you have to count the number of characters in each of your string constants so that you can state the length of the string. However, counting characters is inconvenient and error prone. You can avoid the need to count characters by labeling the location immediately after the last character in the string and using a simple constant expression to determine the number of characters in the string.

Example 5.18   *Show how you can construct a length-plus-value representation for the string "Hello, world." using the byte directive.*

```
my_str:    .byte   last_ch − first_ch      ; just the length
first_ch:  .byte   "Hello, world."
last_ch:                                   ; marking the end
```

Coding Convention—NULL Terminated Strings

For the remainder of this book, we assume that strings are NULL terminated—not because this is the best representation strategy but because C uses this strategy.

Auto-Increment Addressing   We are now ready to consider a simple operation involving strings: a function that computes the length of a NULL terminated string. We will use this example to motivate string processing and auto-increment addressing.

Example 5.19   *Write an assembly language fragment that calculates the length of a NULL terminated string.*

```
        CLEAR    R2          ; R2 is the counter
        MOVE     R3, #str    ; R3 points to the current element
        LOAD.b   R4, @R3     ; load the next character
        BRANCH   test        ; branch to loop exit test
top:
        ADD      R2, R2, #1  ; one more character
        ADD      R3, R3, #1  ; advance the pointer
        LOAD.b   R4, @R3     ; load the next character
test:
        CMP      R4, #0      ; end of string?
        BRNE     top         ; no, process next byte
```

The code starts by establishing R3 as a pointer to the first element of the string and setting the length (stored in R2) to zero. The loop exits when R3 points to the value zero. Every iteration of the loop advances the value of the pointer R3 so that it is pointing to the next element in the string.

The code fragment shown in Example 5.19 illustrates an important characteristic of operations that manipulate strings—the need to process each element in the string in succession. As such, most sections of code that manipulate strings consist of a loop that contains the use of a pointer and the subsequent incrementation of the pointer (used to move to the next element of the string). Because this use of a pointer followed by its incrementation occurs frequently, many machines provide an *auto-increment addressing* mode. In auto-increment addressing, the address given in the instruction is an indirect address. Unlike simple indirect addressing, the effective address calculation does not stop when it determines the value of the address. In auto-increment addressing, the address value is also incremented. Figure 5.16 presents a graphical illustration of post-increment addressing. Note that this addressing mode is composed of two distinct operations: indirection to determine the effective address and incrementation to update the pointer. To

Auto-increment
addressing

emphasize this aspect of auto-increment addressing, it is frequently called *indirect with increment*. The order in which these operations are performed distinguishes two different addressing modes. If the incrementation occurs after the value is used as the effective address, the addressing mode is called *post-increment addressing*; otherwise, it is called *pre-increment addressing*.

Indirect with increment

Post-increment
addressing

Pre-increment
addressing

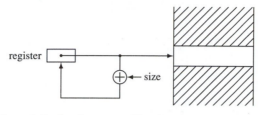

Figure 5.16   Post-increment addressing

Coding Convention—Increment Addressing

We use the notation [addr]+ to denote post-increment addressing and +[addr] to denote pre-increment addressing.

Example 5.20   *Show how you can use post-increment addressing to calculate the length of a NULL terminated string.*

```
        CLEAR    R2            ; R2 is the counter
        MOVE     R3, #str      ; R3 points to the current element
        LOAD.b   R4, [R3]+     ; load the next character
        BRANCH   test          ; branch to loop exit test
top:
        ADD      R2, R2, #1    ; one more character
        LOAD.b   R4, [R3]+     ; load the next character
test:
        CMP      R4, #0        ; end of string?
        BRNE     top           ; no, process next byte
```

A string can be thought of as an array of characters. In C and Pascal, you allocate the space needed for strings by declaring an array of characters. As such, the auto-increment addressing modes provide you with a way to conveniently manipulate every element in an array of characters. In fact, these addressing modes can be used with any array whose elements require only one byte of storage. Because the need to manipulate every element in an array is not limited to arrays whose elements are one byte in length, most machines extend the notion of auto-increment addressing to include incrementation by the size of the memory element being accessed. To make this more general version of auto-increment addressing work as you would like, the machine needs to determine whether to increment the address value by 1, 2, or 4 to determine the address of the next element. Determination of the increment amount is based on the size specifier given in the instruction. For example, if the instruction is LOAD.w, the pointer is incremented by 4. The amount added to a pointer in an auto-increment is frequently called the *stride*.

Stride

Example 5.21   *Show how you can use post-increment addressing to compute the sum of the values in an integer array.*

```
                           .bss
        arr:  .reserve     4*...
    end_arr:

              :

              .text
              CLEAR     R2                 ; R2 is the sum
              MOVE      R3, #arr           ; R3 points to the current element
        top:
              CMP       R3, #end_arr       ; end of the array?
              BREQ      bottom
              LOAD.w    R4, [R3]+          ; load the next value
              ADD       R2, R2, R4         ; add in the next value
              BRANCH    top
    bottom:
```

String Operations   As an alternative to auto-increment addressing, some machines, like the IBM 360 and Intel 8086, provide special instructions to support string processing. These instructions generally incorporate an implicit auto-increment of one or more of their operands. In many cases, these instructions also include an implicit repetition of the basic operation. We ignore the possibility of implicit repetition and concentrate on implicit addressing modes. As an example, the *SCAS (scan string)* operation compares the value of its first operand with the value pointed to by the value of the second operand (setting the condition code register) and increments the second operand.

SCAS (scan string)

Example 5.22   *Show how you can use the SCAS operation to calculate the length of a NULL terminated string.*

```
              MOVE      R2, #-1            ; R2 counts the length
              MOVE      R3, #str           ; R3 is the string pointer
        top:
```

```
ADD     R2, R2, #1    ; increment the count
SCAS.b  #0, R3        ; compare (R3) to 0 and increment R3
BRNE    top           ; no, try again
```

In contrasting these approaches for providing support for strings (special addressing modes versus special string instructions), an important consideration is the independence between operations and operands. Support for a variety of addressing modes emphasizes this independence between operations and operands. In particular, machines that support auto-increment as an addressing mode typically let you combine this addressing mode with any operation supported by the machine. Machines that provide special instructions emphasize a stronger dependence between the operation and the way in which the operands are used.

5.2.5 Stacks—Auto-Decrement Addressing

As you are undoubtedly aware, stacks are an important data structure in many applications. In this section, we will not be concerned with the use of stacks. Rather, we are interested in implementing the operations, push and pop, that define this data structure. A stack of integers can be implemented using an array of integers (to store the values in the stack) and a pointer (to indicate the current top of the stack). To complete this implementation, you need to make two decisions: The first involves the precise meaning of the stack pointer, and the second involves the direction of stack growth.

You can use a stack pointer to identify the cell used by the next push operation or the cell used to store the last value pushed. If you choose the first possibility, the stack pointer is actually a *free-cell pointer* because it identifies a cell that is not currently being used. If you choose the second, the pointer is a *top-of-stack pointer*. These possibilities are illustrated in Figure 5.17. In most applications the choice is arbitrary; however, there is a good reason for choosing a top-of-stack pointer when you are implementing a stack in assembly language. We will discuss the reason for this in a moment.

Free-cell pointer

Top-of-stack pointer

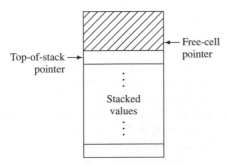

Figure 5.17 Different types of stack pointers

The second issue that we must consider is the direction of stack growth. We begin by making some observations. Because we have chosen to use a top-of-stack pointer, the push operation must start by allocating space for the new element. If the stack grows toward lower addresses, this allocation involves a decrement of the stack pointer. Otherwise, it involves an increment of the stack pointer. In contrast, the decrement or increment of the stack top must occur after the value has been taken from the stack in the pop operation. To summarize: the stack pointer is changed *before* it is used in the push operation and *after* it used in the pop operation. This should remind you of the pre- and post-increment addressing modes that we discussed earlier. As such, a machine might provide a pre-increment addressing mode (used to push items) along with a *post-decrement addressing* mode (used to pop items). In this case, your stacks will grow from lower addresses to higher addresses. Alternatively, many machines provide *pre-decrement addressing* (for pushing values) and post-increment addressing (for popping values). There is no definitive reason for preferring one of these pairs over the other. When the latter pair is used, stacks grow from higher addresses to lower addresses. Graphically, this means that our stacks grow from the bottom of the page to the top of the page as shown in Figure 5.17.

Why did we decide to use a top-of-stack pointer instead of a free-cell pointer? If all of the items that you push onto a stack are the same size, it is possible to know how much space the next element will require and advance the free-cell pointer by that amount after pushing an item onto the stack. However, if you need a stack that has different-sized elements, you cannot predict ahead of time how much space the next item will require, and, as such, you cannot easily maintain a free-cell pointer. By using a top-of-stack pointer instead of a free-cell pointer, you can easily construct a stack that has word and halfword values.

Stacks that mix byte and word (or halfword) values create a special problem on machines that require alignment. We call this problem *stack alignment*. To illustrate this problem, consider the following sequence of instructions:

```
STORE.w    –[R5], R2    ; push a word
STORE.b    –[R5], R3    ; push a byte
STORE.w    –[R5], R4    ; push a word
```

If the first push succeeds, the third will fail because of alignment. If the first push succeeds, the value in R5 must be a multiple of four at the end of the instruction execution. The next push decrements the value in R5 by one. As such, the value in R5 is odd when the third instruction begins execution. The value in R5 is decremented by four and, as such, remains odd when the value in R5 is used as the address to be used in storing the value in R2. This results in an attempt to store a word value at an odd address, which is not legal on an aligned machine. To avoid this problem, you should make sure that your stacks hold only values of a single size (byte, halfword, or word).

Post-decrement addressing

Pre-decrement addressing

Stack alignment

5.2.6 Summary of Addressing Modes

Table 5.1 summarizes the addressing modes that we have discussed. The first column of this table gives the name of the mode, the second column shows the notation that we have introduced for the addressing mode, the third column shows the effective address calculation, and the fourth column shows the value utilized when the addressing mode is used to specify a source operand. Table 5.1 does not give a complete listing of the addressing modes that might be supported by a machine. The actual set of addressing modes provided by a machine is based on a balance between the difficulty of providing the addressing mode and the usefulness of having the addressing mode.

Table 5.1 Addressing modes

Mode	Notation	Effective Address	Value
Immediate	#n	none—not an address	n
Direct register	Rn	Rn	**reg**[n]
Direct memory	addr	addr	**M**[addr]
Register-indirect	@Rn	**reg**[n]	**M**[**reg**[n]]
Memory-indirect	@addr	**M**[addr]	**M**[**M**[addr]]
Register indexed	addr[Rn]	addr + **reg**[n]	**M**[addr + **reg**[n]]
Memory indexed	addr$_1$[addr$_2$]	addr$_1$ + **M**[addr$_2$]	**M**[addr$_1$ + **M**[addr$_2$]]
Register displaced	Rn → disp	disp + **reg**[n]	**M**[disp + **reg**[n]]
Memory displaced	addr→disp	disp + **M**[addr]	**M**[disp + **M**[addr]]
Pre-increment	+[Rn]	**reg**[n] = **reg**[n] + 1 **M**[**reg**[n]]	**reg**[n]
Post-increment	[Rn]+	**M**[**reg**[n]] **reg**[n] = **reg**[n] + 1	**reg**[n]
Pre-decrement	−[Rn]	**reg**[n] = **reg**[n] − 1 **M**[**reg**[n]]	**reg**[n]
Post-decrement	[Rn]−	**M**[**reg**[n]] **reg**[n] = **reg**[n] − 1	**reg**[n]

5.3 THE EFFECTIVE ADDRESS AS A VALUE—LEA

On occasion, you may find yourself in a situation where you need to store the value that is calculated as the effective address (instead of the value stored at the effective address). As we discuss in the next chapter, this is quite common when you are passing parameters to subroutines or procedures. Because the need to perform this task arises frequently, many machines provide a special instruction that simply calculates and stores the effective address of its first operand into the location specified by the second operand.

> **Coding Convention—Load Effective Address (LEA)**
> We use the name LEA for the operation that calculates the effective address.

To illustrate a use of the LEA, consider access to a field of a structure in an array of structures. Figure 5.18 shows a C declaration that declares *dept* as an array of 10 structures. Each structure has three fields: *id, age,* and *salary.*

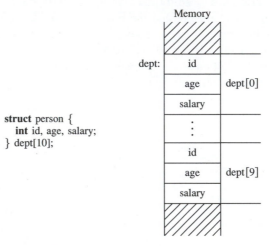

```
struct person {
    int id, age, salary;
} dept[10];
```

Figure 5.18   An array of structures

Example 5.23   *Write an assembly language code fragment to increment the age field of the structure with index* i.

```
        .equate     ID, 0           ; id is at offset 0
        .equate     AGE, 4          ; age is at offset 2
        .equate     SALARY, 8       ; salary is at offset 4
        .equate     P_SIZE, 12      ; the size of each person struct
        .bss
dept:   .reserve    10*P_SIZE       ; allocate space
   i:   .reserve    4
        ⋮
        .text
        LOAD.w      R2, i           ; R2 is going to be an index
        MPY         R2, R2, #P_SIZE ; scale R2 by element size
        LEA         R2, dept[R2]    ; R2 points to the structure
        LOAD.w      R3, R2→AGE
        ADD         R3, R3, #1
        STORE.w     R2→AGE, R3
        ⋮
```

Table 5.2 shows how the LEA operation could be simulated using MOVE, LOAD, and ADD instructions. In examining the first three entries in this table, it is not apparent that the LEA instruction provides a particularly important service. However, the utility of the LEA instruction can be seen by considering the last two entries of this table.

Table 5.2 LEA versus MOVE/LOAD

LEA version	MOVE/LOAD version
LEA R2, 1000	MOVE R2, #1000
LEA R2, @1000	LOAD R2, 1000
LEA R2, @R3	MOVE R2, R3
LEA R2, 1000[R3]	MOVE R2, #1000
	ADD R2, R2, R3
LEA R2, R3→1000	MOVE R2, #1000
	ADD R2, R2, R3

5.4 ADDRESSING MODES IN CONTROL—SWITCH

Up until this point, we have used data structures to motivate the variety of addressing modes found in modern machines. But this is only part of the story; addressing modes can also be used in the implementation of control structures. In this section, we discuss an important technique, the construction of a *branch table*, that can be used in the implementation of a **switch** statement of C (comparable to the **case** statement of Pascal or the **computed goto** of FORTRAN).

Branch table

Figure 5.19 illustrates a simple **switch** statement. This construct is roughly equivalent to the **case** statement of Pascal. In contrast to the **case** statement of Pascal, note the use of the reserved word **case**. In C, the reserved word **case** is used to start a case label. Further, notice the use of the **break** statement in each of the cases. C requires an explicit transfer of control to the end of the **switch** for each of the cases; otherwise, control "falls" into the next case.

```
switch i {
case 1:
    stmt1
    break;
case 2:
case 4:
    stmt2
    break;
case 6:
    stmt3
}
```

Figure 5.19 A sample **switch** statement

Cascaded
comparisons

One way to implement a **switch** is to compare the value of the expression to each of the cases in succession. This strategy is frequently called *cascaded comparisons* because the flow of control "cascades" through a set of comparisons until a match is found or until there are no more values to test.

Example 5.24 *Show how you can implement the* **switch** *statement in Figure 5.19 using cascaded comparisons.*

```
        .text
        LOAD.w   R2, i
        CMP.w    R2, #1
        BRNE     try2
        ⋮
                            ; code for stmt1
        BRANCH   last
try2:
        CMP.w    R2, #2
        BREQ     lab2
        CMP.w    R2, #4
        BRNE     try3
lab2:
        ⋮
                            ; code for stmt2
        BRANCH   last
try3:
        CMP.w    R2, #6
        BRNE     last
        ⋮
                            ; code for stmt3
last:
```

If you write a **switch** statement with a very large number of **case** labels, the cascaded comparisons strategy may result in very slow code. In the branch table approach, the value of the **switch** expression is used as an index into a table (array) of code addresses. Control is transferred directly to the address stored at the index indicated by the value of the **switch** expression. This results in very fast code but requires enough space for a contiguous table of address values.

Example 5.25 *Show how you can implement the* **switch** *statement in Figure 5.19 using a branch table.*

```
        .data
tab:                            ; initialize the branch table
        .word    lab1           ; (i = 1) offset 0 → stmt1
        .word    lab2           ; (i = 2) offset 1 → stmt2
```

```
        .word      last            ; (i = 3) offset 2 → last
        .word      lab2            ; (i = 4) offset 3 → stmt2
        .word      last            ; (i = 5) offset 4 → last
        .word      lab3            ; (i = 6) offset 5 → stmt3
        :

        .text
        LOAD.w     R2, i
        CMP        R2, #1
        BRLT       last            ; nothing to do
        CMP        R2, #6
        BRGT       last            ; nothing to do
        LOAD.w     R2, (tab−4)[R2] ; R2 points to the statement
        BRANCH     @R2
lab1:
        :
                                   ; code for stmt1
        BRANCH     last
lab2:
        :
                                   ; code for stmt2
        BRANCH     last
lab3:
        :
                                   ; code for stmt3
last:
```

5.5 ADDRESSES AND INTEGERS

In our presentation of addressing modes and effective address calculations, we have been fairly casual in our use of arithmetic expressions involving addresses and integers. For example, in displaced addressing, an integer value is added to an address value to form the effective address (an address value). On the one hand, this may seem very natural, as addresses are integers. However, you should remember that addresses are just symbols. Until we have defined what it means to add an integer to an address, adding the integer 4 to an address makes about as much sense as adding 4 to the symbol ↩.

Our choice to use the nonnegative integers as addresses has an important consequence: The nonnegative integers are ordered, and we can use this order to establish an order for addresses. As such, it makes sense to talk about the address that is four addresses after a given address. Table 5.3 presents informal definitions for the operations that we have used involving addresses and integers. In considering the operations shown in Table 5.3, we assume that the "+" operation can be implemented using integer addition and that both of the "−" operations can be implemented using integer subtraction. As such, if we need to perform these operations during the execution of a program, we can make use of the ADD and SUB instructions provided by the machine (as we have done in the examples presented in this section). As we discuss in Chapter 10, these assumptions may be invalid on some architectures.

Table 5.3   Operations on addresses

Operation	Semantics
$a + i$	This operation results in the address value that is i locations after a. If a is greater than $n - i - 1$, the operation is undefined.
$a - i$	This operation results in the address value that is i locations before a. If a is less than i, the operation is undefined.
$a_2 - a_1$	This operation results in the integer value that is the number of locations between a_1 and a_2 including the location labeled by a_1 (if $a_1 \neq a_2$). If a_1 is greater than a_2, the operation is undefined.

where:
a, a_1, and a_2 denote address values.
i denotes a nonnegative integer value.
n is the size of the memory.

It is important to remember that many operations involving addresses and integers do not make sense. For example, it does not make sense to multiply an address by an integer, nor does it make sense to add two addresses together. Should you attempt to perform either of these operations in a constant expression, your assembler will most likely complain about a *nonrelocatable expression*. We will discuss the precise meaning of this message when we consider the translation process in more detail in Chapter 10. Should you attempt to perform one of these operations during the execution of a program (using the MPY or ADD instruction provided by the machine), the machine will not stop you; however, the result is still meaningless!

Nonrelocatable
expression

In reading the definitions presented in Table 5.3, notice that the operations have been defined so that all of the address results are in the range of address values, $0 \ldots n - 1$, or the operation is undefined. We could avoid the need to make the first two operations undefined if we make the ordering of addresses circular, that is, define address 0 to be the address after $n - 1$ and $n - 1$ to be the address before 0. Moreover, as we discuss in Chapter 7, we can still use the ADD and SUB operations provided by the machine to implement these operations (assuming that these operations are based on 2's complement arithmetic and the value of n is appropriate).

5.6 CASE STUDY: ADDRESSING MODES ON THE SPARC

In the previous chapter, we deferred discussion of the addressing fields used in SPARC instructions. We are now ready to consider (most of) these fields. Figure 5.20 recalls the formats used for LOAD and STORE instructions. In this discussion, we are primarily interested in the basic fields used to form the effective address: rs1, rs2, and simm13.

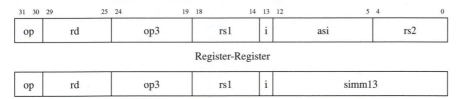

Figure 5.20 Formats for the memory reference instructions on the SPARC

The SPARC architecture only provides support for two addressing modes. Each of the formats in Figure 5.20 supports a different addressing mode.

The first format supports an addressing mode that we call *register-indirect with index*. In this addressing mode, the value in the rs1 field identifies the base register, while the value in the rs2 field identifies the index register. The processor adds the value of the base register with the value of the index register to calculate the effective address.

Register-indirect with index

The second format supports *register-indirect with displacement* addressing. In this addressing mode, the value in the rs1 field identifies the base register. The processor adds the value of the base address register with the sign-extended value in the simm13 field of the instruction to calculate the effective address.

Register-indirect with displacement

Note that the SPARC does not provide direct support for direct-memory addressing or register-indirect addressing. You can easily attain the effect of register-indirect addressing by using R0 as the index register in the first format or by using a displacement of zero in the second format. The lack of direct-memory addressing is related to the lack of support for 32-bit values and, as such, is common to all RISC machines. (Recall the discussion related to the SETHI instruction in Chapter 4.)

To load the value from an arbitrary location in memory on the SPARC, you need to have the processor execute two instructions. The first instruction uses the SETHI operation to load the 22 most significant bits of the memory address into a base register (typically, the register R1 is used for this purpose). The second instruction is the actual LOAD operation. This load operation uses the displaced addressing with the least significant 10 bits of the address as the displacement. While this solution is described in terms of the SPARC instruction set, the structure is common to all RISC machines.

Example 5.26 *Show how you can use the SETHI instruction to implement direct-memory addressing. To be more specific, show how you can use the SETHI instruction to achieve the effect of the statement:*

LOAD.w R2, loc

Where loc *is the label of an arbitrary memory location.*

```
SETHI    R1, #hi(loc )        ; set the high order 22 bits of R1
LOAD.w   R2, R1→lo(loc)       ; load R2 using displaced addressing
```

> **Coding Convention—LOAD/STORE**
> We have and will continue to assume that the assembler converts LOAD and STORE
> instructions that use direct-memory addresses into sequences like the one shown in
> Example 5.26.

5.7 CASE STUDY: ADDRESSING MODES ON THE HP PRECISION

In considering the addressing modes supported by the SPARC, note that this architecture does not support the auto-increment or auto-decrement addressing modes.
Moreover, the SPARC does not provide support for scaling in its indexed addressing. In this respect, the SPARC is representative of many of the RISC machines.
In fact, it has been claimed that the lack of these powerful and complex addressing
modes is a characteristic of RISC machines. When introduced auto-increment addressing, auto-decrement addressing, and scaling, we showed how these addressing
modes reduced the number of instructions in a simple assembly language fragment. A computer architect must weigh the benefits of reducing the number of
instructions executed against the costs associated with the added complexity these
instructions introduce. Here we should note that these decisions cannot be based
on simple examples like the ones we have discussed. Instead, the architect must
examine programs that represent the ways in which the machine will be used.

The designers of the HP Precision architecture decided that the benefits of
these complex addressing modes were greater than the costs that they imposed.
Like the SPARC, the HP Precision architecture does not provide direct support for
direct-memory or register-indirect addressing. You can attain the effect of these
addressing modes using the same techniques that we discussed for the SPARC. The
two addressing modes found on the SPARC provide the basis for the addressing
modes of the HP Precision architecture. However, that is where the similarities
end. In the HP Precision, you can specify whether the base register is modified
by the effective address calculation. In addition, you can specify scaling in the
indexed addressing modes.

5.7.1 Displacement Addressing

The HP Precision provides two basic variations on its *register-indirect with
displacement* addressing: long displacement and short displacement. The long

displacement uses a 14-bit immediate value, while the short displacement uses a 5-bit immediate value. In both cases, you can specify that the base register is to be modified. In the short displacement mode, if the base register is modified, you can also specify whether the effective address is determined before or after the displacement value is added to the base address. In the long displacement mode, the effective address is determined before the displacement is added if the displacement is nonnegative (i.e., post-increment). If the displacement is negative, the effective address is determined after the displacement is added (i.e., pre-decrement). Figure 5.21 illustrates the displacement addressing modes for the HP Precision architecture.

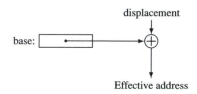

A. Base register not modified

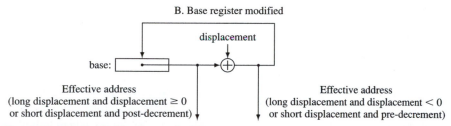

B. Base register modified

Figure 5.21 Displaced addressing on the HP Precision

5.7.2 Indexed Addressing

The HP Precision provides four variations on indexed addresses. The index value can be scaled or not scaled, and the base register can be modified or left unchanged. If you specify that the index is scaled, it will be scaled by the size of the operand (one for byte, two for halfword, and four for word). If you specify modification of the base register, the effective address is the current value of the base register and the base register is set to the result of the index calculation. In other words, when you specify modification of the base register, it becomes *post-index* addressing. Figure 5.22 presents a graphical representation of the indexed addressing modes on the HP Precision architecture.

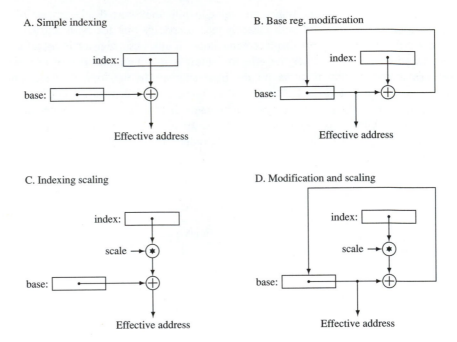

Figure 5.22   Indexed addressing on the HP Precision

5.8 SUMMARY

In this chapter, we have focused on the addressing modes provided by modern computers. The chapter began with a discussion of the assembly process and a small collection of assembler directives. Using these directives and our understanding of the assembly process, we were able to discuss representations for simple data structures (pointers, arrays, records, strings, and stacks). Access to the elements of these simple data structures provided the motivation for the addressing modes that we considered. In addition to the addressing modes, assembler directives, and simple data structures, we covered two topics that are closely related to addressing modes: the LEA instruction and branch tables. As we discussed, the LEA instruction treats the effective address as a value instead of the address of a value. In the next chapter, we will see that this instruction is very useful in the translation of subroutine calls. Branch tables were presented to illustrate that addressing modes can be used in the implementation of control structures as well as data structures. Finally, the chapter concluded with a brief discussion of the similarities and differences between addresses and integers.

In our presentation of addressing modes, each addressing mode has been motivated by considering the memory access patterns that our programs exhibit. For example, we introduced auto-increment addressing by considering the memory access patterns that occur during string processing applications. One of the most difficult aspects of computer design involves the selection of addressing modes to be provided by the machine. Until recently, the trend has been toward providing more and more complex addressing modes. However, with the introduction of the RISC philosophy, many machines are reversing this trend. RISC machines generally provide a very small set of addressing modes, perhaps only direct-memory, direct-register, and indirect-register addressing

5.8.1 Additional Reading

If you want more information about assembler directives, you should consult the books listed in the bibliography under the heading "Assembly Language Programming." In addition, you should consult the User's Manual for any assemblers that are available to you.

If you want more information about addressing modes, you should consult the books listed under the headings "Assembly Language Programming" and "Architecture and Organization." In addition, you should consult the Programmer's Reference Manual for any machines that are available to you.

If you want more information about implementation of the data structures found in high-level languages, you should consult the books listed under the headings "Programming Language Surveys" and "Compiler Construction."

Finally, I highly recommend the tutorial portion of *The C Programming Language* by Kernighan and Ritchie if you want more information about string processing, pointers, and auto-increment/decrement addressing.

5.8.2 Terminology

- Data flow diagrams (bubbles, boxes, and arcs)
- Source code, Object code
- Assembler directives
- Location counter(s)
- The symbol table (insert and lookup), Labels, Symbolic constants
- Forward reference
- Allocation and initialization
- Loading, Relocation, Load-and-go
- Assembler segments (text, data, and bss)
- Implicit segment identification, Explicit segment specification
- Current segment
- Declaration and access
- Addressing modes
- Direct-memory, direct-register, and immediate addressing
- Effective address and effective address calculation

- Register-indirect, memory-indirect addressing
- The address of an address
- Indexed addressing, Relative address, Base address
- Scaled addition
- Zero-based arrays, Nonzero-based arrays, Normalization
- Multidimensional arrays, Array of arrays
- Row major, Column major
- Structures, Records, Displaced addressing
- Length-plus-value, NULL terminated strings
- Auto-increment, Pre-/Post-increment, Indirect with increment
- Auto-decrement, Pre-/Post-decrement, Indirect with decrement
- Stride
- Top-of-stack pointer, Free-cell pointer
- Stack alignment
- Cascaded comparisons, Branch table
- Register-indirect with index
- Register-indirect with scaled index
- Register-indirect with displacement

5.8.3 Review Questions

1. What does the term *forward reference* mean? Give an example of a forward reference.
2. What is the directive used to reserve space? What are the directives used to initialize space? Give an example illustrating the use of each directive.
3. What does the phrase *load-and-go* mean?
4. What is an assembler segment? Explain the difference between implicit and explicit segment identification.
5. Explain the difference between direct-memory addressing and memory-indirect addressing.
6. Explain the difference between memory-indirect addressing and register-indirect addressing.
7. Explain the difference between indexed addressing and displaced addressing.
8. Explain the difference between row major and column major layout for two-dimensional arrays.
9. Explain the difference between pre- and post-increment addressing.
10. What does the term *stride* mean?

11. What does the phrase *scaled addition* mean? In what context is this phrase used?

12. Explain the difference between the *top-of-stack* pointer and a *free-cell* pointer.

13. What is a branch table?

5.9 EXERCISES

1. For each of the following statements, if the statement is true, explain why it must be true; otherwise, describe a counter example. You should assume that the program is loaded starting at memory location zero and that every instruction is four bytes.

    a. During every program execution, the program counter eventually assumes every value assumed by the location counter during the translation of the program.

    b. During program execution, the program counter can only assume values that were assumed by the location counter during the translation of the program.

2. What, if anything, is wrong with the following code fragments? Poor programming style is not wrong, per se; however, comment on poor programming style. In all cases, be certain to distinguish between poor style (that makes the code difficult to understand and modify) and errors (that may lead to difficulties during program execution). As you evaluate these code fragments, assume that the assembler does not provide a distinction between text, data, and bss segments.

    a.

```
        START:
                 :                          ; other instructions
            y:   .reserve   4               ; y needs 4 bytes
                 LOAD.w     R2, y           ; temp = y; (R2 is temp)
            z:   .reserve   4               ; z needs 4 bytes
                 LOAD.w     R3, z           ; R3 is z
                 CLEAR      R4              ; x = 0; (R4 is x)
                 BRANCH     test            ; goto test
          top:
                 ADD        R4, R4, #1      ; x = x + 1;
          test:
                 SUB        R2, R2, R3      ; temp = temp − z;
                 BRGE       top             ; if( temp ≥ 0 ) goto top
            x:   .reserve   4               ; x needs 4 bytes
                 STORE.w    x, R4           ; store the result
```

b.

```
START:
                                        ; other instructions
           LOAD.w   R2, y              ; temp = y; (R2 is temp)
           LOAD.w   R3, z              ; R3 is z
           CLEAR    R4                 ; x = 0; (R4 is x)
           BRANCH   test               ; goto test
    x:     .reserve 4                  ; x needs 4 bytes
    y:     .reserve 4                  ; y needs 4 bytes
    z:     .reserve 4                  ; z needs 4 bytes
  top:
           ADD      R4, R4, #1         ; x = x + 1;
  test:
           SUB      R2, R2, R3         ; temp = temp − z;
           BRGE     top                ; if( temp ≥ 0 ) goto top
           STORE.w  x, R4              ; store the result
```

3.   Suppose your assembler does not provide segments. Moreover, suppose it does not provide any mechanism for beginning execution at any point other than memory location zero. Explain how you could integrate the reserve directives into your programs.

4.   In Example 5.4 we assumed that the location counter was of the form $4x + 2$ (i.e., $n = 4x + 2$) when the assembler encountered the allocation directives. Redraw this diagram assuming that the location counter is of the following form when the assembler encounters these directives:

   a. $4x$.

   b. $4x + 1$.

   c. $4x + 3$.

5.   Rearrange the allocation and alignment directives presented in Example 5.4 to minimize the amount of wasted space, assuming that the location counter is of the following form when the assembler encounters these directives:

   a. $4x$.

   b. $4x + 1$.

   c. $4x + 2$.

   d. $4x + 3$.

6.   What, if anything, is wrong with the following code fragments? Poor programming style is not wrong, per se; however, comment on poor programming style. In all cases, be certain to distinguish between poor style (that makes the code difficult to understand and modify) and errors (that may lead to difficulties during program execution).

   a.

```
           .data                       ; switch to the data segment
    x:     .reserve 4                  ; x needs 4 bytes
    y:     .reserve 4                  ; y needs 4 bytes
    z:     .reserve 4                  ; z needs 4 bytes
```

```
        .text                      ; switch to the text segment
        ⋮                          ; other instructions
        LOAD.w    R2, y            ; temp = y; (R2 is temp)
        LOAD.w    R3, z            ; R3 is z
        CLEAR     R4               ; x = 0; (R4 is x)
        BRANCH    test             ; goto test
top:
        ADD       R4, R4, #1       ; x = x + 1;
test:
        SUB       R2, R2, R3       ; temp = temp − z;
        BRGE      top              ; if( temp ≥ 0 ) goto top
        STORE.w   x, R4            ; store the result
```

b.

```
        .text                      ; switch to the text segment
        ⋮                          ; other instructions
        LOAD.w    R2, y            ; temp = y; (R2 is temp)
        LOAD.w    R3, z            ; R3 is z
        CLEAR     R4               ; x = 0; (R4 is x)
        BRANCH    test             ; goto test
top:
        ADD       R4, R4, #1       ; x = x + 1;
test:
        SUB       R2, R2, R3       ; temp = temp − z;
        BRGE      top              ; if( temp ≥ 0 ) goto top
        STORE.w   x, R4            ; store the result
        ⋮                          ; other instructions
        .bss                       ; switch to the bss segment
x:      .reserve  4                ; x needs 4 bytes
y:      .reserve  4                ; y needs 4 bytes
z:      .reserve  4                ; z needs 4 bytes
```

c.

```
        .text                      ; switch to the text segment
        ⋮                          ; other instructions
        .bss                       ; switch to the bss segment
y:      .reserve  4                ; y needs 4 bytes
        .text                      ; switch to the text segment
        LOAD.w    R2, y            ; temp = y; (R2 is temp)
        .bss                       ; switch to the bss segment
z:      .reserve  4                ; z needs 4 bytes
        .text                      ; switch to the text segment
        LOAD.w    R3, z            ; R3 is z
        CLEAR     R4               ; x = 0; (R4 is x)
        BRANCH    test             ; goto test
```

```
top:
        ADD      R4, R4, #1       ; x = x + 1;
test:
        SUB      R2, R2, R3       ; temp = temp − z;
        BRGE     top              ; if( temp ≥ 0 ) goto top
        .bss                      ; switch to the bss segment
x:      .reserve 4                ; x needs 4 bytes
        .text                     ; switch to the text segment
        STORE.w  x, R4            ; store the result


        ⋮                         ; other instructions
```

7. When we discussed implicit identification of segments, we discussed instructions and the allocation directives, but we did not discuss the align directive.

   a. What special problem does this directive introduce? Explain why this problem does not exist when we use explicit identification of segments?

   b. Suggest how you would deal with alignment in an assembler that performs implicit identification of segments.

8. The following C declarations declare *ch* as a variable of type character and *ptr* as a variable of type pointer to character. Moreover, they initialize *ptr* to point to *ch*. Show how you would translate these declarations into assembly language directives.

   char ch;
   char *ptr = &ch;

9. In C, the following declaration allocates an array of five integers and initializes the elements of this array:

   int my_arr[5] = { 1, 2, 3, 4, 5 };

   Show the directive(s) that you would use to attain the same effect in an assembly language program.

10. An array initializer in C (as described in exercise 9) does not need to specify an initial value for every element in the array. For example, the following is a legal declaration in C:

    int my_arr[20] = { 1, 2, 3, 4, 5 };

    In this case, the first five elements of *my_arr* have been given explicit initial values. Assuming that the remaining elements are left uninitialized, show the directive(s) that you would use to attain the effect of this declaration in an assembly language program.

11. In the text, we described how to introduce a nonzero lower bound in a one-dimensional array. Will a similar technique work for two-dimensional arrays? If so, explain the technique. If not, explain what the problem is.

12. Rewrite the code fragment in Example 5.14, assuming that indexed addresses are scaled.

13. Figure 5.12 shows a two-dimensional array stored in row major order.

    a. Show the storage layout that would result if the array were stored in column major order.

    b. Show an assembly code fragment to assign the value 47 to two_arr[i][j], assuming that the array is stored in column major order.

14. When you have an array of structures, the most obvious representation strategy is to construct a single array in which every element holds an entire structure. However, if the machine you are using requires alignment, you may be better off storing each field in a separate array. This approach to storage layout is called *parallel arrays*.

    a. Give a concrete example that illustrates how the parallel array approach might save memory space on a machine that requires alignment.

    b. Show how you would allocate the space needed for your arrays.

    c. Give an example illustrating how you would access an element of this structure.

15. The parallel array approach is also very useful if the machine you are using provides scaled indexes. Give a concrete example that illustrates how the parallel array approach would be an advantage on a machine that supports indexed addressing with scaling.

16. In Example 5.20, we showed how to calculate the length of a NULL terminated string using post-increment addressing. Rewrite this code fragment to use pre-increment addressing.

17. The code fragments shown in Examples 5.19 and 5.20 increment two registers in the body of the loop. Can you eliminate one of these increments? If so, show how you could rewrite the code fragment in Examples 5.20 so that it uses a single increment. If you cannot eliminate one of the increments, explain why it is not possible.

18. It may seem that Table 5.2 is missing a few entries.

    a. Explain why there is no entry for LEA R2, #1000.

    b. Explain why there is no entry for LEA R2, R3.

    c. What problem would arise if you used pre-increment addressing in the first operand of an LEA instruction? That is, what problem would an instruction of the form LEA R2,+[R3] cause? (Note: any of the auto-increment or auto-decrement addressing modes would present the same difficulty.)

19. Considering the differences between integers and addresses, explain the problem that might arise using the array addressing technique illustrated in Figure 5.11.

20. Indexed and displaced addressing both add an integer with an address to form the effective address. In indexed addressing, the address value is given as a constant. In displaced addressing, the integer is a constant. Under what circumstances is there a significant difference between indexed and displaced addressing? That is, is indexed addressing really just a special case of displaced addressing?

CHAPTER 6

SUBROUTINE CALLING MECHANISMS

In this chapter, we introduce the mechanisms used to implement subroutines. In the first section, we introduce most of the terminology associated with the implementation of subroutines. In introducing these terms, we discuss a simple implementation strategy for subroutines. The second section introduces parameter passing using the registers, covering parameter passing modes (constant and variable) and conventions (value, value/result, and reference). The third section introduces parameter blocks, a technique that allocates space for parameters statically. The fourth section presents the parameter stack and dynamic allocation of subroutine frames; we discuss a stack structure that is appropriate for use with the C programming language.

There are several topics related to subroutine calls that are beyond the scope of our interest. In particular, we will not consider access to nonlocal variables in a language that supports nested subroutine declarations (e.g., Pascal), nor will we consider the procedure copy rule of Algol. The interested reader can find information on these topics in books that survey the principles underlying modern programming languages and in books that cover the principles of compiler construction. In the case of access to nonlocal variables, you should look for a discussion of a data structure called the *display*. In the case of the procedure copy rule, most books discuss this under the general topic of parameter passing and the specific topic of *pass-by-name* parameters.

Many high-level languages distinguish between subprograms that return values, called *functions*, and subprograms that do not return values, called *procedures* or *subroutines*. In this chapter, we use the term *subroutine* to denote a generic subprogram (regardless of whether or not it returns a value). When it is important to note that a subroutine returns a value, we will explicitly note that the subroutine returns a value. In addition to this generic use of subroutine, we also assume that all subroutines are *well structured*. By well structured, we mean that every subroutine has a single entry point and a single exit point. Further, we assume that the entry point is the first statement of the subroutine and the exit point is the last statement of the subroutine.

Functions

Procedures

Subroutines

6.1 BRANCH AND LINK (JUMP TO SUBROUTINE)

Caller

Callee

In discussing subroutines, it is helpful if we identify two separate roles: the caller and the callee. The *caller* is the section of code that initiates the call to a subroutine. The *callee* is the subroutine called by the caller.

We begin by considering the transfers of control needed to implement subroutine invocation. When you call a subroutine, you transfer control to the body of the subroutine. When the subroutine completes, it transfers control back to the instruction immediately following the call. Because you can call the same subroutine from different points in your program, subroutines need to be able to return to different places in your program. The *return address* is the address of the instruction immediately following the instruction that transfers control to the callee. The caller provides the return address to the callee as part of the subroutine linkage. The *subroutine linkage* is a data structure used to share information between the caller and the callee.

Return address

Subroutine linkage

The caller establishes part of the subroutine linkage in a sequence of instructions called the *startup sequence*. The callee establishes the remainder of the subroutine linkage in the *subroutine prologue*. The subroutine prologue may be empty. Because we assume that all subroutines are well structured, the instructions at the end of the subroutine return to the caller. We call this sequence of instructions the *subroutine epilogue*. When control returns to the caller, the caller may need to clean up the subroutine linkage. We call this set of instructions the *cleanup sequence*. The cleanup sequence may be empty. Figure 6.1 presents a graphical illustration of these code sequences.

Startup sequence

Subroutine prologue

Subroutine epilogue

Cleanup sequence

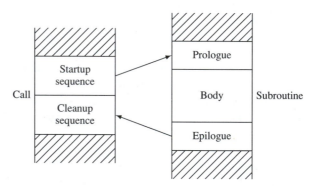

Figure 6.1 Subroutine linkage

The presentation in Figure 6.1 is a bit deceptive. By showing the components of the program side-by-side, it appears that you can see all four code sequences simultaneously. This is seldom the case. The caller and callee may be separated by several pages in a program listing. Moreover, there may be many separate calls to the same subroutine. Because these code sequences are distributed throughout the program, it is not easy to correlate the actions performed by these related sections of code. As such, it is important that you follow a *subroutine calling convention* whenever you write code to call a subroutine or implement a subroutine body. In the remainder of this chapter, we explore a variety of calling conventions.

Subroutine calling convention

In essence, a subroutine calling convention describes the allocation, construction, and deallocation of a subroutine linkage. As we have noted, the subroutine linkage must include the return address. A particularly simple calling convention stores the return address in a register. We will use register R31 to store the return address. Figure 6.2 documents this calling convention by listing the actions performed in each code sequence.

Startup sequence:
    Store the return address in R31.
    Branch to the subroutine.
Subroutine prologue:
    Nothing.
Subroutine epilogue:
    Branch to the address stored in R31.
Cleanup sequence:
    Nothing.

Figure 6.2   A simple calling convention

Example 6.1   *Show how you can realize the calling convention documented in Figure 6.2 in assembly language.*

```
        ⋮                  ; other instructions
        MOVE    R31, #ret  ; the startup sequence
        BRANCH  sub1       ;
ret:
                           ; no cleanup sequence

        ⋮                  ; other instructions

        ⋮                  ; other parts of the program

sub1:
                           ; no prologue

        ⋮                  ; the subroutine body
        BRANCH  @R31       ; the epilogue
```

Coding Convention—Addressing Modes and BRANCH Instructions

Note that the subroutine epilogue in Example 6.1 uses *register-indirect* addressing with a BRANCH instruction. We will use addressing modes with BRANCH instructions in this text. Many machines do not support this use of addressing modes. Instead, they provide special operations, for example, an operation that sets the program counter to the value stored in a register.

Coding Convention—BRANCH Delay Slots

Most RISC machines have a BRANCH delay slot following every BRANCH instruction, including BRANCH instructions used to implement subroutine calling conventions. We will continue to ignore the possibility of BRANCH delay slots in our code examples.

To support subroutines, many machines provide an instruction that stores the return address and branches to the start of the subroutine. Some machines call this operation JSR (jump to subroutine). Others use the name BL (branch and link) because the instruction is a branch instruction that establishes a subroutine linkage. These instructions require three operands: one to specify the return address, another to specify where to store the return address, and a third to specify the starting address of the subroutine. The first operand, the return address, is not typically explicit in the instruction. Instead, this operand is usually assumed to be the address of the next instruction. The second operand, the operand that specifies where the return address should be stored, may be implicit or explicit, depending on the machine. In implicit specification, the machine designates a register as the linkage register. This register stores the return address during the execution of the subroutine call instruction. The final operand, the starting address for the subroutine, is generally an explicit operand in the instruction.

Example 6.2   *Show how you can use a BL instruction in the code fragment presented in Example 6.1*

```
    :                         ; other instructions
    BL          R31, sub1     ; startup sequence
                              ; no cleanup sequence
    :                         ; other instructions

    :                         ; other parts of the program
```

```
sub1:
                        ; no prologue
    :
    :                   ; the subroutine body
    BRANCH   @R31       ; the epilogue
```

6.1.1 Saving the Return Address

If you use this simple calling convention, you need to be careful not to modify the value stored in R31 during the execution of a subroutine. Suppose that you discover that you need to call another subroutine, *sub2,* when you are writing the code for the subroutine *sub1*. Being careful to follow the subroutine calling convention documented in Figure 6.2, you include the following statement in the code for *sub1*:

```
BL   R31, sub2      ; startup sequence
```

Oops! You just destroyed the value stored in R31. In other words, in saving the return address that *sub2* will use, you wrote over the return address that *sub1* needs.

To avoid this problem, you could save the return address upon entry into the subroutine. Figure 6.3 presents a calling convention that saves the return address upon entry into each subroutine.

Startup sequence:
    Branch to the subroutine (storing the return address in R31).
Subroutine prologue:
    Save the value in R31 in a memory location.
Subroutine epilogue:
    Restore the return address and return.
Cleanup sequence:
    Nothing.

Figure 6.3   A simple calling convention (nonleaf subroutines)

Example 6.3   *Show how you can use the calling convention documented in Figure 6.3 to implement a simple subroutine call and return.*

```
    :
    :                        ; other instructions
    BL          R31, sub1    ; the calling sequence
                             ; no cleanup sequence

    :
    :                        ; other instructions

    :
    :                        ; other parts of the program
```

```
            .bss
ret1:       .reserve    4              ; space to save the return address
            .text
sub1:
            STORE.w    ret1, R31      ; the prologue
            ⋮                         ; the subroutine body
            LOAD.w     R31, ret1      ; the epilogue
            BRANCH     @R31
```

Note that the problem of overwriting the return address only occurs in subroutines that call other subroutines. It is useful to distinguish subroutines that never make subroutine calls. We call these subroutines *leaf routines*. Leaf routines can use the calling convention shown in Figure 6.2 while nonleaf routines should use the convention documented in Figure 6.3.

Leaf routines

There is still a potential problem with the code shown in Example 6.3. Suppose that a routine called by *sub1* starts a second call to *sub1* before the first call is complete. A sequence of subroutine calls that includes two or more active calls to the same subroutine is called a *cyclic calling sequence*. A cyclic calling sequence is characteristic of *recursive* subroutines. Some languages, notably FORTRAN 77,[1] do not permit cyclic calling sequences. The calling convention documented in Figures 6.2 and 6.3 is adequate for maintaining the return address in these languages. As we continue our discussion of calling conventions, we assume that subroutines do not exhibit a cyclic calling sequence. In section 6.5, we consider calling conventions that can accommodate recursive subroutines and, as such, cyclic calling sequences.

Cyclic calling sequence

Recursive

6.1.2 Saving Registers

We have seen that modifying R31 during the execution of a subroutine can lead to disaster. What about the other registers? For example, suppose the code in the body of *sub1* moves a value into R2 during a computation. Whether this introduces a problem depends on the assumptions made in the code surrounding the subroutine call. If the caller establishes a value for R2 prior to the call to subroutine *sub1* and expects that R2 is not changed by *sub1*, changing R2 could lead to a disaster. On the other hand, if the caller does not rely on the integrity of the value stored in R2, using R2 in the body of *sub1* will not affect the rest of the program. One way to avoid this problem is to save the registers used in the body of a subroutine in its prologue and restore the registers to their old values in the epilogue. Figure 6.4 documents this calling convention.

---

[1] The newest FORTRAN standard, FORTRAN 90, does support recursive subroutines.

Startup sequence:
  Branch to the subroutine (storing the return address in R31).
Subroutine prologue:
  If nonleaf, save the value in R31 in memory.
  Save the registers used in the body.
Subroutine epilogue:
  Restore the registers saved in the prologue,
  Restore the return address and return.
Cleanup sequence:
  Nothing.

Figure 6.4 Saving and restoring registers

The calling convention documented in Figure 6.4 could be called a *nonintrusive* *strategy* because subroutines do not intrude on the registers used by the caller. You can also develop a *defensive strategy* in which the caller saves the registers that it is using. The code needed to save these registers would be included in the startup sequence and code to restore them would be included in the cleanup sequence.

Nonintrusive

Defensive

Both the nonintrusive and defensive strategies are conservative. The only registers that the caller needs to save are the registers that it is using that are *also* used by the callee. While you could incorporate this strategy in your programs, it is not advisable. To see the difficulty, we note that the register saves need to be in the startup sequence of the caller; otherwise, the callee would need to save any registers it uses that are also used by *any* caller. Now, suppose you need to change a subroutine in such a way that it uses a new register. Are you going to remember to check every call to this subroutine to make sure that this register is saved whenever the caller uses it?

6.2 PARAMETER PASSING—REGISTERS

In Chapter 5, we presented a code fragment to calculate the length of a NULL terminated string (in Example 5.20). Suppose you want to turn this code fragment into a subroutine. Before you do so, there are two issues you need to consider: which string you are going to use in the calculation and how you are going to return the result to the caller. The first problem introduces the issue of parameters. The second introduces the notion of subroutines that return values, that is, functions.

For the moment, we will deal with the second of these issues by adopting a simple convention: subroutines always return their results in register R2. While this convention is sufficient for many applications, it will not handle all possibilities. Suppose you have a subroutine that returns a structure that requires 40 bytes for its representation. You will undoubtedly have a problem trying to fit all 40 bytes in R2! We will return to this problem after we discuss simple parameter passing conventions.

A simple parameter passing convention uses the registers to pass parameter values to a subroutine. As we have noted, this convention will not allow you to pass large structures, but it is adequate for many applications. We use the registers R3 through R30 for parameters. Figure 6.5 illustrates this convention.

Registers

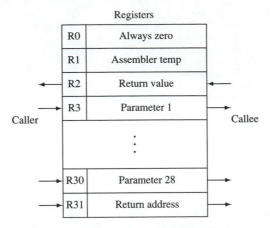

Figure 6.5   Parameter passing—values in registers

Example 6.4   *Show how you would call the routine* strlen, *assuming that the string starts at the memory location labeled* str.

```
MOVE   R3, #str        ; put the parameter in R3
BL     R31, strlen     ; call the subroutine
```

Example 6.5   *Show how you can implement the* strlen *subroutine.*

```
          .bss
save:     .reserve   8                 ; we save 2 registers
          .text
strlen:
          ; the prologue
          STORE.w   save, R3           ; save registers
          STORE.w   save+4, R4

          ; the body
          CLEAR     R2                 ; initialize the result
          LOAD.b    R4, [R3]+          ; load the next character
          BRANCH    test
top:
          ADD       R2, R2, #1         ; one more character
          LOAD.b    R4, [R3]+          ; load the next character
test:
          CMP       R4, #0             ; test for end of string
          BRNE      top
```

```
; the epilogue
LOAD.w    R3, save        ; restore registers
LOAD.w    R4, save+4
BRANCH    @R31            ; return
```

6.2.1 Parameter Passing Conventions

In examining the code presented in Example 6.5, note that the subroutine prologue saves the value of R3 and the epilogue restores its value. On the one hand, the body of *strlen* changes the value of R3, and therefore, the original value of the register should be maintained across the subroutine call. On the other hand, R3 is used to pass a parameter, and it is unlikely that the caller will rely on the fact that the subroutine does not change the value in R3. As such, you might be tempted to remove the instructions that save and restore the value of R3; however, you should not incorporate this kind of optimization into your code.

You should not change the value of R3 because the *strlen* function does not change the string parameter. In this case, the parameter to *strlen* is the address of a string. If *strlen* were to change the address, it would imply that *strlen* moved the string! Some subroutines need to modify their parameters. To distinguish between these uses of parameters, we use the terms *constant parameter* and *variable parameter*. The called subroutine does not alter a *constant parameter*. In contrast, the called subroutine may alter a *variable parameter*.

Constant parameter

Variable parameter

The parameter passing convention that we have been using calls for placing the value of the parameter in a register before calling the subroutine. This parameter passing convention is called *pass-by-value*. Pass-by-value is appropriate for passing (small) constant parameters. In the remainder of this section, we consider two different conventions that can be used to pass variable parameters to subroutines.

Pass-by-value

Pass-by-Value/Result (Copy-In/Copy-Out)   In pass-by-value/result the caller passes *values* to the subroutine. When the subroutine completes its execution, it passes back its *results* by modifying the registers. Figure 6.6 presents a graphical illustration of value/result parameter passing using registers. In this case, the caller can put values into the parameter passing registers and later retrieve results from these registers. Similarly, the subroutine can retrieve values from the parameter passing registers and, upon completion, return results in these registers.

Example 6.6   *To illustrate a pass-by-value/result parameter, we introduce a rather contrived example. In particular, we consider a subroutine that returns the product of its two arguments and modifies the first argument by adding the value of the second to it.*
  Show how you can implement this function using value/result parameter passing.

```
            .text
strange:
            ; the prologue

            ; the body
            MPY        R2, R3, R4      ; calculate the result
            ADD        R3, R3, R4      ; modify the first parameter

            ; the epilogue
            BRANCH   @R31              ; return
```

Example 6.7   *Show how you would implement the call* z = strange(x, y) *for the subroutine shown in Example 6.6.*

```
       .bss
x:     .reserve    4                  ; variables used in the call
y:     .reserve    4
z:     .reserve    4
       .text
       ⋮
       ; z = strange( x, y )
       LOAD.w    R3, x                ; startup sequence
       LOAD.w    R4, y
       BL        R31, strange
       STORE.w   z, R2                ; cleanup sequence
       STORE.w   x, R3
```

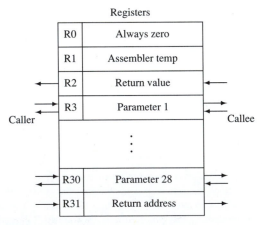

Figure 6.6 Parameter passing—value/result using registers

Pass-by-Reference   Parameter passing based on the value/result convention involves copying values. In Example 6.7, the caller copies the values stored in memory locations x and y into registers prior to the call. Moreover, the caller copies the value in register R3 to memory location x in the cleanup sequence. When you use the pass-by-reference convention, the caller passes the address of the parameter (i.e., a reference to the parameter) instead of its value. Because the subroutine has the address of the parameter, it can manipulate the variable directly and does not need to rely on the caller's cleanup sequence to copy the result back into memory.

Example 6.8   *Rewrite the subroutine* strange *using pass-by-reference for the first parameter (notice, the second parameter is not altered, so we continue to use pass-by-value for this parameter).*

```
        .bss
save2:  .reserve   4              ; we'll need to save a register
        .text
strange:
        ; the prologue
        MOVE     save, R5         ; save registers

        ; the body
        LOAD.w   R5, @R3          ; load the value of the first parameter
        MPY      R2, R4, R5       ; calculate the result
        ADD      R5, R4, R5       ; calculate the sum
        STORE.w  @R3, R5          ; change the first parameter

        ; the epilogue
        LOAD.w   R5, save         ; restore registers
        BRANCH   @R1              ; return
```

Example 6.9   *Show how you would implement the call* z = strange(x, y) *for the subroutine shown in Example 6.8.*

```
    .bss
x:  .reserve   4              ; variables used in the call
y:  .reserve   4
z:  .reserve   4
    .text
    :
    ; z = strange( x, y )
    MOVE     R3, #x           ; the address of x
    LOAD.w   R4, y            ; the value of y
    BL       R31, strange
    STORE.w  z, R2            ; cleanup sequence
```

6.2.2 Summary of Parameter Passing Conventions

There are essentially two types of parameters: constant parameters and variable parameters. The called subroutine does not modify constant parameters but may change the value associated with a variable parameter. We have discussed three parameter passing conventions: pass-by-value, pass-by-value/result, and pass-by-reference. In general, pass-by-value is best suited for the transmission of constant parameters, whereas pass-by-value/result and pass-by-reference are best suited for the transmission of variable parameters. Pass-by-reference is also appropriate for the transmission of large, constant parameters. Note that the *strlen* subroutine uses this technique. In this case, we pass the address of a NULL terminated string to the subroutine, although the subroutine does not modify the string. The size of the string justifies our use of pass-by-reference for a constant parameter—it is unlikely that the value of the string will fit into a register.

The following general points summarize the important issues relating to the three parameter passing conventions that we have introduced in this section:

- Pass-by-value is appropriate for the transmission of small constant parameters.
- In pass-by-value, the subroutine should not alter the value passed in a parameter.
- Pass-by-value/result is appropriate for the transmission of small variable parameters.
- In pass-by-value/result, the caller's cleanup sequence should include code to store the values of any variable parameters.
- Pass-by-reference is appropriate for variable parameters (of all sizes) and large constant parameters.
- In pass-by-reference, the address value passed to the subroutine should not be changed by the subroutine.

The last of these points is based on the following observation:

- Pass-by-reference simply involves passing an address by value.

6.3 SUBROUTINES IN C

We will use subroutines written in C to introduce examples in the remainder of this chapter. In this section, we introduce the C constructs that relate to subroutine definition and use. In the standard terminology of C, subprograms are called functions. We will continue to use the term *subroutine* to be consistent with the remainder of our discussion.

A C subroutine definition consists of a subroutine header and a subroutine body. The subroutine header specifies the type of value returned by the subroutine (if any), along with the names any types of the arguments passed to the routine.

The subroutine body consists of a compound statement that has the executable statements of the subroutine and may declare "local" variables.

In C, parameters are always passed by value. This means that you cannot directly alter any parameter as a result of calling a subroutine. To attain the effect of pass-by-reference you can declare the parameter as a pointer and pass the address of the variable that you want to change.

Example 6.10   *Give a C definition for the function* strange *that we introduced in section 6.2.*

```
int strange( int *p1, int p2 )
{
    int res;

    res = *p1 * p2;
    *p1 = *p1 + p2;
    return res;
}
```

Note that the first argument, *p1,* is declared as a pointer to an integer. Further, whenever we use *p1* in the body of the subroutine, we reference the integer that *p1* points to. In this way, we will change the value in the memory location that *p1* points to.

Example 6.11   *Show a call to the subroutine* strange.

```
{
    int x, y, z;
    ⋮
    z = strange( &x, y );
    ⋮
}
```

By taking the address of *x,* we are passing a pointer to *x* to the subroutine *strange*. As such, this subroutine will be able to change the value associated with *x*.

6.4 PARAMETER BLOCKS—STATIC ALLOCATION

Suppose you need to implement a subroutine that has more parameters than you have registers available. Alternatively, suppose you need to pass a large structure (more than will fit in a register) by value or value/result. In either case, you need to allocate memory space to pass the parameters between the caller and the callee. We use the term *parameter block* to refer to the memory allocated for passing parameters. In effect, a parameter block is a structure. Each parameter starts at a fixed offset from the start of the parameter block. Since we have collected the parameters into a contiguous block, it makes sense to collect the return address and return value in the same block.

Example 6.12 *Give a graphical representation of the parameter block that you would use for the* strange *subroutine introduced in section 6.2.*

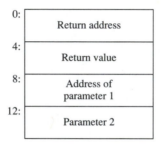

You can associate the parameter block with the caller or the subroutine. If you associate the parameter block with the caller, you need to pass the address of the parameter block to the subroutine. On the other hand, if the parameter block is associated with the subroutine, the caller needs to know the starting address of the parameter block. We will associate the parameter block with the subroutine.

Example 6.13 *Show how you can implement the* strange *subroutine using the parameter block shown in Example 6.12.*

```
          ; symbols used in the parameter block
          .equate    ret, 0              ; the return address
          .equate    res, 4              ; the result value
          .equate    p1, 8               ; the first parameter
          .equate    p2, 12              ; the second parameter
          .equate    pblk_size, 16       ; size of the parameter block

          ; variables
          .bss
str_pblk: .reserve   pblk_size           ; the parameter block
str_save: .reserve   16                  ; register save area
```

```
        .text
strange:
        ; the prologue
        STORE.w    str_pblk, R31        ; save return address
        STORE.w    str_save, R2         ; save registers
        STORE.w    str_save+4, R3
        STORE.w    str_save+8, R4
        STORE.w    str_save+12, R5

        ; the body
        LOAD.w     R2, str_pblk+p1      ; the address of P1 is in R2
        LOAD.w     R3, str_pblk+p2      ; the value of P2 is in R3
        LOAD.w     R4, @R2              ; the value of P1 is in R4
        MPY        R5, R3, R4
        STORE.w    str_pblk+res, R5     ; store the result
        ADD        R4, R3, R4           ; add parameter values
        STORE.w    @R2, R4              ; modify the first parameter

        ; the epilogue
        LOAD.w     R31, str_pblk+ret    ; restore return address
        LOAD.w     R2, str_save         ; restore registers
        LOAD.w     R3, str_save+4
        LOAD.w     R4, str_save+8
        LOAD.w     R5, str_save+12
        BRANCH     @R31                 ; return
```

Example 6.14 *Show how you would write a call to the subroutine presented in Example 6.13.*

```
        .bss
x:      .reserve    4                  ; variables used in the call
y:      .reserve    4
z:      .reserve    4
        .text
          .
          .
          .
        ; z = strange( x, y )
        MOVE       R2, #x              ; pass-by-reference
        STORE.w    str_pblk+p1, R2
        LOAD.w     R2, y               ; pass-by-value
        STORE.w    str_pblk+p2, R2
        BL         R31, strange
        LOAD.w     R2, str_pblk+res    ; the result is in R2
        STORE.w    z, R2               ; complete the assignment
```

The parameter passing technique presented in this section allocates parameter blocks on a subroutine basis, instead of a subroutine call basis. We call this strategy

Static allocation   *static allocation*. In programming contexts, the term *static* indicates that an activity occurs prior to execution. In the case of parameter blocks, the allocation occurs when the loader loads the program. In contrast to the static allocation strategy described in this section, the next section introduces dynamic allocation for parameter blocks. This strategy allocates a new parameter block for each call to a subroutine.

As you examine the code shown in Examples 6.13 and 6.14, note that these code fragments are more complicated than the implementations that we presented earlier. To a large extent, the added complexity is due to the increased generality of the parameter passing technique. Using this technique, you can return structured values of any size and transmit structured parameters by value and value/result. Moreover, there is effectively no limit to the number of parameters that a subroutine can have.

6.5 THE PARAMETER STACK—DYNAMIC ALLOCATION

None of the techniques that we have discussed is capable of dealing with cyclic calling sequences (recursive subroutines). In this section, we discuss the structures that are typically used to support recursion in high-level languages. If you need to write a recursive subroutine or you need to interface an assembly language program with code written in a high-level language, you will need to use structures that are comparable to the structures presented in this section.

The problem with the techniques that we have discussed is that they do not allocate space for the linkage information on every call to a subroutine. If we are going to support recursive subroutines, we need to allocate space to store the linkage every time we call a subroutine. This strategy is called *dynamic allocation* because we allocate the space for the subroutine linkage during the execution of the program. Here we should note that we commonly use static allocation for the pool used for subroutine linkages. The important point is that the space used for a subroutine linkage is allocated, from this pool, during the startup sequence.

Dynamic allocation

6.5.1 The Stack and Stack Frames

A subroutine return always returns from the most recently called subroutine that has not already completed (and returned). This should remind you of the discipline used in a stack: The item popped from the stack is the most recently pushed item that has not been popped from the stack. As such, we can use a stack to manage the memory used to store subroutine linkages. We do not need to implement a general facility for dynamic memory allocation.

Graphical Convention
We will assume that stacks grow from higher numbered addresses to lower numbered addresses. In other words, we will assume that the push operation implements a predecrement on the stack pointer. Graphically, this means that stacks grow toward the top of the page.

The stack used to store subroutine linkages has many names: the subroutine stack, the parameter stack, the run-time stack, or simply the stack. In addition to the linkage information, the stack may be used to save registers and store the local variables used by a subroutine. Every item on the stack is associated with an invocation of a subroutine. The collection of items associated with a single invocation of a subroutine constitutes a unit called the *activation record*. When you call a subroutine, you need to allocate space for the activation record of the called subroutine on top of the stack. When the invocation of a subroutine completes, you need to remove this activation record from the top of the stack and deallocate the space.

Activation record

Example 6.15   *Show the state of the stack after an invocation of subroutine* A *calls subroutine* B, *which calls subroutine* C, *which calls subroutine* A.

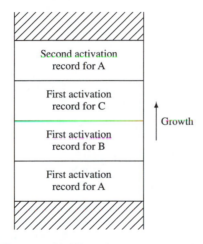

Second activation
record for A

First activation
record for C

First activation
record for B

First activation
record for A

↑ Growth

Because they frame regions of the stack, activation records are frequently called *stack frames*. If you start from the perspective of a high-level language and the notion of subroutine activations, the term *activation record* (i.e., a record that holds the information needed for a subroutine activation) is more appropriate. On the other hand, if you are considering the implementation of subroutines, you are likely to be more interested in the structure of the run-time stack and the term *stack frame* is more appropriate. Considering our perspective, we will use the term *stack frame* for the remainder of this discussion.

Stack frame

There are three types of items that need to be included in the stack frame for a subroutine activation: the parameters, the return linkage (space for the return value and the return address), and space for the local variables. Figure 6.7 illustrates the structure of a stack frame.

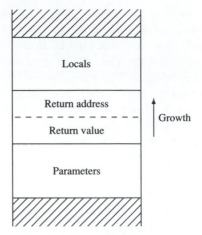

Figure 6.7 The structure of a stack frame

6.5.2 Hardware Support

Many machines provide direct support for the stack and stack frames. For the remainder of this discussion, we assume that the top-of-stack pointer is available for direct manipulation through the special register SP. In addition, we assume that the stack can be manipulated using the instructions described in Table 6.1. In examining the instructions in this table, note that there are no instructions that manipulate the values on the stack (e.g., ADD). Remember, the stack that these instructions support is a parameter stack, not an arithmetic stack as we presented in our discussion of stack machines.

Table 6.1 Stack manipulation instructions

Symbolic instruction	Semantics
PUSH Rn	Push the contents of register n onto the stack.
POP Rn	Pop the top value on the stack into register n.
PUSHEA *addr*	Push the effective address onto the stack.
ALLOC n	Allocate n bytes on top of the stack.
FREE n	Free n bytes from the top of the stack.
JSR *addr*	Jump to the subroutine starting at memory location *addr;* push the return address onto the stack.
RTS	Return from a subroutine by jumping to the address stored on top of the stack and popping this address.

6.5.3 Constructing a Stack Frame

The stack frame is constructed in two pieces. The startup sequence pushes the parameters onto the stack, allocates space for the return value, and jumps to the subroutine, placing the return address on top of the stack. The subroutine prologue constructs the remainder of the stack frame by allocating space for its local variables. In the body of the subroutine, the local variables, parameters, and return value can be accessed using the stack pointer, SP, with displaced addressing. Once the subroutine has completed its activities, the subroutine epilogue needs to free the space allocated for the local variables and return to the caller, popping the return address from the stack. Finally, the cleanup sequence needs to free the space that the caller allocated when it pushed the parameters onto the stack. Figure 6.8 summarizes the activities performed by the various code sequences.

Startup sequence:
   Push the parameters, one at a time.
   Allocate space for the return value.
   Jump to the subroutine, pushing the return address.
Subroutine prologue:
   Allocate space for local variables.
Subroutine epilogue:
   Free the space allocated by the prologue.
   Return to caller popping the return address.
Cleanup sequence:
   Pop the result, if any.
   Free the space used by the parameters.

Figure 6.8 Allocating and deallocating the stack frame

Example 6.16   *Give a graphical representation of the stack frame needed by the* strange *subroutine. Recall, this subroutine needs to save four registers and, as such, needs 16 bytes of local space.*

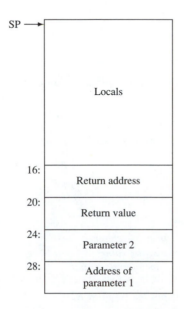

Example 6.17   *Give an implementation of the* strange *subroutine using the stack frame defined in Example 6.16.*

```
              ; stack offsets
              .equate     res, 20         ; offset of the result
              .equate     p2, 24          ; offset of the second parameter
              .equate     p1, 28          ; offset of the first parameter

strange:
              ; the prologue
              PUSH.w      R2              ; save registers
              PUSH.w      R3
              PUSH.w      R4
              PUSH.w      R5

              ; the body
              LOAD.w      R2, SP→p1       ; load the address of p1 into R2
              LOAD.w      R3, SP→p2       ; load the value of p2 into R3
              LOAD.w      R4, @R2         ; load the value of p1 into R4
              MPY         R5, R4, R3      ; calculate the result
              STORE.w     SP→res, R5      ; store the result
              ADD         R4, R3, R4      ; add parameters
              STORE.w     SP→p1, R4       ; modify the first parameter

              ; the epilogue
              POP.w       R5              ; restore registers
              POP.w       R4
              POP.w       R3
              POP.w       R2
              RTS                         ; return
```

Example 6.18   *Show a call to the implementation of the* strange *subroutine given in Example 6.17.*

```
              .bss
x:            .reserve    4               ; variables used in the call
y:            .reserve    4
z:            .reserve    4
              .text
              :
              :
              ; z = strange( x, y )
              PUSHEA      x               ; pass-by-reference
              PUSH.w      y               ; pass-by-value
              ALLOC       4               ; space for the result
              JSR         strange
              POP.w       R2              ; put the result in R2
```

```
STORE.w   z, R2        ; complete the assignment
FREE      8            ; free the parameter space
   .
   .
   .
```

Because we dynamically allocate the space for every variable used in this implementation of *strange,* this version is *reentrant.* A reentrant subroutine can be called before its execution completes. For example, if the body of *strange* contains a recursive call to itself, the new activation of *strange* will reenter the code for this subroutine, before the previous call has completed. Because it is allocated a new stack frame, the recursive invocation will not destroy any of the data needed to complete the current activation. There are essentially two properties that characterize reentrant code. First, the code cannot be self-modifying. Second, the space needed for the subroutine linkage and local variables must be allocated on a per-activation basis.

Reentrant

6.5.4 The Frame Pointer

In our previous examples we allocated the parameters x and y statically using the reserve directive. What if the caller is a subroutine and x and y are local variables that have been allocated space in the stack frame? In this case, we assume that x and y are the names of symbolic constants that are the offsets of the space for these variables from the stack pointer.

Example 6.19 *Show a call to the subroutine* strange, *assuming that the parameters are in the current stack frame.*

```
x:  .equate    ...            ; variables used in the call
y:  .equate    ...
z:  .equate    ...

       .
       .
       .
    ; z = strange( x, y )
    PUSHEA    SP→x          ; pass-by-reference
    PUSH.w    SP→(y+4)      ; pass-by-value
    ALLOC     4             ; allocate space for result
    JSR       strange
    POP.w     R2            ; put the result in R2
    FREE      8             ; free the parameter space
    STORE.w   SP→z, R2      ; complete the assignment

       .
       .
       .
```

Note that the operand to the second push operation is SP→(y+4) instead of SP→y as you might expect. You need the +4 to account for the fact that the stack pointer changed as a result of pushing the first parameter. In general, whenever a subroutine calls another subroutine, there is a potential problem that must be handled in the code. When you push the first argument onto the stack, the offsets for the local variables and parameters of the caller change. This change in offsets is temporary; when you push the next parameter onto the stack, the offsets change again. When the call completes, the cleanup sequence restores the stack pointer to its old value and the original offsets are again valid.

The changing of offsets during a subroutine call is difficult to keep up with, and code that you write to evaluate and pass parameters is likely to be error prone. To avoid the problem of changing offsets, you can introduce another pointer into the stack, the *frame pointer (FP)*. The value of the frame pointer is established in the subroutine prologue and remains fixed throughout the body of the subroutine. If offsets for the locals and parameters are defined relative to the frame pointer, they will not change during a subroutine call.

Figure 6.9 illustrates the use of a frame pointer. In most cases, the frame pointer and the stack pointer point to the same location (the top of the current stack frame). However, when an argument is pushed onto the stack, the stack pointer is moved to reflect the fact that the stack has grown. On the other hand, the frame pointer remains fixed, reflecting the fact that the current stack frame has not moved.

Frame pointer (FP)

A. Before pushing parameters

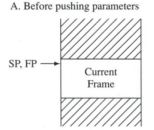

B. After a parameter has been pushed

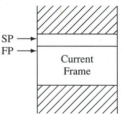

Figure 6.9   Illustrating the frame pointer

Example 6.20   *Show a call to the subroutine* strange *using a frame pointer.*

```
x:   .equate    ...           ; variables used in the call
y:   .equate    ...
z:   .equate    ...

     :
     ; z = strange( x, y )
     PUSHEA   FP→x           ; pass-by-reference
     PUSH.w   FP→y           ; pass-by-value
     ALLOC    4              ; allocate space for result
     JSR      strange
```

```
POP.w      R2              ; put the result in R2
FREE       8               ; free parameter space
STORE.w    FP→z, R2        ; complete the assignment
```

As suggested earlier, the frame pointer is established during the subroutine prologue and remains constant throughout the execution of the subroutine. Because
there is only one frame pointer, the current value of the frame pointer must be
saved whenever a subroutine is called and restored when the called subroutine
completes its execution. Figure 6.10 illustrates the structure of a stack frame
modified to accommodate a frame pointer. In examining Figure 6.10, note that the
frame pointer saved in the stack frame is the frame pointer for the caller. Most of
the remaining information in the stack frame (parameters, return value, locals) is
associated with the called subroutine.

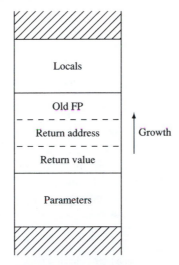

Figure 6.10 A stack frame
including the frame pointer

Example 6.21   *Show how you would alter the implementation of the* strange *subroutine*
to save and restore the frame pointer.

```
; stack offsets
.equate    res, 20         ; offset of the result
.equate    p2, 24          ; offset of the second parameter
.equate    p1, 28          ; offset of the first parameter
```

strange:

```
            ; the prologue
    PUSH.w      FP              ; save the old value of the frame pointer
    PUSH.w      R2              ; save registers
    PUSH.w      R3
    PUSH.w      R4
    PUSH.w      R5
    MOVE        FP, SP          ; establish the frame pointer

            ; the body
    LOAD.w      R2, FP→p1       ; load the address of p1 into R2
    LOAD.w      R3, FP→p2       ; load the value of p2 into R3
    LOAD.w      R4, @R2         ; load the value of p1 into R4
    MPY         R5, R4, R3      ; calculate the result
    STORE.w     FP→res, R5      ; store the result
    ADD         R4, R3, R4      ; add parameters
    STORE.w     FP→p1, R4       ; modify the first parameter

            ; the epilogue
    POP.w       R5              ; restore registers
    POP.w       R4
    POP.w       R3
    POP.w       R2
    POP.w       FP              ; restore the frame pointer
    RTS                         ; return
```

Finally, Figure 6.11 documents a calling convention that includes saving and restoring the value of the frame pointer. Note that this convention distinguishes leaf and nonleaf subroutines. Recall, the frame pointer is only important when a subroutine needs to call another subroutine. In all other cases, you can use the stack pointer instead of the frame pointer. As such, we only save and restore the frame pointer for nonleaf subroutines.

Startup sequence:
    Push the parameters, one at a time.
    Allocate space for the return value.
    Jump to the subroutine, pushing the return address.
Subroutine prologue:
    If nonleaf, push the stack frame pointer.
    Allocate space for local variables.
    If nonleaf, establish the new frame pointer.
Subroutine epilogue:
    Free the space allocated by the prologue.
    If nonleaf, restore the old frame pointer.
    Return to caller popping the return address.
Cleanup sequence:
    Pop the result, if any.
    Free the space used by the parameters.

Figure 6.11 Establishing a frame pointer

6.5.5 Parameter Order

In our examples, we have assumed that the parameters are pushed onto the stack from left to right. As such, the first parameter has the greatest offset from the stack (or frame) pointer. This may seem natural; however, many implementations of the C programming language push the parameters from right to left. C supports the definition of subroutines with a variable number of parameters, that is, the number of parameters passed to the subroutine may be different for different calls to the subroutine. As such, the subroutine does not know how many parameters it will be passed. In general, the first (i.e., leftmost) parameter to a subroutine with a variable number of parameters provides the subroutine with information regarding the number and size of the parameters passed. If this parameter is pushed onto the stack first, the subroutine will not know where the first parameter is until it knows how many parameters there are. However, it cannot know how many parameters there are until it determines the value of the first parameter! If, on the other hand, parameters are pushed from right to left, the first parameter is the top parameter on the stack and has a fixed offset from the top of the stack frame independent of the number of parameters passed to the subroutine. As such, many implementations of C push the parameters from right to left.

6.5.6 Local Variables

We conclude our discussion by considering the allocation and access to local variables. As we have noted, the callee allocates space for its local variables in the stack frame. Up until this point, we have only used this space to store the registers used by the callee. To simplify our examples, we will assume that the caller uses a defensive strategy.

Example 6.22   *Show the organization of the stack frame that you would use for the following C subroutine:*

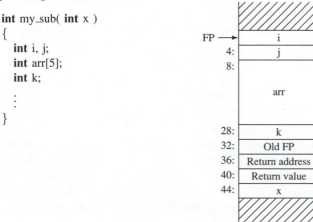

```
int my_sub( int x )
{
    int i, j;
    int arr[5];
    int k;

    :

}
```

Example 6.23   *Given the declarations and stack frame organization shown in the previous example, show how you would translate the statement arr[j] = x + k.*

```
LOAD.w    R3, FP→x
LOAD.w    R4, FP→k
LOAD.w    R5, FP→j
MOVE      R6, #arr
MOVE      R7, #4
ADD       R3, R3, R4      ; calculate x + k
ADD       R6, R6, FP      ; the base of the array
MPY       R5, R5, R7      ; scale the index
ADD       R5, R6, R6      ; the address of arr[j]
STORE.w   @R5, R3         ; complete the assignment
```

In considering this example, note that we used three instructions (a multiply and two additions) to generate the address of arr[j]. Using the addressing modes provided by the SPARC (in particular register-indirect with index), we could merge the second addition into the effective address calculation for the STORE. Using the addressing modes of the HP Precision, we could merge the second addition and the scaling operation into the effective address calculation. Many of the CISC machines provide a special addressing mode that merges both additions and the scaling into the effective address calculation. This addressing mode adds a constant displacement with a scaled index register and the contents of a base register to form the effective address.

6.6 CASE STUDY: SUBROUTINE CONVENTIONS ON THE HP PRECISION

In this section, we present the subroutine calling conventions developed for the HP Precision architecture. In this discussion, we will not consider those portions of the convention that relate to the floating point coprocessor or to the use of millicode routines. Moreover, we will assume that the subroutine is within the range of the BL instruction. The BL instruction on the HP Precision only encodes a 13-bit displacement for the program counter. As such, you cannot use this instruction if the subroutine is too far away from the point of the call. We will discuss a technique that you can use to deal with this problem, *subroutine stubs,* when we consider independent modules in Chapter 10.

Manufacturers publish calling conventions to document the machine features related to subroutine calls and to provide a standard for compiler writers. As an assembly language programmer, you could develop your own subroutine calling convention. However, if you ever need to interface an assembly language routine with code written in a high-level language, you will need to follow the calling convention used by the compiler.

There are two aspects of the calling conventions for the HP Precision architecture that differ from the conventions that we have discussed: the use of registers and the allocation of stack frames. We begin by considering the use of registers. After considering the register conventions, we will discuss the stack conventions.

6.6.1 The Registers

Like most RISC machines, the HP Precision architecture provides 32 general-purpose registers. Figure 6.12 documents the conventional use of these registers. In examining this illustration, note that register R2 holds the return address, register R30 holds the stack pointer, and registers R28 and R29 hold the return value (this makes it easy for functions to return double word values). These conventions are similar to the conventions that we have discussed.

The most interesting aspects of the register usage conventions are the groups of registers identified by the names *callee saves, caller saves,* and *parameters.* Registers R23 through R26 are used to pass the initial parameters to a subroutine. If a subroutine has more parameters than will fit in these registers, you will need to put the remaining parameters on the stack. Using registers to pass parameters can greatly reduce the number of memory accesses needed to call a subroutine.

The callee saves and caller saves regions represent a combination of the defensive and nonintrusive strategies that we discussed in section 6.1. The names of the regions indicate which of the two parties, the caller or the callee, is responsible for saving the register. For example, if the callee needs to use register R4, it must save and restore the value in this register. In other words, the callee cannot intrude on the values in registers R3 through R18. On the other hand, the callee can simply use registers R19 through R22 without needing to save and restore these values.

6.6.2 The Stack

The basic structure of the stack frame is similar to the stack frames that we have discussed. Each (logical) stack frame contains the parameters for the callee, a linkage area, and space for local variables. Here we should note that the stack on the HP grows from lower numbered addresses to higher numbered addresses (i.e., the push operation uses a pre-increment of the stack pointer). We will use the convention that stacks grow from higher numbered addresses to lower numbered addresses to maintain consistency with the other illustrations in this text.

The only significant difference between the HP calling convention and the convention that we outlined earlier is in the allocation of the stack frame. In the convention that we discussed, the caller allocates space for the parameters and part of the linkage area in the *startup* sequence. The callee allocates the remainder of the linkage area along with space for its local variables in the subroutine *prologue*. In the HP convention, each subroutine allocates space for its local variables, space for the parameters for *any* routine it might call, and space for the linkage area in its *prologue*. This approach is illustrated in Figure 6.13.

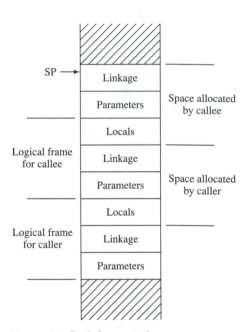

R0	Always 0
R1	Scratch
R2	Return address
R3	
	Callee saves
R18	
R19	
	Caller saves
R22	
R23	
	Parameters
R26	
R27	Other
R28	Return value
R29	
R30	Stack pointer
R31	Other

Figure 6.12 Register usage on the HP Precision architecture

Figure 6.13 Stack frames on the HP Precision architecture

The HP calling convention may waste stack space by forcing routines to allocate parameter space for any routine that they might call; however, this disadvantage is balanced by two advantages. First, each subroutine only allocates stack space one time. In the earlier convention, a subroutine will allocate and deallocate stack space every time it calls another subroutine. The second advantage is that there is no need for a frame pointer. In the HP convention, the stack pointer is only changed in the prologue of the subroutine. The stack pointer is not changed in the body of the subroutine, and, as such, there is no need for a frame pointer.

In closing, we note an interesting interaction between the register conventions and stack conventions. Even though the caller and callee use registers R23 through R26 to pass the first few parameters, the caller is still required to allocate space for these parameters in the stack frame. The caller will not initialize this space; however, the callee may use it to store the contents of the parameter registers if it needs to call another subroutine.

6.7 CASE STUDY: REGISTER WINDOWS ON THE SPARC

The subroutine calling conventions that we have discussed make extensive use of transfers between the registers and the memory. The HP conventions avoid many of these transfers by specifying uses for the registers. However, these conventions may only delay the transfers for nonleaf routines. For example, a subroutine may need to save the parameter values in registers R23 through R26 before it makes a call to another routine.

The SPARC architecture uses the concept of register windows to avoid many of the transfers between the registers and the memory typically associated with subroutine calling conventions. An implementation of the SPARC architecture must provide between 40 and 520 general-purpose registers. At any time, only 32 registers can be accessed. The 32 accessible registers constitute a window into the set of all registers provided by the processor. Eight registers are always accessible. The registers are called R0 through R7. The remaining registers are broken into overlapping sets. Each of these overlapping sets has 24 registers, numbered R8 through R31. When you make a subroutine call, a new set of registers is allocated for the called subroutine. The register set for the caller and the callee are overlapped to facilitate parameter passing. In particular the caller's R8 is the same as the callee's R24. Figure 6.14 illustrates the register sharing between the caller and callee.

Note that the callee's R8 through R23 are distinct from the caller's registers. The callee can use registers R16 through R23 for local variables and temporaries. Moreover, if the callee needs to call another subroutine, it can use its registers R8 through R15 to pass parameters to the new subroutine. The callee does not need to save any registers to call another subroutine. This strategy can greatly reduce the number of transfers between the registers and the memory needed for subroutine calls.

It should be apparent that 16 registers will not be enough to hold the parameters and local variables for every subroutine. As such, you will need to augment the use of register windows with a standard stack convention. Moreover, it is possible that you will not be able to allocate another set of registers when you call a subroutine. In these cases, you will need to copy some of the register sets into memory. Later, you will need to restore these register sets. Between the time you save and restore a register set, you can use it for another subroutine. Note: You only need to save and restore register sets when you have several active subroutines.

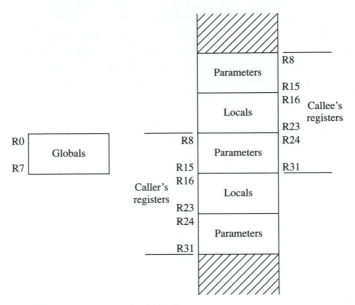

Figure 6.14   Registers on the SPARC

6.8 SUMMARY

In considering subroutines, there are three issues that must be addressed: transmission of the return address, transmission of parameters, and allocation of space for local variables. As we have seen, transmission of the return address is typically supported by a special instruction, BL or JSR. In addition to this instruction, many architectures support a run-time stack for the transmission of parameters. Regardless of whether your machine provides support for a parameter stack, you will need to decide on the structure that you will use to pass parameters to each of your subroutines. Each of the structures that we discussed in this chapter (registers, parameter blocks, and the parameter stack) presents advantages. Moreover, the appropriate structure may be based on a combination of these simple structures. In addition to the general structure used to pass parameters, you need to determine the convention (value, value/result, or reference) to be used for each of the parameters.

6.8.1 Additional Reading

If you are interested in learning more about the material presented in this chapter, you should consult the books listed in the bibliography under the categories "Programming Language Surveys" and "Compiler Construction."

6.8.2 Terminology

- Subroutine, Procedure, Function
- Subroutine linkage

- Return address
- Return value
- Calling convention
- Startup sequence, Cleanup sequence
- Subroutine prologue, Subroutine epilogue
- Caller, Callee
- Branch and link, Jump to subroutine
- Leaf subroutine
- Constant parameter, Variable parameter
- Value, Value/result, and Reference
- Static allocation, Dynamic allocation
- Parameter stack, Subroutine stack, the stack
- Activation record, Stack frame
- Reentrant code
- Stack pointer, Frame pointer
- Register windows

6.8.3 Review Questions

1. What is the purpose of the startup sequence? The cleanup sequence?
2. What actions are performed in the subroutine prologue? The subroutine epilogue?
3. What is the difference between a leaf routine and a nonleaf routine?
4. What is the difference between a stack frame and an activation record?
5. What does value/result mean in the context of parameter passing?
6. What do the terms *static* and *dynamic* mean?
7. What does reentrant mean in the context of subroutines?
8. Is the frame pointer necessary? Explain the purpose of the frame pointer.
9. Why does the calling convention on the HP Precision not require a frame pointer?
10. Why do the register windows in the SPARC overlap?

6.9 EXERCISES

1. Show how you would rewrite the code fragment in Example 6.1 to accommodate a BRANCH delay slot.
2. Consider the following program. Explain what will happen if the program counter starts at the label *main*. Assume that the symbol *exit* labels the first statement in a code sequence that will cause your program to exit gracefully.

```
main:
        BL          R31, sub1     ; call sub1
        BRANCH      exit

sub1:
        BL          R31, sub2     ; call sub2
        BRANCH      @R31          ; return
sub2:
        BRANCH      @R31          ; return
```

3. Explain why a cyclic calling sequence will cause problems when the calling convention documented in Figure 6.3 is used.

4. Suppose that *sub1* uses registers R2, R3, and R5. Modify the code in Example 6.3 so that it adheres to the convention documented in Figure 6.4.

5. In the text, we mentioned the possibility of developing a defensive strategy for saving registers as a contrast to the nonintrusive strategy documented in Figure 6.4.

   a. Document the defensive strategy along the lines of Figure 6.4.

   b. Modify the code shown in Example 6.3 so that it adheres to the defensive strategy. Assume that the caller needs to maintain the values in registers R2, R3, and R5.

   c. Under what circumstances is the nonintrusive strategy better than the defensive strategy? When is the defensive strategy better?

6. The subroutine *count_letter* has a single parameter: the address of a NULL terminated string. This subroutine returns the number of letters (upper- and lowercase) in the string. Write an implementation of *count_letter* and show a call to your subroutine using

   a. Registers to pass parameters.

   b. A parameter block to pass parameters.

   c. A stack frame to pass parameters (the function should not be recursive).

   d. Recursion and stack frames to pass the parameters.

7. The subroutine *stolower* has a single parameter: the address of a NULL terminated string. This subroutine converts every uppercase letter in the string to its lowercase equivalent. Write an implementation of *stolower* and show a call to your subroutine using

   a. Registers to pass parameters.

   b. A parameter block to pass parameters.

   c. A stack frame to pass parameters (the function should not be recursive).

   d. Recursion and stack frames to pass the parameters.

8. In this exercise, we consider the implementation of a simple string processing subroutine, *subch*. The subroutine *subch* has three parameters: the address of a NULL terminated string, and two character values. This subroutine

changes the string by replacing every occurrence of the first character by the second. Write an implementation of *subch* and show a call to your subroutine using

a. Registers to pass parameters.

b. A parameter block to pass parameters.

c. A stack frame to pass parameters (the function should not be recursive).

d. Recursion and stack frames to pass the parameters.

9. As we noted in the text, the parameter block can be associated with the caller or the subroutine. The code in Example 6.13 associates the parameter block with the subroutine. In this exercise, we explore the possibility of associating the parameter block with the caller. As you answer these questions, remember that the caller can use the same parameter block for all of the subroutines that it calls.

a. Explain why the start of the parameter block must be passed to the subroutine when it is associated with the caller but can be accessed directly by the caller when it is allocated by the subroutine.

b. Rewrite the code shown in Example 6.13 so that the parameter block is associated with the caller.

c. Under what circumstances is it better to associate parameter blocks with the caller? When is it better to associate parameter blocks with the subroutine?

10. Suppose you are working on a machine that does not provide the operations shown in Table 6.1 but does provide access to the stack pointer using SP and auto-increment and auto-decrement addressing. For each of the instructions listed in Table 6.1, show how you could realize the instruction on your machine.

11. Given the instructions presented in Table 6.1, explain why the return value must be placed below the return address in the stack frame, as shown in Figure 6.7.

12. Our implementation of the *strange* subroutine in section 6.5 is based on the assumption that the first parameter is passed by reference. In this exercise, we explore the possibility of passing this parameter by value/result using the same linkage structures.

a. Show how the subroutine implementation would change from the implementation shown in Example 6.17 if the first parameter is to be passed by value/result instead of reference.

b. Show how the subroutine call (calling sequence and cleanup sequence) would change from the implementation shown in Example 6.17 if the first parameter is to be passed by value/result instead of reference.

13. In our presentation of the stack, we ignored the issue of *stack overflow*. Suppose the following assembler directives are used to allocate space for the stack. Explain how you would test for stack overflow.

```
        stack_end:
                    .reserve    1024
        stack_top:
```

14. Consider the following subroutine:

```
     int sub1( int p1, int p2, int p3 )
       {
       int l1, l2;
       int l_arr[6];

       l1 = sub2( p1, p3 );
       arr[l1] = sub3( p2 );
       l2 = sub4( p1+p2, p2, p1, p3, l1 );
       return l1 + l2;
       }
```

Using the calling convention described in Section 6.5,

a.   Show the stack frame that you would use for this subroutine.

b.   Show how you would translate the subroutine into assembly language using a frame pointer.

c.   Show how you would translate the subroutine into assembly language without using a frame pointer.

15. Repeat exercise 14 using the calling convention for the HP Precision architecture.

16. Repeat exercise 14 using register windows on the SPARC architecture. (You will need to augment the SPARC register windows with a stack convention. Be certain to clearly document your use of the stack.)

NUMBER REPRESENTATION

REPRESENTING INTEGERS

CHAPTER 7

In this chapter, we address the problem of representing integer values in a fixed number of bits. We begin by considering the representation and manipulation of unsigned integers. We then consider the representation and manipulation of signed integers.

7.1 UNSIGNED INTEGERS

The most obvious technique for representing unsigned integers, the n-bit binary representation, is also the most reasonable. If the binary representation of x requires more than n bits, we say that x is outside of the *range* of the representation. In this case, the range of the representation should be obvious. We can represent any integer, x, such that

Range

$$2^n - 1 \geq x \geq 0$$

In the remainder of this section, we discuss implementations of the operations needed for unsigned integers: addition, subtraction, multiplication, and division. In discussing implementations of these operations, we concentrate on the most obvious strategy. It is important to note that the most obvious strategy is not usually the most efficient or the most common. In some cases, we will discuss the nature of the inefficiencies and hint at ways in which the implementation could be improved, but we will not discuss these improvements in detail.

7.1.1 Addition of Unsigned Values

When you first learned to add numbers, you probably memorized an addition table. The addition table tells you the result of adding any two digits. To add numbers with more than one digit, you had to learn how to *carry* a one. The addition algorithm that you use is so familiar that you probably have not thought much about it since you learned it. Before we consider mechanical implementations of addition, we should take a moment and review the algorithm that we use. To add two m-digit numbers, you start by adding the rightmost digit of each number to determine the rightmost digit of the result (this is simply a table lookup). If the sum

Carry

of the two rightmost digits is greater than nine, you need to carry a one into the next step of the addition; otherwise, you carry a zero into the next step. The next step in the addition adds the next digits from the original numbers and the carry from the previous step to form the next digit and a new carry (again, this is simply a table lookup). In general, every step of the addition takes three inputs—the carry from the previous step and the two digits from the inputs to the addition—and produces two outputs—the carry into the next step and a new digit for the result. (The first step of the addition has the same form if we assume that the initial carry is zero.)

Figure 7.1 illustrates a simple two-digit adder. The three inputs are labeled x_i, y_i and c_{in}. The outputs are labeled z_i and c_{out}. In effect, the adder shown in Figure 7.1 implements the table lookup step in our algorithm. To complete the implementation of our algorithm, we will use n copies of our simple adder—one adder per bit in the numbers to be added. Figure 7.2 illustrates how these simple adders can be connected to implement our simple addition algorithm when $n = 4$.

Ripple-carry adder

The connection scheme shown in Figure 7.2 is called a *ripple-carry adder* because the carry bits must ripple through the entire adder. In particular, the ith full adder cannot produce a valid output on its c_{out} output (or its z_i output for that matter) until the previous full adder has produced a valid output on its c_{out} output. As such, the maximum time needed to complete the addition operation is proportional to the number of bits to be added.

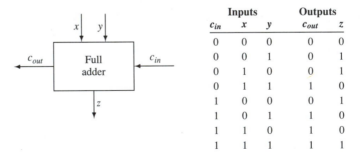

Inputs			Outputs	
c_{in}	x	y	c_{out}	z
0	0	0	0	0
0	0	1	0	1
0	1	0	0	1
0	1	1	1	0
1	0	0	0	1
1	0	1	1	0
1	1	0	1	0
1	1	1	1	1

Figure 7.1   A full adder

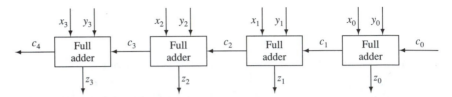

Figure 7.2   A 4-bit ripple-carry adder

Building Faster Adders   The ripple-carry adder mimics the addition algorithm we learned in grammar school. While this is probably the most obvious way to implement binary addition, it is not the fastest. In this subsection, we consider two approaches that have been used to improve the speed of binary addition: conditional sum and lookahead-carry adders. Both of these techniques represent attempts to uncover *parallelism* in binary addition. In particular, the goal is to perform the bitwise additions independently of one another. The intent of this subsection is to point out that the simple approach is not necessarily the fastest and to hint at how the speed of the operation can be improved.

     Parallelism

   A *conditional sum adder* has $\log_2 n + 1$ stages, where n is the number of bits in the two operands. Each stage results in a collection of conditional sums. The last stage results in a single conditional sum. Each conditional sum has two values: We construct one value assuming that the sum to the right will generate a carry; we construct the other value assuming that the sum to the right will not generate a carry. Later, when the adder determines whether the sum to the right will actually generate a carry, it can discard one of the values in the final conditional sum. In other words, the condition of a conditional sum adder is whether the sum to the right generates a carry.

     Conditional sum adder

   In the first stage, a conditional sum adder constructs a conditional sum for each pair of bits from the input values. The rightmost sum in the conditional sum assumes that the sum to the right does not generate a carry, the leftmost sum assumes that the sum to the right generates a carry.

Example 7.1   *Show how you would construct a conditional sum from the pair of bits 0 and 1.*

In constructing the rightmost value in the conditional sum, we assume that there is no carry into the sum; as such, the rightmost value is

$$0'1$$

Here we use the symbol "'" to separate the result from the carry bit. In this case, the result is 1 and the carry bit is 0. In constructing the leftmost value, we assume that there is a carry into the sum. In this case, the value is

$$1'0$$

We write the result as

$$\langle 1'0, 0'1 \rangle$$

Example 7.2   *Show the conditional sums that would be generated by the first stage of a conditional sum adder in adding 01101110_2 to 01010101_2.*

x	0	1	1	0	1	1	1	0
y	0	1	0	1	0	1	0	1

$$\langle 0'1, 0'0 \rangle \quad \langle 1'1, 1'0 \rangle \quad \langle 1'0, 0'1 \rangle \quad \langle 1'0, 0'1 \rangle \quad \langle 1'0, 0'1 \rangle \quad \langle 1'1, 1'0 \rangle \quad \langle 1'0, 0'1 \rangle \quad \langle 1'0, 0'1 \rangle$$

The remaining stages in a conditional sum adder have a common structure. Each of these stages combines pairs of conditional sums from the previous stage into a single conditional sum. Given a pair of conditional sums, combining them into a single conditional sum is relatively easy. Suppose that we need to combine the conditional sum $\langle s_3, s_2 \rangle$ with the conditional sum $\langle s_1, s_0 \rangle$. We begin by constructing the rightmost sum in the resulting conditional sum. We construct this value by considering the carry bit of s_0. If the carry bit of s_0 is 0, we concatenate the result part of s_0 (i.e., s_0 without the carry bit) onto the end of s_2 and use this as the rightmost pair in the final conditional sum. Otherwise, if the carry bit of s_0 is 1, we use s_3 instead of s_2. Similarly, we use the carry bit of s_1 to determine if we concatenate the value part of s_1 onto the end of s_2 or s_3 to construct the leftmost value in the resulting conditional sum.

Example 7.3   *Show how you would combine the conditional sum $\langle 0'11, 0'10 \rangle$ with the conditional sum $\langle 1'00, 0'11 \rangle$.*

In this case s_0 is $0'11$. Because the carry bit is 0, we concatenate the value part of s_0 (11) onto the end of s_2 to get $0'1011$ as the rightmost value in the result. Because the carry bit of s_1 ($1'00$) is 1, we concatenate the value part of s_1 (00) onto the end of s_3, resulting in $0'1100$ as the leftmost value in the resulting conditional sum. The final result is:

$$\langle 0'1100, 0'1011 \rangle$$

Example 7.4   *Example 7.2 presents the first stage in adding 01101110_2 to 01010101_2. Show the remaining stages.*

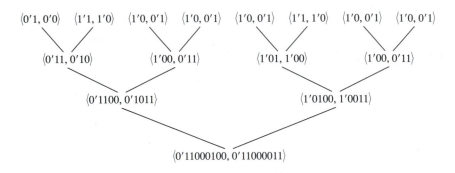

After the first stage, each stage in the conditional sum adder combines pairs of sums from the previous stage into a single pair of sums. In this way each stage reduces the number of pairs by half (and doubles the number of bits in each sum). As such, the result will be available after $\log_2 n$ stages. Because each stage can be completed in a fixed amount of time (independent of the number of bits in the sum), the time required to complete the entire addition is proportional to $\log_2 n + 1$.

A *lookahead-carry adder* uses two stages to complete an addition. The first stage constructs all of the carries in a fixed amount of time (independent of the number of bits to be added). Once all of the carries have been constructed, the individual bit additions can be performed in parallel (independently of one another). Figure 7.3 illustrates the stages in a lookahead-carry adder.

Lookahead-carry adder

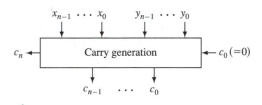

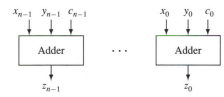

Figure 7.3 The stages in a lookahead-carry adder

Example 7.5 *Give a Boolean expression in disjunctive normal form that computes the third carry bit, c_2, from the inputs.*

We begin by using a fairly obvious definition of c_2:

$$c_2 = x_2 y_2 + c_1(x_2 + y_2)$$

Next, we substitute for c_1 to obtain

$$c_2 = x_2 y_2 + (x_1 y_1 + c_0(x_1 + y_1))(x_2 + y_2)$$

Distributing c_0 gives

$$c_2 = x_2 y_2 + (x_1 y_1 + c_0 x_1 + c_0 y_1)(x_2 + y_2)$$

Finally we get

$$c_2 = x_2 y_2 + x_1 y_1 x_2 + x_1 y_1 y_2 + c_0 x_1 x_2 + c_0 x_1 y_2 + c_0 y_1 x_2 + c_0 y_1 y_2$$

Lookahead-carry adders are the fastest, but most complex, of the adders. The maximum size of lookahead-carry adders is limited by the *fan-out* problem. To see the degree of fan-out, consider the number of uses of y_2 in the previous example; there will be twice as many uses of this input in constructing the value for c_3. In contrast, ripple-carry adders have simple implementations but may be too slow. The conditional sum adders are somewhere in between. It is common to combine these techniques in the design of actual adders. For example, a 16-bit adder might be constructed using four 4-bit lookahead-carry adders connected in a ripple-carry fashion.

Overflow—The Carry Bit(s)   Regardless of the technique used to implement the addition, Figure 7.4 presents a reasonable abstraction of an n-bit adder. The adder accepts two n-bit inputs, x and y, and produces an n-bit result, z. In addition, the

Carry-input bit

adder accepts a carry-input bit, c_0, and produces a carry-out bit, c_n. The *carry-input bit* is used as the carry into the least significant bit and will typically be set to zero. As we will see, there are situations when the carry-input bit needs to be set to something other than zero; as such, it is an input to the n-bit adder. The

Carry-out bit

carry-out bit is the carry out of the most significant bit.

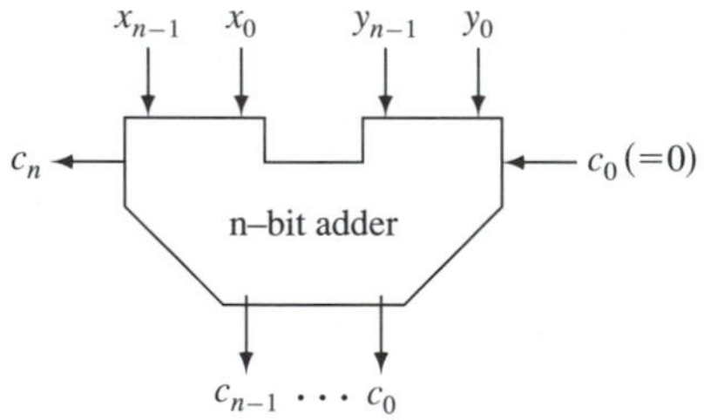

Figure 7.4   An n-bit adder

If the carry-out bit is set at the end of an addition, it means that the result is greater than or equal to 2^n; that is, the result is outside of the range of the repre-

Overflow

sentation. This situation is called an *overflow* because the value of the result has overflowed the space allocated for it. Notice that the carry-out bit is equivalent to overflow—if it is set, overflow has occurred; otherwise, the result did not overflow the representation.

Exception

On some machines, overflow causes an *exception*. We consider exceptions and exception handling in Chapter 11. For the present, we restrict our attention to

Carry bit

machines that use a bit in the condition code register, the *carry bit*, based on the value of the carry-out bit. Instructions following an addition operation can test the value of the carry bit to determine if an overflow has occurred. Conditional branching based on the value of the carry bit is generally provided by two opera-

BROC

tions, that we call *BROC* (branch on carry) and *BRNC* (branch no carry).

BRNC

The occurrence of an overflow (i.e., having the carry bit set after an addition) is not necessarily an indication of an error. In some instances, the programmer may want an addition modulo 2^n (e.g., in the code for a random number generator). In these cases, simply ignore the carry-out if the addition is correct.

Example 7.6   *Suppose you have an application that requires the addition of two 64-bit values but your machine only provides 32-bit arithmetic. Show how you can implement a 64-bit addition using the BROC and BRNC operations. You should assume that two 64-bit values are in registers R2, R3, R4, and R5. Your code fragment should implement the operation:*

$$\langle R3, R2 \rangle \leftarrow \langle R3, R2 \rangle + \langle R5, R4 \rangle$$

where R3 and R5 hold the most significant parts of the values.

```
          ADD    R2, R2, R4     ; add the least significant parts
          BRNC   add_high       ; test the carry bit
          ADD    R3, R3, #1     ; add carry to most significant part
          BROC   overflow       ; now it is too big!
add_high:
          ADD    R3, R3, R5     ; add the most significant parts
          BROC   overflow       ; now it is too big!
          ⋮
overflow:
```

You may wonder why the *n*-bit adder shown in Figure 7.4 provides a *carry-input* input. During a normal addition, this line is set to 0, a constant, so it hardly seems necessary to show an explicit input for this value. However, the second, third, and fourth statements in the code presented in Example 7.6 are only used to add the carry bit into the second step in the addition. Many machines provide an *add-with-carry* operation, *ADDC*, that sets the value of the carry-input to the current value of the carry bit.

Carry-input

ADDC

Example 7.7   *Show how you can simplify the code presented in Example 7.6 using the ADDC operation.*

```
          ADD    R2, R2, R4     ; add the least significant parts
          ADDC   R3, R3, R5     ; add the most significant parts
          BROC   overflow       ; now it is too big!
          ⋮
overflow:
```

The *carry bit* seems to indicate that it will only be updated during an addition; however, if you examine the instruction set of most machines, you will find that the carry bit gets updated by many of the instructions. As we discussed in Chapter 4, the carry bit is also updated by the *shift* and *rotate* instructions. In addition, the carry bit is also updated by the subtraction operation, SUB.

7.1.2 Subtraction of Unsigned Integers

Subtraction of unsigned numbers is, for the most part, just like the addition of unsigned numbers, with one exception—the operation is different! This statement is not as absurd as you might expect. If you think back to when you first learned how to subtract numbers, you will recognize that the basic algorithm is the same as it was for addition, start with the rightmost digit and proceed to the left, one digit at a time. Moreover, each step in this algorithm has three inputs and produces two outputs—just like addition. The names of the inputs and outputs are usually different (e.g., the name *borrow* is used in the place of *carry*), but that is a simple matter of relabeling. The important difference is the way in which input values are mapped to the output values. Figure 7.5 summarizes the mapping for a binary subtractor.

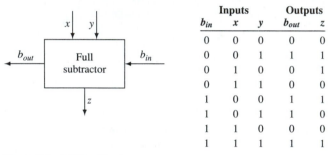

	Inputs		Outputs	
b_{in}	x	y	b_{out}	z
0	0	0	0	0
0	0	1	1	1
0	1	0	0	1
0	1	1	0	0
1	0	0	1	1
1	0	1	1	0
1	1	0	0	0
1	1	1	1	1

Figure 7.5 A full subtractor

Given our basic subtraction algorithm, we could consider the direct construction of different types of subtractors, that is, *ripple-borrow* subtractors, *conditional-borrow* subtractors, and *borrow-lookahead subtractors*. However, Figure 7.6 shows how you can construct a full subtractor from a full adder. Figure 7.7 then shows how this approach can be generalized to construct an *n*-bit subtractor from an *n*-bit adder.

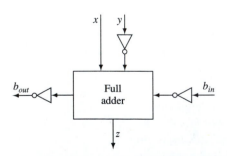

Figure 7.6 Constructing a full subtractor from a full adder

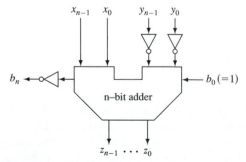

Figure 7.7 An *n*-bit subtractor

An n-bit subtractor accepts a borrow-in input and produces a borrow-out output. Typically, the borrow bit is stored in the carry bit of the condition code register. In addition to the basic unsigned subtraction operation, most machines provide a *subtract-with-borrow* operation, *SUBB*. This operation sets the borrow-in input to the current value of the carry bit in the condition code register.

SUBB

Before we leave this discussion, there is a minor point of terminology that is frequently confusing. If an unsigned binary subtraction generates a value that is outside the range of the representation, the result is called an *overflow*. Importantly, it is *not* called an *underflow*. The term *underflow* has a specific meaning, which we will discuss when we consider floating point representations. Overflow means that the value is not within the range of the representation—it does not indicate whether the value is too large or too small.

Overflow

Underflow

7.1.3 Multiplication and Division of Unsigned Integers

Existing processors provide varying degrees of support for multiplication and division of unsigned integers. Most of the newer CISC machines (e.g., the Motorola 680x0 and Intel 80x86 machines) have integer multiplication and integer division operations. At least one RISC machine, the MIPS processor, has integer multiplication and division operations. Another RISC machine, the Motorola 88100, uses the floating point coprocessor to implement integer multiplication and division (we discuss this approach at greater length in the Chapter 8). Still other RISC machines, the HP Precision and the SPARC, provide special instructions that you can use to implement simple and efficient algorithms for integer multiplication and division.

Besides the varying degrees of support, integer multiplication and division operations are complicated by the results that they generate. Multiplication of two 32-bit integers could result in a 64-bit value. If all of the registers are 32 bits wide, some provision needs to be made for the result. One approach involves the notion of *register pairs*. In this approach, the result is stored in two consecutive registers (e.g., R3 and R4). We used this approach in Example 7.7 when we illustrated the ADDC operation. Another approach simply stores the least significant 32 bits and sets an overflow flag if the result requires more than 32 bits. The Motorola 88100 processor uses this approach. The MIPS processor illustrates another approach. In addition to a set of thirty-two 32-bit general-purpose registers, the MIPS processor has two special-purpose 32-bit registers called *hi* and *lo*. The machine provides special operations that transfer values between the general-purpose registers and the hi and lo registers. The multiply operation loads the lo register with the least significant 32 bits of the result and loads the hi register with the most significant 32 bits of the result. Subsequent instructions may transfer the values in the lo and hi registers into the general-purpose registers where they can be manipulated.

Integer division is complicated by the fact that a 32-bit division operation may result in a 32-bit quotient and a 32-bit remainder. In essence, the problem is the same as the problem introduced by integer multiplication, and the solutions are closely related. In the *register pair* approach, the quotient is stored in one of the registers while the remainder is stored in the other. The Motorola 88100 simply stores the 32-bit quotient and does not make the remainder available after an integer division. The MIPS processor stores the remainder in the lo register and uses the lo register for the quotient.

In the remainder of this section, we will consider simple algorithms for implementing binary multiplication and division for unsigned values. Our goal is to motivate the special operations provided by the HP Precision and SPARC architectures. We begin by considering two examples. The first illustrates the algorithm that we use to implement decimal multiplication. The second shows how we can simplify this algorithm for binary multiplication.

Example 7.8   *Show how you would compute 476 * 529.*

The standard multiplication algorithm yields the following computation:

$$476 * 529 = (4 * 529) * 100 + (7 * 529) * 10 + (6 * 529) * 1$$

To complete this multiplication, you can expand each of the nested products, for example,

$$4 * 529 = (4 * 5) * 100 + (4 * 2) * 10 + (4 * 9) * 1$$

You can implement this computation using (*a*) table lookup for the nested multiplications (e.g., $4 * 5 = 20$), (*b*) left shifts with zero fill for the multiplications involving powers of 10 (e.g., $20 * 100 = 2000$), and (*c*) a simple adder to compute the final sum.

Example 7.9   *Show how you would compute $010_2 * 101_2$.*

$$010 * 101 = (0 * 101) * 100 + (1 * 101) * 10 + (0 * 101) * 1$$

Note that the nested products are multiplications by 1 or 0 and, as such, are trivial to evaluate. Thus, there is no need to decompose this computation any further.

To develop an algorithm for binary multiplication, we can rearrange this computation slightly:

$$010 * 101 = 0 * (101 * 100) + \{1 * (101 * 10) + [0 * (101 * 1)]\}$$

This reorganization provides the basis for the algorithm presented in Figure 7.8. In this case, the multiplier is 010 and the multiplicand is 101. In this algorithm, we use left shifts to implement multiplications by powers of two; we use right shifts to examine the bits of the multiplier one at a time.

one of the operands is called the *multiplier*
the other is called the *multiplicand*

product = 0
for(i = 0 ; i < n ; i++) {
if(the least significant bit of the multiplier is 1) {
        product = product + multiplicand
    }
    shift the multiplicand to the left
    shift the multiplier to the right
}

Figure 7.8 An algorithm for *n*-bit binary
multiplication

Example 7.10 *Illustrate how the algorithm presented in Figure 7.8 will compute 1011_2 *
1010_2.*

	Product	Multiplicand	Multiplier
Initial	00000000	1011	1010
After step 1	00000000	10110	101
After step 2	00010110	101100	10
After step 3	00010110	1011000	1
After step 4	01101110	10110000	0

Example 7.11 *Give an assembly language code fragment that implements the algorithm
presented in Figure 7.8. You should assume that the values to be multiplied are in R2
and R3 and that the result should be stored in R4. You may assume that the result can
be stored in 32 bits and you may alter the contents of any registers that you need to use.*

```
        CLEAR   R4              ; initialize the result
        MOVE    R5, #31         ; 32 bits in a word
top:
        SRZ     R3, R3, #1      ; shift multiplier—set carry bit to LSB(R3)
        BRNC    no_add          ; if LSB(R3)
        ADD     R4, R4, R2      ; add in multiplicand
no_add:
        SLZ     R2, R2, #1      ; left shift multiplicand
        ADD     R5, R5, #−1     ; decrement the counter
        BRGT    top             ; branch to top if more bits
```

The body of the loop shown in this example consists of two shift operations, an
addition operation, and a conditional branch (the loop control includes an addition

and a conditional branch). The SPARC architecture provides a special operation that combines the operations in the body of the loop into a single operation called *MULS* (multiply step).

The actual MULS operation is based on the algorithm shown in Figure 7.9. Recognizing that the product may need twice as many bits as the multiplier or multiplicand, this algorithm partitions the product into two parts: *product high* and *product low*. The multiplicand is always added into the product high using a 32-bit addition. If this addition generates a carry-out, the carry bit will be shifted back into the product high on the next combined shift. In examining this algorithm, note that the multiplicand is not shifted to the left; instead, the product is shifted to the right. Because we always add into the high part of the product, shifting the product to the right has the same effect as shifting the multiplicand to the left.

```
one of the operands is called the multiplier
the other is called the multiplicand

product high = 0;
product low = 0;
for( i = 0 ; i < n ; i++ ) {
    if( the least significant bit of the multiplier is 1 ) {
        combined shift product high and product low to the right
            (fill the most significant bit with the carry bit)
        product high = product high + multiplicand
    }
    shift the multiplier to the right
}
combined shift product high and product low to the right
    (fill the most significant bit with the carry bit)
```

Figure 7.9 A second algorithm for *n*-bit binary multiplication

Example 7.12   *Illustrate how the algorithm presented in Figure 7.9 will compute $1011_2 * 1010_2$.*

| | Product | | | |
	High	Low	Multiplicand	Multiplier
Initial	0000		1011	1010
After step 1	0000	0	1011	101
After step 2	1011	00	1011	10
After step 3	0101	100	1011	1
After step 4	1101	1100	1011	
After final shift	0110	1110	1011	

In considering this example, note that the number of bits needed to represent the product low grows by one on each iteration, while the number of bits needed to represent the multiplier is reduced by one. The SPARC MULS operation takes advantage of this observation by storing the product low and the multiplier in a single 32-bit register.

One final aspect of the algorithm shown in Figure 7.9 is of interest. Using the MULS operation, the body of the loop consists of a single instruction. The loop control, on the other hand, requires two instructions—an addition and a conditional branch. Because the number of loop iterations is fixed (i.e., *definite iteration*) it is common to write this algorithm as a sequence of 32 MULS instructions followed by a combined right shift (that can be implemented using a MULS instruction).

As was the case for binary multiplication, binary division is much easier than division in base 10 because we only have two cases to consider at each step. Figure 7.10 illustrates the standard division algorithm for two binary numbers. We leave the development of a division algorithm (similar to the multiplication algorithm shown in Figure 7.8) as an exercise.

```
            1001
      ┌─────────
1010 │ 1011110
       1010
       ────
       0011
       0000
       ────
        0111
        0000
        ────
         1110
         1010
         ────
          100
```

Quotient 1001; remainder 100

Figure 7.10 Long division of binary numbers

7.2 THE REPRESENTATION OF SIGNED INTEGERS

There are 2^n different patterns that can be formed using n bits. In the representation of signed integers, approximately half of these patterns are used to represent positive integers; the other half are used to represent negative integers. The essential problem is to determine how signed integer values are mapped into these patterns. In this section, we consider four representations (mappings) for signed integers: signed magnitude, excess, 2's complement, and 1's complement. We emphasize the 2's complement representation because this is the most commonly used representation for signed integers.

In contrasting these mappings, we need to consider how the various operations (negation, addition, subtraction, multiplication, and so forth), can be implemented on the bit patterns. We concentrate on the simple arithmetic operations: absolute value, negation, addition, and subtraction. In particular, we will not consider multiplication and division within the representation.

In addition to the simple arithmetic operations, we consider another pair of operations: *size extension* and *size reduction*. As we noted in Chapter 3, the memory subsystem can provide data values in a variety of sizes (8-bit, 16-bit, 32-bit, and so forth). As we will discuss, the mapping functions make use of the number of bits allotted for the value. The size extension and reduction operations deal with changing the number of bits used in the representation of a signed integer value.

Size extension

Size reduction

7.2.1 Signed Magnitude

Perhaps the most obvious technique for representing signed integers is to use the most significant bit of the representation as a *sign bit* (i.e., a bit to indicate whether the value is negative or positive) and the remaining bits to represent the magnitude of the number. This representation technique is called *signed magnitude* (or sign and magnitude). In effect, this is the technique that we use to write signed integers (where the + or − is to the left of the digits). The only decision that we need to make is whether to use 0 to represent the symbol + or the symbol −. It is

Sign bit

Signed magnitude

common to use 0 to represent $+$, and we will follow this convention. We can summarize the signed magnitude representation as:

$$\text{rep}(x) = \begin{cases} 0\,\text{bin}(x) & \text{if } 2^{n-1} > x \geq 0 \\ 1\,\text{bin}(|x|) & \text{if } -2^{n-1} < x < 0 \end{cases} \tag{7.1}$$

where bin(x) denotes the binary representation of x.

Example 7.13   *Give the 5-bit signed magnitude representation of -5 and the 5-bit signed magnitude representation of 5.*

$$\text{rep}(-5) = 10101; \ \text{rep}(5) = 00101$$

Note that the bit pattern $100\cdots0$ is not associated with any value. It is common to treat this pattern as a representation of zero. To distinguish it from the true representation of zero, it is common to refer to this pattern as *negative zero*.

Negation and Absolute Value in Signed Magnitude   If you think about it for a moment, you can probably guess how to implement the negation and absolute value operations in signed magnitude. But how do you know that your operations are correct? In this section, we describe how to implement the signed magnitude negation and absolute value operations and present a technique that can be used to verify that these implementations are correct. We begin by considering examples of the negation and absolute value operations.

Example 7.14   *Give the 5-bit, signed magnitude representation for the values 5, -5, 3, -3, 14, -14, and 0. In addition, give the representation for the negative and absolute value for each of these values.*

x	**rep(x)**	**rep($-x$)**	**rep($|x|$)**
5	00101	10101	00101
-5	10101	00101	00101
3	00011	10011	00011
-3	10011	00011	00011
14	01110	11110	01110
-14	11110	01110	01110
0	00000	00000	00000

In examining this table, note that the representation of a number and the representation of its negation only differ in the most significant bit position. In particular, if you invert the most significant representation of a number you will obtain the representation of the negation of the number. The only exception to this rule is zero—negating the representation of zero does not affect the most significant bit in the representation. From these observations, we conclude that the signed magnitude negation operation can be implemented by inverting the most significant bit in the representation of the number, unless the pattern is the representation of zero. If the pattern is a representation of zero, it should not be altered. The signed magnitude absolute value operation is simpler because it does not have a special case for zero. This operation can be implemented by setting the most significant bit in the representation of the number to zero.

How can we be certain that our observations regarding the signed magnitude negation and absolute value operations are correct? In this discussion, we only consider the negation operation; justification of the absolute value operation is similar. In the case of the negation, there is one relationship that must be preserved by the negation operation: If you map a number to its representation and then apply the signed magnitude negation operation, you must end up with the same bit pattern that you would get if you started with the negative of the number and mapped this value to its representation. Algebraically, we have:

$$\sim \text{rep}(x) = \text{rep}(-x) \tag{7.2}$$

where $\sim$ is the signed magnitude negation operator. A graphical interpretation of this relationship is shown in Figure 7.11. In the graphical interpretation, starting in the lower left-hand corner is equivalent to selecting x. Moving to the right and then up is equivalent to negating x and then mapping $-x$ into the representation, that is, $\text{rep}(-x)$. Moving up and then to the right is equivalent to mapping x into the representation and negating this value using the signed magnitude negation operation, that is, $\sim \text{rep}(x)$. It does not matter which path you take, you will end up at the same point.

It is important to note that *any* operation that preserves this relationship can be used as an implementation of the signed magnitude negation operation. To see the significance of this statement, consider -5 and its negation, 5. As we have seen, the (5-bit signed magnitude) representation of -5 is 10101 and the representation of 5 is 00101. As such, the signed magnitude negation operation must map 10101 to 00101; moreover, any operation that maps 10101 to 00101 implements the signed magnitude negation operation at the point 10101.

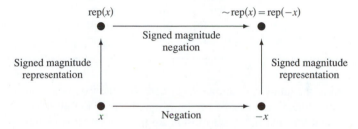

Figure 7.11 Negation in the representation

Now, we are in a position to justify our implementation of the signed magnitude negation operation. To justify this implementation, we only need to verify that the implementation preserves the relationship stated in equation 7.2 at every point (i.e., for every value within the range of the representation). We verify this property by considering the cases:

$x = 0$. If x is zero, the representation of x is all zeros and the representation of $-x$ is also all zeros. This is the special case for our negation operation—our operation correctly maps the pattern of all 0's to itself.

x **is positive.** If x is a positive number, the most significant bit in the representation of x is 0 and the remaining bits will be the binary representation of $|x|$. The representation of $-x$ is exactly the same except the most significant bit is 1 instead of 0. As such, inverting the most significant bit correctly preserves the essential relationship.

x **is negative.** If x is a negative number, the most significant bit in the representation of x will be 1 and the remaining bits will be the binary representation of $|x|$. Again, the representation of $-x$ will be exactly the same except that the most significant bit will be 0 instead of 1. Again, inverting the most significant bit correctly preserves the essential relationship.

Because the signed magnitude representation is symmetric about 0, the signed magnitude operation cannot result in an overflow. As such, there is no need to detect overflow in the implementation of this operation.

Addition and Subtraction in Signed Magnitude   We now consider implementations for the signed magnitude addition and subtraction operations. In implementing these operations, we will use the unsigned adders and subtractors described in section 7.1 whenever possible. We begin by considering sample additions.

Example 7.15   *Show the 5-bit, signed magnitude representations for the following sums:*
$5 + 7$, $-5 + -7$, $-5 + 7$, and $5 + -7$.

x	y	rep(x)	rep(y)	rep($x + y$)
5	7	00101	00111	01100
-5	-7	10101	10111	11100
-5	7	10101	00111	00010
5	-7	00101	10111	10010

In examining the table in Example 7.15, note that the first two sums can be implemented using binary addition of the representations of the numbers (the second sum requires that the sign bit be set to indicate that the result is negative). In more general terms, signed magnitude addition can be implemented using $n-1$ bit binary addition whenever the signs of the two numbers are the same. Otherwise, if the signs of the two numbers are different, signed magnitude addition is implemented using $n - 1$ bit binary subtraction. For the moment, we will defer the details of how the binary subtraction is invoked and rely on a simple algebraic identity, $x + y \equiv x - (-y)$. These statements can be summarized as follows:

$$\text{rep}(x) \oplus \text{rep}(y) = \begin{cases} \text{rep}(x) + \text{rep}(y) & \text{if } x, y \geq 0 \\ \sim (|\text{rep}(x)| + |\text{rep}(y)|) & \text{if } x, y < 0 \\ \text{rep}(x) \ominus \sim \text{rep}(y) & \text{otherwise} \end{cases} \quad (7.3)$$

where $+$ denotes unsigned, $(n - 1)$-bit binary addition; $\sim$ and $|\ |$ denote the signed magnitude negation and absolute value operations, respectively; and $\oplus$ and $\ominus$ denote the signed magnitude addition and subtraction operations, respectively. You can implement the predicates in equation 7.3 by testing the most significant bit in the representation of the number. Overflow of signed magnitude addition is equivalent to overflow of the $(n - 1)$-bit binary addition.

As was the case for the addition operation, if the signs of the values are the same, the subtraction operation can be implemented using $n-1$ bit unsigned binary subtraction. Otherwise, we can use another simple identity, $x - y \equiv x + (-y)$, that transforms the subtraction into an addition. The only tricky part is to make sure that the unsigned binary subtraction does not result in a negative value (i.e., an overflow). An implementation of the signed magnitude subtraction operation is summarized as follows

$$\text{rep}(x) \ominus \text{rep}(y) = \begin{cases} \text{rep}(x) - \text{rep}(y) & \text{if } x \geq y \geq 0 \\ \sim [\text{rep}(y) - \text{rep}(x)] & \text{if } y > x \geq 0 \\ \sim (|\text{rep}(x)| - |\text{rep}(y)|) & \text{if } x < y < 0 \\ |\text{rep}(y)| - |\text{rep}(x)| & \text{if } y < x < 0 \\ \text{rep}(x) \oplus \sim \text{rep}(y) & \text{otherwise} \end{cases} \quad (7.4)$$

where $-$ denotes unsigned, $(n - 1)$-bit binary subtraction; $\sim$ and $|\ |$ denote the signed magnitude negation and absolute value operations, respectively; and $\oplus$ and $\ominus$ denote the signed magnitude addition and subtraction operations, respectively. Overflow of the signed magnitude subtraction operation is equivalent to overflow of the $(n - 1)$-bit binary subtraction.

To justify that our implementations of signed magnitude addition and subtraction are correct, we would need to verify that each operation preserves a simple relation. In particular, we would need to verify that the addition operation preserves the relation

$$\text{rep}(x + y) = \text{rep}(x) \oplus \text{rep}(y) \quad (7.5)$$

and that the subtraction operation preserves the relation

$$\text{rep}(x - y) = \text{rep}(x) \ominus \text{rep}(y) \quad (7.6)$$

Verification that these relationships are preserved is straightforward.

Size Extension/Reduction in Signed Magnitude   The size extension/reduction operations address the problem of mapping the representation of a number from its n-bit representation to its m-bit representation. If $n < m$, we are increasing the number of bits used to represent the value—a size extension operation. In signed magnitude, size extension is accomplished by moving the sign bit, so it becomes the most significant bit in the m-bit representation, and clearing the bits in between the old sign bit and the new one (including the old sign bit). Size reduction ($n > m$) is also accomplished by moving the sign bit. If any of the bits between the old sign bit and the new sign bit (including the bit replaced by the new sign bit) is nonzero, the value cannot be represented in m bits.

7.2.2 Excess

Bias

In the remaining representations (excess, 2's complement, and 1's complement), the representation of signed integers is a two-step process. In the first step, the value is mapped to a nonnegative integer. In the second, the nonnegative integer is mapped to its binary representation. In an excess representation, the first step consists of adding a value, called the *bias*, to the number being represented. The result of this step must be a nonnegative number less than 2^n; otherwise, the number is outside of the range of the representation. The excess representation is summarized by the following equation (where b is the bias):

$$\text{rep}(x) = \text{bin}(x + b) \qquad (-b \le x < 2^n - b) \qquad (7.7)$$

For the remainder of this discussion, we will assume that the bias, b, is greater than or equal to zero and less than 2^n (this assumption allows us to use n-bit adders and subtractors to add in or take out the bias). It is common to use a bias of 2^{n-1} or $2^{n-1} - 1$. Using either of these biases means that the range of the representation is almost symmetric about zero and may simplify the implementation of many of the operations.

Example 7.16   *Show the 3-bit excess 4 ($4 = 2^{3-1}$) representation.*

x	-4	-3	-2	-1	0	1	2	3
$x + 4$	0	1	2	3	4	5	6	7
$\text{rep}(x)$	000	001	010	011	100	101	110	111

Example 7.17   *Show the 3-bit excess 3 ($3 = 2^{3-1} - 1$) representation.*

x	-3	-2	-1	0	1	2	3	4
$x + 3$	0	1	2	3	4	5	6	7
$\text{rep}(x)$	000	001	010	011	100	101	110	111

In examining the tables in Examples 7.16 and 7.17, note that most significant bit in the representation of every negative number is 0 and the most significant bit in the representation of every positive number is 1. In general, when the bias is 2^{n-1} or $2^{n-1} - 1$, the most significant bit in the excess representation of a number acts as an *inverse sign bit*. If the value being represented is negative, $x + 2^{n-1}$ will be less than 2^{n-1}, and hence, the most significant bit will be 0. Otherwise (if x is nonnegative), $x + 2^{n-1}$ and $x + 2^{n-1} - 1$ will be greater than or equal to 2^{n-1}; as such, the most significant bit will be 1. Notice that the two biases treat 0 differently. If the bias is 2^{n-1}, zero appears to be a positive number (the most significant bit in the representation of zero is 1). On the other hand, if the bias is $2^{n-1} - 1$, zero appears to be a negative number (the most significant bit in the representation of zero is 0).

Inverse sign bit

Negation and Absolute Value in Excess   Given a number x, we know that x is represented by the binary representation of $b + x$ and $-x$ is represented by the binary representation of $b - x$. For example, the excess 4 representation of -3 is the binary representation of 1, and the excess 4 representation of 3 is the binary representation of 7. As such, the excess 4 negation operation needs to map the binary representation of $b + x$ [for example, $4 + (-3)$] to the binary representation of $b - x$ [for example, $4 - (-3)$]. To implement this mapping, we first need to determine the value of x. At first, it may seem that we could use the calculation $\text{rep}(x) - b$ to determine (the binary representation of) the value of x. Unfortunately, it is not quite that simple—if x is negative, the binary subtraction will overflow (i.e., result in a negative number). A careful implementation of the negation operation is shown below:

$$\sim \text{rep}(x) = \begin{cases} b - (\text{rep}(x) - b) & \text{if } x \geq 0 \\ b + (b - \text{rep}(x)) & \text{if } x < 0 \end{cases} \tag{7.8}$$

where $\sim$ denotes the excess negation operator and $+$ and $-$ denote n-bit binary addition and subtraction, respectively.

If $b = 2^{n-1}$, the comparison to zero used in equation 7.8 can be implemented by testing the most significant bit in the representation of x. If the bias is not 2^{n-1}, this test must be implemented by comparing the value to the bias, that is, a subtraction followed by a test of the borrow bit. Moreover, the first subtraction in the first line of the implementation can be implemented by setting the most significant bit to zero. Similarly, the addition in the second line of the implementation can be implemented by setting the most significant bit to one.

It is possible for the negation operation to result in an overflow. Overflow in the negation operation is equivalent to overflow of the last binary operation.

There is no particularly simple way to implement the absolute value operation; about all you can do is to negate the representation of negative values.

Addition and Subtraction in Excess   If we simply add the representations of two numbers using binary addition, we will end up with the representation of the sum plus the bias, that is,

$$\text{rep}(x) + \text{rep}(y) = \text{bin}(b + x) + \text{bin}(b + y)$$
$$= \text{bin}(b + x + b + y)$$
$$= \text{bin}(b + x + y) + \text{bin}(b)$$
$$= \text{rep}(x + y) + \text{bin}(b)$$

As such, the excess-b addition operation can be implemented by adding the representations of the two values (using binary addition) and subtracting the binary representation of the bias, that is,

$$\text{rep}(x) \oplus \text{rep}(y) = \text{rep}(x) + \text{rep}(y) - \text{bin}(b) \tag{7.9}$$

Similarly, subtraction can be implemented by subtracting the two values and adding in the bias, that is,

$$\text{rep}(x) \ominus \text{rep}(y) = \text{rep}(x) - \text{rep}(y) + \text{bin}(b) \tag{7.10}$$

Unfortunately, it is not quite that simple. In particular, you need to consider the possibility of overflow in the intermediate steps. As was the case for the negation operation, you need to be careful about the order in which the operations are performed. We will leave this as an exercise.

Size Extension/Reduction in Excess The size extension/reduction operators associated with excess are trivial if the bias is not changed when the size is changed. Extension is accomplished by filling the most significant bits with zeros, while reduction is accomplished by discarding the most significant bits. However, in most cases, the bias is determined by the number of bits used in the representation and is not independent of the size of the representation. When the bias changes from b to b' as the size changes, size extension requires that the value $b' - b$ be added to the representation. In size reduction, the value $b - b'$ must be subtracted from the representation.

7.2.3 2's Complement

As was the case for excess representations, complement representations start by mapping the number to a value between 0 and $2^n - 1$ (inclusive) and using the binary representation of this value as the representation of the number. Unlike the excess representations, complement representations map nonnegative numbers to themselves. Negative numbers are mapped by adding a bias that is larger than any nonnegative value in the range of the representation. These statements can be summarized as:

$$\text{rep}(x) = \begin{cases} \text{bin}(x) & b > m \geq x \geq 0 \\ \text{bin}(b + x) & 0 > x > -(b - m) \end{cases} \tag{7.11}$$

where b is the bias and m is the largest number in the representation. Complement representations are defined by two parameters: the bias and the maximum value.

Note that the value a number is mapped to could be as large as $b - 1$, where b is the bias. As such, the bias must be less than or equal to 2^n. Moreover, it makes sense to select a bias of 2^n; otherwise, the bit patterns that correspond to values between $b - 1$ and $2^n - 1$ can never be used in the representation of a signed number. To make the range of the representation (almost) symmetric about zero, the maximum should be about 2^{n-1}. Selecting a maximum of $2^{n-1} - 1$ simplifies the implementation of many operations. The representation that results from selecting a bias of 2^n and a maximum of $2^{n-1} - 1$ is called *2's complement*. 2's complement
We summarize the 2's complement representation as:

$$\text{rep}(x) = \begin{cases} \text{bin}(x) & 2^{n-1} > x \geq 0 \\ \text{bin}(2^n - |x|) & 0 > x \geq -2^{n-1} \end{cases} \tag{7.12}$$

Example 7.18   *Show the 3-bit 2's complement representation.*

x	0	1	2	3	−4	−3	−2	−1
rep(x)	000	001	010	011	100	101	110	111

In examining this table, you will notice that the most significant bit in the representation of every nonnegative value is 0 while the most significant bit in the representation of every negative value is 1. In essence, the most significant bit in the representation of a value acts as an *effective sign bit*. In contrast to the signed Effective sign bit
magnitude representation, where the most significant bit was set aside as a sign bit, the sign bit that arises in the 2's complement representation is a consequence of the representation.

Two's complement is an instance of a more general representation scheme called *radix complement*. It happens that we are using a radix of 2 (binary); however, Radix complement
the properties that we will discuss for 2's complement hold for any radix, r, if the bias is selected as r^n and the maximum is selected as $r^{n-1} - 1$.

Negation and Absolute Value in 2's Complement   In Chapter 1, we described a simple negation operation for 2's complement: To negate the representation of x, invert all of the bits in the representation of x and add 1.

Example 7.19   *Show how to negate the 5-bit 2's complement representation of 5.*

$$
\begin{array}{rl}
\text{rep(5)} & 00101 \\
\text{invert the bits} & 11010 \\
\text{add 1} & \underline{+1} \\
\text{rep(}-5\text{)} & 11011
\end{array}
$$

Carry-in

Carry-out

Because the 2's complement representation is not symmetric about zero, it is possible that the negation operation will result in an overflow. Overflow can be detected by comparing the carry into the most significant bit (*carry-in*) to the carry out of the most significant bit (*carry-out*) during the second step of the negation operation. If the carry-in is not the same as the carry-out, the negation results in a number that is outside the range of the representation.

Example 7.20   *Show what will happen if you negate the 5-bit 2's complement representation of* −16.

$$
\begin{array}{rlll}
 & & 01111 & \text{Carry bits} \\
\text{rep(}-16\text{)}\quad 10000 & \text{invert} & 01111 & \\
 & \text{add 1} & \underline{+1} & \\
\text{rep(}-16\text{)} & & 10000 &
\end{array}
$$

In this case, the carry-in is 1 and the carry-out is 0, which indicates an overflow.

As was the case for the excess representations, there is no particularly easy way to implement a 2's complement absolute value operation. About the only thing that you can do is to test the effective sign bit and negate the value if the sign bit indicates that the value is negative.

Why does this simple algorithm for 2's complement negation and overflow detection work? Intuitively, negation can be implemented by subtracting the representation of the value from 2^n (using binary subtraction). To see why this works, consider the cases. If x is positive, x is represented by the binary representation of x and its negation is represented by the binary representation of $2^n - x$. On the other hand, if x is negative, x is represented by the binary representation of $2^n - |x|$ and its negation is represented by the binary representation of $|x|$. Because $2^n - (2^n - |x|) = |x|$, we get the correct result.

Example 7.21   *Show how you can negate the 3-bit 2's complement representation of* −3 *using subtraction from* 2^3.

$$
\begin{array}{rl}
2^3 & 1000 \\
\text{rep}(-3) & -101 \\
\hline
& 011 \qquad \text{rep}(3)
\end{array}
$$

This intuitive explanation is missing an important case, $x = 0$, and does not tell us how to detect overflow. We will return to these issues in a moment. Right now, we need to address another interesting problem. The binary representation of 2^n requires $n + 1$ bits; as such, it appears as though we will need an $n + 1$ bit binary subtractor to implement our negation operation. However, if we rearrange the operations used in the implementation, we can make sure that all of the operations can be carried out in n bits:

$$\sim \text{rep}(x) = \big[(2^n - 1) - \text{rep}(x)\big] + 1 \tag{7.13}$$

where $+$ and $-$ denote n-bit binary addition and subtraction, respectively.

How efficient is this implementation of the 2's complement negation operation? It appears to require a subtraction followed by an addition. However, the subtraction is particularly simple. Note that the binary representation of $2^n - 1$ is all 1's. As such, subtracting any nonnegative value less than or equal to $2^n - 1$ from $2^n - 1$ will not generate a borrow during the calculation of any of the binary digits. This means that we can perform all of the bitwise subtractions in parallel. Thus, each bit of the result can be determined by inverting the corresponding bit in the original value. These observations explain the basic algorithm used to implement 2's complement negation.

Now we return to the two issues that we dropped while we considered the normal cases: negating zero and overflow. We first consider how our negation algorithm handles zero. Suppose we apply our negation algorithm to the representation of zero. What will happen? As it turns out, our simple algorithm will produce the correct result.

Example 7.22   *Show how our negation algorithm works with the 5-bit 2's complement representation of 0.*

$$
\begin{array}{rl}
\text{rep}(0) & 00000 \\
\text{invert bits} & 11111 \\
\text{add 1} & +1 \\
\hline
\text{rep}(0) & 00000
\end{array}
$$

Because the range is (slightly) asymmetric about zero, it is possible that the negation of a number will result in an overflow. In particular the number -2^{n-1} is within the range of the representation; however, the negation of this number, 2^{n-1}, is not. As such, applying our simple algorithm to the representation of -2^{n-1} could not produce a correct result.

Example 7.23   *Show what happens if you try to negate the n-bit 2's complement representation of -2^{n-1}.*

$$
\begin{array}{rl}
\text{rep}(-2^{n-1}) & 1\,\underbrace{0\cdots0}_{n-1} \\[2mm]
\text{Invert bits} & 0\,\underbrace{1\cdots1}_{n-1} \\[2mm]
\text{Add 1} & \dfrac{+1}{1\,\underbrace{0\cdots0}_{n-1}}
\end{array}
$$

In this case, the carry-in is 1 and the carry-out is 0. Because the carry-in is not the same as the carry-out, our overflow detection rule indicates that an overflow occurred during the negation operation.

To complete the justification of our overflow detection rule, we need to demonstrate that the carry-in is the same as the carry-out whenever x and $-x$ are within the range of the representation. This demonstration is straightforward and is left as an exercise.

Addition and Subtraction in 2's Complement   An important aspect of the 2's complement representation is that all additions can be implemented using a simple n-bit, unsigned binary adder. It does not matter if either or both of the operands are negative; the result will be correct! Moreover, subtraction can be implemented by adding the negative. Overflows in an addition or subtraction can be detected by the simple overflow detection rule used for the 2's complement negation operation: carry-in $\neq$ carry-out $\equiv$ overflow.

Example 7.24   *Show how you would calculate rep(4) + rep (−2), where rep is the 4-bit 2's complement representation.*

$$
\begin{array}{rrl}
 & 1100 & \text{Carry bits} \\
\text{rep}(4) & 0100 & \\
\text{rep}(-2) & +1110 & \\
\hline
\text{rep}(2) & 0010 &
\end{array}
$$

Here, the carry-in and carry-out are both 1, and there is no overflow. Note that we ignore the carry-out in determining the final result.

Example 7.25 *Show how you would calculate rep(2) − rep(4), where rep is the 4-bit 2's complement representation.*

			0000	Carry bits
		rep(2)	0010	
rep(4)	0100	negate	+1100	
		rep(−2)	1110	

Here the carry-in and carry-out are both 0, and there is no overflow.

Example 7.26 *Show how you would calculate rep(−4) + rep (−5) where rep is the 4-bit 2's complement representation.*

	1000	Carry bits
rep(−4)	1100	
rep(−5)	+1011	
rep(7)	0111	

Here, the carry-in is 0, and the carry-out is 1. As such, the result is an overflow.

To see why all 2's complement additions can be implemented using simple binary addition, consider the cases. For the moment, we will ignore the possibility of overflow and assume that the result is in the range of the representation.

x **and** y **are nonnegative.** In this case, x and y are represented by their binary representations and their sum will be represented by its binary representation. Clearly, binary addition can be used to implement this addition.

x **is negative,** y **is nonnegative.** In this case, x is represented by the binary representation of $2^n - |x|$, and y is represented by its binary representation. Binary addition of these values results in: $2^n - |x| + y$. Now, we have two subcases to consider:

  $y - |x| \geq 0$. Here, the result is positive. We can rearrange the terms in the result indicated above to obtain $2^n + (y - |x|)$. By our assumptions, this sum is greater than or equal to 2^n. Hence, the addition will generate a carry-out (of the most significant bit) and the n-bit result will be $(y - |x|)$.

  $|x| - y > 0$. Here, the result is negative and represented by $2^n + (y - |x|)$, which is the result indicated earlier (after rearranging terms).

x **is nonnegative,** y **is negative.** This case is identical to the previous case, exchanging x and y.

x **is negative,** y **is negative.** In this case, x is represented by $2^n n - |x|$ and y is represented by $2^n - |y|$. The binary addition will result in $2^n + 2^n - (|x| + |y|)$. Because $|x| + |y| < 2^n$ (otherwise, the result would be an overflow), the result of the binary addition is greater than 2^n. As such, the addition will generate a carry, and the result of the addition will be $2^n - (|x| + |y|)$—the representation of $x + y$.

To see why our overflow rule works, we again consider the cases:

carry-in = 0, carry-out = 0. Because there is no carry-in and no carry-out, at most one of the most significant bits could be 1. In other words, we could be adding a negative value and a nonnegative value or two nonnegative values. If we are adding a negative and a nonnegative, we cannot encounter overflow. If we are adding two nonnegative values, the sum must be less than 2^{n-1} (carry-in = 0) and hence there is no overflow.

Apparent change in sign

carry-in = 0, carry-out = 1. In this case, we must be adding two negative values (i.e., the most significant bit of both must be 1). The most significant bit of the result will be 0, indicating that the result is nonnegative. This *apparent change in sign* clearly indicates overflow.

carry-in = 1, carry-out = 0. Because there is a carry-in and no carry-out, the most significant bit of both numbers must have been 0; that is, they were both nonnegative numbers. The fact that there is a carry into the most significant bit indicates that the result is greater than or equal to 2^{n-1}. (Note: This is also an apparent change in sign.)

carry-in = 1, carry-out = 1. Because there is a carry-out, at least one of the values must have a most significant bit of 1. If only one of the values has a most significant bit of 1, we are adding a negative value and a nonnegative value, and no overflow could occur. If both values have a most significant bit of 1, we are adding two negative values. Because there is a carry into the most significant bit, the most significant bit of the result will be 1. As such, the result of the addition will result in a number between $2^n - 1$ and 2^{n-1} (inclusive). This implies that the value being represented is between -1 and -2^{n-1}, and there is no overflow.

Implementation of Addition and Subtraction   Before leaving our discussion of addition and subtraction in 2's complement, we should consider implementation of these operations in detail. We begin by summarizing what we know:

- Negation can be implemented by inverting the bits and adding 1.
- Addition can be implemented using an n-bit binary adder.
- Subtraction can be implemented by negating the second argument and adding the negated value to the first.

If we simply substitute the first two rules into the second, it would seem that we should complete the negation (i.e., invert the bits and add 1) *before* starting the binary addition of the two values in the implementation of the subtraction operation. We can improve the performance of the subtraction operation if we combine the add 1 stage of the negation with the addition stage in the subtraction operation. Figure 7.12 illustrates how this can be done. In this case, we show how a simple *n*-bit adder can be extended to support both addition and subtraction of integers represented using 2's complement.

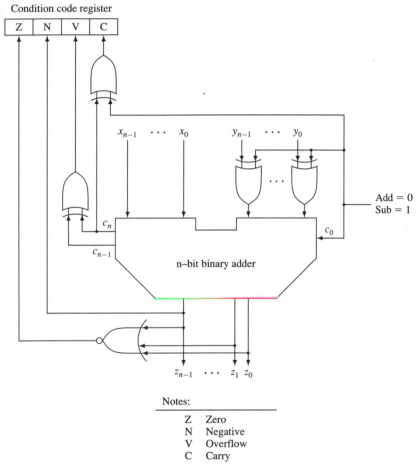

Figure 7.12 A 2's complement adder/subtractor

Condition code register

Notes:

Z	Zero
N	Negative
V	Overflow
C	Carry

The input on the right side of Figure 7.12 controls the operation performed. We will call this input the *operation input*. If the operation input is 0, the circuit shown in Figure 7.12 will add the x and y inputs; otherwise, this circuit will subtract the y input from the x input. In an addition operation, the y input is unaltered by the array of *xor* gates and the carry into the binary adder is 0. Hence, this circuit will implement 2's complement addition. On the other hand, in a subtraction, the y input will be inverted by the array of *xor* gates and the carry into the binary

Operation input

addition will be set to 1 and. In this case, the circuit implements 2's complement subtraction.

In addition to the data outputs (z_0 through z_{n-1}), the circuit in Figure 7.12 illustrates four common condition codes. The *zero (Z)* flag is set if the result is zero. The *negative (N)* flag is set if the result is negative. The *overflow (V)* flag is set if there is an overflow in a signed operation. The *carry (C)* flag is set if the operation generates a carry (unsigned addition) or borrow (unsigned subtraction).

It is important to note that the circuit shown in Figure 7.12 also implements unsigned addition and subtraction. It should be obvious that it implements unsigned addition. To see that it implements unsigned subtraction, you should compare this circuit with the circuit shown in Figure 7.7.

Size Extension/Reduction in 2's Complement   Suppose you need to change the number of bits used in the 2's complement representation of x from n bits to m bits. If m is less than n (i.e., a size reduction), then the m-bit representation of x is the least significant m bits of the n-bit representation of x. The only concern is the potential for overflow. If any of the $n + 1 - m$ most significant bits in the n-bit representation of x are different than the most significant bit in the n-bit representation, the value cannot be represented in m bits. It is helpful to think of this as a *sign compression operation* (where the most significant $n + 1 - m$ bits are compressed into a single sign bit).

Sign compression operation

On the other hand, if m is larger than n, then the least significant n bits will be the same as they were in the n-bit 2's complement representation and the most significant $m - n$ bits will be set to the most significant bit in the n-bit representation of x. Because the sign bit is replicated into the new bit positions during size extension, this operation is frequently called a *sign extend operation* (in concept, the sign bit is extended as the representation size is extended).

Sign extend operation

7.2.4 1's Complement

While 2's complement is an example of the *radix complement* representation technique, 1's complement is an example of the *diminished radix complement* representation technique. In diminished radix complement, negative values are biased by $r^n - 1$; that is, the bias used in radix complement is diminished by 1. As such, we can define the representation as follows:

Diminished radix complement

$$\text{rep}(x) = \begin{cases} \text{bin}(x) & 2^{n-1} > x \geq 0 \\ \text{bin}((2^n - 1) - |x|) & 0 > x > -2^{n-1} \end{cases} \tag{7.14}$$

In considering the 1's complement representation, note that no value is mapped to $2^n - 1$. In other words, the bit pattern consisting of n 1's is not used by the 1's complement representation. It is common to refer to this pattern as a representation of zero, that is, *negative zero*.

Negative zero

Example 7.27   *Show the 3-bit 1's complement representation.*

x	0	1	2	3	-3	-2	-1	-0
rep(x)	000	001	010	011	100	101	110	111

Negation and Absolute Value in 1's Complement   One of the primary motivations for using 1's complement is the simplicity of the negation operation. Negation can be implemented by subtracting the value from $2^n - 1$:

$$\sim \text{rep}(x) = \left[(2^n - 1) - \text{rep}(x) \right] \qquad (7.15)$$

As we have discussed, this operation can be implemented by inverting the bits in the representation of x. Because the range of the representation is symmetric about zero, negation cannot result in an overflow. The only special case involves zero—the representation of zero should not be altered by the negation operation.

As was the case in 2's complement, the absolute value operation can be implemented by testing the effective sign bit and negating the value if the sign bit indicates that the value is negative.

Addition and Subtraction in 1's Complement   In essence, 1's complement addition can be implemented using binary addition; however, the simple adder must have two extensions to support 1's complement addition. First, if the addition results in the binary representation of $2^n - 1$ (i.e., the representation of -0), the result must be adjusted back to zero. This extension is not difficult to provide, but does complicate the addition process. Second, the binary addition must be augmented with an *end-around carry*—if the binary addition of the two numbers produces a carry-out of the most significant bit, the result needs to be adjusted by adding in a 1. In concept, the carry-out of the most significant bit is brought around and added back into the result.

End-around carry

Example 7.28   *Show how to add rep(5) and rep(9), where rep is the 5-bit 1's complement representation.*

```
                  00001     Carry bits
        rep(5)    00101
        rep(9)   +01001
        rep(14)   01110
```

In this case the carry-out is 0, so there is no end-around carry.

Example 7.29   *Show how to add rep(5) and rep (−9), where rep is the 5-bit 1's com-plement representation.*

	00100	Carry bits
rep(5)	00101	
rep(−9)	+10110	
rep(−4)	11011	

Again the carry-out is 0, so there is no end-around carry.

Example 7.30   *Show how to add rep(5) and rep(−5), where rep is the 5-bit 1's comple-ment representation.*

	00000	Carry bits
rep(5)	00101	
rep(−5)	+11010	
adjust	11111	
rep(0)	00000	

Here, the simple binary addition results in the representation for −0. This result must be adjusted to the representation of 0.

Example 7.31   *Show how to add rep(−5) and rep (−9), where rep is the 5-bit 1's complement representation.*

	11110	Carry bits
rep(−5)	11010	
rep(−9)	+10110	
	10000	
end-around	+1	
rep(−14)	10001	

Here, the carry-out is 1, so there is an end-around carry.

Example 7.32   *Show how to add rep(−5) and rep (9), where rep is the 5-bit 1's comple-ment representation.*

	11000	Carry bits
rep(−5)	11010	
rep(9)	+01001	
	00011	
end-around	+1	
rep(4)	00100	

Here, the carry-out is 1, so there is an end-around carry.

To see why binary addition with an end-around carry can be used in the implementation of 1's complement addition, we consider the cases:

x and y are positive. Since x and y are both represented by their binary representations, binary addition of these values results in the representation of $x + y$. The addition will not generate a carry-out of the most significant bit because the most significant bit in the representation of x and the most significant bit in the representation of y are both zero.

x and y are negative. The binary addition produces

$$[(2^n - 1) - |x|] + [(2^n - 1) - |y|] = 2^n + 2^n - (|x| + |y|) - 2$$

Because $|x| + |y| - 1 < 2^n$, the result of this addition is greater than 2^n. As such, this computation will produce a carry-out of the most significant bit. The value actually computed is equal to

$$2^n - (|x| + |y|) - 2$$

with a carry-out of 1. When the end-around carry is completed, the result will be

$$2^n - (|x| + |y|) - 1$$

which is the representation of $x + y$.

x is positive, y is negative, $x > |y|$. In this case, the binary addition produces

$$|x| + (2^n - 1) - |y| = 2^n + (x - |y|) - 1$$

Because $|x| > |y|$, this addition produces a result that is greater than $2^n - 1$. The n-bit result is

$$x - |y| - 1$$

with a carry-out. After the end-around carry, the result is

$$x - |y|$$

which is the representation of $x + y$.

x is positive, y is negative, $x \leq |y|$. In this case, the binary addition produces

$$|x| + (2^n - 1) - |y| = 2^n - (|y| - x) - 1$$

which is the representation of $x + y$. Note that the result of the addition is less than 2^n (because $x \leq |y|$) and, as such, will not produce a carry-out of the most significant bit.

The overflow rule for 1's complement addition is essentially the same as the overflow rule for 2's complement: Overflow is equivalent to (carry-in $\neq$ carry-out). We will explore this overflow rule in more depth in the exercises.

Size Extension/Reduction The size extension and reduction operations for 1's complement are the same as they were for 2's complement. Size reduction uses a sign compression operation, while size extension uses a sign extend operation.

7.2.5 Contrasts

In this section, we have covered the four techniques commonly used in the representation of signed integers. Tables 7.1 and 7.2 summarize the 3-bit signed integer representations. In examining these tables, note that two of the representation techniques, signed magnitude and 1's complement, present a range that is symmetric about zero. Both of these representations have an unused bit pattern. In most contexts, this unused bit pattern can be treated as a representation of 0 (i.e., -0).

Table 7.1 3-bit representations (pattern to value)

	000	001	010	011	100	101	110	111
Signed magnitude	0	1	2	3	-0	-1	-2	-3
Excess 4	-4	-3	-2	-1	0	1	2	3
Excess 3	-3	-2	-1	0	1	2	3	4
2's complement	0	1	2	3	-4	-3	-2	-1
1's complement	0	1	2	3	-3	-2	-1	-0

Table 7.2 3-bit representations (value to pattern)

	-4	-3	-2	-1	0	1	2	3	4
Signed magnitude	—	111	110	101	000	001	010	011	—
Excess 4	000	001	010	011	100	101	110	111	—
Excess 3	—	000	001	010	011	100	101	110	111
2's complement	100	101	110	111	000	001	010	011	—
1's complement	—	100	101	110	000	001	010	011	—

In examining Table 7.1, you will notice that the excess representations have an interesting property: As the number gets larger, the binary number used to represent the number also increases. This aspect of excess representations makes them ideally suited for representing the exponent of a floating point number.

In contrasting the representation techniques, an important consideration is the efficiency of the operations within the representation. That is, how fast is the 2's complement negation operation relative to the negation operation that would be needed to implement negation in an excess representation? It turns out that none of the representation techniques is best at all operations. For example, the signed magnitude representation permits the most efficient negation operation (simply invert the sign bit); however, the 2's complement representation permits the most efficient addition and subtraction operations (recall that signed magnitude and excess both require a binary adder and a binary subtractor). Table 7.3 presents a relative ranking for each of the representations and each of the simple arithmetic operations.

Table 7.3   Ranking the representation techniques

	Negate	Add/subtract	Reduce/extend
Signed magnitude	1	3	1
Excess	4	3	4
2's complement	3	1	2
1's complement	2	2	2

In examining Table 7.3, it should be obvious that the excess representation technique is not particularly efficient in any of the simple arithmetic operations we have discussed. The signed magnitude representation is clearly superior in its implementation of these operations. When contrasting signed magnitude with the complement techniques, signed magnitude offers the advantages of an efficient negation operation and efficient reduction/extension operations. However, the efficiency of these operations must be contrasted with the costs associated with the addition and subtraction operations. Signed magnitude requires the presence of a binary adder as well as a binary subtractor. When the complement techniques are used, both addition and subtraction can be implemented using only a binary adder (no subtractor is needed). The complement techniques are more widely used because the costs associated with the negation and size change operations are outweighed by the costs associated with introducing a separate subtractor.

In contrasting 1's complement with 2's complement, we first note that both representations use the same size extension/reduction operations. The 1's complement negation operation, that requires only a bitwise inversion of the value, offers the more efficient negation operation (negation in 2's complement requires a bitwise inversion plus a step in which 1 is added to the result). In contrast, 2's complement offers a more efficient addition/subtraction operation. Thus, if the only concern is providing operations for signed integers, the decision to use 1's complement versus 2's complement hinges on the expected number of negations versus the expected number of additions and subtractions. If you need to support both signed and unsigned integers, the balance clearly swings to 2's complement. The circuit shown in Figure 7.12 will support unsigned addition and subtraction as well as signed addition and subtraction.

7.2.6 Arithmetic Shift Operations

We conclude our discussion of signed integer representations by considering the arithmetic shift operations typically provided by modern computers. If you consider the representation of unsigned integers, the right and left shift operations can be used to implement divisions and multiplications by powers of two. (Shifting to the right can be used for divisions; shifting to the left can be used for multiplications.) It turns out that this technique can be used for signed integers if the shift operations are modified slightly. Many machines provide *arithmetic shifts* that incorporate the needed modifications.

Multiplying a signed number by a power of two can be accomplished by shifting the 2's complement representation of the value to the left and filling the vacated bit positions with zero. Hence, an arithmetic shift to the left can be implemented using a left shift with zero fill. The only modification needed involves the detection of overflow. If the sign bit ever changes during this shifting operation, the value cannot be stored in the space that has been allotted for it. Therefore, the overflow flag (V) should be set if the sign bit ever changes during an arithmetic shift to the left.

Sign extension

Dividing a signed number by a power of two can be accomplished by shifting the 2's complement representation of the value to the right and filling the vacated bit positions with the old value of the sign bit. For obvious reasons, this is called a right shift with *sign extension*. There is one case that is not covered by this operation. Suppose you divide the representation of -1 by 2 using an arithmetic shift to the right. The result will be the representation of -1, not the representation of 0 as it should be. It is not difficult to deal with this problem if you remember that the basic right-shift operation stores the value of the last bit shifted out of the word in the carry flag (C). We will leave this as an exercise.

7.3 SUMMARY

The most important aspect of number representations is a perspective. Representations must be studied by considering the format of the representation and the implementation of the operations that will be used to manipulate values stored in the representation. A representation format cannot be studied without also studying the effect of the format on manipulations.

The second most important aspect of number representations is that they are finite. In the case of integer representations, this means that operations may result in overflow. It also means that simple properties of operations (e.g., associativity of addition) do not necessarily hold.

Beyond these issues, we also discussed why 2's complement is the most popular technique for representing signed integers. Along these lines, the fact that the same hardware can be used for signed and unsigned operations is an important advantage of the 2's complement technique.

7.3.1 Additional Reading

Much of the presentation in this chapter has been based on the material contained in *Introduction to Arithmetic for Digital Systems Designers* by Shlomo Waser and Michael J. Flynn (Holt, Rinehart & Winston, 1982). If you are interested in learning more about number representations, I highly recommend this book. In addition, *Seminumerical Algorithms* (the second volume in the series) by Donald Knuth (Addison-Wesley Publishing 1968, 1973) will provide you with more background on the material presented in this chapter.

7.3.2 Terminology

- Range and overflow
- Carry
- Ripple-carry adders, Conditional sum adders, Lookahead-carry adders
- Carry-in, Carry-out
- Size extension, Size reduction
- Sign bit, Signed magnitude
- Negative zero
- Bias, Excess
- Complement, Radix complement, Diminished radix complement
- 2's complement, 1's complement
- Effective sign bit, Inverse sign bit
- End-around carry
- Apparent change in sign

7.3.3 Review Questions

1. How is a conditional sum adder an improvement on a ripple-carry adder?
2. What is a lookahead-carry adder? What are the advantages and disadvantages of a lookahead-carry adder?
3. What is the purpose of an add-with-carry instruction?
4. Explain the difference between an overflow and an underflow.
5. What does the term *negative zero* mean? Which representations have a negative zero?
6. To what extent do 2's complement and 1's complement have a sign bit?
7. State the overflow detection rule for 2's complement.

7.4 EXERCISES

1. Show the conditional sums that would be generated in adding 11001100 to 10101101 using a conditional sum adder. You should structure your answer along the lines of Examples 7.2 and 7.4.
2. Prove that the circuit shown in Figure 7.6 correctly implements a full subtractor.
3. Using induction on n, the number of bits, prove that the circuit shown in Figure 7.7 correctly implements an n-bit binary subtractor.
4. Example 7.11 assumes that the result will fit in a 32-bit register. Show how you could rewrite the code shown in Example 7.11 without this assumption.

Assume that all registers are 32 bits and that the ALU provides a 32-bit addition operation.

5. In this exercise, we consider the development of a division algorithm for unsigned integers.

   a. Give an algorithm for unsigned binary division along the lines of the multiplication algorithm shown in Figure 7.8

   b. Show how you could implement your algorithm in assembly language.

6. Show the 4-bit excess 24 representation. Why do you think it would not be a good idea to use excess 24 with a word size of 4 bits?

7. When we discussed negation in excess representations, we pointed out that overflow is equivalent to overflow in the last binary operation performed. We also pointed out that when the bias is 2^{n-1} we do not need to use the full binary subtraction in the negation of a negative number. Explain how overflow can be detected in this case.

8. In this exercise, we consider addition in an excess representation.

   a. Show how to perform addition in excess carefully (i.e., without overflow in the intermediate operations).

   b. Given your addition algorithm, how could you detect overflow?

   c. Can your addition algorithm be simplified if the bias is 2^{n-1}? If so, explain the simplification.

9. As we discussed in the text, the radix complement technique can be used with any radix. In this exercise, we examine radix complement with a radix of 8, that is, 8's complement. Suppose each word consists of four octal digits.

   a. Give the representation for each of the following numbers:
      1.) 22
      2.) −22
      3.) 15
      4.) −15

   b. What is the range of the representation?

10. Repeat exercise 9 using a radix of 10.

11. The diminished radix complement technique can also be used with any radix. In this exercise, we consider using this representation technique with a radix of 8, that is, 7's complement. As with the previous exercise, suppose each word consists of four octal digits.

    a. Give the representation for each of the following numbers:
       1.) 22
       2.) −22
       3.) 15
       4.) −15

    b. What is the range of the representation?

12. Repeat exercise 11 using a radix of 10.

13. Prove (using induction on n) that subtracting any nonnegative value less than or equal to $2^n - 1$ from $2^n - 1$ using an n-bit binary subtractor will not generate a borrow in any binary digit.

14. Explain why our simple algorithm for implementing the 2's complement negation operation will result in the same value for the carry-in and carry-out whenever the number and its negation are within the range of the representation. (It may be helpful to notice that the carry-in and carry-out are both 0, unless the value being negated is zero.)

15. Explain the difficulties that would be encountered if a designer tried to use a conditional sum adder to implement 2's complement addition.

16. Explain why the circuit shown in Figure 7.12 will generate an overflow ($c_{n-1} \neq c_n$) only if the naive algorithm (the algorithm that completes the negation before starting the addition) generates an overflow.

17. It is possible that the circuit shown in Figure 7.12 will not generate an overflow when the naive algorithm would generate an overflow. In particular, it is possible that the negation step might overflow if it is completed before starting the addition step. Explain, using detailed examples, how it would be possible for the circuit shown in Figure 7.12 to "miss" an overflow. Is it possible that these "missed" overflows would prove to be a problem?

18. Explain why our implementation of the 2's complement size extension operation (which is based on a sign extend) works correctly. In writing this explanation, it may be helpful to introduce some more notation. In particular, you need to be a bit more careful about indicating the number of bits used in the representation. For example, you might use $\text{rep}_n(x)$ to denote the n-bit 2's complement representation of x. By explicitly indicating the number of bits used in the representation, you can describe the size extension operation as a mapping from $\text{rep}_n(x)$ to $\text{rep}_m(x)$, where $m > n$.

    In explaining why our implementation of size extension is correct, you should consider two cases: x is negative, and x is nonnegative.

19. In the text, we suggested that the overflow rule for 1's complement is essentially the same as that for 2's complement: overflow $\equiv$ carry-in $\neq$ carry-out. In this rule does carry-in mean the carry into the most significant bit during the first binary addition or during end-around carry?

20. Explain why the overflow detection rule works for 1's complement. (Present a case analysis of 1's complement addition.)

21. Suppose that you are working on a 2's complement machine that provides an arithmetic right-shift operation. This operation performs a "right shift with sign extension." Explain how this operation can be used to implement integer division by a power of two. Be certain to consider $-9/2^3$, which should result in -1, and $-9/2^4$, which should result in 0.

22. Suppose you need to implement 2's complement multiplication using unsigned multiplication. You could simply negate the operands if they are

negative, multiply the positive values, and negate the result if the signs of the operands are different. However, there is a faster algorithm that you can use for 2's complement. The algorithm is based on the algorithm presented in Figure 7.8. To accommodate signed values, the multiplicand is initially sign extended to $2n$ bits. In addition, the **for** loop is only executed $n - 1$ times. After the loop completes, if the multiplier is 1 (i.e., the original multiplier was negative), the final value of the multiplicand is subtracted from the product.

Using Example 7.10 as a guide, show how this algorithm will compute each of the following products when n is 4:

a.   Multiplicand = -2; multiplier = 3

b.   Multiplicand = 2; multiplier = -3

c.   Multiplicand = -2; multiplier = -3

23.   Describe how you would modify the algorithm shown in Figure 7.9 to accommodate signed numbers. Illustrate how your algorithm will compute the products indicated in exercise 22.

24.   Explain why the algorithm described in exercise 22 works correctly. You should approach this exercise by considering the four possible cases for the operands. Warning: the cases in which the multiplicand is negative are complicated by the need to ignore the high-order bits that are generated during the addition steps.

FLOATING POINT NUMBERS

CHAPTER 8

In Chapter 7, we considered techniques for representing signed and unsigned integer values. In this chapter, we consider the representation of values with fractional parts, for example, 3½. We begin by introducing fixed point representations, a generalization of simple integer representations. We then consider floating point representation techniques with an emphasis on the IEEE (Institute of Electrical and Electronics Engineers) 754 floating point standard. We conclude with a brief discussion of floating point coprocessors.

8.1 FIXED POINT REPRESENTATIONS

Suppose you have an application that requires fractional values, for example, ½, ¾, ⁻⅞. Alternatively, suppose you have an application that requires very large integers—larger than the largest integer on the machine that you are using. As long as you do not need to use very small numbers and very large numbers in the same application, you could scale all of the numbers in your program by an appropriate constant and use integers for their representation.

In general, the number n is represented by $n \times s$, where s is the *scale factor*. **Scale factor** This representation technique is called *fixed point* because it is as if there were a radix point at a fixed location in the representation of every number. If the scale factor is larger than 1, this technique can be used to represent fractional values. If the scale factor is less than 1, this techniques can be used to represent very large values. Finally, integers are simply fixed point numbers with a scale factor of 1. Figure 8.1 illustrates the concept of a fixed radix point.

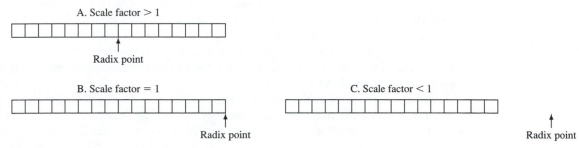

Figure 8.1   Fixed point representations

Example 8.1   *Suppose you have an application that needs to manipulate values between 1 and −1 (noninclusive). Further, suppose that your application needs to store each value in one byte (8 bits). Explain how you would represent these values.*

The 8-bit 2's complement representation provides a range of −128 to 127. Using this representation with a scale factor of 128, provides a range from −1 to 127/128. The following table gives a short list of values and their decimal representations (the binary representations are defined by the 8-bit 2's complement representations).

Value	Representation (in signed decimal)
1/64	2
3/32	12
7/32	28
−5/32	−20
−5/16	−40
1/2	64

Example 8.2   *Suppose you have an application that needs to manipulate nonnegative numbers that may be close to 2048. Further, suppose that your application needs to store each value in one byte (8 bits). Explain how you would represent these values.*

The 8-bit unsigned binary representation provides a range of 0 to 255. Using a scale factor of 1/8 (.125), we obtain a range of 0 to 2040. The following table give a short list of values and their decimal representations.

Value	Representation (in signed decimal)
96	12
320	40
1200	150

In considering the representations described in Examples 8.1 and 8.2, note that there are numbers within the range of the representation that do not have an exact representation. For example, the representation scheme described in Example 8.2 does not provide a representation for 100. The closest numbers that have exact representations are 96 and 104. In this case, 100 falls in the gap between 96 and 104. Given a representation scheme, the *gap* is the distance between successive values that have exact representations. In a fixed point representation, the gap is simply the inverse of the scale factor.

Gap

When a value falls in the gap between two numbers that have exact representations, the value must be represented by one of the numbers that has an exact representation. The mapping from a number that does not have an exact representation to a number that does is called *rounding*. Rounding introduces inaccuracies in the representation. *Precision* refers to the degree to which a representation can accurately represent values. Precision is characterized by the number of bits used in the representation.

Example 8.3 *Characterize the representations described in Examples 8.1 and 8.2 in terms of gap and precision.*

Both representations have a precision of 8 bits. The representation described in Example 8.1 has a gap of $1/128$, while the representation described in Example 8.2 has a gap of 8.

If two numbers are represented using the same scale factor, addition, subtraction, and negation can be implemented using the basic addition, subtraction, and negation value operations provided by the machine. In contrast, the results of multiplication and division operations must be corrected. These corrections are performed by dividing or multiplying by the scale factor after performing the multiplication or division. If the scale factor is a power of two, these corrections can be performed efficiently using shift operations. The relevant identities are presented in Table 8.1.

Table 8.1 Identities associated with fixed point representations

$$(a \times s) + (b \times s) = (a + b) \times s$$
$$(a \times s) - (b \times s) = (a - b) \times s$$
$$-(a \times s) = -a \times s$$
$$((a \times s) \cdot (b \times s))/s = (a \cdot b) \times s$$
$$((a \times s)/(b \times s)) \cdot s = (a/b) \times s$$

Example 8.4 *Using the representation described in Example 8.1, describe how to perform the following calculations*

1. $3/32 - 5/16$.
2. $1/2 \cdot 5/16$.

1. The representation of 3/32 is 12, and the representation of 5/16 is 40. As such, the calculation proceeds by subtracting 40 from 12, which results in -28, the representation of $-7/32$.
2. The representation of 1/2 is 64, and the representation of 5/16 is 40. Multiplying 64 by 40, we obtain 2560. At this point we need to correct the result by dividing by 128 (the scale factor). This division results in the value 20, the representation of 5/32.

8.2 FLOATING POINT NUMBERS

Fixed point representations may be adequate for many applications, but the limited range may be unacceptable in other applications. In particular, you cannot represent numbers with very large and very small magnitudes using a simple fixed point representation unless you are willing to use a very large number of bits in the representation. In this section, we consider an alternative to fixed point representations—floating point representations—which has been developed to increase the range of numbers that can be represented using a "reasonable" number of bits. Floating point representations are similar to scientific notation. As such, we begin our coverage of floating point representations by reviewing scientific notation.

8.2.1 Scientific Notation

In scientific work, numbers with very large magnitudes arise frequently: the speed of light (in meters per second), the number of atoms in a mole, the number of microseconds in a year, and so forth. Similarly, numbers with very small magnitudes arise frequently: the mass of a helium atom (in grams), the volume of a helium atom (in cubic centimeters), and so forth. Scientific notation was developed to deal with the problems associated with discussing numbers that have very large or very small magnitudes, in particular, with the problem of describing such numbers in a succinct fashion. In scientific notation, numbers are written as a product of a decimal number and an integer power of 10. The convenience of scientific notation is easily demonstrated by considering how difficult it would be to write the number 3.45×10^{78} using a simple positional notation.

One potential problem associated with scientific notation is the lack of a unique representation. For example, 3.45×10^{78} and $.000345 \times 10^{82}$ are both valid representations for the same number. This complicates the implementation of arithmetic operations and comparisons. The problem is usually avoided by introducing a *normal form*, which defines a unique representation. In scientific notation, it is common to insist that the decimal number have exactly one nonzero digit to the left of the decimal point, unless the number being represented is zero.

Because zeros are not used as place holders when numbers are written in scientific notation, they can be used to express the *precision* of the number. For example, suppose a friend tells you that there were 2,000 people at the last meeting of your local ACM (Association for Computing Machinery) chapter. Does that mean that there were *about* 2,000 people there or *exactly* 2,000 people? Knowing how people use numbers, you might guess that your friend means about 2,000. Does "about 2,000" mean more than 1,500 but less than 2,500 or more than 1,950 but less than 2,050? In particular, how precise is the number? Scientific notation avoids this difficulty by introducing the concept of *significant digits*. For example, the following are all representations of 2,000:

- 2.0×10^3
- 2.00×10^3
- 2.000×10^3

Normal form

Precision

Significant digits

In writing 2.0, you imply that the number is between 1.95 and 2.05 (numbers smaller than 1.95 would be rounded to 1.9, numbers larger than 2.05 would be rounded to 2.1). In writing 2.00, you imply that the number is between 1.995 and 2.005. In this way, you can express the accuracy of a number by the number of significant digits you write.

8.2.2 Early Floating Point Formats

In this section, we introduce the two of the early floating point formats: the format used on the IBM 360/370 and the format used in the DEC PDP/11 and Vax. These formats provide background for the format used in the IEEE 754 floating point standard that we will discuss in the next section.

Every number written in scientific notation is really a triple: the decimal number, the base of the exponent, and the exponent. For example, 3.45×10^{78} is the triple $\langle 3.45, 10, 78 \rangle$. For the remainder of this discussion, we will call these numbers the *significand*, the *base*, and the *exponent*, respectively. The names *base* and *exponent* should be obvious. The name *significand* comes from the fact that this number is used to express the number and value of the significant digits. In the case of the number 3.45×10^{78}, 3.45 is the significand, 10 is the base, and 78 is the exponent. In many contexts, the exponent is called the *characteristic*, and the significand is called the *mantissa*.

Significand

Base

Exponent

Characteristic

Mantissa

The representation of floating point numbers becomes a problem of representing the significand, the base, and the exponent. Typically, the base is a constant fixed by the representation and, as such, does not need to be stored explicitly with the value. In scientific notation, for example, we use a base of 10. In general, the significand is a signed fixed point number, while the exponent is a signed integer.

IBM System 360/370   The IBM System 360/370 (short) format is shown in Figure 8.2. In this case, the base of the exponent is 16, the exponent is represented using excess 64, and the significand is stored as a fractional value represented using signed magnitude.

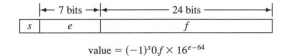

$$\text{value} = (-1)^s 0.f \times 16^{e-64}$$

Figure 8.2   The IBM System 360/370 floating point format

Example 8.5   *Show how you would represent −7.6875 using the IBM 360/370 floating point format.*

$$7.6875_{10} = 111.1011_2$$
$$= 0.01111011_2 \times 16^1$$
$$= 0.01111011_2 \times 16^{65_{10} - 64_{10}}$$
$$= 0.01111011_2 \times 16^{1000001_2 - 64_{10}}$$

As such, the fraction, f, is $0111110110\cdots0$ and the exponent, e, is 1000001. Because the significand is negative, the sign bit, s, is 1. Thus -7.6875_{10} can be represented by:

| 1 | 1000001 | 01111011000000000000000 |

Example 8.6   *Show how you would represent 0.0390625 using the IBM 360/370 floating point format.*

$$0.0390625_{10} = 0.0000101_2 \times 16^0$$
$$= 0.0000101_2 \times 16^{64_{10} - 64_{10}}$$
$$= 0.0000101_2 \times 16^{1000000_2 - 64_{10}}$$

which leads to the following bit pattern:

| 0 | 1000000 | 00001010000000000000000 |

Normal form

It turns out there are many different bit patterns that we could have used to represent these two numbers. Just like scientific notation, there is a *normal form* for the IBM 360 floating point representation. In the IBM representation, normal form requires that there be a 1 in the first 4 bits of the fraction unless the number being represented is zero. As such, the first example is in normal form; however, the second is not.

Example 8.7   *Show how you would represent 0.0390625 in normal form using the IBM 360/370 floating point format.*

$$0.0390625_{10} = 0.0000101_2$$
$$= 0.101_2 \times 16^{-1}$$
$$= 0.101_2 \times 16^{63_{10} - 64_{10}}$$
$$= 0.101_2 \times 16^{0111111_2 - 64_{10}}$$

Thus, 0.0390625_{10} can be represented by

| 0 | 0111111 | 10100000000000000000000000 |

DEC PDP 11/Vax   The DEC single-precision, 32-bit, floating point format is shown in Figure 8.3. This format is used on both the PDP 11 and the Vax. As was the case in the IBM format, the DEC format uses excess notation (in this case, excess 128) to store the exponent, and the significand is stored using signed magnitude. There are two important differences between the IBM and DEC formats. First, note that DEC uses a base of 2 (in contrast, IBM uses a base of 16). Second, note the 1 that appears directly to the right of the radix point in the significand—this bit does not appear explicitly in the fraction and is called the *hidden bit*.

Hidden bit

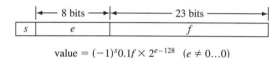

$$\text{value} = (-1)^s 0.1f \times 2^{e-128} \quad (e \neq 0...0)$$

Figure 8.3   The DEC (single-precision) floating point format

Example 8.8   *Show how you would represent 7.6875 using the DEC single-precision floating point representation.*

$$7.6875_{10} = 111.1011_2$$
$$= 0.1111011_2 \times 2^3$$
$$= 0.1111011_2 \times 2^{131_{10} - 128_{10}}$$
$$= 0.1111011_2 \times 2^{10000011_2 - 128_{10}}$$

As such, the fraction, f, is $1110110\cdots0$ (note that the bit just to the right of the radix point is not stored in the fraction) and the exponent, e, is 10000011. Because the number is positive, the sign bit is 0.

| 0 | 10000011 | 11101100000000000000000 |

Example 8.9   *Show how you would represent 0.0390625 using the DEC single-precision floating point format.*

$$0.0390625_{10} = 0.0000101_2$$
$$= 0.101_2 \times 2^{-4}$$
$$= 0.101_2 \times 2^{124_{10} - 128_{10}}$$
$$= 0.101_2 \times 2^{01111100_2 - 128_{10}}$$

As such, the fraction, f, is $0100 \cdots 0$ (again, the 1 immediately to the right of the radix point has been dropped) and the exponent, e, is 01111100. Because the number is positive, the sign bit is 0.

0	01111100	01000000000000000000000

In effect, the hidden bit forces normalization of values stored using this format. In particular, we had no choice in determining the values for the fields in the DEC representation. The hidden bit does introduce one minor problem: How do you represent zero? The problem is that zero does not have a 1 to hide. In the DEC format, if the exponent, e, is all 0's and the sign bit, s, is 0, the pattern represents zero (regardless of the bits in the fraction, f). The pattern with an exponent of 0 and sign bit of 1 is reserved (it is not a representation of -0).

8.2.3 The IEEE 754 Floating Point Standard

Figure 8.4 shows the 32-bit, single-precision format of the IEEE 754 floating point standard. As you can see, this format is very similar to the DEC format. In examining this format, there are two obvious differences between this format and the DEC format: The hidden bit of the IEEE format is to the left of the radix point, and the IEEE format stores the exponent using excess 127 instead of excess 128. Beyond these differences, the IEEE format includes a representation for -0, a mechanism for representing values that are very close to zero ("denormals"), representations for ∞ and $-\infty$, and bit patterns that are specifically disallowed in the representation of numbers (NaNs).

Unlike the DEC format, the representation of 0 in the IEEE format is very specific—in addition to an exponent field of 0's, all bits in the fraction must be

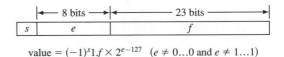

$$value = (-1)^s 1.f \times 2^{e-127} \quad (e \neq 0...0 \text{ and } e \neq 1...1)$$

Figure 8.4   IEEE 754 standard single-precision floating point format

0. If the sign bit is 1 and all other bits are zero, the pattern represents -0. The remaining patterns with an exponent field of 0's are called *denormals*. The value represented by a denormal is given by the following formula:

Denormals

$$\text{value} = (-1)^s 0.f \times 2^{-126}$$

Notice that the hidden bit is no longer present in the formula. Denormals provide a mechanism for representing values that are very close to zero. They are called denormals because the values are not represented in the normalized format (with a 1 to the left of the radix point).

Bit patterns with an exponent field of $1 \ldots 1$ represent reserved patterns. If the exponent field is all 1's and the fraction field is all 0's, the pattern is interpreted as ∞ (the sign bit is used to distinguish between $+\infty$ and $-\infty$). If the exponent field is all 1's and the fraction field is anything other than all 0's, the pattern is not a valid number representation. These patterns are commonly called NaNs for *not a number*. NaNs arise during illegal operations (e.g., $\sqrt{-5}$). Table 8.2 summarizes these aspects of the IEEE 754 format and contrasts the IEEE format and the DEC format.

NaN $\equiv$ not a number

Table 8.2 The IEEE 754 and DEC floating point formats

s	e	f	IEEE	DEC
1	$1 \ldots 11$	$1 \ldots 11$		
$\vdots$	$\vdots$	$\vdots$	NaN	
1	$1 \ldots 11$	$1 \ldots 11$		
1	$1 \ldots 11$	$1 \ldots 11$	$-\infty$	numbers
1	$1 \ldots 10$	$1 \ldots 10$		
$\vdots$	$\vdots$	$\vdots$	numbers	
1	$1 \ldots 01$	$1 \ldots 01$		
1	$0 \ldots 00$	$1 \ldots 11$		
$\vdots$	$\vdots$	$\vdots$	denormals	reserved
1	$0 \ldots 00$	$0 \ldots 01$		
1	$0 \ldots 00$	$0 \ldots 00$	-0	
0	$0 \ldots 00$	$0 \ldots 00$	$+0$	
0	$0 \ldots 00$	$0 \ldots 01$		
$\vdots$	$\vdots$	$\vdots$	denormals	0
0	$0 \ldots 00$	$1 \ldots 11$		
0	$0 \ldots 01$			
$\vdots$	$\vdots$	anything	numbers	
0	$1 \ldots 10$			
0	$1 \ldots 11$	$0 \ldots 00$	$+\infty$	numbers
0	$1 \ldots 11$	$0 \ldots 01$		
$\vdots$	$\vdots$	$\vdots$	NaN	
0	$1 \ldots 11$	$1 \ldots 11$		

8.2.4 Simple Arithmetic Operations

Pre-normalization

For the most part, the algorithms used to perform simple arithmetic operations are the same as the algorithms that you would use given two numbers in scientific notation. Figure 8.5 presents a simple algorithm to multiply two numbers in scientific notation. The first step, normalize the operands, is often called *pre-normalization*. This step is not needed if both operands are already in normal form.

1   Normalize the operands.
2   Add the exponents.
3   Multiply the significands.
4   Normalize the result.

Figure 8.5 Floating point multiplication

Example 8.10   *Show how to multiply 57 and 2.3 × 10⁴ using the algorithm shown in Figure 8.5.*

$$57 \cdot (2.3 \times 10^4)$$

1	Normalize the operands.	$(5.7 \times 10^1) \cdot (2.3 \times 10^4)$
2	Add the exponents.	$(5.7 \cdot 2.3) \times 10^5$
3	Multiply the significands.	13.11×10^5
4	Normalize the result.	1.3×10^6

Extended precision

Note that the result of the multiplication (step 2) contains four significant digits while the operands are specified with two significant digits. The multiplication is performed in *extended precision*. In the last step, normalization, the number of significant digits is reduced as the exponent is adjusted to put the number into normal form.

Figure 8.6 illustrates how our multiplication algorithm could be implemented for the IEEE 754 standard, single-precision, floating point format. To simplify the illustration, we assume that both operands are valid numbers, that neither operand is zero, that neither operand is a denormal, and that neither operand is infinite. Because the operands are already in normal form, there is no need for a pre-normalization step. The sign of the result is determined by taking the exclusive or of the sign bits from the two operands. The add and subtract operations implement the addition of the exponents (using excess-127 arithmetic). The multiply operation implements the multiplication of the significands. Note that the hidden bit is introduced just prior to the multiplication. The multiplication is simple unsigned integer multiplication. Only the most significant 25 bits of the multiplication are retained. Discarding the low-order 23 bits is equivalent to dividing the result by 2^{23}. This division is needed because we are really implementing a fixed point multiplication with a scale factor of 2^{23}. The 8-bit exponent and the most significant 25 bits of the multiplication are passed to a component that normalizes the result. We leave the details of the normalization process as an exercise.

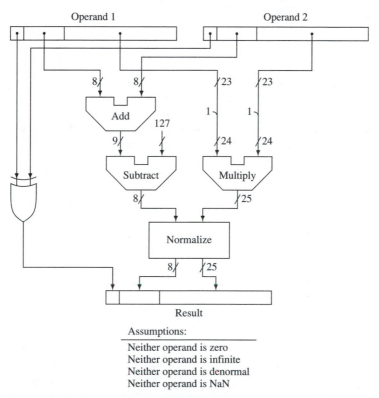

Figure 8.6 Multiplication for the IEEE 754 standard (most common case only)

Addition and subtraction are complicated by the fact that the exponents of the two numbers must be the same before you can manipulate the significands. Figure 8.7 presents an algorithm to add two numbers in scientific notation. Like the multiplication algorithm, this algorithm begins with a pre-normalization step that is not needed if the numbers are already in normal form.

1. Normalize the operands.
2. Obtain a common exponent.
3. Add the significands.
4. Normalize the result.

Figure 8.7 Floating point addition

Example 8.11   *Show how to add 9.8×10^4 and 3.4×10^3 using the algorithm presented in Figure 8.7.*

1.	Normalize the operands.	$(9.8 \times 10^4) + (3.4 \times 10^3)$
2.	Obtain a common exponent.	$(9.8 \times 10^4) + (.34 \times 10^4)$
3.	Add the significands.	(10.14×10^4)
4.	Normalize the result.	(1.0×10^5)

Note that we adjust the number with the smaller exponent to obtain a common exponent in step 2. Remember that the significand is stored in a fixed number of bits. As such, adjusting the exponent may result in the loss of bits in the significand. Here it is better to lose bits in the significand of the number with the smaller exponent because these bits are not as significant in the result.

Figure 8.8 presents a code fragment that adjusts the number with the smaller exponent so that both numbers have the same exponent. Because the exponents are typically stored using an *excess* representation, these numbers can be treated as unsigned numbers in this code.

Excess

```
/* let s1 and s2 be the (fixed point) significands and
      e1 and e2 be the exponents (in excess) */
if( e1 > e2 ) {
    swap( e1, e2 );
    swap( s1, s2 );
}
/* shift the first significand by e2 − e1 */
s1 = s1 >> (e2 − e1);
```

Figure 8.8   Adjusting numbers during a floating point add

8.2.5 Consequences of Finite Representation

When you work with floating point numbers, it is important to remember that the representation is finite. The finite aspect of floating point representations has three important consequences that we express in terms of range, precision, and gap.

Range and Overflow   As with any technique for representing numbers, the range of a floating point representation is defined by the smallest and largest values that can be represented. Because floating point formats use a signed magnitude representation, we only need to specify the largest value—the smallest is determined by negating the largest.

Example 8.12   *What is the largest number in the single-precision format of the IEEE 754 standard?*

In the single-precision format, the largest exponent is established by setting the e field to seven 1s followed by a single 0 (11111110_2)—recall, patterns in which the e field is all 1s are reserved by the representation. This binary value corresponds to the decimal value 254. Because exponents are stored in excess 127, we conclude that the largest exponent that can be represented using the single-precision format is 127.

The largest fractional part is established by setting the f field to twenty-three 1s. This represents a fractional part of $1 - 2^{-23}$. For most practical purposes, 2^{-23} is so close to zero that it can be ignored. As such, we can think of the fractional part as 1. Recalling the hidden bit, we conclude that the largest number that can be represented using the IEEE 754 single-precision floating point format is slightly less than

$$2 \times 2^{127} = 2^{128}$$

As this example illustrates, the range of a floating point representation is effectively determined by the number of bits reserved for the representation of the exponent. As was the case with fixed point representations, overflow occurs when the result of an operation exceeds the range of the representation.

Precision, Gap, Rounding, and Underflow   Just as the precision of a number given in scientific notation is determined by the number of significant digits, the *precision* of a number given in a floating point representation is determined by   Precision
the number of bits allocated for the significand. As such, the IEEE 754 single-precision format provides 24 bits of precision (23 bits for denormals).

Single-precision refers to the number of bits used in the representation of a floating point value. In contrast to the single-precision formats that we have discussed, most floating point representations have a corresponding *double-precision* format.   Double-precision
As an example, Figure 8.9 presents the IEEE 754 double-precision format. In this case, the single-precision format uses 32 bits, while the double-precision format uses 64 bits (i.e., double-precision doubles the number of bits used in the representation). In further contrasting the single- and double-precision formats, note that the number of bits used in the representation of the significand, that is, the precision, has more than doubled (from 23 bits to 52 bits). This has a significant impact on the precision of the representation, and, as such, it is reasonable to emphasize the increase in precision by referring to this representation as *double-precision*.

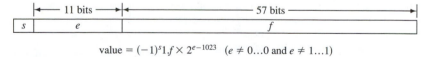

value = $(-1)^s 1.f \times 2^{e-1023}$ ($e \neq 0...0$ and $e \neq 1...1$)

Figure 8.9   IEEE 754 standard double-precision floating point format

The notion of precision is closely related to the gaps present in the representation. The *gap* is the difference between successive numbers in a floating point   Gap
representation. In fixed point representations, the gap is fixed as the inverse of the

scale factor. In floating point representations, the gap depends on the position of the numbers within the range. For example, the gap in the IEEE 754 floating point standard is determined by the following formula

$$\text{gap}(x) = 2^{e-23} \tag{8.1}$$

where e is the exponent used in the representation of x.

Example 8.13   *What is the number immediately after 1.5 in the single-precision format of the IEEE 754 standard?*

$1.5_{10} = 1.1_2$, and, as such, the exponent, e, in the single-precision format is zero and the gap is 2^{-23}. Thus, the next number is $1.5 + 2^{-23}$.

Example 8.14   *What is the number immediately after 10.5 in the single-precision format of the IEEE 754 standard?*

$1.5_{10} = 1010.1_2 = 1.010 \times 2^3$, and, as such, the exponent, e, in the single-precision format is 3 and the gap is 2^{-20}. Thus, the next number is $10.5 + 2^{-20}$.

In this case, if a number smaller than 2^{-20} is added to 10.5, the significant digits in the smaller number will be lost when the exponent is adjusted to the value of the larger exponent.

Our discussion of the gap has emphasized the gap between successive numbers. Alternatively, the gap can be related to the fact that there is a fixed number of values between any two powers of 2. For example, in the IEEE 754 single-precision format, there are 2^{23} numbers between any two powers of 2. In other words, there are 2^{23} numbers between 1/2 and 1 and 2^{23} numbers between 1024 and 2048.

Rounding

When an operation results in a value that is in the gap between two consecutive numbers in the representation, the result must be mapped to one of the numbers. This mapping is called *rounding*. Four different techniques for rounding a number are described in Table 8.3.

Table 8.3   Rounding modes

Rounding mode	Description
Unbiased	Round to the nearest number in the representation. In the case of a tie, round to the even number.
Truncation	Round toward zero.
Round up	Round toward $+\infty$.
Round down	Round toward $-\infty$.

Underflow

When a rounding operation maps a nonzero value to zero, it is called an *underflow*. The denormals of the IEEE 754 standard were introduced to reduce the gap for numbers that are very close to zero and, hence, to reduce the possibility of underflow. Without denormals, the number immediately after zero in the single-precision format would have been 1.0×2^{-126}. In other words, the gap at 0 would have been 2^{-126}. However, the gap at 1.0×2^{-126} is $2^{-126-23} = 2^{-149}$. The least significant bits of the significand cannot be used to distinguish numbers from zero, but they can be used to distinguish numbers in all other situations—this is an immediate consequence of the hidden bit. In the IEEE 754 standard, denormals do not have a hidden bit, and, as such, the immediate successor to zero is $2^{-126-23} = 2^{-149}$.

Extended Temporaries   The IEEE 754 floating point standard recommends that floating point operations be performed using *extended precision temporaries*. The standard recommends two extended precision formats, one for the single-precision format and another for the double-precision format. Figure 8.10 presents an extended precision format based on the recommendations associated with the single-precision format. In contrasting this format with the single-precision format shown in Figure 8.4, note that the number of bits allocated for the exponent has been increased from 8 to 11 and that the number of bits used for the fractional part of the significand has been increased from 23 to 31. In addition, note that the hidden bit is explicit. (The illustration shows the hidden bit as 1; however, this will be 0 whenever the number is a *denormal*.) Finally, note that this representation uses 44 bits. This might create a problem if there were a need to store these values into the memory of the machine (44 is not a multiple of 8 or 16). However, this representation is intended to be used as a temporary format during floating point operations and, as such, should not need to be stored in memory.

Extended precision temporaries

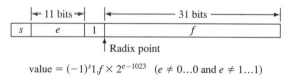

$$\text{value} = (-1)^{s} 1.f \times 2^{e-1023} \quad (e \neq 0...0 \text{ and } e \neq 1...1)$$

Figure 8.10   An extended precision format

Extended temporaries are intended to be used for sequences of operations. Because they increase the range of the representation, using extended temporaries may mask overflows that would otherwise occur. Because they increase the precision of the representation, using extended temporaries may mask underflows and accumulated rounding errors that would otherwise occur.

To illustrate the masking of an overflow, consider the operations that need to be performed to compute

$$(A * B) * C$$

Assume that A and B are very large—large enough that $A * B$ will overflow the basic representation used for floating point numbers. Further, assume that $C = 1/B$. Now, if we perform the preceding computation using the basic (single-precision) representation, the result will be ∞—$A * B = \infty$ (because of the overflow) and $\infty * C = \infty$. On the other hand, if we use extended temporaries in the calculation, we should get a result that is very close to A. In this case, the calculation of $A * B$ will be close to the actual value (perhaps not exactly $A * B$ because of rounding) and, as such, multiplying by C will result in a value that is very close to A.

8.3 FLOATING POINT COPROCESSORS

A coprocessor is a processor that provides a special set of functions. A floating point (or math) coprocessor provides a collection of operations that manipulate floating point values. Coprocessors are like the CPU in that they provide local storage (registers or an operand stack) and they are capable of performing data manipulation tasks. However, coprocessors are unlike the CPU in that they do not fetch their own instructions or data values. Instructions and operands are fetched by the CPU and presented to the coprocessor. Because coprocessors do not fetch their own instructions or operands, they are not complicated by the need to provide addressing modes or flow of control instructions.

Figure 8.11 illustrates the relation between the CPU and a coprocessor. As shown in Figure 8.11, there are three types of communication between the CPU and the coprocessor: data, addresses, and control. Data communications are used to transfer values between the CPU and the coprocessor. Address communications are used to specify the operands to be manipulated. Control communications to the coprocessor are used to specify the operation to be performed.

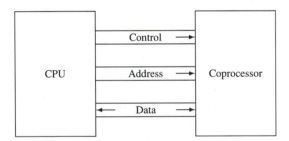

Figure 8.11   A floating point coprocessor

Internally, floating point processors provide a set of registers (or an operand stack) to store values and logic to support the manipulation of floating point values. Floating point coprocessors typically provide the standard arithmetic operations (addition, subtraction, multiplication, and division), some more complex operations (e.g., square root), and a collection of conversion operations. The conversion operations convert between integer and floating point representations and between the different floating point representations supported by the coprocessor (e.g., single-precision, double-precision, extended precision, and so forth). Floating point operations are performed by loading values in the registers of the coprocessor and instructing the coprocessor to perform the operation. When the floating point operation is complete, you can store the result for future use.

Modern processors use three different strategies for accessing the registers associated with the floating point coprocessor. The Motorola 88100 does not provide a separate set of floating point registers. In this machine, the floating point coprocessor simply uses the general-purpose registers. This strategy simplifies the design of the coprocessor and simplifies the design of the instruction set because there are no special instructions to load or store the floating point registers. The MIPS and Intel i860 provide a separate set of registers for the floating point coprocessor. These machines provide operations to transfer values between the memory and the floating point registers as well as operations to transfer values between the general-purpose registers and the floating point registers. Here, we should note that the effective address calculations always use the general-purpose registers. The SPARC and HP Precision architectures are also based on separate floating point registers; however, these machines do not provide operations to transfer values directly between the floating point registers and the general-purpose registers. To transfer a value from a general-purpose register to a floating point register, you must first store the value into the memory and then load it into the floating point register. Figure 8.12 illustrates these strategies.

Table 8.4 presents a sample set of floating point operations. These operations are prefixed with an "F" to distinguish them from the similar operations that manipulate integer values. The operations presented in Table 8.4 are not complete. Many other operations will be supported by a floating point coprocessor. In particular, most floating point coprocessors provide a collection of comparison operations and a collection of transcendental function (e.g., sine, cosine, logarithm).

Table 8.4 Sample floating point operations

Symbolic instruction	Semantics
FLOAD FRd, $addr$	Load the floating point register FRd with the value stored in the memory location or general-purpose register denoted by $addr$.
FSTORE $addr$, FRd	Store the value in floating point register FRd into the memory location or general-purpose register denoted by $addr$.
FITOS FRd, FRs	Convert the value stored in the floating point register FRs from integer representation to the single-precision format, and store the result in the floating point register FRd.
FSTOI FRd, FRs	Convert the value stored in the floating point register FRs from the single-precision format to integer representation (truncate any fractional part), and store the result in the floating point register FRd.
FADD FRd, FRs_1, FRs_2	Add the value stored in the floating point register FRs_1 to the value stored in the floating point register FRs_2, and store the result in the floating point register FRd.
FSUB FRd, FRs_1, FRs_2	Subtract the value stored in the floating point register FRs_2 from the value stored in the floating point register FRs_1, and store the result in the floating point register FRd.
FMPY FRd, FRs_1, FRs_2	Multiply the value stored in the floating point register FRs_1 with the value stored in the floating point register FRs_2, and store the result in the floating point register FRd.
FDIV FRd, FRs_1, FRs_2	Divide the value stored in the floating point register FRs_2 by the value stored in the floating point register FRs_1, and store the result in the floating point register FRd.

A. Shared register (the Motorola 88100)

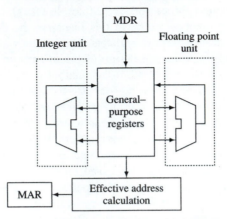

B. Separate register sets (MIPs and i860)

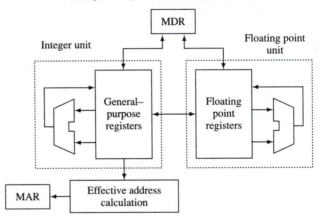

C. Independent register sets (SPARC and HP Precision)

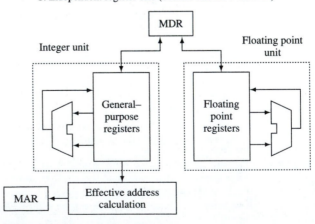

Figure 8.12   Floating point coprocessors

Example 8.15   *Using the operations shown in Table 8.4, show how to calculate* $y = x^i$ *where* x *and* y *are single-precision floating point values and* i *is an integer value.*

We begin by writing a pseudo-code version of the algorithm that we will use.

int i;
float x, y;

⋮

x = 1.0;
while(i > 0){
  x = x * y;
  i = i − 1;
}

Next we translate the pseudo-code into assembly language.

```
        FLOAD.w   FR1, y          ; FR1 is y
        LOAD.w    R2, i           ; R2 is i
        MOVE      R3, #1          ; R3 = 1
        FLOAD.w   FR2, R3         ; FR2 is x, x = 1
        FITOS     FR2, FR2        ; x = 1.0
        BRANCH    test

top:
        FMPY      FR2, FR1, FR2   ; x = x * y;
        ADD       R2, R2, #-1     ; i = i − 1;

test:
        CMP       R2, #0
        BRGT      top             ; while( i > 0 )

        FSTORE.w  FR2, x
```

An important aspect of the coprocessor organization is that floating point operations can proceed in *parallel* with the other operations performed by the CPU. Parallel The benefit of this parallel execution is illustrated in Figure 8.13. The first part of this figure shows how long it would take to execute two iterations of the loop shown in Example 8.15 if all operations were performed in a strictly sequential fashion. The second part illustrates how long it will take to execute the same two iterations, this time assuming that the coprocessor operations are performed in parallel with the actions of the CPU. Note that the CPU must still perform some initialization of the floating point operation (fetching the instruction and issuing a command to the coprocessor).

In Figure 8.13, we assumed that the floating point operation completed before the CPU completed the remaining operations and issued the next floating point operation. What if it were the other way around? What if the floating point operations took a lot more time? In this case, the CPU would need to

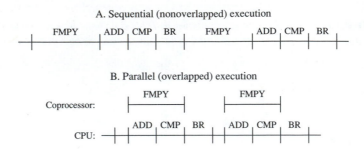

Figure 8.13   Parallel operation of the CPU and coprocessor

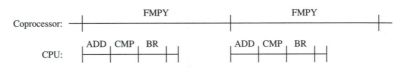

Figure 8.14   Waiting for the coprocessor

delay the start of the next floating point operation until the previous floating point operation had completed. Figure 8.14 illustrates the waiting that the CPU must perform when the floating point operation takes more time than the remaining operations.

Real estate

Three factors have motivated the development of floating point coprocessors: available real estate, end user economics, and concurrency. Until recently, the *real estate* available on a single chip was not sufficient to hold the gates needed to implement the instruction set of a typical microprocessor and the operations needed to support floating point numbers. By separating the floating point operations from the rest of the processor, the manufacturers could implement the processor on a single chip (the coprocessor would be implemented on a separate chip).

The added cost of floating point hardware could be avoided by providing software implementations of these operations. Implementing the floating point operations in software reduces the cost of the processor but increases the time required to perform these operations. The trade-off between hardware and software implementations is not as straightforward as one would like. Moreover, the decision to adopt one approach over the other may change, depending on the context in which a computer is going to be used. By adopting the coprocessor approach, manufacturers can package the coprocessor as a separate component and offer the end user the option of purchasing a coprocessor.

Finally, the fact that even hardware implementations of floating point operations are potentially slow when compared with the other operations performed by the CPU has also led to the development of floating point coprocessors. As we have seen, execution of floating point operations can be overlapped with other activities that are performed by the CPU. Ultimately, this may be the only reason that floating point operations are performed by a separate processor in future machines. Current manufacturing technology can provide enough gates on a single chip to implement a complete (integer) instruction set, a coprocessor, and more! Moreover, the cost of both processors is not significantly greater than the cost of the main processor.

8.4 SUMMARY

When you consider the representation of integers (signed or unsigned), the most important consideration is the range of the representation. It is reasonable to assume that every integer value in the range of the representation will have an exact representation. When we consider the representation of numbers with fractional parts, we can no longer assume that every value in the range has an exact representation. In this chapter, we introduced the terms *gap* and *precision* to characterize the inexact nature of fixed and floating point representations.

Fixed point representations use an integer representation and a scale factor. These representations are appropriate when you need to represent numbers with very large magnitudes or numbers with very small magnitudes. When you need to represent numbers with very large and very small magnitudes in the same application, you will need to use a floating point representation. Floating point representations encode both a significand (a scaled integer value) and an exponent. In effect, the exponent is a variable scale factor that is explicitly stored in the floating point value.

In the last section of this chapter, we covered the essential aspects of floating point coprocessors. While they were originally motivated by three factors, the primary motivation for coprocessors in modern machines is the provision for parallel execution. Coprocessors represent a very simple form of parallel execution. We will consider a variety of other forms of parallel execution in Chapter 13 when we study parallel machines.

8.4.1 Additional Reading

As with the previous chapter, much presentation in this chapter has been based on the material contained in *Introduction to Arithmetic for Digital Systems Designers* by Shlomo Waser and Michael J. Flynn (Holt, Rinehart & Winston, 1982). If you are interested in learning more about number representations, I highly recommend this book. In addition, *Seminumerical Algorithms* (the second volume in the series) by Donald Knuth (Addison-Wesley Publishing, 1968, 1973) will provide you with more background on the material presented in this chapter.

8.4.2 Terminology

- Fixed point, Scale factor
- Normal form, Normalization, Pre-normalization
- Significand, Base, Exponent

- Precision, Significant digits
- Hidden bit
- NaN
- Single-precision, Double-precision, Extended temporaries
- Rounding, Underflow, Gap
- Real estate
- Parallel, Overlapped

8.4.3 Review Questions

1. What is the scale factor in a fixed point representation?
2. How is the gap characterized? How can you calculate the gap in a fixed point representation?
3. How is precision characterized?
4. How does the gap in a floating point representation differ from the gap in a fixed point representation?
5. What is the hidden bit?
6. What is the relationship between a hidden bit and normalization?
7. What is the difference between the hidden bit in the DEC floating point format and the IEEE 754 standard floating point format?
8. What does NaN stand for?
9. Why do most floating point representations use an excess representation for the exponent?
10. Describe the steps needed to add two floating point numbers.
11. Describe the steps needed to multiply two floating point numbers.
12. What is the primary benefit provided by a floating point coprocessor?

8.5 EXERCISES

1. For each of the following numbers, show how the number would be represented using the IEEE 754 single-precision floating point format. (Only show the 10 most significant bits of the f field.)
   a. 37.55.
   b. 0.000565.
   c. 0.6.
   d. −432.78.
   e. 5,000,000,401.
2. Repeat exercise 1 using the DEC single-precision floating point format.

3. Repeat exercise 1 using the IBM 360/370 floating point format.

4. What is the largest number that can be represented using the DEC single-precision floating point format?

5. What is the largest number that can be represented using the IBM 360/370 representation? Would your answer change if we required that the number be normalized?

6. Consider the DEC single-precision floating point format.

    a. What is the gap at 0?

    b. What is the gap at the number immediately after 0?

    c. What is the gap at 2^{15}?

7. Repeat exercise 6 for the IBM 360/370 format, assuming that values do *not* need to be stored in normal form.

8. Repeat exercise 6 for the IBM 360/370 format, assuming that values *must* be stored in normal form.

9. The term *denormal* seems to indicate that numbers no longer need to be represented in normal form. In other words, there may be two different representations for the same number. Is this the case? If so, describe two different representations for a number using the single-precision format of the IEEE 754 standard. If not, explain why two different representations for the same number are impossible.

10. In this exercise, we consider structure of the Normalize component shown in Figure 8.6.

    a. Given the assumptions stated in the figure, explain why at least one of the two most significant bits of the 25-bit value passed to the Normalize component must be 1.

    b. If the most significant bit is 1, how should the final exponent and 23-bit significand be determined?

    c. If the most significant bit is 0, how should the final exponent and 23-bit significand be determined?

11. Explain, using an example, how it is possible that $a + b = a$, even though $b \neq 0$.

12. Explain, using an example, why the addition algorithm always adjusts the number with the smaller exponent.

13. In discussing the extended formats recommended by the IEEE 754 standard, we illustrated how the use of extended temporaries might mask an overflow. Explain, using an example, how the use of extended temporaries might mask an underflow.

14. Write an assembly language fragment to compute the sum of the elements in an array of floating point values. The array will have *n* elements and starts in the memory location labeled by *arr*. After writing your code fragment, indicate where the CPU can overlap its activities with the coprocessor.

15.   Consider the binary pattern: 01010000010010000100010100000000. What
      does this pattern represent?
      a.   As an ASCII string.
      b.   As an integer.
      c.   As part of a program for the simple computer described in Chapter 3.
      d.   As an IBM 360/370 format floating point number.
      e.   As an IEEE 754 standard single-precision floating point number.

INSTRUCTION REPRESENTATION

PART FOUR

INSTRUCTION INTERPRETATION CHAPTER 9

In Chapter 3, we discussed the direct hardware interpretation of a simple instruction set. In this chapter, we review the principles of direct interpretation and introduce two other techniques associated with instruction interpretation: pipelining and microprogramming. Pipelining increases the rate of instruction execution and provides the basis for modern RISC machines. Microprogramming increases the flexibility of the basic hardware and was used extensively in CISC machines.

Section 9.1 introduces the instruction set for a simple machine and discusses a direct implementation of this instruction set. Section 9.2 covers the techniques that have been developed to fetch instructions from memory. Section 9.3 covers pipelining and concludes by discussing a pipelined implementation of the simple machine described in section 9.1. Section 9.4 covers superpipelining and superscalar organizations. Finally, section 9.5 covers microprogramming and concludes with a microprogrammed implementation of the simple machine introduced in section 9.1.

9.1 DIRECT IMPLEMENTATIONS

In this section, we review the principles of direct implementation by introducing a simple machine and sketching a direct implementation of its instruction set. Our simple machine is based on a 16-bit word. The machine has 16 general-purpose registers named R0 through R15; R0 is hardwired to the value 0. The instruction set includes data transfer operations, data manipulation operations, support for immediate values, and conditional branching instructions. The machine language is based on three formats: a format for instructions that use three registers, a format for the instructions that use immediate values, and a format for the branching instructions.

9.1.1 The Instruction Set

The data migration (LOAD and STORE) and the data manipulation (ADD, SUB, and so forth) operations use the three-register format. This format has a 4-bit opcode and three 4-bit register addresses. The registers are called d, s_1, and s_2. There are four data transfer operations: load word (LDW), load byte (LDB), store word (STW), and store byte (STB). In these operations, two of the registers (s_1 and s_2) specify the effective address, and the third register (d) specifies the register involved in the transfer. The LDB operation sign extends the 8-bit value fetched from the memory to fill the 16-bit register. The STB operation only stores the least significant 8 bits of the register. There are six data manipulation operations: integer addition, integer subtraction, bitwise and, bitwise or, bitwise exclusive or, and bitwise exclusive or not. In these operations, two of the registers specify the source operands while the third specifies the destination. Table 9.1 summarizes the three register instructions.

Table 9.1 The three register instructions

Format: | op | d | s_1 | s_2 |

Operation	Semantics	Name	Opcode
Load word	$R[d] \leftarrow M[\ R[s_1]+R[s_2]\ ]_{16}$	LDW	0000
Load byte	$R[d] \leftarrow M[\ R[s_1]+R[s_2]\ ]_8$	LDB	0001
Store word	$M[\ R[s_1]+R[s_2]\ ] \leftarrow R[d]_{16}$	STW	0010
Store byte	$M[\ R[s_1]+R[s_2]\ ] \leftarrow R[d]_8$	STB	0011
Integer add	$R[d] \leftarrow R[s_1] + R[s_2]$	ADD	0100
Integer subtract	$R[d] \leftarrow R[s_1] - R[s_2]$	SUB	0101
Bitwise and	$R[d] \leftarrow R[s_1]\ \&\ R[s_2]$	AND	0110
Bitwise or	$R[d] \leftarrow R[s_1]\ |\ R[s_2]$	OR	0111
Bitwise xor	$R[d] \leftarrow R[s_1] \oplus R[s_2]$	XOR	1000
Bitwise xor not	$R[d] \leftarrow R[s_1] \oplus \sim R[s_2]$	XORN	1001

There are two *set register* operations: set high (SETHI) and set low (SETLO). These operations set the most and least significant 8 bits in the destination register, respectively (the remaining 8 bits are not affected by the operation). The format used to encode these operations has a 4-bit opcode, a 4-bit register address, and an 8-bit immediate value. Table 9.2 summarizes the set register instructions.

Table 9.2 The set register instructions

Format: | op | d | immed 8 |

Operation	Semantics	Name	Opcode
Set high	set the high byte of R[d] to $immed_8$	SETHI	1010
Set low	set the low byte of R[d] $immed_8$	SETLO	1011

Our simple machine provides one unconditional and six conditional branching operations. Branching operations are encoded with a 5-bit opcode and an 11-bit offset. When the branch is taken, the 11-bit offset is sign extended to 16 bits, multiplied by 2, and added to the program counter. Table 9.3 summarizes the branching instructions.

Table 9.3 The branching instructions

Format: | op | offset_{11} |

Condition	Semantics	Name	Opcode
Always	$PC \leftarrow PC + \text{offset}_{11}$	BRA	11000
Equal	if(Z) $PC \leftarrow PC + \text{offset}_{11} \times 2$	BREQ	11001
Not equal	if(!Z) $PC \leftarrow PC + \text{offset}_{11} \times 2$	BRNE	11010
Less	if(N & !Z) $PC \leftarrow PC + \text{offset}_{11} \times 2$	BRLT	11011
Less or equal	if(N | Z) $PC \leftarrow PC + \text{offset}_{11} \times 2$	BRLE	11100
Greater	if(!N & !Z) $PC \leftarrow PC + \text{offset}_{11} \times 2$	BRGT	11101
Greater or equal	if(!N | Z) $PC \leftarrow PC + \text{offset}_{11} \times 2$	BRGE	11110

9.1.2 A Direct Implementation

Figure 9.1 illustrates the set of data paths, registers, and combinational circuits we use to implement the instruction set of our simple machine. This implementation uses three buses: two source buses (buses 1 and 2) and a result bus (bus 3). The *shifter* and *ALU* use the source buses for their inputs and can send their results to the result bus. Most of the registers load values from the result bus and can send their values to one of the source buses. The MDR (memory data register) and PC (program counter) are exceptions to this rule. The MDR loads its value from one of the source buses (bus 2) and can send its value to the result bus. This structure is based on the use of the MDR. This register holds the result of a memory read operation and is used as the source for a memory write operation. The PC is unique in that it can be used as a result (during an instruction fetch) or a source (during a branching operation).

The two temporary registers, temp_1 and temp_2, can be used to store temporary results during the interpretation of an instruction. Notice that the value of temp_1 can only be transmitted along bus 1, while the value of temp_2 can only be transmitted along bus 2. In addition, the value of the PC can only be transmitted along bus 2, and constant values can only be transmitted along bus 1. These constraints may affect which of the temporary registers should be used to store a value.

Figure 9.2 presents the basic structure for the ifetch loop used to implement the instruction set for our simple machine. In this illustration, each box represents a sequence of control activities. Each iteration of the loop begins by fetching the next instruction, storing it in the instruction register, and incrementing the program counter. Once the instruction has been fetched, its opcode is examined to determine which sequence is performed next. Figure 9.2 illustrates a separate sequence for each type of operation.

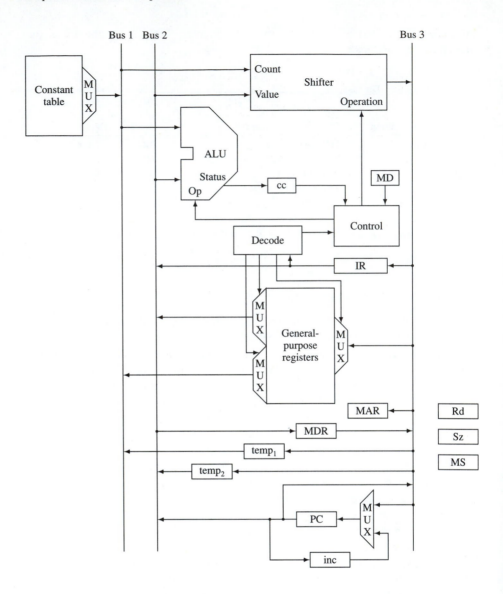

Component	Description	Component	Description
MD	Memory done	IR	Instruction register
MAR	Memory address register	PC	Program counter
MDR	Memory data register	inc	Increment by 2
MS	Memory select	Shifter	A combinational shifter
Rd	Memory read	ALU	Arithmetic and logic unit
Sz	Memory size	cc	condition code register
Constant table	A table of constant values	temp$_1$, temp$_2$	Temporary registers

Figure 9.1   Data paths for a direct implementation of the simple machine

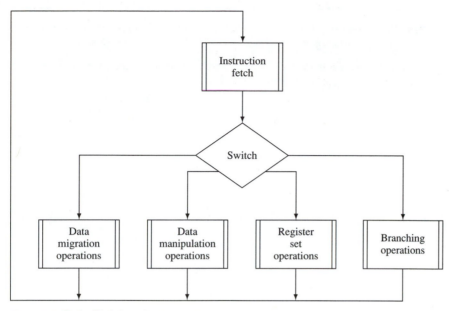

Figure 9.2 Basic ifetch loop for the simple machine

Example 9.1   *Describe how you could use the data paths shown in Figure 9.1 to implement the instruction fetch sequence.*

Cycle	Activities
1	PC → bus 3, load MAR
	clear MD, set MS, set Rd, set Sz
$2 \ldots n-1$	wait **while** MD == 0
n	MDR → bus 3, load IR
	inc → PC, load PC
	clear MS

Example 9.2   *Assuming that the instruction has already been fetched, describe how you could use the data paths shown in Figure 9.1 to implement the data manipulation instructions.*

Cycle	Activities
$n+1$	Reg[src$_1$] → bus 1
	Reg[src$_2$] → bus 2
	select ALU op
	ALU → bus 3
	load Reg[dest]

Example 9.3   *Assuming that the instruction has already been fetched, describe how you could use the data paths shown in Figure 9.1 to implement the branching instructions.*

Here we assume that the immediate values 5 and 4 are stored in the constant table. Notice how these values are used in cycles $n + 1$ and $n + 2$.

Cycle	Activities
$n + 1$	IR $\rightarrow$ bus 2
	#5 $\rightarrow$ bus 1
	Select left shift with zero fill
	Shifter $\rightarrow$ bus 3
	Load $temp_2$
$n + 2$	$temp_2 \rightarrow$ bus 2
	#4 $\rightarrow$ bus 1
	Select right shift with sign extend
	Shifter $\rightarrow$ bus 3
	Load $temp_1$
$n + 3$	$temp_1 \rightarrow$ bus 1
	PC $\rightarrow$ bus 2
	Select ALU add operation
	ALU $\rightarrow$ bus 3
	Load PC **if** branch condition met

9.2 INSTRUCTION SEQUENCING

Pipelining, superpipelining, and superscalar organizations make it possible to design processors that can interpret hundreds of millions of instructions per second. However, the memories that store these instructions are only capable of delivering tens of millions of words per second. For example, a processor may be capable of interpreting 100 million instructions per second; however, a memory with a 20-nanosecond cycle time is only capable of delivering 50 million words per second. The difference between these rates is called the *memory latency problem.*

Memory latency problem

In this section, we consider four techniques that have been developed to deal with the memory latency problem. We begin by considering *wide memories.* In this technique, two or more instructions are stored in a single memory word (a word is the unit of memory access). *Interleaving* is a technique that allows overlapping memory operations. In this approach, the memory is divided into two or more *banks;* each bank can perform an operation on a different word at the same time. The third technique we consider is *instruction prefetching.* This technique is most appropriate when instruction interpretation takes a varying number of processor cycles. The fourth technique we consider is *instruction caching.* This technique uses a small, high-speed memory, called a *cache,* to store instructions as they are fetched from *primary memory.* Instruction caching is based on the *principle of locality.* According to the principle of locality, once an instruction is fetched, it is likely that it will be fetched again in the near future. The importance of caching is

Principle of locality

not limited to instruction caching. Caching can also be used to improve the time needed to access data. As such, we conclude this section with a brief discussion of data caching.

9.2.1 Wide Memories

Suppose that the memory cycle time is four times the processor cycle time. To keep the processor operating at full speed, we need to design a memory system that can provide four instructions on each memory cycle. One way to do this is to increase the width of the memory. If an instruction is 32 bits, we can make the memory 128 bits wide. Thus, when we fetch an instruction, we actually get four instructions. In ideal circumstances, the processor can interpret these instructions while it is fetching the next set of four instructions.

Note that using a wide memory does not reduce the time required to fetch an instruction from memory. However, this technique does improve the *instruction bandwidth*—the number of instructions delivered per second.

Instruction bandwidth

While wide memories present a simple solution to the memory latency problem, this approach has two important disadvantages. First, as you will recall from the discussion in Chapter 3, wide memories complicate the write operation[1] (see exercise 7). Second, considering the frequency of branching instructions and the problem of alignment, it is unlikely that the processor will actually interpret all four instructions in a set of four instructions. Despite these difficulties, wide memories have been used in a number of machines. Wide memories are typically used in combination with other techniques. For example, the IBM RS/6000 uses 128-bit words in its instruction cache. The 128-bit word allows the RS/6000 to fetch and begin the interpretation of four instructions at one time. We will discuss this machine in greater detail when we consider superscalar approaches in section 9.4.

9.2.2 Interleaving

In interleaving, the memory is divided into two or more banks. Each bank is capable of delivering another instruction on each memory cycle. If the activities of the different memory banks are overlapped, the entire memory system will be able to deliver more than one word of memory every memory cycle. The term *interleaving* emphasizes the way in which addresses are assigned to the memory banks. Because most instruction fetches are sequential, an interleaved memory assigns consecutive addresses to different memory banks. The first word is stored in the first bank, the second word is stored in the second bank, and so on. (See Figure 3.8 for an example of interleaved addresses.)

---

[1] This is not a significant consideration if you are only concerned about instruction fetches.

Example 9.4   *Suppose that the memory cycle time is twice the processor cycle time. Further suppose that the memory has been divided into two banks. How many processor cycles will it take to fetch the following sequence of instructions:* $i_0, i_1, i_2, i_3, i_7, i_8$?

Without interleaving, it would take 2 processor cycles to fetch each instruction or 12 processor cycles to fetch all 6 instructions. The following illustration shows that it only takes 8 processor cycles when the memory is interleaved using 2 banks.

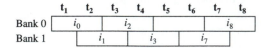

This scheme makes it possible to deliver an instruction on every processor cycle. However, consecutive accesses to the same memory bank cause a bubble in the delivery of the next instruction. In particular, no instruction is delivered at processor cycle t_6.

Like the use of wide memories, interleaving does not decrease the time required for individual memory operations, but can decrease the time required for a sequence of memory operations. To benefit from memory interleaving, the processor must start to fetch the next instruction before it begins execution of the current instruction.

9.2.3 Instruction Prefetching

Instruction buffer

In instruction prefetching, we put a *first-in, first-out* queue, called the *instruction buffer*, between the logic that fetches instructions and the logic that interprets instructions. Figure 9.3 illustrates this arrangement. Whenever there is an available slot in the instruction buffer and the memory is idle, the instruction fetch logic initiates the fetch of another instruction. In this way, the instruction fetch logic can fetch instructions before they are needed by the instruction interpretation logic.

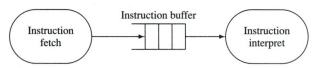

Figure 9.3   Instruction prefetching

Branching instructions create problems for systems that support instruction prefetching. In simple systems, the instruction (pre)fetch logic fetches instructions, one after the other, from the memory system. When a branch is taken, the instructions in the instruction buffer are incorrect. In these systems, the instruction buffer is cleared whenever the instruction interpretation logic executes a branch.

Like the previous techniques, this approach does not decrease the time required for an individual memory operation. The advantage of instruction prefetching is that it keeps the memory operating at its full capacity. This technique is most appropriate when some instructions require more time to execute than a memory fetch. When the processor is busy executing one of these instructions, the prefetch logic can put another instruction in the instruction buffer.

We can reduce the number of times the instruction buffer is cleared by including decode logic in the instruction fetch logic. Using this decode logic the instruction fetch logic can alter its program counter whenever it detects an unconditional branch instruction. In this way, the instruction fetch logic will fill the instruction buffer with the correct instructions.

Several machines take the decode logic one step further. These machines include a branch predictor in their conditional branch instructions. The branch predictor indicates whether the branch is likely or not. For example, it is likely that the conditional branch at the bottom of a loop will be taken. Using these branch predictors, the instruction fetch (and decode) logic can fetch the instructions that are likely to be needed, thus reducing the number of times the instruction buffer is cleared.

9.2.4 Instruction Caching

Modern RISC machines use instruction caching to improve instruction bandwidth. In instruction caching, a small instruction memory, called the *instruction cache* is built into the processor. Because the cache is built using the same technology as the processor, it can operate at the same speed as the processor. When the processor needs to fetch an instruction, it first checks the cache to determine if the instruction is already in the cache. If the instruction is in the cache, the processor fetches the instruction from the cache and continues. Otherwise, the processor fetches the instruction from primary memory. Whenever the processor fetches an instruction from primary memory, it saves the instruction in the instruction cache, expecting that it will need to interpret the instruction again in the near future. Figure 9.4 presents a graphical illustration of instruction caching.

To see the advantage of instruction caching, consider the execution of a small loop—one that is small enough to fit in the instruction cache. During the first iteration of the loop, the processor fetches the instructions in the loop, interprets them, and writes them to the instruction cache. On subsequent iterations of the loop, the processor finds the instructions in the cache and immediately begins their interpretation.

Functionally, the instruction cache is similar to primary memory. In particular, the instruction cache provides a read operation and a write operation. However,

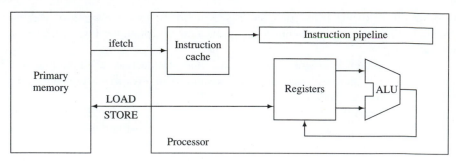

Figure 9.4   Instruction caching

Cache miss

Cache hit

Tag bits

Fully associative

Direct mapping

in contrast to the read operation for primary memory, the read operation for an instruction cache can fail. When the read operation fails, it is called a *cache miss*. When the read operation succeeds, it is called a *cache hit*.

In considering implementations of the read and write operations for an instruction cache, it is important to recognize that instruction cache does not have a unique location for every address in primary memory—several primary memory addresses may be mapped to the same location in the instruction cache. The instruction cache implements an *association* between primary memory addresses and values. Each word of the instruction cache holds an instruction and a collection of *tag bits* that identify the address of the instruction stored in the cache word. The tag bits may also record useful information about the cache word. As a minimum, the cache will use one tag bit to indicate if the cache word holds a valid instruction. This bit is initially clear and is set whenever an instruction is loaded into the cache.

If every primary memory address can be mapped to every cache address, the cache is *fully associative*. In this case, the cache must check the tag bits for every word when it performs a lookup. In contrast to the fully associative approach, a *direct mapping* maps each primary address to a single cache address. Several memory addresses may be mapped to the same cache address. The tag bits are used to identify the memory address currently associated with the cache word (if any). Direct mapping simplifies the lookup operation because the cache only needs to check one set of tag bits. However, it may lead to conflicts when two (or more) addresses that map to the same cache word need to be stored in the cache.

Example 9.5   *Develop a direct mapping for a primary memory with 16-bit addresses and a cache with 32 locations.*

In this case, we use the least significant 5 bits of the memory address as the cache address and the remaining 11 bits as the tag bits. The following diagram illustrates the data paths needed to implement the read operation.

Memory address

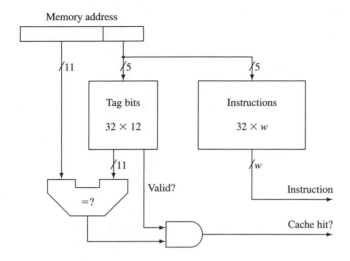

Most instruction caches are based on a *set associative* approach. In this ap-   Set associative
proach, each memory address is mapped to a small set of cache addresses. In
contrast to the direct mapping approach, the set associative approach reduces conflicts by providing alternative locations for memory addresses that map to filled
cache locations. In contrast to the fully associative approach, the set associative
approach reduces the complexity of the lookup logic by limiting the number of
tag bits that need to be checked. Set associative caches typically map memory
addresses to 2, 4, 8, or 16 cache addresses. A cache that maps each memory   *n*-way set associative
address to *n* cache addresses is called an *n-way set associative cache*.   cache

When memory addresses are mapped to two or more cache locations, you will
need to select which location to use when writing a value in the cache. If any of
the locations is open (i.e., does not hold a valid value), an open location should be
used. However, if every location holds a valid value, one of these values is replaced
by the write operation. Several strategies can be used to select the value that is
replaced. In *least recently used (LRU) replacement*, the value that was referenced   Least recently used
the farthest in the past is replaced. In *first in, first out (FIFO) replacement*, the   (LRU) replacement
value that was written first is replaced. In *random replacement*, a random value is   First in, first out
selected for replacement. We will not consider these or other replacement strategies   (FIFO) replacement
in any further depth in this text.

Random replacement

9.2.5 Data Caching

Caching is also used to improve data access. Figure 9.5 illustrates how a data cache
can be added to a processor based on the load/store architecture. In this case, the
data cache is between the registers and the primary memory. Whenever a value is
loaded into a register, it is also written into the data cache. Similarly, whenever a
value is stored into the primary memory, it is also written in the data cache.

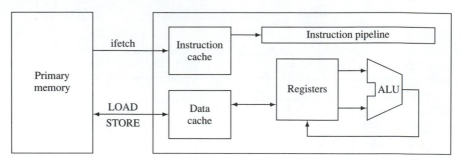

Figure 9.5   Instruction and data caching

As you might guess, data caching is similar to instruction caching; however, there are two aspects of data caching that are distinct from instruction caching. First, data access patterns are not usually as simple as instruction access patterns. Because the patterns are not as simple, it is reasonable to expect that there will be more cache conflicts in the data cache. Two strategies are commonly used to reduce conflicts in the data cache: increasing the size of the cache and the degree of associativity. For example, the IBM RS/6000 uses a two-way set associative cache that holds 8 Kbytes for its instructions cache, but uses a four-way set associative cache that holds 64 Kbytes for its data cache.

The second difference is related to the fact that data can be modified and written back into the memory. Cache designers have developed two strategies for writing values into memory: store-through and store-back. When a register value is stored in primary memory, its value is always written into the data cache as part of the store operation. In a *store-through* system, the store operation also initiates a write operation to primary memory. In a *store-back* system, the value is not written to the primary memory until the cache needs to use the location where the value is stored. The store-through strategy simplifies the cache structure and makes sure that the memory always has the newest values. The store-back strategy reduces the number of memory accesses that are needed when values are updated frequently. Most of the newer systems use a store-back strategy.

Store-through

Store-back

9.3 PIPELINING

The goal of pipelining is to interpret an instruction on every processor cycle. Pipelining is based on overlapping the execution of several instructions. We have already discussed the use of overlapping to improve execution time in other contexts. In Chapter 7, we discussed how overlapping could be used to improve the speed of unsigned integer addition. In Chapter 8, we discussed the speed improvement attained by overlapping coprocessor operations with the other operations performed by the CPU. In section 9.2, we discussed how memory interleaving uses overlapping to improve instruction bandwidth.

To pipeline the ifetch loop for a machine, we divide the body of the loop into several pieces. Each piece is called a *pipeline stage*. The stages are joined together, one after the other, to form a sequence called the instruction interpretation pipeline. As an example, we might divide the body of the ifetch loop into two pieces: one piece to fetch the next instruction and another to decode and interpret the previously fetched instruction. Thus, the CPU can fetch the next instruction **while** it is executing the current instruction.

Pipeline stage

Figure 9.6 illustrates how the ifetch loop for our simple machine could be divided into four pipeline stages. The first stage—instruction fetch—fetches the next instruction. Once the instruction has been fetched, it is passed to the second stage—instruction decode and source fetch. This stage decodes the instruction and obtains the source operands from the source registers. The third stage of the pipeline—ALU—performs the operation encoded in the instruction. The fourth and final stage—save result—saves the result in the destination register.

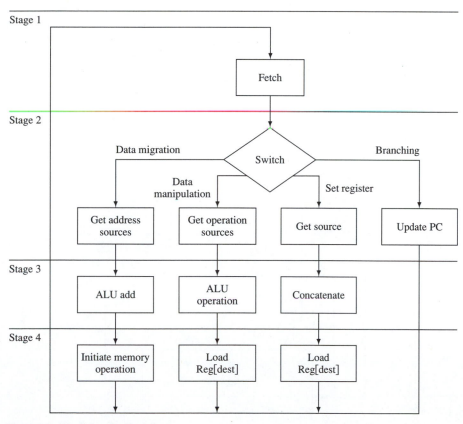

Figure 9.6 Pipelining the ifetch loop

Figure 9.7 illustrates the basic circuits, data paths, and registers needed to implement this four-stage pipeline. Note that there is a register between each stage in the pipeline. These registers are used to hold the values passed between the stages in the pipeline. In addition to the pipeline stages, Figure 9.7 illustrates the data paths associated with the ALU. Again, note that there are temporary registers between the stages. In the data manipulation instructions the second stage of the pipeline loads the input registers for the ALU (labeled A and B in the illustration). The third stage uses these values and loads the ALU output register (labeled C). The fourth stage loads one of the general-purpose registers with the value stored in the ALU output register.

For the LOAD and STORE instructions, the second and third stages calculate the effective address while the fourth stage initiates the appropriate memory operation (read or write). Note that the actual memory operation is detached from the interpretation of the instruction. This means that the pipeline can continue interpreting instructions while the memory operation is being performed. We will consider this aspect of pipelining in greater detail when we discuss register interlocking later in this section.

BRANCH instructions are typically designed so that they can be interpreted in the second stage of the pipeline. This means that the program counter will be updated after the first stage of the pipeline has fetched one instruction following the BRANCH instruction. Note that this requires a separate adder to add the offset

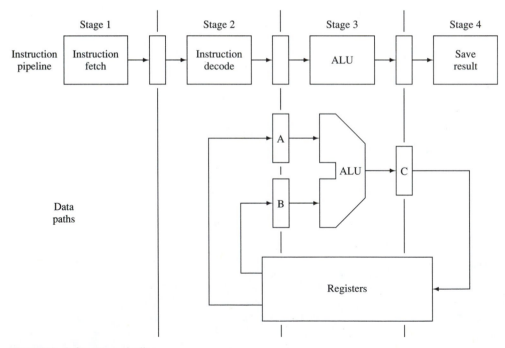

Figure 9.7 A four-stage pipeline

value and the program counter. We will return to the interpretation of BRANCH instructions when we consider delay slots and instruction nullification.

Pipelining is based on a *data-oriented perspective*. In contrast, flowcharts and procedural programming languages are based on a *control-oriented perspective*. The difference in these perspectives is best illustrated by considering the kinds of questions that make sense. Given an executing program, it makes sense to ask where the machine is in its interpretation of the program. However, given an executing pipeline, it does not make sense to ask where the machine is in its interpretation of the pipeline. In this case, the machine is everywhere—each stage of the pipeline is a separate machine.

Data-oriented perspective

Control-oriented perspective

Given an executing pipeline, it does make sense to ask where an instruction is in the pipeline, that is, which stage is processing the instruction. However, if you write a program to implement the ifetch loop, it would not make sense to ask where an instruction is during the execution of this program.

Instructions are the data for an instruction execution pipeline. In designing the pipeline, you need to focus on the flow of data (instructions) through the pipeline. Here it is often useful to think of the pipeline as a *conveyor belt*. Instructions are placed on the conveyor belt by the first stage of the pipeline. Once they are on the conveyor belt, instructions pass by each stage of the pipeline.

Conveyor belt

9.3.1 The Efficiency of Pipelining

Pipeline execution is based on processor cycles. On each processor cycle, the first stage of the pipeline fetches a new instruction, the instruction in the last stage of the pipeline is removed from the pipeline, and every other instruction in the pipeline advances to the next stage. To gain the maximum benefit from pipelining, each stage in the pipeline should take roughly the same time. If one stage takes much longer than the rest, it means that the other stages will spend a great deal of time waiting. Similarly, if one stage is much shorter than the other stages, it means that the short stage will spend a great deal of time waiting. As you might imagine, designing an efficient pipeline is a difficult task.

Figure 9.8 illustrates the overlap in instruction execution provided by our four-stage pipeline. In this illustration, the boxes represent instructions. Each instruction is divided into four smaller boxes that indicate the stage that the instruction is passing through. For example, at time t_4, instruction i_1 is in the save stage, instruction i_2 is in the ALU stage of the pipeline, instruction i_3 is in the decode stage of the pipeline, and instruction i_4 is in the fetch stage of the pipeline. Note that every stage of the pipeline has an instruction. When this happens, we say that the pipeline is *full*.

If each stage in the pipeline takes roughly the same amount of time, we can conclude that the execution of a single instruction would take approximately four processor cycles. As such, it would take approximately 20 processor cycles to interpret five instructions using a standard ifetch loop. However, as Figure 9.8 illustrates, we only need eight processor cycles to interpret five instructions using our four-stage pipeline.

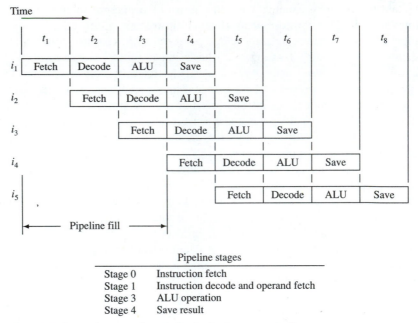

Pipeline stages

Stage 0	Instruction fetch
Stage 1	Instruction decode and operand fetch
Stage 3	ALU operation
Stage 4	Save result

Figure 9.8   Instruction execution overlap in the four stage pipeline

Example 9.6   *Develop a formula for the time needed to execute* n *instructions using our four-stage pipeline, where* t *is the time for a processor cycle.*

In examining Figure 9.8, note that starting with time t_4, an instruction execution is completed at the end of each processor cycle. The first three cycles are needed to fill the pipeline (alternatively it takes three cycles for the first instruction to reach the fourth stage of the pipeline). These observations lead to the following formula

$$\text{Time} = (3 + n)t$$

In considering the efficiency of pipelining, it is important to remember that pipelining does not decrease the time required to interpret an individual instruction. In fact, if the pipeline stages do not all require the same amount of time, pipelining may increase the time required to interpret an instruction. Pipelining does, however, improve the throughput of instruction interpretation. *Throughput* is measured by the number of instructions interpreted in a given time, for example, the number of instructions interpreted per second.

Throughput

9.3.2 Pipeline Stalls

You cannot always ensure that every stage of a pipeline takes the same amount of time for every instruction. Some pipeline stages may take longer for different instructions. As an example, fetching an instruction may take a short amount of time (when the instruction is found in the instruction cache) or it may take a relatively long amount of time (when the processor has to go to primary memory). When a stage in the pipeline takes more time than a single processor cycle, the remaining stages must be delayed until the instruction fetch has been completed. This delay is called a *pipeline stall*. Table 9.4 illustrates a pipeline stall. In this case, the fetch for the third instruction requires three pipeline steps instead of one.

Table 9.4   A pipeline stall

Stage	t_1	t_2	t_3	t_4	t_5	t_6	t_7	t_8	t_9	t_{10}
Fetch	i_1	i_2	i_3	Stall	Stall	i_4	i_5	—	—	—
Decode	—	i_1	i_2	Stall	Stall	i_3	i_4	i_5	—	—
ALU	—	—	i_1	Stall	Stall	i_2	i_3	i_4	i_5	—
Save	—	—	—	Stall	Stall	i_1	i_2	i_3	i_4	i_5

Any memory access, not just instruction fetches, may take a long time when contrasted to a processor cycle. In the *load/store architecture*, only the LOAD and STORE instructions access data values stored in memory. From the perspective of the instruction interpretation pipeline, these instructions have been interpreted when the appropriate memory operation is initiated. In particular, once the memory operation has been initiated, the pipeline can continue with the execution of the next instruction. (In a moment, we will discuss a technique, *register interlocking*, that blocks instructions that use values that have not yet been read from memory.) If data manipulation instructions could reference values stored in memory (without needing to load those values into registers), we would expect more pipeline stalls during the interpretation of an arbitrary code sequence. The load/store architecture is a consequence of the instruction interpretation pipeline used in RISC processors.

Load/store architecture

9.3.3 Register Forwarding and Interlocking

While pipelining generally improves the speed of program execution, it introduces two difficulties that the pipeline designer must address: data dependencies and delay slots. First, we consider the problem of data dependencies. There are two types of data dependencies that affect the design of an instruction interpretation pipeline: write/read dependencies and write/write dependencies. In a *write/read dependency*, one instruction writes a result into a register and a later instruction uses (i.e., reads) the value stored in the register. Because the second instruction is after the first instruction, the value read by the second instruction must be the value written by the earlier instruction.

Write/read dependency

Example 9.7   *Give a simple code sequence that has a write/read dependency.*

```
ADD   R2, R3, R4    ; R2 ← R3 + R4
ADD   R2, R2, R5    ; R2 ← R2 + R5
```

In this case, the first instruction writes a value to R2 and the second instruction uses this value.

Write/write
dependency

    In a *write/write dependency*, two instructions write their results to the same register. Because the second instruction follows the first, only the value written by the second instruction can be read by later instructions. Note that the instructions presented in Example 9.7 represent a write/write dependency because both instructions write their results to R2.

Example 9.8   *Give an example of a code sequence that has a write/write dependency that does not include a write/read dependency.*

```
ADD   R2, R3, R4    ; R2 ← R3 + R4
ADD   R2, R4, R5    ; R2 ← R4 + R5
```

In this case, both instructions write their results to R2.

    In examining the code presented in Example 9.8, note that the first of these instructions could be eliminated without altering the result. This is true of any write/write dependency that does not also involve a write/read dependency. In this sense, write/read dependencies are more fundamental than write/write dependencies. However, the pipeline designer must be aware of write/write dependencies, just in case a programmer writes a code fragment like the one shown in Example 9.8

    In a purely sequential execution of instructions, write/read and write/write dependencies do not present a significant problem because every instruction completes its execution before the next one starts. However, in a pipelined machine, the first instruction may not be finished executing before the second instruction starts its execution.

Example 9.9   *Suppose that registers R2, R3, R4, and R5 hold the values 2, 3, 4, and 7, respectively. Show how a simple pipelined execution of the instructions shown in Example 9.7 leads to an incorrect result.*

The following table illustrates a simple pipelined execution of the instructions given in Example 9.7:

$$i_1 = \text{ADD R2, R3, R4}$$

$$i_2 = \text{ADD R2, R2, R5}$$

	t_1	t_2	**Time step** t_3	t_4	t_5
Stage 1	Fetch i_1	Fetch i_2			
Stage 2		R3→A	R2→A		
		R4→B	R5→B		
Stage 3			A+B→C	A+B→C	
Stage 4				C→R2	C→R2
General-	R2 = 2	R2 = 2	R2 = 2	R2 = 7	R2 = 9
purpose	R3 = 3	R3 = 3	R3 = 3	R3 = 3	R3 = 3
registers	R4 = 4	R4 = 4	R4 = 4	R4 = 4	R4 = 4
	R5 = 7	R5 = 7	R5 = 7	R5 = 7	R5 = 7
ALU	A = ?	A = 3	A = 2	A = ?	A = ?
registers	B = ?	B = 4	B = 7	B = ?	B = ?
	C = ?	C = ?	C = 7	C = 9	C = ?

These instructions should put the sum of the registers R3, R4, and R5 in the register R2. In particular, the final value stored in R2 should be 14; however, R2 ends up with the value 9. The error occurs in step t_3. During this step, stage 2 of the pipeline places the *old* value of R2 in the A register of the ALU. The correct value is not stored in register R2 until the end of step t_4.

There are two techniques that have been developed to deal with data dependencies: register forwarding and register interlocking. In *register forwarding*, the result of an instruction is used by a later instruction *before* it is stored in the destination register. When *register interlocking* is used, later instructions are blocked until their source registers hold the results from earlier instructions. Register interlocking provides a general solution to the data dependency problem but may impose unnecessary delays in the interpretation of simple instruction sequences.

Register forwarding

Register interlocking

Figure 9.9 illustrates the data paths needed to support register forwarding. Given the data paths shown in this illustration, we can transfer any of the general-purpose registers to either input of the ALU. In addition we can transfer the result of a previous ALU operation to either input of the ALU. The path labeled *forward 1* is used to transfer the result of the previous instruction into an ALU input. This is the path needed by our example. The path labeled *forward 2* can be used to transfer the result of the instruction before the previous instruction (i.e., the instruction in stage 4 of the pipeline) to one of the ALU inputs.

In addition to the data paths shown in Figure 9.9, register forwarding requires knowledge of the destination register for the instructions being processed in stages

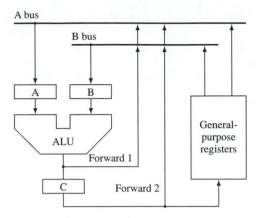

Figure 9.9 Data paths needed for register forwarding

3 and 4 of the pipeline. Given this information, stage 2 of the pipeline can determine if either (or both) of the source operands needs to be forwarded or taken from the general-purpose registers. To avoid problems associated with write/write dependencies, stage 2 should get its source operands from the earliest stage possible.

Example 9.10 *Show how register forwarding can be used to ensure correct execution of the instructions presented in Example 9.7.*

$$i_1 = \text{ADD R2, R3, R4}$$

$$i_2 = \text{ADD R2, R2, R5}$$

	t_1	t_2	t_3	t_4	t_5
			Time step		
Stage 1	Fetch i_1	Fetch i_2			
Stage 2		R3→A	A+B→A		
		R4→B	R5→B		
Stage 3			A+B→C	A+B→C	
Stage 4				C→R2	C→R2
General-	R2 = 2	R2 = 2	R2 = 2	R2 = 7	R2 = 14
purpose	R3 = 3	R3 = 3	R3 = 3	R3 = 3	R3 = 3
registers	R4 = 4	R4 = 4	R4 = 4	R4 = 4	R4 = 4
	R5 = 7	R5 = 7	R5 = 7	R5 = 7	R5 = 7
ALU	A = ?	A = 3	A = 7	A = ?	A = ?
registers	B = ?	B = 4	B = 7	B = ?	B = ?
	C = ?	C = ?	C = 7	C = 14	C = ?

The change occurs in step t_3, where stage 2 forwards the correct value to the A input of the ALU.

Register interlocking can also be used to handle write/read dependencies. This technique uses a single bit for each of the general-purpose registers. The bit indicates whether the register holds an accurate value. If the bit is clear, the register holds an accurate value; otherwise, the register holds an invalid value. The value is invalid because an instruction in the pipeline is going to update the register. No instruction can read a register when its bit is 1. As such, we say that the register is *locked*. The register bits are updated in stages 2 and 4 of the pipeline and examined   Locked
in stage 2. When an instruction enters stage 2 of the pipeline, it is blocked until the bits associated with its source registers are clear at the start of a pipeline step. As it completes the processing of an instruction, stage 2 sets the bit associated with the destination register. This indicates that this instruction will change the value of the register. Stage 4 clears the bit associated with the destination register to indicate that the register has been updated. To avoid problems associated with write/write dependencies, stage 2 should also block instructions whenever their destination register is locked.

Example 9.11 *Show how register interlocking could be used to ensure correct execution of the instructions presented in Example 9.7.*

				Time step			
	t_1	t_2	t_3	t_4	t_5	t_6	t_7
Stage 1	Fetch i_1	Fetch i_2					
Stage 2		R3→A	Slip	R2→A			
		R4→B		R5→B			
Stage 3			A+B→C	Slip	A+B→C		
Stage 4				C→ R2	Slip	C→R2	
Locked	None	R2	R2	None	R2	R2	None

In this case, register R2 is locked when the first instruction reaches stage 2 (at step t_2) and remains locked until the instruction leaves stage 4 (at step t_4). When register R2 is unlocked, stage 2 of the pipeline continues its execution of the second instruction (at time step t_5).

Notice that we use the term *slip* to denote the idle steps for the stages in the   Slip
pipeline. In a stall, the entire pipeline is stopped. In a slip, instructions ahead of the blocked instruction are allowed to proceed through the pipeline. In this case, we must allow the earlier instructions to complete their activities so the blocked instructions can obtain their results.

As the last two examples indicate, register forwarding is the most efficient solution in terms of time. As such, register forwarding is commonly used in instruction interpretation pipelines. However, register forwarding can only be used when the values needed by later instructions are already in the pipeline. Register interlocking, on the other hand, provides a general solution to the write/read data dependency problem. This technique can be used when values are loaded into registers from memory locations. In addition, register interlocking can be used to ensure that *coprocessor instructions* are issued at the correct time.

9.3.4 Branch Delay Slots and Nullification

Data dependencies represent one type of problem the pipeline designer must address. In addition, the pipeline designer must recognize that branching instructions have a delayed effect. By the time the program counter is altered by the branch instruction (during stage 2), stage 1 of the pipeline will have fetched the next instruction. One solution is to *nullify* any instruction in an earlier stage of the pipeline whenever the program counter is altered by a branch instruction. When a pipeline stage receives a nullified instruction, it simply forwards the instruction to the next stage of the pipeline. The pipeline stage is idle when it processes a nullified instruction. Each nullified instruction creates a *bubble* in the pipeline.

Nullify

Bubble

Nullification presents the programmer with a simple model of program execution but may be very inefficient in terms of pipeline utilization. Every bubble in the pipeline represents an instruction that could have been executed by the pipeline. It has been estimated that 20 percent of the instructions executed by a processor are branching instructions. As such, nullifying the instruction following every branch instruction results in a 20 percent degradation in the number of instructions executed. For example, if you design a pipeline that is capable of executing 20 million instructions per second, you should only expect that it will execute 16 million instructions per second.

To avoid the loss in the number of instructions that can be executed, most RISC processors use *branch delay slots*. The instruction slot immediately following a branching instruction is called the branch delay slot. The instruction in the branch delay slot is executed whenever the branch instruction is executed. As we have seen, many machines provide nullification for the instruction in the delay slot of a conditional branch when the branch is not taken.

Branch delay slots seem to assume that branch instructions are interpreted in the second stage of the pipeline. If branch instructions are not interpreted until the third stage of the pipeline, the first stage of the pipeline will fetch two instructions before the program counter is updated by the branch instruction. In this case, the designer might use a two-instruction delay slot; however, it is very difficult to structure programs to accommodate two branch delay slots. Here, it is more reasonable to assume that the designer will use a single instruction delay slot and nullification of the second instruction after the branch.

9.3.5 A Pipelined Implementation of Our Simple Machine

We conclude this section by describing a pipelined implementation of our simple machine. Recall that our simple machine supports four types of operations: data migration operations (load and store), data manipulation operations (integer addition, bitwise and, and so forth), set register operations (set high and set low), and branching operations.

9.3.6 Pipeline Stages

Table 9.5 summarizes the activities performed in each pipeline stage for the instructions supported by our simple machine. Stage 1 always fetches the next instruction and increments the program counter. In the data manipulation operations, stage 2 decodes the operation and loads ALU registers with the values in the source registers; stage 3 performs the actual operations; and stage 4 saves the result. The stages for the set register operations are similar to the stages for the data manipulation operations. In the data transfer operations, the second and third stages calculate the effective address and the fourth stage initiates the memory operation. The branching operations only use the first two stages of the pipeline. The second stage checks the condition and updates the program counter. This makes it relatively easy to implement a single branch delay slot following each branching instruction.

Table 9.5 Pipeline stages for our simple machine

Operation	Stage 1	Stage 2	Stage 3	Stage 4
Data manipulation	Fetch instruction; increment PC	Decode operation; load ALU regs	Perform operation	Save result
Set register	Fetch instruction; increment PC	Decode operation; get register	Set bits	Save result
Data transfer	Fetch instruction; increment PC	Decode operation; load ALU regs	ALU add	Start memory operation
Branching	Fetch instruction; increment PC	Test condition; update PC	Nothing	Nothing

9.3.7 Data Paths

Figure 9.10 illustrates the basic data paths needed to implement the data manipulation instructions. This diagram does not show the paths needed for data forwarding or the paths needed to implement any form of pipeline delay or nullification.

Whenever you determine a value in one stage of the pipeline and use the value as the instruction is processed by a later stage of the pipeline, the value must be saved in a register. For example, the address of the destination register is determined at the end of the first stage, when the instruction is fetched. Because this value is not used until the instruction is in the fourth stage, it must be saved in a separate register at the end of the second stage and at the end of the third stage. Similarly, the decode logic in stage 2 of the pipeline determines the ALU operation that is performed when the instruction enters the third stage of the pipeline. As such, we store the value of the ALU operation in a register at the end of the second stage.

The *save cc register* determines whether the condition code register is updated by the current instruction. All of the data manipulation operations update the condition code register, cc. As such, the save cc register and associated data paths shown in Figure 9.10 are not strictly necessary if we limit our attention to data manipulation operations. However, the other operations do not update the condition code

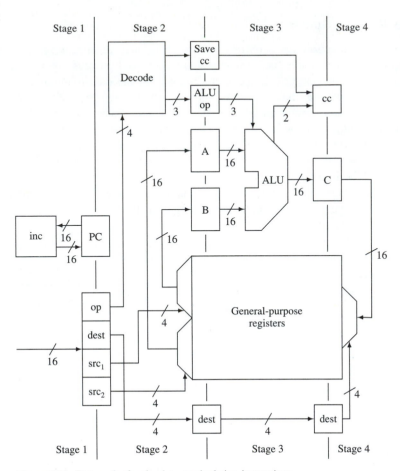

Figure 9.10   Data paths for the data manipulation instructions

register and, as such, the mechanism implemented by this register would need to be added when we considered those operations.

9.3.8 Pipeline Delays and Nullification

In considering pipeline delays, we need to focus on the registers used to pass values between the stages. With the exception of the first stage, every pipeline stage has a set of input registers. With the exception of the last stage, every pipeline stage has a set of output registers. For example, stage 2 in Figure 9.10 has the instruction register in its set of input registers and A in its output register set. A pipeline stage cannot proceed until its input registers are full and its output registers are empty.

In considering the pipeline for our simple machine, the third and fourth stages of this pipeline can always complete their activities in a single processor cycle. As such, the registers in their input sets are always empty at the end of a processor cycle. The situation for the second stage of the pipeline is not as simple. Even when its input register (the instruction register) is full, the second stage of the pipeline may not be able to complete its activities in a single processor cycle. In the case of a data manipulation or data migration operation, the second stage may need to wait until a register has been loaded from the memory (register interlocking). In the case of a branching operation, the second stage may need to wait until the previous instruction updates the condition code register.

Whenever a pipeline stage can introduce a delay, it is important to make sure that the previous stage does not write over the input registers while the later stage still needs these values. Unfortunately, this constraint can make the pipeline very inefficient. Therefore, the output registers of one stage are usually the same as the input registers for the next stage. In our example, the instruction register is the output register for the first stage of the pipeline and the input register for the second stage of the pipeline. Because the instruction register is an output register for the first stage, the first stage cannot initiate its activities until this register is empty. However, the second stage does not know if it will empty the instruction register until it has had a chance to run. This leads to a situation in which each stage is only working on alternate cycles. If the first stage fills the instruction register on one processor cycle, it needs to wait during the next cycle while the second stage determines if it can empty the instruction register. When the second stage is finished with the instruction register, it needs to wait during the next processor cycle while the first stage fetches the next instruction.

Double buffering provides a mechanism to avoid this inefficiency. In double buffering, the registers that are shared between two stages in the pipeline are duplicated. This means that the output registers for one stage are no longer the input registers to the next stage. Whenever the later stage finishes using its input registers, it copies the output registers from the previous stage into its input registers. In this way the output registers for the previous stage will be empty while the later stage determines if it is finished using its input registers.

Double buffering

Figure 9.11 illustrates how double buffering can be used to implement the delays needed in the pipeline shown in Figure 9.10. This illustration assumes that the first stage of the pipeline can always complete its activities in a single processor cycle. We will consider delays introduced by the first stage in the exercises.

In addition to the two instruction registers (labeled IR_1 and IR_2), this illustration includes a combinational circuit (labeled *done?*) and three 1-bit registers (labeled *Empty*, $Full_3$, and $Full_4$). The combinational circuit determines if the second stage of the pipeline will complete its processing of the instruction in IR_2 during the current processor cycle. The $Full_3$ and $Full_4$ registers indicate if the input registers for stages 3 and 4 are full. These stages will not perform any processing when their Full registers are clear. The Empty register controls the activity of the first stage. The first stage will not initiate the fetch of the next instruction when the Empty register is clear.

Given a structure like the one shown in Figure 9.11, it is relatively simple to implement instruction nullification. For example, to nullify the instruction that is

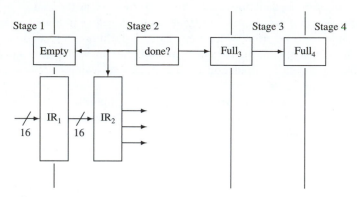

Figure 9.11 Double buffering in the pipeline

currently being processed by the second stage of the pipeline, you can simply clear the $Full_3$ register at the end of the current processor cycle. This forces stage 3 to be idle during the next processor cycle. In addition, because the value of $Full_3$ is simply forwarded to $Full_4$, it forces stage 4 to be idle during the processor cycle following the next cycle.

9.4 SUPERPIPELINED AND SUPERSCALAR MACHINES

In this section, we consider two techniques that are aimed at interpreting more than one instruction per processor cycle. In superpipelining, each processor cycle is divided into two or more subcycles and a new instruction interpretation is initiated on each subcycle. A superscalar machine has multiple functional units, each of which can complete an operation in a single processor cycle. We begin by considering the superpipelined approach.

9.4.1 Superpipelining

The goal of superpipelining is to complete the interpretation of more than one instruction in each processor cycle. As we noted previously, superpipelining involves dividing the processor cycle into two or more subcycles. Figure 9.12 illustrates the advantage of superpipelining. In this case, our four-stage pipeline has been divided into eight stages, each of which requires half of a processor cycle. The original pipeline requires eight processor cycles to interpret five instructions, while the superpipelined version only requires six processor cycles to interpret the same five instructions. Starting with processor cycle t_5, the superpipelined version completes the interpretation of two instructions on each processor cycle. Note that each instruction requires the same number of processor cycles for its interpretation. The primary advantage of superpipelining is that each instruction starts sooner relative to the previous instruction.

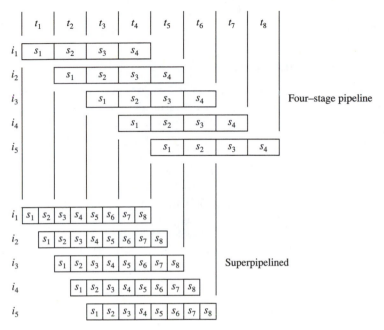

Figure 9.12 Superpipelining

As an example, Table 9.6 presents a brief description of the pipeline stages used in the MIPS R4000 processor. In examining this table, note that all memory accesses have been split into two stages. Stages 1 and 2 are used to fetch the next instruction, while stages 5 and 6 are used to initiate a memory read or write operation (as part of a load or store operation).

Table 9.6 Pipeline stages in the MIPS R4000

Stage	
Stage 1	Instruction fetch, first half
Stage 2	Instruction fetch, second half
Stage 3	Decode instruction and fetch source values
Stage 4	Execute operation
Stage 5	LOAD/STORE, first half
Stage 6	LOAD/STORE, second half
Stage 7	Check LOAD/STORE
Stage 8	Write back (save result)

While superpipelining increases the throughput of the pipeline, increasing the number of pipeline stages increases the problems associated with data dependencies and branch delays. For example, branch instructions on the MIPS R4000 do not update the program counter until stage 4 of the pipeline. By the time the program counter is updated, the first stage of the pipeline has already initiated the fetch for three additional instructions. The first of these instructions is in the branch delay slot and is always executed. However, the other two instructions must be nullified if the branch is taken.

9.4.2 The Superscalar Approach

Figure 9.13 presents a block diagram of the major components used in the IBM RS/6000 architecture. The RS/6000 is based on three primary functional units: a branch unit, an integer unit, and a floating point unit. The *branch unit* fetches instructions, interprets branch instructions, and interprets instructions that manipulate the values in the condition registers. The branch unit forwards floating point instructions to the *floating point unit*. It also forwards load instructions, store instructions, and integer arithmetic instructions to the *integer unit*. Under ideal circumstances, the RS/6000 can interpret four instructions in a single processor cycle. The branch unit can interpret a branch instruction and a condition manipulation instruction in a single processor cycle. The integer unit could complete the interpretation of a load, store, or arithmetic operation in the same processor cycle. Finally, the floating point unit could complete the interpretation of a floating point instruction in the same processor cycle.

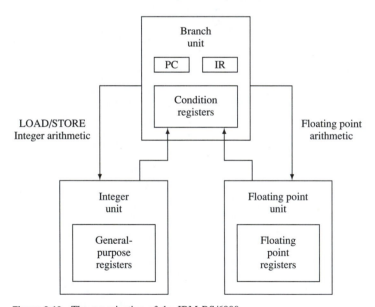

Figure 9.13   The organization of the IBM RS/6000

Before concluding this section, we should take a closer look at the structure of the IBM RS/6000. In particular, we consider the mechanisms related to conditional branching.

All conditional branching is based on the bits in the condition registers. The RS/6000 provides eight 4-bit condition registers. Condition register zero is the standard condition code register that is (optionally) updated by the integer arithmetic operations. In addition, the RS/6000 provides integer and floating point comparison operations that can save their results in any of the condition registers. These comparison instructions have three explicit addresses: two source registers (either general-purpose registers or floating point registers) and a destination register (a condition register). There are two conditional branch instructions: branch on true and branch on false. These instructions test a single bit in a condition register and branch if the bit matches the branch condition (1 matches *true*). The RS/6000 also provides a full set of Boolean operations for manipulating the bits in the condition registers. For example, the RS/6000 provides an operation that examines two bits in the condition registers, form the *exclusive or* of these bits, and save the result in one of the condition registers.

The RS/6000 uses register interlocking to make sure that the bits in the condition registers are examined and set in the correct sequence. Whenever the branch unit forwards an instruction that updates a condition register to the integer unit or the floating point unit, it locks the appropriate condition register. When the unit that interprets the instruction completes its interpretation of the instruction, it unlocks the condition register. The branch unit blocks any instructions that use bits in a locked condition register. In particular, it will block conditional branch instructions and instructions that perform Boolean operations on the bits in a condition register.

9.5 MICROPROGRAMMING

As the examples at the end of section 9.1 illustrated, the control unit simply generates sequences of control signals. In the remainder of this section, we introduce microprogramming as a technique for implementing the control unit, that is, for generating a sequence of control signals. In microprogramming, the sequence of control signals generated by the control unit is described by a microprogram. As we will discuss, the microprogram can base its actions (i.e., the signals that it generates) on the values of the status registers. The microprogram itself is stored in a special memory called the *control store*.

Control store

Before we discuss the details of microprogramming, it is worth considering the advantages that microprogramming offers over a direct implementation. The primary advantage is flexibility. In general, it is easier to modify or extend software than it is to modify or extend complex hardware. If you need to modify the instruction set for a microprogrammed machine, you only need to edit the microprogram, reassemble it, and load it into the control store. In a microprogrammed machine, it is unlikely that you will ever need to modify the hardware because only the simplest and most useful operations are implemented in hardware. This does not imply that modifying the microprogram for a machine is as simple as modifying an assembly language program. The degree of difficulty of modifying the microprogram for a machine lies between the degree of difficulty of modifying an assembly language program and that of modifying the hardware of the machine. For this reason, microprograms are frequently classified as *firmware* to emphasize the fact that microprograms represent a middle ground between software and hardware.

Firmware

One of the more interesting aspects of microprogramming is the fact that a single piece of hardware could run several different microprograms and thus, provide several different machine languages. For example, one microprogram might provide an implementation of the PDP 11 instruction set while another might provide an implementation of the IBM 360 instruction set. Simply changing the microprograms would change the machine seen by the assembly language programmer. While it is unlikely that one would want this much variation in a single piece of hardware, it is possible—at least in concept.

9.5.1 Data Paths

In the remainder of this section, we consider a microprogrammed implementation of the simple machine introduced in section 9.1. Figure 9.14 illustrates the data paths that we will use in this implementation. In comparing the data paths shown in this illustration with those shown in Figure 9.1, note that we have removed the *decode* and *control* components. These components have been replaced by a microprogrammed controller.

The microprogrammed controller has six primary components: a microbranch register (μBR), a branch mapping table (*MAP*), a microprogram counter (μPC), a control store, a microinstruction register (μIR), and a microcontrol unit ($\mu control$). As we have noted, the control store holds the instructions in a microprogram. The microprogram counter holds the address of the current microinstruction. At the end of each processor cycle, the value of the microprogram counter is used to identify the next instruction. The selected instruction is stored in the microinstruction register and the microcontrol unit decodes the microinstruction to generate the specified control signals.

In addition to generating the appropriate control signals, the microcontrol determines a new value for the microprogram counter. The multiplexer in the microprogrammed controller selects the value loaded into the microprogram counter at the end of the current processor cycle. This multiplexer can select the value determined by the microinstruction control or it can select the value determined by the mapping table. The mapping table, in conjunction with the microbranch register, provides a mechanism for implementing multiway branches in the microprogram. The mapping table maps the value in the microbranch register to an address in the microprogram that can be loaded into the microprogram counter. Programming the microprogrammed controller involves loading the control store, the map table, and the constant table.

In addition to the microprogrammed controller, Figure 9.14 introduces three new registers: src_1, src_2, and *dest*. These 4-bit registers hold the addresses of general-purpose registers used in an instruction.

9.5.2 A Microassembly Language

A microprogram is written in a microassembly language and translated into micromachine language version that can be loaded into the control store. We use a

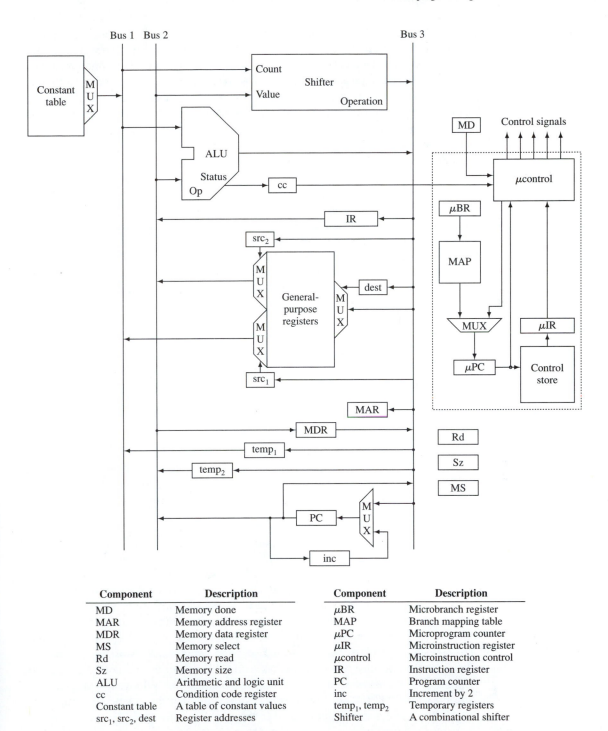

Component	Description	Component	Description
MD	Memory done	μBR	Microbranch register
MAR	Memory address register	MAP	Branch mapping table
MDR	Memory data register	μPC	Microprogram counter
MS	Memory select	μIR	Microinstruction register
Rd	Memory read	μcontrol	Microinstruction control
Sz	Memory size	IR	Instruction register
ALU	Arithmetic and logic unit	PC	Program counter
cc	Condition code register	inc	Increment by 2
Constant table	A table of constant values	$temp_1$, $temp_2$	Temporary registers
src_1, src_2, dest	Register addresses	Shifter	A combinational shifter

Figure 9.14 Data paths for a microprogrammed implementation of the simple machine

simple microassembly language to describe the microprogrammed implementation of our simple machine. A microprogram is a list of microassembly instructions followed by a list of values to store in the mapping table. Each microassembly language instruction has four fields: a label definition field, followed by a control field, followed by an operation field, followed by a branch field. Any or all of these fields may be omitted. A single microassembly language instruction may span several lines in the assembly language program. Anything following a semicolon up to the end of the line is treated as a comment.

Labels in our microassembly language are similar to labels in standard assembly language programs. A label definition consists of an identifier followed by a colon. The value of the label is the address of the next instruction in the microassembly language program. Labels are used to specify unconditional transfers within the microprogram and to specify the values stored in the mapping table.

The control field starts with the word **if** or the word **while**, followed by a condition. If the control field is omitted, the microcontrol logic performs the operations specified in the microinstruction. If the control field is an **if** condition, the microcontrol logic only performs the operations specified in the operation field if the condition is true. If the control field is a **while** condition, the microcontrol logic repeatedly performs the operations specified in the microinstruction while the condition is true. You can use this construct to block execution of the microprogram until the condition is false. Table 9.7 summarizes the conditions that can be used in the control field of a microassembly instruction. (Note that there is no condition to test if the MD register is set.)

Table 9.7 Microconditions

Condition	Meaning
N	The N bit of the condition code register is set
!N	The N bit of the condition code register is clear (not N)
Z	The Z bit of the condition code register is set
!Z	The Z bit of the condition code register is clear (not Z)
N | Z	N or Z
!(N|Z)	Not (N or Z)
!MD	MD register is clear (not MD)

The operation field consists of a comma separated list of micro-operations. Figure 9.15 presents a grammar for micro-operations. According to this grammar, a micro-operation is a memory operation, a register operation, an increment of the program counter, or mapping the microprogram counter. Memory operations include read and write operations involving words and bytes. Register operations are defined by the bus they use to transmit the result value. Most operations use bus 3 for their results; however, we can load a value into the memory data register using bus 2. Constant values needed in the microassembly language program are specified by a "#" followed by a value. We assume that the assembler arranges to have all of the constant values stored in the constant table when the microprogram is loaded.

⟨micro op⟩ :: ⟨mem op⟩ | ⟨reg op⟩ | inc PC | MAP μBR

⟨mem op⟩ :: READ word | READ byte |
WRITE word | WRITE byte

⟨reg op⟩ :: ⟨bus 3 source⟩ → ⟨bus 3 dest ⟩ |
⟨bus 2 source⟩ → MDR

⟨bus 3 source⟩ :: ⟨shift res⟩ | ⟨alu res⟩ | MDR | PC
⟨bus 3 dest⟩ :: μBR | IR | src₂ | dest | Reg[dest] | src₁ |
MAR | temp₁ | temp₂ | PC

⟨shift res⟩ :: SHIFT ⟨shift op⟩ (⟨bus 1 source⟩, ⟨bus 2 source⟩)
⟨shift op⟩ :: left | right | right arith.

⟨alu res⟩ :: ALU ⟨alu op⟩ (⟨bus 1 source⟩, ⟨bus 2 source⟩)
⟨alu op⟩ :: add | sub | and | or | xor | xorn |
add.cc | sub.cc | and.cc | or.cc | xor.cc | xorn.cc

⟨bus 1 source⟩ :: ⟨constant⟩ | Reg[src₁] | temp₁
⟨bus 2 source⟩ :: IR | Reg[src₂] | temp₂ | PC
⟨constant⟩ :: #n

Figure 9.15 A grammar for micro-operations

You cannot have any conflicts in the micro-operations specified in a single microinstruction. A *resource conflict* is an attempt to use a single resource for two different activities in the same microinstruction. Most resource conflicts involve the use of a bus to transmit more than one value.

Resource conflict

When present, a branch field contains the word **branch** followed by a label. Every microinstruction includes the address of the next instruction. If the branch field is omitted, the microassembler fills this field with the address of the next instruction. In other words, sequence is implicit. Branching is unconditional; when it completes the execution of a microinstruction, the microcontrol unit sends the address in the branch field to the microprogram register.

Example 9.12 *Write a microassembly language code fragment to implement instruction fetch.*

```
    ifetch:
(1)    PC → MAR, READ word        ; start the memory read
(2)    while !MD                   ; wait for memory read
(3)    MDR → IR, inc PC            ; load the instruction register
```

The first instruction copies the value of the program counter to the memory address register and initiates the read of a memory word. The second instruction waits until the memory operation is complete. The third instruction copies the value of the memory data register to the instruction register.

Example 9.13 *Describe how you would implement a multiway branch based on the opcode of the instruction in the instruction register.*

(4)   SHIFT left(#11, IR) → μBR   ; *5-bit opcode to μBR*
(5)   MAP μPC   ; *switch*

The first of these instructions copies the opcode of the current instruction to the micro-branch register. The next instruction sets the microprogram register based on the value of the opcode.

For the remainder of these examples, we will assume that the mapping table has been loaded with the following list of labels:

MAP TABLE
ldw, ldw, ldb, ldb, stw, stw, stb, stb, add, add, sub, sub, and, and, or, or, xor, xor, xorn, xorn, sethi, sethi, setlo, setlo, bra, breq, brne, brlt, brle, brgt, brge, illegal

Combining this table with the previous example indicates that opcodes 00000 and 00001 are associated with the label *ldw* and so on. We will define the labels used in the mapping table as we write code fragments to handle the various instructions. Note that most of the labels are duplicated in the mapping table. Most instructions use a 4-bit opcode; however, the microprogram extracts a 5-bit opcode (so it can distinguish the branching instructions).

Example 9.14   *The opcode 11111 does not correspond to a legal opcode in our simple machine. Show how you can ignore instructions that have an opcode of 11111.*

    illegal:
(6)   **branch** ifetch

This instruction simply returns to the top of the ifetch loop.

Example 9.15   *Show how you would implement the BRLE instruction.*

    brle:
(7)   SHIFT left(#5, IR) → $temp_2$; *extract the offset field*
(8)   SHIFT right arith.(#4, $temp_2$) → $temp_1$; *sign extend and multiply by 2*
(9)   **if** N|E ALU add($temp_1$, PC) → PC **branch** ifetch ; *conditionally update the PC*

The first of these instructions stores the offset in the most significant 11 bits of $temp_2$. The next instruction stores the sign extended offset in $temp_1$. The last instruction adds the program counter with $temp_1$ and stores the result back into the program counter. Note that this instruction will not update the program counter if the N and Z flags are both 0.

Example 9.16   *Show how to implement the ADD instruction.*

add:

 ; *decode the remaining fields of the instruction*
(10) ALU and(#7, IR) → src$_2$; *extract the src$_2$ field*
(11) SHIFT right(#4, IR) → temp$_2$; *throw out the least significant 4 bits*
(12) ALU and(#7, temp$_2$) → src$_1$; *extract the src$_1$ field*
(13) Shift right(#4, temp$_2$) → temp$_2$; *throw out the least significant 4 bits*
(14) ALU and(#7, IR) → dest ; *extract the dest field*

 ; *perform the operation*
(15) ALU add.cc(Reg[src$_1$], Reg[src$_2$]) → Reg[dest] **branch** ifetch

Instructions 10 through 14 are used to decode the instruction. In particular, these instructions extract the src$_1$, src$_2$, and dest fields of the instruction. The last instruction performs the actual operation.

9.5.3 Implementing the Microarchitecture

In his book, *A Brief History of Time*, Stephen Hawking begins the first chapter with the following story:

> A well-known scientist (some say it was Bertrand Russell) once gave a public lecture on astronomy. He described how the earth orbits around the sun and how the sun, in turn, orbits around the center of a vast collection of stars called our galaxy. At the end of the lecture, a little old lady at the back of the room got up and said: "What you have told us is rubbish. The world is really a flat plate supported on the back of a giant tortoise." The scientist gave a superior smile before replying, "What is the tortoise standing on?" "You're very clever, young man, very clever," said the old lady. "But it's turtles all the way down!"

By now you may feel a bit like the scientist in Stephen Hawking's story. When you look to see how the machine is implemented, you find that it is implemented by another programming language (turtle). Well, it is not "turtles all the way down." In the remainder of this section, we discuss a hardware implementation of the microarchitecture that we used to implement our simple machine. We begin by presenting a format for encoding microinstructions, that is, a micromachine language.

Figure 9.16 presents a format for microinstructions. There are three fields in every microinstruction: the control field, the branch field, and the operation field. The control field encodes the condition specified in the microassembly instruction. The branch field encodes the address of the next microinstruction. The operation field encodes the control signals specified in the microassembly instruction.

Figure 9.16 A microinstruction format

The control field needs to encode the type of condition (**if** or **while**) along with the condition. We use a single bit to encode the type of the condition (1 for **while**). Table 9.8 presents the encodings that we use for the conditions.

Figure 9.17 shows how the control field can be used to control the updating of the microprogram counter. This circuit uses three multiplexers. The first determines the value of the condition encoded in the microinstruction. In addition to controlling the generation of the control signals, this value is the control input for the second multiplexer. The second multiplexer selects between the branch field in the microinstruction and the current value of the microprogram counter. If the **while** flag of the control field is set and the condition is true, the multiplexer selects the old value of the microprogram counter. In this way, the machine will reexecute the same microinstruction while the condition is true. Otherwise, the multiplexer selects the branch field of the microinstruction. The final multiplexer selects between the mapped value of the microbranch register and the value determined by the previous multiplexer. This multiplexer is controlled by a standard control signal (we use the micro-operation "map μPC" to denote this signal in our microassembly language).

The operation field is used to encode the micro-operations to be performed during the execution of the microinstruction. There are three techniques used to encode the control signals in a microinstruction: horizontal microprogramming, vertical microprogramming, and nanoprogramming. We limit our consideration to horizontal and vertical microprogramming.

Table 9.9 summarizes the control signals needed to control the registers and combinational circuits shown in Figure 9.14. In *horizontal microprogramming,* the operation field of the microinstruction has one bit for every control signal. This approach leads to fast execution of microinstructions because there is no need to decode the operation field of the microinstruction. It is called horizontal microprogramming because the microinstructions tend to be very wide.

Table 9.10 presents an alternative summary of the control signals. In this presentation, the control signals are grouped to permit encoding. For example, all of the

Table 9.8 Encoding conditions

Condition	Encoding
N	000
!N	001
Z	010
!Z	011
N | Z	100
!(N|Z)	101
true	110
!MD	111

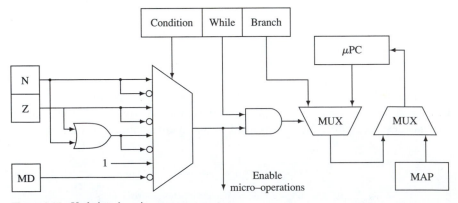

Figure 9.17 Updating the microprogram counter

signals that gate values onto bus 2 form an encoding group. There are four signals in this group. In horizontal microprogramming, these signals would require 4 bits in the microinstruction; however, they can be encoded using two bits. This approach is called vertical microprogramming to contrast it with horizontal microprogramming.

Table 9.9 Microcontrol signals

General registers		Memory Registers		Other registers	
0	Load src_1	6	Load MAR	16	Inc $\rightarrow$ PC
1	Load src_2	7	Load MDR	17	Load PC
2	Load dest	8	MDR $\rightarrow$ bus 3	18	PC $\rightarrow$ bus 2
3	Reg[src_1] $\rightarrow$ bus 1	9	Set Rd	19	PC $\rightarrow$ bus 3
4	Reg[src_2] $\rightarrow$ bus 2	10	Clear Rd	20	Load IR
5	Load Reg[dest]	11	Set Sz	21	IR $\rightarrow$ bus 2
		12	Clear Sz	22	Load $temp_1$
		13	Set MS	23	$Temp_1$ $\rightarrow$ bus 1
		14	Clear MS	24	Load $temp_2$
		15	Clear MD	25	$Temp_2$ $\rightarrow$ bus 2

ALU and shifter		Miscellaneous	
26–28	Select ALU operation	34	Load μBR
29	ALU $\rightarrow$ bus 3	35	MAP $\rightarrow$ μPC
30	Load cc	36	CT $\rightarrow$ bus 1
31–32	Select SHIFT operation	37–40	Select CT[0]–CT[15]
33	Shifter $\rightarrow$ bus 3		

Table 9.10 Microcontrol signals—encoded

To bus 1 (0–1)		To bus 2 (2–3)		To bus 3 (4–5)	
00	CT $\rightarrow$ bus 1	00	IR $\rightarrow$ bus 2	00	Shifter $\rightarrow$ bus 3
01	Reg[src_1] $\rightarrow$ bus 1	01	Reg[src_2] $\rightarrow$ bus 2	01	ALU $\rightarrow$ bus 3
10	$temp_1$ $\rightarrow$ bus 1	10	$temp_2$ $\rightarrow$ bus 2	10	MDR $\rightarrow$ bus 3
		11	PC $\rightarrow$ bus 2	11	PC $\rightarrow$ bus 3

Register loads (6–9)		Memory ops (10–11)		Other signals	
0000	Load IR	00	Read word	12–14	Select ALU op
0001	Load src_1	01	Read byte	15	Load cc
0010	Load src_2	10	Write word	16–17	Select SHIFT op
0011	Load dest	11	Write byte	18	MAP $\rightarrow$ μPC
0100	Load Reg[dest]			19–22	Select CT[0]–CT[15]
0101	Load MAR			23	inc $\rightarrow$ PC
0110	Load MDR				
0111	Load $temp_1$				
1000	Load $temp_2$				
1001	Load PC				
1010	Load μBR				

Vertical microprogramming schemes have much shorter microinstructions. For example, our horizontal scheme would require 41 bits in the operation field while our vertical scheme only requires 24 bits. This advantage is balanced by the added cost of decoding and a possible limitation of parallelism. To see the limitation of parallelism, consider the control signals in the register loads group. Because all of the register loads are in a single group, each microinstruction can load at most one register. This limitation is not present in the horizontal scheme. In the horizontal scheme, we could load a value into several registers in the same microinstruction. In our vertical scheme, we would need one microinstruction for each register that needs to be loaded.

The primary differences between horizontal and vertical microprogramming are summarized in Table 9.11 and illustrated in Figure 9.18.

Table 9.11   Horizontal versus vertical microprogramming

	Horizontal	Vertical
Instruction width	Very wide ($-$)	Reasonable ($+$)
Signal decode	Minimal ($+$)	Significant ($-$)
Parallelism	Excellent ($+$)	Moderate ($-$)

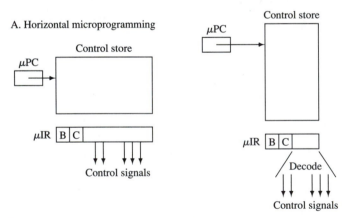

Figure 9.18   Horizontal versus vertical microprogramming

9.6 SUMMARY

In this chapter, we have discussed three techniques for implementing the instruction set of a machine: direct implementation, pipelining, and microprogramming. In addition, we have discussed several techniques aimed at improving instruction bandwidth.

Historically, direct implementation was the preferred approach, and machines had very simple instruction sets. However, as processors became faster, instruction bandwidth became the bottleneck in instruction interpretation. To reduce the impact of the instruction bandwidth bottleneck, many designers increased the complexity of the instructions in the instruction set. The goal was to decrease the number of instructions in an assembly language program by increasing the amount of work performed by each instruction.

As instructions became increasingly complicated, designers began to use microprogramming to reduce the complexity of processor design. As we have discussed, microprograms are (relatively) easy to extend and modify. In this way, microprogramming made it possible to develop very complex instruction sets. Instruction sets became so complicated that it was difficult to determine how effective the instruction set was. Many of the most complex instructions were used so infrequently that their benefit was questionable. Perhaps the most important concern was that most compilers were not able to make use of the increasingly complex instructions.

The RISC approach to processor design is based on the use of very simple instructions. The instruction set is simple enough to permit a direct, pipelined implementation. In fact, much of the instruction set is tailored to the pipelined implementation. The instruction set is simple enough to permit quantitative studies of the trade-offs in the instruction set. Many of the problems associated with instruction pipelining (in particular instruction scheduling) are relatively easy to handle in a compiler. Instruction caching is used to overcome the instruction bandwidth problem. While it is apparent that the RISC approach will continue to be the preferred implementation technique, it is also apparent that future generations of RISC machines will increase the complexity of their instruction sets and begin to look much more like CISC machines.

9.6.1 Additional Reading

If you would like a different perspective on this material, you should read the books listed under the category of *Computer Organization*. Among these books, I recommend *Computer Architecture, a Quantitative Approach* by Hennesy and Patterson; *Computer Organization* by Hamacher, Vranesic, and Zaky (3rd edition); *Structured Computer Organization* (3rd edition) by Andrew S. Tanenbaum; and *Computer Architecture: A Modern Synthesis* by Dasgupta. If you are interested in a more comprehensive presentation of microprogramming, I recommend *Computer Design and Architecture* by Pollard.

9.6.2 Terminology

- Memory latency, Instruction bandwidth
- Instruction interleaving, Instruction prefetch, Instruction buffer, Branch predictors
- Fully associative cache, Direct mapping cache, Set associative cache
- Cache hit, Cache miss, Tag bits

- Store-through, Store-back
- Pipelining, Pipeline stage
- Data-oriented perspective, Control-oriented perspective
- Read/write dependency, Write/write dependency
- Pipeline stall, Pipeline slip, Pipeline bubble
- Register forwarding, Register interlocking
- Double buffering
- Superpipelining, Superscalar
- Control store, Firmware
- Resource conflict
- Horizontal microprogramming, Vertical microprogramming

9.6.3 Review Questions

1. What does the term *instruction bandwidth* mean? Explain why you cannot always compute instruction bandwidth as the inverse of the memory cycle time.
2. Explain how branch predictors are used in instruction prefetch.
3. What is the principle of locality? Why is this principle important in instruction caching?
4. Explain the difference between a fully associative cache, a direct mapping cache, and a set associative cache. Explain what it means to say that a cache is four-way set associative.
5. Explain the difference between the terms *store-back* and *store-through.*
6. Explain why we say that pipelining is based on a data-oriented perspective. Explain the conveyor belt analogy for pipelining.
7. Give an example of a read/write dependency.
8. Explain the difference between a pipeline stall, a pipeline slip, and a pipeline bubble.
9. Why is register interlocking a more general solution than register forwarding?
10. Explain how the load/store architecture simplifies pipelining.
11. What does superpipelining mean? What does superscalar mean?

9.7 EXERCISES

1. Assuming that the instruction has already been fetched, describe how you could use the data paths shown in Figure 9.1 to implement
   a. Load instructions.
   b. Store instructions.

c.   Setlo instruction.

d.   Sethi instruction.

2.   In Example 9.3, we note that the PC is updated **if** the condition is met. Design a combinational circuit that will produce a 1 if the condition is met and a 0 otherwise. Your circuit should use the N (negative) and Z (zero) flags of the condition code register along with the 5 most significant bits of the opcode as inputs.

3.   In Example 9.5 we used the least significant 5 bits to identify the cache address. Explain why it would not be a good idea to use the most significant 5 bits.

4.   Draw a diagram that illustrates the data paths needed to implement a write operation for the cache structure described in Example 9.5.

5.   You can build a two-way set associative cache from two direct mapping caches. Using a diagram, show the data paths needed to implement the read operation for a system with a 16-bit memory address and a two-way set associative cache with a total of 64 elements (i.e., two 32-element direct mapping caches).

6.   Consider the instructions

     ADD R2, R3, R4
     ADD R2, R4, R5
     ADD R3, R2, R6

     Suppose that the registers R2, R3, R4, R5, and R6 start with the values 2, 3, 4, 5, and 6, respectively. Show what will happen if you execute this instruction sequence on our four-stage pipeline, assuming that the pipeline uses register interlocking but does not block instructions when their destination register is locked.

7.   Adapt Figure 9.10 to implement the *store* operations. At the end of stage 3, these instructions should set three registers: the memory address register, MAR; the memory data register, MDR; and the size register SZ. (The size register indicates the size of the operation—byte or word.)

8.   Adapt Figure 9.10 to implement the register set operations. To implement these operations, you need to add some combinational logic to stage 3 of the pipeline. In particular, you will need to add the logic that determines the new value of the destination register.

     In drawing your solution, you do not need to reproduce all of the data paths shown in Figure 9.10. In particular, you can omit the data paths related to the ALU. However, you should include enough information to indicate how your data paths can be integrated with the data paths shown in Figure 9.10. For example, you will probably need a multiplexer on the data path leading into the general-purpose registers to select between the ALU result and the set register result.

9. Adapt Figure 9.10 to implement the branching operations. In designing your solution to this exercise, there are two things that you will need to consider. First, the conditional branching operations use the condition code register, cc, to determine whether to update the program counter, PC. Second, by the time the second stage of the pipeline has determined the new value of the program counter, the first stage will have fetched the next instruction and will be ready to save a new value in the program counter.

10. Considering the data paths and registers shown in Figure 9.10, explain how you would implement data forwarding for the data manipulation operations. You do not need to show how you would modify this illustration, but you should explain how you would examine the registers to determine which value to forward. To simplify your explanation, you may assume that src_1 is the only register that could be forwarded.

11. Considering the data paths shown in Figure 9.10, explain how you could implement the conditional pipeline slip needed for the branching operations.

12. Figure 9.11 assumes that the first stage of the pipeline always completes its activities in a single processor cycle. Show how you would alter this illustration if the first stage is not completed in a single processor cycle. In particular, the register IR_1 may not be full when the second stage has completed its use of the value in IR_2.

13. Write a microassembly language fragment that implements:

    a. The load word instruction.

    b. The store byte instruction.

    c. The set high instruction.

    d. The set low instruction.

14. The code fragment shown in Example 9.15 performs two operations before it determines if the branch should be taken. Rewrite this code sequence so that it determines if the branch will be taken before it performs any meaningful work. (Hint: you will need to conditionally map the microprogram counter.)

THE TRANSLATION PROCESS

CHAPTER 10

In the first section of Chapter 5, we introduced a simple model of the translation process. In this chapter, we elaborate on that model. The translation process is divided into three stages: the assembly process (implemented by the *assembler*), the linkage process (implemented by the *linker*), and the loading process (implemented by the *loader*).

The assembler performs the initial translation of an assembly language module into machine code (a module is a file that contains part of a program). The input for the assembler is called a *source module*—it is the source of the translation. The output of the assembler is called an *object module*—it is the object of the translation. The assembler is not able to complete the translation into machine code if the module uses a symbol (label) that is defined in another module or library.

Source module

Object module

The linker performs the next stage in the translation process by linking assembled modules and libraries to form a complete program. The primary task that the linker performs is to *resolve external references*. In particular, if one module uses a symbol that is defined in another module or defined in a library, the linker will match the use of the symbol with its definition. Having matched the use of a symbol with its definition, the linker can complete the translation of any instructions that use the symbol. The linker reads several object modules and libraries and constructs an *executable file*.

Executable file

The loader performs the final stage in the translation process—loading the program into memory where it can be executed. In some systems, the loader simply copies the executable program into the appropriate memory locations. In these systems, the loader does not have a role in translation. However, in other systems, the loader must be capable of loading the program into different memory locations at different times. Loading a program into different locations at different times is called *relocation*. To provide this relocation, the loader must adjust many of the addresses used in a program to reflect the actual location of the program. In other words, the loader must perform a final translation of the addresses used in a program.

Relocation

Figure 10.1 illustrates the relationships between the processes involved in the translation process (i.e., the assembler, linker, and loader) and the types of files (i.e., source, object, and executable) they manipulate. Each object file is produced by running the assembler on a separate source file. Several object files and libraries can be combined by the linker to produce a single executable file. The executable file is read by the loader and loaded into memory prior to execution.

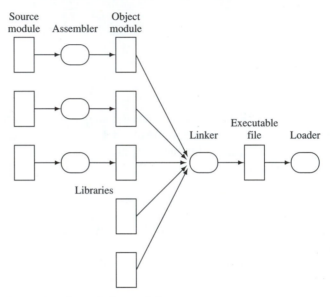

Figure 10.1   Stages in the translation process

10.1 ASSEMBLY

We begin by considering the structure of an assembler. In this section, we concentrate on the basic translation process and ignore the possibility of external references. In particular, we only consider the resolution of names that are defined and used in the same file. We consider external references when we discuss linking in the next section. In addition to ignoring the possibility of external references, we also ignore the fact that most assemblers support multiple assembler segments (e.g., text, data, and bss) in our initial discussions. We consider the impact of assembler segments after we have discussed the basic structures.

Assemblers perform a line-oriented translation. In other words, an assembler translates an assembly language program one line at a time. Figure 10.2 presents pseudocode for a simple assembler. The assembler begins by constructing an empty symbol table and initializing the value of the location counter to LOAD_ADDR, the memory address where the program will be loaded. The main loop reads a line from the source file, enters any new label definitions into the symbol table, translates the instruction (if any) into machine language, and writes it to the object file.

```
void main( void )
{
    /* construct an empty symbol table */
    make_empty_table( sym_tab );

    /* initialize the location counter */
    location = LOAD_ADDR;

    /* process each line in the source file */
    while( !eof(source_file) ) {
        read_line( source_file, this_line );

        /* check for a new label definition on this line */
        label = new_label( this_line );
        if( label ≠ NULL ) enter( sym_tab, label, location );

        /* translate the instruction on this line */
        mach_inst = translate( this_line, location );
        if( mach_inst ≠ NULL ) {
            write( object_file, mach_inst );
            location = location + size_of( mach_inst );
        }
    }
}
```

Figure 10.2   Pseudocode for a simple assembler

The translate function translates a line from the source file into machine language. If the line contains an assembly language instruction, the translate function returns the corresponding machine language instruction. If the line from the source file contains an assembler directive, the translate function interprets the directive. The special machine language instruction NULL is used to indicate that the line did not contain an assembly language instruction and, as such, translate cannot produce a machine language instruction. If the translate routine returns a non-NULL machine language instruction, the assembler writes the machine language instruction to the object file and updates the location counter.

Example 10.1   *To illustrate the basic assembly process, we consider the following code fragment. This code fragment sums the values in an array of integers.*

```
(1)       array:   .reserve    20*4            ; 20 integers
    :
(2)   code_start:                              ; execution starts here
    :
(3)              CLEAR    R2              ; R2 holds the result
(4)              MOVE     R3, #array      ; R3 points to current element
(5)              MOVE     R4, #20         ; R4 number of elements left
```

(6)	top:			
(7)		LOAD.w	R5, [R3]+	; *get the next value*
(8)		ADD	R2, R2, R5	; *update the result*
(9)		ADD	R4, R4, #−1	; *one less element*
(10)		BRGE	top	; *process the next element*

When the assembler encounters definitions for the labels *array* and *code_start* on lines 1 and 2, it enters these definitions in the symbol table. To translate the instruction on line 3, the assembler constructs a machine language instruction using the appropriate instruction format. (In this case, the assembler will use an OR instruction to simulate the CLEAR operation.) To translate the next instruction on line 4, the assembler needs to look up the value associated with the label *array* in the symbol table.

Translation of the code fragment presented in Example 10.1 is simple because every label is defined before it is used. In particular, every instruction that uses a label uses a label that was defined earlier in the program. When the use of **Backward reference** a label refers to a previously defined label, it is called a *backward reference*. When the use of a label refers to a label that is defined later in the code, it is **Forward reference** called a *forward reference*. Forward references present a problem to the assembler because the assembler does not know the value of the label when it is translating the instruction that uses the label. In the remainder of this section we consider two techniques—a two-pass approach and the use of a patch list—to handle the difficulties introduced by forward references.

Example 10.2   *To illustrate the difficulty introduced by forward references, we consider a slight modification to the code fragment presented Example 10.1. The following code fragment sums the* positive *values in an array of integers.*

(1)	array:	.reserve	20*4	; *20 integers*
(2)	code_start:			; *execution starts here*
(3)		CLEAR	R2	; *R2 holds the result*
(4)		MOVE	R3, #array	; *R3 points to current element*
(5)		MOVE	R4, #20	; *R4 number of elements left*
(6)	top:			
(7)		LOAD.w	R5, [R3]+	; *get the next value*
(8)		BRLE	dec	; *do not add negative values*
(9)		ADD	R2, R2, R5	; *update the result*
(10)	dec:			
(11)		ADD	R4, R4, #−1	; *one less element*
(12)		BRGE	top	; *process the next element*

When the assembler starts to translate the BRLE instruction on line 8, it cannot complete the translation of this instruction because it has not seen the definition for the label *dec*. The assembler will not see the definition for this label until it reaches line 10.

10.1.1 The Two-Pass Approach

In the two-pass approach, the assembler makes two separate passes over the source file. During the first pass, the assembler builds a symbol table that has an entry for every symbol defined in the source file. During the second pass, the assembler uses the information stored in the symbol table to translate the instructions in the source file. The assembler does not attempt to translate instructions during the first pass over the source file; it simply determines the value of every symbol defined in the source file. The actual translation of instructions is performed during the second pass—after the value of every symbol has been recorded in the symbol table. The two-pass strategy works because the assembler can determine the size of every instruction without needing to translate them into machine language.

Figure 10.3 presents pseudocode for a two-pass assembler. In contrasting the pseudocode shown in Figure 10.3 with the pseudocode for the simple assembler (Figure 10.2), note that the two-pass assembler separates the single loop of the

```
void main( void )
{
    /*********** the first pass ***********/
    make_empty_table( sym_tab );
    location = LOAD_ADDR;
    while( !eof(source_file) ) {
        this_line = read_line( source_file );

        label = new_label( this_line );
        if( label ≠ NULL ) enter( sym_tab, label, location );

        location = location + bytes_needed( this_line );
    }

    /*********** the second pass ***********/
    rewind_file( source_file );
    location = LOAD_ADDR;
    while( !eof(source_file) ) {
        this_line = read_line( source_file );

        mach_inst = translate( this_line, location );
        if( mach_inst ≠ NULL ) {
            write( object_file, mach_inst );
            location = location + size_of( mach_inst );
        }
    }
}
```

Figure 10.3 Pseudocode for a two-pass assembler

simple assembler into two loops. The first loop constructs the symbol table, while the second constructs the object file. The function "bytes_needed" determines the number of bytes needed to translate an assembly language instruction into machine language. This function does not translate the assembly language instruction; it only determines the number of bytes that will be used when the instruction is actually translated.

Example 10.3 *Consider the following code fragment. Suppose that each instruction requires four bytes and that the location counter has the value 0 when it starts. Give the value for each label defined in this code. (This is the code fragment presented in Example 10.2 to add up the positive values in an array of integers.)*

```
(1)    array:   .reserve   20*4           ; 20 integers
(2)  code_start:                          ; execution starts here
(3)           CLEAR      R2              ; R2 holds the result
(4)           MOVE       R3, #array      ; R3 points to current element
(5)           MOVE       R4, #20         ; R4 number of elements left
(6)    top:
(7)           LOAD.w     R5, [R3]+       ; get the next value
(8)           BRLE       dec             ; don't add negative values
(9)           ADD        R2, R2, R5      ; update the result
(10)   dec:
(11)          ADD        R4, R4, #-1     ; one less element
(12)          BRGE       top             ; process the next element
```

Label	Value
array	0
code_start	80
top	92
dec	104

We should note that the assembler does not need to make two passes over the original source file to qualify as a two-pass assembler. Many two-pass assemblers copy the essential parts of the source file to a temporary file as they are making the first pass over the source file. During the second pass, the assembler reads the temporary file rather than the original source file. By omitting nonessential items like comments from the temporary file, the assembler may be able to process the temporary file much faster than it would be able to process the original source file. In addition to omitting nonessential items, the assembler may perform a simple translation as it writes the assembly language instructions to the temporary file. As an example, consider the mnemonics used to specify the operation in an assembly language instruction. While you and I find the use of mnemonics convenient, they complicate the assembly process because the assembler must first identify the start and end of the mnemonic and then look up the mnemonic in a table to determine the meaning of the mnemonic. From the assembler's perspective, translation would be much easier if every assembly language instruction began with an operation *number*. The assembler could then simply read the number and use it as an index into an array to determine the meaning of the operation number. In a two-pass assembler, the assembler might translate operation mnemonics to operation numbers[1] during the first pass in an attempt to simplify the I/O processing that must be done during the second pass.

10.1.2 Using a Patch List

An alternative to the two-pass assembler involves the construction and use of a patch list. In this approach, the assembler makes a single pass over the source file but makes two passes over the object file. During the first pass, the assembler deposits partially translated instructions one after the other into the object file. Instructions that have forward references are not completely translated; however, the assembler allocates enough space in the object file so that it can complete the translation on the second pass.

After the assembler completes the first pass, it will have determined all of the label values. It can then "patch" all of the instructions that used forward references. Note that the second pass is over the object file instead of the source file. Moreover, the second pass is driven by the patch list that was constructed during the first pass. In both approaches, the first pass is driven by the lines in the source file. In a two-pass assembler, the second pass is also driven by the lines in the source file.

A patch list is a list of patch entries. Each *patch entry* records the location of an instruction that needs to be patched. In addition, each patch entry has a pointer to the symbol table entry that (eventually) holds the definition of the symbol. Patch entries are constructed (and added to the patch list) whenever the assembler encounters a forward reference.

Patch entry

The first time the assembler encounters a reference to an undefined label, it creates an entry for the label in the symbol table along with the patch entry that is added to the patch list. The assembler sets a flag in the symbol table entry to indicate that the symbol is not defined. When the assembler encounters other forward references, it will find the entry for the symbol in the symbol table. Because it is still undefined, the assembler generates a patch entry for the current instruction. When the assembler encounters a definition for the label, it sets the flags in the symbol table entry to indicate that the symbol is defined and will then set the value field of the symbol table entry.

---

[1] These operation numbers do not necessarily have any relationship to the operation codes of the machine language.

Example 10.4   *To illustrate the patch list approach, we once again consider our code fragment that sums the positive values in an array.*

(1)	array:	.reserve	20*4	; *20 integers*
(2)	code_start:			; *execution starts here*
(3)		CLEAR	R2	; *R2 holds the result*
(4)		MOVE	R3, #array	; *R3 points to current element*
(5)		MOVE	R4, #20	; *R4 number of elements left*
(6)	top:			
(7)		LOAD.w	R5, [R3]+	; *get the next value*
(8)		BRLE	dec	; *don't add negative values*
(9)		ADD	R2, R2, R5	; *update the result*
(10)	dec:			
(11)		ADD	R4, R4, #−1	; *one less element*
(12)		BRGE	top	; *process the next element*

In this case, the assembler needs to construct a single patch list entry for the forward reference in line 8 of the code. When the assembler starts its translation of the ADD instruction on line 9, the patch list and symbol table will have the following structure:

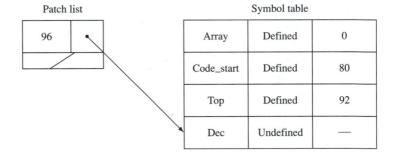

Figure 10.4 presents pseudocode for an assembler using a patch list. Before starting the first pass, the assembler creates an empty patch list. The assembler creates a patch list entry for any instruction that cannot be completely translated. During the second pass, the assembler uses the entries in the patch list to update the object file. If a patch list entry points to a symbol table entry that is still undefined, the assembler produces an error message.

While a two-pass assembler and a patch list assembler both use a symbol table, they use different implementations of the *insert* and *lookup* operations. Table 10.1 contrasts the implementations used by the two approaches. The insert operation is invoked whenever the assembler encounters the definition of a label. In particular, the *enter* operation used in the pseudocode presented in Figures 10.3 and 10.4 will invoke an insert operation for the symbol table. The lookup operation is invoked whenever the assembler encounters the use of a label. In particular, the *translate*

```
void main( void )
{
    /*********** the first pass ***********/
    make_empty_tab( sym_tab );
    location = LOAD_ADDR;
    make_empty( patch_list );
    while( !eof(source_file) ) {
        this_line = read_line( source_file );

        label = new_label( this_line );
        if( label ≠ NULL ) enter( sym_tab, label, location );

        mach_inst = translate( this_line, location );
        if( mach_inst ≠ NULL ) {
            if( incomplete(mach_inst) ) {
                patch_item = make_patch( mach_inst, location );
                add_to_end( patch_list, patch_item );
            }
            write( object_file, mach_inst );
            location = location + size_of( mach_inst );
        }
    }

    /*********** the second pass ***********/
    while( !is_empty(patch_list) ) {
        patch_item = remove_first( patch_list );
        apply_patch( object_file, patch_item );
    }
}
```

Figure 10.4 Pseudocode for an assembler using a patch list

Table 10.1 Symbol table operations

Operation	Two-pass	Patch list

Insert	**if** symbol present
	    error
	else
	    add symbol
		if symbol present
		    if not defined
		        update symbol entry
		    else
		        error
		else
		    add symbol

Lookup	**if** symbol present
	    get value
	else
	    error
		if symbol present
		    if defined
		        get value
		else
		    insert symbol (not defined)
		    generate patch entry

operation used in Figures 10.3 and 10.4 will invoke the lookup operation during the translation of an instruction.

We begin by considering the differences in the insert operations. In the two-pass approach, symbol entries are only added to the symbol table when the symbol is defined, hence the assembler produces an error message ("multiple definitions of symbol") if the symbol is already in the table when the insert operation is invoked. In the patch list approach a symbol table entry is added the first time the assembler encounters the symbol. Because the first time the symbol appears in the source file may be a use (instead of a definition), it is possible that the assembler will find that the symbol is already present in the symbol table when it encounters the definition of a symbol. In this case, it is only an error if the symbol is already in the symbol table *and* the flag indicates that the symbol is defined.

The lookup operation used in the two-pass assembler is also very simple. In this case, the assembler can simply produce an error message ("symbol not defined") whenever it fails to find a symbol when it is translating instructions during the second pass. In contrast, the lookup operation for a patch list assembler must insert the symbol if it is not already present in the symbol table. (Remember, the patch list assembler produces error messages about undefined symbols when it processes the patch list.)

10.1.3 Assembler Segments

You may be interested in the ways that the assembler segments (text, data, and bss) interact with the assembly approaches we have discussed. As we discussed in Chapter 5, the assembler maintains a separate location counter for each segment and deposits values for the text and data segments in separate temporary files. After the entire program has been translated, the assembler concatenates the data segment onto the end of the text segment and prepends a file header that, among other things, specifies the size of the bss segment.

Figure 10.5 presents pseudocode for a simple assembler that includes support for assembler segments. This code begins by assuming that the assembler already knows the length of the text and data segments. Given this (magic) information, the assembler can compute the base address for each segment and initialize a location counter for each segment. Before entering its main loop, the assembler establishes the text segment as the default segment. The body of the loop is essentially the same as it was for the simple assembler; only a few lines of code have been changed. Most of the changes reflect the fact that *location* and *object_file* are no longer simple variables, but arrays indexed by the current segment. The only significant change in the body of the loop involves the calculation of the label address in the call to the function *enter*. The address of the label is calculated by adding the base address of the current segment with the location counter for the current segment. The code following the main loop is used to create the final output file by concatenating the text and data segments onto the file header.

The major complication introduced by assembler segments is the need to compute the final address for each label by adding the segment base address to the offset of the label within the segment. This is not a problem for labels defined in text segment because the base address of the text is a fixed constant, LOAD_ADDR; however, the base address of the data segment is determined by the length of the text segment, and the base address of the bss segment is determined by the length of the text and data segments.

```
void main( void )
{
    /* setup segment base addresses — this is MAGIC */
    base[text] = LOAD_ADDR;
    base[data] = base[text] + length[text];
    base[bss]  = base[data] + length[data];

    /* we need a location counter for each segment */
    location[text] = 0;
    location[data] = 0;
    location[bss] = 0;

    make_empty_table( sym_tab );
    cur_seg = text;
    while( !eof(source_file) ) {
        this_line = read_line( source_file );

        label = new_label( this_line );
        if( label ≠ NULL )
            enter( sym_tab, label, base[cur_seg] + location[cur_seg] );

        mach_inst = translate( this_line, location[cur_seg], cur_seg );
        if( mach_inst ≠ NULL )
            if( cur_seg ≠ bss ) write( object_file[cur_seg], mach_inst );

        location[cur_seg] = location[cur_seg] + size_of( mach_inst );
    }

    /* now we build the final output file */
    write_header( final_output );
    rewind( object_file[text] );
    copy_file( object_file[text], final_output );
    rewind( object_file[data] );
    copy_file( object_file[data], final_output );
}
```

Figure 10.5 Pseudocode for an assembler with segments

The assembler cannot determine the length of the text or data segments until it has made a complete pass over the source file. At this point, you might consider developing a three-pass assembler. The first pass determines the length of each segment, the second determines the address of every label, and the third translates the source code. A better approach involves using *offsets* instead of addresses in the   Offsets symbol table. In this approach, the symbol table associates a segment and an offset with each label. During the first pass, the assembler determines the segment and offset for each label as well as the length of the text, data, and bss segments. As such, whenever a label is used during the second pass, the assembler can determine the final address for the label from the information stored in the symbol table.

Example 10.5   *Consider the following code fragment. Show the part of the symbol table that results when a two-pass assembler completes its first pass over this code. Unless otherwise noted, assume that every assembly language instruction requires four bytes.*

```
        .bss
v1:     .reserve    20*4        ; space for 20 integers
v2:     .reserve    4           ; space for a single integer

        .data
i:      .word       0           : initialized variables
j:      .word       0

        .text
        LOAD.w      R2, i       ; initialize the looping register
        LOAD.w      R3, #20     ; initialize the termination test
        LOAD.w      R4, #v1     ; pointer initialization
        CLEAR       R5          ; initialize the result
        BRANCH      test
loop:
        LOAD.w      R6, [R4]+   ; get the next array value
        ADD         R5, R5, R6  ; add it into the running sum
        ADD         R2, R2, #1  ; increment the control register
test:
        CMP         R2, R3
        BRNE        loop
```

Label	Segment	Offset
v1	bss	0
v2	bss	40
i	data	0
j	data	4
loop	text	20
test	text	32

Adapting the patch list approach to accommodate multiple assembler segments is also relatively straightforward. As with the two-pass approach, the symbol table records segment and offset pairs instead of addresses. During the first pass, the assembler constructs the symbol table along with two patch lists, one for the text segment and another for the data segment. The patch list for the text segment records patch locations within the text segment, while the patch list for the data segment records patch locations within the data segment. After the assembler completes its initial translation of the source file, it can complete the translation by first applying the patches in the text segment patch list and then applying the patches in the data segment patch list.

One surprising aspect of using the patch list approach with assembler segments is that the combined patch lists will be much larger than the single patch list was for the simple (single segment) case. As we noted, every forward reference will generate an entry on a patch list. Moreover, many backward references (uses of symbols that have already been defined) will also generate entries on the patch lists. Remember, a patch list entry is generated whenever the assembler does not have enough information to complete the translation of the instruction during the first pass.

Example 10.6   *Consider the code fragment presented in Example 10.5. Which statements will generate patch list entries?*

The LOAD.w R4, #v1, and BRANCH test instructions will generate patch list entries. The first instruction uses a backward reference; however, the address of *v1* will not be known until the assembler completes the first pass.

   Note that the BRNE loop instruction does not generate a patch list entry. By the time the assembler encounters this instruction, it will know the address associated with the label *loop*. Moreover, this instruction will most likely be encoded using a relative address (i.e., an offset from the program counter). As such, the assembler does not need to know the value of the label, only the difference between the address of the current instruction and the value of the label.

10.2 LINKING

The primary task of the linker is to resolve external references, that is, to match symbols that are defined in one file with the uses of these symbols in other files. In addition to resolving external references, the linker must also merge several object and library files into a single executable file. It turns out that a variation on the patch list approach provides an effective basis for the linker. In this approach, the assembler simply completes the first pass over the source file, constructing a first approximation of the text and data segments, the symbol table, and two patch lists. All of this information, along with a file header, is written to the *object file*.   Object file
Processing the patch lists (updating the text and data segments) is left for the linker. In contrast to the previous version, the assembler needs to create a patch entry whenever a symbol is used as an address in the program (including uses of previously defined symbols in the text segment).

   In the remainder of this section, we consider the structure of the object file produced by the assembler and the process used to link object files. We begin by introducing the assembly language directives associated with external references. After we discuss these directives, we consider the information stored in the symbol table entries used by the assembler and linker. Next, we consider the structure of the object file produced by the assembler. In particular, we consider how the data structures (symbol table and patch lists) are stored in the object file. After presenting the structure of the object file, we turn our attention to the actual linking process. We conclude our discussion of linking by considering multiple object files and libraries.

10.2.1 The Import and Export Directives

Modules

Linking allows the programmer to divide a large program into several files, called *modules*, that can be assembled separately and linked together at a later time. An important aspect of linking is the sharing of symbol definitions—a symbol defined in one module may be used in other modules. This brings up an interesting problem: Can every symbol defined in every module be used in any other module? Most of the symbols that you use in an assembly language program have a very small range of use (the top or bottom of a loop, the else part of a conditional, and so forth) and would never be needed by other modules. As such, there is no need to make the definitions for these symbols available for use in another module. In an attempt to protect the programmer from accidently using a symbol defined in another module, most assemblers require the use of special directives to share symbol definitions among different modules. By default, any symbol used in an assembly language file must be defined in that file.

Coding Convention—Import and Export (Public and Private)

We will use two assembler directives to express shared symbols: import and export. The import directive is used to declare that a symbol (or list of symbols) is defined in another file, that is, the symbol definition is to be imported. The export directive is used to declare that a symbol (or list of symbols) defined in the current file is to be made available to other files. Symbols that are defined in a file, but not exported are called *private* symbols while symbols that are exported are called *public* symbols.

Example 10.7   *Show how you would use the import and export directives to define a pseudorandom number generator in a separate file.*

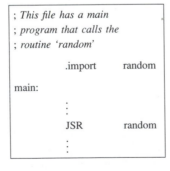

There are two (rather obvious) rules associated with imported and exported symbols. Every symbol in an export must be defined in the file that contains the export list. The symbols in an import list cannot be defined in the file that contains the import list.

10.2.2 Symbol Table Entries

The nature of the import/export directives has a direct impact on the structure of symbol table entries. Up until this point, we have identified four fields in a symbol table entry: a field that holds the name of the symbol, a field that holds the segment for the symbol (text, data, or bss), a field that holds the offset of the symbol, and a field that indicates if the symbol is defined. To support linking, we need to add two new fields. These fields indicate whether the symbol is imported or exported. Figure 10.6 presents a C structure declaration that summarizes the fields in a symbol table entry. This figure includes an enumeration that lists the three types of segments: text, data, and bss. The structure declares a name field (implemented as a pointer to a character), a segment field, an offset field, a defined field, an imported field, and an exported field. The last three fields are implemented as *bit fields*. Each of these fields uses a single bit. When a new symbol table entry   Bit fields
is created, the defined, imported, and exported flags are all set to *false* (0). If the symbol is defined, the defined flag is set to *true* (1). If the symbol appears in an import list, the imported flag is set to *true*. If the symbol appears in an export list, the export flag is set to *true*.

```
/* first, an enumeration of the segment types */
enum segment {text, data, bss};

struct sym_entry {
    char *name;                /* a string */
    unsigned int offset;       /* the offset of the symbol */
    enum segment seg;          /* the segment */
    unsigned int defined :1;   /* defined/undefined flag */
    unsigned int imported :1;  /* imported flag */
    unsigned int exported :1;  /* exported flag */
};
```

Figure 10.6   The structure of a symbol table entry

After a file has been assembled, there is no need to separate the imported and exported flags—a single flag could be used to indicate whether the symbol is public or private. However, during the assembly process, the separation of these fields can be used to detect errors. Table 10.2 summarizes the use of these flags in detecting errors. As shown in Table 10.2, there are only three acceptable configurations of the three flags in a symbol table entry. The configuration on line 3 corresponds to an exported symbol—every exported symbol must be defined.

Table 10.2 Detection of errors involving symbol definitions

	Defined	Imported	Exported	
(1)	T	T	T	Error
(2)	T	T	F	Error
(3)	T	F	T	OK (exported symbol)
(4)	T	F	F	OK (private symbol)
(5)	F	T	T	Error
(6)	F	T	F	OK (imported symbol)
(7)	F	F	T	Error
(8)	F	F	F	Error

The configuration on line 6 corresponds to an imported symbol—imported symbols cannot be defined. The configuration on line 4 corresponds to a private symbol—symbols that are neither exported nor imported must be defined.

Many of the error conditions indicated in Table 10.2 can be checked whenever a flag in a symbol table entry is changed during the assembly process. However, because of the possibility of forward references, the error conditions indicated in lines 7 and 8—an undefined exported symbol and an undefined private symbol—cannot be checked until the entire source file has been assembled. These error conditions must be checked by examining each symbol table entry after the entire source file has been processed. As we will discuss, this check can be performed as the symbol table is written to the object file and, as such, does not require a separate pass over the entries in the symbol table.

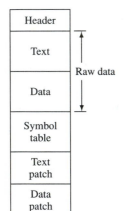

Figure 10.7 The basic structure of an object file

Raw data

10.2.3 The Object File Format

Figure 10.7 illustrates the basic structure of an object file. The file begins with a header record that describes the remainder of the file and other information needed by the linker. The file header is followed by the text and data segments. These sections of the object file are frequently called the *raw data* because they are not interpreted by the linker. The text and data segments are followed by the symbol table and the two patch lists.

The Symbol Table   There are several aspects of the file structure shown in Figure 10.7 that merit further discussion. We begin by considering how the symbol table can be written to a file. To this point we have said very little about the structure of the symbol table. The symbol table might be implemented as a binary search tree, a hash table, or some other data structure. The data structure used to implement the symbol table is not important as long as we are able to insert new symbols into the table and look up the attributes of symbols in the table. It is reasonable to assume that the data structure used to implement the symbol table is memory oriented and that it would be difficult to write this structure directly to a file. To avoid this difficulty, the assembler can simply write the symbol table entries one after the other to the object file and let the linker reconstruct any data structures (e.g., hash table or binary search tree) that it needs. Figure 10.8

illustrates this strategy. In this case, the assembler transforms a binary search tree into a sequence using a level-by-level traversal. The linker then reads the sequential version of the symbol table and builds a hash table. As the assembler writes each symbol table entry to the object file, it is a simple matter to check for the error conditions presented in Table 10.2. In particular, the error conditions presented on lines 7 and 8 cannot be checked until the entire file has been processed.

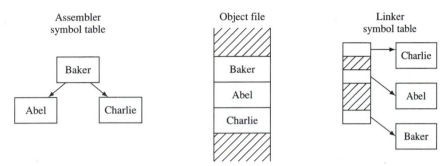

Figure 10.8 Writing the symbol table to the object file

This brings us to the symbol table entries themselves. The major complication introduced by the symbol table entries is the need to store the name of every public symbol (either imported or exported) in the object file. (Note: The names of private symbols do not need to be recorded in the object file.) The names of the symbols may be stored in the symbol table entry, or they may be stored in a separate string pool. When the names of the symbols are stored in a separate string pool, each symbol table entry records the start of the name (an offset in the string pool) and the length or end of the name.

Figure 10.9 illustrates these approaches. In this illustration, the symbol table entries in part B record the start along with the end of each symbol. The advantage

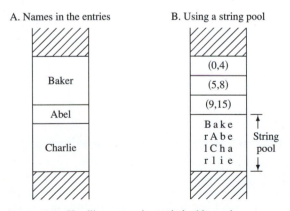

Figure 10.9 Handling names in symbol table entries

of the string pool approach is that every symbol table entry is the same size. When the name of the symbol is stored with the symbol table entry, the size of each symbol table entry depends on the length of the name. Some systems avoid the difficulty associated with variable-length records by setting a limit on the maximum length of a symbol name and allocating enough space for the maximum in every symbol table entry. This simplifies the structure of the object file but imposes an arbitrary limit on the number of significant characters in a symbol.

Patch Lists   The patch lists represent the final difficulty in the structure of the object file. The difficulty associated with patch lists involves the individual entries in the patch lists. In particular, each patch list entry has a pointer to a symbol table entry. Pointers are memory addresses; as such, it does not make much sense to write them to a disk file. Instead, we assign each symbol table entry a unique index and use this index instead of the pointer when we write the patch list entries to the object file. The indexes can easily be assigned as the assembler writes the symbol table entries to the object file. Before it begins writing the symbol table entries to the object file, the assembler initializes an index variable to zero. As it writes each symbol table entry to the object file, the assembler records the value of the index variable in the current symbol table entry (in a new field of the symbol table entry) and increments the index variable. Now, whenever a patch list entry needs to be written to the object file, the assembler simply writes the index of the symbol table entry in place of the pointer. Figure 10.10 illustrates the transformation from pointers to indexes. In this case, the symbol table entries are written in the order Baker, Abel, Charlie. The only remaining pointers in the patch list entries are used to indicate the next element in the patch list. These pointers are not needed if the patch list entries are written to the object file in the correct order.

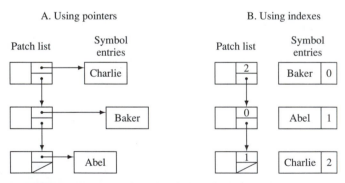

Figure 10.10   Changing pointers into indexes in the patch lists

10.2.4 Linking Object Files

Initially, we limit our discussion to the problem of linking two object files to form an executable file. We will discuss approaches to linking multiple object files after we have considered this problem. The actual linking process is performed in three steps. In the first step, the text, data, and bss segments from the two object files are merged into a single executable file. In the second step, the linker builds three symbol tables: a private symbol table for each of the object files and a public symbol table. The public table provides access to all of the symbols exported by either of the object files. In the third step, the patch lists are applied to the executable file. It is not until the third step that external references are actually resolved.

Figure 10.11 illustrates the basic merge operation. In effect, the segments of the two files are shuffled so that the two text segments are combined into a single text segment, the two data segments are combined into a single data segment, and the two bss segments are (logically) combined into a single bss segment. In examining Figure 10.11, note that the text segment from the second object file is not at the beginning of the text segment in the executable file. This segment has been displaced by the text segment from the first object file. Similarly, the data segment from the second object file has been displaced by the data segment from the first object file. Although not shown, the bss segment from the second object file has also been displaced by the bss segment from the first object file.

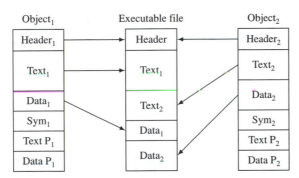

Figure 10.11   Merging two object files

The second step of the linking process involves the construction of three symbol tables. The linker builds two private symbol tables (one for each object file) and a public symbol table. The public symbol table includes the exported symbols from both of the object files. The private symbol tables are accessed through the entries in the patch lists. As we have discussed, the patch list entries use indexes to reference symbol table entries. As such, the private symbol tables can be implemented by arrays that map the symbol index to the symbol table entry (i.e., an array of pointers). Every exported symbol is entered in the public symbol table when it is entered in the appropriate private symbol table. In contrast to the private symbol tables, the public symbol table must map names to symbol table entries. As such, the public symbol table needs to be implemented using a binary search tree, hash table, or similar data structure.

Example 10.8   *Suppose that one object file defines a private symbol* y, *defines and exports the symbols* yy *and* zz, *and imports the symbol* xx. *In addition, suppose that the other object file defines a private symbol* y, *defines and exports the symbols* vv *and* xx, *and imports the symbol* yy. *Show the symbol table structure that the linker creates when it begins processing these object files.*

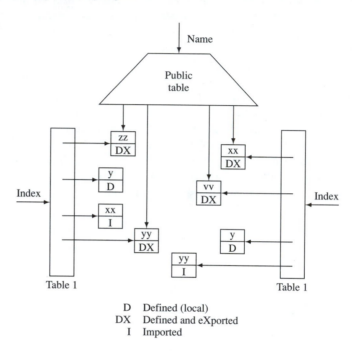

D	Defined (local)
DX	Defined and eXported
I	Imported

Construction of the symbol tables involves reading the symbol table entries from each of the object files. As the entries from the first file are processed, the first private table is constructed. In addition, any symbols that are exported by the first file are entered into the public symbol table. Processing the symbol table entries from the second file is similar except that the offset fields of each symbol table entry in the second object file need to be adjusted to reflect the fact that the segments in the second object file have been displaced by the segments in the first object file. Only the symbols defined in the second object file need to be adjusted. The adjustment involves determining the segment for the symbol (by examining the segment field of the symbol table entry) and adding in the size of the corresponding segment in the first object file to the offset field.

The final step in the linking process involves applying the patches indicated in the patch lists. The step is accomplished by processing the text patch list from the first file, followed by the text patch list from the second file, followed by the data patch list from the first file, followed by the data patch list from the second file.

Processing the patch lists in this order means that all of the patches are applied in a single pass over the executable file.

Processing a patch entry involves determining the offset of the patch (in the executable file) and determining the final value of the symbol referenced by the patch entry. Recall that each patch entry has the offset of the patch within the segment that the patch list was built for. Determination of the file offset involves adding the offset field of the patch entry to the size of the file header and adding in the size of any segments in front of the segment being patched. Table 10.3 summarizes the calculations used to determine the file offset of a patch.

Figure 10.12 illustrates the steps taken to determine the patch value. In the first step, the symbol index is determined by examining the patch list entry. In the

Table 10.3 Calculation of a patch offset

Patch list	Calculation
$text_1$	$off + fh$
$text_2$	$off + fh + t_1$
$data_1$	$off + fh + t_1 + t_2$
$data_2$	$off + fh + t_1 + t_2 + d_1$

Notes: off Offset field of the patch entry
fh Size of the file header
t_1 Size of the text segment from the first file
t_2 Size of the text segment from the second file
d_1 Size of the data segment from the first file

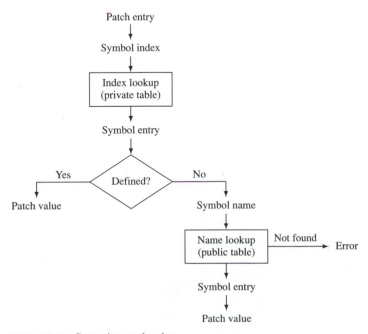

Figure 10.12 Generating patch values

second step, the symbol index value is used to look up the symbol table entry in the appropriate private symbol table. If the symbol table entry indicates that the symbol is defined, the patch value is determined by examining the symbol table entry. Otherwise, the symbol referenced by the patch is an imported symbol and the linker initiates a lookup in the public symbol table. If the symbol is not found during this search, the linker issues an error message and stops processing this patch entry. When the appropriate symbol table entry is found, the patch value is determined by adding the base address of the segment for the symbol with the offset (stored in the symbol table entry).

Example 10.9   *Given the symbol table structure shown in Example 10.8, describe the steps that the linker performs when a patch list entry in the second object file references the imported symbol* yy.

The linker begins by determining the symbol index from the patch list entry. The linker uses this value, say 32, as an index into the private symbol table for the second object file. This identifies a pointer to a symbol table entry as shown below:

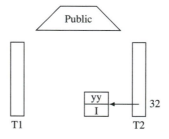

At this point, the linker knows the name of the symbol, *yy,* and can use this name to look up the symbol definition in the public symbol table. This is shown in the following illustration:

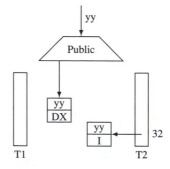

Finally, the linker can update the symbol entry in the private table for the second object module so that it does not need to look up the symbol in the public symbol table. This step is not strictly necessary but will improve the efficiency of the linker.

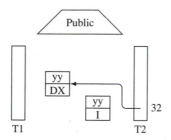

10.2.5 Case Study: External References on the SPARC

External labels could be used in three types of instructions in the SPARC: the subroutine call instruction, load and store instructions, and conditional branch instructions. We limit our consideration to the first two possibilities. While it is possible to have a conditional branch to an external label, it is not very common.

We begin by considering subroutine call instructions. Figure 10.13 presents the format of the subroutine call instruction for the SPARC. (This format was presented in Figure 4.5 in Chapter 4 along with the formats for the remaining SPARC instructions.) In most contexts, SPARC addresses use 32 bits. However, subroutine labels must be aligned on a word address. Because there are four bytes per word, the last 2 bits of every subroutine address must be zero. As such, the subroutine call instruction only stores the most significant 30 bits of the program counter displacement. When a patch list entry identifies a subroutine call instruction, the linker needs to fill in the low-order 30 bits of the instruction with the most significant 30 bits of the program counter displacement.

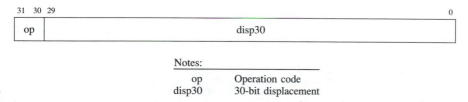

Figure 10.13   Format for the subroutine call instruction on the SPARC

The load and store instructions are not quite as simple. As we have discussed, direct-memory addressing requires two instructions on the SPARC, a SETHI instruction followed by a LOAD instruction. The SETHI instruction sets the most significant 22 bits of a register (usually R1) with the most significant 22 bits of the address. The LOAD instruction uses the register set by the SETHI instruction as the base address in a displaced address. To illustrate this aspect of the SPARC instruction set, we reproduce Example 5.26.

Example 10.10   *Show how you can use the SETHI instruction to implement direct-memory addressing. To be more specific, show how you can use the SETHI instruction to achieve the effect of the statement:*

LOAD.w   R2, loc

where loc *is the label of an arbitrary memory location.*

```
SETHI     R1, #hi(loc)        ; set the high order 22 bits of R1
LOAD.w    R2, R1→lo(loc)      ; load R2 using displaced addressing
```

Figure 10.14 presents the formats for the SETHI and LOAD (with displaced addressing) instructions. Given these formats, we can describe the activities performed by the linker. When a patch list entry indicates a LOAD instruction, the linker needs to patch two instructions, the SETHI instruction and the LOAD instruction. The linker patches the SETHI instruction by setting the least significant 22 bits of the instruction to the most significant 22 bits of the label value. The linker patches the LOAD instruction by setting the least significant 13 bits of the instruction to the least significant 10 bits of the label value.

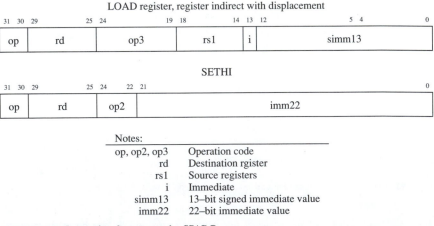

Figure 10.14   Instruction formats on the SPARC

10.2.6 Linking Several Object Files

If we need to link several object files, we can simply extend the basic linker so that it processes several object files. The new linker starts by merging all of the object files into a single executable file. Then it builds a private symbol table for each object file along with the public symbol table. Finally, it applies the patch lists from each object file to the executable file to complete the linking process. A direct extension of the basic linker is likely to have all of the object files open during the entire linking process—all of the object files are opened during the first step (merging), and none is closed until its patch lists have been applied during the last step. Having all of the object files open at any time during the linking process may prove to be a problem, depending on your operating system and the number of files that need to be linked. Most operating systems impose a limit on the number of files that can be open at any time. Because the number of files to be linked may exceed the maximum number of open files, we must be careful to ensure that the number of open files is kept small.

We consider two approaches to minimizing the number of object files that need to be open at any one time. The first is simply a careful implementation of the approach we have just described. The second constructs the executable file incrementally, by successively linking pairs of object files.

In our first algorithm, only two files need to be opened at any time; however, the linker needs to make two passes over the list of files being linked. During the first pass over the list of object files, the linker constructs the public symbol table and text segment of the executable file. During the second pass, the linker constructs the data segment and applies the patches indicated in the patch lists.

The linker begins by creating the executable file and writing an uninitialized header to this file. Then the linker makes a first pass over the list of object files. For each file in the list of object files, the linker opens the file and reads the header, the text segment, and the symbol table of the object file and closes the object file. From the header, the linker determines the size of the text, data, and bss segments and the number of entries in the symbol table. Using this information, the linker can update its information regarding the sizes of the segments in the executable file and determine where each section of the object file begins. After reading the header for the object file, the linker reads the text segment for this file and concatenates it onto the end of the executable file. The linker also reads the symbol table looking for exported symbols. All exported symbols are added to the public symbol table. After the linker has completed the first pass over the list of object files, it will have constructed the public symbol table and the text segment for the executable file.

During the second pass, the linker processes each object file by opening the file; reading the file header, data segment, the symbol table, and patch lists; and then closing the file. During the second pass, the linker constructs the data segment for the executable file by concatenating the individual data segments onto the end of the executable file. In addition, the linker reads the symbol table entries from the object file and builds the private symbol table for the object file. The linker then applies the patches indicated by the patch lists in the object file. Once these patches have been applied, the linker can deallocate the space used by the private symbol table and close the object file. After every object file has been processed, the linking process is completed by updating the header of the executable file.

Our second algorithm uses several invocations of the linker to complete the linking process. This algorithm is illustrated in Figure 10.15. In this case, the linker needs to link three object files, A, B, and C. The linker begins by *merging* the object files A and B to produce the object file AB. After the linker has produced the object file AB, it can *link* AB with C to produce the executable file ABC. The object file AB is an example of a *temporary file*; it is created during the linking process and destroyed when the linker is done with it.

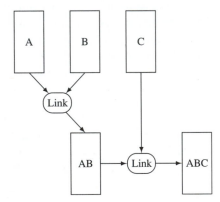

Figure 10.15   Linking multiple object files

Unlike the basic merge operation that we presented earlier, the merge operation shown in Figure 10.15 must produce a complete object file. In particular, this merge operation must merge the symbol tables and patch lists in addition to the text and data segments. The symbol tables and patch lists can be merged by concatenating the appropriate part of the second object file onto the end of the corresponding part from the first object file. For example, the text patch list of the second object file is concatenated onto the end of the text patch list from the first file to form the text patch list for the final object file. As the patch lists from the second file are concatenated onto the end of the patch lists from the first file, the patch offsets recorded in the patch entries need to be adjusted to reflect the fact that the text, data, and bss segments of the second object file have been displaced by the corresponding segments in the first object file.

Merging the symbol tables introduces two minor problems. First, the indexes for the entries in the second symbol table will change because of the symbols in the first symbol table. As such, the patch list entries in the second object file need to be adjusted to reflect these new indexes. Second, a symbol that is imported by one of the object files and exported by the other will appear in both symbol tables.

It may seem that the two symbol table entries for this symbol should be merged into a single symbol table entry as the symbol tables are merged; however, this would complicate the adjustment of symbol indexes and probably is not worth the effort. Instead, it is easier to realize that two or more symbol table entries (for the same private symbol table) may have the same name. Because they all have different indexes and at most one of the entries actually reflects a definition of the symbol, this should not be difficult to handle in the linker.

This algorithm only requires that three files be opened at any given time: the executable or temporary file being produced and the two files being merged or linked.

10.2.7 Libraries

A library is nothing more than a collection of object files with an index. The index indicates which symbols are exported by the object files in the library. Whenever a search of the public symbol table fails to resolve an external reference, the linker looks in the index of the library to see if an object file in the library exports the symbol. If an object file exports the symbol, the object file is extracted from the library and linked with the other object files. When the symbols defined by the object file are entered into the public symbol table, the linker ignores duplicate symbol definitions; that is, symbols that are exported by the library module but already defined in the public symbol table are not entered in the public symbol table. It is important to note that only those portions of the library that are referenced by other parts of the program are actually included in the final executable file.

10.3 LOADING

Once a source program has been translated and linked, it must be loaded into memory before it can be executed. In essence, the loader copies text and data segments from an executable file into the memory of the machine. Figure 10.16 presents pseudocode for a simple loader. In this code, the loader begins by reading the header portion of the executable file. Among other things, the header for the executable file contains the start address, that is, the address of the first instruction to be executed. After it has read the header, the loader enters a loop in which the remaining bytes of the executable file (the text and data segments) are copied into the memory of the machine. Finally, the loader returns the value of the start address field of the file header. Presumably, this value is used as the target of a branch (or jump to subroutine) instruction when it is time to execute the program.

Two aspects of the loader program require further explanation: the variable *byte_addr* and the field *start_addr*. We begin by considering the variable *byte_addr*. This variable is declared as a pointer to a character, that is, the address of a character. It is reasonable to assume that a character is stored using a byte of memory and, as such, the variable *byte_addr* holds the address of a byte of memory. This variable is initialized to the constant value LOAD_ADDR (the value used by the

```
/*** define the structure of the header record ***/
struct exec_head {
    unsigned int start_addr;

    /* other parts of the executable file header */
};

/*** prototypes for functions used by the loader ***/
struct exec_head read_header( FILE * );
char get_byte( FILE * );


/*** ———the loader——— ***/
char *load( FILE *exec_file )
{
    struct exec_head header;
    char *byte_addr;

    /* read the file header */
    header = read_header( exec_file );

    /* copy the text and data segments into the memory */
    byte_addr = LOAD_ADDR;
    while( !eof(exec_file) ) {
        *byte_addr = get_byte( exec_file );
        byte_addr = byte_addr + 1;
    }

    return( (char *)header.start_addr );
}
```

Figure 10.16   Pseudocode for a simple loader

assembler in the previous section). On each iteration of the **while** loop, the memory location identified by *byte_addr* is assigned the next byte from the executable file. Then the value of *byte_addr* is incremented by one.[2]   In this way, the contents of the executable file are copied into consecutive memory locations starting at LOAD_ADDR.

We now consider the declaration and use of the field *start_addr*. As its name suggests, this field holds the address of the first instruction in the program; however, it is declared as an unsigned integer. This reflects an important set of conventions regarding addresses, pointers, and unsigned integers. Addresses and pointers are equivalent when used in a program. However, it does not make sense to store memory addresses in a file. As such, when we need to store an address value in a file, we convert the address value to an unsigned integer before writing it to the file. Conversely, whenever we read an address value from a file, we need to convert

---

[2] In C, incrementing a pointer by one moves the pointer so that it points to the next object of the type that the pointer points to. In this case, *byte_addr* points to a byte, so incrementing *byte_addr* makes it point to the next memory location.

the value from an unsigned integer to a pointer. This convention is based on the assumption that pointers and unsigned integers are both the same size. It is the responsibility of the loader to perform the conversion from unsigned integer to address. In this case, the conversion is performed by a type cast[3] in the return statement:

return((char *)header.start_addr);

The loader shown in Figure 10.6 is called an *absolute loader* because it loads the executable program in a fixed location. In some absolute loaders, the load address is determined by a field in the header of the executable file. While this approach is a bit more general than the use of a predefined constant, the location used for the program is still determined when the program is assembled and linked. Absolute loaders are sufficient for many applications; however, they are not appropriate for many others. In particular, it is not always reasonable to assume that a program can be loaded into the same memory locations every time it is executed. In the remainder of this section, we discuss relocation, a technique that allows a program to be loaded at an arbitrary location in memory.

Absolute loader

When relocation is used, the assembler and linker translate every program as if the program were going to be loaded starting at memory location zero; that is, LOAD_ADDR is set to zero. When the program is loaded, the loader determines where the program is loaded and alters the program so that it can run in its newly assigned location. In other words, the loader relocates the program. While relocation offers many advantages, it does introduce a significant problem: If you simply pick up a program and move it to a different location in memory, it will probably not work correctly. In particular, many of the addresses used in the program depend on the location of the program.

Example 10.11 *Consider the following code fragment:*

```
          .data
    arr:  .reserve    50*4        ; space for 50 integers
      i:  .reserve    4           ; a simple integer
          .text
            :
            :
(1)       LOAD.w    R2, i         ; R2 ← i
(2)       MOVE      R3, #arr      ; R3 ← &arr
(3)       MPY       R4, R2, #4    ; scale the index
(4)       ADD       R3, R4, R3    ; R3 ← &arr[i]
(5)       STORE.w   R2, @R3       ; arr[i] ← i
```

---

[3] In C, whenever an expression is preceded by a type designator in parentheses, it is called a *type cast*. Type casts are used to change the type of an expression—in this case, from unsigned integer to pointer to character.

If the assembler and linker (assuming that the program is loaded starting at memory location zero) determine that *arr* is stored in memory locations 1,000 through 1,199 and that *i* is stored in memory locations 1,200 through 1,103, they will produce code equivalent to

(1)	LOAD.w	R2, 1200	; *R2 ← i*
(2)	MOVE	R3, #1000	; *R3 ← &arr*
(3)	MPY	R4, R2, #4	; *scale the index*
(4)	ADD	R3, R4, R3	; *R3 ← &arr[i]*
(5)	STORE.w	R2, @R3	; *arr[i] ← i*

Now suppose that the loader determines that the program should be loaded starting at memory location 20,000 instead of location zero. When the program is moved from memory location zero to location 20,000, the address of *arr* changes from 1,000 to 21,000 and the address of *i* changes from 1,200 to 21,200. To ensure correct execution of the program, the loader needs to arrange to have the addresses used in the program translated to reflect the actual location of the program in memory.

Address space

Logical address space

Physical address space

To discuss the relocation process we introduce two terms, the logical address space and the physical address space. An *address space* provides a context for the interpretation of addresses. The *logical address space* represents the view taken from the perspective of the program. In this view, the only objects that need addresses are the objects referenced by the program. The assembler and linker both use the logical address space to complete their stages of the translation process. The *physical address space* represents the view taken from the perspective of the memory on the machine. In this view, every memory location has an address. The loader completes the translation process by mapping program addresses from the logical address space to the physical address space. Figure 10.17 illustrates the mapping from logical addresses to physical addresses.

Static relocation

Dynamic relocation

Two techniques can be used to ensure that programs execute correctly after they have been moved: static relocation and dynamic relocation. The *static* in *static relocation* refers to the fact that programs can only be relocated before they have begun their execution. When *dynamic relocation* is used, programs can be relocated at any time (even after they have begun their execution), hence the name dynamic relocation.

In examining Figure 10.17, note that the instructions in the physical address space use an unusual addressing notation. For example, the first instruction uses the direct address (2)1200. This notation indicates that the address may be altered as the program is mapped into the physical address space. For example, in static relocation, the loader maps the address from 1200 (a logical address) to 21200 (the physical address). In contrast, dynamic relocation does not alter the addresses used in the program but uses special address-mapping hardware to map logical addresses into physical addresses during program execution.

Static relocation requires that the linker provide additional relocation information in the executable file. As we will discuss, this relocation information consists of a patch list that tells the loader which program locations need to be modified

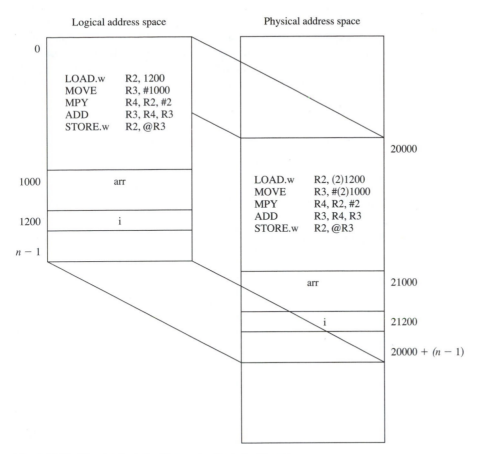

Figure 10.17　Mapping logical addresses to physical addresses

when the program is moved. Dynamic relocation is simpler and more flexible than static relocation but requires address-mapping hardware. If the required address-mapping hardware is not provided, static relocation must be used.

10.3.1 Dynamic Relocation—Address Mapping

In dynamic relocation, the addresses used in a program are mapped to physical addresses whenever they are used during the execution of the program. The logical addresses generated by the assembler and linker are not altered during loading. We begin by considering a simple scheme in which the program is loaded into *contiguous memory locations*; that is, the program is not scattered throughout memory. Figure 10.18 presents a simple loader that can be used with dynamic relocation. In this case, the loader reads the header from the executable file and determines the amount of space needed for the program. The loader then allocates enough space for the program and copies the executable file into memory. When

Contiguous memory locations

the program is loaded into the memory, the loader establishes the mapping for the program by passing the load address and the size of the program to a routine called *set_mapping*. In reading this code, note that the load function returns an unsigned integer instead of a pointer. This reflects the fact that the start address is a logical address and not a physical address.

```
struct exec_head {
    unsigned int start_addr;
    unsigned int text_size, data_size, bss_size;
    /* other fields in the header record */
};

/* prototypes for functions used by the loader */
struct exec_head read_header( FILE * );
char get_byte( FILE * );
char *get_memory( unsigned int );
void set_mapping( char *, unsigned int );


/*** ———the loader——— ***/
unsigned int load( FILE *exec_file )
{
    struct exec_head header;
    char *byte_addr, *load_addr;
    unsigned int pgm_size;

    header = read_header( exec_file );

    /* determine the size of the program and allocate space for it */
    pgm_size = header.text_size + header.data_size + header.bss_size;
    load_addr = get_memory( pgm_size );

    /* copy the text and data segments */
    byte_addr = load_addr;
    while( !eof(exec_file) ) {
        *byte_addr = get_byte( exec_file );
        byte_addr = byte_addr + 1;
    }

    /* set up the address mapping */
    set_mapping( load_addr, pgm_size );

    return( header.start_address );
}
```

Figure 10.18   Pseudocode for a simple loader (dynamic relocation)

This brings us to the address-mapping hardware. Figure 10.19 illustrates the address-mapping hardware. Whenever the CPU needs to perform a memory access (read or write), it presents the result of the effective address calculation to the address-mapping hardware. The address-mapping hardware translates the logical address into a physical address.

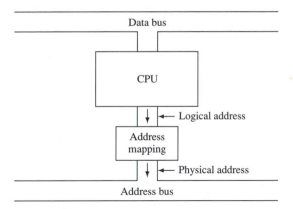

Figure 10.19 An operational view of address mapping

Because our simple loader loads programs into contiguous memory, the address-mapping hardware only needs to add the load address to each logical address to form the corresponding physical address. The address-mapping hardware may also check to see if the logical address is legal, that is, less than the size of the program, and generate an addressing exception if it is not. This form of address mapping is called *base-and-bound mapping* because the logical addresses used by the program are interpreted relative to a *base* address determined by the loader and there is a *bound* on the magnitude of a logical address.

Base-and-bound mapping

Example 10.12 *To illustrate base-and-bound address mapping, we consider the code from Example 10.11*

```
(1)  LOAD.w   R2, 1200      ; R2 ← i
(2)  MOVE     R3, #1000     ; R3 ← &arr
(3)  MPY      R4, R2, #4    ; scale the index
(4)  ADD      R3, R4, R3    ; R3 ← &arr[i]
(5)  STORE.w  R2, @R3       ; arr[i] ← i
```

Suppose that this program is loaded starting at location 20,000. When the machine executes the first instruction, it will present the address-mapping hardware with the logical address 1,200. The address-mapping hardware adds the base address to the logical address to obtain the physical address 21,200.

When the machine executes the second instruction, it simply puts the value 1,000 into register R3. All address calculations are performed using *logical* addresses. The calculated address is not mapped to a physical address until the fifth instruction when it is used in a STORE instruction.

Example 10.13 *To illustrate the dynamic aspect of dynamic relocation, suppose that this program needs to be moved to memory location 40,000 after it has started its execution. All that needs to be done is to copy the program from memory location 20,000 to 40,000* *and change the base address value to 40,000. Thereafter, every logical address is mapped to a physical address based at 40,000 instead of 20,000.*

Figure 10.20 summarizes the stages in an address translation. The translation begins with an address descriptor. An address descriptor contains the information needed to complete the effective address calculation. The effective address calculation transforms an address descriptor into a logical address. The logical address is transformed into a physical address by the address-mapping stage.

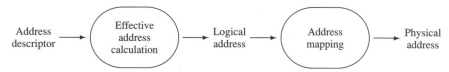

Figure 10.20   The stages of address translation

Before we consider techniques that support noncontiguous memory allocation, we need to discuss a bit of magic in the code for the loader shown in Figure 10.18. For this code to work correctly, the memory references that it generates must not be mapped by the address-mapping hardware. To see the problem, assume that the loader is loaded starting at memory location 3,000. In addition, assume that the call to *get_memory* returns the value 10,000; that is, the user's program is loaded starting at memory location 10,000. When the loader attempts to load the first byte of the user's program it will initiate a memory write to location 10,000. If address mapping is enabled, the physical address will be calculated as 13,000 and the program will be loaded starting at physical memory location 13,000 instead of location 10,000! We could avoid this problem by subtracting the base address of the loader from the value returned by *get_memory* and thus cancel the addition that is performed by the address-mapping hardware. However, this solution will not work when more sophisticated techniques are used. Instead, we simply assume that the loader is loaded in an absolute location and the memory references generated by the loader are not subject to address mapping.

Segmentation   In segmentation, every logical address is specified by a segment number and an offset. We use the notation ⟨*segment, offset*⟩ to denote a logical address. The mapping from logical to physical addresses is based on a segment-mapping table. The *segment-mapping table* stores a base-and-bound pair for every segment in the program. Whenever a logical address is used to access memory, the segment number is used as an index into the segment-mapping table to determine the base address and bound for the segment. If the offset is within the range specified by the bound, the offset is added to the segment base address to form the physical address. Address translation using a segment-mapping table is illustrated in Figure 10.21.

⟨segment, offset⟩

Segment-mapping table

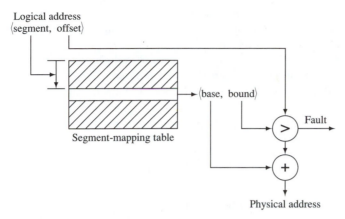

Figure 10.21 The segment-mapping table

Segmentation is frequently called *two-dimensional addressing*. In this context, the segment number defines the first dimension and the offset defines the second. The analogy to Cartesian coordinates is simple if you imagine that the segments in a program are placed side by side. This perspective is illustrated in Figure 10.22. In contrast to the two-dimensional addressing structure imposed by segmentation, other techniques are based on a *flat address space*. In a flat address space, the items in the address space are associated with a single range of addresses [that is, 0 to $(n-1)$].

Two-dimensional addressing

Flat address space

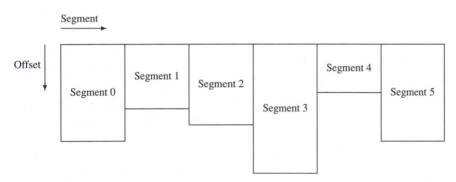

Figure 10.22 Illustrating the two dimensions of segmentation

Construction of the segment mapping table requires some minor modifications to the assembler, linker, and loader. We begin by considering the changes to the assembler. To simplify the presentation, we ignore the linker and assume that the assembler generates an executable file. The assembler determines segment numbers and offsets for all of the objects (e.g., labels) that are referenced in a program. Up until this point, we have assumed that the assembler merges all of the segments initiated by a data directive into one large data segment, all of the segments initiated by a text directive into one large text segment, and all of the segments initiated by a bss directive into one large bss segment. However, the assembler could create a new segment and assign it a new segment number whenever it encounters a segment directive in an assembly language program.

Figure 10.23 contrasts these approaches. The center of the figure depicts an assembly language source program with six segment directives. The left side of the figure depicts the structure of the executable file that would be created by a conventional assembler. The right side of the figure depicts the structure of the executable file that would be created by an assembler that supports segmentation. As with the standard file, the segmented file begins with a header that describes the contents of the remainder of the file. However, the header is followed by a collection of segment header/body pairs instead of the text and data segments. The number of segment header/body pairs is specified in the file header. Each segment header specifies the type of the segment (text, data, or bss) and the size of the segment body. Note that no space is allocated for the body of a bss segment; however, space is allocated for the header of a bss segment.

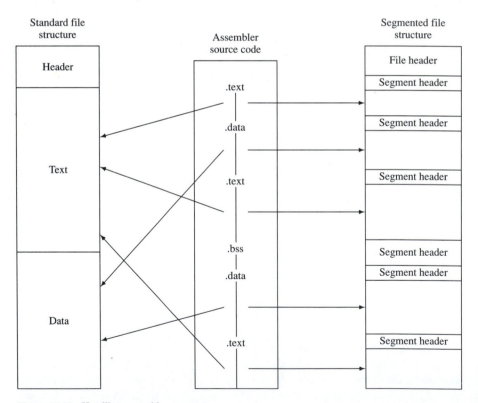

Figure 10.23 Handling assembler segments

Example 10.14   *To illustrate segmentation, we consider a modified version of the code fragment introduced in Example 10.11:*

```
            .data
    arr:    .reserve    50*4            ; space for 50 integers
      i:    .reserve    4               ; a simple integer
            .text
              ⋮
(1)         LOAD.w      R2, i           ; R2 ← i
(2)         MPY         R3, R2, #4      ; scale the index
(3)         STORE.w     R2, arr[R3]     ; arr[i] ← i
```

Suppose that the assembler has already encountered 23 segment directives (assigning the segment numbers 0 through 22 to these segments) before it begins to translate this code. As such, the assembler will assign the segment initiated by the data directive on the first line segment number 23. Moreover the labels *arr* and *i* will be associated with the logical addresses $\langle 23, 0 \rangle$ and $\langle 23, 200 \rangle$ respectively. In this case, the instructions in the text segment are equivalent to:

```
(1)         LOAD.w      R2, ⟨23, 200⟩     ; R2 ← i
(2)         MPY         R3, R2, #4        ; scale the index
(3)         STORE.w     R2, ⟨23, 0⟩[R3]   ; arr[i] ← i
```

Suppose that segment 23 has been loaded into physical memory addresses 20,000 through 20,203. Execution of the first instruction begins by fetching the value stored at the logical address $\langle 23, 200 \rangle$. The address-mapping hardware determines that segment 23 begins at physical address 20,000 and, as such, determines that the appropriate physical address is 20,200.

Execution of the third instruction begins by calculating the effective address. In this case, the effective address is determined by adding the contents of register R3 to the logical address $\langle 23, 0 \rangle$. If R3 holds the value 24, the effective address calculation results in the logical address $\langle 23, 24 \rangle$. Note that the effective address calculation never alters the segment number—the effective address calculation only affects the offset used in the logical address.

Figure 10.24 presents a collection of C declarations that define the structures needed to support the segmented file structure. These declarations begin with an enumeration of the different types of segments and a declaration that specifies the structure of a logical address. In our declaration of the logical address structure, *logical_addr*, we presume that the segment number and offset portions of a logical address are stored as unsigned integers. The remaining declarations specify the structure of the file and segment headers. Note that the file header, *exec_head*, only contains the starting address and the number of segments in the executable file; it does not contain the lengths of the segments. The lengths of the segments along with their types are stored in the segment headers.

Finally, Figure 10.25 presents pseudocode for a loader that supports segmentation. The loader is responsible for loading the segments into memory and

```
/* There are three basic segment types. */
enum seg_types {text, data, bss};

/* A logical address consists of a segment number and an offset. */
struct logical_addr {
    unsigned int seg, offset;
};

/* The file header only has the start address (a logical address) and
 * the number of segments in the executable file.
 */
struct exec_head {
    struct logical_addr start_addr;
    unsigned int num_segs;
};

/* Each segment header indicates the type of segment (text, data, or
 * bss) and the size of the segment.
 */
struct seg_head {
    enum seg_types type;
    unsigned int size;
};
```

Figure 10.24   Types used to support segmentation

constructing the segment-mapping table. The segment-mapping table, *seg_map,* is declared as an array of segment entries. Each segment entry consists of a base address and a bound. The main body of the loader consists of two nested **for** loops. The outer loop processes the segments in the executable file one at a time. The processing for each segment consists of four steps: reading the segment header, allocating space for the segment, entering information into the segment mapping table, and loading the segment into memory.

Paging   Paging is another technique that enables noncontiguous memory allocation. In paging, the program is assembled and linked as if it were going to be loaded into contiguous memory locations starting at location zero; however, as it is loaded, the program is divided into fixed-sized units called pages. The size of a page is fixed by the address-mapping hardware of the machine (256 bytes, 512 bytes, 1,024 bytes, and 2,048 bytes are typical page sizes). Paging simplifies the memory management task because memory is always allocated one page at a time.

Whenever a page of memory is allocated, it is always allocated at an address that is an integer multiple of the page size. Because they are always allocated in fixed locations, the locations used to allocate pages are frequently called *page frames*; that is, these locations "frame a page of memory."

Page frames

Paging does not require any modification to the basic assembler we described in section 10.1. Only the loader needs to be altered. In principle, the loader builds a program image from the executable file and divides this image into pages. In contrast to the executable file, the program image does not have a header and it does have space allocated for the bss segment.

```
struct seg_entry {
    char *base;
    unsigned int bound;
};

/* prototypes for functions used by the loader */
struct exec_head read_exec_header( FILE * );
struct seg_head read_seg_header( FILE * );
char get_byte( FILE * );
char *get_segment( unsigned int );
void set_mapping( struct seg_entry map[], int );

struct logical_addr load( FILE *exec_file )
{
    struct exec_head file_header;
    struct seg_head seg_header;

    struct seg_entry seg_map[MAX_SEGS];

    char *byte_addr;
    unsigned int seg_num;
    unsigned int byte_num;

    /* read the file header and process each segment */
    file_header = read_exec_header( exec_file );
    for( seg_num = 0 ; seg_num < file_header.num_segs ; seg_num++ ) {
        seg_header = read_seg_header( exec_file );      /* read segment header */
        byte_addr = get_segment( seg_header.size );   /* allocate segment space */

        /* update the segment mapping table */
        seg_map[ seg_num ].base = byte_addr;
        seg_map[ seg_num ].bound = seg_header.size;

        /* load the segment—nothing to copy if it's a bss segment */
        if( seg_header.type ≠ bss ) {
            for( byte_num=0 ; byte_num< seg_header.size ; byte_num++ ) {
                *byte_addr = get_byte( exec_file );
                byte_addr = byte_addr + 1;
            }
        }
    }

    set_mapping( seg_map, file_header.num_segs );
    return( file_header.start_addr );
}
```

Figure 10.25   Pseudocode for a loader supporting segmentation

Figure 10.26 illustrates how a program image is divided into pages. In dividing the program image into pages, the loader does not pay attention to segment boundaries; it is only concerned with the number of bytes in each page. In most cases, the size of the program image is not an exact multiple of the page size. As such, part of the last page may not be used by the program image. In Figure 10.26, note that the last part of page 4 is not used by the program image. Once it has determined the number of pages needed for the program image, the loader allocates memory for the pages one at a time. As with segmentation, there is no relationship between the base addresses of the pages used in a program. The translation from logical addresses to physical addresses is based on a page-mapping table.

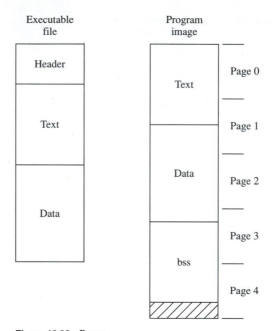

Figure 10.26   Pages

Example 10.15   *To illustrate paging, we again consider the code fragment introduced in Example 10.11:*

(1)	LOAD.w	R2, 1200	; *R2 ← i*
(2)	MOVE	R3, #1000	; *R3 ← &arr*
(3)	MPY	R4, R2, #4	; *scale the index*
(4)	ADD	R3, R4, R3	; *R3 ← &arr[i]*
(5)	STORE.w	R2, @R3	; *arr[i] ← i*

Suppose that each page is 512 bytes. As such, page 0 holds logical addresses 0–511, page 1 holds logical addresses 512 through 1,023, page 2 holds logical addresses 1,024 through 1,535, and so on. Recall that the assembler allocates (logical) memory locations 1,000 through 1,199 for the array *arr* and (logical) memory locations 1,200 and 1,203 for the variable *i*. Here it is worth noting that the array *arr* starts on page 1 continues into page 2.

In executing the first instruction, the logical address 1,200 needs to be translated into a physical address. Because each page is 512 bytes, this logical address refers to page 2, offset 176. As such, the physical address is determined by adding 176 to the base address for page 2.

In mapping a logical address to a physical address, the address-mapping hardware must first determine the page number and offset that the address refers to. The page number and offset can be determined by dividing the logical address by the page size—the quotient is the page number, and the remainder is the offset. If the page size is a power of 2, for example, 2^n, this division can be implemented by splitting the binary representation of the address—the least significant n bits are the offset, and the remaining bits are the page number. The address mapping proceeds by using the page number as an index into the page-mapping table. This determines the base address of the page frame used to store the page. The physical address is formed by adding the page base address with the offset. If the page size is a power of 2, for example, 2^n, the least significant n bits of the page base are always zero, and, as such, the physical address can be formed by concatenating the page frame number (the most significant bits of the page base address) with the offset. Figure 10.27 illustrates the translation from a logical address to a physical address when paging is used. In this illustration, we have assumed that the page size is a power of 2.

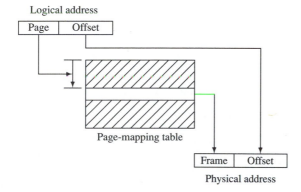

Figure 10.27   The page-mapping table

Figure 10.28 presents pseudocode for a loader that supports paging. The loader is responsible for dividing the program into pages, allocating space for each page, initializing the contents of the pages (as appropriate), and constructing the page-mapping table used by the address-mapping hardware. Note that the page-mapping table only has a base address for each page. In particular, there is no bound stored in the page-mapping table. Because every page is the same size, this information does not need to be explicitly stored in the page-mapping table. The loader begins by determining the number of pages needed for the program image and enters a **for** loop to allocate the needed page frames. This loop is followed by a loop that initializes the page frames associated with the text and data segments. The loader completes its activities by setting the mapping information and returning the start address.

```
struct exec_head {
    unsigned int start_addr;
    unsigned int text_size, data_size, bss_size;
    /* other fields in the header record */
};

/* prototypes for functions used by the loader */
struct exec_head read_header( FILE * );
char get_byte( FILE * );
char *get_page_frame( void );
void set_mapping( char *map[], int );

unsigned int load( FILE *exec_file )
{
    struct exec_head header;
    char *page_map[MAX_PAGES], *byte_addr;
    unsigned int npages, page_num, pgm_size, offset;

    /* read header, calculate program size and number of pages */
    file_header = read_header( exec_file );
    pgm_size = header.text_size + header.data_size + header.bss_size;
    npages = (pgm_size + PAGE_SIZE - 1) / PAGE_SIZE;

    /* allocate all of the page frames needed */
    for( page_num = 0 ; page_num$<$npages ; page_num++ ) {
        page_map[ page_num ] = get_page_frame();
    }

    /* copy the text and data segments into page frames */
    for( page_num = 0 ; !eof(exec_file) ; page_num++ ) {
        byte_addr = page_map[ page_num ];
        for( offset = 0 ; offset<PAGE_SIZE && !eof(exec_file) ; offset++ ) {
            *byte_addr = get_byte( exec_file );
            byte_addr = byte_addr] + 1;
        }
    }

    set_mapping( page_map, npages );
    return( file_header.start_addr );
}
```

Figure 10.28   Pseudocode for a loader supporting paging

10.3.2 Static Relocation

In static relocation, the program is actually modified as it is loaded into memory. Figure 10.29 illustrates the structure of an executable file that supports static relocation. In addition to the header, the text segment, and the data segment, the assembler includes a patch list in the executable file. The patch list is used by the loader to determine which locations in the program image need to be fixed after the program has been loaded. Each element in the patch list is the (logical) address of a location in the code or data segment that holds a logical address. These locations are fixed by adding the load address into the logical address (this is the same fix that is performed by the address-mapping hardware in dynamic relocation).

Figure 10.30 presents pseudocode for a simple loader that performs static relocation. This code is based on the assumption that an address and an unsigned integer are the same size (e.g., 32 bits). After the loader has copied the text and data segments into the memory space allocated for the program, it begins to process the patch list. Processing the patch list is relatively straightforward; the loader gets the logical address of the next patch, adds in the load address to determine the physical address that needs to be patched, and patches this location by adding in the load address.

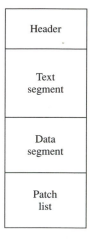

Figure 10.29
An executable file structure to support static relocation

```
struct exec_head {
    unsigned int start_addr;
    unsigned int text_size, data_size, bss_size;
    unsigned int patch_size;
    /* other fields in the header record */
};

/* prototypes for functions used by the loader */
struct exec_head read_header( FILE * );
char get_byte( FILE * );
char *get_memory( unsigned int );

unsigned int load( FILE *exec_file )
{
    struct exec_head header;
    char *byte_addr, *load_addr;
    unsigned int pgm_size;
    unsigned int *patch_addr;
    unsigned int offset, patch_num;

    /* read the file header, determine the program size and allocate space */
    header = read_header( exec_file );
    pgm_size = header.text_size + header.data_size + header.bss_size;
    load_addr = get_memory( pgm_size );

    /* copy the text and data segments into memory */
    byte_addr = load_addr;
    for( offset = 0 ; offset<header.text_size+header.data_size ; offset++ ) {
        *byte_addr = get_byte( exec_file );
        byte_addr = byte_addr + 1;
    }

    /* apply the patches to the code and data segments */
    for( patch_num = 0 ; patch_num < header.patch_size ; patch_num++ ) {
        patch_addr = load_addr + get_patch( exec_file );
        *patch_addr = *patch_addr + (unsigned int)load_addr;
    }

    return( header.start_address + (unsigned int)load_addr );
}
```

Figure 10.30 Pseudocode for a simple loader (static relocation)

The code used to perform the actual patch might be a bit confusing:

*patch_addr = *patch_addr + (unsigned int)load_addr;

The expression on the right-hand side of the assignment fetches the value currently stored in the physical address identified by patch_addr and adds in the value of load_addr. However, before the value of load_addr is added to the value indicated by patch_addr, this value is converted from an address to an unsigned integer. In this case, the purpose of the type cast is to convince the C compiler that it should use unsigned integer arithmetic to compute the value of the expression on the right-hand side. Without the type cast, the compiler would use pointer arithmetic because load_addr is a pointer.

You may be curious about the possibility of relocating a program after it has begun its execution. When one of the dynamic relocation techniques is used, it is easy to relocate a program after it has begun its execution—simply adjust the address-mapping tables. If you are using static relocation, it may seem that you could simply move the program and reapply the patch list after the program has been moved. However, there is a problem associated with this solution. Should the contents of the registers (or variables) be altered during the relocation? In general, this question cannot be answered because you do not know how the program will use the value stored in the register. The value in a register might be used as an address (e.g., indirect-register addressing) or it might be used as a simple integer. If the value is used as an address, it should be altered; otherwise, it should not be altered. Note that the dynamic relocation techniques avoid this problem by waiting until the value is actually used. If the value is used as an address, it is mapped by the address-mapping hardware; otherwise, it is not altered.

10.3.3 Bootstrapping

How is the loader loaded into memory? If you think about it, this creates a bit of a problem. We need a loader to load the loader. The loader that is used to load the loader is a program, and, as such, it also needs to be loaded into memory. It seems that we are in a nasty cycle here. In modern computing systems this cycle is broken by storing a primitive loader (perhaps an absolute loader) in ROM. This primitive loader is always loaded in memory and does not need to be explicitly loaded. To answer our original question, the loader is loaded into memory when the ROM is programmed. This primitive loader can be used to load a more sophisticated loader, that can in turn be used to load a collection of operating system utilities.

Bootstrapping

Booting

The process of starting with a primitive loader and using this loader to load a more sophisticated loader is called *bootstrapping*. In many contexts, the term is shortened to *booting*, and it is now common to talk about "booting the operating system." The original term, *bootstrapping,* refers to the notion of "pulling oneself up by the bootstraps." Long ago, young boys were told that if they pulled hard enough on their bootstraps they could make themselves taller. In the context of loaders, the analogy is rather weak—if the loader keeps loading, it will eventually grow into a real loader. However, the visual image of pulling on your bootstraps to make yourself taller carries enough appeal to make bootstrapping a part of the terminology associated with loading.

You may wonder how the primitive loader was loaded in the "good old days" before ROM was an effective solution (high-speed, inexpensive ROM is a fairly recent development). We begin by introducing the control panel. Figure 10.31 illustrates a simple control panel. The panel consists of two sets of toggle switches (labeled ADDRESS and DATA), a set of LEDs (labeled DATA), three flip switches (labeled READ, WRITE, and PC), and a RUN/HALT switch.

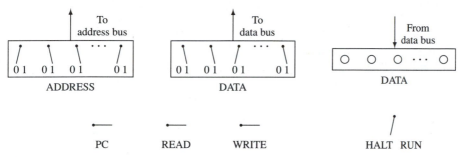

Figure 10.31   A simple control Panel

When the RUN/HALT switch is in the RUN position, the machine executes its ifetch loop, fetching instructions from memory. When this switch is in the HALT position, the machine is halted and does not continue to fetch instructions. The flip switches are used to control the operations that can be performed from the control panel. Depressing the flip switch labeled READ causes the value stored in the memory location identified by the address toggle switches to be displayed in the data LEDs. Depressing the WRITE flip switch causes the value indicated by the data toggle switches to be loaded into the memory location indicated by the address toggle switches. The PC flip switch is used to load the program counter. Using the switches on the control panel, the operator can load a program into memory. A primitive loader may be as small as 5 to 10 instructions, and, as such, it not particularly difficult to load using the control panel.

10.4 SUMMARY

In this chapter, we have considered the three processes involved in the translation process: assembly, linking, and loading. The first of these processes, assembly, initiates the translation of an assembly language source-code module. Because a source-code module may use symbols that are defined by other source-code modules, the assembler cannot complete the translation of the source-code module. Instead, the assembler constructs an object-code file that includes the translated instructions and data values along with information needed by the linker, the symbol table, and patch lists. The linker combines several object-code modules (and libraries) into a single executable file. The linker completes the translation initiated by the assembler. The executable file produced by the linker is based on a logical address space, an address space defined for the program. The addresses in the logical address space must be translated into physical addresses, addresses defined for the physical memory of the machine. This translation of addresses may be implemented by the loader (static relocation) or by special address translation hardware (dynamic relocation).

The translation of individual instructions is relatively straightforward. The major difficulty involves the use of labels, in particular, the association of a label with a physical address. This is called the *binding* of an address with a label. *Binding time* refers to the time at which this binding is established. In general, it is better to delay this binding as long as possible. The later the binding, the more flexibility you have in running programs. In our simple assemblers and linkers, we assumed that the load address for the code was known to the assembler and linker. This allows us to build a complete executable image but means that the program has to be loaded in the same memory locations every time it is run. A loader that supports static relocation defers the final binding of addresses with labels until the program is loaded. This means that the program can be loaded into different locations when it is run, but once it is loaded, it cannot be moved. The techniques that support dynamic relocation (base-and-bounds addressing, segmentation, and paging) defer the final binding until a value is used as an address. In these systems, the assembler and linker bind labels to logical addresses, and the address translation hardware binds the logical addresses to physical addresses.

Binding

Binding time

10.4.1 Additional Reading

Most of the books listed in the sections "Architecture and Organization," "Assembly Language Programming,""Operating Systems," and "Programming Language Surveys" have a discussion of the translation process. The architecture and organization texts along with the assembly language programming texts cover the essential aspects of the three processes used in translation. The operating system texts give a more comprehensive treatment of segmentation and paging. The programming language survey texts emphasize the translation of high-level languages into assembly language and frequently include a discussion of binding times.

10.4.2 Terminology

- Source module (file), Object module (file), Executable file
- Forward reference, Backward reference
- Two-pass assembler
- Patch list
- Import, Export
- Public symbol table, Private symbol table
- Relocation, Static relocation, Dynamic relocation

- Absolute loader
- Logical address, Physical address
- Address-mapping hardware
- Contiguous memory location
- Base-and-bound mapping
- Segmentation, Segment-mapping table, Two-dimensional addressing
- Paging, Page frame, Page-mapping table
- Bootstrapping

10.4.3 Review Questions

1. What is the difference between a source file, an object file, and an executable file?
2. What does the linker translate? What does the loader translate (assume static relocation)?
3. Explain the difference between a forward reference and a backward reference. Which type of reference creates a more significant problem for the assembler? Why?
4. In a two-pass assembler, what does the assembler do during the first pass?
5. Why does each patch list entry store a pointer to a symbol table entry?
6. During linking, how are values found in the private symbol table? How are they found in the public symbol table?
7. Explain the difference between static and dynamic relocation.
8. What is the general difference between the terms *static* and *dynamic?*
9. Explain how base-and-bound address mapping works.
10. Why is segmentation called two-dimensional addressing?
11. What information is stored in a segment-mapping table?
12. What is a page frame?
13. What information is stored in a page-mapping table?

10.5 EXERCISES

1. Consider the pseudocode shown in Figure 10.2.
   a. Describe an example in which the *translate* routine needs to use the value of *location* to translate an instruction.
   b. Is it possible that the *translate* routine will need to change the value of *location?* Be certain to support your answer.
2. Consider the following code fragment. This code fragment computes the length of a null-terminated string and was introduced in Example 5.19.

```
(1)           str:  .reserve   150          ; space for the string
(2)    code_start:                           ; execution starts here
(3)                 CLEAR      R2            ; R2 is the counter
(4)                 MOVE       R3, #str      ; R3 points to the element
(5)                 LOAD.b     R4, @R3       ; load the next character
(6)                 BRANCH     test          ; branch to loop exit test
(7)           top:
(8)                 ADD        R2, R2, #1    ; one more character
(9)                 ADD        R3, R3, #1    ; advance the pointer
(10)                LOAD.b     R4, @R3       ; load the next character
(11)          test:
(12)                CMP        R4, #0        ; end of string?
(13)                BRNE       top           ; no, process next byte
```

a. For each instruction that uses a label, determine whether the use is a forward reference or a backward reference.

b. Assuming that the location counter starts at 0 and that each instruction requires four bytes, show the symbol table that a two-pass assembler would construct during its first pass.

c. Using the assumptions from part b, show the patch list and symbol table that a patch list assembler would create when it is assembling the LOAD instruction on line 10 of this code fragment.

3. Consider the following code fragment. This code counts the number of uppercase characters in a null-terminated string.

```
(1)           str:  .reserve   150          ; space for the string
(2)    code_start:                           ; execution starts here
(3)                 CLEAR      R2            ; R2 is the counter
(4)                 MOVE       R3, #str      ; R3 points to the element
(5)           top:
(6)                 LOAD.b     R4, @R3       ; load the next character
(7)                 ADD        R3, R3, #1    ; advance the pointer
(8)                 CMP        R4, #'A'      ; compare to the letter A
(9)                 BRLT       test          ; check for end of string
(10)                CMP        R4, #'Z'      ; compare to the letter Z
(11)                BRGT       test          ; check for end of string
(12)                ADD        R2, R2, #1    ; it must be an uppercase letter
(13)          test:
(14)                CMP        R4, #0        ; end of string?
(15)                BRNE       top           ; no, process next byte
```

a. For each instruction that uses a label, determine whether the use is a forward reference or a backward reference.

b. Assuming that the location counter starts at 0 and that each instruction requires four bytes, show the symbol table that a two-pass assembler would construct during its first pass.

c. Using the assumptions from part *b,* show the patch list and symbol table that a patch list assembler would create when it is assembling the ADD instruction on line 12 of this code fragment.

4. Consider the following code fragment (this is the code fragment from exercise 2 using segments).

```
(1)              .bss
(2)     str:     .reserve    150             ; space for the string
(3)              .text
(4)              CLEAR       R2              ; R2 is the counter
(5)              MOVE        R3, #str        ; R3 points to the element
(6)              LOAD.b      R4, @R3         ; load the next character
(7)              BRANCH      test            ; branch to loop exit test
(8)     top:
(9)              ADD         R2, R2, #1      ; one more character
(10)             ADD         R3, R3, #1      ; advance the pointer
(11)             LOAD.b      R4, @R3         ; load the next character
(12)    test:
(13)             CMP         R4, #0          ; end of string?
(14)             BRNE        top             ; no, process next byte
```

a. Assuming that each location counter starts at 0 and that each instruction requires four bytes, show the symbol table that a two-pass assembler would construct during its first pass.

b. Using the assumptions from part *a,* show the patch lists and symbol table that a patch list assembler would create when it is assembling the LOAD instruction on line 11 of this code fragment.

5. Consider the following code fragment (this is the code fragment from exercise 3 using assembler segments).

```
(1)              .bss
(2)     str:     .reserve    150             ; space for the string
(3)              .text
(4)              CLEAR       R2              ; R2 is the counter
(5)              MOVE        R3, #str        ; R3 points to the element
(6)     top:
(7)              LOAD.b      R4, @R3         ; load the next character
(8)              ADD         R3, R3, #1      ; advance the pointer
(9)              CMP         R4, #'A'        ; compare to the letter A
(10)             BRLT        test            ; check for end of string
(11)             CMP         R4, #'Z'        ; compare to the letter Z
(12)             BRGT        test            ; check for end of string
(13)             ADD         R2, R2, #1      ; it must be an uppercase letter
(14)    test:
(15)             CMP         R4, #0          ; end of string?
(16)             BRNE        top             ; no, process next byte
```

    a.   Assuming that each location counter starts at 0 and that each instruction requires four bytes, show the symbol table that a two-pass assembler would construct during its first pass.

    b.   Using the assumptions from part *a,* show the patch lists and symbol table that a patch list assembler would create when it is assembling the ADD instruction on line 13 of this code fragment.

6.   Explain why the assembler does not need a patch list for the bss segment.

7.   Explain why you would want to use a separate patch list for text and data segments if your assembler supports multiple assembler segments. In other words, explain the problems you would encounter if you tried to use a single patch list.

8.   When assembler writes symbol table entries to the object file, does it need to write the index of the symbol table entry to the object file? Explain your answer.

9.   In Example 5.18 we introduced the following code fragment to initialize a string using the length-plus-value representation technique:

```
my_str:   .byte   last_ch − first_ch      ; just the length
first_ch: .byte   "Hello, world."
last_ch:                                  ; marking the end
```

    a.   Explain why the subtraction in the first line can be performed by the assembler and does not need to be changed by the linker or loader.

    b.   Explain why the assembler would not let you change the subtraction in the first line into an addition.

    c.   Explain how a two-pass assembler would translate this code fragment.

    d.   What complication does this code fragment introduce for a two-pass assembler? Explain how the assembler could overcome this difficulty.

10. In Example 5.13 we introduced the following code fragment to deal with a nonzero-based array (in this case, the array has a lower bound of 15 and an upper bound of 34):

```
            .bss
            .align      4
i:          .reserve    4
real_base:  .reserve    (34-15+1)*4              ; 4 bytes per integer
            .equate     my_arr, real_base − 15*4

            .text
            MOVE        R2, #432
            LOAD.w      R3, i
            MPY         R3, R3, #4               ; scale the index
            STORE.w     my_arr[R3], R2
```

    a.   To what extent can the assembler perform the subtraction used to define the symbol *my_arr* in the equate directive of this code fragment.

    b.   Would it make any difference to the assembler if the equate directive used an addition (instead of a subtraction) to define the symbol *my_array?* Explain your answer.

    c.   Suppose that the location counters for the bss and text segments are both zero when the assembler begins its translation of this code fragment. Show the symbol table that a two-pass assembler would generate during its first pass over the source code.

    d.   Given the assumptions stated in part *c* show the patch lists and symbol table that a patch list assembler would generate in translating this code fragment.

11.   Consider the following code fragment:

```
.import   real_base
.equate   my_arr, real_base − 15*4
```

Explain why the assembler would have a difficult time attaining a useful definition for the symbol *my_arr.*

12.   Consider the following source modules:

Module 1:

(1)		.import	str	; *the string is imported*
(2)		.export	str_len	; *we will export the function*
(3)		.text		
(4)	str_len:			
(5)		CLEAR	R2	; *R2 is the counter*
(6)		MOVE	R3, #str	; *R3 points to the element*
(7)		LOAD.b	R4, @R3	; *load the next character*
(8)		BRANCH	test	; *branch to loop exit test*
(9)	top:			
(10)		ADD	R2, R2, #1	; *one more character*
(11)		ADD	R3, R3, #1	; *advance the pointer*
(12)		LOAD.b	R4, @R3	; *load the next character*
(13)	test:			
(14)		CMP	R4, #0	; *end of string?*
(15)		BRNE	top	; *no, process next byte*
(16)		RTS		; *return to the caller*

Module 2:

(1)		.export	str	; *we will export a string*
(2)		.import	str_len	; *we will use the function*
(3)		.data		
(4)	str:	.byte	"Hello.", 0	; *allocate space for the string*
(5)		.text		
(6)		JSR	str_len	; *call the function*

    a.   Assuming that each location counter starts at 0 and that each instruction requires four bytes, show the patch lists and symbol table that an assembler would create for each of these source modules.

b.   Illustrate the public and private symbol tables that the linker will construct as it links these two modules.

c.   Explain how the linker will process each entry in the patch lists as it links these two modules.

13.   Suppose that the segment-mapping table has the following information:

Base	Bound
1,230	548
3,432	198
9,480	150
8,710	132
2,094	580

In other words, the program has access to five segments that have logical addresses 0 through 4. For each of the following logical addresses, give the corresponding physical address. If a logical address is invalid, explain why it is invalid.

a. $\langle 2, 42 \rangle$.

b. $\langle 0, 142 \rangle$.

c. $\langle 4, 652 \rangle$.

d. $\langle 3, 100 \rangle$.

e. $\langle 5, 48 \rangle$.

f. $\langle 0, 18 \rangle$.

g. $\langle 2, 200 \rangle$.

h. $\langle 3, 57 \rangle$.

i. $\langle 1, 92 \rangle$.

j. $\langle 4, 98 \rangle$.

14.   Suppose that each page is 512 bytes long. Further, suppose that the page-mapping table has the following values:

Page frame
20
15
12
43
60
16
18
30
25

In this case, the program uses nine pages (page 0 through page 8). For each of the following logical addresses, give the corresponding physical address. In performing this translation, be certain to identify the page number and offset for each logical address. If any of the logical addresses is invalid, be certain to explain why the address is invalid.

a.   1,000.

b.   92.

c.   1,024.

d.   4,090.

e.   5,000.

f.   4,000.

g.   3,000.

h.   3,101.

i.   2,045.

j.   2,001.

k.   104.

l.   432.

m.   999.

INPUT/OUTPUT STRUCTURES

PART FIVE

EXTENDED OPERATIONS AND EXCEPTIONS

An operating system is a collection of routines that manage the resources of a computing system. Most computing systems provide a variety of resources: one or more CPUs, memory, a keyboard, a monitor, a printer, and so forth. Management of these resources encompasses two important aspects: providing convenient access to the resources and protecting these resources from intentional and accidental abuses. We begin by considering convenient access. After we have addressed the issues related to convenient access, we will turn our attention to protection and the mechanisms used to control access to the resources of a computing system.

The loaders we discussed in the previous chapter are examples of operating system routines. In this case, the loader is involved in the management of the memory resource, in particular, the memory used by application programs. Another important set of routines are the routines that provide access to the input/output (I/O) devices. These routines are collectively called the basic I/O system (or *BIOS*). Figure 11.1 illustrates the BIOS. In this case, the BIOS provides access to four devices: a keyboard, a monitor, a printer, and a disk drive. The BIOS contains routines that can be used to control the I/O. When you write an application program, you can use the routines in the BIOS instead of writing code to directly control these devices.

BIOS

From a functional perspective, the routines in the BIOS provide an extension of the instruction set. In extending the instruction set, the BIOS routines provide a uniform interface to the I/O devices and may extend the basic capabilities of these devices. The extensions implemented by the BIOS should simplify the task of the application programmer.

In Chapter 3, we presented a brief overview of I/O devices. As you will recall, there are three registers associated with each I/O device: a data register, a control register, and a status register. To send a character to the printer, for example, you must first wait until the printer is ready to receive a character. You can implement this wait by testing the appropriate bit in the printer status register until it indicates that the printer has finished the last request. When the printer is ready, you can send the character by putting its representation in the data register and setting the appropriate bit(s) in the control register. As this example illustrates, you must

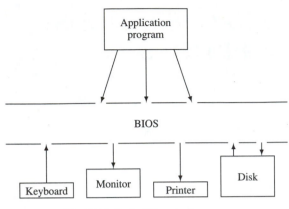

Figure 11.1   The BIOS (basic I/O system)

remember a few details to use the printer: the addresses of the device registers for the printer and the meanings associated with the bits in the status and control registers. If you want to send a character to the monitor, you will need to know the same details about the monitor registers. The BIOS can simplify your task by providing a uniform and convenient interface to the I/O devices. As an example, the BIOS may provide a single routine—*put_char*—with two parameters—a character and a device identifier—that can be used to send a character to the printer or the monitor. When you use this routine, the only detail you need to remember is the identifier for the device.

Reading characters from the keyboard introduces a new problem. What if the keyboard needs to send characters when the application program is not ready to read them? In other words, what happens if the user types when the application program is performing a calculation? If the application program is not ready to receive a character, some of the characters typed by the user may get lost. To avoid this difficulty, the BIOS may provide a *keyboard buffer* (a circular queue) to save the characters the user types until the application program requests them. When the application program needs the next character, it can call the BIOS routine that returns the next character from the keyboard buffer. If there are no characters in the keyboard buffer, the BIOS routine will wait until the user types a character. Figure 11.2 illustrates the keyboard buffer.

In addition to the keyboard buffer, Figure 11.2 shows a printer buffer. Printer buffers are used because printers are generally much slower than the CPU. When the BIOS provides a printer buffer, the routine used to send a character to the printer puts the character in the printer buffer and returns to the application. Later, when the printer is ready to accept the next character, the BIOS will send the next character. While the BIOS is waiting to send the character to the printer, the application program can continue with its calculations. The application only needs to wait when it needs to print a character and there is no room in the printer buffer.

Keyboard buffer

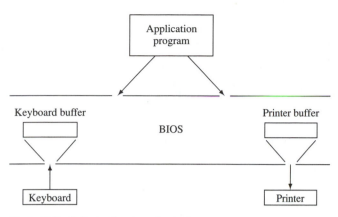

Figure 11.2 Buffering inputs and outputs

In thinking about the structure of the BIOS, there are two interfaces that need to be considered: the interface between the application program and the routines of the BIOS and the interface between the BIOS and the I/O devices. These interfaces are shown as horizontal lines in Figures 11.1 and 11.2. In this chapter, we discuss the interface between the application program and the BIOS. In particular, we consider the mechanisms that are used to call the routines in the BIOS. In Chapter 12, we discuss the mechanisms that are used to implement the interface between the BIOS and the I/O devices.

In section 11.1, we introduce the basic mechanism used to invoke operating system routines. In section 11.2, we discuss basic protection mechanisms. Finally, in section 11.3 we discuss exceptions, the mechanism used to identify and control abuses of the resources provided by a computing system.

11.1 THE RESIDENT MONITOR

Knowing that the operating system (OS) is a collection of routines, you might suspect that it is implemented as a library, as shown in Figure 11.3. In this case, the code for an application program is linked with the operating system routines that it uses. This produces an executable file that can be loaded and executed.

While this approach may seem natural, it is inefficient. Many of the routines in the operating system will be used by almost every application program. As such, the loader will spend a great deal of time reloading these routines whenever an application program is loaded. Moreover, if there are several application programs in memory at the same time, each will have its own copy of the operating system routines.

To avoid these costs, many operating systems keep the most commonly used routines resident in the memory of the machine. The two approaches, the OS as a library and the resident OS, are contrasted in Figure 11.4. In this case, two application programs, application 1 and application 2, have been loaded into

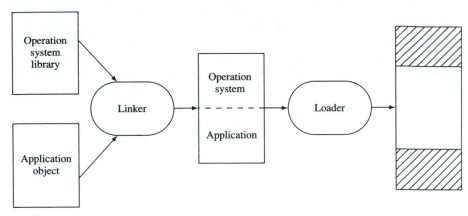

Figure 11.3   The OS as a library

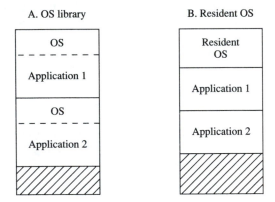

Figure 11.4   Resident OS routines

memory. In Figure 11.4A, each program has its own copy of the operating system routines that it uses. In Figure 11.4B, these applications share the resident OS routines.

Among other things, the resident OS routines monitor the I/O devices in the computing system (e.g., checking the keyboard for keystrokes) as well as the execution of application programs. For these reasons these routines are collectively called the *resident monitor*. Routines that are not used as frequently do not need to be resident in the memory of the machine. These routines can be loaded when they are needed by the application program. In contrast to the resident routines, these routines are called *transient routines* because they are only loaded when they are needed. When a transient routine is no longer needed, the space that the routine was using can be used to hold another program or a different transient routine.

Making (portions of) the operating system resident introduces an interesting problem: How can application programs link to the operating system routines?

Resident monitor

Transient routines

Once all of the operating system routines have been compiled, assembled, and linked, it is possible to determine where each routine will be loaded when the operating system is loaded. As such, the developers of the operating system could publish the starting address for every operating system routine. Application programmers could then use these addresses in their programs to invoke the operating system routines. For example, if the *put_char* routine is known to start at memory location 246, then an application program might include the statement JSR 246 (after establishing the parameter values). While this solution will work, it is impractical when you consider the fact that operating systems change. When the operating system is changed and a new version is released, the starting addresses for many of the routines will change. This means that every application program will need to be edited, reassembled, and relinked before it can be used with the new release of the operating system. When you have hundreds or even thousands of application programs, this situation is not reasonable.

11.1.1 A Dispatch Routine

The problem of changing addresses in the operating system stems from the fact that changes to one routine will affect the starting addresses of other routines. While it is difficult to fix the starting addresses for several routines, it is not difficult to fix the starting address for a single routine. As such, the operating system designers might choose to provide a single entry point for the operating system. This single entry point is frequently called a *dispatch routine*. When an application program needs to invoke an operating system routine, instead of calling the operating system routine directly, the program calls the dispatch routine. Along with the parameters needed by the operating system routine, the application program passes an identifier for the operating system routine that it needs to invoke. (Routine identifiers are typically small nonnegative integer values.) The dispatch routine simply transfers control to the appropriate operating system routine using the routine identifier passed by the application program. The name for the dispatch routine is based on the fact that this routine does not do any real work. It simply forwards the work to the appropriate operating system routine. In other words, the dispatch routine dispatches requests made by an application program. Figure 11.5 illustrates the flow of control that results from using a dispatcher.

Dispatch routine

If you are using a dispatch routine and the operating system is changed but the location of the dispatch routine remains fixed, application programs will not need to be reassembled or relinked. Any changes in the addresses of the operating system routines will only be reflected in the dispatch routine and will not be known to the application programmer. In this way, the routine identifiers remain fixed even if the addresses of the operating system routines change.

11.1.2 Vectored Linking

If you need to implement the dispatch routine, the branch table that we discussed at the end of Chapter 5 is the perfect construct. As you will recall, a branch table

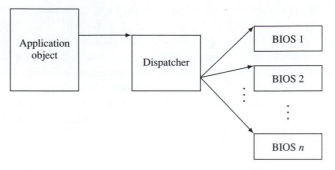

Figure 11.5   The dispatcher

is simply an array of addresses. Branch tables are used to implement multiway branches.

Example 11.1   *Present the code needed to implement the dispatch routine, assuming that the operation identifier is in register R2. In writing this code, assume that the start of the branch table is labeled by* os_routines *and that each operation identifier is an index into the branch table.*

```
                .data
routine_ptrs:   .word      . . .                ; initialization for the table
                .text
    dispatch:                                    ; the dispatch routine
                MOVE     R8, #routine_ptrs       ; R8 holds the base address
                MPY      R2, R2, #4              ; scale the index
                ADD      R2, R8, R2              ; R2 holds the table address
                LOAD.w   R2, @R2                 ; R2 holds the routine address
                BRANCH  @R2
```

Seen in this light, it hardly seems worth the effort of having a dispatch routine. If the operating system publishes the address of the branch table used in the dispatch routine instead of the address of the dispatch routine, application programs could jump to the routine through the branch table. Then when the operating system is changed, the developers only need to make sure that the branch table, *routine_ptrs,* has a fixed starting location and is initialized with the starting addresses of the appropriate operating system routines whenever the operating system is loaded.

Example 11.2   *Given the branch table* routine_ptrs, *write an assembly language code fragment jump to the operating system routine identified by the value 5.*

```
.import      routine_ptrs          ; address of the table
.text
MOVE         R2, #routine_ptrs     ; R2 holds the base address
ADD          R2, R2, #20           ; R2 holds the table address
LOAD.w       R2, @R2               ; R2 holds the routine address
JSR          @R2
```

The branch table is simply an array of routine addresses. One-dimensional arrays are called *vectors* and, as such, the branch table is a vector of routine addresses. In many contexts, this approach is called *vectored linking*. As you will recall, the essential problem that we are trying to solve is linking an application program with the operating system routines. Our solution calls for linking the application routine with the address of a vector. The vector table introduces a level of indirection between the application program and the operating system routines.

Vectored linking

Most of the RISC machines support a variation on the approach we have discussed. In these machines, the vector does not hold the address of an OS routine; instead, it holds the first few instructions of the routine. The vector holds the same number of instructions for each routine, and, as such, the routine addresses can be calculated using a simple index calculation. In some cases, the entire routine fits in the vector; in others, the code in the vector concludes with a branch to the remainder of the routine.

Example 11.3 *Suppose that the OS vector holds four instructions (16 bytes) for each routine. Moreover, suppose that the vector start is labeled by the symbol os_routines. Show the code needed to call the OS routine identified by the value 5.*

```
.import      os_routines          ; address of the table
.text
MOVE         R2, #os_routine      ; R2 holds the base address
ADD          R2, R2, #5*16        ; R2 holds the routine address
JSR          @R2
```

In comparing the code fragments presented in Examples 11.2 and 11.3, note that the code in Example 11.3 saves one memory reference (LOAD.w R2, @R2). In considering the RISC approach, this is a significant savings.

11.1.3 XOPs, Traps, and Software Interrupts

Most machines provide direct support for resident routines by providing a special operation that implements vectored linking. We call this operation XOP, for

Extended operation
(XOP)

XOP vector

Processor status word
(PSW)

extended operation. In a sense, the resident routines extend the operations supported by the base architecture. Different machines use different names for this operation. For example, the operation is called *TRAP* on the SPARC, *SYSCALL* (for system call) on the MIPS 4000 and *SVC* (for supervisor call) on the IBM RS/6000.

An XOP instruction consists of the name of the operation, XOP, followed by a nonnegative integer. The nonnegative integer is used to specify the index of an entry in the *XOP vector*. As we have discussed, this entry may point to an operating system routine or it may be the first few instructions of the operating system routine.

Figure 11.6 illustrates the sequence of events that occur when an application program executes an XOP instruction. The left side of the illustrations assumes that the XOP vector holds routine addresses, while the right side assumes that the XOP vector holds the actual routines. To execute an XOP instruction, the machine first determines the address of the operating system routine that handles the XOP. This may involve a lookup in the XOP vector (if the XOP vector holds routine addresses), or it may involve a simple index calculation (if the XOP vector holds instructions). Next, the current state of the processor is saved. The state of the processor involves the program counter and the *processor status word (PSW)*. (We will discuss the information stored in the processor status word in a moment.)

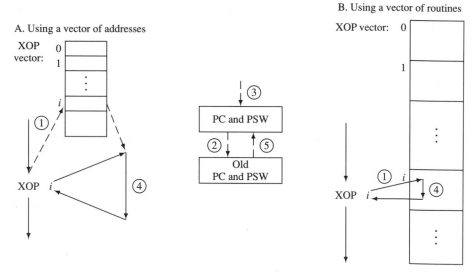

Notes:
1. Find entry *i* in the XOP vector table.
2. Save the PC and PSW.
3. Update the PC and PSW.
4. Execute the OS routine.
5. Restore the PC and PSW.

Figure 11.6 Execution of an XOP

The ordering of the first two steps is not important—they may in fact be done together. When these steps are complete, the processor status word and the program counter are updated, transferring control to the operating system routine. When the operating system routine completes, it restores the processor status word and the program counter. Restoring the program counter returns control to the application program.

The different names used by the different machines emphasize different aspects of vectored linking. As we have indicated, XOP stands for extended operation. In this case, the name emphasizes the fact that the routines in the operating system extend the basic instruction set of the machine by introducing new operations that manage I/O devices and other resources. The name SVC (used on the IBM RS/6000 for supervisor call) has a similar emphasis.

The name *trap* (used on the SPARC) is related to exceptions. When an application program encounters an exception (e.g., division by zero), the operating system traps the execution of the program to handle the exception. As we will discuss later in this chapter, most machines use the same mechanism for exceptions and XOPs. In this context, an XOP can be viewed as a voluntary trap into the operating system.

XOPs are frequently called *software interrupts*. In most contexts, the term *interrupt* refers to a signal generated by an I/O device. As we will discuss in the next chapter, most machines use the same mechanism to handle hardware interrupts and XOPs. In this context, the execution of the operating system routine can be viewed as an interrupt in the execution of the application program.

Software interrupts

11.1.4 The Processor Status Word

In addition to the program counter, the XOP operation typically saves a more detailed record of the processor state called the processor status word. Figure 11.7 presents the processor status word for the SPARC. In this case, the processor status word is 32 bits and includes the condition code register (the N, Z, V, and C fields). In addition to the condition code register, the processor status word includes an interrupt mask (the PIL field), a supervisor bit (the S field), the previous value of the supervisor bit (the PS field), a trap enable bit (the ET field), and a current register window pointer (the CWP field). The remaining fields in the processor status word are beyond the scope of this discussion. The current register window is related to the use of register windows on the SPARC (recall the discussion of register windows in section 6.7). The enable traps bit can be used to disable traps (in particular, exceptions and interrupts) during the execution of a trap handler. We will discuss the supervisor and previous supervisor bits when we discuss basic protection mechanisms later in this chapter. We will discuss the interrupt mask when we discuss interrupts and interrupt handling in Chapter 12.

Updating the processor status word during an XOP operation varies from machine to machine. On the PDP 11, each entry in the XOP vector table contains a new value for the processor status word in addition to the new value for the program counter. Most machines specify a fixed updating of the bits in the processor

Field	Bits	Meaning
impl ident	24–32	Identifies the implementation and version of the processor
N	23	The N (negative) bit of the condition code
Z	22	The Z (zero) bit of the condition code
V	21	The V (overflow) bit of the condition code
C	20	The C (carry) bit of the condition code
EC	13	Coprocessor enable
EF	12	Floating point coprocessor enable
PIL	8–11	Processor interrupt level
S	7	Supervisor mode
PS	6	Old value of the S bit
ET	5	Trap enable
CWP	0–4	Current (register) window pointer (see section 6.7)

Figure 11.7   SPARC processor status word

status word. The SPARC, for example, performs three updates of the processor status word: It clears the ET bit (thus disabling further traps), it copies the current value of the S (supervisor) field to the PS (previous supervisor) field and sets the S field to one, and it updates CWP field to allocate a new register window.

Here we should note that the SPARC does not automatically save the processor status word at the start of an XOP (i.e., it does not save the PSW in step 2 of Figure 11.6). When the XOP handler completes its activities, the SPARC will reverse the steps it performed in updating the processor status word. If the XOP handler takes any other action that might change the processor status word (e.g., enabling traps), it must save the value of the processor status word.

11.1.5 Subroutines and XOPs

The XOP operation is similar to the JSR (jump to subroutine) operation. Both operations save the current value of the program counter before transferring control to a different location in memory. As with the JSR operation, the application programmer needs to make sure that the parameters have been set up for the XOP handler; that is, stored in registers or pushed onto the stack, before issuing an XOP instruction. The XOP handler itself is similar to a subroutine; the XOP handler performs a specific task and returns to the point from which it was called.

While there are many similarities, there are three important differences between the JSR and XOP mechanisms. First, there is no branch delay slot following an XOP instruction. Second, transferring control to the XOP handler is based on the XOP vector table instead of using a name or address for the subroutine. Third, the JSR operation only saves the program counter before transferring control to the called subroutine. In contrast, the XOP operation saves and updates the processor status word and saves the program counter before transferring control to the XOP handler. Because the XOP saves more information, the operation used to return from an XOP needs to restore more information than the RTS (return from subroutine) operation. Importantly the RTS operation cannot be used to return from an XOP handler. If your machine provides an XOP operation, you can expect that it will also provide a special operation, RTX, to return from the XOP handler. On the SPARC, this instruction is called RETT (return from trap).

Whenever you write an XOP handler, there are a few points that you need to keep in mind:

- You need to select an XOP number and determine the location of the XOP vector for this number.
- You need to store the address of your XOP handler or the first few lines of the handler in the XOP vector.
- You need to terminate your XOP handler with an RTX instruction instead of an RTS instruction.

Example 11.4 *Write an XOP handler that will calculate the length of a null-terminated string. Assume that the starting address of the string is in R3 and you should put the result in R2.*

```
strlen:
        CLEAR     R2          ; R2 is the counter
        BRANCH    ldch        ; branch to loop exit test
    top:
        ADD       R2, R2, #1  ; one more character
    ldch:
        LOAD.b    R4, [R3]+   ; load the next character
        CMP       R4, #0      ; end of string?
        BRNE      top         ; no, process next byte
        RTX                   ; XOP return
```

Example 11.5 *Suppose that the XOP vector starts a memory location 128 and that the XOP vector holds the address for each XOP handler. Write an assembly language fragment to install the routine presented in Example 11.4 as XOP 14.*

```
.equate    xop_base, 128            ; base address for XOP table
    :
MOVE    R2, #(xop_base+14*4)    ; R2 holds the vector address
MOVE    R3, #strlen             ; R3 holds the routine address
STORE.w @R2, R3                 ; install the vector
    :
```

Example 11.6   *Suppose that the XOP vector starts a memory location 128 and that the XOP vector holds the first eight bytes (two instructions) for each XOP handler. Explain how you would install the routine presented in Example 11.4 as XOP 14.*

Here, you need to assemble the following instructions and make sure they are loaded in locations $128 + 14*8$ and $128 + 14*8 + 4$. These instructions clear the counter and branch to the middle of the loop that calculates the string length.

```
BRANCH ldch              ; branch to loop exit test
CLEAR  R2                ; this is the BRANCH DELAY SLOT
```

In this case, the code for the XOP handler can be simplified to

```
top:
      ADD      R2, R2, #1      ; one more character
ldch:
      LOAD.b   R4, [R3]+       ; load the next character
      CMP      R4, #0          ; end of string?
      BRNE     top             ; no, process next byte
      RTX                      ; XOP return
```

Example 11.7   *Write an assembly language fragment that uses XOP 14.*

```
         .bss
my_str:  .reserve  100              ; allocate space for the string
         .text
         ⋮                          ; initialize the string
         MOVE   R3, #my_str         ; initialize the parameter
         XOP    #14                 ; call the XOP
         ⋮                          ; use R2
```

11.1.6 XOPs (Traps) on the SPARC

We conclude this section by considering the implementation of XOPs on the SPARC. As we have already noted, XOPs are called traps on the SPARC. Moreover, the XOP vector is called the *trap table*. Each entry in the trap table contains the first four instructions (16 bytes) of the handler. The trap table consists of 256, 16-byte entries for a total of 4,096 bytes (4 Kbytes). The first 128 entries (0 through 127) are reserved for exceptions and interrupts identified by the hardware. We will consider these when we discuss exceptions and interrupts. The remaining 128 entries (128 through 255) are used for trap instructions.

A trap instruction consists of an operation (TA for trap always) and a trap identifier. The trap identifier may be specified using an immediate value or an effective address (register indirect with index). In either case, the processor only uses the least significant 7 bits of the value. These bits are interpreted as an unsigned integer and added to the value 128 (the start of the software trap entries). The 8-bit result is used as an index into the trap table.

The trap table is not in a fixed location on the SPARC. When a TA instruction is executed on the SPARC, the trap base register (TBR) is used to determine the address of the XOP handler. Figure 11.8 illustrates the fields in the trap base register. The TBA (trap base address) field provides the most significant 20 bits of the handler address. These bits can be set using the WRTBR (write TBR) instruction. In effect, the TBA field identifies the base address of the trap table. The TT (trap type) field completes the address for the trap handler. When a TA instruction is executed, the TT field is set to the 8-bit index calculated by adding 128 to the trap identifier (a number between 128 and 255).

32	12 11	4 3	0
TBA	TT	Zero	

Field	Bits	Meaning
TBA	12–32	Trap table base address
TT	4–11	Trap type
Zero	0–3	Always zero

Figure 11.8 The trap base register (TBR) on the SPARC

Example 11.8 *Summarize the actions performed by a SPARC processor when it executes the instruction* TA #14.

1. First, the processor adds 128 to the immediate value 14, obtaining the value 132.
2. Second, the processor sets the TT field of the TBR to the value 132.
3. Finally, the processor uses the value of the TBR as the address of the next instruction. If, for example, the TBA field of the TBR is 0 (a reasonable assumption), the next instruction will be fetched from memory location 2,012.

Example 11.9 *Explain how you would install the handler presented in Example 11.4 as the handler for trap 14 on the SPARC. Assume that the TBA field of the TBR is 0.*

First, you would need to load following the instructions into memory starting at location 2,012 (these instructions will only use 8 of the 16 available bytes):

```
BRANCH   ldch          ; branch to loop exit test
CLEAR    R2            ; this is the BRANCH DELAY SLOT
```

The SPARC does not support post-increment addressing, so we would need to alter the body of the routine slightly:

```
top:
        ADD       R2, R2, #1       ; one more character
ldch:
        LOAD.b    R4, [R3]         ; load the next character
        ADD       R3, R3, #1       ; increment the address
        CMP       R4, #0           ; end of string?
        BRNE      top              ; no, process next byte
        RTX                        ; XOP return
```

11.2 ACCESS CONTROL

In this section, we turn our attention to protection, in particular, to access control. Protection is an essential aspect of any computing system. Without protection of the resources in a computing system, the operating system cannot implement or enforce any of its resource management policies. In particular, the operating system must be able to control access to the resources of the computing system. The access control mechanisms implemented in modern computing systems are based on the notion of privilege level. Some machines, like the Motorola 88100, the IBM RS/6000, and the SPARC, only distinguish two levels of privilege—supervisor and user. Other machines, like the Intel 80386, DEC Vax, and HP Precision, provide more than two levels of privilege. We begin by considering the notion of privilege levels. Once we have considered this aspect of protection, we will discuss the details of access control. In particular, we consider the mechanisms that are used to control access to memory, the CPU, and the I/O devices. We conclude this section with a discussion of the access control mechanisms implemented by the HP Precision architecture.

11.2.1 Levels of Privilege

Access control is based on privilege level: different privilege levels are subject to different access control policies. In this section, we consider the mechanisms that are used to establish and enforce privilege levels. Initially, we limit our discussion to a simple two-level scheme. In this scheme, the machine distinguishes two levels of privilege, called supervisor mode and user mode. When the machine is in *supervisor mode*, it can access every resource in the system. When the machine is executing in *user mode*, it may have limited access to the resources of the system. In terms of access control, the basic idea is simple: Operating system routines should be executed in supervisor mode, while application programs should be executed in user mode with the appropriate access controls. We need to ensure that application programs are never executed in supervisor mode.

Supervisor mode

User mode

Privilege (or supervisor) bit

Implementation of this two-level scheme is based on a single bit, the *privilege (or supervisor) bit*, that is usually stored in the processor status word. When the value of the privilege bit is 0, the processor is in user mode. When the privilege bit is 1, the processor is in supervisor mode. The CPU should be in supervisor mode whenever it is executing an instruction from an operating system routine and in user mode whenever it is executing an instruction from an application program. The value of the privilege bit is maintained according to the following rules:

- When the processor starts up (after a reset or power on signal), the privilege bit is set to 1.
- Whenever an operating system routine is called (using the XOP mechanism), the privilege bit is set to 1.
- When an operating system routine completes and returns to the point of invocation (using the RTX instruction), the privilege bit is restored to its previous value.

If we can ensure that the privilege bit is cleared (to 0) whenever an application program starts, these rules ensure that the CPU will only be in supervisor mode when it is executing instructions from an operating system routine. Clearing the privilege bit when an application program is started involves a bit of a trick. After the first application program (perhaps a command line interpreter) has been loaded, the operating system constructs a "saved" program counter and a "saved" processor status word. The privilege bit in the saved processor status word is set to 0, while the saved program counter is simply the address of the first instruction in the application program. These saved values are stored in the location that the RTX instruction uses to restore the program counter and processor status word. Then, to start the application program, the operating system simply executes an RTX instruction. Now, whenever an application program starts its execution, the privilege bit will be set to 0.

We should note that the XOP instruction can always be executed. It does not matter whether the CPU is in user mode or supervisor mode. On the other hand, the RTX operation must be restricted so that it can only be executed when the CPU is in supervisor mode. Otherwise, an application program could use our trick to have the CPU execute an application program when the CPU is in supervisor mode.

11.2.2 Resource Protection

Resource protection is implemented using two tools: privileged operations and protection agents. A *privileged operation* is an operation that can only be performed when the CPU is in supervisor mode. The RTX operation is an example of a privileged operation. A *protection agent* is an agent of the operating system that enforces the resource management policies of the operating system.

Privileged operation

Protection agent

Figure 11.9 illustrates the role of the protection agent. In principle, the protection agent surrounds the resource—every request to access the resource must go through the protection agent. Given the access request and the privilege level of the processor, the protection agent determines whether the request should be allowed or disallowed. If the request is allowed, it is forwarded to the resource and the resource performs the requested operation. Otherwise, the protection agent generates an exception. We will consider exceptions and exception handling in the next section. In this section, we simply identify the nature of the exceptions that result from invalid accesses. In the remainder of this discussion, we consider the implementation of protection agents for the basic resources provided by a computing system. In particular, we consider the implementation of protection agents for the memory, CPU, and I/O devices of a computing system. To enforce the resource management policies of the operating system, these protection agents must reflect the allocation strategies of the operating system.

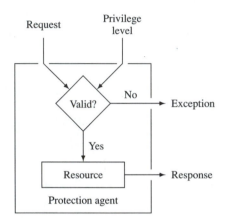

Figure 11.9   A protection agent

Memory Protection   As a minimum, the CPU protection agent must ensure that application programs cannot modify the XOP vectors or the operating system routines. Without such protection, it would be easy to trick the CPU into executing an application program in supervisor mode. In most systems, memory protection is implemented in the address-mapping hardware. Frequently, this hardware is implemented as a coprocessor called the *memory management unit (MMU)*.

Memory management unit (MMU)

Memory requests are specified by an operation and an address. We will consider three types of operations involving memory: instruction fetch (and execute), data read (i.e., LOAD register), and data write (i.e., STORE register). The memory protection agent must ensure that each request is valid given the memory allocation and mapping strategy. In particular, the memory protection agent must ensure that the application program is constrained to the blocks of memory that the loader allocated for the program. To perform this task, the agent must check every memory access performed by the application program. If the access is legal, the application program is allowed to continue its activities. Otherwise, the memory access is aborted and control is transferred to the operating system (using the exception mechanism described in the next section).

The access check depends on the address-mapping hardware being used. We begin by considering the protection agent needed for the base-and-bound address-mapping scheme that we discussed in Chapter 10 (see section 10.3.1). Figure 11.10 presents the logic that the memory protection agent needs to implement. In this case, memory accesses are always permitted when the processor is in supervisor mode. Moreover, these accesses are not mapped (note that the base value is not added into the address). When the processor is in user mode, memory accesses are only permitted if the (logical) address is less than the bound value. Note that we have ignored the type of operation (ifetch, read, or write) being performed. The operations used to set the base-and-bound values must be privileged operations; otherwise, an application program could easily circumvent the access control provided by this protection agent.

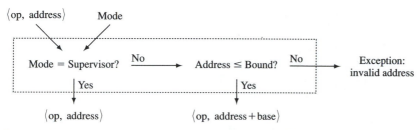

Figure 11.10 A memory protection agent for base-and-bound addressing

If address translation is based on paging, the primary test that the memory protection agent must check is to be certain that page number in the logical address is valid. This can be implemented by comparing the page number with the size of the page-mapping table. To implement a more sophisticated access control policy, we can store access control bits in the page-mapping table (along with the page frame). This would allow the memory protection agent to enforce different access control policies to different pages of the application program. Figure 11.11 illustrates the structure of a memory protection agent for paged addressing.

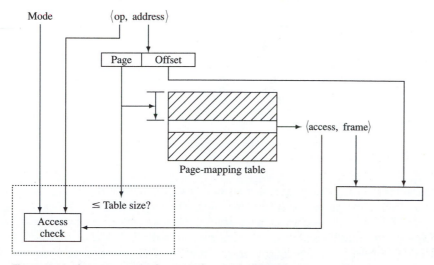

Figure 11.11 A memory protection agent for paged addressing

Example 11.10   *Suppose that each page table entry has two access bits. Describe how you could use those bits to control access.*

Bits	Permitted access
00	Read only
01	Read or execute
10	Read or write
11	Read, write, or execute

CPU Protection   Memory is allocated in blocks of cells, and the memory protection agent must ensure that application programs are constrained to the blocks of cells that have been allocated for them. The CPU, on the other hand, is allocated for a block of time. As such, the CPU protection agent must ensure that the application program does not use more time than it was allocated.

Implementing CPU protection is quite simple. When an application program is granted the CPU resource, a timer is started. The timer is set to generate an interrupt at the end of the time block for the application. When the interrupt hits, an operating system routine will take over the CPU and remove the application program. Figure 11.12 illustrates this form of CPU protection. In this case, it is interesting to note that the CPU protection agent does not check each access to the CPU (i.e., each instruction execution) but, instead, ensures that it can regain control of the resource when further use of the resource by the application program would be invalid.

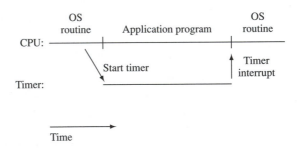

Figure 11.12   Using a timer to implement CPU protection

I/O Devices   The remaining resources are accessed through the I/O system. Operating systems use two distinct allocation strategies for I/O devices: indirect access and direct access. In indirect access, the application program is required to use an OS routine whenever it needs to access the I/O device; that is, access to the I/O device is mediated by an OS routine. This situation is illustrated in Figure 11.13.

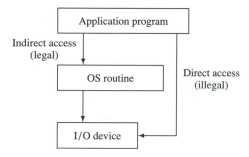

Figure 11.13 Indirect access

In this case, the I/O device protection agent must ensure that access to the I/O devices is granted only if the processor is in supervisor mode. Implementation of this protection agent depends on the I/O structure of the machine. If the machine provides special I/O operations, the I/O device protection agent can be implemented by making the I/O operations privileged operations. If I/O devices are mapped into memory, you only need to ensure that the regions of memory used for I/O devices cannot be accessed by application programs. In this case, the I/O device protection agent can be integrated into the memory protection agent.

While indirect access is appropriate for many I/O devices (like the keyboard and printer), it may be inappropriate for other I/O devices. In particular, indirect access may incur too much overhead for I/O devices that are used frequently. For example, some displays require a large number of commands from the application program in a very short period of time to display an image. In this case, the operating system needs to allow the application program direct access to the I/O device, but it must be able to control when this access is granted. To maintain the needed control, the application program must invoke an operating system routine to acquire direct access to the device before it can use the device. When the operating system routine gives the application program access to the device, it notifies the device protection agent. Once the application program has been granted access rights for the device, it can access the device directly (without needing to invoke an operating system routine). These steps are illustrated in Figure 11.14.

This allocation policy is effectively the same as the policy used to allocate to memory. Implementation of the protection agent again depends on the I/O structures provided by the machine. If the I/O devices are memory mapped, the protection agent is provided by the memory protection agent. On the other hand, if the I/O devices are isolated (i.e., the machine has special I/O operations), the I/O device protection agent must be able to selectively enable and disable direct access to the cells in the I/O space. In the Intel 80386, this control is implemented by an I/O permission bitmap. In principle, the I/O device protection agent maintains a bit for every cell in the I/O address space. When an application program attempts to perform an I/O operation, the I/O device protection agent checks the corresponding bit in the I/O permission bitmap. If the bit is 0, the access is allowed; otherwise, the I/O device protection agent generates an exception.

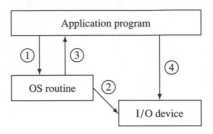

Notes:
1. The application program requests use of the I/O device.
2. The OS allocates the device and informs the protection agent.
3. The OS returns to the application program.
4. The application program uses the I/O device.

Figure 11.14   Direct access

11.2.3 Separate Stacks

Code that runs in supervisor mode uses the same basic instructions and programming techniques as the code in an application program. As such, operating system routines may use a parameter stack to pass parameters to other routines in the operating system. The stack used by routines in the operating system should be distinct from the stacks used by application programs. If the operating system routines simply use the stack allocated by an application program, they may inadvertently overwrite protected regions of memory. As an example, suppose the application program sets the stack pointer to point into the XOP vector before calling an OS routine. If the OS routine uses the application stack pointer, it will overwrite the values store in the XOP vector. For the remainder of this discussion, we will distinguish between the *user stack* (the stack used when the processor is executing in user mode) and the *supervisor stack* (the stack used when the processor is executing in supervisor mode).

User stack

Supervisor stack

Most of the newer, RISC-style architectures do not automatically switch to a supervisor stack when an XOP handler is invoked. These machines save the PC (program counter) and PSW (processor status word) in internal CPU registers during the execution of an XOP. The values stored in these internal registers are used to restore the PC and PSW by the RTX operation. If an XOP handler needs to invoke another OS routine, it must establish a supervisor stack and save the values of the old PC and old PSW into memory location. This strategy is based on the observation that most OS routines do not need to call other operating system routines. Given this observation, it would be wasteful if the machine automatically established a supervisor stack and saved the PC and PSW in memory locations.

In contrast to the RISC approach, most of the CISC machines do establish a supervisor stack when an XOP is invoked. Figure 11.15 illustrates the steps performed by the Motorola 68000. Before it executes an XOP instruction, the application program pushes its parameters onto the user stack. When the XOP is executed, the PC and PSW are pushed onto the supervisor stack, the privilege bit in the PSW is set to 1, and control is transferred to the OS routine. The OS routine can obtain the parameters using special operations that access the user stack. Any subroutine calls made by the OS routine use the supervisor stack. When the operating system routine is complete, it returns to the application by executing an RTX instruction. The RTX restores the PC and PSW from the supervisor stack.

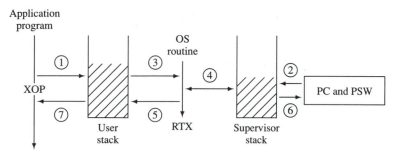

Notes:

1. The application program pushes arguments onto the user stack.
2. The current PC and PSW are saved on the supervisor stack.
3. The OS routine retrieves and processes the arguments.
4. The OS routine uses the supervisor stack.
5. The OS routine puts the result on the user strack.
6. The old PC and PSW are restored from the supervisor stack.
7. The application program retrieves the result from the user stack.

Figure 11.15 Separate stacks

11.2.4 Multiple Levels—Rings and Gates

While the simple two-level scheme provides adequate protection for the operating system, it may not reflect the protection structure *within* the operating system (and related utilities). As such, several machines extend the simple two-level scheme to multiple levels of privilege. In these systems, privilege levels are called *rings* be- Rings
cause they can be imagined as concentric rings. Lower numbered rings correspond to higher levels of privilege. Instead of a single bit, two or more bits are used to record current privilege level or the number of the current ring. Usually routines executing in lower numbered rings (higher privilege level) can access resources defined in the higher numbered rings (lower privilege level). However, routines executing in the higher numbered rings cannot directly access resources defined in lower numbered rings. Figure 11.16 illustrates a system with four rings.

In many cases, changing privilege levels in a ring-oriented system is based on the XOP mechanism. In particular, XOP instructions are used to increase the privilege level. The privilege level is restored to its previous value when the called routine returns using an RTX instruction. In ring-based systems, the vectors used to identify the routines in the inner rings are called *gates*. In concept, the rings Gates
are walls that protect resources and the gates are openings in these walls.

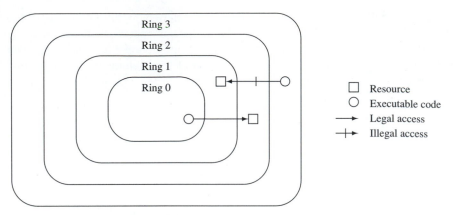

Figure 11.16   Rings of privilege

The generalization to more than two privilege levels introduces three new problems. First, how is the RTX instruction restricted? Second, how is the privilege level of the called routine determined? Third, can any routine call any other routine?

As we have noted, the RTX instruction restores the privilege level of the processor based on a value stored on the current stack. In the simple two-level scheme, an RTX instruction can only be executed when the processor is in supervisor mode. In a ring-based system, the RTX instruction cannot be restricted to the highest privilege level. In particular, it must be possible for a routine in ring 2 to return to a routine in ring 3 using the RTX instruction. In this case, it is reasonable to expect that the RTX instruction is restricted in such a way that the resulting privilege level is no greater than the privilege level in effect when the RTX instruction is executed. In other words, the RTX instruction cannot be used to increase the privilege level. On a related note, most systems that provide multiple privilege levels require that the privilege level that results from the execution of an XOP be at least as high as the privilege level in effect before the XOP. Executing an XOP that lowers the privilege level cannot be used to defeat the basic protection mechanism; however, the called routine could not return to the caller using the RTX instruction.

In the simple two-level scheme, the privilege level is always set to "supervisor." In a system that has more than two privilege levels, any privilege level that is higher than the current privilege level could be used as the new privilege level. In some systems, for example, the Intel 80386, the new privilege level is determined by the routine being called. The new privilege level can be stored in the gate or associated with the routine. In other systems, for example, the DEC Vax, there are separate operations (and separate gate tables) for each ring. In this case, the privilege level is determined by the operation.

In the simple two-level system, there is no restriction on the use of the XOP instruction. In particular, an application program can call any of the operating system routines. In a system that supports multiple privilege levels, the ability to call any routine from any privilege level may be restricted. While the DEC Vax does not restrict which routines can be called from the various privilege levels, other machines, like the Intel 80386, do. In the case of the 80386, each gate has a privilege level. To use a gate, the privilege level of the processor must be at least as high as the privilege level of the gate. The privilege level of the gate should be lower than the privilege level of the routine that it points to, but there is no other relation between the two privilege levels.

Figure 11.17 illustrates several uses of gates. In this illustration, we assume that gate access is determined by the privilege level of the gate (as in the Intel 80386). The arrow from a gate to a routine represents the vectored aspect of gates (each gate points to a routine). The arrows that lead from routines to gates represent calls using the gate (i.e., XOPs). In all cases, the privilege level of the routine or gate is illustrated by the position of the routine or gate within the rings.

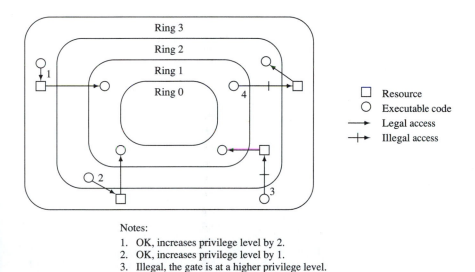

Notes:
1. OK, increases privilege level by 2.
2. OK, increases privilege level by 1.
3. Illegal, the gate is at a higher privilege level.
4. Illegal, this would decrease the privilege level by 1.

Figure 11.17 Using gates

The first access in Figure 11.17 illustrates a routine executing in ring 3 using a gate in ring 3 to call a routine in ring 1. This type of access, where the current routine and the gate are at the same privilege level, is the most common use of gates. The next access illustrates a routine in ring 2 using a gate in ring 3 to call a routine in ring 1. Because the privilege level of the gate is lower than the current routine and the privilege level of the called routine is higher than the privilege level of the called routine, this represents a legal access. The third access illustrates an illegal use of a gate. In this case, the privilege level of the gate is higher than the privilege level of the current routine and, as such, the current routine cannot use this gate. The fourth access is also illegal. In this case, the gate is in ring 3 while the current routine is in ring 1, so there is no problem with the current routine accessing the gate. However, the called routine is at a lower privilege level than the current routine so this access is not allowed.

11.2.5 Access Control on the HP Precision

We conclude our discussion of access control by considering the access control mechanisms provided by the HP Precision architecture. To simplify the presentation we will ignore the *protection id* mechanism and concentrate on the access rights mechanism. The HP Precision provides four levels of privilege. The current privilege level, PL, is stored in the least significant 2 bits of the program counter. (Because instructions must be aligned on word boundaries, these bits are not used when an instruction is fetched.) Lower values of PL are associated with less restrictive access controls. Level zero is the most privileged level.

The HP Precision does not provide special I/O operations, so all of the resources (except the CPU) are accessed through the memory. Memory accesses are mapped using a page-mapping table. Each entry in the page-mapping table includes a 7-bit access rights field. The structure of the access rights field is shown in Figure 11.18.

Page type	PL1	PL2
3	2	2

Figure 11.18   The access rights field on the HP Precision

The HP Precision distinguishes three types of memory access: read, write, and execute. Table 11.1 shows the privilege check performed by the HP Precision given the *type* field from the page table and the type of the operation requested. In examining this table, note that read and write access always have an upper bound for PL. This aspect of the privilege check reflects the fact that larger values for PL imply less access. In contrast to read and write access, execute accesses have an upper *and*

Table 11.1   Interpretation of access rights on the HP Precision

Type	Page type	Read	Write	Execute
			Privilege check	
000	Read only	$PL \leq PL1$	Illegal	Illegal
001	Read and write	$PL \leq PL1$	$PL \leq PL2$	Illegal
010	Read and execute	$PL \leq PL1$	Illegal	$PL2 \leq PL \leq PL1$
011	Read, write, and execute	$PL \leq PL1$	$PL \leq PL2$	$PL2 \leq PL \leq PL1$
100	Gateway 0	Illegal	Illegal	$PL2 \leq PL \leq PL1$
101	Gateway 1	Illegal	Illegal	$PL2 \leq PL \leq PL1$
110	Gateway 2	Illegal	Illegal	$PL2 \leq PL \leq PL1$
111	Gateway 3	Illegal	Illegal	$PL2 \leq PL \leq PL1$

lower bound for PL. As with the read and write accesses, the upper bound reflects the fact that larger values for PL imply less access. The lower bound reflects the fact that some executable pages may not be trusted to hold "safe" instructions.

To see the problem with "unsafe" instructions, consider a page that can be written and executed. If the page can be written by an application program and executed by an OS routine, it is possible that the application program will assemble and write an unsafe instruction into the page. Later, this instruction might be executed by an OS routine, compromising the integrity of the access control policy. The fourth line of Table 11.1 makes it impossible for the processor to execute an instruction that might have been written by an application program.

The last four lines of Table 11.1 represent the *gateway mechanism* used on the HP Precision. Unlike most machines, the HP Precision does not rely on vectored linking (i.e., the XOP/RTX mechanism) to change privilege levels. Because the privilege level is stored in the program counter, operations that change the program counter could change the privilege level. Simple branch instructions can only demote the privilege level (i.e., increase the PL value). As such, a standard subroutine return operation can be used to demote the privilege level when an OS routine completes its activities.

Gateway operations must be used to promote the privilege level. A gateway operation is a branch operation that includes a possible promotion of privilege level. To promote the privilege level, the gateway instruction must appear on a page that has a type field between 100 and 111. When the gateway instruction is executed, the privilege level may be promoted to the value represented by the last 2 bits in the type field for the page holding the gateway instruction. Gateway instructions cannot be used to demote the privilege level. As such, if the current PL value is less than the value represented by the last 2 bits of the type field, the privilege level is not changed.

Gateway mechanism

11.3 EXCEPTIONS

An exception is an invalid use of a resource. As an example, division by zero is an invalid use of the ALU resource. In section 11.2, we introduced two other exceptions: a violation of the memory protection policy, *invalid address,* and execution of a privileged operation in user mode, *illegal operation.* When an exception is detected, control is transferred to an operating system routine using a mechanism like the XOP mechanism. The program counter and processor status word are saved and the privilege bit is set before control is transferred to the routine. Operating system routines that are called when exceptions are detected are called *exception handlers*.

Exception handlers
Exception vector

The exception handlers (or their addresses) are stored in an *exception vector.* Each exception is associated with a nonnegative integer. For example, the divide-by-zero exception might be associated with the integer 5. When an exception is detected, the number associated with the exception is used as an index into the exception vector. In many cases, the exception vector and the XOP table are distinct. On other machines, these vectors are combined into a single vector. Figure 11.19 presents a graphical representation of exception handling.

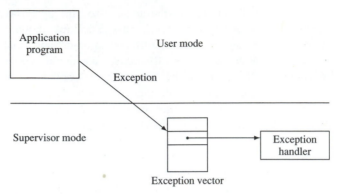

Figure 11.19   Handling an exception

There are two important differences between exceptions and XOPs. First, XOPs are *explicit* in the code of a program. In contrast, exceptions are *implicit*—an exception is implied by the instruction and the context in which the instruction is executed. For example, if R0 contains the value 0, then an instruction that divides R1 by R0 will generate an exception. Second, the action taken by the operating system routine is likely to be different for exceptions and extended operations. In particular, operating system routines that handle exceptions do not usually return to the instruction immediately following the instruction that generated the exception. Instead, exception handlers typically print a message and abort the execution of the application program.

In the remainder of this section, we consider five issues that are related to exceptions and exception handling: traps, user-defined handlers, break-point debugging, exception priorities, and synchronization. In section 11.3.1, we begin by considering traps—exceptions that are explicitly tested by special instructions in an application program. After considering traps, we consider the possibility of user-defined exception handlers in section 11.3.2. In section 11.3.3, we consider an interesting application of exception handling—the design of a break-point debugger. When an instruction can generate more than one exception, on most machines an exception priority scheme is used to determine which exception is signaled. In section 11.3.4, we consider exception priorities. Finally, in section 11.3.5, we consider the fact that several instructions may be in the instruction interpretation pipeline when an exception is identified.

11.3.1 Traps—Explicit Exceptions

Some exceptions cannot be checked by the hardware and must be checked by instructions in the application program. For example, exceeding the bounds of an array in a Pascal program is an exception; however, use of an invalid index only generates an invalid address if the final (indexed) address is outside the range of addresses allocated for the program. However, the hardware does not know the sizes or locations of the arrays in the application program and, as such, cannot check the validity of array indexes.

To simplify the code needed to check for these exceptions, many machines provide operations, called *traps*, that generate an exception if a condition is met. For example, the Motorola 88100 provides a variety of trap operations. One trap operation generates an exception if a specific bit in a register is set. Another operation generates an exception if a specific bit is clear. Another operation generates an exception by comparing the value in a register to zero. Still another operation generates an exception if the value in a register is greater than a specified value. This last operation can be used to implement array bounds checking.

Traps

The SPARC and many of the CISC machines provide a special trap operation to check for integer overflow in the previous arithmetic operation. This approach stems from the fact that signed and unsigned operations frequently use the same circuit but have different overflow detection rules. These machines provide a single version of the integer arithmetic operations and let the application program determine if the result is an overflow. In contrast, most of the RISC machines (excluding the SPARC) provide two sets of arithmetic operations (e.g., add signed and add unsigned). In these machines, the signed operations generate an exception if the result is an overflow.

11.3.2 User-Defined Exception Handlers

Suppose that you are writing an application program that will perform several thousand divisions. Moreover, you know that, at most, one or two of the divisions may end up dividing by zero. When this happens, you would simply like to ignore the error and continue with the execution of your program. One way to deal with this situation is to carefully check the denominator before each division and avoid the division whenever the denominator is zero. This solution works, but it complicates your code and makes it inefficient. The inefficiency stems from the fact that the number of divisions is large and the probability of dividing by zero is very small.

A better way to deal with this situation is to convince the operating system to ignore division by zero exceptions when they occur during the execution of your program. In other words, the exception handler for the divide-by-zero handler should simply execute an RTX (return from extended operation) instruction and allow your program to continue its execution. While it is reasonable to assume that the operating system would provide two types of exception handlers—one that aborts the application program and another that ignores the instruction that generated the exception—it is not reasonable to assume that the operating system will provide an exception handler that is perfect for every application. As such, the operating system may provide a routine that allows users to provide their own exception handlers.

Figure 11.20 presents a graphical representation of the activities that are performed to invoke a user-defined exception handler. When the exception is detected,

Upcall

control is transferred to the operating system exception handler. This OS routine transfers control to the user-defined exception handler using an *upcall*. Unlike an ordinary procedure call, an upcall demotes the privilege level. In a two-level system, this changes the mode from supervisor to user. When the user-defined exception handler completes its activities, it returns directly to the application program (without returning to the OS exception handler).

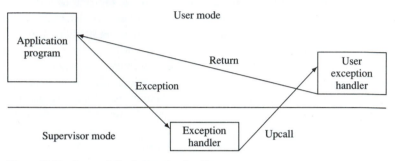

Figure 11.20   A user-defined exception handler

11.3.3 Break-Point Debugging

Break-point debugger

Many operating systems provide a *break-point debugger*. In a break-point debugger, the debugger first loads the application program and then allows the user to establish break points in the code for the program. The application program is executed after the programmer has established a set of break points. When execution crosses a break point, the application program is suspended and control is returned to the debugger. When control returns to the debugger, the programmer can examine the state of the registers and the memory. After examining the state of the computation, the programmer can resume the execution of the program. The programmer will again be able to examine the state of the computation when the program crosses another break point.

To implement a break-point debugger, you need to identify an instruction that generates an exception. Many machines provide a special break-point instruction for this purpose. If the machine does not provide a break-point operation, you need to devise an illegal instruction. We call this instruction the *break-point instruction*. Moreover, we call the exception generated by the break-point instruction the *break-point exception*. The debugger needs to install a handler for the break-point exception.

When the programmer inserts a break point in the code, the debugger saves the instruction where the break point is to be inserted and replaces this instruction by the break-point instruction. In this way, the application program will generate a break-point exception and invoke the handler installed by the debugger whenever it crosses a break point in the code.

If the programmer can set several break points, the debugger must determine which break point was crossed when the exception was generated. This is typically done by maintaining a list of break-point records. Each break-point record contains the location of the break point and the original instruction in the break point. When a break-point exception occurs, the debugger (i.e., the handler for the break-point exception) uses the value of the saved program counter to search its list of break-point records. If the debugger finds a break-point record with the same location as the saved program counter, it has determined the correct break point. If no such record exists, the debugger must forward the exception to the actual handler for the exception. If, for example, the break-point debugger is using the divide-by-zero exception as its break-point exception, it will forward the exception to the real divide-by-zero exception handler.

11.3.4 Exception Priorities

It is possible that a single instruction could generate several exceptions. For example you might attempt to execute an instruction that has a privileged operation and an invalid memory address when the processor is in user mode. Executing this instruction could generate two exceptions: an illegal instruction exception and a data address exception. Most machines resolve this difficulty by establishing priorities among the exceptions that are detected. In this case, it would be natural to assign a higher priority to the illegal instruction exception and ignore the illegal address exception.

The Intel i860 has an interesting approach to multiple exceptions. The i860 supports a single exception handler. When an exception occurs, a bit is set in the processor status word and control is transferred to the exception handler. There is a bit in the PSW for each exception that can be detected by the machine. If multiple exceptions occur, multiple bits will be set before control is transferred to the exception handler.

11.3.5 Synchronization

As we have noted, most machines do not have a branch delay slot following an XOP instruction. When the processor determines that it is executing an XOP instruction, it stops fetching new instructions until it determines the address of the XOP handler. The processor then completes its execution of all instructions in the pipeline before it changes the mode of the processor (from user mode to supervisor mode) and transfers control to the XOP handler.

Unfortunately, exceptions are not as well behaved as XOPs. Some exceptions cannot be detected until the processor has already fetched and begun execution of one or more instructions that follow the invalid instruction. Moreover, some of these instructions may have updated CPU registers. To avoid the difficulties associated with undoing these partial results, most processors complete the execution of all instructions in the pipeline whenever an exception is detected. This means that the program counter that is saved when control is transferred to the exception handler may not identify the invalid instruction. Instead, the saved program counter may identify an instruction that was executed several instructions after the invalid instruction. In addition, any of the instructions in the pipeline before the exception is detected may generate exceptions. These aspects of exception handling and pipelining make it very difficult to debug programs.

To simplify the programmer's task, most machines provide an explicit synchronization operation. This operation introduces a delay in the pipeline that ensures that all instructions in the pipeline are completed before the processor starts its execution of the next instruction. These operations slow down the execution of the program but simplify the task of identifying the invalid instruction.

11.4 SUMMARY

In this chapter, we covered vectored linking and three related topics: resident OS routines, exception handlers, and changes in privilege level. Most machines use vectored linking to transfer control to resident operating system routines and exception handlers. Vectored linking provides a level of indirection between the caller and the called routine and usually includes a promotion of privilege level. The level of indirection simplifies the invocation of resident OS routines because the caller only specifies the index of the routine, not its address. The level of indirection also simplifies the invocation of exception handlers. In this case, vectored linking makes it easy for the machine to determine the address of the exception handler when it detects an exception while providing users with the ability to change exception handlers.

Most machines automatically promote the privilege level of the processor when an operating system routine or exception handler is called (using vectored linking). In many cases, the invoked XOP or exception handler needs to access protected resources. In these cases, the promotion of privilege level is appropriate; however, there are situations when the handler does not need to run at a higher privilege level. In these cases, it is important that the programmer demote the privilege level as soon as possible. There have been several violations of security that stem from exception handlers that run at an unnecessarily high privilege level.

11.4.1 Additional Reading

Most of the books listed under the categories of "Operating Systems" and "Architecture and Organization" cover the essential aspects of vectored linking. In addition, some of the books in the "Assembly Language Programming" section address this topic. Texts on operating systems also cover the topic of computer security and security mechanisms in more depth. If you are interested in more details about the vectored linking mechanisms, you will need to consult the processor reference manuals for the specific machines you are interested in.

11.4.2 Terminology

- BIOS, Resident monitor, Transient routines
- Dispatching, Vectored linking
- Extended operations (XOPs), Traps, and Software interrupts
- XOP vector, XOP handler
- Processor status word (PSW)
- Privilege level, Supervisor mode, User mode
- Privileged operation
- Protection agent
- User stack, Supervisor stack
- Rings and gates
- Exception, Exception vector, Exception handler
- Trap
- Upcall
- Break point, Break-point debugger

11.4.3 Review Questions

1. Describe the purpose of the BIOS.
2. Explain the differences between a standard library routine and a resident routine.
3. What are the two basic approaches to vectored linking? Explain the advantages and disadvantages of each approach.
4. Explain why the XOP vector needs to be protected from modification by an application program.
5. What are the fields that you would expect to find in a processor status word?
6. Give an example of a privileged operation and explain why it must be a privileged operation.
7. What is the relationship between protection agents and exceptions?
8. Why does a protection agent need to know the mode that the processor is in?
9. Why it is important to have two stacks, a user stack and a supervisor stack?
10. Why does the 80386 not let a routine call a routine at a lower privilege level using a gate?
11. Explain the problem of "unsafe" instructions. How does the HP Precision handle unsafe instructions?
12. What is an exception? Give three examples of exceptions.
13. What is an upcall?
14. What is a break point?

11.5 EXERCISES

1. The memory protection agent shown in Figure 11.10 does not examine the requested operation. Explain how you could extend this memory protection agent so that it examines the requested operation.

2. What is the benefit of distinguishing different types of memory operations in a memory protection agent? On the one hand, the memory has been allocated to the application program and, as such, the application program should be able to access it in any way it chooses. What is wrong with this position?

3. Design a sequential circuit that implements the access check shown in Figure 11.11 using the access bits presented in Example 11.10. Your circuit should produce a logic 0 when the access is permitted. Be certain to document your assumptions about the encodings used for the *mode* and *op* inputs.

4. In discussing ring-based systems, we noted that the privilege level of the called routine is determined by the gate (or the routine itself). It might seem reasonable to simply increase the privilege level one ring from the current level. Why is this not usually done?

5. Most machines do not provide direct support for the upcall shown in Figure 11.20. Explain how you would implement an upcall. In other words, given the address of the user-defined exception handler, explain how you would implement the exception handler in the OS so that it transfers control to the user-defined exception handler. In designing this implementation, your goal is to make it appear as if the application program called the user-defined exception handler. You must make it possible for the user-defined exception handler to return to the application program.

6. The upcall mechanism (illustrated in Figure 11.20 and discussed in exercise 5) may seem overly complicated. It may seem that it would be better if the operating system simply let the application program change selected entries in the exception vector. Explain why this is not a good idea.

7. The microcode shown in Example 9.14 simply returns to the top of the ifetch loop when it detects an illegal opcode. In this exercise, we explore different ways to transfer control to the appropriate exception handler. In all cases, describe the changes that you need to make to the data paths shown in Figure 9.14 and provide microcode to implement the described mechanism. In all cases, ignore the need to save the PSW and change the privilege level; simply implement the described transfer of control.

   a. Suppose that the code for the exception handler starts at memory location 128.

   b. Suppose that memory location 128 holds the address of the exception handler.

c. Suppose that memory location 128 is the starting address of the exception handler, the illegal opcode exception is exception 8, and each entry in the exception vector holds the first four instructions of the exception handler.

d. Suppose that memory location 128 is the starting address of the exception handler, the illegal opcode exception is exception 8, and each entry in the exception vector holds the address of the exception handler.

8. Give C (Pascal, or Ada) declarations for the structures needed by a break-point debugger. Explain how you would search this data structure in the break-point exception handler (assume that you know the address of the instruction that generated the break point).

9. Given the pipeline stages presented in Table 9.5 give a detailed example showing

a. How one or more instructions might be fetched before an exception is detected.

b. How it is possible for two or more instructions to generate exceptions before the first is handled.

CHAPTER 12

DEVICE COMMUNICATION AND INTERRUPTS

In Chapter 11, we discussed the interface between application programs and the operating system. In particular, we discussed the mechanisms that are used to make the I/O devices accessible yet protected, using resident operating system routines. In this chapter, we explore the interface between the operating system routines and the I/O devices. We begin by considering simple, programmed I/O. After we present programmed I/O, we will introduce interrupts and interrupt handling. We conclude this chapter by considering DMA (direct-memory access) transfers and bus structures.

12.1 PROGRAMMED I/O

In this section, we present a simple I/O strategy, called programmed I/O because the I/O is directly controlled by a program. We begin by introducing a common I/O device—the UART (universal asynchronous receiver/transmitter). After considering the uses of UARTs and their basic structure, we will discuss code fragments that can be used to send and receive character values through a UART.

12.1.1 UARTs

A UART is an I/O device that encapsulates the transmit and receive functions used in asynchronous serial communication. Appendix B covers asynchronous serial communication in some detail. In this chapter, we simply note that UARTs are used to transmit characters between a computing system and its external devices using serial communication. UARTs are used to communicate with simple, character-oriented devices, for example, a keyboard, a printer, or a modem. As the name suggests, a UART is actually two devices, a receiver and a transmitter, in one package. Figure 12.1 illustrates the logical structure of a UART. As shown, a UART has four registers: a control register, a status register, a transmit register, and a receive register. The transmit and receive registers are the data registers for the transmitter and receiver. The *transmit (data) register* holds the next character

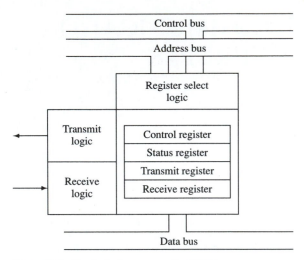

Figure 12.1   The logical structure of a UART

to be sent from the UART to the attached device. The *receive register* stores the most recently received character.

Because the transmitter and receiver are in the same package, they can share the same status and control registers. The *control register* controls the communication functions implemented by the UART. Bits in this register control the speed of the transmission, the parity checking, the number of data bits transmitted per value (5, 6, 7, or 8), and so forth. The control register is usually set once, when the UART is initialized, and not altered after communication has been established.

The *status register* maintains the status of the UART. One of the bits in the status register, the *receive register full* bit, indicates if there is a new character in the receive register. Another, the *transmit register empty* bit, indicates if the transmit register is empty. Other bits in the status register are used to indicate errors in the reception of a character. For example, Table 12.1 summarizes the function of the bits in the status register for the Intel 6851A PCI (programmable communications interface). Of these bits, we will only consider bits 0, 1, and 4 in the remainder of this chapter. The remaining bits are discussed in Appendix B.

Table 12.1   The status register of the Intel 6851A

Bit	Meaning when bit = 1
0	Transmit register empty
1	Receive register full
2	Transmission complete
3	Parity error
4	Overrun error
5	Framing error
6	SYNC character detected
7	DSR active

Before we discuss how the registers of a UART are accessed in an assembly language program, we need to consider how the UART uses these registers. When the UART is initialized, the transmit register empty bit in the status register is set to 1 and the remaining bits in the status register are cleared. When the transmit logic completes a transmission, it checks the transmit register. If there is a new value in the transmit register, the transmit logic copies the value and sets the *transmit buffer empty* bit in the status register. Otherwise, the transmit logic waits until a value is written to the transmit register. When a character value is written into the transmit register, the UART clears the transmit buffer empty bit in the status register.

When the receive logic receives a new value, it copies the value to the receive register and sets the receive register full bit in the status register. If any errors were detected during the reception of the value, the receive logic sets the appropriate error bits in the status register. Whenever the value is read from the receive register, the receive register full bit and the error bits in the status register are cleared. Table 12.2 summarizes the updates to the transmit register empty and receive register full bits in the status register.

Table 12.2 Updating bits in the status register

	Transmit register empty	Receive register full
Cleared by	Write to transmit register	Read from receive register
Set by	Transmit logic	Receive logic

In part, access to the registers of a UART depends on the machine that uses the UART. If the UART is mapped into the memory space of the machine, it will occupy two or more addresses in the memory. In this case, the registers can be accessed using LOAD and STORE operations. In a machine that provides separate I/O operations, like the Intel 8086, the UART will occupy two or more addresses in the I/O address space. In this case, registers can be accessed using the I/O instructions of the machine. Because the elements in the I/O address space are used to access the environment outside the computing system, they are frequently called *ports*. Using this terminology, the UART occupies two or more I/O ports in the machine.   Ports

You may be curious about the fact that a UART may occupy as few as two locations in the memory or I/O space of a machine. Because there are four registers, it may seem that the UART should occupy four locations—one for each register. However, you can only write values to the control and transmit registers, and you can only read values from the status and receive registers. As such, the control and status registers can share the same address, while the transmit and receive registers can share the same address. Registers that share the same address are distinguished by the operation performed (read/get or write/put). A possible mapping of the UART registers is shown in Table 12.3. In this case, the two addresses used for the UART are denoted by *addr0* and *addr1*.

Now we are ready to consider I/O using a UART. In *programmed I/O*, the   Programmed I/O
program repeatedly reads and examines the status register until the bits indicate

Table 12.3 Mapping the UART registers

	addr0	addr1
Write/put	Control register	Transmit register
Read/get	Status register	Receive register

that the UART is ready to perform the desired operation (send or receive). This is called programmed I/O because the program is in direct control of the transfer of data between the UART and the CPU registers.

Example 12.1   *Write a code fragment that will send the 8-bit value in register R3 to the device attached to a UART. In writing this code, assume the UART has been initialized (e.g., you do not need to set the control register) and that bit 0 in the status register is the receive register full bit. Moreover, you should assume that the UART registers are mapped into the memory and that the labels UART_STAT and UART_XMT have been defined as the addresses of the UART status and transmit registers respectively.*

```
        ; wait until the transmit register is empty
wait_send:
        LOAD.b   R2, UART_STAT    ; read the status register
        AND      R2, R2, #1       ; test bit 0 of the status register
        BREQ     wait_send        ; if zero, try again
        ; write the character in R3 to the transmit register
        STORE.b  UART_XMT, R3
```

Example 12.2   *Write a code fragment that will load R3 with the next character from a UART. In this case, assume that the label UART_RCV is defined as the address of the UART receive register and that bit 1 of the status register indicates that a new character has been received.*

```
        ; wait until the transmit register is empty
wait_rcv:
        LOAD.b   R2, UART_STAT    ; read the status register
        AND      R2, R2, #2       ; test bit 1 of the status register
        BREQ     wait_rcv         ; if zero, try again
        ; read the character in the receive register
        LOAD.b   UART_RCV, R0
```

12.1.2 Device Register Addresses

The fact that many device registers are 8 bits wide and the data bus on most machines is 16 or 32 bits wide has an impact on the addresses used for the device registers. Because the device registers are only 8 bits wide, many I/O devices are designed for use with an 8-bit data bus. These devices can be used in a system with a 16- or 32-bit data bus by attaching the device to the least significant 8 bits of the data bus. Because the I/O devices are attached to the least significant 8 bits of the address bus, they can only receive bytes sent to even addresses. As such, I/O devices typically occupy consecutive *word* addresses in the memory or I/O space of a machine. For example, the registers of a UART might be mapped to the addresses 20 and 24.

12.1.3 Volatile Values and Caching

The delay loops at the start of the code fragments in Examples 12.1 and 12.2 create a bit of a problem in light of the data caching techniques we discussed in Chapter 9. In particular, if the UART status register is cached, these loops will not work correctly. The first time the code reads the value of the UART status register, it will load this value into the data cache. Subsequent attempts to read the status register will determine that the value has been stored in the cache, and the processor will use the value in the cache. As such, the CPU will not reread the UART status register.

The code in these examples relies on the fact that the status register changes when the state of the UART changes. Values like the UART status register that change independently of the CPU are called volatile values. Caching systems must have a mechanism for dealing with volatile values. In the case of device registers, not caching the values is probably the most appropriate solution.

12.2 INTERRUPTS—PROGRAM STRUCTURES

Suppose you need to write an application program that performs a calculation and reads characters typed at a keyboard. Suppose further that the keyboard is connected to a UART. What happens if the user types several characters while your program is in the middle of its calculation? The UART can only store the most recently received character in the receive register. If a new character is received before your program reads the previous character, the new character will overwrite the previous character in the receive register. When characters are lost in this fashion, it is called an *overrun error*. In effect, the newer character overruns the character in the receive register. Most UARTs provide a bit, the *overrun* bit, in the status register that can be examined to determine if characters were lost due to overruns (in the Intel 6851A, bit 4 is used to indicate overruns).

Overrun error

Now, it seems that you are in a difficult position. If you simply write code to perform the calculation, you may lose characters typed by the user. To avoid this problem, you might consider writing your code so that it periodically checks the UART status register to see if the user typed another character. While it is possible to make this solution work, it is difficult to program and error prone. A great deal of the difficulty stems from the fact that you are trying to do two things at once: perform the calculation and read characters. In this section, we introduce interrupts and show how they can be used to read characters from the UART *while* your program performs a calculation.

12.2.1 Interrupt Handlers

An interrupt is a signal generated by an I/O device controller when the controller needs the attention of the CPU. For example, UARTs can usually be configured to generate an interrupt whenever the receive register is loaded with a new character. In this case, the UART needs to have the CPU read the character from the receive register. Because there are situations when the UART should not be able to generate an interrupt, we need a mechanism to enable and disable interrupts from the UART. Typically, this control is provided by bits in the control register—one bit for each interrupt the UART can generate. Figure 12.2 illustrates the generation of the UART receive interrupt. Note that the UART will only generate an interrupt signal when the appropriate bit in the control register is set and when the receive register full bit in the status register is set.

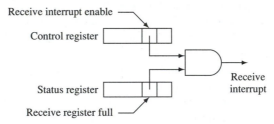

Figure 12.2   Interrupt generation on a UART

Interrupt handler

When the CPU detects an interrupt signal, it suspends the task it is currently executing and transfers control to routine called an *interrupt handler*. The interrupt handler is responsible for servicing the device that generated the interrupt. When the interrupt handler completes its activities, the CPU can resume the task that it suspended when it detected the interrupt. In this way, execution of the interrupt handler interrupts the execution of the current task. Figure 12.3 illustrates the control transfer involved in the execution of an interrupt handler.

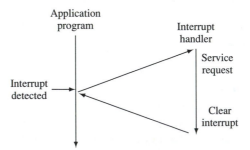

Figure 12.3   Execution of an interrupt handler

In considering interrupts, it is important to recognize that an interrupt signal could be detected at any point during the execution of an application program.

Interrupts are not synchronized with the execution of the application program. If the program is rerun at a later time, interrupt signals will occur at different points during the execution of the program. As such, it is important that the mechanism used to invoke the interrupt handler and the interrupt handler itself make it appear as if nothing happened when the interrupt was serviced. Imagine the problems that would arise if the interrupt handler changed a bit in the condition code register. During one run of the application program, the interrupt handler might execute between a comparison operation and a conditional branch operation causing the program to produce an incorrect result. This type of bug is very difficult to find because it is difficult to reproduce.

The CPU does not constantly check to see if an external device has generated an interrupt. Instead, the CPU examines the interrupt status line(s) after the execution of each instruction. If the interrupt status line(s) indicates that a device needs attention, the CPU transfers control to the interrupt handler using the XOP mechanism that we discussed in Chapter 11. As such, the program counter and processor status word (including the condition code register) are saved before control is transferred to the interrupt handler.

Because the time it takes to execute an instruction may vary from instruction to instruction, devices must maintain their interrupt signals until they are certain that the CPU has detected them. Most devices maintain their interrupt signals until they are explicitly cleared by an instruction executed by the CPU. In the case of a UART, the interrupt generated when the receive register is loaded is cleared by reading the value of the receive register. The fact that devices maintain their interrupt signals until they are explicitly cleared creates a bit of a problem. In general, you cannot structure interrupt handlers so that the first instruction of the interrupt handler clears the interrupt. As such, the processor may detect the interrupt after the first instruction of the interrupt handler and initiate another transfer to the interrupt handler. Two techniques are used to avoid this problem: interrupt masking and edge-triggered interrupts.

When *interrupt masking* is used, there is a bit in the processor status word, called the interrupt mask bit, which is used to indicate if interrupts are allowed. When the interrupt mask bit is 1, interrupts are enabled and the processor will transfer control to the interrupt handler whenever it detects an interrupt on the interrupt status line. When the interrupt mask bit is 0, interrupts are disabled and the processor ignores the interrupt status line(s). Privileged operations are used to set and clear the interrupt mask bit.

Interrupt masking

Coding Convention—SETIM
We use a single instruction, SETIM (set interrupt mask), with a single operand (#0 or #1) to set the interrupt mask bit.

In machines that use interrupt masking, the mask bit is typically cleared as the privilege bit is set when control is transferred to the interrupt handler. When the interrupt handler clears the interrupt, it can reenable interrupts using a SETIM instruction or implicitly by returning to the application program using an RTX instruction.

Edge-triggered interrupts

When *edge-triggered interrupts* are used, once the CPU has detected an interrupt, it will not recognize another interrupt until the interrupt signal is dropped and reasserted. They are called edge-triggered interrupts because the interrupt is only detected after the state of the line has changed, that is, on the edge of the interrupt signal. Many machines combine both approaches. For example, the Intel 8086 CPU recognizes two interrupt signals: a *maskable interrupt* signal and a *nonmaskable interrupt* signal. As its name implies, the maskable interrupt signal can be masked by a bit in the processor status word. In contrast nonmaskable interrupts cannot be masked. Because they cannot be masked, nonmaskable interrupts must be edge triggered.

Maskable interrupt

Nonmaskable interrupt

12.2.2 An Example—Buffered Input

With this background, we are ready to consider a fairly extensive example: buffered input. In buffered input, characters received from a UART are stored in an input buffer as they are received. Characters in the input buffer can be retrieved by an application program at a later time. Figure 12.4 presents a graphical illustration of buffered input. When the UART generates an interrupt, the interrupt handler reads the character from the UART and places it in the input buffer, *in_buf*. An application program can retrieve an input character by issuing the appropriate XOP. The XOP handler, called *get_ch,* removes a character from the input buffer and returns it to the application program.

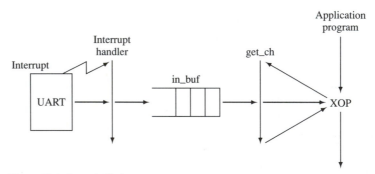

Figure 12.4   Input buffering

We consider the implementation of buffered input in three parts. First, we consider the directives needed to allocate space for the input buffer. Second, we consider the code that handles receive interrupts from the UART. Third, we consider the code that allows a user to receive the next character from the input buffer.

Example 12.3 *Give directives to allocate an input buffer.*

```
            .bss
ibuf_start: .reserve  256              ; space for the buffer
ibuf_end:

            .data
            .align    4
icount:     .word     0                ; number of values in buffer
ihead:      .word     #ibuf_start      ; head pointer
itail:      .word     #ibuf_start      ; tail pointer
```

Example 12.4 *Write an interrupt handler that reads a character from the UART and adds it to the buffer described in Example 12.3. If the buffer is full, your handler should simply return. Assume that interrupts are disabled while the interrupt handler executes.*

```
            .equate   UART_RCV, xxx    ; UART receive register
            .bss
regs1:      .reserve  3*4              ; space to save 3 registers
            .text
rcv_int:    ; save the registers used by the interrupt handler
            STORE.w   regs1, R1
            STORE.w   regs1+4, R2
            STORE.w   regs1+8, R3

            ; read the character in the UART receive register
            LOAD.b    R2, UART_RCV

            ; increment the count—there will be one more character
            LOAD.w    R3, icount
            CMP       R3, #256         ; is the buffer full?
            BREQ      done1            ; buffer full, give up
            ADD       R3, R3, #1       ; increment count
            STORE.w   icount, R3

            ; put the character in the buffer and update the head pointer
            LOAD.w    R3, ihead
            STORE.w   [R3]+, R2
            CMP       R3, #ibuf_end
            BRNE      no_wrap1
            MOVE      R3, #ibuf_start
no_wrap1:
            STORE.w   ihead, R3

done1:      ; restore the saved registers and return
            LOAD.w    R1, regs1
            LOAD.w    R2, regs1+4
            LOAD.w    R3, regs1+8
            RTX
```

The code in Example 12.4 begins by saving the registers used in the interrupt handler. Next, the interrupt handler reads the character from the UART receive register, thereby clearing the UART interrupt. After it reads the character, the interrupt handler checks to see if there is space in the input buffer. If there is space, the handler increments the count variable and saves the character in the input buffer while it increments the head pointer. If the head pointer points past the end of the buffer, the code sets the head pointer back to the start of the buffer. In this way, the interrupt handler implements a circular buffer.

If the input buffer is full, the interrupt handler returns and the character read from the UART will be lost. You might think that the interrupt handler should enter a loop, waiting until the application program removes a character from the buffer. However, this could never happen. Remember, the application program is suspended until the interrupt handler finishes processing the interrupt. Thus, interrupt handlers can never wait for an action that will be performed by the application program. In a real system, the interrupt handler might set a flag to indicate that it lost a character.

Example 12.5   *Write an XOP handler that will get a character from the input buffer. If the buffer is empty, the handler should wait until a value is placed in the buffer. Your handler should return the character in register R31. Assume that interrupts are enabled when your XOP handler is invoked.*

```
            .bss
regs2:      .reserve    3*4                 ; space to save 3 registers
            .text
get_ch:
            ; save the registers used by the XOP
            STORE.w   regs2, R1
            STORE.w   regs2+4, R2
            STORE.w   regs2+8, R3

            ; wait until the value of count is nonzero
wait:
            LOAD.w    R2, icount
            CMP       R2, #0
            BREQ      wait

            ; decrement the count—there will be one fewer character
            SETIM     #0                    ; disable interrupts
            LOAD.w    R2, icount
            ADD       R2, R2, #-1           ; decrement count
            STORE.w   icount, R2
            SETIM     #1                    ; reenable interrupts

            ; get the next character and update the tail pointer
            LOAD.w    R2, itail
            LOAD.b    R31, [R2]+
```

```
             CMP       R2, #ibuf_end
             BRNE      no_wrap2
             MOVE      R2, #ibuf_start
no_wrap2:
             STORE     itail, R2

             ; restore the saved registers and return
             LOAD      R1, regs2
             LOAD      R2, regs2+4
             LOAD.w    R3, regs2+8
             RTX
```

The XOP handler begins by waiting until there is a character in the buffer. The XOP handler executes on behalf of the application program, and it can wait until the interrupt handler puts another character in the buffer. When the UART receives a character, the execution of the application program (in this case the XOP handler) will be interrupted and the interrupt handler will put the character received by the UART into the buffer. When the application program is resumed, it will detect that there is a character in the buffer. Once the code has determined that there is a character in the input buffer, it decrements the count variable and retrieves the next character from the buffer.

Note that the decrement of the count variable in the *get_ch* routine is bracketed by an instruction that disables interrupts and another that reenables interrupts. The instructions ensure that the *count* variable has a valid value after it is incremented.

Example 12.6 *Show how the variable* count *could end up with an invalid value if the instructions that disable and reenable interrupts were omitted in Example 12.5.*

Suppose that *count* has the value 4 when the application program makes a call to the XOP handler. The following table summarizes the actions that would occur if the XOP handler were interrupted between the instruction that decrements the count variable and the instruction that stores the new value.

XOP handler		R2	count	R3	Interrupt handler	
		?	4	?		
LOAD.w	R2, count	4	4	?		
ADD	R2, R2, #-1	4	4	?		
		—interrupt—				
		?	4	?	STORE.w	reg_save1+4, R2
		?	4	4	LOAD.w	count, R3
		?	4	5	ADD	R3, R3, #1
		?	5	5	STORE.w	count, R3
		3	5	5	LOAD	R2, reg_save1+4
		3	5	?	RTX	
STORE.w	count, R2	3	3	?		

Note that *count* should end up with the value 4—one value was removed and another value was added. Instead, however, count has final value of 3.

12.2.3 Another Example—Buffered Output

So far, we have concentrated on interrupts associated with the availability of input. UARTs can also be configured to generate an interrupt whenever the transmit buffer is empty. This capability can be used to implement buffered output. Before we present an implementation of buffered output, we verify that buffered output is indeed useful.

Example 12.7   *Suppose that a UART is transmitting characters at 9,600 bits per second. How many instructions could the CPU execute while the UART is sending a character?*

First, we calculate the time it takes the UART to send a character. In this calculation, it is reasonable to assume that the UART must send 10 bits for each character (a start bit, 7 data bits, a parity bit, and a stop bit), so it will take the UART

$$\frac{1}{9,600}\frac{\text{sec}}{\text{bit}} \times 10\frac{\text{bit}}{\text{char}} = \frac{1}{960}\frac{\text{sec}}{\text{char}} \approx \frac{1}{1,000}\frac{\text{sec}}{\text{char}}$$

If the CPU can execute 1 million instructions per second, we get

$$1,000,000\frac{\text{inst}}{\text{sec}} \times \frac{1}{1,000}\frac{\text{sec}}{\text{char}} = 1,000\frac{\text{inst}}{\text{char}}$$

This calculation demonstrates that there is plenty of time for the CPU to perform another task while the UART transmits a character. As such, buffered output, which allows an application program to put a character in the output buffer and continue its execution, may improve the execution efficiency of the application program. Figure 12.5 presents a graphical illustration of buffered output. In this case, the

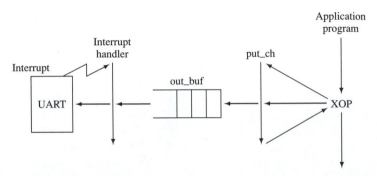

Figure 12.5   Output buffering

application program uses a *put_ch* routine to put a character in the buffer. If the buffer is not full, the application program will be able to continue its activities without waiting. When the UART completes the transmission of a character and empties the transmit buffer, it generates a *transmit interrupt*. The handler for the transmit interrupt removes the next character from the output buffer and sends it to the UART. If the output buffer is empty, the interrupt handler simply clears the interrupt.

Example 12.8   *Give directives to allocate an output buffer.*

```
            .bss
obuf_start: .reserve  256              ; space for the buffer
obuf_end:

            .data
            .align    4
ocount:     .word     0                ; number of values in buffer
ohead:      .word     #obuf_start      ; head pointer
otail:      .word     #obuf_start      ; tail pointer
busy:       .word     0                ; busy flag
```

In addition to the buffer, these directives allocate space for a *busy* flag. As we will discuss, this flag indicates when the UART is busy sending a character.

Example 12.9   *Write an interrupt handler for the transmit interrupt.*

```
          ; symbols that need to be defined
          .equate     UART_XMIT, xxx    ; address of UART transmit buffer
          .equate     UART_CREG, xxx    ; address of UART control register
          .equate     CLR_INT, xxx      ; clear transmit interrupt enable bit

          .bss
regs3:    .reserve    3*4               ; space for 3 registers

          .text
xmt_int:

          ; save the registers used by the interrupt handler
          STORE.w   regs3, R1
          STORE.w   regs3+4, R2
          STORE.w   regs3+8, R3

          ; check if there is another character to send
          LOAD.w    R2, ocount
          CMP       R2, #0
          BRNE      send_next
          MOVE      R2, #CLR_INT        ; no more characters to send
```

```
              STORE.w    UART_CREG, R2        ; clear the UART interrupt
              STORE.w    busy, R0             ; clear the busy flag
              BRANCH     done3

              ; send the next character
send_next:    ADD        R2, R2, #-1          ; decrement and save count
              STORE.w    ocount, R2

              LOAD.w     R2, otail
              LOAD.b     R3, [R2]+            ; get character from buffer
              STORE.w    UART_XMIT, R3        ; send the character
              CMP        R2, #obuf_end        ; check for wraparound
              BRNE       no_wrap3
              MOVE       R2, #obuf_start
no_wrap3:     STORE.w    otail, R2

    done3:

              ; restore the saved registers and return
              LOAD.w     R1, regs3
              LOAD.w     R2, regs3+4
              LOAD.w     R3, regs3+8
              RTX
```

When a transmit interrupt is detected, the interrupt handler first determines if the output buffer is empty. If the buffer is empty, the interrupt handler clears the interrupt at the UART, clears the busy flag, and returns. Otherwise, the interrupt handler moves the next character in the output buffer into the UART transmit register.

Example 12.10   *Write an XOP handler for the* put_ch *routine. Assume that the character to be added to the buffer is in register R2.*

```
              ; symbols that need to be defined
              .equate    UART_XMIT, xxx       ; address of UART transmit buffer
              .equate    UART_STAT, xxx       ; address of UART status register
              .equate    UART_CREG, xxx       ; address of UART control register
              .equate    ENBL_INT, xxx        ; set transmit interrupt enable bit

              .bss
    regs4:    .reserve   3*4                  ; space for 3 registers

              .text

    put_ch:

              ; save the registers used by the XOP handler
              STORE.w    regs4, R1
              STORE.w    regs4+4, R3
              STORE.w    regs4+8, R4
```

```
                ; wait for space in the output buffer
buf_full:   LOAD.w    R3, count
            CMP       R3, #256
            BREQ      buf_full

            SETIM     #0                     ; disable interrupts

                ; see if the UART is busy
            LOAD.w    R3, busy
            CMP       R3, #0
            BREQ      send

                ; increment the count—there will be one more character
            LOAD.w    R3, ocount
            ADD       R3, R3, #1             ; increment count
            STORE.w   ocount, R3

                ; add the character to the buffer
            LOAD.w    R3, ohead
            STORE.b   [R3]+, R2
            CMP       R3, #obuf_end
            BRNE      no_wrap4
            MOVE      R3, #obuf_start
no_wrap4:   STORE.w   ohead, R3
            BRANCH    done4

    send:
                ; send the character to the UART and enable interrupts
            STORE.w   UART_XMIT, R2
            MOVE      R3, #ENBL_INT
            STORE.w   UART_CREG, R3

                ; set the busy flag to indicate that the UART is busy
            MOVE      R3, #1
            STORE.w   busy, R3

done4:      SETIM     #1                     ; reenable interrupts
                ; restore the saved registers and return
            LOAD.w    R1, rsave4
            LOAD.w    R3, rsave4+4
            LOAD.w    R4, rsave4+8
            RTX
```

The *put_ch* routine starts by waiting until there is space in the output buffer. When there is space, the routine checks to see if the UART is busy. If the UART is busy, the *put_ch* routine adds the character to the output buffer. Otherwise, it sends the new character to the UART, enables UART interrupts, and sets the busy flag. The busy flag represents an important part of the communication between the interrupt handler and the *put_ch* routine. In considering the code for these routines, you should convince yourself of the following claim: The busy flag is 1 if and only if the UART will generate a transmit interrupt.

12.2.4 Combining Buffered Input and Buffered Output

So far, we have studied input and output buffering as independent problems. If we combine input and output buffering, we create a bit of a problem. Our code assumes that we know which interrupt (transmit or receive) the interrupt handler is processing. However, most UARTs only have a single interrupt line. This line combines the receive and transmit interrupts as shown in Figure 12.6. In this case, the interrupt handler must first determine which interrupt occurred and then proceed to handle that interrupt. The interrupt handler can determine which interrupt occurred by inspecting the appropriate bits in the status register.

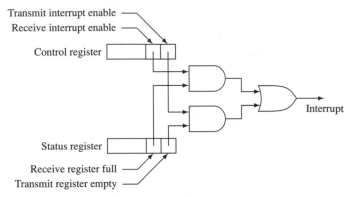

Figure 12.6   Combined interrupt generation on a UART

As we have noted, UARTs combine two separate devices, a receiver and a transmitter, in a single device. This combination is useful because many communication applications require both transmission and reception. As an example, most terminals are connected to computing systems using a bidirectional communication link. This link is usually implemented using a UART at each end and a pair of wires in between, as shown in Figure 12.7. (In addition to the two transmission wires, a third, common, wire is also needed but not shown in this illustration.)

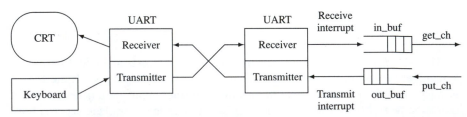

Figure 12.7   Connecting a terminal to a computing system

Because there is a direct relationship between the transmitter and the receiver in the UART, it is reasonable to consider relationships between the input buffer and the output buffer. In many systems, characters in the input buffer are copied to the output buffer. This copying of characters into the output buffer is called *echoing* because the characters you type are echoed to your CRT.

Echoing

Figure 12.8 contrasts two forms of echoing. Unix uses the version shown in Figure 12.8A. In this case, characters are copied to the output buffer as they are entered in the input buffer. This form of echo gives you immediate feedback when you type characters at the keyboard. This feedback is independent of the application program. DOS uses the version shown in Figure 12.8B. In this case, characters are not echoed until they are removed from the input buffer. This means that you do not see your keystrokes until the application program reads them from the buffer. The DOS approach makes it easy to write programs that do not echo their input—simply write another OS routine that gets a character from the input buffer without echoing the character. In contrast, the Unix approach requires that you change the behavior of the interrupt handler.

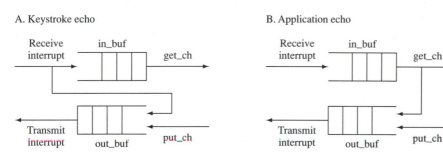

Figure 12.8 Echoing input

12.3 INTERRUPTS—HARDWARE STRUCTURES

In this section, we consider approaches for connecting the interrupt lines of several devices to the CPU. We classify these approaches by the way that interrupts are sent to the CPU. From the perspective of the CPU, the simplest approach is to provide a single interrupt line. This approach simplifies the logic of the CPU, but complicates the external logic and/or software needed to support I/O devices. In addition to the single-line approach, we consider two other approaches: interrupt encoding and interrupt mapping. Before discussing the approaches, we introduce the issues that we need to consider in contrasting the different approaches.

When more than one device can interrupt the CPU, there are four issues that must be addressed: selective masking, device identification, simple priorities, and dispatching. *Selective masking* is used to (temporarily) disable interrupts from selected devices while leaving interrupts from other devices enabled. *Device identification* selects a device that has an enabled and unserviced interrupt. When more than one device has an enabled and unserviced interrupt, a *simple priority* scheme determines which device is identified. Finally, *dispatching* involves the transfer of control to the section of code that handles interrupts from the identified device.

So far, we have assumed that interrupts are masked and unmasked using a single interrupt mask bit in the processor status word. When the mask bit is 0, interrupts from external devices are disabled; otherwise, interrupts from external devices are enabled. Thus, the mask enables or disables interrupts from *all* external devices. There are situations when you may need a finer degree of control over the masking of interrupts. As an example, suppose you have a device that generates an interrupt every 200 microseconds and another device that does not generate interrupts very often but has a very long interrupt handler. If the interrupt handler, for the second device takes 300 microseconds, a simple interrupt mask may not be sufficient. If you disable all interrupts during the long interrupt handler, you may lose an interrupt from the fast device (i.e., the fast device might generate two interrupts while the interrupt handler is executing). On the other hand, if you cannot clear the interrupt on the second device until the end of the interrupt handler, you will not be able to reenable interrupts during the execution of the long interrupt handler. In this situation, you need to be able to disable interrupts from the second device while interrupts from the first devices remain enabled.

Direct masking

Leveled masking

There are two two approaches for providing selective masking: direct masking and leveled masking. In *direct masking*, each device (or group of devices) is associated with a bit in an *interrupt mask register.* When its associated bit is 0, interrupts from the device (or group) are masked. In *leveled masking*, each device (or group of devices) is assigned an interrupt level. While the CPU is handling an interrupt, only devices with interrupt levels that are greater than the level of the device being serviced are enabled.

12.3.1 A Single Interrupt Signal

From the perspective of the CPU, the simplest strategy is to provide a single interrupt line. This strategy simplifies the logic of the CPU but requires additional logic between the I/O devices and the CPU. Figure 12.9 illustrates the relationship between the devices, the external logic, and the CPU.

We consider three approaches to the external logic: minimal logic, a daisy chain, and an interrupt controller. We conclude this discussion by considering how an interrupt acknowledge cycle can be used to improve the speed of device identification

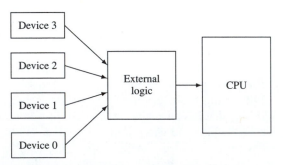

Figure 12.9   A single interrupt line to the CPU

and dispatching. In a minimal configuration, the external logic simply provides a logical *or* of the interrupt signals from the I/O devices. In this strategy, selective masking, device identification, simple priorities, and dispatching are implemented in software. A daisy chain establishes an order for the devices. This order provides selective masking and simple priorities; device identification and dispatching are still performed in software. An interrupt controller encapsulates most of the activities related to device interrupts (selective masking, device identification, and simple priorities) but still requires that dispatching be performed in software. Several processors use a single interrupt line with an interrupt acknowledge cycle to provide direct support for device identification and dispatching.

Minimal Logic—Software Polling   As a minimum, the external logic must provide a logical *or* of the interrupt signals from the I/O devices. Figure 12.10 illustrates a system with minimal external logic. This strategy is easy to implement, but it requires that selective interrupt masking, device identification, simple priorities, and dispatching be performed in software. Selective masking can be implemented by setting the mask bits in the control register for each masked device. As we noted earlier, device identification can be implemented by examining the bits in the status register for each device that could have generated an interrupt. This approach is commonly called *software polling* because the interrupt   Software polling
handler checks each device to see if it generated an interrupt. Once a device has been identified, dispatching can be implemented by branching to the appropriate routine.

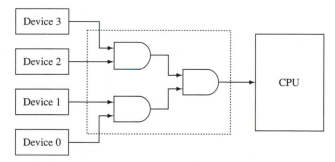

Figure 12.10   Minimal external logic

Software polling and dispatching can be implemented using three parallel arrays. One array maintains the address of the status register for each device. A second identifies the bit in the status register to test when polling the device. A third array maintains the address of the routine that handles the interrupt from the device identified by the first two arrays. When an interrupt is detected, the interrupt handler scans the status register bits identified by the first two arrays until it finds the device that generated the interrupt. When it finds the device, the interrupt handler transfers control to the routine identified by the third array. The

order in which the interrupt handler scans the arrays looking for the device that
generated the interrupt establishes a simple priority among the devices.

Daisy Chaining   Figure 12.11 illustrates the structure of a daisy chain. As shown,
the interrupt signal of each device is connected to a component called the *chain
logic*. Each unit of the chain logic communicates with its left and right neighbors.
The chain logic sends interrupt signals to the right and *interrupt-in-service signals*
to the left. The *chain control* logic interfaces the daisy chain with the CPU.

Interrupt-in-service
signals

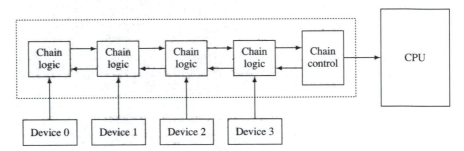

Figure 12.11   The structure of a daisy chain

The daisy chain provides simple priorities and selective masking based on
leveled masking. The simple priority and level of each device is determined by
its distance from the CPU. Devices that are closer to the CPU have higher simple
priorities and are associated with higher interrupt levels. The daisy chain does not
provide direct support for device identification or dispatching.

When a device generates an interrupt, the interrupt signal is propagated through
the chain logic components to the chain control logic and finally to the CPU.
When the CPU detects the interrupt, it transfers control to the interrupt handler.
The interrupt handler begins by notifying the chain control logic that it has started
to service the interrupt. The chain control logic sends an interrupt-in-service signal
to the chain logic. The chain logic components propagate this signal to the device
that generated the interrupt.

The chain logic components implement selective masking and simple priorities
by the way that they propagate interrupt and interrupt-in-service signals. The chain
logic is a sequential circuit that can be in one of three states: no interrupt, interrupt
pending, or interrupt-in-service. Initially, the chain logic is in the *no interrupt* state.
When it is in this state, the chain logic propagates interrupt and interrupt-in-service
signals. When the device generates an interrupt, the chain logic switches to the
interrupt pending state. While it is in the interrupt pending state, the chain logic
sends an interrupt signal to its neighbor and waits for an interrupt-in-service signal.
When it receives an interrupt-in-service signal, the chain logic enters the *interrupt-
in-service* state. In this state, the chain logic drops its interrupt request and masks
any interrupt signals it receives. When the interrupt has been processed and the
device drops its interrupt signal, the chain logic returns to the no interrupt state.

Interrupt Controller   Figure 12.12 illustrates the structure of a programmable interrupt controller. A programmable interrupt controller encapsulates the functionality of the daisy chain and simplifies the task of device identification. The interrupt line for each device is connected to a separate input line of the interrupt controller. There is a single interrupt line from the interrupt controller to the CPU. Internally, the interrupt controller maintains three registers: an interrupt mask register, an interrupt-in-service register, and a device id register. The CPU can read values from the device id register and write values to the interrupt mask register.

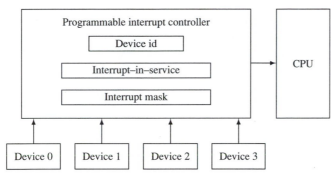

Figure 12.12   A programmable interrupt controller

The *device id* register simplifies the task of device identification. Because the interrupt controller records the identifier of the device that generated the interrupt, the interrupt handler does not need to poll the devices to determine which device generated the interrupt. Instead, the interrupt handler simply reads the device id register in the interrupt controller

Selective masking is provided by the *interrupt mask* and *interrupt-in-service* registers. These registers have a bit for each device. Using these registers, the interrupt controller combines both forms of selective masking: direct masking and leveled masking. Direct masking is implemented using the interrupt mask register. By changing the value of the interrupt mask register, the CPU can selectively mask interrupts from the devices attached to the interrupt controller.

The interrupt-in-service register implements leveled masking. The level of a device is determined by the line on the interrupt controller that the device is attached to. When the CPU reads the device id register, the interrupt controller sets the bit in the interrupt-in-service register that is associated with the device in the device id register. This bit is cleared when the device drops its interrupt signal. The interrupt controller only forwards interrupts from devices with interrupt levels that are greater than the level of the highest device whose interrupt-in-service bit is set.

Interrupt Acknowledge Cycle   As we have seen, the interrupt handler usually begins by identifying the device that generated the interrupt. After it identifies the device, the interrupt handler dispatches the interrupt by branching to the section of code that handles interrupts from the identified device. In an effort to simplify the device identification and dispatching tasks, several processors (including the Motorola 68000 and Intel 80x86) use an interrupt acknowledge cycle. The interrupt acknowledge cycle consists of three steps. The first step starts when the processor detects an interrupt. During this step, the processor generates an *interrupt acknowledge* signal. When the external logic receives this signal, it places the device identifier on the data bus and signals the processor. In the third step, the processor reads the device identifier from the data bus and dispatches the interrupt by using the device identifier as an index into a vector of interrupt handlers.

Figure 12.13 illustrates the steps performed during an interrupt acknowledge cycle. A processor with an interrupt acknowledge cycle can be used with a daisy chain or an interrupt controller.

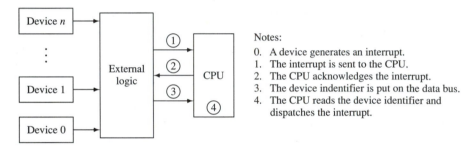

Notes:
0. A device generates an interrupt.
1. The interrupt is sent to the CPU.
2. The CPU acknowledges the interrupt.
3. The device indentifier is put on the data bus.
4. The CPU reads the device identifier and dispatches the interrupt.

Figure 12.13   Steps in an interrupt acknowledge cycle

12.3.2 Interrupt Encoding

Figure 12.14 illustrates interrupt encoding. In contrast to the previous approaches, in this strategy the CPU provides several interrupt lines. When a device generates an interrupt, the device identifier is encoded and sent to the CPU on the interrupt lines. The device identifier is used for selective masking, simple priorities, selective masking, and dispatching.

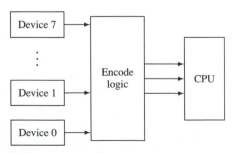

Figure 12.14   Interrupt encoding

Selective masking is based on leveled masking. The CPU maintains an interrupt mask register. (Usually this register is part of the processor status word.) When the CPU detects a nonzero value on its interrupt lines, it compares the value on the interrupt lines to the value in the interrupt mask register. If the value on the interrupt lines is greater than the value in the interrupt mask register, the interrupt is enabled. Simple priority is implemented by the interrupt encode logic. If two or more devices generate an interrupt, the encode logic selects the device with the highest identifier. Finally, the CPU dispatches the interrupt by using the value on the interrupt lines as an index into an array of interrupt handlers.

12.3.3 Interrupt Mapping

Several RISC machines (including the HP Precision, the IBM RS/6000, and the MIPS R4000) map interrupt signals into an *interrupt status register* (ISR). In these systems, an *interrupt mask register* (IMR) provides selective interrupt masking. Figure 12.15 illustrates this strategy. Each device is associated with a bit in the interrupt mask and status registers. When a device has an unserviced and unmasked interrupt, the bit in the ISR associated with the device is set. The CPU detects an interrupt when there is a bit set in the ISR.

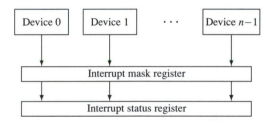

Figure 12.15   Interrupt mapping

When it detects an interrupt, the CPU transfers control to the interrupt handler. The interrupt handler can identify the device(s) that generated the interrupt by examining the bits in the interrupt status register. In this strategy, simple priority is determined by the way that the interrupt handler examines the bits in the interrupt status register.

In addition to the ISR and IMR, systems that use interrupt mapping usually provide an interrupt mask bit in the processor status word. This bit is used to mask all interrupts while an OS routine is executing. The interrupt mask bit is set to disable interrupts just before control is transferred to an OS routine.

12.4 DMA TRANSFERS AND BUS STRUCTURES

The techniques that we have discussed are appropriate for character-oriented devices. A *character-oriented device* transfers one character or word at a time. In

Character-oriented device

Block-oriented device

contrast, a *block-oriented device* transfers hundreds or thousands of bytes in a single transfer. While a UART is a good example of a character-oriented device, a disk is a good example of a block-oriented device. Whenever you access a disk, you must read or write an entire block of data. The size of the block is determined by the disk format.

While block-oriented devices logically transfer a block of data, the transfer is actually performed by transferring one word at a time between the disk and the disk controller. Given the structures that we have discussed, the CPU would need to transfer the words from the disk controller into memory.

Example 12.11   *Write an assembly language code fragment that will transfer a block of 512 words from the disk controller into memory, starting at the memory location labeled by the symbol* buf.

```
        ; symbols related to the disk controller
        .equate    DISK_STAT            ; status register
        .equate    RDY_MASK             ; mask to check status register
        .equate    DISK_RCV             ; disk receive data register

        .text
        ; initialize registers
        MOVE       R2, #buf             ; R2 points to the next memory location
        MOVE       R3, #512             ; R3 number of words to transfer

        ; wait until the disk has transferred the next word
wait:
        LOAD.w     R4, DISK_STAT        ; read the disk status register
        AND        R4, #RDY_MASK        ; check the ready bit
        BREQ       wait

        LOAD.w     R4, DISK_RCV         ; read the next word
        STORE.w    [R2]+, R4
        ADD        R3, #-1
        BRNE       wait
```

This approach represents a poor use of the CPU. To improve the utilization of the CPU, controllers for block-oriented devices are designed to access memory directly—without going through the CPU. This arrangement is called *direct-memory access (DMA)*. In direct-memory access, the controller transfers each data value directly into memory instead of storing it in a data register until the CPU transfers the value to memory. Figure 12.16 contrasts these two approaches: CPU-controlled I/O and direct I/O. In the first case, the CPU controls the transfer between the controller and the memory. In the second, the controller initiates and controls the transfer into memory.

Direct-memory access (DMA)

A device controller that uses DMA implements the block transfer routine presented in Example 12.11. When the CPU needs to have a block of data read

A. CPU-controlled input

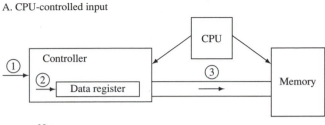

Notes:
1. A data value arrives at controller.
2. The data value is saved in the controller's data register.
3. The CPU transfers the value to memory.

B. Direct input

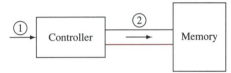

Notes:
1. A data value arrives at controller.
2. The controller transfers the data value to memory.

Figure 12.16   CPU-controlled input versus direct input

from (or written to) the device controlled by the DMA controller, it initiates the transfer by loading the control registers in the DMA controller. When the DMA controller completes the transfer, it generates an interrupt, indicating that the transfer is complete.

Figure 12.17 presents the logical structure of a DMA controller. Before the DMA controller starts to transmit data values, the CPU must initialize the *address* and *count* registers in the controller. Initialization of these registers is comparable to the initialization performed in the first two lines of code in Example 12.11. The body of the loop shown in Example 12.11 is implemented by the DMA controller. Whenever the controller receives a data value and the value in its count register is nonzero, it stores the data value in the memory location identified by the current value of its address register. As the value is being stored in memory, the controller can increment the value in its address register and decrement the value in its count register. If the value of the count register becomes zero, the DMA controller generates an interrupt for the CPU.

12.4.1 Arbitration

The existence of DMA controllers introduces an interesting shift in perspective. Up until this point, we have assumed that the CPU is the focal point of a computing system. In most contexts, this is a reasonable perspective. However, in considering

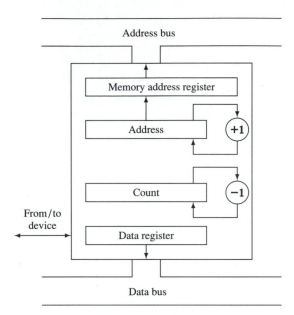

Figure 12.17   The logical structure of a DMA controller

DMA transfers, it is better to focus on the memory system. Figure 12.18 illustrates this perspective. In this case, the memory system provides a shared storage for two DMA controllers (DMA_1 and DMA_2) and a CPU. Note that the CPU is just like a DMA controller from the perspective of the memory system. Like a DMA controller, the CPU can only request that the memory system perform fetch and store operations.

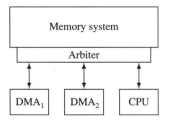

Figure 12.18   Focus on the memory system

Arbiter

   In examining Figure 12.18, note that the CPU and the DMA controllers are connected to an *arbiter*. The arbiter resolves conflicts involving memory accesses because the memory system can only service one request at a time. If two components (e.g., the CPU and a DMA controller) request a memory access at the same time, the arbiter will decide the order in which the requests are passed to the memory system.

Memory arbitration is not usually implemented by the memory system as shown in Figure 12.18. Most computing systems use a single memory bus, and, as such, the need for arbitration arises in the use of the buses. For the remainder of this discussion, we will use the term bus to refer to the three buses (address, data, and control). Once a component has acquired use of the bus, it can use the memory (or any other resource on the bus). Because the component has exclusive access to the bus, it also has exclusive access to the memory (and other resources). Figure 12.19 illustrates this perspective.

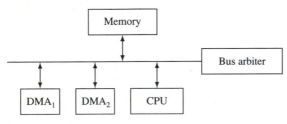

Figure 12.19 Bus arbitration

Any component that can acquire the bus is commonly called a *bus master*.   Bus master
Note that a bus master only controls the bus after it has acquired exclusive access. Acquisition of the bus is typically implemented by a handshake involving two signals: *bus request* and *bus grant*. A third signal, *bus grant acknowledge,* may be used in some systems. When a bus master needs to acquire the bus, it asserts its bus request signal to inform the bus arbiter that it needs the bus. After requesting the bus, the bus master waits until the request is acknowledged on its bus grant signal. If only two signals are used, the bus master continues to assert its bus request signal until it has completed its use of the bus. Otherwise, if the bus grant acknowledge signal is used in addition to the bus request and bus grant signals, the bus master drops its bus request signal and asserts its bus grant acknowledge signal when it receives a bus grant signal.

Figure 12.20 illustrates two strategies for connecting bus masters to the bus arbiter. In the first, the bus arbiter provides a separate pair of signals for each bus master. This strategy allows the arbiter to respond directly to the appropriate bus master. The second strategy uses a daisy chain to respond to the requesting bus master. A third alternative, distributed arbitration, is not shown in Figure 12.20. There is no centralized arbiter in this approach; instead, the arbitration logic is distributed among the bus masters.

12.4.2 DMA Transfers and Caching

When we discussed device registers at the beginning of this chapter, we noted that the volatile nature of device registers has an impact on memory caching. At the time, we suggested that the device registers should not be cached. DMA transfers that write data blocks into memory introduce a similar problem. In this

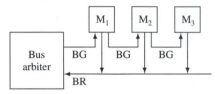

A. Parallel arbitration

B. Daisy chain arbitration

Notes:

M_i The ith bus master.
BR Bus request.
BG Bus grant.

Figure 12.20 Bus arbitration strategies

Snoopy cache

case, the data cache in the CPU may hold a value that is being updated by the DMA transfer. This difficulty is typically handled by using a *snoopy cache*, which monitors the address lines of the memory bus. Whenever a snoopy cache observes a store operation involving a memory location held in the cache, it invalidates the cache entry. The next time the processor attempts to read the cached value, it will determine that the cached value is invalid and initiate a memory load operation to fill the cache entry.

12.5 SUMMARY

In this chapter, we have covered the basic aspects of device communication. In an effort to keep the I/O systems as simple as possible, we have assumed an emphasis on computation with infrequent I/O. While this perspective is appropriate for personal computers and scientific workstations, many large computing systems are dominated by I/O with relatively little computation. Consider, for example, the kind of computing done by a bank. Banks do not perform long or complex computations, but they do use a large number and variety of I/O devices. Importantly, the computations performed by a bank are dominated by I/O considerations. You should expect that these systems will have more complex I/O systems than the simple systems that we have considered in this chapter.

In our presentation, we began by considering simple programmed I/O in which the program controls the entire I/O operation. Programmed I/O is characterized by loops that repeatedly read the device status registers until they indicate that the

I/O operation can be performed. These loops are frequently called *polling loops*   Polling loops
because the CPU is asking the device controller if the I/O can be completed.

After discussing programmed I/O, we introduced *interrupt-driven I/O*. In interrupt-driven I/O, the device controller generates a special interrupt signal when it needs to be serviced by the CPU. The CPU examines its interrupt status line(s) after it completes the execution of each instruction. If the CPU detects an interrupt, it transfers control to an interrupt handler, using a mechanism that is similar to the XOP mechanism introduced in Chapter 11.

To motivate interrupts and interrupt handlers, we discussed buffered I/O. Buffered input lets the operating system collect input values (keystrokes) while the application programming is performing a calculation. The application program does not need to periodically poll the I/O devices to determine if they need to be serviced. Buffered output can be used to compensate for temporary differences in output rates. In this case, the application program can continue with its computation while its output is being processed.

After introducing interrupts, we considered several hardware structures related to interrupt processing. In discussing these approaches, we considered four important issues: selective masking, simple priorities, device identification, and dispatching. The basic approaches that we considered were: use of a single interrupt line, interrupt encoding, and interrupt mapping. Using a single interrupt line simplifies the design of the CPU but complicates the external logic and software needed for the I/O devices. Interrupt encoding may reduce the complexity of the external hardware and software, but it decreases the flexibility of the interrupt system. Interrupt mapping seems to be the favored approach in the newer machines. This approach requires very little external hardware, and simple systems do not require very complex software for their interrupt handlers. However, very few decisions are built into the hardware, so this approach offers a great deal of flexibility.

We concluded our presentation of device communication with a brief consideration of direct-memory access (DMA). DMA is used with block-oriented devices like tape drives and disks. In contrast to character-oriented devices, controllers for these devices transfer blocks of data between the device and the memory. Because these devices must compete with the CPU for memory accesses, there needs to be some form of memory arbitration to decide which component is granted access to the memory. Usually this arbitration is done when a bus master acquires the memory bus.

12.5.1 Additional Reading

Most of the texts listed in the category of "Architecture and Organization" cover the basics of device communication and interrupt structures. If you are interested in the details of I/O devices and simple I/O systems, you should consult the data sheets for specific devices. In addition, *Microprocessor Systems: The 8086/8088 Family* by Liu and Gibson, and *Computer Design and Architecture* by Pollard cover a number of details related to I/O devices and systems.

The most important topic that we have introduced in this chapter is *concurrency*. Concurrency involves multiple activities in a single time frame. For example, we considered the possibility that an application program could be performing a computation while an I/O operation was in progress. Concurrency is covered in depth in the texts listed in the area of "Operating Systems."

12.5.2 Terminology

- UART
- Receive register full, Transmit register empty
- Programmed I/O
- Volatile values
- Overrun error
- Interrupt, Interrupt handler
- Interrupt masking, Edge-triggered interrupts
- Buffered input, Buffered output
- Character echo, Keystroke echo, Application echo
- Selective masking, Device identification, Simple priority, Dispatching
- Leveled masking, Direct masking
- Software polling
- Daisy chain, Interrupt-in-service
- Interrupt controller
- Interrupt acknowledge cycle
- Interrupt encoding
- Interrupt mapping
- Character-oriented device, Block-oriented device
- CPU-controlled I/O, DMA
- Cycle stealing
- Arbitration
- Parallel arbitration, Daisy chain arbitration

12.5.3 Review Questions

1. What functionality is encapsulated in a UART? Identify the four registers in a UART. Explain the purpose of each register.
2. Explain how the receive register full and transmit register empty bits in the status register of a UART are set and cleared.
3. Explain how programmed I/O works.
4. What is a volatile value? Give an example of a volatile value.
5. What is an overrun error? Explain how an overrun error might occur.

6. What are the basic activities performed by an interrupt handler?

7. How are interrupts detected? What is the purpose of interrupt masking? What is the difference between a level-triggered interrupt and an edge-triggered interrupt?

8. What is the advantage of buffered input? What kinds of errors are avoided by buffered input? What is the purpose of buffered output?

9. What does character echoing mean? Explain the difference between keystroke echo and application echo.

10. There are four activities related to interrupt handling: selective masking, device identification, simple priorities, and dispatching. Explain what each of these activities accomplishes.

11. Selective masking can be based on leveled masking or direct masking. Explain the difference between these forms of masking. Are they mutually exclusive or can the two forms of masking be combined?

12. Which activities are performed by software polling? What are the primary advantages and disadvantages of software polling?

13. Which activities are performed by a daisy chain? Explain how priority and masking levels are determined in a daisy chain.

14. Which activities are performed by an interrupt controller?

15. What is the purpose of an interrupt acknowledge cycle?

16. Which form of interrupt masking is usually associated with interrupt encoding?

17. Which form of interrupt masking is usually associated with interrupt mapping?

18. What is the difference between a character-oriented device and a block-oriented device? If block-oriented devices actually transfer a single word at a time, why do we not treat them like character-oriented devices?

19. What is DMA? What is the primary advantage of DMA?

20. Explain the term *cycle stealing*.

21. What is bus arbitration? Describe two forms of bus arbitration.

12.6 EXERCISES

1. In reading an assembly language program, a friend came across an instruction that enabled interrupts followed immediately by an instruction that disabled interrupts, that is,

   ```
   SETIM  #1     ; enable interrupts
   SETIM  #0     ; disable interrupts
   ```

   Your friend claims that this is silly, pointing out that the chance of an interrupt occurring between these two instructions is so small it is not worth the effort of checking. What is wrong with your friend's logic? Assume that interrupts are disabled when these instructions are executed.

2. Buffering is used to compensate for temporary differences rates. For example, an application program can rapidly fill an output buffer and then continue with its computation while the slower UART sends the characters to the device. However, if the application program continues to produce characters at a faster rate than the UART, the program will eventually be slowed to the rate of the UART and the buffer will not be useful.

   a. Suppose you have an application program that periodically generates 10,000 characters in a 0.1-second interval. If the UART is sending 960 characters per second, how long does the application need to compute (on average) between its output bursts? Be certain to show your work.

   b. Suppose you have an application program that generates 1,500 characters in a 0.01-second interval every minute. How fast does the UART need to be to keep up with this application?

   c. For parts *a* and *b* of this exercise, how big would you make the output buffer? Explain your answer.

   d. If you know that your application program is always going to have characters to transmit, is it possible that the programmed output routine shown in Example 12.1 would be significantly better than the buffered output routines presented in Examples 12.8 through 12.10? Justify your answer.

3. Consider the busy flag used in Examples 12.8 through 12.10. It might seem that you could use the *count* variable to accomplish the same task. What problems will you encounter if you try to eliminate the *busy* flag and only use the *ocount* variable?

4. Write the code needed to implement an interrupt handler that performs software polling. Assume that the three arrays have been allocated and initialized and are called *Dev_Addr*, *Dev_Bit,* and *Dev_Routine.* In addition, assume that the symbol *N_Dev* specifies the number of devices in these arrays. Implement a circular scan of the devices.

5. Consider the arrays used in software polling. Is is possible that a single device would need to be in these arrays more than once? In other words, would you ever need to duplicate an entry in the first array (the address array)? If so, describe the circumstances when this might be needed. Explain why you might want to duplicate a device entry even if it is not strictly necessary.

6. Design a circuit that could be used to encode interrupts from seven devices. In essence, this is simply an encoder like the ones discussed in Chapter 2; however, there is an important twist. You need to be certain that the CPU never sees an inconsistent value from the encoder. In particular, if only devices 1 and 2 have interrupts, it must never appear as if device 3 has an interrupt.

7. In Chapter 3, we used timing diagrams to illustrate the handshake between the CPU and the memory. Draw a timing diagram to illustrate the handshake between the CPU and the interrupt encode logic when an interrupt acknowledge cycle is used (as presented in Figure 12.13). In drawing this timing diagram, assume that the interrupt encode logic drops the interrupt signal to indicate that it has placed the device identifier on the data bus. Be certain to indicate when the device identifier is valid on the data bus.

8. What are the criteria that should be used in determining the priority level for a device? In other words, given several devices, what information would you need to establish the interrupt level for each device? In addition to identifying the criteria, be certain to explain how you will use them to determine the level of a device.

9. Consider the following interrupt encode circuit. What is the simple priority of each device? Explain why this circuit should not be used in a machine that implements selective masking based on the encoded interrupt number.

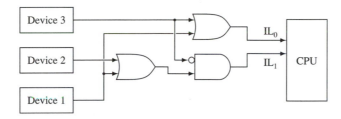

10. When an interrupt controller is used, interrupts can be masked at the interrupt controller and at the CPU.

    a. Explain why interrupt handlers should always run with interrupts enabled at the CPU when an interrupt controller is used.

    b. It may seem that interrupts should always be enabled when an interrupt controller is used, and, as such, the ability to mask interrupts is not needed. Describe a situation in which the ability to mask interrupts is needed.

11. Suppose you have a disk drive that is capable of transferring 400,000 words per second and a memory system with an external access time of 80 nanoseconds. What percentage of the available memory cycles will the disk controller use?

CURRENT TOPICS

PART SIX

CHAPTER 13
PARALLEL MACHINES

PARALLEL MACHINES

CHAPTER 13

We have previously discussed three different forms of parallelism. In Chapter 7, we discussed how a parallel implementation could reduce the time required for binary addition. In particular, we discussed *conditional sum* and *lookahead-carry* adders to illustrate parallel implementations of binary addition. In Chapter 8, we discussed the parallel execution provided by floating point coprocessors. Finally, in Chapter 9, we discussed the use of pipelining to improve the time required for instruction interpretation. In this chapter, we consider the principles of parallel machines in a general context.

In the not-so-distant past (about a decade ago), parallel machines were rare and access to most of these machines was strictly limited. In the recent past, parallel processing has become an integral part of computing, and there are strong indications that parallel processing will become much more important in the next decade.

We introduce the motivations and basic issues related to parallelism by considering a simple example. Suppose you live in city A and need to deliver a package to city B and another package to city C. Further suppose that the distance between A and B is 90 miles, the distance between A and C is 70 miles, and the distance between B and C is 130 miles. If you drive from city A to city B, then to city C, and return to city A, you will cover a total of 290 miles. This is called a *sequential* *implementation* because you perform the subtasks (visiting the different cities) in a sequence. If you average 25 miles per hour, the trip will take 11.6 hours. On the other hand, if you hire a friend to deliver the package to city C and return *while* you deliver the package to city B and return, your friend will complete a trip of 140 miles while you complete a trip of 180 miles. This is called a *parallel* *implementation* because you and your friend are visiting the cities *in the same time frame*. If you both average 25 miles per hour, your friend will return in 5.6 hours while your trip will take 7.2 hours. Thus, you will have finished the entire task in 7.2 hours, saving 4.4 hours. Figure 13.1 illustrates this situation.

This example illustrates an important motivation for parallelism: *speedup*. In our example, we indicated speedup by the amount of time you saved by using a parallel implementation—4.4 hours. The problem with using *time saved* as a

> Sequential implementation
>
> Parallel implementation
>
> Speedup

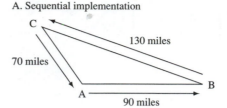

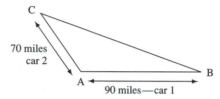

Figure 13.1 Illustrating parallel execution

measure of speedup is that it does not include any indication of the time taken for the sequential implementation. For example, if I save 1 minute on a task, it does not seem as significant as saving 4.4 hours. However, if a sequential implementation of the task took 2 minutes, then saving 1 minute is quite significant. For this reason, speedup is calculated as follows

$$\text{Speedup} = \frac{\text{Time for sequential implementation}}{\text{Time for parallel implementation}}$$

In our example, the speedup is $\frac{11.6}{7.2} = 1.611$; that is, using twice as many cars lets you complete the task 1.611 times as fast. Exercise 2 explores another important measure, *parallel efficiency.*

Economic considerations also play an important role in motivating the development of parallel machines. Returning to our example, suppose you buy a car that lets you make your deliveries at an average rate of 50 miles per hour. Using this car, you can complete your deliveries in 5.8 hours. Thus, having a car that is twice as fast is better than having two slow cars. As long as your cars are relatively slow, two cars may even cost more than one fast car. However, when you approach the fastest cars, you will reach a point when a single fast car costs more than two slow cars. For example, Formula One race cars cost on the order of $1 million and can be driven at speeds of 250 miles per hour. However, you could easily purchase a car that will go 150 miles per hour for less than $100,000.

This dramatic increase in cost is not unique to high-performance automobiles. Figure 13.2 illustrates the typical relation between cost and performance. Initially, the curve is linear; however, as you approach the (current) limits of the technology, the cost increase becomes dramatic.

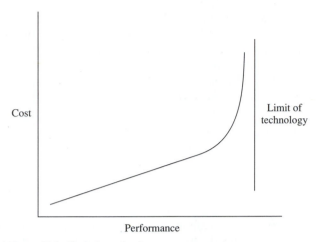

Figure 13.2   Typical cost/performance curve

Economic considerations have lead to the concept of *massively parallel* ma-   Massively parallel
chines. These machines have thousands of processors selected from the right end
of the linear portion of the cost/performance curve. Because they are constructed
from relatively inexpensive processors, massively parallel machines cost much less
than a single processor that offers 100 times the performance of the processors
used in the massively parallel machine (assuming that such a processor could
be built). Moreover, the massively parallel machine may be able to offer more
performance than the single processor.

   Our goal in this chapter is to consider the approaches to developing massively
parallel machines. As we discuss these approaches, you should remember that the
construction of massively parallel machines does not ensure their utility. In particular, it is not always obvious how thousands of processors can be used to solve a
given problem. In fact, some problems cannot benefit from additional processors.
Consider our problem of making deliveries to two different cities. In this case you
will not be able to make your deliveries any faster with more than two cars.[1]

   In the remainder of this chapter, we briefly survey the issues and models of
parallel execution. Because every model of parallel execution has an implicit
parallel machine, we use the terms *parallel model* and *parallel machine* inter-
changeably in this discussion. In section 13.1, we consider two computationally
oriented examples of parallel implementations: matrix multiplication and sorting.
As we introduce these examples, we introduce a simple model of parallel execution:
vector parallelism. In section 13.2, we consider Flynn's classification of parallel
machines, which is based on the number of instruction and data streams provided
by a parallel machine. To illustrate this characterization, we introduce two models of parallel programming: *pipeline machines* and *data parallel programming*.

---

[1] You may want to use two cars on each route (for a total of four cars) to prevent problems
associated with breakdowns, but having more than two cars will not improve your delivery times.

In section 13.3, we consider another characterization of parallel machines: synchronization. To illustrate this characterization, we introduce two more models of parallel programming: *systolic machines* and *data flow machines*. Section 13.4 considers the issue of granularity—the size of the unit for parallel execution. We illustrate granularity by introducing a model based on *cooperating processes*. In section 13.5, we consider memory structures for parallel machines. To illustrate this issue, we introduce a model based on *communicating processes*. Finally, section 13.6 considers the issues related to the design of processor interconnection networks to support the communication and synchronization needed by the processors in a parallel machine.

13.1 TWO EXAMPLES

We begin by introducing two computationally oriented examples: matrix multiplication and sorting. We use these examples in the remainder of this chapter to motivate and contrast the different approaches to parallel execution.

Example 13.1   *Consider the matrix multiplication:* $C = A \times B$ *where*

$$A = \begin{bmatrix} a_{00} & a_{01} \\ a_{10} & a_{11} \\ a_{20} & a_{21} \end{bmatrix} \quad and \quad B = \begin{bmatrix} b_{00} & b_{01} \\ b_{10} & b_{11} \end{bmatrix}$$

and, as such,

$$C = \begin{bmatrix} a_{00} \cdot b_{00} + a_{01} \cdot b_{10} & a_{00} \cdot b_{01} + a_{01} \cdot b_{11} \\ a_{10} \cdot b_{00} + a_{11} \cdot b_{10} & a_{10} \cdot b_{01} + a_{11} \cdot b_{11} \\ a_{20} \cdot b_{00} + a_{21} \cdot b_{10} & a_{20} \cdot b_{01} + a_{21} \cdot b_{11} \end{bmatrix}$$

Give a sequential code fragment to calculate the elements of C.

```
for( i = 0 ; i < 3 ; i++ ) {
    for( j = 0 ; j < 2 ; j++ ) {
        C[i][j] = 0;
        for( k = 0 ; k < 2 ; k++ ) {
            C[i][j] = C[i][j] + A[i][k]*B[k][j];
        }
    }
}
```

13.1.1 Model: Vector Parallelism

One way to provide parallel expression is to define high-level operations that have parallel implementations. This is the approach taken by *vector parallel machines*.

Many of the applications that could benefit from parallel processing use *vectors* (one-dimensional arrays) and *matrices* extensively. Several operations on vectors and matrices (e.g., multiplication by a scalar, dot product, and so forth) have obvious and simple parallel implementations. As such, it is reasonable to develop a vector processing unit that provides a collection of vector operations.

Example 13.2   *Describe how you would implement the matrix multiplication presented in Example 13.1 using vector operations.*

Each element of *C* is formed by taking the dot product of a row from *A* and a column from *B*. In the C programming language, a two-dimensional array is stored as an array of rows. As such, *A*[*i*] refers to the *i*th row of the matrix *A*. To get the columns of *B*, we construct the transpose of *B* (remember the rows of a transposed matrix are the columns from the original matrix).

```
/* BT (B Transpose) is an array of the columns of  B */
double BT[2][2];

/* initialize  BT.  This may be a parallel operation */
transpose( BT, B, 2, 2 );

for( i = 0 ; i < 3 ; i++ ) {
    for( j = 0 ; j < 2 ; j++ ) {
        /* dot product is a parallel operation */
        C[i][j] = dot_product( A[i], BT[j], 2 );
    }
}
```

Because the vector operations have parallel implementations, the vector unit provides the benefit of parallel execution without requiring that the programmer learn much about parallel execution. As the previous example illustrates, the programmer only needs to learn how to use the operations provided by the vector unit. While vector processing units are an important source of parallel execution, they do not provide a sufficient degree of parallelism for many applications. In the remainder of this chapter, we consider models that provide explicit expression of parallel execution.

Example 13.3   *Describe how you could use multiple processors to perform the matrix multiplication indicated in Example 13.1.*

We distinguish the approaches by the number of processors available:

- With 2 processors, you can have each processor compute a column of the *C* matrix.
- With 3 processors, you can have each processor compute a row of the *C* matrix.

- With 6 processors, you can have each processor compute an element of the C matrix.
- With 12 processors, you can adopt a two-step approach. In the first step, each processor computes one of the multiplications needed for an element of C. In the next step, only 6 of the processors are used; each of these processors computes an element of C by adding two of the results from the previous step.

Matrix multiplication is an example of a problem that is *embarassingly parallel;* there are many different ways to utilize additional processors to improve the performance of matrix multiplication. Many algorithms do not lend themselves to parallel implementations because of *data dependencies.* Two operations have a **Data dependency** *data dependency* if one operation uses the value produced by the other operation. Data dependencies limit parallelism because they force sequential ordering—the second operation cannot begin until the first operation produces the value that it needs. In the matrix multiplication example, we only observe a data dependency in the last approach when the additions cannot be started until the multiplications have completed.

Our second example, sorting, has many more data dependencies. In particular, an array is only sorted (in ascending order) when the first element in the array is less than the second, the second is less than the third, and so on. Given this requirement, it might seem that you need to determine the first element before you can determine the second. However, we simply need to ensure that this relation holds when the array is sorted. The actual data dependencies depend on the sorting algorithm that you use.

Example 13.4   *Describe how you could use multiple processors to sort an array of numbers.*

We can develop a parallel implementation of bubble sort or a parallel implementation of merge sort.

- To develop a parallel implementation of *bubble sort,* we use $n/2$ processors, where n is the number of elements to be sorted. Each processor is assigned to three elements of the array, as shown in the following illustration. Sorting requires $n + 1$ steps. On odd-numbered steps, each processor makes sure that the left pair of its elements is in order. On even steps, each processor makes sure its right pair of elements is in order.

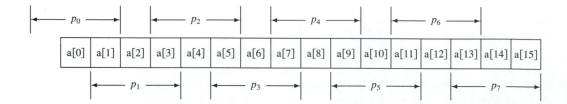

■ You can develop a parallel version of *merge sort* using two processors. Initially, each processor sorts half of the array. When the processors have finished sorting their halves of the array, one of the processors needs to merge the two sorted halves into a single array. If you have more than two processors, you can use the additional processors when you sort the halves of the array.

13.2 ISSUE: INSTRUCTION AND DATA STREAMS

In 1966, Michael Flynn described a simple classification scheme for parallel processors. While it is commonly recognized that Flynn's classification does not address several important issues in the design of modern parallel processors, it does provide a useful starting point for our study of parallel processors. Moreover, the terminology introduced by Flynn's taxonomy is still commonly used.

Flynn's classification is based on instruction and data streams. To execute a program, a processor needs a source of instructions and a source of data values. Flynn's classification is based on the number of instruction streams and the number of data streams used by a machine. Sequential and vector machines have a single instruction stream and a single data stream. Parallel machines may have multiple instruction streams, multiple data streams, or both. Figure 13.3 illustrates the categories of machines identified by Flynn's scheme.

A. Single instruction, single data

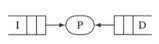

B. Multiple instruction, single data

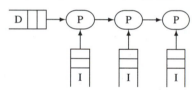

C. Single instruction, multiple data

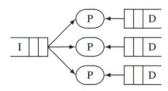

D. Multiple instruction, multiple data

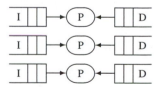

Figure 13.3 Flynn's classification

Flynn's scheme is the basis for a set of commonly used acronyms: SISD (single instruction, single data), MISD (multiple instruction, single data), SIMD (single instruction, multiple data), and MIMD (multiple instruction, multiple data). In verbal communication, these acronyms are usually pronounced and not spelled. Thus, we refer to a "SIM-Dee" machine instead of an "S-I-M-D" machine.

13.2.1 Model: Pipelines (MISD)

Pipelines and assembly lines are examples of MISD machines. In this case, each stage in the pipeline or assembly line is implemented by a processor. The data stream is passed from processor to processor, and each processor has a separate instruction stream. The instruction pipelines presented in Chapter 9 have fixed stages and, as such, do not require explicit instruction streams for each stage in the pipeline. Instead, the instruction streams are incorporated in the logic used to implement the pipeline stages.

In considering instruction execution pipelines, it is important to remember that the instructions executed by the pipeline are the data for the pipeline. In particular, while pipelining falls into the MISD category, instruction pipelines are used to implement SISD machines.

Pipelines can be used to implement parallel solutions to many problems—not just instruction interpretation. To describe a pipeline program, you must specify a program for each stage in the pipeline. Each of these programs must specify how the processor produces an output value whenever it gets an input value. In addition, you must describe the structure of the data stream.

Example 13.5 *Describe a pipeline algorithm to sort a stream of integers. When your program completes, the smallest value should be in the first processor, the second smallest value should be in the second processor, and so on. Assume that there are as many processors in the pipeline as there are numbers in the data stream.*

To solve this problem, we will have each processor in the pipeline execute the following program:

```
int smaller = INT_MAX, current, larger;

/* get the next input value */
input current;

/* keep the smaller value, send the larger value */
larger = max( smaller, current );
smaller = min( smaller, current );

/* send the larger value */
output larger;
```

In this case, we have chosen to have every processor execute the same program. Other pipeline programs could have different processors executing different programs. If there are *n* items in the data stream, this program requires at most $2n$ pipeline steps to sort the elements in the data stream.

13.2.2 Model: Data Parallel (SIMD) Programming

SIMD machines have given rise to a style of programming called *data parallel programming*. In most programming contexts, a program specifies how the program counter is updated during execution. Given this perspective, one way to provide parallel execution is to provide multiple program counters—as was the case for the pipeline model. This approach is called *control parallel programming*. In data parallel programming, the idea is to have the instructions of a single program applied to many different data values. In other words, parallelism in the data provides parallelism in the execution.

Control parallel programming

Figure 13.4 illustrates the basic structure of a SIMD machine. The *control processor* executes a data parallel program by broadcasting instructions to the

Control processor

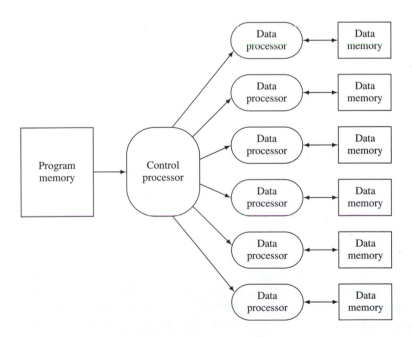

Figure 13.4 The structure of a SIMD machine

Data processors

data processors. After it broadcasts an instruction to the data processors, the control processor waits until all of the data processors have executed the instruction before it broadcasts the next instruction. SIMD machines have been built with thousands of processors. For example, when it was being built, the Thinking Machines CM2 could be configured with as many as 65,536 processors.

Example 13.6   *Describe how you would implement the matrix multiplication presented in Example 13.1 using a SIMD machine. Your solution should use a processor for each element of C.*

The following code fragment describes the sequence of instructions to be broadcast to the data processors. In this code, the variables *row* and *col* are local to each data processor and *PID* is the identifier of the data processor (a number between 0 and 5). In the first two statements, each data processor uses its processor identifier to determine its position in the matrix.

int row, col;

```
row = PID / 2;
col = PID % 2;
C[row,col] = A[row,0]*B[0,col] + A[row,1]*B[1,col];
```

Example 13.7   *Describe a data parallel implementation of bubble sort.*

As described in Example 13.4, our solution uses $n/2$ processors, where n is the number of elements in the array to be sorted. The following code fragment describes the program executed by the control processor:

int i, arr[n];

```
for( i = 0 ; i < n ; i++ ) {
    if( PID ≠ 0 && arr[PID*2-1] > arr[PID*2] ) {
        swap( arr[PID*2], arr[PID*2+1] );
    }
    if( arr[PID*2] > arr[PID*2+1] ) {
        swap( arr[PID*2], arr[PID*2+1] );
    }
}
```

Virtual processors

The second example introduces two interesting aspects of data parallel programming. First, if n (the number of elements in the array) is very large, it is likely to be larger than the number of data processors in a SIMD machine. To avoid this problem, programming environments for SIMD machines provide *virtual processors*. Each data processor of the SIMD machine simulates several virtual processors. When an instruction is broadcast to a data processor, it executes the instruction several times—once for each virtual processor.

The second aspect of data parallel program introduced in Example 13.7 is the way in which control structures are executed. The **for** loop is used to control the instructions that are broadcast to the processors, and, as such, the instructions needed to implement this loop are not broadcast to the data processors. On the other hand, the **if** statements in the body of the **for** loop depend on data that is local to the data processors (i.e., PID); as such, these statements control which processors receive the broadcast instructions. In principle, each data processor evaluates the condition of the **if** statement. If the condition for a data processor is *true,* the processor executes the instructions in the body of the **if** statement as they are broadcast from the control processor; otherwise, the data processor waits until the control processor finishes the body of the **if** statement.

13.3 ISSUE: SYNCHRONOUS VERSUS ASYNCHRONOUS

Synchronization refers to the need for one processor to wait until another processor has completed an activity. Parallel machines can be classified as either *synchronous* or *asynchronous.* Synchronous machines execute programs in discrete steps. At the start of a step, each processor is assigned a task. A step is complete when every processor has completed its task. No processor can start the next step until all processors have completed the current step. In this way, the completion of a step represents a *global synchronization* point. In this context, *global* means that the synchronization point applies to all processors.

This form of synchronization is frequently called *barrier synchronization* because the completion of a step represents a barrier. No processor may cross the barrier until every processor is ready to cross the barrier. Figure 13.5 presents a graphical illustration of barrier synchronization. The vertical lines represent barriers. In this example processor P_2 determines the length of the first step while processors P_0 and P_3 determine the length of the second step.

Global synchronization

Barrier synchronization

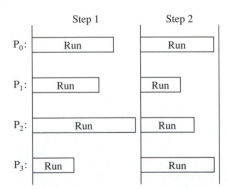

Figure 13.5 Illustrating barrier synchronization

In contrast to synchronous machines, asynchronous machines are not based on global synchronization points. Programs written for asynchronous machines may need to synchronize the activities of two or more processors; however, global synchronization of the processors is infrequent.

The pipeline and SIMD models are examples of synchronous models. In the remainder of this section, we introduce systolic arrays and data flow machines. Systolic arrays provide an example of synchronous MIMD machines, while data flow machines provide an example of asynchronous MIMD machines.

13.3.1 Model: Systolic Arrays (Synchronous MIMD)

Pipeline machines have a strong analogy to the cardiovascular system. At every pipeline step, every stage of the pipeline receives a shared timing signal called the *heartbeat*. In concept, the heartbeat pushes data values (blood) through the pipeline (an artery). This analogy to the cardiovascular system led to the name *systolic machine*.

Generalizing the pipeline structure to two dimensions yields a class of machines called *systolic arrays*. A pipeline is a linear sequence of pipeline stages. Each stage in the pipeline accepts an input value and produces an output value that serves as the input to the next stage. Each node in a systolic array accepts two input values (one from above and one from the left) and produces two output values (one down and one to the right). Figure 13.6 illustrates the structure of a pipeline and the structure of a systolic array.

Heartbeat

A. The organization of a pipeline

B. The organization of a systolic array

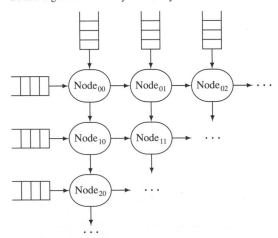

Figure 13.6   Pipeline and systolic array organizations

Like the stages in a pipeline, each node in a systolic array executes an independent program. To simplify the illustration, the multiple instruction streams are not shown in Figure 13.6. Unlike a pipeline, a systolic array has multiple data streams. As shown in Figure 13.6, a systolic array has a data stream for each row and each column in the array of processors. As such, systolic arrays are examples of synchronous MIMD machines.

Describing a systolic array program is similar to describing a pipeline program. You need to specify a program for each processor in the array, and you need to specify the structure of the data streams. When you specify the data streams, you need to be careful to ensure that the data values arrive at the processors at the right times. In considering the nodes shown in Figure 13.6, notice that $Node_{11}$ does not receive any input values in the first step of the execution. Processors only execute their programs on steps when they receive an input value. Nodes that are not on the main diagonal of the processor array always receive one input value before the other. For example, $Node_{01}$ gets an input from above on the first step, but it does not get an input from the right until the second step. These nodes must consume any input values they receive so that the sending processors can send values on the next step.

Example 13.8   *Describe how you would implement the matrix multiplication presented in Example 13.1 using a systolic array. Your solution should use a processor for each element of C.*

Our solution uses the following arrangement of processors and data streams:

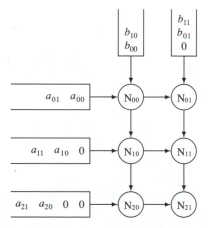

The following code fragment describes the program executed by each processor. In this code the variables *a, b,* and *c* are local to the processors in the array.

```
double a, b, c = 0.0;

/* get input values */
a = left;
b = top;

c = c + a*b;

/* copy inputs to outputs (for next processor) */
right = a;
bottom = b;
```

As with Example 13.5 (using a pipeline to sort a stream of numbers), we have chosen to have every processor execute the same program. This is not a requirement of systolic arrays. Different processors in the array can execute different programs.

In considering this solution, note the leading zeros in the data streams. These values are used to make sure that the processors receive the data values as pairs from the matrix. The following table traces the activities of processor N_{11}.

Step	Left	Top	C (at end of step)
start	—	—	0
1	—	—	0
2	0	0	0
3	a_{10}	b_{01}	$a_{10} \cdot b_{01}$
4	a_{11}	b_{11}	$a_{10} \cdot b_{01} + a_{11} \cdot b_{11}$
5	—	—	$a_{10} \cdot b_{01} + a_{11} \cdot b_{11}$

13.3.2 Model: Data Flow (Asynchronous MIMD)

To illustrate asynchronous MIMD machines, we introduce the *data flow model*. We begin by considering data flow programs—in particular, data flow graphs. While most programs specify how the program counter is updated, a data flow program specifies how its input values are transformed into output values, that is, how the data flows from the inputs to the outputs.

In this text, we use data flow graphs to specify data flow programs. A data flow graph is a directed graph. Nodes that do not have input edges or output edges denote program inputs and outputs, respectively. In many contexts, input nodes are called *source nodes* (because they are the source of data values) and output nodes are called *sink nodes* (everything goes down a sink). All other nodes represent operations. The arcs connecting nodes represent the paths taken by data values as the program executes.

Execution of a data flow graph is based on *tokens* and *operator firings*. Data values are represented by tokens as they move through a data flow graph. Most operators are *strict*, requiring tokens on all of their inputs to fire. When an operator fires, it consumes a token from each of its inputs and produces a token on one or more of its outputs.

Source nodes

Sink nodes

Tokens

Operator firings

Strict

Example 13.9 *Give a data flow graph for the matrix multiplication problem described in Example 13.1.*

The following graph illustrates the portion of the program that computes c_{00} and c_{01}. This data flow graph is based on the last parallel implementation described in Example 13.3

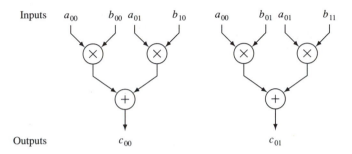

In addition to the standard operators (addition, subtraction, multiplication, and so forth), there are two important operators used in data flow graphs: the *merge* operator, and the *conditional* operator. Figure 13.7 illustrates the operation of these operators. Note that the merge operator is not strict. To be able to fire, this operator only requires a token on one of its inputs. Whenever a token arrives on either of the inputs to a merge node, the token is simply copied to the output of the merge operator. The conditional operator is similar to the conditional operator of C. This operator takes two inputs: a data input and a control input. If the control input is *T (true)* the data input is copied to the left output of the operator; otherwise, the data token is copied to the right output of the operator.

A. The merge operator

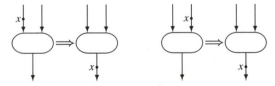

B. The conditional operator

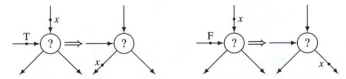

Figure 13.7 Merge and conditional operators for data flow graphs

Example 13.10   *Give a data flow graph to compute* res $= \sum_{i=1}^{n} i$.

The following data flow graph implements the following code fragment:

```
res = n;
while( n ≠ 0 ){
    res = res + n;
    n = n − 1;
}
```

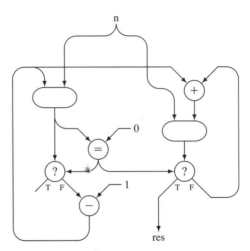

The important aspect of data flow graphs is that they expose a great deal of low-level parallelism. During the interpretation of a flow graph, several operator nodes may have their required input values. These operators can be fired (executed) in parallel.

13.4 ISSUE: GRANULARITY

The next issue we consider is granularity. *Granularity* refers to the size of the operation each processor performs before it needs to synchronize its activities with other processors. In concept, the program is partitioned into grains for parallel execution. Parallel machines are classified in three categories based on granularity: *fine grain, medium grain,* and *large* (or *coarse*) *grain.*

The SIMD and data flow models are based on fine-grain parallel execution. At each step, each SIMD processor executes a single (machine level) instruction. The unit of execution in the data flow model is also a single (machine level) operation. In contrast, systolic arrays are based on medium-grain parallel execution. At each step, each processor in a systolic array executes a relatively small program, typically on the order of a few statements, in a high-level language. Other parallel machines are based on large-grain parallel execution. On these machines, the processors execute relatively independent programs and do not synchronize their activities very frequently.

13.4.1 Model: Cooperating Processes

To illustrate the large-grain asynchronous MIMD model, we consider a model called *cooperating processes*. In this model, each processor is given a sequential program, called a *process,* to execute. There is no implicit synchronization between the processes and different processors may be given different programs to execute. For the moment, we assume that the processors share a global memory.

Because there is no implicit synchronization, any synchronization between the processes must be explicit in their code. We use *semaphores* to express synchro-   Semaphores nization. Semaphores are manipulated by two operations, *wait* and *signal* (also called P and V). When a process executes the wait operation, it is blocked, waiting for a signal from another process. Signals have memory, so if the signal has already been sent, the process that executed the wait is not blocked. Each signal operation unblocks a single process.

Example 13.11   *Describe how you could implement parallel merge sort for an array of* n *elements, using cooperating processes. Assume that* n *is a power of 2.*

In developing a parallel implementation of merge sort, we start from the bottom up. In particular, we start by creating $n/2$ processes. Each process sorts a pair of adjacent values in the array. When these processes finish this task, half of them terminate. The remaining processes merge the pair they sorted with the pair sorted by the (terminated) process to their right. These processes partition the array into subarrays containing four sorted elements. This process continues until only one process remains.

The following diagram presents a graphical illustration of this approach for an array with 16 elements. Initially p_0 sorts the first two elements of the array. When p_0 has sorted the first two elements and p_1 has sorted the next two elements, p_0 merges these segments to sort the first four elements of the array.

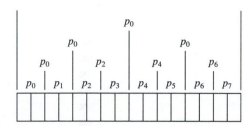

The following code fragment presents a parallel implementation of merge sort. The main function starts by creating $n/2$ merge processes with identifiers from 0 to $n/2 - 1$. Each merge process uses its identifier to determine which chunks of the array it should merge.

After merging its part of the array, the merge process uses its identifier to determine if it should continue. If it is not going to continue, it signals that it has completed its task and exits. If the merge process is going to continue, it waits for the process to its right to complete before merging the next two chunks of the array.

```
int arr[n];
semaphore sorted[n/2], finished;

void merge( int pid )
{
    int p1, p2, temp[n], done = FALSE, chunk = 1;

    while( !done && chunk ≠ n ) {
        /* every process gets two chunks to sort */
        p1 = (2*chunk) * pid;
        p2 = p1 + chunk;

        /* merge the two chunks starting at indices p1 and p2 */
        ...

        /* odd numbered processes terminate on each iteration */
        if( pid%2 == 1 ) {
            done = TRUE;
            signal( sorted[ pid ] );  /* let your neighbor know you have finished */
        } else {
            wait( sorted[pid+1] );  /* wait for your neighbor to finish */
            pid = pid/2;
            chunk = chunk*2;
        }
    }
    if( pid == 0 ) signal( finished );
}

void main( void )
{
    int i;

    for( i = 0 ; i < n/2 ; i++ ) {
        create process merge( i );
    }
    wait( finished );
}
```

13.5 ISSUE: MEMORY STRUCTURE

In the last example, we assumed that the processors shared a common memory. As such, each process could directly access elements of the array as needed. In considering the memory structure for a multiprocessor, there are three approaches: physically shared memory, logically shared, physically distributed memory, and distributed memory.

In a physically shared memory multiprocessor, all processors share a common memory. Processes running on different processors can communicate by reading and writing values in the shared memory. In a distributed memory multiprocessor, each processor has its own memory. Processors cannot directly access the memory of other processors. As such, processes running on other processors must exchange messages to communicate with one another. Multiprocessors with logically shared, physically distributed memories represent a compromise between the two approaches. In these machines, each processor has a local memory (in other words, the memory is physically distributed) that can be accessed directly by other processors (in other words, the memory is logically shared). Figure 13.8 illustrates these structures.

13.5.1 Physically Shared Memory

In contrasting these approaches, multiprocessors with *physically shared memory* provide a convenient programming environment but do not scale very well. To gain the benefit of multiprogramming, the programmer/compiler only needs to partition the control portion of the program into independent processes that manipulate the shared data structures. The data structures are stored in the shared memory where they can be accessed by any of the processors. However, this structure can only support systems with a few tens of processors. When too many processors are added to the system, the shared memory becomes a *bottleneck*— many of the processors will be idle, waiting to perform a transaction on the shared memory bus.

Bottleneck

To a small extent, a cache in each processor can overcome the shared memory bottleneck. The caches reduce the number of memory operations performed by each processor, thereby reducing the contention for the shared memory. While caching increases the number of processors that can be connected to a shared memory, memory contention still limits the number of processors that can be used with this structure.

The use of local caches introduces a *cache coherence* problem. Because any processor can update any memory location, it is possible that a processor will update a memory location that is currently cached by another processor. The problem is similar to the problem introduced by DMA controllers and can be resolved using a *snoopy cache*. There is an important difference between the DMA situation and the multiprocessor situation. When a processor performs a memory write, it may write the new value to the memory (and its cache) or it may simply update the entry in its cache, delaying the actual memory operation. A *store-through cache* updates the primary memory whenever a value is stored in the cache. In contrast, a *store-back cache* only writes a value in the primary memory when the cache location used to hold the value is needed for another value.

Cache coherence

Snoopy cache

Store-through cache

Store-back cache

A. Physically shared memory

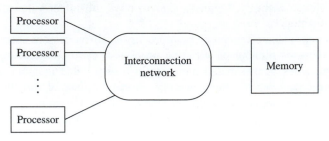

B. Physically distributed/logically shared memory

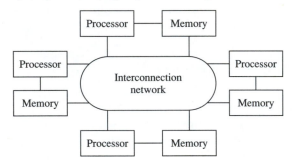

C. Distributed memory

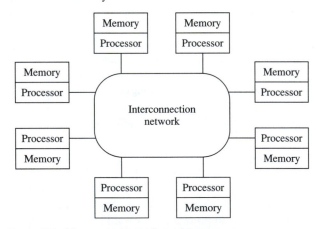

Figure 13.8   Memory structures for multiprocessors

13.5.2 Logically Shared Memory (NUMA)

To avoid the bottleneck associated with a physically shared memory, several machines have been designed with a *logically shared, physically distributed memory.* Instead of a physically shared memory, the memory is partitioned and distributed among the processors. The entire memory is still addressed with a single set of addresses. Thus, any program written for a shared memory multiprocessor could be run on this type of machine.

Example 13.12   *Consider a multiprocessor with 16 processors and a 16-bit address space (i.e., each address is 16 bits and there is a total of 64 Kbytes in the memory). Explain how you would distribute the memory to the 16 processors.*

The following table presents a reasonable distribution of the memory to processors:

Processor	Addresses	Processor	Addresses
0	0–4095	8	32768–36863
1	4096–8191	9	36864–40959
2	8192–12287	10	40960–45055
3	12288–16383	11	45056–49151
4	16384–20479	12	49152–53247
5	20480–24575	13	53248–57343
6	24576–28671	14	57344–61439
7	28672–32767	15	61440–65535

This distribution means that we can use the 4 most significant bits of an address to identify the processor and the remaining bits to identify location within the memory assigned to the processor.

The memory assigned to a processor is called *local* memory, the rest is *remote*. There is a significant difference between the time it takes to access local memory and the time it takes to access remote memory. For this reason, these machines are frequently called *nonuniform memory access (NUMA)* machines, while machines with a physically shared memory are called *uniform memory access (UMA)* machines.

Nonuniform memory access (NUMA)

Uniform memory access (UMA)

13.5.3 Distributed Memory (NORMA)

In a *distributed memory multiprocessor,* all access to the memory associated with a processor must go through the processor. Because these machines do not provide direct access to remote memory (memory associated with another processor), they are frequently called *no remote memory access (NORMA)* machines. To access the memory of another processor, the processor initiating the request must interact with the remote processor.

No remote memory access (NORMA)

13.5.4 Model: Communicating Processes

NORMA machines have lead to a programming model in which processes communicate by exchanging messages. We use the operations *send* and *receive* to exchange messages. The send operation identifies the value to be sent and the destination process. The receive operation identifies the location to use in storing the message and the source (or originating) process. The receive operation is blocking; that is, when a process attempts to receive a message from another process, its execution is blocked until a message is available from the sending process.

Example 13.13   *Describe how to sort an array of positive numbers using communicating processes.*

Again, we base our solution on merge sort. In this case, the main program constructs a tree of processes as shown in the following illustration. Each leaf process gets an element of the array that it sends to its parent. The internal processes produce a sorted output stream by merging the streams produced by their children. Note that each process sends a 0 to signal the completion of its stream.

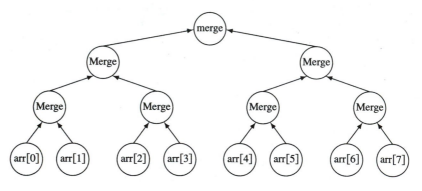

```
void merge( process creator, process l_child, process_rchild )
{
    int p1, p2;
    process parent;

    receive parent from creator;

    receive p1 from l_child;
    receive p2 from r_child;

    while( p1 > 0 && p2 > 0 ) {
        if( p1 < p2 ) {
            send p1 to parent;
            receive p1 from l_child;
        } else {
            send p2 to parent;
            receive p2 from r_child;
        }
    }
```

```
    while( p1 > 0 ) {
        send p1 to parent;
        receive p1 from l_ch; c1++;
    }
    while( p2 > 0 ) {
        send p2 to parent;
        receive p2 from r_ch; c2++;
    }
    send 0 to parent;
}

void leaf( int val, process creator )
{
    process parent;

    receive parent from creator;

    send val to parent;
    send 0 to parent;
}

void main( void )
{
    process lc, rc, par, root;
    process_queue Q;
    int arr[ n ];

    Q.make_empty();

    /* create the leaves */
    for( i = 0 ; i < n ; i++ ) {
        Q.add( create process leaf( arr[i], me ) );
    }

    chunk = 1;
    /* create the internal nodes */
    while( Q.size() > 1 ) {
        lc = Q.remove();
        rc = Q.remove();
        par = create process merge( me, lc, rc );

        /* let the children know who their parent is */
        send par to lc; send par to rc;

        Q.add( par );
    }
    root = Q.remove;
    send me to root;
```

```
for( i = 0 ; i < n ; i++ ) {
    receive arr[i] from root;
}
}
```

13.6 ISSUE: MULTIPROCESSOR INTERCONNECTIONS

In this section, we consider the design of interconnection networks for multiprocessor machines. In section 13.5, we indicated the need for an interconnection network either between the processors of a multiprocessor (NORMA) or between the processors and the memories of a multiprocessor (UMA and NUMA). In addition, a multiprocessor may use an interconnection network to issue control signals. For example, a SIMD machine needs an interconnection network to broadcast instructions and to note when all of the data processors have completed their tasks.

Processor interconnection networks are constructed from switches and links. Links carry the messages through the network, while the switches route messages to the different links in the network. Different networking strategies are distinguished by their topologies—the relation between switches and links. In the remainder of this section, we discuss four network topologies: the shared bus topology, the fully connected (or crossbar) topology, the hypercube topology, and the butterfly topology. As we introduce these types of networks, we consider the trade-off between contention and cost. Contention arises whenever two processors need to use the same link in the same time frame. As a general rule, you can reduce network contention by adding more links to the network. To add more links, you need to increase the number or complexity of the switches used in the network. These factors tend to increase the cost of the network.

13.6.1 The Shared Bus Topology

A shared bus consists of a single link and a simple switch for every processor and memory module connected to the network. This strategy easily supports processor-to-processor communication as well as processor-to-memory communications. Figure 13.9 shows how the shared bus strategy can be used to support processor-to-processor communications. Like the (physically) shared memory described in section 13.5, the shared bus represents a point of contention if there are more than a few tens of processors connected to the network.

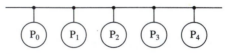

Figure 13.9   The shared bus topology

13.6.2 The Fully Connected Topology and Crossbar Switch

In a fully connected network, every processor has a direct link to every other processor. Figure 13.10 illustrates a fully connected network of five processors. When you use a fully connected network, the network does not introduce any contention because each processor has an independent path to every other processor. However, every processor must have a switch that can send messages to any other processor in the network. If you try to construct a network with a few thousand processors, these switches will be very expensive. Moreover, a fully connected network with n processors will have $n(n-1)/2$ links (see exercise 11).

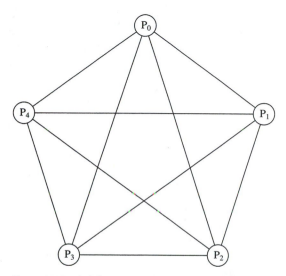

Figure 13.10 A fully connected topology with five processors

If you only need to connect processors to memory modules, a fully connected network will provide many unnecessary memory-to-memory and processor-to-processor connections. In this situation, you can use a crossbar switch. Figure 13.11 illustrates a crossbar switch. The horizontal and vertical links shown in this illustration are only connected by the switches. Each switch can create a connection between a vertical link and a horizontal link. Because each memory and each processor has an independent link, the crossbar switch does not introduce any contention that is not present in the application. However, if you have n processors and m memory modules, the crossbar switch will require $n \cdot m$ switches and $n+m$ links.

13.6.3 The Hypercube Topology

The shared bus and fully connected (or crossbar) topologies are at opposite ends of the spectrum of interconnection networks. A shared bus is inexpensive but it introduces a great deal of contention. A fully connected network (or crossbar

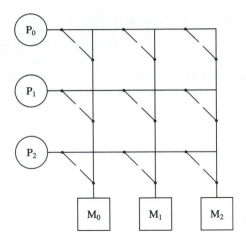

Figure 13.11   A 3 × 3 crossbar switch

switch) is prohibitively expensive but it does not introduce any contention. In the remainder of this section, we consider two related interconnection topologies: the hypercube and butterfly. These topologies fall between the shared bus and fully connected topologies. They introduce less contention than the shared bus but do not cost as much as a fully connected strategy. We begin by considering the hypercube topology.

A hypercube is a recursive topology. The simplest hypercube consists of a single node—this is a called a hypercube of degree 0. If you have two hypercubes of degree n, you can construct a hypercube of degree $n + 1$ by connecting the corresponding nodes in these two hypercubes. Figure 13.12 illustrates the construction of a degree-three hypercube.

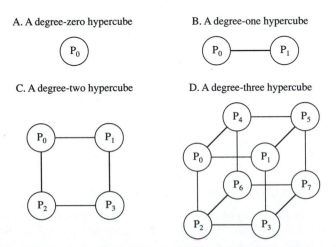

Figure 13.12   Constructing a degree-three hypercube

Hypercubes have many interesting properties, such as the following:

- Every processor in a hypercube of degree n ($n \neq 0$) is directly connected to $n - 1$ other processors.
- Every hypercube of degree n has 2^n nodes (see exercise 12).
- Every hypercube of degree n has $n(n - 1)/2$ links (see exercise 13).

To better see the contrast between a hypercube and a fully connected network, assume that you need to construct a network of 2^n nodes. If you use a fully connected topology, you will need $2^n(2^n - 1)/2$ links and each processor will need to be connected to $2^n - 1$ other processors. On the other hand, if you use a hypercube topology, you will only need $n(n - 1)/2$ links and each processor will only be connected to $n - 1$ other processors.

While hypercube networks are clearly less expensive than fully connected networks, hypercubes may introduce contention that was not present in the original application. The possibility of contention is illustrated by assigning nodes in the application graph to processors in the processor interconnection network. This assignment is called an *embedding* of the application graph in the processor interconnection network. When two arcs in the application graph share the same link in the processor interconnection network, the embedding may introduce contention.

Example 13.14 *The application graph in Example 13.13 is an example of a complete binary tree with 15 nodes. Show how to embed the complete binary tree with 7 nodes in a hypercube of degree three.*

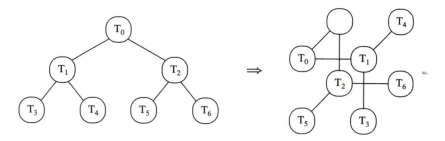

In this case, the topology does not introduce any contention; however, note that messages between the root (T_0) and its right child (T_2) must go through an intermediate node in the hypercube.

When one processor needs to send a message to another processor in a hypercube, it may need to *route* the message through other processors before it reaches its destination. A *routing algorithm* specifies how this path is constructed. The length of the route is the number of processors in the route, excluding the processor that originated the message. In a hypercube of degree n, there is always a route of length n or less between any two processors in the hypercube (see exercise 14).

13.6.4 The Butterfly Topology

While the switches used in the hypercube are much less complicated than the switches used for a fully connected network with the same number of processors, they may become prohibitively expensive if they are used in networks with millions of processors. To minimize the cost of the switches, we would like to use switches with a fixed number of inputs and outputs. Figure 13.13 illustrates a simple butterfly network. This network is constructed using switches with two inputs and two outputs. In this case, the network connects a set of processors with an equal number of memory modules. Unlike the other networks that we have considered, the switches in the butterfly network are not all associated with processors (or memory modules).

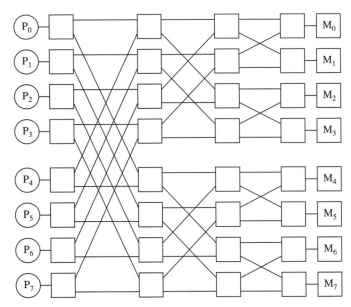

Figure 13.13   An 8×8 butterfly network

You cannot use the simple butterfly network shown in Figure 13.13 to construct a network consisting only of processors. However, a simple modification makes this network well suited to this requirement. The modification involves joining the endpoints of the butterfly (i.e., joining M_0 with P_0, M_1 with P_1, and so on). The network that results from this merging is called a *wrapped butterfly*.

Wrapped butterfly

Like the hypercube, the butterfly is actually a recursive structure. Figure 13.14 illustrates the recursive nature of the butterfly network by showing that the 8 × 8 butterfly is constructed from two 4 × 4 butterfly networks.

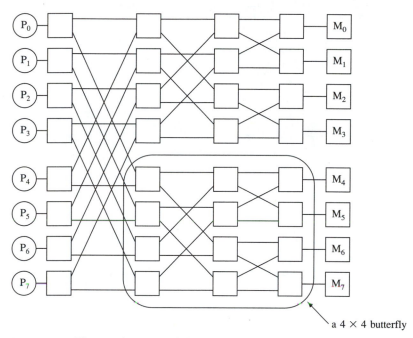

a 4 × 4 butterfly

Figure 13.14 The recursive nature of the butterfly network

Perhaps the most interesting aspect of the butterfly network is its relation to the hypercube. If you think of each level in the butterfly network as a node in a hypercube, you will notice that the levels provide the same connections that the hypercube provides. In this way, the butterfly network can be thought of as a distributed implementation of the switches needed for a hypercube. Figure 13.15 illustrates this aspect of the butterfly network.

13.7 SUMMARY

Parallel programming and the development of parallel machines are relatively new and rapidly growing areas in the field of computing. It seems that there are announcements of new machines every month or so. With this rate of change, any survey of actual machines is bound to be outdated before it is published. In fact, the only machine mentioned by name in the body of this chapter, the Thinking Machines CM2 (a SIMD machine), was replaced by the CM5 (a MIMD machine) before this chapter was written. Some machines, like the nCUBE-2, will be replaced by newer versions in the near future (in this case the nCUBE-3,

A. Turn every row into a single node

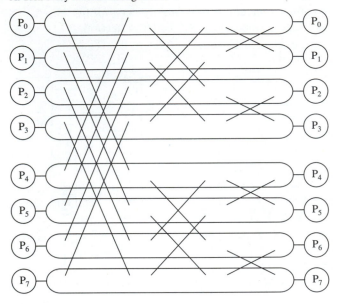

B. Remove redundant connections

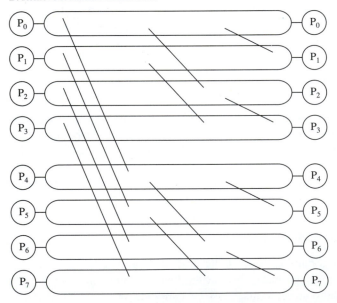

Figure 13.15 The relationship between the butterfly network and the hypercube

which should be out in late 1993). To avoid problems associated with describing out-of-date machines, we have emphasized the models underlying the machines. For the most part, the models are derived from actual machines (i.e., machines that were constructed and run). However, that is not particularly important. What is important is that the different models emphasize different aspects of parallel computations. In some applications, the potential for parallel execution may be more apparent in one model than another.

If there is a current trend in the development of parallel machines, it seems that many vendors are building machines that easily support the large-grain MIMD model. While the fine-grain approaches offer many conceptual advantages, machines based on fine-grained parallel execution spend a great deal of time controlling the execution of millions of very small operations. In contrast, machines based on the large-grain model have fewer operations to control and, as such, can dedicate their resources to performing the relatively large operations. The trend toward MIMD machines is based on convenience. Programmers may want to have different programs running on different processors. It is worth noting that many programs do not take advantage of the capability to have multiple programs (consider the examples presented in this chapter). In fact, a new acronym, SPMD (for single program multiple data), has been coined to characterize this style of programming.

13.7.1 Additional Reading

There are a number of excellent books that survey the development of parallel machines, models, and algorithms. Among these books, I highly recommend *Introduction to Parallel Algorithms and Architectures: Arrays, Trees, Hypercubes* by Thomas Leighton. While this text provides an exceptional coverage of parallel computing, it may be too theoretical for some readers. For these readers, I recommend *Parallel Processing: Principles and Practice* by Krishnamurthy and *High Performance Computer Architecture* by Harold Stone. In addition, most of the texts listed in the area of "Computer Architecture and Organization" will have a section or chapter that provides a survey of parallel processing.

13.7.2 Terminology

- Sequential implementation, Parallel implementation
- Speedup, Parallel efficiency
- Massively parallel
- Vector parallelism
- Data dependency
- SISD, MISD, SIMD, MIMD
- Pipeline machine, Systolic array, Heartbeat
- Data parallel programming, Control parallel programming
- Control processor, Data processor, Program memory, Data memory

- Virtual processor
- Synchronous machine, Asynchronous machine
- Global synchronization
- Data flow, Input node, Source node, Output node, Sink node
- Tokens, Operator firings
- Strict
- Fine grain, Medium grain, Large (coarse) grain
- Semaphore
- UMA, NUMA, NORMA
- Write-through cache, Write-back cache
- Shared bus, Fully connected, Crossbar
- Hypercube, Butterfly network, Wrapped butterfly
- Embedding

13.7.3 Review Questions

1. Explain the advantages and disadvantages of vector parallel machines.
2. What is a data dependency? Give a concrete example of a data dependency.
3. Give an example to illustrate the difference between data parallel programming and control parallel programming.
4. What are the major components of a SIMD machine?
5. In the context of SIMD machines, what is a virtual processor? Are virtual processors only applicable to SIMD machines? If not, list the other machines that could benefit from virtual processors.
6. What does global synchronization mean? What is the difference between a synchronous machine and an asynchronous machine?
7. What happens when an operator fires in a data flow graph? What is the difference between a strict and a nonstrict operator in a data flow graph?
8. What is a semaphore? What are the operations defined for semaphores?
9. Explain the difference between the UMA, NUMA, and NORMA memory structures.
10. What is the difference between a write-through cache and a write-back cache?
11. What is the primary disadvantage of the shared bus topology?
12. What is the primary advantage of a fully connected topology? What is the primary disadvantage?
13. Draw a hypercube of degree four.
14. What does it mean to embed an application graph in an interconnection network?

13.8 EXERCISES

1. Suppose that each basic operation (multiplication or addition) takes the same amount of time. Calculate the speedup provided by each of the approaches described in Example 13.3, and draw a graph that shows the relation between speedup and the number of processors.

2. In the text we discussed speedup as an important measure for evaluating a parallel implementation. Parallel efficiency, defined by the following formula, is another measure that is commonly used to evaluate parallel implementations.

$$\text{Efficiency} = \frac{\text{Speedup}}{\text{Number of processors}}$$

   a. Calculate the parallel efficiency for each implementation described in Example 13.3.
   b. Give a simple interpretation for parallel efficiency.

3. Consider the pipeline sorting algorithm presented in Example 13.5.
   a. Explain how this program could require $2n$ pipeline steps when the input has n values.
   b. Suppose that you need to sort $4n$ items but you only have n processors. Explain how you would adapt the pipeline sorting algorithm.

4. Describe how you would write a pipeline program to compute the first n primes. When your program completes, the first prime (2) should be in the first processor, the second prime (3) should be in the second processor, and so on. (Hint: Processors do not need to produce an output value on each pipeline step.)

5. Example 13.6 presents a data parallel implementation of a simple matrix multiplication. In this implementation each processor calculates an element of the result. Describe a SIMD implementation in which each processor computes
   a. A column of the result.
   b. A row of the result.

6. Write a data parallel program that determines which values in the range $2-n$ are prime.

7. In Example 13.8 we traced the activities performed by the processor N_{11}. Using a similar table, trace the activities performed by the processors:
   a. N_{21}.
   b. N_{20}.
   c. N_{00}.

8. A *wavefront* machine combines the data flow approach with a systolic array. A node in a wavefront processor only "fires" when it has both of its inputs.

    a. How would you change the solution presented in Example 13.8 for a wavefront machine?

    b. Trace the execution of the N_{11} and N_{20} nodes for your solution.

9. In example 13.12, we distributed contiguous blocks of memory to 16 processors. We could have interleaved the addresses across the processors. In this scheme, byte 0 would be assigned to processor 0, byte 1 to processor 1, and so on.

    a. Explain how you would determine which machine has the desired memory value given the address.

    b. What kinds of problems would this approach introduce?

10. Design a data flow graph that will sort eight input values. Your graph should be structured so that the smallest value is on the leftmost output.

11. Using induction on the number of processors, prove that a fully connected network of *n* processors has $n(n-1)/2$ links.

12. Using induction on the degree of the hypercube, prove that a hypercube of degree *n* has 2^n processors.

13. Using induction on the degree of the hypercube, prove that a hypercube of degree *n* has $n(n-1)/2$ links.

14. Using induction on the degree of the hypercube, prove that there is always a route whose length is at most *n* between any two processors in a hypercube of degree *n*.

15. Show how you can embed the fully connected graph with five nodes in a hypercube of degree three.

16. Consider the hypercube of degree three.

    a. Identify all routes between processor P_0 and processor P_7 with length three.

    b. Identify all routes between processor P_0 and processor P_6 with length two.

17. Describe a routing algorithm for the hypercube. In particular, when a message arrives at a processor in the hypercube, describe how to use the address of the message destination (and the address of the processor) to determine the next processor the message should be sent to. Your algorithm should ignore contention and simply find a route with the shortest length through the hypercube. (Hint: Consider what happens if you take the exclusive or between the processor identifier and the destination address.)

18. In the text, we described how to construct a hypercube. Describe how to construct a butterfly network.

19. Draw a wrapped butterfly with eight processor nodes.

20. Describe a routing algorithm for a butterfly network. In particular, given the destination address, describe how to set the switches in the network so

the message is sent to the correct destination. (Hint: Look at the binary representation of the destination.)

21. The following network is called a perfect shuffle network. Describe a routing algorithm for this network.

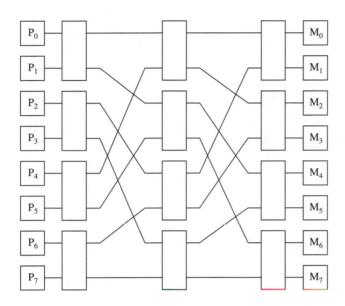

ASSEMBLY LANGUAGE CONVENTIONS

This appendix summarizes the assembly language conventions introduced and used in this text.

A.1 ASSEMBLER DIRECTIVES

Assembler directives are instructions to the assembler that control the translation of an assembly language program. When they appear in an assembly language program, assembler directives start with a period ("."). Assembler directives can be used to establish the default assembler segment (bss, data, and text); to reserve initialized space (byte, word, and halfword); to reserve uninitialized space (reserve); to define a symbolic constant (equate); and to define and use global symbols (export and import). The following table summarizes the assembler directives used in this text:

Directive	Page	Definition
.bss	170	Make the bss segment the default segment.
.data	170	Make the data segment the default segment.
.text	170	Make the text (code) segment the default segment.
.byte	166	Initialize one or more bytes of memory.
.halfword	166	Initialize one or more halfwords of memory.
.word	166	Initialize one or more words of memory.
.align	167	Align the location counter on a word address.
.reserve	165	Reserve a block of uninitialized memory.
.equate	163	Define a named constant.
.export	364	Make a symbol available to other modules.
.import	364	Use a symbol defined in another module.

A.2 LOAD/STORE OPERATIONS

The LOAD and STORE operations are used to transfer values between the registers and memory of a machine. In addition to the basic LOAD and STORE operations, the text introduces three related operations: an operation to load the effective address (LEA), an operation to clear the contents of a register (CLEAR), and an operation to load a register with a value (MOVE). The following table summarizes these operations:

Operation	Page	Definition
LOAD	127	Load a register from a memory location.
STORE	127	Store a register into a memory location.
LEA	191	Load a register with the effective address.
CLEAR	130	Clear a register to zero.
MOVE	130	Copy the source value to the target register.

In addition to the operation name, the LOAD and STORE operations have size specifiers (see page 131). The following table summarizes the size specifiers used in the text:

Specifier	Meaning
.b	Byte (8 bits).
.h	Halfword (16 bits).
.w	Word (32 bits).

The memory address in a LOAD or STORE operation can be specified using the following addressing modes. These modes are described in Chapter 5.

Mode	Notation	Effective address	Value
Immediate	#n	None—not an address	n
Direct register	Rn	Rn	**reg**[n]
Direct memory	addr	addr	**M**[addr]
Register indirect	@Rn	**reg**[n]	**M**[**reg**[n]]
Memory indirect	@addr	**M**[addr]	**M**[**M**[addr]]
Register indexed	addr[Rn]	addr + **reg**[n]	**M**[addr + **reg**[n]]
Memory indexed	$addr_1[addr_2]$	$addr_1 + \mathbf{M}[addr_2]$	$\mathbf{M}[addr_1 + \mathbf{M}[addr_2]]$
Register displaced	$Rn \to disp$	disp + **reg**[n]	**M**[disp + **reg**[n]]
Memory displaced	addr→disp	disp + **M**[addr]	**M**[disp + **M**[addr]]
Pre-increment	+[Rn]	**reg**[n] = **reg**[n] + 1 **M**[**reg**[n]]	**reg**[n]
Post-increment	[Rn]+	**M**[**reg**[n]] **reg**[n] = **reg**[n] + 1	**reg**[n]
Pre-decrement	−[Rn]	**reg**[n] = **reg**[n] − 1 **M**[**reg**[n]]	**reg**[n]
Post-decrement	[Rn]−	**M**[**reg**[n]] **reg**[n] = **reg**[n] − 1	**reg**[n]

A.3 ARITHMETIC OPERATIONS

The following table summarizes the basic arithmetic operations introduced in the text. The binary operations (ADD, SUB, and MPY) have three register operands: the destination register followed by two source registers. The instruction *op Ra, Rb, Rc* performs the assignment *Ra = Rb op Rc*.

Operation	Page	Definition
ADD	127	Integer addition.
ADDC	251	Integer addition with carry.
SUB	127	Integer subtraction.
SUBB	253	Integer subtraction with borrow.
MPY	127	Integer multiplication.
MULS	256	Integer multiplication step.
NEG	130	Integer negation.

A.4 BRANCHING OPERATIONS

Operation	Page	Definition
BB	147	Branch if bit set.
BRANCH	133	Unconditional control transfer.
BREQ	138	Branch equal to.
BRGE	138	Branch greater than or equal to.
BRGT	138	Branch greater than.
BRLE	138	Branch less than or equal to.
BRLT	138	Branch less than.
BRNE	138	Branch not equal.
BROC	250	Branch on carry.
BRNC	250	Branch no carry.
CMP	139	Comparison (sets condition code register).
NOP	129	No operation.

A.5 BIT MANIPULATION OPERATIONS

Operation	Page	Definition
AND	145	Bitwise *and* operation.
ANDN	145	Bitwise *and not* operation.
OR	145	Bitwise *or* operation.
ORN	145	Bitwise *or not* operation.
XOR	145	Bitwise *xor* operation.
BCLR	147	Bit clear.
BSET	147	Bit set.
ROTL	148	Rotate left.
SLO	148	Left shift, one fill.
SLZ	148	Left shift, zero fill.

A.6 SUBROUTINE OPERATIONS

Operation	Page	Definition
BL	213	Branch and link (save return address).
JSR	226	Jump to subroutine.
RTS	226	Return from subroutine.
ALLOC	226	Allocate space on the parameter stack.
FREE	226	Free space on the parameter stack.
POP	226	Pop a value from the parameter stack.
PUSH	226	Push a value on the parameter stack.
PUSHEA	226	Push the effective address on the parameter stack.

A.7 REGISTER USAGE

Register	Use
R0	The constant value 0.
R1	Assembler temporary.

ASYNCHRONOUS
SERIAL COMMUNICATION

In Chapter 12, we discussed the basic function of a UART. In this appendix, we consider the details of the function implemented by a UART: asynchronous serial communication. In addition to asynchronous serial communication, we consider modems and the RS-232 standard.

B.1 CHANNELS

A channel provides the medium for transmitting signals (information) between two parties. The channel includes the physical medium used to transmit the signals (perhaps a wire) and the hardware needed to put the signals on the medium.

In considering communication channels, there are three types of channels: simplex, half-duplex, and full-duplex. In a *simplex channel*, one party acts as the transmitter and the other acts as the receiver. In other words, a simplex channel provides a one-way communication link between the two parties. In a *half-duplex channel*, the two parties can change their roles; however, at any instant in time, one party is acting as the transmitter and the other is acting as the receiver. In other words, a half-duplex channel provides a two-way (bi-directional) link between the two parties; however, the two parties must execute a *turnaround protocol* to change the direction of the link. In a *full-duplex channel*, both parties can act as transmitters and receivers simultaneously. A full-duplex channel can be constructed from two simplex channels.

Simplex channel

Half-duplex channel

Turnaround protocol

Full-duplex channel

Example B.1 *Most modern workstations include a pointing device, such as a mouse or trackball. What type of channel would you use to connect a pointing device to a workstation?*

In this case, the pointing device always sends signals to the workstation, so a simplex channel should be sufficient. If you have an intelligent pointing device (i.e., a pointing device that can be configured for different modes of operation), you may need a half- or full-duplex channel so that the workstation can send configuration commands to the pointing device.

Example B.2   *Give an example of a half-duplex channel.*

Walkie-talkies and intercom systems are examples of half-duplex channels. When you press the talk button on a walkie-talkie or an intercom, you become the transmitter and you cannot receive signals from the other party. In this case, the turnaround protocol is usually initiated by a verbal cue (e.g., "over") from the current transmitter.

Example B.3   *Simple computer terminals have a keyboard and a display (more sophisticated terminals may include pointing devices and printers). Explain how you would connect a terminal to a computer.*

Because we need bi-directional communication (from the keyboard to the computer and from the computer to the display), we could use a half- or full-duplex channel. The following diagram illustrates a common strategy for connecting a terminal to a computer using a full-duplex channel. Note that characters typed on the keyboard are sent to the computer and processed before they are sent back to your display where you see them.

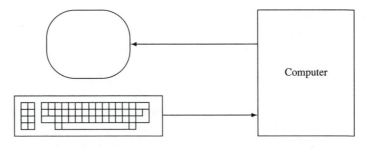

B.2 SERIAL COMMUNICATION

In most cases, the channel between a terminal and a computer is implemented using asynchronous serial communication. We begin by considering serial communication. In serial communication, the bits used to represent a value are transmitted one bit at a time. When an ASCII character is transmitted, the least significant bit is transmitted first.

Example B.4   *Using a graphical representation, show how the ASCII representation of "Q" would be transmitted using serial communication.*

Recall, the ASCII representation of "Q" is 1010001. This leads to the following illustration.

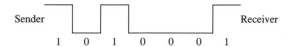

It may seem obvious that the illustration shown in Example B.4 represents the transmission of the bit pattern 1010001. However, it is not as obvious as you might expect. For example, how do you know that it does not represent the transmission of the 8-bit pattern 10100001 (i.e., the character "!" with an extra "garbage" bit)? Moreover, how do you know that it does not represent the 14 bits 11001100000011?

We rule out these possibilities by two "obvious" assumptions. First, we assume that each bit has the same width (or duration). This assumption rules out the possibility that Example B.4 represents the bit pattern 10100001_2, because the relatively long string of 0's is three times the width of the shorter marks. Second, because you know that the character "Q" is being transmitted, you can easily deduce the width of a bit. This rules out the possibility that this illustration represents the transmission of 14 bits.

Although not absolutely necessary, these two assumptions are embedded in almost every serial communication scheme. All bits have the same duration, and the duration of a bit is known to both the sender and the receiver. The duration of a bit is called the *bit time*. In most cases, the bit time is given as a rate, the *bit rate*, that indicates the number of bits transmitted per second. Bit rates of 2,400, 4,800, 9,600 and, 19,200 are common in modern computing systems.

Bit time

Bit rate

B.3 START AND STOP BITS

Because the communication line is a two-state device, it must be in the state corresponding to 0 or 1 when there are no characters to transmit. It is common to hold the communication line in the state corresponding to 1 when it is idle.

Example B.5   *Using a graphical representation, show how you would transmit "Q" followed by "U".*

Recall, the ASCII representation of "Q" is 1010001 and the ASCII representation of "U" is 1010101. This leads to the following illustration.

While transmission of the bits is relatively straightforward, receiving the correct bits is not quite as simple. In particular, if the receiver starts recognizing bits too early or too late, it may recognize the wrong value.

Example B.6   *Consider the transmission pattern shown in Example B.5. Show what happens if the receiver starts too early in its recognition of the second value.*

If the receiver starts one bit too soon, it will recognize the character "+" (the ASCII representation of "+" is 0101011) instead of the "U" that the transmitter intended.

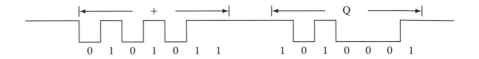

Example B.7   *Consider the transmission pattern shown in Example B.5. Show what happens if the receiver starts too late in its recognition of the second value.*

If the receiver starts one bit too late, it will recognize the character "j" (the ASCII representation of "j" is 1101010) instead of the "U" that the transmitter intended.

To ensure that the receiver starts recognizing bits at the correct time, a start bit is sent before any of the bits in the character representation. The start bit has a value of 0 (to distinguish it from the idle state) and is the same duration as any other bit. In effect, the start bit synchronizes the sender and receiver for the transmission of a single character.

Example B.8   *Show how you would transmit "Q" followed by "U" including start bits.*

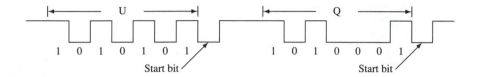

B.3.1 Sampling Points

In asynchronous communication, the sender and receiver do not share a common clock. Each component has its own clock. The sender uses its clock to determine how long to hold the communication line low when sending a 0 (or high when sending a 1). The receiver uses its clock to determine when to sample the communication line for the next bit. Between character transmissions, the receiver is constantly observing the state of the communication line. When the receiver detects a *1/0 transition*, it waits for half a bit time and resamples the communication line. 1/0 transition If the line is still 0, the receiver assumes that it has seen the start of the next character (instead of noise on the line) and begins sampling the communication line every bit time to determine the next bit. When the receiver has sampled enough bits for a character, it returns its initial state and waits for the next start bit.

Example B.9   *Consider the transmission illustrated in Example B.8. Show the sampling points for the receiver.*

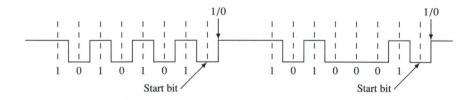

Figure B.1 presents pseudocode for an asynchronous receiver. This code uses the function Sample and the procedure Wait. The *Sample* function samples the Sample communication line and returns the value 0 or 1. The *Wait* procedure causes the receiver to wait for the specified number of clock ticks. The code for the Wait

```
/* BIT_TIME is the number of clock ticks per bit this value is determined by
   the clock frequency and the bit rate */
#define BIT_TIME ...

/* The Sample function samples the communication line and returns 1 if the
   line is high; otherwise, 0 */
int Sample( void );

/* The Wait function causes the calling function to delay for the given number
   of clock ticks */
void Wait( int ticks );

/* the character buffer is available to other parts of the system */
unsigned char Char_buf;

void async_receiver( void )
{
  int i, valid_start;

  while( TRUE ) {
    /* wait for a start bit */
    valid_start = FALSE;
    while( !valid_start ) {
      /* wait until the line enters the idle state between characters */
      while( Sample( ) == 0 ) /* nothing */;

      /* wait for a 1/0 transition, indicating the start of a start bit */
      while( Sample( ) == 1 ) /* nothing */;

      /* confirm that this is a start bit */
      Wait( BIT_TIME / 2 );
      valid_start = (Sample( ) == 0);
    }

    /* read the bits in the character */
    Char_buf = 0;
    for( i = 0 ; i < 7 ; i++ ) {
      Wait( BitTime );
      Char_buf = (Char_buf>>1) | Sample( )<<6;
    }
  }
}
```

Figure B.1   The receiver program

asynchronous receiver is an infinite loop. On each iteration, the receiver waits until it detects a valid start-bit. After detecting a valid start bit, the receiver reads seven bits into the *Char_buf* variable.

B.3.2 Stop Bits

It is important to note that the receiver returns to its initial state (waiting for a start bit) after it has recognized a complete character. In particular, the receiver waits until the line returns to the idle state (1) before it starts to look for a stop bit. This creates a problem if characters are sent "back to back" (with no delay). In particular, if the first character transmission ends with a 0, the receiver will not detect a 1/0 transition for the start of the start bit and, as such, will not receive the correct character.

Example B.10   *Show what happens if the sender sends a "1" followed immediately by another "1."*

The following illustration shows the pattern that the sender sends.

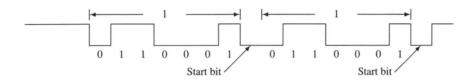

However, the receiver will recognize a different pair of characters: a "1" followed by an "l" (lowercase ell).

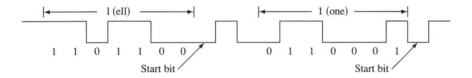

To avoid this problem, a stop bit is sent after each character. The stop bit has the value 1 and is at least as long as one bit time. Unlike the start bit, the stop bit can be longer than a single bit time. If the duration of the stop bit is longer than a single bit time, it is common to think of the stop bit as multiple bits—1, 1.5, and 2 stop bits are commonly used. The presence of the stop bit(s) ensures that the receiver detects a 1/0 transition when the start bit is sent (and thus recognizes the correct starting point of the next character).

Example B.11   *Show how you would transmit a "1" followed immediately by another "1" including stop bits.*

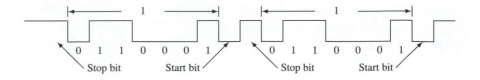

B.3.3 Clock Drift

At this point, you may wonder why stop bits are needed. It might seem that the receiver could sample the communication line at the end of each character and determine its behavior based on the value sampled. If the receiver sees a 0 immediately after the last bit of a character, it would assume that the 0 represents the start bit of the next character and continue sampling the communication line at one bit time intervals. On the other hand, if the receiver sees a 1, it would assume that the sender is not transmitting another character and wait for the next 1 to 0 transition. In a perfect world, this scheme would work—that is, stop bits are not a logical necessity of asynchronous serial communication. However, our world is not perfect.

If you have two clocks in your house, you know that they need to be reset every so often so they both show the same time. One of your clocks is undoubtedly a bit faster than the other. This phenomenon is called clock drift and can be expected with any two clocks. In particular, the sender's clock and the receiver's clock will not run at exactly the same rates. This generally is not a problem for the transmission of a single character because the rates of the two clocks are pretty close (assuming that they agree on the bit rate). However, during the transmission of a long sequence of back-to-back characters, clock drift will eventually lead to incorrect character recognition. In effect, the stop and start bits are used to resynchronize the sender and receiver on a character-by-character basis during the transmission of long sequences of characters.

B.4 ERROR DETECTION

As noted eariler, we do not live in a perfect world. As such, errors are bound to happen. In particular, no one can guarantee perfect reliability in serial communication. In section B.3 we discussed how the receiver protocol (resynchronization after a stop/start bit transition) can mask minor differences in the two clocks that might otherwise lead to a communication failure. Note: This scheme does not preclude the possibility of communication failures that result from clock drift but greatly reduces the possibility of these failures.

In this section, we consider the two error detection schemes that are frequently used in asynchronous serial communication: parity and framing. As we discuss these mechanisms, remember that they are only intended to detect errors. As such, they do not specify the actions (if any) needed to correct the situation once an error has been detected.

B.4.1 Parity

We introduced parity bits in section 1.4. Most serial communication schemes include a parity bit to detect a single bit flip during the transmission of a character. A parity bit is a single bit sent immediately after the 7-bit character code. Because the bit patterns for characters are sent from least significant to most significant, it is common to think of the parity bit as the most significant bit in an 8-bit character value. When even parity is used, the parity bit is set to 1 or 0 to ensure that an even number of 1's are sent in the transmission of the character (including the parity bit). When odd parity is used, the parity bit is set to 1 or 0 to ensure that an odd number of 1's are sent in the transmission of the character (including the parity bit).

The parity bit can be used to detect single bit changes in the transmission of a character. If a single bit is changed between the sender and the receiver, the parity will change and the receiver can announce a parity error. The actions that the computer or terminal takes when it detects a parity error depend on a number of factors. In the case of the computer, a primary consideration is the program that the user is running. In the case of the terminal, it is common to display a special character that indicates that a parity error was detected.

You can disable parity checking on most terminals and computers by setting the parity switch to "none." The exact meaning of none seems to vary among manufacturers. In some cases, it means that no parity bit is sent or expected by the receiver (i.e., only the 7 bits plus start and stop bits are sent). We call this *no parity*. In other cases, a parity bit is expected; however, the last bit is ignored, and no parity errors are detected. We call this *ignore parity*.

People who make computers, terminals, and terminal emulation software frequently adopt a very liberal interpretation for the meaning of the parity bit. While these "abuses" of terminology are potentially confusing, they are convenient in many instances. Mark parity (the parity bit is always set to 1) and space parity (the parity bit is always set to 0) are not really parity settings, but they are often selectable on a parity switch. In point of fact, these "parity" settings are actually extensions of the intercharacter resynchronization presented in the previous section.

Table B.1 summarizes the parity settings we have discussed. Note that only the first two of these settings (even and odd parity) support the detection of transmission errors.

B.4.2 Framing

Although it is not absolutely necessary, most receivers check the stop bits (1, 1.5, or 2) that are supposed to be sent. If the receiver detects a 0 when it is expecting a stop bit, it can announce a framing error. In this sense, the character value is

Table B.1   Parity settings

Name	Meaning
Even parity	The parity bit is set to 1 or 0 to ensure that the total number of 1's in the character and the parity bit is even.
Odd parity	The parity bit is set to 1 or 0 to ensure that the total number of 1's in the character and the parity bit is odd.
No parity	The parity bit is not sent (or received), only 7 bits are transmitted—sometimes called none.
Ignore parity	A parity bit is sent (and received), but its value is ignored—sometimes called none.
Mark parity	The parity bit is always set to 1.
Space parity	The parity bit is always set to 0.

framed by the start bit, parity bit (if any), and the stop bit. Framing errors are extremely rare. When they occur, framing errors can usually be traced to a failure to make sure that the sender and receiver are set to the same bit rate. Framing errors can also occur if the sender and receiver are not set to generate (expect) the same number of stop bits.

Break key

An interesting use of framing errors is illustrated by the use of the break key on most terminals. Unlike the other keys on a terminal keyboard, the *break key* does not generate an ASCII character. Instead, this key causes the communication line to enter a "break condition" in which the communication line is held low (0) for a longer time than it takes to send a character. This causes the receiver to detect a framing error. In many systems, the announcement of a framing error causes the system to abort the execution of the program that is currently being executed for the terminal that generated the framing error.

B.5 UARTS

A UART (universal asynchronous receiver/transmitter) is an electronic device that encapsulates the transmit and receive functions used in asynchronous serial communication. UARTs are widely available and inexpensive. There is a UART in your terminal and another UART in the computer that your terminal is connected to. Like the terminal, a UART is actually two independent devices in one: a receiver and a transmitter. Figure B.2 illustrates how these UARTs are connected. Note that the send and receive lines between the terminal and the computer are crossed. This crossing is needed in a null modem connection—we will discuss modems and null modem connections in section B.7.

Given the binary representation of a character, the transmitter portion of a UART generates the start bit, the character bits, the parity bit (if any), and the stop bit(s) needed to send the character to the receiver portion of another UART. The receiver portion of the UART samples the communication line and checks for parity and framing errors in the reception of a character. Once a character has been received, only the binary representation of the character is made available to the other components in the device. In particular, the display and the computer never

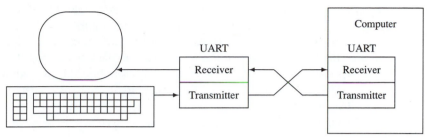

Figure B.2 UARTs

see the start bit, the parity bit, or the stop bit(s). These bits are only communicated between the UARTs to achieve reliable communication.

UARTs are universal in the sense that they can be configured for use in almost any situation that requires asynchronous, serial communication. You can set the bit rate, the number of stop bits, and the number of data bits. Additionally, you can set the UART to detect parity and framing errors.

Typically, four registers define the external interface of a UART: a control register, a status register, a received data register, and a transmit data register. By changing the values in the control register, you can alter the details of the function performed by the UART. The UART reports status information (e.g., parity errors, completed transmission of a character, reception of a new character, and so on) in the status register. Characters to be transmitted by the UART are placed in the transmit data register—transmission starts when a value is written into this register. Characters received by the UART are available in the received data register. Figure B.3 shows the block diagram for a typical UART.

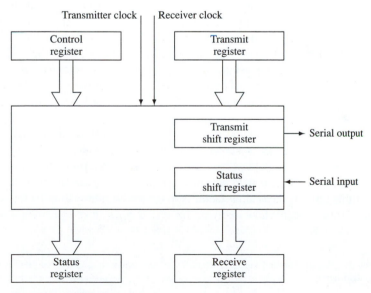

Figure B.3 UART block diagram

The two shift registers shown in Figure B.3 are internal to the UART. When the UART starts to transmit the character in the transmit register, it copies the value into its internal shift register and starts the transmission. When it completes this transmission, the UART checks for a new character in the transmit register. If it finds a new character, it repeats the transmission process; otherwise, it waits for a new character. The receive shift register has a similar function. As the UART is receiving a character, it constructs the new character in this internal register. When the UART completes the reception of a character, it copies the contents of its receive shift register into the receive register.

If you write characters in the transmit register faster than the UART can send them, you will write over one or more of the characters and they will not be transmitted. To avoid this problem, one of the flags in the UART status register is set whenever the UART copies the contents of the transmit register to its internal transmit shift register. You can examine this flag to know when it is safe to put another character in the transmit register.

What happens if the receiver portion receives characters faster than you take them out of the receive register? The UART cannot tell the other end to stop sending characters (remember, this is a full-duplex connection). If the UART receives characters faster than you take them out of the receive register, the UART writes over the character in the receive register and sets a flag in the status register to indicate that an overrun error has occurred.

B.5.1 The Texas Instruments TMS 9902 ACC

Texas Instruments makes a UART called the TMS 9902 Asynchronous Communications Controller (ACC). A simplified diagram of the TMS 9902 control register is shown in Figure B.4 (several of the fields have been omitted and the logical structure has been flattened[1] to simplify the presentation). As show in Figure B.4, you can set the UART to generate or expect 1, 1.5, or 2 stop bits. By setting the two bits in the parity field, you can configure the TMS 9902 for even, odd, or no parity. Additionally, you can configure the chip to generate or receive 5, 6, 7, or 8 data bits. The receiver interrupt enable (RIEN) field is used to enable receiver interrupts from the UART. In addition, as we will discuss, this field is used to indicate when the value in the receive register has been read.

The TMS 9902 uses a single clock input (not a separate clock input for the receiver and transmitter as is shown in Figure B.3) and the 11-bit value in the transmit (or receive) rate field of the control register to determine the bit time. The most significant bit of each field specifies a scaling factor for the input clock frequency. If this bit is 1, the scaling factor is 8; otherwise, the scaling factor is 1. The remaining 10 bits specify how many of the scaled clock ticks constitute a bit time.

---

[1] Actually, the transmit rate and the receive rate fields are overlayed, and a mode field is used to select the field being set.

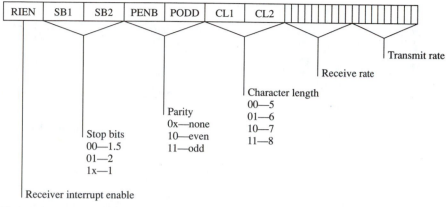

Figure B.4 The TMS 9902 control register

If you prefer to think in terms of bit rates (instead of bit times), you can use the following formula to calculate the bit rate on the TMS 9902. In this formula, MSB stands for the most significant bit in the transmit or receive rate field and VALUE stands for the value in the remaining 10 bits of the field.

$$\text{Bit rate} = \frac{\text{Basic clock rate}}{2 \cdot 8\text{MSB} \cdot \text{VALUE}}$$

Example B.12 *Suppose that the input clock frequency is 1 Mhertz (1,000,000 cycles per second). How would you set the transmit rate field to attain a bit rate of 9600 bits per second?*

We start by solving the following equation:

$$9600 = \frac{1,000,000}{2x}$$

This gives us

$$x = \frac{500,000}{9600} \approx 52$$

As such, we should set the most significant bit of the transmit rate field to 0 and the remaining bits to the binary representation of 52.

Example B.13 *Suppose that the input clock frequency is 1 Mhertz (1,000,000 cycles per second). How would you set the transmit rate field to attain a bit rate of 300 bits per second?*

We start by solving the following equation:

$$300 = \frac{1,000,000}{2x}$$

This gives us

$$x = \frac{500,000}{300} \approx 1667 \approx 8 \cdot 208$$

As such, we should set the most significant bit of the transmit rate field to 1 and the remaining bits to the binary representation of 208.

Note, the TMS 9902 ACC does not directly support mark, space, or ignore parity. If you want one of these parity settings, you can set the number of data bits to 8 (assuming 7-bit ASCII characters) and deal with the parity bits externally.

Figure B.5 illustrates the status register of the TMS 9902 (again, several flags have been left out to simplify the presentation). The UART sets the flags to 1 to indicate that the condition is true or 0 to indicate that the condition is false. For example, if the PE flag is 1, the receiver has detected a parity error. Four of the flags, RBRL, FE, OE, and PE, are related to the receiver function of the UART. The other two fields, XSRE and XBRE, are related to the transmitter function.

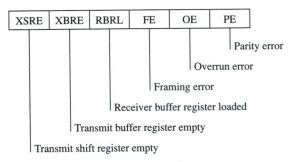

Figure B.5 The TMS 9902 status register

First, we examine the status bits set by the receiver portion of the TMS 9902. The error flags, FE, OE, and PE are always set to reflect errors detected during the reception of the most recent character. The UART sets the RBRL (receiver buffer register loaded) flag to 1 whenever there is a valid character in the receive register. When you read a character from the receive register, you need to write a bit (either a 1 or a 0) to the RIEN field of the control register to inform the UART that you have read the character. If the receiver receives a character before you tell it that you have read the previous character, it will write the new character over the character in the receive register and set the OE (overrun error) flag to indicate

```
/* The 9902 Control Register */
extern struct {
  unsigned int RIEN:1;         /* Receiver interrupt enable */
  unsigned int SB:2;            /* Stop bits */
  unsigned int PTY:2;           /* Parity setting */
  unsigned int CL:2;            /* Character length */
  unsigned int RRATE:10;        /* Receive rate */
  unsigned int XRATE:10;        /* Transmit rate */
} control;

/* The 9902 Status Register */
extern struct {
  unsigned int XSRE:1;          /* Transmit shift register empty */
  unsigned int XBRE:1;          /* Transmit buffer register empty */
  unsigned int RBRL:1;          /* Receiver buffer register loaded */
  unsigned int FE:1;            /* Framing error */
  unsigned int OE:1;            /* Overrun error */
  unsigned int PE:1;            /* Parity error */
} status;

/* The 9902 Receive Buffer */
extern char Receive_Buf;

char read_ch( void )
{
  char temp;

  /* check for overrun errors */
  if( status.RBRL && status.OE ) Announce( "Overrun Error" );

  /* wait for the next character */
  while( status.RBRL ≠ 1 ) /* nothing */ ;

  /* check error conditions */
  if( status.FE ) Announce( "Framing Error" );
  if( status.PE ) Announce( "Parity Error" );

  /* read the character and tell the UART that the character has been read */
  temp = Receive_Buf;
  control.RIEN = 0;

  return( temp )
}
```

Figure B.6 Reading a character from the TMS 9902

that an overrun error has occurred. A pseudocode function illustrating how to read a character from the TMS 9902 is shown in Figure B.6.

You can examine the remaining flags in the status register, XSRE and XBRE, to determine the status of character transmissions. The XSRE (transmit shift register empty) flag indicates whether or not the transmitter is currently transmitting a character (when the transmitter is done, the shift register is empty). Note: The XSRE flag is not all that important—once the UART has accepted the character, it will eventually complete the transmission. The XBRE (transmit buffer register empty) flag is important because it tells you when it is safe to put another character

```
/* The 9902 Status Register */
extern struct {
  unsigned int XSRE:1;        /* Transmit shift register empty */
  unsigned int XBRE:1;        /* Transmit buffer register empty */
  unsigned int RBRL:1;        /* Receiver buffer register loaded */
  unsigned int FE:1;          /* Framing error */
  unsigned int OE:1;          /* Overrun error */
  unsigned int PE:1;          /* Parity error */
} status;

/* The 9902 Transmit Buffer */
extern char Transmit_Buf;

void write_ch( char ch )
{
  /* wait until the transmit register is empty */
  while( status.XBRE ≠ 1 ) /* nothing */ ;

  Transmit_Reg = ch;
}
```

Figure B.7   Writing a character to the TMS 9902

into the transmit register. A pseudocode procedure to write a character is shown in Figure B.7.

B.5.2 The Motorola MC 6850 ACIA

In most respects, the TMS 9902 and the Motorola MC 6850 ACIA (asynchronous communications interface adapter) are very similar. However, two aspects of the MC 6850 are different than what we saw with the TMS 9902. Unlike the TMS 9902, the MC 6850 does not require explicit notification that the character in the receiver register has been read—when you read the character, the MC 6850 notes that the character has been read.

The second contrast involves the way in which you set the bit rate on the MC 6850. Unlike the TMS 9902 (and like the general UART shown in Figure B.3), the MC 6850 needs two input clock signals—one for the transmitter and one for the receiver. It is expected that the actual frequencies of these two clocks can be configured; however, this configuration is not part of the MC 6850 specification. In configuring the MC 6850, you can specify (using a field in the control register) whether the bit time is to be 16 or 64 times the clock signal (the multiplier applies to both clock signals).

For example, if you want the MC 6850 to transmit at 9600 bits per second and receive at 300 bits per second, you can set the multiplier to 16 and configure the transmitter clock to a frequency of 156,600 (16×9600) cycles per second and the receiver clock to a frequency of 4800 (16×300) cycles per second.

B.6 SYNCHRONOUS COMMUNICATION

Noticing our emphasis on asynchronous serial communication, you might wonder if there is another form of serial communication—yes, there is something called synchronous communication. In synchronous communication, characters are transmitted one after the other with no gaps. Because both ends of the connection know when to expect the next character, there is no need for start and stop bits. By leaving off start and stop bits, you can transmit 20 percent more data in the same time frame using the same bit rate (assuming a single stop bit). However, synchronous communication introduces three problems. First, you need a *startup* *protocol* to synchronize the transmitter and receiver when the communication channel is established. Second, you need to determine how to handle idle periods in the communication (i.e., times when the transmitter does not have anything to transmit). Third, you need to address the clock drift problem that we introduced in our earlier discussion of stop bits.

Startup protocol

One way to initially synchronize both ends of the communication channel is to transmit a character that is known to both ends. The ASCII synchronization character (SYNCH, 0010110) can be used for this purpose. This character has the important property that its binary representation cannot be found in any sequence of SYNCH characters, unless you start at the first bit of a character. As such, if the sender sends a stream of SYNCH characters, the two parties are synchronized when the receiver recognizes a SYNCH character.

When you do not have anything to send, you still need to send something. Here, you need a special character to let the receiver know that you really do not want to send anything (so that the receiver will not attempt to interpret the character you sent). Traditionally, the ASCII SYNCH character is also used as an idle character. However, this brings up another problem. Suppose you really do want to send the character that the receiver thinks is the idle character. To get around this problem, you can introduce an escape character (ASCII has the DLE, data link escape, character for this purpose). Now, to really send the idle character (or the DLE for that matter), you just precede the character by the DLE character.

To avoid the clock drift problem, we need to find a way to have the receiver "recover" the sender's clock during the transmission of a long sequence of characters. The receiver can recover a bit sampling point whenever it detects a 0/1 or 1/0 transition (just wait half a bit time and use that as the new sampling point). However, this little trick will not work if the transmitter sends a long sequence of NULs (all 0s) or a long sequence of DELs (all 1s) because the receiver will not see any transitions for a long time. This difficulty can be overcome by periodically transmitting the synchronization character. The need to transmit this resynchronization character decreases the effective transfer rate and complicates the communication hardware. In section B.7.4, we discuss another way that the sender's clock can be reconstructed by the receiver.

B.7 MODEMS AND THE EIA-232-D STANDARD

If you have a terminal (or personal computer) at home, you are probably familiar with an important use for modems. They let you use a telephone line to establish a connection between your terminal (or PC) and a computer system. The use of a modem for this purpose may seem natural; you probably could not afford the cost of running a cable from your house to the computer, and the phone company has already run one for you. However, even if you could afford a direct connection between your terminal and the computer, you would still need a modem! As a rule, you cannot run a 9600 bit per second line more than about 250 feet before the noise on the line makes communication unreliable (at 1,200 bits per second, you might be able to run a line of about 5,000 feet). So, if your house is more than 250 feet from the computer, you'll need some special data communication equipment (DCE) to enable reliable data transmission. In most cases, a pair of modems are used for "long-distance" data communication. Figure B.8 illustrates how modems are used in a long-distance connection.

Notes:

1. DTE stands for data terminal equipment. In this case, the word "terminal" can mean the terminal or the computer—both are at terminal ends of the communication channel.

2. DCE stands for data communication equipment. A modem is an example of the communication equipment used in such a connection.

Figure B.8   Modems for long-distance communication

Modem is actually an acronym for *mo*dulator/*dem*odulator. Modems communicate modulating (and demodulating) data values onto (or off of) a carrier (or base) signal. This modulation involves a modification of the carrier signal for each bit of information. You can think of the carrier signal as a sine wave. As such, this signal is described by three parameters: amplitude, frequency, and phase. Different types of modems modify different parameters of the carrier signal to transmit information. Modern modems use a combination of amplitude and phase shifting to achieve bits rates of 2,400 bits per second and greater.

To establish a full-duplex channel, the two modems use different carrier signals for sending information. Which modem uses which frequency? It depends on which modem originated the connection and which modem answered the call. Regardless of how they modulate the data, once an asynchronous, full-duplex channel has been established, modems use the data transmission protocols [start bit, stop bit(s), parity bit, and data bits] that we discussed in the preceding sections.

B.7.1 Channel Control

If you look carefully at the cable that goes between your terminal and the computer, notice that the connector on this cable has more than three pins (the minimum needed for a full-duplex serial connection). In many cases, you will find a 25-pin connector. This connector reflects another standard used in asynchronous serial communication—the Electronics Industry Association (EIA) Standard EIA-232-D interface.[2] Some of the lines used in these connectors are shown in Table B.2.

Table B.2 EIA-232-D channel control signals

Pin	Symbol	Function	Direction
1	AA	Equipment ground	
7	AB	Signal ground	
2	BA	Transmit data (TD)	DTE $\rightarrow$ DCE
3	BB	Receive data (RD)	DTE $\leftarrow$ DCE
6	CC	DCE ready	DTE $\leftarrow$ DCE
20	CD	DTE ready	DTE $\rightarrow$ DCE
8	CF	Received line signal detector (RLSD)	DTE $\leftarrow$ DCE

In examining this table, note that it is organized by function rather than pin number. The first group (pins 1 and 7) are the ground signals. Of these pins, only pin 7, signal ground (AB), is absolutely necessary. Pin 1, equipment ground (AA), is a protective equipment ground. (In many cases, pins 1 and 7 are connected together.)

The second group (pins 2 and 3) are the data transmission lines. Note that pins 2 and 3 are directed and both parties know which line is which. In particular, a modem knows that it is supposed to receive data on pin 2 and send data on pin 3. Hence, there is no need to cross the wires from pins 2 and 3 when you connect a modem to a terminal or a computer.

The third group contains three signals: DCE ready (pin 6), DTE ready (pin 20), and received line signal detector (RLSD, pin 8).[3] The signals in this group are used to establish and maintain a communication channel between the two end points (e.g., your terminal and a computer).

The ready signals, DTE ready and DCE ready, are used to indicate that the corresponding piece of equipment is turned on and operational. These signals do not imply anything about the status of the communication channel. On the other hand, the RLSD signal does indicate that the local modem has received a line signal (carrier signal) from the remote modem. This signal indicates that the channel has been established and is operational. Table B.3 presents the actions that take place in establishing a communication channel.

---

[2] This standard used to be called the RS-232-C standard.

[3] In the RS-232-C standard, the signals DCE ready and DTE ready were called data set ready (DSR) and data terminal ready (DTR), respectively.

Table B.3 Establishing a channel

1. When you turn on your modem and terminal, they assert their respective ready signals.
2. When you instruct your modem to initiate a connection (after you have dialed the number for the computer's modem), your modem sends a carrier signal to the computer's modem.
3. When the computer's modem detects this carrier signal, it responds to your modem with its own carrier signal. (In this example, your terminal's modem is the originator and will use the "originate frequency" for its carrier signal. The computer's· modem will use the "answer frequency" for its carrier signal.)
4. Once the modems have established the channel, they both assert their RLSD signals.

Once the communication channel has been established, your terminal and the computer can transmit characters through the channel. Many DTEs will not transmit data to the DCE unless they see both the DCE ready and RLSD signals. When you are done talking with the computer, the communication channel must be taken apart. The steps taken during this channel teardown are described in Table B.4.

Table B.4 Channel teardown

1. When you turn your terminal off, it drops its DTE ready signal.
2. When the terminal's modem no longer detects DTE ready, it drops its carrier signal to the remote modem.
3. When the computer's modem detects this loss of carrier (for an extended period), it drops its RLSD signal to the computer.

B.7.2 Null Modem Connections

Our discussion to this point has assumed that you were using modems to make a long-distance connection between your terminal and a computer (as shown in Figure B.8). The EIA-232-D standard was developed for this type of connection. However, if your terminal is relatively close to the computer, you do not need to use modems to establish this connection. Because there are no modems, this connection is called a null modem connection.

In designing a cable to support null modem connections, we need to make both ends of the connection (the terminal and the computer) think that there are modems in the connection (to maintain compatibility with the EIA-232-D standard). Figure B.9 illustrates this minimal null modem cable. You need to cross lines 2 and 3 (send and receive) so that the terminal will receive what the computer sends and vice versa. You also need to connect line 7 (signal ground) for each end of the cable, so that the computer and terminal share a common signal ground.

As you know from our earlier discussion, there is more to the establishment of a communication channel than the ability to send and receive data. How does the computer know when you initiate a connection (turn your terminal on) or when you break the connection (turn your terminal off)? If we really want to make your terminal and computer think that there are modems between them, we need to add

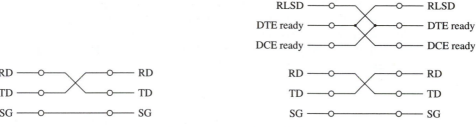

Figure B.9   A minimal null modem cable   **Figure B.10**   A null modem cable with channel control

a few more wires to our null modem cable. Figure B.10 illustrates a null modem cable with channel control.

In examining Figure B.10, note that the DTE ready signal is connected to both the DCE ready and RLSD signals on the other end of the connection. As such, when you turn on your terminal, the computer sees the DEC ready and RLSD signals. When you turn off your terminal, the computer no longer sees either of these signals. This is exactly the behavior that the computer would have seen if there were modems between the computer and the terminal.

B.7.3 Modem Control

Once the modems have established a communication channel, the computer and terminal can continue to transmit characters as long as the DSR signal is asserted, right? No. Some modems require that they be notified before you start sending characters so they can turn on their transmitter circuits. These modems expect to go through a "handshake" protocol before you start sending characters. Special signals have been included in the EIA-232-D standard for the implementation of this handshake protocol. These signals are shown in Table B.5.

Table B.5   EIA-232-D modem control signals

Pin	Symbol	Function	Direction
4	CA	Request to send (RTS)	DTE $\rightarrow$ DCE
5	CB	Clear to send (CTS)	DTE $\leftarrow$ DCE

When a terminal or computer (DTE) wants to send values through a modem, it asserts the request to send signal (RTS, pin 4). When the modem sees this signal, it turns on its transmitter and prepares to modulate the signal it receives on the transmit data line (TD, pin 2). When the modem is ready to modulate transmissions, it asserts the clear to send signal (CTS, pin 5). When the DTE and modem have completed this handshake protocol, the DTE can transmit data until it drops the RTS signal.

If there are no modems between the DTEs (your terminal and the computer), there is no need to complete the RTS handshake. However, the DTEs may be configured to complete the handshake protocol (because they do not know that the modems have been removed). As such, our null modem cable should be constructed so that the DTEs are able to complete the handshake protocol even though there is no modem to respond to the RTS signal. To accomplish this, we simply connect the RTS signal for each DTE back to its CTS signal—whenever the DTE sets its RTS signal, it will see that its request has been granted. Figure B.11 illustrates the construction of a null modem cable with modem control signals.

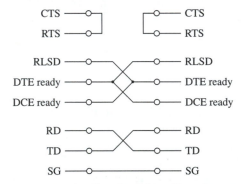

Figure B.11   A null modem cable with modem control

B.7.4 Synchronous Communication

We concluded section B.6 by describing a technique for encoding clock signals needed in synchronous communication in the characters being transmitted. Another way to deal with the clock drift problem is to introduce a separate line to encode the sender's clock. The EIA-232-D standard includes signals for encoding clock signals. These signals are shown in Table B.6. The first signal in this table (DA) is used to encode the clock on the DTE when it is sending data to the modem. The modem can use the ON to OFF transitions on this signal to determine when to sample the data being transmitted (on pin 2). The last signal (DD) has an analogous function for encoding the modem's clock.

Table B.6   EIA-232-D timing signals

Pin	Symbol	Function	Direction
24	DA	Transmitter signal element timing	DTE → DCE
17	DD	Receiver signal element timing	DTE ← DCE

B.8 ADDITIONAL READING

A great deal of the material presented in this chapter is based on *Technical Aspects of Data Communication* (3rd ed.) by John McNamara. If you want to learn more about this subject, I highly recommend McNamara's book.

BIBLIOGRAPHY

C.1 ARCHITECTURE AND ORGANIZATION

[1] Dasgupta, Subrata. *Computer Architecture: A Modern Synthesis*. New York: John Wiley & Sons, 1989.

[2] De Blasi, Mario. *Computer Architecture*. Reading, Mass.: Addison-Wesley Publishing, 1990.

[3] Dewar, Robert B. K., and Matthew Smosna. *Microprocessors: A Programmer's View*. New York: McGraw-Hill, 1990.

[4] Gear, C. William. *Computer Organization and Programming: With an Emphasis on the Personal Computer*. 4th ed. New York: McGraw-Hill, 1985.

[5] Gorsline, George W. *Assembly and Assemblers: The Motorola 68000 Family*. Englewood Cliffs, N.J.: Prentice Hall, 1988.

[6] _____. *Computer Organization: Hardware/Software*. 2nd ed. Englewood Cliffs, N.J.: Prentice Hall, 1986.

[7] Hamacher, V. Carl; Zvonko G. Vranesic; and Safwat G. Zaky. *Computer Organization*. 3rd ed. New York: McGraw-Hill, 1990.

[8] Hennesy, John L., and David A. Patterson. *Computer Architecture: A Quantitative Approach*. Morgan Kaufmann Publishers, Inc., 1990.

[9] Hoshino, Tsutomu. *PAX Computer: High Speed Parallel Processing and Scientific Computing*. Reading, Mass.: Addison-Wesley Publishing, 1989.

[10] Kain, Richard Y. *Computer Architecture: Software and Hardware*. Englewood Cliffs, N.J.: Prentice Hall, 1989.

[11] Karam, Gerald M., and John C. Bryant. *Principles of Computer Systems*. Englewood Cliffs, N.J.: Prentice Hall, 1992.

[12] Lippiatt, Arthur G., and Graham G. L. Wright. *The Architecture of Small Computer Systems*. 2nd ed. Prentice Hall International UK LTD, 1985.

[13] Liu, Yu-cheng, and Glenn A. Gibson. *Microcomputer Systems: The 8086/8088 Family: Architecture, Programming, and Design*. 2nd ed. Englewood Cliffs, N.J.: Prentice Hall, 1986.

[14]   Lorin, Harold. *Introduction to Computer Architecture and Organization.* New York: John Wiley & Sons, 1989.

[15]   Mano, M. Morris. *Computer System Architecture.* 2nd ed. Englewood Cliffs, N.J.: Prentice Hall, 1982.

[16]   Pfleeger, Charles P. *Machine Organization: An Introduction to the Structure and Programming of Computing Systems.* New York: John Wiley & Sons, 1982.

[17]   Pollard, L. Howard. *Computer Design and Architecture.* Englewood Cliffs, N.J.: Prentice Hall, 1990.

[18]   Schneider, G. Michael. *The Principles of Computer Organization.* New York: John Wiley & Sons, 1985.

[19]   Scragg, Greg W. *Computer Organization: A Top-down Approach.* New York: McGraw-Hill, 1992.

[20]   Siewiorek, Daniel P.; C. Gordon Bell; and Allen Newell. *Computer Structures: Principles and Examples.* New York: McGraw-Hill, 1982.

[21]   Stone, Harold S. *High-Performance Computer Architecture.* Reading, Mass.: Addison-Wesley Publishing, 1990.

[22]   _____. *Introduction to Computer Architecture.* Chicago: Science Research Associates, 1975.

[23]   Tanenbaum, Andrew S. *Structured Computer Organization.* 3rd ed. Englewood Cliffs, N.J.: Prentice Hall, 1990.

[24]   Toy, Wing, and Benjamin Zee. *Computer Hardware/Software Architecture.* Englewood Cliffs, N.J.: Prentice Hall, 1986.

[25]   Wakerly, John F. *Microcomputer Architecture and Programming: The 68000 Family.* New York: John Wiley & Sons, 1989.

[26]   Ward, Stephen A., and Robert H. Halstead, Jr. *Computation Structures.* New York: McGraw-Hill, 1990.

C.2 PROCESSOR REFERENCE MANUALS

[1]   Digital Equipment Corporation. *Alpha Architecture Handbook,* prelim. ed., February 1992.

[2]   Hewlett-Packard Company. *HP 3000/930 and HP 9000/840 Computers Procedure Calling Conventions Manual.* November 1986.

[3]   Hewlett-Packard Company. *HP Precision Architecture and Instruction Set Reference Manual.* 3rd ed., April 1989.

[4]   Intel Corporation. *i860 64-bit Microprocessor Programmer's Reference Manual.* 1990.

[5]   International Business Machine Corporation. *IBM RISC System 6000 Technology.* 1990.

[6]   MIPS Computer Systems, Inc. *MIPS R4000 Microprocessor User's Manual.* 1991.

[7]   Motorola, Inc. *MC88100 RISC Microprocessor User's Manual.* 1988.

C.3 LOGIC DESIGN

[1] Mano, M. Morris. *Digital Design*. Englewood Cliffs, N.J.: Prentice Hall, 1984.

C.4 ASSEMBLY LANGUAGE PROGRAMMING

[1] Able, Peter. *IBM PC Assembly Language and Programming*. 2nd ed. Englewood Cliffs, N.J.: Prentice Hall, 1991.
[2] El-Asfouri, Souhail; Olin Johnson; and Willis K. King. *Computer Organization and Programming: VAX-11*. Reading, Mass.: Addison-Wesley Publishing, 1984.
[3] Ford, William, and William Topp. *MC68000 Assembly Language and Systems Programming*. Lexington, Mass.: D.C. Heath, 1988.
[4] Kapps, Charles, and Robert L. Stafford. *VAX Assembly Language and Architecture*. Prindle, Weber and Schmidt, 1985.
[5] King, Tim, and Brian Knight. *Programming the 68000*. 2nd ed. Benjamin/Cummings Publishing, 1987.
[6] Levy, Henry M., and Richard H. Eckhouse, Jr. *Computer Programming and Architecture: The VAX*. 2nd ed. Digital Press, 1989.
[7] Nelson, Ross P. *The 80386 Book*. Microsoft Press, 1988.

C.5 NETWORKS AND COMMUNICATION

[1] Comer, Douglas E. *Internetworking with TCP/IP*. 2nd ed. Englewood Cliffs, N.J.: Prentice Hall, 1991.
[2] McNamara, John E. *Technical Aspects of Data Communication*. 3rd ed. Digital Press, 1988.
[3] Tanenbaum, Andrew S. *Computer Networks*. 2nd ed. Englewood Cliffs, N.J.: Prentice Hall, 1988.
[4] Walrand, Jean. *Communication Networks: A First Course*. Aksen Associates, 1991.

C.6 OPERATING SYSTEMS

[1] Hansen, Per Brinch. *Operating System Principles*. Englewood Cliffs, N.J.: Prentice Hall, 1973.
[2] Comer, Douglas. *Operating System Design: The XINU Approach*. Englewood Cliffs, N.J.: Prentice Hall, 1984.
[3] Davis, William S. *Operating Systems: A Systematic View*. 4th ed. Benjamin/Cummings Publishing, 1992.
[4] Deitel, Harvey M. *An Introduction to Operating Systems*. 2nd ed. Reading, Mass.: Addison-Wesley Publishing, 1990.

[5] Finkel, Raphael A. *An Operating Systems Vade Mecum.* 2nd ed. Englewood Cliffs, N.J.: Prentice Hall, 1988.

[6] Krakowiak, Sacha. *Principles of Operating Systems.* Cambridge, Mass.: MIT Press, 1988.

[7] Leffler, Samuel J.; Marshall Kirk McKusick; Michael J. Karels; and John S. Quarterman. *The Design and Implementation of the 4.3BSD Unix Operating System.* Reading, Mass.: Addison-Wesley Publishing, 1989.

[8] Maekawa, Mamoru; Arthur E. Oldehoeft; and Rodney R. Oldehoeft. *Operating Systems: Advanced Concepts.* Benjamin/Cummings Publishing, 1987.

[9] Milenković, Milan. *Operating Systems: Concepts and Design.* New York: McGraw-Hill, 1987.

[10] Nutt, Gary J. *Centralized and Distributed Operating Systems.* Englewood Cliffs, N.J.: Prentice Hall, 1992.

[11] Organick, Elliott I. *The Multics System: An Examination of Its Structure.* Cambridge. Mass.: MIT Press, 1972.

[12] Show, Alan C. *The Logical Design of Operating Systems.* Englewood Cliffs, N.J.: Prentice Hall, 1974.

[13] Silberschatz, Abraham; James L. Peterson; and Peter B. Galvin. *Operating Systems Concepts.* 3rd ed. Reading, Mass.: Addison-Wesley Publishing, 1991.

[14] Stallings, William. *Operating Systems.* New York: Macmillan, 1992.

[15] Tanenbaum, Andrew S. *Operating Systems: Design and Implementation.* Englewood Cliffs, N.J.: Prentice Hall, 1987.

C.7 PARALLEL COMPUTING

[1] Akl, Selim G. *The Design and Analysis of Parallel Algorithms.* Englewood Cliffs, N.J: Prentice Hall, 1989.

[2] Gibbons, Alan, and Wojciech Rytter. *Efficient Parallel Algorithms.* Cambridge University Press, 1990.

[3] Hatcher, Philip J., and Michael J. Quinn. *Data-Parallel Programming on MIMD Computers.* Cambridge, Mass.: MIT Press, 1991.

[4] JáJá, Joseph. *An Introduction to Parallel Algorithms.* Reading, Mass.: Addison-Wesley Publishing, 1992.

[5] Krishnamurthy, E. V. *Parallel Processing: Principles and Practice.* Reading, Mass.: Addison-Wesley Publishing, 1989.

[6] Leighton, F. Thomson. *Introduction to Parallel Algorithms and Architectures: Arrays, Trees, Hypercubes.* Morgan Kaufmann Publishers, 1992.

C.8 PROGRAMMING LANGUAGE SURVEYS

[1] Friedman, Linda Weiser. *Comparative Programming Languages: Generalizing the Programming Function.* Englewood Cliffs, N.J.: Prentice Hall, 1991.

[2] Ghezzi, Carlo, and Mehdi Jazayeri. *Programming Language Concepts*. 2nd ed. New York: John Wiley & Sons, 1987.

[3] MacLennan, Bruce J. *Principles of Programming Languages: Design, Evaluation, and Implementation*. 2nd ed. New York: Holt, Rinehart & Winston, 1987.

[4] Sebesta, Robert W. *Concepts of Programming Languages*. Benjamin/Cummings Publishing Company, 1989.

[5] Sethi, Ravi. *Programming Languages: Concepts and Constructs*. Reading, Mass.: Addison-Wesley Publishing, 1989.

C.9 COMPILER CONSTRUCTION

[1] Aho, Alfred V.; Ravi Sethi; and Jeffrey D. Ullman. *Compilers: Principles, Techniques, and Tools*. Reading, Mass.: Addison-Wesley Publishing, 1986.

[2] Barret, William A.; Rodney M. Bates; David A. Gustafson; and John D. Couch. *Compiler Construction: Theory and Practice*. 2nd ed. Chicago: Science Research Associates, 1986.

[3] Fischer, Charles N., and Richard J. LeBlanc, Jr. *Crafting a Compiler*. Benjamin/Cummings Publishing Company, 1988.

[4] Tremblay, Jean-Paul, and Paul G. Sorenson. *The Theory and Practice of Compiler Writing*. New York: McGraw-Hill Book Company, 1985.

C.10 PROGRAMMING

[1] Abelson, Harold, and Gerald Jay Sussman. *Structure and Interpretation of Computer Programs*. Cambridge, Mass.: MIT Press, 1985.

[2] Bently, Jon. *Programming Pearls*. Reading, Mass.: Addison-Wesley Publishing, 1986.

[3] Bently, Jon Louis. *Writing Efficient Programs*. Englewood Cliffs, N.J.: Prentice Hall, 1982.

[4] Harbison, Samuel P., and Guy L. Steele Jr. *C: A Reference Manual*. Englewood Cliffs, N.J.: Prentice Hall, 1984.

[5] Kernighan, Brian W., and Dennis M. Ritchie. *The C Programming Language*. 2nd ed. Englewood Cliffs, N.J.: Prentice Hall, 1988.

[6] Knuth, Donald E. *The Art of Computer Programming: Fundamental Algorithms,* vol. 1. 2nd ed. Reading, Mass.: Addison-Wesley Publishing, 1973.

[7] ———. *The Art of Computer Programming: Sorting and Searching,* vol. 3. Reading, Mass.: Addison-Wesley Publishing, 1973.

[8] ———. *The Art of Computer Programming: Seminumerical Algorithms,* vol. 2. 2nd ed. Reading, Mass.: Addison-Wesley Publishing, 1981.

[9] Koenig, Andrew. *C Traps and Pitfalls*. Reading, Mass.: Addison-Wesley Publishing, 1989.

C.11 MISCELLANEOUS

[1]   Eves, Howard. *An Introduction to the History of Mathematics*. 3rd ed. New York: Holt, Rinehart & Winston, 1969.

[2]   Hawking, Stephen W. *A Brief History of Time: From the Big Bang to Black Holes*. Bantam Books, 1988.

[3]   Hofstadter, Douglas R. *Gödel, Escher, Bach: An Eternal Golden Braid*. Vintage Books, 1979.

GLOSSARY

1's complement: An encoding technique used for signed integer values. In 1's complement, a negative value, x, is represented using the binary representation of $2^n - |x| + 1$. Related terms: 2's complement, signed magnitude, excess, and BCD. Introduced in section 7.2.

2's complement: An encoding technique used for signed integer values. In 2's complement, a negative value, x, is represented using the binary representation of $2^n - |x|$. Related terms: 1's complement, signed magnitude, excess, and BCD. Introduced in section 1.2; discussed in depth in section 7.2.

ACM: Association for Computing Machinery. A professional society for people involved in computing.

ALU: Arithmetic and logic unit. A combinational circuit that performs arithmetic and logical operations. Introduced in section 3.2.

ASCII: American Standard Code for Information Interchange. A fixed length code for representing character values. Introduced in section 1.3.

absolute loader: A loader that loads executable programs in a predetermined location in memory. The location may be fixed, or it may be specified in the header of the executable file. Related terms: loader, relocation, dynamic relocation, and static relocation. Introduced in section 10.3.

access time: The time interval from the start of a read operation until the requested value is available. Related terms: cycle time and transaction access time. Introduced in section 3.1.

accumulator: A register used to accumulate intermediate results during a sequence of arithmetic operations. Introduced in section 3.2.

address space: A mapping from address values to objects.

address translation: The process of translating a logical address to a physical address. Related terms: logical address, physical address, and dynamic relocation. Introduced in section 10.3.

aligned: The requirement that multiple-unit values start at an address that is a multiple of the number of units in the object. Introduced in section 3.1.

assembler: A tool that translates source modules (assembly language) into object modules (machine language). Related terms: source module, object module, linker, and loader.

assembler directive: A directive to the assembler. Assembler directives are used to allocate space, define symbols, align data objects, and initialize data. Introduced in section 5.1.

backward reference: Use of a label (symbol) that was defined earlier in the program. Related term: forward reference. Introduced in section 10.1.

bandwidth: The rate at which values can flow through a communication channel. For example, a bus might have a bandwidth of 20,000 bytes per second. Related term: instruction bandwidth. Introduced in section 3.4.

barrier synchronization: A form of synchronization in which no processor may cross the synchronization point until all processors are ready to cross it. Introduced in section 13.3.

base-and-bound mapping: A dynamic address mapping scheme in which the logical address is compared to a bound to check for validity. If the logical address is valid, it is added to a base value to form the physical address. Related terms: address translation, logical address, physical address, relocation, dynamic relocation, and loader. Introduced in section 10.3.

BCD: Binary-coded decimal. A technique used to encode integer values. In this strategy, each digit in the decimal representation is encoded in 4 bits. In addition to the encodings for the digits, there are encodings for the symbols "+" and "−." Related terms: 1's complement, 2's complement, signed magnitude, and excess. Introduced in section 1.2.

bias: The value added to each number in an excess representation scheme. Related term: excess. Introduced in section 7.2.

Big Endian: Refers to a machine in which the most significant byte of a multibyte value is stored in the lowest address; that is, you get the big end first. Related term: Little Endian. Introduced in section 3.1.

binding: The association of a label (symbol) with a value. Related term: binding time. Introduced in section 10.4.

binding time: The time at which the association between a label (symbol) and its value is fixed. There are four important binding times associated with the translation and execution of an assembly language program: assembly time, link time, load time, and execution time. Introduced in section 10.4.

BIOS: Basic I/O system. Introduced in Chapter 11.

block-oriented device: An I/O device that transfers hundreds or thousands of bytes in each transfer. Related terms: DMA and character-oriented device. Introduced in section 12.4.

bootstrapping: The process of initializing a computing system. Introduced in section 10.3.

branch delay slot: On most RISC machines, the instruction following a BRANCH instruction is always executed. The instruction slot following a BRANCH operation is called the branch delay slot. Related terms: delay slot and load delay slot. Introduced in section 4.5.

break point: Used in debugging. Break points are associated with memory locations. When the execution of the program crosses a break point, execution of the program is suspended and control is returned to the debugger. Introduced in section 11.3.

buffering: A communication technique that uses a queue of buffers (memory locations or registers) between the sender and the receiver. The buffers allow the sender to continue sending even though the receiver has not consumed all of the previous messages. Related terms: double buffering and instruction buffer. Introduced in sections 9.2 and 12.2.

burst-mode transaction: A single bus transaction in which several values are transmitted. Introduced in section 3.4.

bus: A collection of wires used to transmit values between the components of a computing system. An internal bus is internal to the CPU. Internal buses are controlled in a centralized fashion; the control unit determines which components use the internal buses. External buses are external to the CPU and are effectively controlled by the components attached to the bus. Related term: bus transaction. Introduced in section 3.4.

bus arbitration: The process of selecting the next bus master when several bus components may be competing to initiate a bus transaction. Related terms: bus transaction, transaction master, and transaction slave. Introduced in section 3.4.

bus master: See transaction master.

bus slave: See transaction slave.

bus transaction: The transfer of one or more data values between two components on a bus. Related terms: burst-mode transaction, transaction master, and transaction slave. Introduced in section 3.4.

butterfly: A processor-to-memory interconnection topology constructed from simple switches. A related topology, the wrapped butterfly can be used to connect processors to processors. The wrapped butterfly topology is directly related to the hypercube topology. Related terms: wrapped butterfly hypercube, fully connected topology, and shared bus topology. Introduced in section 13.6.

byte: Eight bits of storage. Related terms: word, half-word, and byte addressable. Introduced in sections 3.1 and 4.3.

byte addressable: Memory in which every address is associated with a byte. Introduced in section 3.1.

CCR: Condition code register. A set of bits that are set to reflect the result of the last arithmetic operation. These bits are used in conditional control transfers. Introduced in section 4.5.

CISC: Complex instruction set computer. Related term: RISC. Introduced in Chapter 4.

CS: Chip select. The signal used to select a memory chip. Introduced in section 3.1.

cache: A relatively small, high-speed storage that operates at processor speeds. Caches are used to hold the instruction and data values needed by the CPU during the execution of a program. Related terms: instruction cache, data cache, set-associative cache, and fully associative cache. Introduced in section 9.2.

cache hit: When the read operation on a cache succeeds; that is, when the value being read is found in the cache. Related term: cache miss. Introduced in section 9.2.

cache miss: When the read operation on a cache fails; that is, when the value being read is not found in the cache. In this case, the read operation is completed by accessing the primary memory. Related term: cache hit. Introduced in section 9.2.

cache tag bits: Bits associated with a word in the cache to identify the address of the value in primary memory. Introduced in section 9.2.

carry bit: When two n-bit values are added together, the result is an $n + 1$ bit value. The most significant bit of this result is called the carry bit. The carry bit is usually stored in the condition code register (CCR) of the processor status word (PSW). In addition, the carry bit of the CCR is frequently used to store the last bit shifted out of a register during a shift operation. Introduced in section 7.1 (addition and subtraction) and section 4.6 (shift and rotate operations).

character-oriented device: An I/O device that transfers a single character in each transfer. Related term: block-oriented device. Introduced in section 12.4.

characteristic: Another term for exponent.

chip: A small piece of silicon (a "chip") used to implement a combinational or sequential circuit. Introduced in section 2.1.

communicating processes: A model of parallel execution in which processes communicate by sending messages. Related terms: NORMA and coordinated processes. Introduced in section 13.5.

conditional sum adder: An adder that produces pairs of sums at each stage. One sum in each pair is produced assuming that the carry in will be 1, the other is produced assuming that the carry in will be 0. Related terms: ripple-carry adder and lookahead-carry adder. Introduced in section 7.1.

conjunctive normal form: A standard form for writing Boolean expressions. In this form, the Boolean expression is written as a product of sums. Introduced in section 2.1.

constant table: A table of constants stored in memory. Introduced in section 4.4.

control parallel: A model of parallel execution in which parallelism is provided by multiple threads of control. Related term: data parallel programming. Introduced in section 13.2.

control processor: The processor that broadcasts instructions to the data processors in a SIMD machine. Related terms: SIMD, data parallel programming, and data processor. Introduced in section 13.2.

control register: The register in an I/O device used to control the activities of the device. Related terms: data register and status register. Introduced in sections 3.3 and 12.1.

control store: Storage in the CPU used to hold a microprogram. Related term: microprogram. Introduced in section 9.5.

cooperating processes: A model of parallel execution in which processes communicate using shared memory. Related terms: UNMA, NUMA, semaphores, and communicating processes. Introduced in section 13.4.

coprocessor: A processor that operates in conjunction with the CPU. Unlike the CPU, coprocessors do not usually fetch their own instructions or operands. They are usually "slave" processors whose activities are controlled by the CPU. Most machines use coprocessors to perform floating point operations, and some use coprocessors to perform memory-mapping and management operations. Introduced in section 8.2.

crossbar switch: A processor-to-memory interconnection strategy in which each processor has an independent link to each memory module. Related terms: fully connected topology, shared bus, hypercube, butterfly. Introduced in section 13.6.

cycle time: The time from the start of one operation until the next operation can begin. Related terms: access time and transaction cycle time. Introduced in section 3.1.

DIP: Dual in-line package. Introduced in section 2.1.

DMA: Direct-memory access. In DMA, data values are transferred directly between an I/O device and the memory without intervention from the CPU. Introduced in section 12.4.

DRAM: Dynamic RAM. Refers to a memory system that must have its value refreshed on a regular basis; that is, the memory must be dynamically refreshed. Related term: SRAM. Introduced in section 3.1.

daisy chain: A simple communication scheme that provides fixed priorities and selective masking based on levels. In this text, daisy chains are used in the context of device interrupts and bus arbitration. Related terms: interrupt, interrupt priority, selective interrupt masking, leveled interrupt masking, software polling, interrupt acknowledge cycle, interrupt controller, and bus arbitration. Introduced in section 12.3.

data dependency: When an operation uses the result of another operation. Introduced in section 13.1.

data flow: A fine grain, asynchronous, MIMD model of parallel execution. Data flow programs are expressed as data flow graphs. Data flow graphs emphasize the data dependencies among the operations in a program. Related terms: data flow graphs, MIMD, and granularity. Introduced in section 13.3.

data flow graph: A directed graph in which the nodes represent operators and the arcs represent data paths between the operations (i.e., the arcs represent data dependencies). Related terms: data token, source node, sink node. and strict. Introduced in section 13.3.

data parallel programming: A model of parallel execution in which parallelism in execution derives from parallelism in the data. Related terms: SIMD and control parallel programming. Introduced in section 13.2.

data processor: The processor that manipulates data values in a SIMD machine. Related terms: SIMD, data parallel programming, control processor, and virtual processor. Introduced in section 13.2.

data register: An I/O device register used to hold data values. Related terms: control register and status register. Introduced in sections 3.3 and 12.1.

data token: The representation of a data value in the execution of a data flow graph. Related terms: data flow graph and operator firing. Introduced in section 13.3.

delay slot: Some instructions (e.g., BRANCH instructions) have a delayed affect. The instructions following the delayed instructions will be executed as if the delayed instruction had not been executed. The instruction slot following a delayed instruction is called a delay slot. Related terms: branch delay slot and load delay slot. Introduced in section 4.2.

denormal: In the IEEE 754 floating point standard, values whose magnitudes are small are not stored in normal form. These values are called denormals. Related terms: normal form, normalization, and gradual underflow. Introduced in section 8.2.

destination operand: The operand that specifies the location to store the result of an operation. Related term: source operand. Introduced in section 4.1.

diminished radix complement: A general strategy for representing signed integer values in a fixed number of digits in any base. The 1's complement representation scheme is an example of diminished radix complement with a base of 2. Related terms: 1's complement and radix complement. Introduced in section 7.2.

direct access: A memory in which the cells can be accessed directly; that is, you do not need to access intermediate memory cells. Related terms: sequential access and RAM. Introduced in section 3.1.

direct interrupt masking: A selective interrupt masking strategy in which each device (or group of devices) is associated with a bit in the interrupt mask. Related terms: selective interrupt masking, leveled interrupt masking, interrupt masking. Introduced in section 12.3.

direct mapping cache: A cache in which each address in the primary memory is mapped to a single cache address. Related terms: set-associative cache and fully associative cache. Introduced in section 9.2.

directive: See assembler directive.

disjunctive normal form: A standard form for writing Boolean expressions. In this form, the Boolean expression is written as a sum of products. Introduced in section 2.1.

dispatch routine: A routine that determines which routine should handle a request and transfers control to that routine. Introduced in section 11.1.

double buffering: A buffering technique that uses two buffers. While one buffer is being filled, the other can be emptied. Introduced in section 9.3.

double precision: A floating point representation in which the number of bits used in the representation is twice the number of bits used in the default, single-precision representation. Related terms: precision, single precision, and extended precision. Introduced in section 8.2.

dynamic: An activity that is performed during program execution. Related term: static. Introduced in section 6.5.

EEPROM: Electrically erasable programmable read only memory. Related terms: ROM, PROM, and EPROM. Introduced in section 3.1.

EPROM: Erasable programmable read only memory. Related terms: ROM, PROM, and EEPROM. Introduced in section 3.1.

echo: When the characters typed at the keyboard are displayed on the display. In keystroke echoing, the characters are echoed as they are typed. In application echoing, the characters are displayed as they are processed by the application program. Introduced in section 12.2.

edge-triggered: Activities that are initiated by a transition in a control signal. Related terms: flip-flop and level-triggered. Introduced in section 2.2.

effective sign bit: In the 1's and 2's complement representation schemes, the most significant bit in the representation of a value indicates the sign of the value. In these cases, the sign bit is a consequence of the representation, not part of the definition. Related terms: 1's complement, 2's complement, sign bit, and inverse sign bit. Introduced in section 7.2.

end-around carry: In the 1's complement representation, addition is performed using binary addition; however, after the basic addition is performed, the carry bit is added into the result. This final step is called the end-around carry. Related term: carry bit. Introduced in section 7.2.

exception: An invalid use of a resource. Related terms: XOP and trap. Introduced in section 7.1 and discussed in section 11.3.

exception handler: The routine that is invoked when an exception occurs. Related terms: exception, interrupt handler, and XOP handler. Introduced in section 11.3.

exception vector: An array of exception handlers or exception handler addresses. Related terms: exception handler, interrupt vector, XOP vector. Introduced in section 11.3.

excess: An encoding technique used for signed integer values. In excess, a value, x, is represented using the binary representation of $x + b$ where b is the bias of the representation. Related terms: bias, 1's complement, 2's complement, signed magnitude, and BCD. Introduced in section 7.2.

executable file: A file that contains an executable program. Related terms: source module, object module, library, linker, and loader. Introduced in Chapter 10.

export: An assembler directive used to indicate that a symbol (label) defined in the current module can be used by other modules. In concept, the symbol is exported by the module. Related term: import. Introduced in section 10.2.

extended-precision: A floating point format used during arithmetic calculations. The extended-precision format is larger than either the single-precision format or the double-precision format. Using this format can prevent some overflows and underflows that would otherwise occur. Related terms: precision, single precision, and double precision. Introduced in section 8.2.

external bus: See bus.

Flynn, Michael: In 1966, Michael Flynn introduced a taxonomy of parallel machines based on the number of instruction and data streams provided by the machine. This taxonomy includes SISD (single instruction, single data), MISD (multiple instruction, multiple data), SIMD (single instruction, multiple data), and MIMD (multiple instruction, multiple data). Related terms: SISD, MISD, SIMD, and MIMD. Introduced in section 13.2.

fan-out: The number of places a signal is sent to. A signal can only be routed to a small number of gate inputs before it loses its integrity. Introduced in section 2.1.

fetch: Get a value from a memory location. Related terms: store and read.

firmware: A name for microcode. Related term: microprogram. Introduced in section 9.5.

flat address space: An address space in which the addresses form a single sequence. Related terms: paging and two-dimensional address space. Introduced in section 10.3.

flip-flop: The basic unit of storage. Flip-flops are edge-triggered devices. Related terms: edge-triggered and latch. Introduced in section 2.2.

forward reference: Use of a label (symbol) that is defined later in the program. Related terms: backward reference, two pass assembler, and patch list assembler. Introduced in section 10.1.

full adder: A combinational circuit that takes two 1-bit inputs along with a 1-bit carry and produces the sum and carry. Related terms: half adder and ripple-carry adder. Introduced in section 2.1.

fully associative cache: Refers to a cache in which any address in the primary memory can be associated with any location in the cache. Related terms: direct mapping cache and set-associative cache. Introduced in section 9.2.

fully connected topology: A processor-to-processor interconnection topology in which every processor has a direct link to every other processor. The fully connected topology is appropriate for connecting processors to processors, while the crossbar switch is appropriate for connecting processors to memory modules. Related terms: crossbar switch, shared bus topology, hypercube, and butterfly. Introduced in section 13.6.

gap: The distance between consecutive values in a fixed or floating point representation scheme. Related terms: precision, significant digits, and underflow. Introduced in sections 8.1 and 8.2.

gate: simple Boolean function. Introduced in section 2.1.

gradual underflow: In the IEEE 754 standard, values with a magnitude that is smaller than the smallest magnitude that can be represented in normal form can be represented as denormals. This means that values that would otherwise result in an underflow can be represented within the representation. Related terms: IEEE 754 standard, precision, denormal, gap, and underflow. Introduced in section 8.2.

granularity: Refers to the amount of work performed by a unit of parallel execution. In a fine-grain machine, parallelism is at the level of a machine operation. In a medium-grain machine, parallelism is based on a small collection of operations. In a coarse- or large-grain machine, parallelism is based on relatively independent programs. Introduced in section 13.4.

Hamming distance: Given two bit patterns of the same length, the Hamming distance between the two patterns is the number of bits that are different between the two patterns. Introduced in section 1.4.

half adder: A combinational circuit that takes two 1-bit inputs and produces the sum and carry. Related term: full adder. Introduced in section 2.1.

halfword: A unit of storage that is half the size of a word. Typically 16 bits. Related terms: byte and word. Introduced in sections 3.1 and 4.3.

heartbeat: The global synchronization signal that initiates the start of a step in systolic and pipeline machines. Related terms: pipeline and systolic machines. Introduced in section 13.3.

hertz: Cycles per second.

hidden bit: In the DEC PDP 11/Vax and IEEE 754 floating point representations, the most significant bit of the significand is not explicitly stored in the representation. This bit is called the hidden bit because it is not visible in the representation. Introduced in section 8.2.

hypercube topology: A processor-to-processor interconnection topology. A hypercube of degree n has 2^n processors, and each processor has a link to n other processors. Hypercubes represent a compromise between fully connected topologies and shared bus topologies. Related terms: butterfly switch, shared bus topology, and fully connected topology. Introduced in section 13.6.

IC: Integrated circuit. Introduced in section 2.1.

IEEE: Institute of Electrical and Electronics Engineers. A professional society for electrical engineers and computer scientists.

IEEE 754 Standard: A standard for floating point representation. Related terms: denormal, hidden bit, gradual underflow, and extended precision. Introduced in section 8.2.

IR: Instruction register. The register holds the value of the current instruction as it is being interpreted. Introduced in section 3.2.

ifetch loop: The instruction fetch/execute loop. Introduced in section 3.2.

import: An assembler directive used to indicate that a symbol (label) used in the current module is defined in another module. In concept, the symbol is imported by the module. Related term: export. Introduced in section 10.2.

internal bus: See bus.

interrupt: An external request for service. When an I/O device requires service, it generates an interrupt signal for the CPU. When the CPU detects the interrupt signal, it suspends its current processing and services the device that generated the interrupt signal. After servicing the device, the CPU returns to its previous activity. Related terms: interrupt masking and interrupt handler. Introduced in section 12.2.

interrupt I/O: When I/O transfers between a device and the CPU are initiated in response to an interrupt from the I/O device. Related terms: receive interrupt, transmit interrupt, and programmed I/O. Introduced in section 12.2.

interrupt acknowledge cycle: A strategy used to identify the device that generated an interrupt signal. After the CPU detects an interrupt, it enters an interrupt acknowledge cycle. During the interrupt acknowledge cycle, the device that generated the interrupt sends its identifier to the CPU. Related terms: software polling, daisy chain, and interrupt controller. Introduced in section 12.3.

interrupt controller: A programmable device that encapsulates the priority and device identification associated with interrupts from I/O devices. Related terms: software polling, daisy chain, and interrupt acknowledge cycle. Introduced in section 12.3.

interrupt encoding: An interrupt identification strategy in which the interrupting device sends its (encoded) identifier to the CPU when it generates an interrupt. The value sent to the CPU signals an interrupt and identifies the device that generated the interrupt. Related term: interrupt. Introduced in section 12.3.

interrupt handler: The code that services an interrupt from an I/O device. Related terms: interrupt, exception handler, and XOP handler. Introduced in section 12.2.

interrupt mapping: An interrupt identification and masking strategy in which each device (or group of devices) is associated with a bit in an interrupt status register (ISR) and an interrupt mask register (IMR). In this strategy, the interrupt signal for each device is continuously *and*ed with the appropriate bit in the IMR and stored in the appropriate bit in the ISR. Related terms: interrupt, interrupt masking, and selective interrupt masking. Introduced in section 12.3.

interrupt masking: Disabling the detection of interrupts from I/O devices. Related terms: selective interrupt masking, maskable interrupts, and nonmaskable interrupts. Introduced in section 12.3.

interrupt vector: An array of interrupt handlers or interrupt handler addresses. Related terms: interrupt handler, exception vector, and XOP vector. Introduced in section 12.2.

instruction bandwidth: Number of instructions delivered to the CPU per second. Related term: bandwidth. Introduced in section 9.2.

instruction buffer: A buffer used to hold instructions before they are executed. Related terms: instruction prefetch and buffering. Introduced in section 9.2.

instruction prefetch: Fetching instructions before they are needed by the CPU. Related terms: instruction buffer and instruction bandwidth. Introduced in section 9.2.

instruction scheduling: Arranging instructions to reduce the delays introduced by memory accesses. Related term: register interlock. Introduced in section 4.2.

interleaving: When consecutive memory addresses are associated with different memory banks. Introduced in sections 3.1 and 9.2.

isolated I/O: In isolated I/O, the I/O devices are in a separate address space from the memory cells. To support isolated I/O, the machine must provide special operations for I/O. Related term: memory-mapped I/O. Introduced in section 3.2.

inverse sign bit: In the excess representation schemes, the most significant bit can act as an inverse sign bit (i.e., the bit is 0 when the value is negative). Related terms: sign bit and effective sign bit. Introduced in section 7.2.

keyboard buffer: A buffer used to hold characters typed on the keyboard. Introduced in Chapter 11.

Little Endian: Refers to a machine in which the least significant byte of a multi-byte value is stored in the lowest address; that is, you get the little end first. Related term: Big Endian. Introduced in section 3.1.

LSI: Large-scale integration. Related terms: SSI, MSI, and VLSI. Introduced in section 2.1.

latch: A basic unit of storage. In contrast to flip-flops, latches are level-triggered devices. Latch is frequently used as a verb to denote the act of loading (latching) a value into a register. Related terms: level-triggered and flip-flop. Introduced in section 2.2.

latency: The time interval between the start of an operation to the completion of the operation. In contrast to access time, latency is measured by the initiator of the request while access time is measured by the provider of the service. Related term: access time. Introduced in section 3.1.

leading edge: The 0-to-1 transition at the start of a timing pulse. Related term: trailing edge. Introduced in section 2.2.

leveled interrupt masking: A selective interrupt masking strategy in which each device (or group of devices) is assigned a level. When the CPU is servicing an interrupt, only devices with an interrupt level greater than the level of device being serviced are enabled. Related terms: selective interrupt masking and direct interrupt masking. Introduced in section 12.3.

level-triggered: Activities that are initiated by the value of a control signal. Related terms: latch and edge-triggered. Introduced in section 2.2.

linker: A translation tool that combines several object modules and libraries into a single executable file. Related terms: object module, library, executable file, assembler, and loader. Discussed in section 10.2.

locality: When an instruction or data value is fetched from memory, there is a good chance that it will be used again in the next few instructions. The more general principle states that values close to the fetched value will be used. Introduced in section 9.2.

load: Put a value in a register. Related term: store.

load delay slot: On the MIPS R3000 processor, the instruction following a LOAD operation cannot reference the value being loaded. In this machine, the instruction slot following a LOAD instruction is called the load delay slot. Related terms: delay slot and branch delay slot.

logical address space: The address space from the perspective of the program. Related terms: physical address space and address translation. Introduced in section 10.3.

lookahead-carry adder: An adder in which all of the carries are generated during the first step and the additions are performed (in parallel) during the second step. Related terms: conditional sum adder and ripple-carry adder. Introduced in section 7.1.

MAR: Memory address register. This register holds the address during a memory access. Introduced in section 3.2.

MDR: Memory data register. This register holds the data value during a memory access. Introduced in section 3.2.

Mhertz: Megahertz, a measure equaling millions of cycles per second.

MIMD: Multiple instruction streams, multiple data streams. See Flynn, Michael.

MISD: Multiple instruction streams, single data stream. See Flynn, Michael.

MMU: Memory management unit. Introduced in section 11.2.

MSI: Medium-scale integration. Related terms: SSI, LSI, and VLSI. Introduced in section 2.1.

mantissa: See significand.

maskable interrupt: An interrupt signal that can be masked (i.e., disabled). Related terms: interrupt, interrupt masking, nonmaskable interrupt. Introduced in section 12.2.

massively parallel: Parallelism in which there are thousands or tens of thousands of processors. Introduced in Chapter 13.

memory-mapped I/O: In memory-mapped I/O, the I/O devices are mapped into the same address space as the memory cells. Any machine can support memory-mapped I/O; some machines require memory-mapped I/O because they do not provide special I/O operations. Related term: isolated I/O. Introduced in section 3.2.

microprogram: The program executed by the micro-programmed controller. Related term: control store. Introduced in section 9.5.

microsecond: 10^{-6} seconds.

multiplex: Using the same object for different things at different times. Introduced in section 3.1 (in the context of pin multiplexing).

NORMA: No remote memory access. Refers to a multiprocessor in which the memory modules do not provide remote access. In these systems, the processors must communicate using messages. Related terms: communicating processes, UMA, and NUMA. Introduced in section 13.5.

NUMA: Nonuniform memory access. Refers to a multiprocessor in which the memory modules provide remote access, but remote accesses may take longer than local memory accesses. Related terms: UMA and NORMA. Introduced in section 3.1.

NaN: Not a number. The result of an illegal operation (e.g., taking the square root of -5). Related term: IEEE 754 standard. Introduced in section 8.2.

nanosecond: 10^{-9} seconds.

negative zero: In the signed magnitude and 1's complement representation schemes, there is a pattern that does not correspond to any value. These patterns are the same as the pattern used to represent zero, except the sign bit indicates that the value is negative. These patterns are called negative zero. Introduced in section 7.2.

normal form: A standard form for values stored in a floating point representation. Related terms: normalization, denormal, hidden bit, and IEEE 754 standard. Introduced in section 8.2.

normalization: The process of transforming a floating point value into normal form. Related term: normal form. Introduced in section 8.2.

nullify: To ignore the results of an operation. When an operation is nullified, it is as if the operation was not performed. Introduced in sections 4.5 and 9.3.

OPCODE: The binary encoding of an operation. Introduced in section 3.2.

object module: The result of translating a source module. Related terms: source module, assembler, and linker. Introduced in Chapter 10.

operator firing: A step in the execution of a data flow graph. An operator node in a data flow graph can be fired when it has data tokens on its inputs. Strict operators require data tokens on all of their inputs before they can fire. When an operator is fired, it consumes the data tokens on its inputs and produces data tokens on its outputs. Related terms: data flow graph and data token. Introduced in section 13.3.

overflow: When a value is outside the range of the representation. Related terms: range, exception, and underflow. Introduced in section 7.1.

overrun: When a new value arrives and overwrites an old values before the old value is processed. Introduced in section 12.2.

PC: Program counter. The register that holds the address of the next instruction. Introduced in section 3.2.

PIC: Programmable interrupt controller. See interrupt controller.

PROM: Programmable read only memory. Related terms: ROM, EPROM, and EEPROM. Introduced in section 3.1.

PSW: Processor status word. Introduced in section 11.2.

page frame: A collection of memory locations used to hold a page from a program. Related term: paging. Introduced in section 10.3.

paging: A technique that allows noncontiguous memory allocation for programs. In paging, the program is partitioned into fixed-sized blocks called pages. The pages are then loaded into page frames in the memory. Related terms: flat address space and segmentation. Introduced in section 10.3.

parallel: When several activities are performed in the same time frame.

parallel efficiency: Measures the utilization of the processors in a parallel implementation. Parallel efficiency is calculated by dividing the speedup by the number of processors used in the parallel implementation. Related term: speedup. Introduced in Chapter 13.

parity: The parity of a bit pattern is determined by counting the number of 1's in the pattern. If the number of 1's is even, the pattern has even parity; otherwise, the pattern has odd parity. Introduced in section 1.4.

patch list assembler: An assembler that uses a patch list to translate instructions that use forward references. When the assembler encounters an instruction that uses a forward reference, it adds an entry to its patch list. When the assembler finishes reading the source module, it then processes the patch list to complete the translation of the instructions that use forward references. Related terms: forward reference and two-pass assembler. Introduced in section 10.1.

physical address space: The address space from the perspective of the physical memory. Related terms: logical address space and address translation. Introduced in section 10.3.

pin limitation: While the number of transistors that can be placed on a chip is proportional to the area of the chip, the number of pins that can be attached to the chip is proportional to the circumference. As such, the functionality implemented by the transistors on the chip must increase as the number of transistors is increased. Introduced in section 2.1.

pipeline: A technique for improving throughput. In pipelining, the activity to be performed is divided into a fixed collection of smaller activities called pipeline stages. Because each stage in the pipeline can operate on a different object, the entire pipeline can process more objects in a time period. Related terms: pipeline bubble, pipeline slip, pipeline stall, register forwarding, and throughput. Introduced in section 9.3 in the context of instruction execution pipelines. A more general discussion is presented in section 13.2.

pipeline bubble: When an instruction in the instruction execution pipeline is nullified, the pipeline stages following the nullification do not perform any work. This creates a bubble in the pipeline. Related terms: pipeline, pipeline slip, and pipeline stall. Introduced in section 9.3.

pipeline slip: When a pipeline stage waits for a value that will be produced by a later stage in the pipeline. Related terms: pipeline, pipeline bubble, and pipeline stall. Introduced in section 9.3.

pipeline stall: When all of the stages in a pipeline are delayed until a stage in the pipeline can complete its operation. Related terms: pipeline, pipeline bubble, and pipeline slip. Introduced in section 9.3.

precision: The accuracy of a number. Related terms: significand, single precision, and double precision. Introduced in section 8.2.

privilege level: Specifies the operation and access controls placed on the processor. Related terms: privileged operation, supervisor mode, and user mode. Introduced in section 11.2.

privileged operation: An operation that can only be performed when the processor is in a privileged mode. Related terms: privilege level and supervisor mode. Introduced in section 11.2.

product of sums: See conjunctive normal form.

programmed I/O: Performing I/O by constantly polling (examining) the status register of an I/O device. Related terms: status register and interrupt I/O. Introduced in section 12.1.

propagation delay: The amount of time that it takes for the output signals of a circuit to stabilize after the inputs have changed. Introduced in section 2.1.

pseudo-operation: An operation this is not defined by the machine but is translated by the assembler into another operation or sequence of operations. Pseudo-operations are also called synthetic operations. In some contexts, the name pseudo-operation is used to denote an assembler directive. Introduced in section 4.2.

RAM: Random access memory. Related terms: direct access and sequential access. Introduced in section 3.1.

RISC: Reduced instruction set computer. Related term: CISC. Introduced in Chapter 4.

ROM: Read only memory. Related terms: PROM, EPROM, and EEPROM. Introduced in section 3.1.

radix complement: A general strategy for representing signed integer values using any base. The 2's complement representation scheme is an example of radix complement in which the base is 2. Related terms: 2's complement and diminished radix complement. Introduced in section 7.2.

range (of representation): The set of values that can be represented in a fixed number of bits using a specified representation technique. Introduced in sections 1.2, 7.1, and 7.2.

read: Get a value from a memory location. Related terms: write and fetch.

real estate: Refers to the amount of space available on a chip. Space is measured by the number of gates that can be placed on the chip.

receive interrupt: An interrupt generated by an I/O device when it has received a value. Related terms: interrupt I/O and transmit interrupt. Introduced in section 12.2.

refresh logic: The logic used to periodically read and rewrite the values stored in a dynamic RAM. Related terms: DRAM and SRAM. Introduced in section 3.1.

register: A collection of flip-flops controlled by a single clock signal. Introduced in section 2.2.

register forwarding: When the result of an instruction is used before it is stored in the destination register. Related terms: pipeline and register interlock. Introduced in section 9.3.

register interlock: The value in a register cannot be used until the value being loaded into the register has been fetched from memory or computed. Register interlocking is used to delay the execution of any instruction that needs the value in a register until the register has been loaded. Related terms: register forwarding and instruction scheduling. Introduced in section 4.2.

relocation: Moving a program to a different location in the memory of a machine. Related terms: static relocation, dynamic relocation, and loader. Introduced in section 10.3.

resident monitor: The operating system routines that remain in primary memory. Introduced in section 11.1.

resource conflict: An attempt to use that same object for two different purposes at the same time. Introduced in section 9.5.

ripple-carry adder: An adder constructed from a collection of full adders. The carry output of each full adder is connected to the carry input of the next full adder. In concept, the carry "ripples" through the full adders. Related terms: conditional sum adder, lookahead-carry adder, and full adder. Introduced in section 7.1.

rounding: Transforming the result of a floating point operation into a value in the representation. Related terms: gap and precision. Introduced in section 8.2.

SIMD: Single instruction stream, multiple data streams. See Flynn, Michael.

SISD: Single instruction stream, single data stream. See Flynn, Michael.

SIP: Single in-line package. Introduced in section 2.1.

SRAM: Static RAM. Refers to a memory system that retains its values as long as it has power; that is, memory that does not need to be refreshed. Static is a contrast to the dynamic nature of DRAM. Related term: DRAM. Introduced in section 3.1.

SSI: Small-scale integration. Related terms: MSI, LSI, and VLSI. Introduced in section 2.1.

scale factor: In a fixed point representation, every value is multiplied by a scale factor and then represented as an integer. Introduced in section 8.1.

segmentation: A technique that allows noncontiguous memory allocation for programs. In paging, the program is partitioned into logical units called segments. Segmentation introduces two-dimensional addressing. Related terms: two-dimensional addressing and paging. Introduced in section 10.3.

selective interrupt masking: The ability to disable interrupts from selected devices while enabling interrupts from other devices. Related terms: direct interrupt masking and leveled interrupt masking. Introduced in section 12.3.

semaphore: A data structure used for explicit synchronization. Semaphores are manipulated by two operations: wait and signal. Related term: coordinated processes. Introduced in section 13.4.

sequential access: A memory in which the cells must be accessed in sequence; that is, you must pass over intermediate storage cells to the desired cell. Magnetic tape is an example of sequential access storage. Related terms: direct access and RAM. Introduced in section 3.1.

set-associative cache: Refers to a cache in which an address in the primary memory can be associated with a set of locations in the cache. Related terms: direct mapping cache and fully associative cache. Introduced in section 9.2.

shared bus: A processor-to-processor or processor-to-memory interconnection strategy in which every component (processor or memory) is connected to a single bus. Related terms: fully connected topology and hypercube. Introduced in section 13.6.

sign bit: In the signed magnitude representation the most significant bit is a sign bit: 1 indicates that the value is negative, 0 indicates that the value is nonnegative. Related terms: signed magnitude, effective sign bit, and inverse sign bit. Introduced in sections 1.2 and 7.2.

sign extend: Replicating the sign bit of a value stored in 1's or 2's complement representation. This replication preserves the value being represented when the size used in the representation is increased. Introduced in sections 1.2 and 7.2.

signed magnitude: An encoding technique used for signed integer values. In signed magnitude, values are represented using a sign bit followed by the binary representation of the magnitude. Related terms: 1's complement, 2's complement, excess, and BCD. Introduced in section 1.2; discussed in depth in section 7.2.

significand: The significant bits (digits) of a number in a floating point representation. Introduced in Chapter 8.

single precision: The default floating point representation. Related terms: precision, double precision, and extended precision. Introduced in section 8.2.

sink node: A node in a data flow graph that only consumes data tokens; that is, a node that does not produce any tokens. Related terms: data flow graph, source node, data token. Introduced in section 13.3.

snoopy cache: A cache that monitors the address lines of the memory bus and invalidates any entry in the cache when its associated memory value is updated by a DMA transfer or another processor. Introduced in sections 12.4 and 13.5.

software interrupt polling: A interrupt device identification strategy in which the interrupt handler examines (polls) the status registers of the devices that could have generated an interrupt to identify the device that generated the interrupt. Related terms: daisy chain, interrupt acknowledge cycle, and interrupt controller. Introduced in section 12.3.

source module: An assembly language module. Related terms: assembler, object module, and executable file. Introduced in Chapter 10.

source node: A node in a data flow graph that only produces data tokens; that is, a node that does not produce any tokens. Related terms: data flow graph, sink node, and data token. Introduced in section 13.3.

source operand: An operand that provides a value for an operation. Related term: destination operand. Introduced in section 4.1.

speedup: Measures the extent to which a parallel implementation improves the execution time used for a sequential implementation. Speedup is calculated by dividing the time required for the sequential implementation by the time required for the parallel implementation. Related term: parallel efficiency. Introduced in Chapter 13.

static: An activity that is performed prior to program execution. Related term: dynamic. Introduced in section 6.5.

status register: The register in an I/O device used to indicate the status of the device. Related terms: control register and data register. Introduced in sections 3.3 and 12.1.

store: Put a value in a memory location. Related terms: load, fetch, and write.

store-back cache: A cache in which values are only written to memory when their cache entries are replaced. Related term: store-through cache. Introduced in section 9.2.

store-through cache: A cache in which values are written to memory whenever they are updated in the cache. Related term: store-back cache. Introduced in section 9.2.

sum of products: See disjunctive normal form.

superpipeline: In a superpipelined machine, the processor can complete the interpretation of multiple instructions in each processor cycle. Related terms: pipeline and superscalar. Introduced in section 9.4.

superscalar: A processor that uses multiple functional units to attain multiple instruction executions per processor cycle. Related term: superpipeline. Introduced in section 9.4.

supervisor mode: A privilege level that grants complete access to the processor. Related terms: privilege level and user mode. Introduced in section 11.2.

synthetic operation: See pseudo-operation.

temporary: A register or memory location used to hold an intermediate result during a calculation. Introduced in section 4.1.

throughput: A measure of the number of objects processed in a time interval. For example, the number of instructions executed per second. Related term: pipeline. Introduced in section 9.3.

trailing edge: The 1-to-0 transition at the end of a timing pulse. Related term: leading edge. Introduced in section 2.2.

transaction access time: The time interval between the time the transaction slave recognizes the operation and the time it asserts the Done signal. Introduced in section 3.4.

transaction cycle time: The time interval between subsequent requests for the same device. Introduced in section 3.4

transaction master: The initiator of a bus transaction. Introduced in section 3.4.

transaction slave: The target of a bus transaction. Introduced in section 3.4.

transmit interrupt: An interrupt generated by an I/O device when it has transmitted a value. Related terms: interrupt I/O and receive interrupt. Introduced in section 12.2.

trap: An operation that generates an exception if a condition is met. In addition, many machines (including the SPARC) use the term *trap* in reference to an XOP. Related terms: exception and XOP. Introduced in section 11.3.

two-dimensional address space: The address space imposed by segmentation. The address space consists of a collection of sequences. Related terms: segmentation and flat address space. Introduced in section 10.3.

two pass assembler: An assembler that makes two passes over the source module to resolve forward references. Related terms: forward reference and patch list assembler. Introduced in section 10.1.

UART: Universal asynchronous receiver transmitter. A programmable device that encapsulates asynchronous serial communication. Introduced in section 12.1.

UMA: Uniform memory access. Refers to a multiprocessor in which memory accesses require a uniform amount of time. Related terms: NUMA and NORMA. Introduced in section 3.1.

underflow: When the magnitude of a value represented using a floating point representation falls in the gap between 0 and the smallest magnitude that can be represented. Related terms: gap, overflow, denormals, and gradual underflow. Introduced in section 8.2.

upcall: The process of calling a user level function from a supervisor level function. Introduced in section 11.3.

user mode: A privilege level that grants limited access to the processor. Related terms: privilege level and supervisor mode. Introduced in section 11.2.

VCR/LCR: Vertical redundancy check/longitudinal redundancy check. A simple error correction technique. Introduced in section 1.4.

VLSI: Very large scale integration. Related terms: SSI, MSI, and LSI. Introduced in section 2.1.

volatile: A memory system that does not retain its values in the absence of power. Most RAM memories are volatile. ROMs are nonvolatile. Introduced in section 3.1.

vector parallelism: Refers to a machine that provides vector operations that are implemented in parallel. Introduced in section 13.1.

virtual processor: A simulated data processor in a SIMD machine. When there is more data than data processors, a single data processor may simulate several virtual processors. Related term: data processor. Introduced in section 13.2.

wait state: Bus cycles introduced when the slave is unable to respond within the standard time for a bus cycle. Introduced in section 3.4.

word: The unit of memory access. Can be defined in several ways: (a) smallest addressable memory unit, (b) collection of cells manipulated by a single word select line (also called physical word), (c) unit provided by a memory chip (also called logical word), (d) the width of data path between the memory and the CPU, (e) the width of the internal data paths, and (f) the width of the registers in the CPU.

wrapped butterfly: A butterfly network in which the endpoints have been joined. Related term: butterfly. Introduced in section 13.6.

write: Put a value in a memory location. Related terms: read and store.

XOP: Extended operation. Related terms: exception, trap, and interrupt. Introduced in section 11.1.

XOP handler: The routine that is invoked when an XOP is called. Related terms: XOP, exception handler, and interrupt handler. Introduced in section 11.1.

XOP vector: An array of XOP handlers or XOP handler addresses. Related terms: XOP handler, exception vector, interrupt vector. Introduced in section 11.1.

INDEX